Conceptualizations and Mental Processing in Language

Cognitive Linguistics Research
3

Editors
René Dirven
Ronald W. Langacker

Mouton de Gruyter
Berlin · New York

Conceptualizations and Mental Processing in Language

Edited by

Richard A. Geiger
Brygida Rudzka-Ostyn

1993
Mouton de Gruyter
Berlin · New York

Library
University of Texas
at San Antonio .

Mouton de Gruyter (formerly Mouton, The Hague)
is a Division of Walter de Gruyter & Co., Berlin

Library of Congress Cataloging in Publication Data

Conceptualizations and mental processing in language ; includ-
ing a selection of papers from the First International Cognitive
Linguistic Conference, Duisburg, Germany, March/April
1989 / edited by Richard A. Geiger and Brygida Rudzka-
Ostyn.
     p. cm. — (Cognitive linguistic research ; 3)
Conference held Mar. 28 – Apr. 4, 1989.
  Includes about a third of the 65 papers presented at the
Conference, most of which have also been revised for publi-
cation.
Includes bibliographical references and index.
ISBN 3-11-012714-8
  1. Cognitive grammar — Congresses. 2. Psycholingu-
istics — Congresses. I. Geiger, Richard A., 1939 – .
II. Rudzka-Ostyn, Brygida. III. International Cognitive Lin-
guistics Conference (1st ; 1989 ; Duisburg, Germany) IV. Series.
P165.C86 1993
415 – dc20   93-19401
                             CIP

Die Deutsche Bibliothek — Cataloging in Publication Data

Conceptualizations and mental processing in language / ed. by
Richard A. Geiger ; Brygida Rudzka-Ostyn. — Berlin ; New
York : Mouton de Gruyter, 1993
 (Cognitive linguistics research ; 3)
 ISBN 3-11-012714-8
NE: Geiger, Richard A. [Hrsg.]; GT

Printing: Werner Hildebrand, Berlin
Binding: Dieter Mikolai, Berlin
Printed in Germany

Contents

Preface

The contributions to this volume come from two sources. Some were invited by the editors especially for this collection. Most of them, however, were originally presented at the 14th International L.A.U.D. Symposium (the *First International Cognitive Linguistics Conference*), which was held in Duisburg, Germany, from March 28 through April 4, 1989, and represent less than a third of the over 65 papers read at that meeting. All were selected for inclusion only after a lengthy process of refereeing and, in many cases, extensive revising. Thus, despite its subtitle, this volume is not in the usual sense the publication merely of the "proceedings" of a conference.

Those in attendance at the symposium were overwhelmingly agreed that an exciting new cognitive paradigm in linguistics (see Introduction) had successfully been launched internationally in the 1980s. Signs of this international success are, in addition to the First International Cognitive Linguistics Conference itself and the second conference (held in July/August 1991 in Santa Cruz, California), the many studies in cognitive linguistics which have recently been published in major publishing houses, the new journal *Cognitive Linguistics (CL)*, the new monograph series *Cognitive Linguistics Research (CLR)*, the new professional organization *International Cognitive Linguistics Association (ICLA)*, the *ICLA Newsletter* and the rapidly expanding bibliography by Rainer Schulze and René Dirven, *The non-annotated bibliography of cognitive linguistics: The second update, L.A.U.D. Paper* A 289 (1990).

The editors of this volume would like to acknowledge a great debt of gratitude to the several groups of persons who made its publication possible - the contributors, the editors and the publishers of *CLR*, Rüdiger Schütz and Birgit Smieja of the Duisburg L.A.U.D. team, whose midwifing skills enabled their computer to become the surrogate mother of the volume, and especially René Dirven, our ever-willing advisor and friend.

Above all, we want to thank the following individuals who acted as our additional referees, advising the contributors as well as the editors, some of whom were generous enough to review more than one of the papers offered to us for inclusion in the collection: Werner Abraham (Groningen, The Netherlands), Geert Adriaens (Leuven, Belgium), Eugene H. Casad (Tucson, AZ, USA), Kenneth W. Cook (Honolulu, HI, USA), Paul Deane

(Orlando, FL, USA), Renaat Declerck (Kortrijk, Belgium), René Dirven (Duisburg, Germany), Dirk Geeraerts (Leuven, Belgium), Ronald Geluykens (Oxford, UK), Louis Goossens (Antwerp, Belgium), Barbara Gorayska (Oxford, UK), John Haiman (St. Paul, MN, USA), Bruce W. Hawkins (Normal, IL, USA), Richard Hudson (London, UK), Yoshihiko Ikegami (Tokyo, Japan), Laura A. Janda (Rochester, NY, USA), Robert S. Kirsner (Los Angeles, CA, USA), Tomasz P. Krzeszowski (Gdansk, Poland), Béatrice Lamiroy (Leuven, Belgium), Paul Pauwels (Antwerp, Belgium), Günter Radden (Hamburg, Germany), Gisa Rauh (Wuppertal, Germany), Waltraud Ressel (Göttingen, Germany), Rainer Schulze (Essen, Germany), Hansjakob Seiler (Cologne, Germany), Chris Sinha (Risskov, Denmark), Michael B. Smith (Rochester, MI, USA), Pierre Swiggers (Leuven, Belgium), John R. Taylor (Johannesburg, South Africa), Mark Turner (Chicago, IL, USA), Frank Van Eynde (Leuven, Belgium), Willy Van Langendonck (Leuven, Belgium), Johan Vanparys (Namur, Belgium) and Anna Wierzbicka (Canberra, Australia). Whatever merit the volume as a whole is found to have in the eyes of its readers will have been due in no small measure to the expertise of these scholars.

Richard A. Geiger   Brygida Rudzka-Ostyn
Göttingen, Germany   Leuven, Belgium

List of contributors

Geert ADRIAENS
Department of Linguistics
University of Leuven
Leuven, Belgium

Eugene H. CASAD
Summer Institute of Linguistics
Tucson, Arizona, USA

Haruko Minegishi COOK
Department of East Asian Languages & Literatures
University of Hawaii at Manoa
Honolulu, Hawaii, USA

Kenneth W. COOK
English Foundations Program
Hawaii Pacific University
Honolulu, Hawaii, USA

Dirk GEERAERTS
Department of Linguistics
University of Leuven
Leuven, Belgium

Richard A. GEIGER
Department of English/Linguistics
University of Göttingen
Göttingen, Germany

Ronald GELUYKENS
The Queen's College
Oxford University
Oxford, UK

Yoshihiko IKEGAMI
Department of Foreign Languages
College of Arts and Sciences
University of Tokyo
Tokyo, Japan

Theo A. J. M. JANSSEN
Department of Linguistics
Free University of Amsterdam
Amsterdam, The Netherlands

Robert S. KIRSNER
Department of Germanic Languages
University of California at Los Angeles
Los Angeles, California, USA

Zoltán KÖVECSES
Department of American Studies
Eötvös Loránd University
Budapest, Hungary

Tomasz P. KRZESZOWSKI
Institute of English
University of Gdansk
Gdansk-Oliwa, Poland

Béatrice LAMIROY
Department of Linguistics
University of Leuven
Leuven, Belgium

Gerda E. LAUERBACH
Institute of English and American Studies
University of Frankfurt
Frankfurt/Main, Germany

John NEWMAN
Department of Modern Languages
Massey University
Palmerston North, New Zealand

Yoshiki NISHIMURA
Jissen Women's University
Tokyo, Japan

Wolf PAPROTTÉ
Department of Linguistics
University of Münster
Münster, Germany

Paul PAUWELS
Department of English
Catholic Flemish Institute of Higher Education
Antwerp, Belgium

Brygida RUDZKA-OSTYN
Department of Linguistics
University of Leuven
Leuven, Belgium

Rainer SCHULZE
Department of Literature and Linguistics
University of Essen
Essen, Germany

Hansjakob SEILER
UNITYP Research Group
University of Cologne
Cologne, Germany

Anne-Marie SIMON-VANDENBERGEN
Department of Linguistics
University of Ghent
Ghent, Belgium

Chris SINHA
Institute of Psychology
University of Aarhus
Risskov, Denmark

Michael B. SMITH
Department of Linguistics
Oakland University
Rochester, Michigan, USA

Pierre SWIGGERS
Department of Linguistics
University of Leuven
Leuven, Belgium

Elżbieta TABAKOWSKA
Institute of English
Jagiellonian University
Cracow, Poland

John R. TAYLOR
Department of Linguistics
University of the Witwatersrand
Johannesburg, South Africa

Savas L. TSOHATZIDIS
Department of Linguistics
Aristotelian University
Thessaloniki, Greece

Mark TURNER
Department of English
University of Chicago
Chicago, Illinois, USA

Anna WIERZBICKA
Department of Linguistics
Australian National University
Canberra, Australia

Introduction

Brygida Rudzka-Ostyn

The picture that we get of recent cognitive-linguistic research is one of great diversity with respect to the analytical tools used, the points emphasized, and the perspectives adopted.* What lends coherence to this research and justifies our talking about the "cognitive paradigm" is a set of common views on language and cognition which depart from those advocated within other paradigms.[1] Here are some of these views in a nutshell, along with a few basic findings:

- as one domain of human cognition, language is intimately linked with other cognitive domains and as such mirrors the interplay of psychological, cultural, social, ecological, and other factors; thus, a fuller understanding of this linkage cannot be effected without interdisciplinary research;
- linguistic structure depends on (and itself influences) conceptualization, the latter being conditioned by our experience of ourselves, the external world and our relation to that world;
- language units are subject to categorization which commonly gives rise to prototype-based networks; much of it critically involves metaphor and metonymy;
- grammar is motivated by semantic considerations;
- the meaning of a linguistic unit is a conceptual structure conventionally associated with this unit; an essential aspect of it is imagistic, i.e. relating to the particular mental construal (favored over other possible construals) of the given situation or object; these and other factors indicate that meanings are language-specific, not universal;
- meanings can be characterized with respect to relevant knowledge structures (variously labelled as "conceptual domains", "scenes", "folk models", or "cognitive models"); in terms of the figure-ground opposition, these knowledge structures provide the conceptual ground against which meanings receive figure-like prominence;

- given the interaction among language subcomponents as well as the interaction between language and other domains of cognition, the various autonomy theses and dichotomies proposed in the linguistic literature have to be abandoned; a strict separation of syntax, morphology and lexicon is untenable; furthermore, it is impossible to separate linguistic knowledge from extra-linguistic knowledge.

These views find varying implementation within the diverse cognitive-linguistic approaches. The present volume is representative inasmuch as it reflects not only points of convergence but also differences. The particular proposals made by George Lakoff, Ronald Langacker, Leonard Talmy, Anna Wierzbicka, Charles Fillmore, or Gilles Fauconnier are all present. An enriching dimension is added by appealing to theories developed within other cognitive disciplines.

While sharing the concerns and expectations of other cognitively-oriented linguists, the contributors to *Conceptualizations and mental processing in language* raise a number of fundamental issues, stake out territories for further research, identify the challenges posed by familiar data, and test the cognitive framework's explanatory power by applying it to a wide range of language phenomena. The following sections of the Introduction will present some of the contributors' main claims and findings and relate them to research carried out elsewhere.

The material brought together in this volume intersects along several parameters and might easily have been arranged differently. The present arrangement was chosen in order to highlight the great variety of problems treated as well as different perspectives adopted and different conclusions drawn. Part I takes up a number of general issues both theoretical and methodological. Note that the emphasis on theory is not absent in other sections of the book, but there the focus is more on specific types of problems. Thus, Part II concentrates, on the one hand, on questions related to mental representation, sense and reference and, on the other, on problems of metaphorization. Part III explores lexico-syntactic phenomena in different languages, confining itself usually to the word or sentence level. A discourse perspective is adopted in most of the contributions of Part IV, where, in addition, cross-language and cross-culture considerations play an important role.

**Part I: The cognitive paradigm:
Goals, frameworks, implications**

In the context of the many trends and orientations characteristic of pre-sent-day linguistics, it is important to ask ourselves some basic questions concerning the status and the ultimate goals of linguistic research. What is or should be its primary domain? What are our main purposes in ap-proaching this domain? Which of the different methods and tools pro-posed offer serious potential for achieving them? Given our commit-ment to interdisciplinarity, what are the implications of our findings for other disciplines? And how do their insights relate to ours? Although not absent in the remaining sections of the volume, these questions re-ceive special prominence in Part I.

In her article on the "alphabet" of human thoughts, Anna Wierzbicka raises several fundamental issues, reminding us that the proper domain of linguistics is, in the first place, the study of languages, and the various methods and theoretical constructs we devise should be evaluated in the light of "the results they produce in actually describing languages". But what is language? "Essentially a tool for expressing meaning", Wierzbicka assures us, forcing us to reflect on the nature of meanings encoded by different languages and on the properties required of a framework within which they can adequately be described.

Meanings are found to be, by and large, language-specific, and the analytical tools she proposes are the outcome of a wide-scale empirical search for conceptual primes out of which all other concepts arise and in terms of which all complex meanings can be defined. This search has yielded about a dozen universally valid concepts and a few whose validity is still being tested. The semantic metalanguage based on the universal concepts already identified offers a language-independent, culture-free, and self-explanatory framework for the description and comparison of all natural languages,[2] and as such can render great ser-vice to other human sciences as well. Yet it is not only first-hand infor-mation about this metalanguage that the reader receives in the course of the discussion. Ever quick to diagnose fallacies and abuses, Wierzbicka also brings our attention to the peculiar mixture of dogma-tism and cavalierism which occasionally creeps into our treatment of the notion of family resemblance and of the "fuzziness" of human thought and language.

Other issues of a foundational nature are brought into focus by Dirk Geeraerts' contribution. His concern is with the epistemological posi-tion of Cognitive Semantics. To define this position, Geeraerts juxtaposes Cognitive Semantics with Continental non-analytical philosophies of mind and knowledge. From this perspective, it becomes clear that, in addition to experientialism (Lakoff 1987), the epistemological position of Cognitive Semantics also embraces paradigmatism (Geeraerts 1985). Experientialism and paradigmatism are complementary in that the former accounts for the grounding of language in human experience in and of the world, whereas the latter handles the "expectational nature" of language categories as reflected in their prototypical structure. Put somewhat differently, paradigmatism accounts for the interpretation and acquisition of what is new and as yet not fully grasped in terms of existing concepts and categories. It is due to this complementariness that Cognitive Semantics overcomes the post-Cartesian empiricist-rationalist split.

Setting Cognitive Semantics against philosophical epistemology brings to light interesting affinities between the former and the phenomenological orientation in philosophy (consider e.g. Merleau-Ponty's emphasis on the embodiment of consciousness) and undermines certain basic views held by post-structuralists, including Derrida's denial of the epistemological role of the human subject. The big challenge posed by Geeraerts' investigation involves, among other things, a psychological verification of the epistemological position emerging from the confrontation of linguistics with philosophy.

Not only interdisciplinarity, intradisciplinary crossing of boundaries between alternative theories, too, can be enriching and illuminating. Such cross-theory work is undertaken by Robert Kirsner, who contrasts Cognitive Grammar with the Columbia School framework. The ensuing discussion concentrates on problems of semantics, specifically on the way language users are assumed to infer messages from meanings. Unlike Cognitive Grammar, which stresses a "bleaching view of communication", in which literally inappropriate meanings can be used metaphorically and details irrelevant to the intended message disregarded, the Columbia School emphasizes a "fill-in view of communication". According to the latter, linguistic meanings are no more than "imprecise hints" from which concrete messages can be gleaned by inferring the relevant information via contextual clues both linguistic and extralinguistic.

An analysis of the Dutch demonstratives brings out the weaknesses of each of the two approaches. In the first place, it questions the adequacy of the Columbia School treatment of meaning as purely directional or instructional. Serious doubts also arise about the status of strategies, i.e. conventionalized associations of meanings with particular messages. When the Cognitive Grammar framework is adopted, Kirsner's analysis raises questions about the somewhat uncontrolled appeal to conceptual metaphors, the criteria by which cognitive domains can be identified, and the non-uniqueness exhibited by descriptions relying on this framework. Moreover, from the Columbia School vantage point, cognitive grammarians pay insufficient attention to the discourse mechanisms involved in the communicative use of meanings. While this last challenge is already being met (see the contributions to Part IV), it remains to be seen which of the others are real challenges.

Speaking of challenges, few notions have inspired more research than that of prototype, which comes as no surprise given its manifestations in various domains. Corrigan, Eckman & Noonan (1989), Geeraerts (1989), Taylor (1989) and Tsohatzidis (1990), to mention only some of the more recent publications, all bear witness to the continued attraction of this phenomenon. However, in Hansjakob Seiler's opinion, we have not yet arrived at a truly comprehensive theory of prototypes. His contribution to this volume presents an attempt in this direction. Seiler's proposal is particularly promising as it integrates research on prototypicality with research on language universals and language typology. Central to his theory of prototypes is the notion of "function", i.e. the relation between universal concepts arrived at by abduction, and language-specific meanings arrived at by inductive generalization. A prototype is here considered to be the result of the language user's mental operations, specifically of those operations that optimize a function. It is in the prototype that the optimal values of the parameters defining the given category converge. As his discussion of prototypization in phonology, morphosyntax, speech acts, the lexicon, and one universal functional dimension suggests, his integrated approach should allow us to pinpoint the relevant parameters involved in categorization at all levels of linguistic structure. It holds potential, moreover, for a coherent handling of the relationship between conceptualizations and meanings.

Very different problems are taken up by Geert Adriaens in his article on natural language understanding. The perspective adopted here is that of cognitive science as the meeting ground of Artificial Intelligence, psychology and linguistics, and the main question tackled is: How can language use in general and language understanding in particular be accounted for from this broad perspective? Drawing on recent findings in the three disciplines, Adriaens outlines an appropriate framework and formulates the demands that a cognitive-scientific approach to language and language use should meet. Above all, he argues, it must fulfill the requirements of computational realizability and psychological validity.

If one takes these requirements seriously, one is inevitably led to accept the anteriority of process (over structure) thesis and to abandon the notion of "competence" as knowledge of linguistic structure in favor of the notion of "processing competence" as "a set of *processing universals*, strong cognitive constraints on and characteristic of processes active during language *understanding, producing* and *learning*". With respect to language understanding, Adriaens' investigation reveals that it is a "robust, incremental, lexically driven, semantic/pragmatic interactive process". In addition, his study has important implications for linguistic theory in presenting evidence against various autonomy theses, specifically against attempts to construe a syntactic knowledge module independent of semantic/pragmatic considerations.

From a similarly broad interdisciplinary perspective, Wolf Paprotté investigates requirements for the design of a computational lexicon. The main question he asks is: What can the organization and working of man's mental lexicon tell us about these requirements? Underlying this question is the assumption that a computational lexicon can and should be designed as a functional model of the mental one. On the basis of insights from current linguistic and psychological research, Paprotté identifies the properties of the mental lexicon. In addition to sensitivity to contextual clues, they include the ability to learn and expand, to store and activate encyclopedic knowledge structures, to establish interconnections among the manifold entries, and to accommodate linguistic information of all sorts. A computational lexicon that is to simulate the mental lexicon should, Paprotté argues, display all these properties. Unlike researchers who take computer programs as models of human cognition, Paprotté reverses the perspective and thereby opens up new vistas for the construction of such programs.

Another area where cognitive-linguistic research has much to contribute is foreign-language teaching. The advances made in regard to linguistic categorization, its experiential basis and its metaphoric dimension enable designers of teaching materials to arrange them more appropriately and to explain the different uses of linguistic units in a more satisfactory way. If, as psychological experiments indicate,[3] spatial arrangements are so important to the formation of mental images and the latter are critically involved in the processing and retention of knowledge, exploitation of image schemata should provide the learner with powerful memory aids.[4]

The relevance of cognitive-linguistic findings to the teaching of foreign languages is probed in a systematic way by John Taylor. Having identified the peculiar needs of a pedagogical grammar as opposed, for instance, to one meant for professional linguists, Taylor provides a basis against which the usefulness of cognitive-linguistic insights can be assesssed. As follows from the many concrete examples discussed, such insights enable the learner to perceive what motivates the foreign-language system and help him to understand why a given expression or construction is as it is and why it combines with some but not other constructions. Moreover, they unveil for the learner the logic behind idiosyncratic conceptualizations coded in the foreign language.

Part II: Meaning and meaning extension

Questions relating to meaning recur throughout the volume, but in Part II they receive special attention. The first three papers center around problems of mental representation, sense and reference, whereas the last three focus on meaning extension, specifically on the structure and workings of metaphor.

As cognitive-linguistic research into meaning did not start at point zero, questions about its relation to past semantic theories will long be raised.[5] It is certainly legitimate to ask whether there is a way of reconciling Cognitive Semantics, with its emphasis on subjective experience, with aspects of what Lakoff and Johnson identify as objectivist semantics. And if so, with which ones. Can, for instance, Frege's distinction between sense and reference be accommodated? How can, or should, this and other distinctions proposed in the past be approached from an interdisciplinary cognitive perspective?

Such a perspective is adopted by Chris Sinha. Meaning, as Sinha points out, is the sole area where the concerns of the relevant disciplines are bound to meet. Why this should be so becomes evident when we realize that meaning is the dimension which "structures, organizes and is implicated in all aspects of human behavior, human cognition and human language which are the object of studies in the human sciences". An adequate theory of meaning is then of primary importance, but it is precisely in this domain where a crisis has taken place, partly as a result, in Sinha's opinion, of the previous excessive emphasis on formalization without due attention to the "specifically semiotic dimension of human language and human cognition".

To resolve the crisis, Sinha proposes reformulating the concept of "representation". His reformulation stresses its intersubjectivity, its derivative nature and the asymmetry obtaining between representation and signification. Individual mental representations are said to derive from discursive representations, the latter being "articulated upon the world, and not just upon our ideas upon the world". On the basis of this reformulation, Sinha reworks Frege's sense-reference distinction and outlines a new theory of meaning. While supporting Frege's claim about the primacy of sense over reference, this theory departs from Frege's doctrine in that the analysis of sense and reference presented relies heavily on "the completion of conditions upon successful intersubjective action in a discursive context, rather than upon the truth conditions attaching to isolated expressions". Interesting in this context are Kövecses' arguments against Frege's doctrine as well as Geiger's discussion of the many problems arising from the very notion of reference itself.

Concentrating on word meanings, Zoltán Kövecses points out that for many semanticists sense rather than reference is the proper domain of lexical semantics. Sense is thereby assumed to represent the core of a word's meaning, and as such to be more important than connotation. Unlike connotation, sense is also often found to be objective and structured, and therefore capable of being studied in a principled way. When identified with core meaning, sense is said to determine reference.

Taking issue with all of these views, Kövecses argues that the primacy of sense over both reference and connotation is an illusion. In fact, there are good reasons, he feels, for giving up the dichotomies altogether. First, in most cases it is impossible to separate core meaning from residual meaning, i.e. connotation. (See in this connection Krzeszowski's arguments against the denotation-connotation distinction.) Moreover, elements of the so-called "core" often do not reflect objective reality but rather the way human beings understand and conceptualize it, and are thus no less subjective than residual meanings. Finally, as both core and residual meanings are associated with cognitive models, which are highly structured, they can both be subjected to systematic and principled investigation. It is via such models rather than by the core alone that reference is determined. This being the case, semantics should concern itself not with "minimal meaning" but with "full meaning" as embodied by cognitive models.

Problems related specifically to reference are the focus of Richard Geiger's study. In an attempt to systematize current theories of reference assessment (cf. also the papers by Krzeszowski and Pauwels & Simon-Vandenbergen), Geiger proposes a framework for a unified ap-

proach to all reference-related phenomena. Crucial to the framework
are three "metacognitive" parameters: perspective, (degree of) recursiveness, and gradation. Under closer scrutiny, the notion of reference
as the relationship between language and "objective" reality is found to
be inadequate and is rejected in favor of a notion of reference as a relationship "between minds using language or some other semiotic system".

Passing now to meaning extension, one of the focal points of the ever
intensifying research in this area, inspired in large measure by Lakoff
and Johnson, has been the structure and functioning of metaphor.
Without systematizing a great deal, metaphor can be said to be at work
when one domain is structured in terms of another. The correspondences established between such domains give rise to innumerable
metaphoric expressions and, what is more, motivate categorial extension in the field of grammar (see below).

But what does it mean for one domain to be structured in terms of
another? What is or is not preserved in the course of a metaphoric
mapping? What constrains a cross-domain transfer? A number of specific factors facilitating or blocking metaphorization have been suggested by students of metaphor,[6] but what is the superordinate, the
most general constraint? Despite the great attention it has received
from linguists, philosophers and psychologists,[7] this question remains a
vexing one. Recently an answer, first suggested in Lakoff & Turner
(1989), has explicitly been formulated as the "Invariance Hypothesis" in
Lakoff (1989, 1990). This hypothesis claims that "metaphorical mappings preserve the cognitive topology (that is, the image-schema structure) of the source domain" (Lakoff 1990: 54).

Re-examining this claim, Mark Turner argues in this volume that it is
the image-schematic structure of the target domain that matters. This
structure must be preserved, and the image-schematic structure of the
source domain that participates in the mapping must be "consistent
with that preservation". Turner further hypothesizes that the constraint
as formulated by him governs all types of conceptual metaphor. A very
powerful hypothesis, and one that will no doubt inspire further research. Turner himself suggests lines along which the research should
be carried out, pointing to the need for a theory of image schemata,
their origin and their use in the structuring of concepts.

An important component of numerous metaphors and the underlying
schemata relates to values. Some aspects of this component are explored by Tomasz Krzeszowski. Krzeszowski concentrates on preconceptual image schemata, arguing that all such schemata must include

the axiological PLUS-MINUS parameter. In support of this claim hosts of metaphorical expressions, both conventional and novel, are investigated. It is suggested that the axiological parameter lends special dynamism to the use of preconceptual schemata in metaphorization.

The role of values in metaphoric extensions is also explored, from a different angle, by Paul Pauwels and Anne-Marie Simon-Vandenbergen. Focusing on metaphoric projections from the domain of body-parts onto that of linguistic action, the authors attempt to identify the elements which determine a negative or positive value judgment. Among them, an important variable is found to be the presence or absence of control, which leads the authors to suggest a modification to Johnson's schemata. The status of the schemata and their interaction as well as their relation to cognitive domains is further found to be in need of re-examination and specification with greater precision. The very notion of value judgment needs, in the authors' opinion, closer examination, and might best be carried out in a broader pragmatic context including politeness and other culture-bound factors.

It is becoming increasingly clear that metaphor plays a major role in lexical extension, grammaticalization and related processes. Disregarding the complexities involved, we can say that lexical categories grow by "encroaching" on new cognitive domains. Very similar mechanisms are activated in the case of other linguistic categories, morphophonemic, morphological, or syntactic; their development also involves acquisition of new values by extensions into new territories, as studies in this area richly document.

The present volume (in Parts III and IV) offers its own views of the role of metaphor in categorization. Haruko Minegishi Cook points to the *container-participant* schema as a factor sanctioning the extended uses of the Japanese nominal particles *ga* and *wa*. Rainer Schulze notes the role of prototypical figure-ground configurations in the extensions of English *(a)round*. John Newman discusses metaphoric instantiations of the *control* schema as coded by the Mandarin verb *gěi*. Michael Smith traces the working of metaphor in the category of case. And Béatrice Lamiroy and Pierre Swiggers probe the extension of diverse linguistic units into the domain of discourse and mobilization signals. The metaphoric mechanisms behind the evolution of many of the categories discussed in this volume, however, still await detailed examination.[8]

Part III: Lexico-syntactic phenomena

While in the earlier stages cognitively-oriented research concentrated more on the lexicon, now other levels of linguistic structure are coming under scrutiny. One result of this research has been a growing awareness that language is much more complex than some linguists would have us believe. What we once viewed as lexical or grammatical atoms turn out to be whole constellations of elements. To complicate matters further, these constellations interact with each other, giving rise to intricate networks of interconnections and interdependencies.[9] Whether syntactic, morphological or lexical in nature, linguistic units emerge as complex categories repeatedly found to be prototype-based. A fundamental role in establishing many of the interconnections within and across these categories is, as already mentioned, played by metaphor and metonymy.

The papers included in Part III continue this line of research and focus primarily on the structure and functioning of lexical and morphosyntactic units. Grammar is found to be motivated by semantics, including different dimensions of imagery such as the speaker's vantage point, directionality, or the orientation of one entity vis-à-vis another.

In her study, Haruko Minegishi Cook relies on the schematic network model to account for the manifold uses of the Japanese particles *wa* and *ga*. Cook argues convincingly that these uses can be analyzed as instantiations of schemata which in turn instantiate the superordinate *container-participant* schema. The schematic network model enables her not only to describe in a unified manner the otherwise puzzling behavior of *wa* and *ga* but, more importantly, to explain their behavior.

This model is also used by Rainer Schulze, who probes the semantic structure of *(a)round* in its various grammatical realizations. His analysis demonstrates that the variants of *(a)round* are all members of a complex prototype-based category held together by two image schemata. Inherent in each of the schemata is a particular figure-ground configuration which motivates extensions into non-spatial domains. In Schulze's opinion the category's "prototypical core meaning may be identified as the image-schema at the highest level of abstraction, less prototypical meanings may be located at a lower level".

Among the notorious phenomena that find elegant and revelatory solutions within the cognitive framework is the semantics of giving in Mandarin as expressed by the very complex verb *gěi*. As John Newman's investigation indicates, the verb can be used to mean 'give', 'to', 'for the benefit of' and 'to permit' or to mark agents in passive constructions. A case of accidental homonymy? Polysemy, argues Newman. To explain these disparate uses of *gĕi*, he shows how its various senses relate to the frame emerging from the experience of giving and what is associated with it. His study also offers insights into iconic relationships as manifested by the instantiations of the *prior-subsequent* schema and, as already noted, into the mechanisms of metaphorization.

Yoshiki Nishimura tests the descriptive and explanatory potential of cognitive grammar in his research into thematic roles, primarily that of Agent. With regard to English, the investigation reveals that Agent should be treated as a complex category covering "a spectrum with a volitional entity directly effecting an event (the prototypical Agent) at one extreme and an inanimate or abstract entity as ultimate or relevant cause of an event at the other". The situation is very different in Japanese, where only nominals with animate, typically human, referents assume the agentive role. This fact correlates nicely with other restrictions noted which Yoshihiko Ikegami (this volume) attributes to culture-bound differences in conceptualization.

Starting from the assumption that conceptual categorization manifests itself not only via lexical items but also via grammatical units, Michael Smith studies the behavior of the dative and accusative cases in German. The results of his inquiry challenge the view that morphological cases are mere grammatical markers devoid of meaning. His analysis demonstrates that, on the contrary, they form complex networks of interrelated meanings where the more peripheral senses can be viewed as extensions from the prototypical ones. To take the accusative as an example, its prototype "centers on the fundamental conceptual notion of one entity coming into physical contact with another entity". And it is this *contact* image which, like the two images proposed by Schulze for *(a)round*, determines the accusative's extension into more abstract domains.

In Kenneth Cook's study of Samoan, interesting problems arise with respect to the status of *galo* and *lavea* verbs, the former expressing forgetting, understanding and responsibility, and the latter profiling events that affect a terminal participant or the states that result from such events. Cook argues that contrary to what has been claimed, these verbs cannot be subsumed under the common denominator of "stative verbs". Instead, they form two separate classes, which is borne out by their semantic structure and syntactic framing. An important difference between them involves their behavior vis-à-vis the rules of Clitic Placement and Equi. Cook's analysis strongly supports the claim that case marking indicates semantic roles and that phenomena like Clitic

Placement are best captured in terms of such roles rather than in terms of grammatical relations.

Like Kenneth Cook's study, Eugene Casad's research into the Cora verb challenges some current views on case relations, especially those identified as Locative, Path, Source, and Goal. In Cora each of these constitutes a conceptual complex for which the *Directed Path* schema functions as a superordinate category. This schema can be instantiated by both verb stems and verbal prefixes. What is interesting is that the same prefix sequence may be used to indicate either Source, Goal, or Path, which proves that the latter are not "local" cases or case markers. Rather they are best characterized as aspects of the *Directed Path* schema. This schema subsumes no less than six interrelated families of more specific variants, each giving rise to its own network of path-related concepts. The overall network represents what Lakoff (1987) identifies as a "radial" category.

A number of topics for further research emerge from the above studies. To confine ourselves to case relations, future research will have to determine how the facts described by Michael Smith and others relate to other "case" languages as well as to languages devoid of formal case markers. What are, for instance, the correspondences between Nominatives, Accusatives or Datives and the thematic roles identified as Agent, Patient or Goal in languages that do not mark them morphologically? Closely related to the above is the problem of correlations between the conceptual domain to which a given verb pertains and the thematic roles it selects. Moreover, how do case/thematic roles relate to the categories of e.g. subject or object? Another important area involves the evolution of case categories and their formal markers. Why did cases develop the way they did in particular languages? Why did some but not other case markers merge? Coincidence, or a cognitively driven process? Despite all the work already done in this area, many intriguing questions remain.[10]

Part IV: A broader perspective:
Discursive, cross-linguistic, cross-cultural

Although it has concentrated more on the word and sentence levels, cognitively oriented research has not lost sight of the importance of discourse for linguistic analysis. In Chafe (1987), for example, a cognitive model of the information flow in discourse production and comprehension has been presented. Appealing to aspects of this model, Fox and

Thompson (1989, 1990) have explained a number of skewings in the grammar of English relative clauses. The distribution of such clauses is shown to relate to speaker knowledge as it is affected by an ongoing conversational exchange. Cognitive principles relating to the flow of information and the dictates of figure-ground alignment are also at the base of, for instance, word-order phenomena (Penhallurick 1984, Delbecque 1990) and dative shift. With respect to the latter, Thompson (1989) has demonstrated that variations in the rendition of Recipients in English are "determined by considerations of how speakers manage the flow of information". But the principles underlying this management become apparent only when larger pieces of discourse, not just isolated sentences, are taken into account.

Such broader considerations unite the contributions in Part IV. In several of them, the discourse perspective is coupled with a crossing of language boundaries. The first three papers employ, in addition, authentic conversational data.

In the case of numerous grammatical constructions, essential aspects of their semantics cannot be determined unless such data are brought in. Very instructive in this respect is Béatrice Lamiroy and Pierre Swiggers' study of the discourse function of the imperative in Romance languages. A closer look at this function reveals a set of strategies which correlate with appropriate positional patterns whose primary goal is to mobilize interlocutors in a verbal exchange. Like other discourse signals examined by the authors, the imperative is found to have undergone a major functional and categorial shift. It has lost part of its referential and syntactic potential, but at the same time has acquired properties which fit mobilization patterns. These patterns constitute one of the components that a comprehensive theory of speech events will have to take into account. An outline of such a theory is put forward.

An interesting question concerning strategies used in verbal interaction is what constrains them. In addressing this question Gerda Lauerbach states that they are constrained by participants' purposes and the cognitive models conventionally associated with a given type of discourse. To substantiate her claim, she examines two such models - the *disarm* and the *appease* schemata - as they emerge from her data base, and explores their relation to rules of clarity and politeness as well as to face or identity of speaker and hearer. She finds evidence for subconscious or semiconscious conversational routines, which language users generally develop as conventionalized "rhetorical" schemata.

In like manner, Ronald Geluykens uses conversational data to formulate generalizations about the behavior and categorial status of constructions often subsumed under the rubric of "left-dislocations". These constructions are shown to mark the introduction of a new referent for further development as a new discourse topic. Like so many other linguistic structures, left-dislocations form a complex, prototype-based category. What is more, their very functions in discourse can, as Geluykens argues, be described advantageously in terms of prototypical and peripheral values.

A broader context of speech events is also invoked in Savas Tsohatzidis' contribution, though not via textual analyses, since its objective is very different. His concern is with the standard approach to orders and threats as epitomized in Searle & Vanderveken (1985). Taking issue with this approach, Tsohatzidis argues that it is mistaken in treating orders and threats as independent categories of illocutionary acts. The mistake can be corrected, he feels, by distinguishing between foregrounded and backgrounded elements in conceptual organization. Both orders and threats confront the hearer with the same choice situation, but while orders foreground the speaker's directive intention and background everything else, threats bring to the fore the speaker's commissive intention. These findings have wider implications inasmuch as they shed new light on a constraint operating in a very different area, namely in that of disjunctive coordination.

A domain in which context and cotext similarly play an essential role is that of deixis. This domain receives special attention from Robert Kirsner and Theo Janssen. As already pointed out, Kirsner concentrates on demonstratives and uses his discussion as a springboard for raising general theoretical issues, whereas Janssen's concern is mainly with a theory of deixis. By pursuing certain parallels between tenses and demonstratives in Dutch, Janssen shows that they are in fact variants of a single linguistic category. Critical to the analysis of both are three factors: (1) the speaker's vantage point, (2) the salience of the given event/object from the speaker's vantage point, and (3) the speaker's actual vs. disactual referential concern for the event/object.

Assuming that the meaning of a linguistic expression is indicative of how speakers of the given language conceptualize reality, a cross-language analysis should reveal interesting differences in conceptualizations. As attested by many recent studies, the cognitive framework offers useful tools here in the form of e.g. explicitly formulated parameters of scene construal such as vantage point, figure-ground alignment, levels of specificity/schematicity, backgrounding, foregrounding, and others.

Relying on some of these tools, Elżbieta Tabakowska examines the expression of (in)definiteness in English and Polish and the problems it poses for translators. As a conceptual category, (in)definiteness is found to be intimately linked with the parameters of scene construal. While English grammaticalizes these parameters by means of articles, Polish relies on the interaction of all textual components in its expression of definiteness or indefiniteness. Having no articles, it offers the addressee more freedom in terms of the objectification or subjectification of what has been communicated. Interesting questions to be explored in the context of Tabakowska's study would be how the differences noted correlate with other features of the two languages and whether they form a system reflecting deep-seated cultural differences.

The latter question is taken up by Yoshihiko Ikegami, albeit with respect to other types of linguistic structures and languages. Ikegami compares English with Japanese. What distinguishes the two languages is, among other things, the lack of number distinction for nouns in Japanese. This is not a chance property; on the contrary, it can be related to other cases of neutralization characteristic of Japanese, for instance, the blurring of the distinction between the achievement and non-achievement senses of action verbs, a distinction clearly marked in English. Such differences in grammar reflect, in Ikegami's opinion, differences in conceptualization: while English favors the *individuum* schema (which reinforces the figure-ground opposition), Japanese is closer to the *continuum* schema (which blurs the opposition). Underlying these typological differences are cultural differences: in contrast to its Anglo-American counterpart, the Japanese culture stresses the concept of the individual as dissolved in the group and merged with nature.

Culture-bound distinctions also emerge from other studies presented in this volume. Wierzbicka's observations on Russian and Thai as well as the data discussed by Nishimura, Newman and Casad all suggest different cultural contexts. Casad's contribution together with his (1988) study points, moreover, to the ecological conditioning of human conceptualization and its expression in language. To mention just one obvious example, consider the role that the notion *hill* plays in the structure of Cora.

A systematic study integrating all such conditioning will no doubt open up many other areas for cognitively oriented research. In keeping with the spirit of the cognitive paradigm, RESEARCH IS A JOURNEY in which progress is clearly being made by cognitivists. The milestones of that journey which have already been reached should be an inspiration to chart the innumerable intertwining paths toward the still very distant goal of understanding human conceptualization and mental processing in language.

Notes

*	I owe a special word of thanks to Dick Geiger for his very helpful comments and suggestions.
1.	The differences also involve, of course, views on the nature of the linguistic inquiry itself. For discussion of the points of departure from mainstream linguistics see Lakoff (1982, 1987, 1988), Langacker (1982, 1987, 1990a,b), and several articles in Rudzka-Ostyn (1988). It should be noted that the cognitivists' views are compatible with many assumptions underlying e.g. Richard Hudson's Word Grammar and the theories developed by M.A.K. Halliday, Simon Dik, T. Givón, the Columbia School or the Prague School.
2.	Cf. e.g. Wierzbicka (1988).
3.	The relevant experiments are reviewed in Kelly (1985).
4.	For a discussion or exemplifications of the applicability of cognitive-grammar concepts and tools to foreign-language teaching, see Dirven (1989a, 1989b, to appear) and Rudzka, Ostyn & Godin (in press).
5.	See in this connection Geeraerts (1986, 1988), Johnson (1987), Lakoff (1987, 1988), and Swiggers (1988).
6.	Cf. e.g. Kittay & Lehrer (1981), Kittay (1987), Lehrer (1974, 1978, 1983), and Paprotté & Dirven (1985).
7.	Cf. Honeck & Hoffman (1980), Johnson (1981), Kittay (1987), Miall (1982), and Paprotté & Dirven (1985).
8.	Regarding the diachronic dimension, important findings emerge from the work of Claudi and Heine (1986), Heine, Claudi & Hünnemeyer (1990), Nikiforidou (to appear), Sweetser (1988, 1990), and Traugott (1982, 1988, 1990). Claudi, Heine, Sweetser, and Traugott have documented, for instance, the role of metaphor in grammaticalization, that is, the process by which lexical items become grammatical markers. The process involves abstraction and consequent loss of semantic content with a simultaneous acquisition of new values. By appealing to cross-domain metaphorical connections, Sweetser was able to explain a host of otherwise puzzling facts in the area of perception verbs, modality, conjunction and conditionals. Diachronic changes of metaphorical patterns are being investigated by Dirk Geeraerts.
9.	See Schulze & Dirven (1990) for references. An annotated version of this bibliography is in preparation. See also Davidse (in press, to appear), Grondelaers (to appear), and Langacker (1990a, in press).
10.	Some of the problems mentioned will be examined within the framework of the *Case and thematic relations* project launched at Leuven University.

References

Casad, Eugene H.
1988   "Conventionalization of Cora locationals", in: Brygida Rudzka-Ostyn
            (ed.), 345-378.
Chafe, Wallace
1987   "Cognitive constraints on information flow", in: Russell Tomlin (ed.),
            21-51.
Claudi, Ulrike & Bernd Heine
1986   "On the metaphorical base of grammar", *Studies in Language* 10: 297-
            335.
Corrigan, Roberta, Fred Eckman & Michael Noonan (eds.)
1989   *Linguistic categorization.* Amsterdam: Benjamins.
Davidse, Kristin
in press   "Transitivity/ergativity: The Janus-headed grammar of actions and
            events", in: Martin Davies & Louise Ravelli (eds.), *Selected papers
            from the Seventeenth International Systemic Congress.* London: Pinter.
to appear   Categories of experiential grammar. [Ph.D. Dissertation, University of
            Leuven.]
Delbecque, Nicole
1990   "Word order as a reflection of alternate conceptual construals in
            French and Spanish: Similarities and divergencies in adjective
            position", *Cognitive Linguistics* 1: 349-416.
Dirven, René
1989a   "Cognitive linguistics and pedagogic grammar", in: Gottfried
            Graustein & Gerhard Leitner (eds.), *Reference grammars and modern
            linguistic theory.* Tübingen: Niemeyer, 56-75.
to appear   "Grammar as the scaffolding of a community's conceptual world",
            Fremdsprachen Lehren und Lernen.
Dirven, René (ed.)
1989b   *A user's grammar of English.* Frankfurt: Lang.
Eco, Umberto, Marco Santambrogio & Patrizia Violi (eds.)
1988   *Meaning and mental representations.* Bloomington: Indiana University
            Press.
Fox, Barbara & Sandra A. Thompson
1989   "Discourse and cognition: Relative clauses in English conversation".
            Duisburg: L.A.U.D.
Fox, Barbara & Sandra A. Thompson
1990   "A discourse explanation of the grammar of relative clauses in English
            conversation", *Language* 66: 297-316.
Geeraerts, Dirk
1985   *Paradigm and paradox: Explorations into a paradigmatic theory of
            meaning and its epistemological background.* Leuven: Leuven University
            Press.
1986   *Woordbetekenis: Een overzicht van de lexicale semantiek.* Leuven: Acco.
1988   "Cognitive grammar and the history of lexical semantics", in: Brygida
            Rudzka-Ostyn (ed.), 647-677.
Geeraerts, Dirk (ed.)
1989   *Prospects and problems of prototype theory.* Special issue of *Linguistics*
            [27.4.].

Grondelaers, Stefan
  to appear   The semantics of Dutch *er* from a synchronic and diachronic perspective.
Heine, Bernd, Ulrike Claudi & Friederike Hünnemeyer
  1990   From cognition to grammar: Evidence from African languages. [MS.]
Honeck, Richard P. & Robert R. Hoffman (eds.)
  1980   *Cognition and figurative language*. Hillsdale, N.J.: Erlbaum.
Johnson, Mark
  1987   *The body in the mind: The bodily basis of meaning, imagination, and reason*. Chicago: University of Chicago Press.
Johnson, Mark (ed.)
  1981   *Philosophical perspectives on metaphor*. Minneapolis: University of Minnesota Press.
Kelly, Peter
  1985   A dual approach to FL vocabulary learning: The conjoining of listening comprehension and mnemonic practices. [Unpubl. Ph.D. Dissertation, University of Louvain.]
Kittay, Eva F.
  1987   *Metaphor: Its cognitive force and linguistic structure*. Oxford: Oxford University Press.
Kittay, Eva F. & Adrienne Lehrer
  1981   "Semantic fields and the structure of metaphor", *Studies in Language* 5: 31-63.
Lakoff, George
  1982   "Categories: An essay in cognitive linguistics", in: Linguistic Society of Korea (eds.), *Linguistics in the morning calm*. Seoul: Hanshin, 139-193.
  1987   *Women, fire, and dangerous things: What categories reveal about the mind*. Chicago: University of Chicago Press.
  1988   "Cognitive semantics", in: Umberto Eco, Marco Santambrogio & Patrizia Violi (eds.), 119-154.
  1989   "The invariance hypothesis: Do metaphors preserve cognitive topology?" Duisburg: L.A.U.D.
  1990   "The invariance hypothesis: Is abstract reason based on image-schemas?", *Cognitive Linguistics* 1: 39-74.
Lakoff, George & Mark Turner
  1989   *More than cool reason: A field guide to poetic metaphor*. Chicago: University of Chicago Press.
Langacker, Ronald W.
  1982   "Space grammar, analysability, and the English passive", *Language* 58: 22-80.
  1987   *Foundations of cognitive grammar*. Vol. 1: *Theoretical prerequisites*. Stanford: Stanford University Press.
  1990a   *Concept, image, and symbol: The cognitive basis of grammar*. Berlin: Mouton de Gruyter.
  1990b   "The rule controversy: A cognitive grammar perspective", *CRL Newsletter* [Center for Research in Language, UCSD] 4.3: 4-15.
  in press   *Foundations of cognitive grammar*. Vol. 2: *Descriptive application*. Stanford, California: Stanford University Press.
Lehrer, Adrienne
  1974   *Semantic fields and lexical structure*. Amsterdam: North-Holland.
  1978   "Structures of the lexicon and transfer of meaning", *Lingua* 45: 95-123.

1983   *Wine and conversation*. Bloomington: Indiana University Press.
Miall, David S. (ed.)
1982   *Metaphor: Problems and perspectives*. Hassocks, Sussex: Harvester Press.
Nikiforidou, Vassiliki
    to appear   "The meanings of the genitive: A case study in semantic structure and semantic change", *Cognitive Linguistics*.
Paprotté, Wolf & René Dirven (eds.)
1985   *The ubiquity of metaphor: Metaphor in language and thought*. Amsterdam: Benjamins.
Penhallurick, John
1984   "Full-verb inversion in English", *Australian Journal of Linguistics* 4: 33-56.
Rudzka, Brygida, Paul Ostyn & Pierre Godin
in press   *Woordkunst*. Brussels: Plantyn.
Rudzka-Ostyn, Brygida (ed.)
1988   *Topics in cognitive linguistics*. Amsterdam: Benjamins.
Schulze, Rainer & René Dirven
1990   *The non-annotated bibliography of cognitive linguistics: The second update*. Duisburg: L.A.U.D.
Searle, John R. & Daniel Vanderveken
1985   *Foundations of illocutionary logic*. Cambridge: Cambridge University Press.
Sweetser, Eve E.
1988   "Grammaticalization and semantic bleaching", *BLS* 14: 389-405.
1990   *From etymology to pragmatics: Metaphorical and cultural aspects of semantic structure*. Cambridge: Cambridge University Press.
Swiggers, Pierre
1988   "Grammatical categories and human conceptualization: Aristotle and the Modistae", in: Brygida Rudzka-Ostyn (ed.), 621-646.
Taylor, John R.
1989   *Linguistic categorization: Prototypes in linguistic theory*. Oxford: Oxford University Press.
Thompson, Sandra A.
1989   "Information flow and 'Dative Shift' in English discourse". Duisburg: L.A.U.D.
Tomlin, Russell S. (ed.)
1987   *Coherence and grounding in discourse*. Amsterdam: Benjamins.
Traugott, Elizabeth Closs
1982   "From propositional to textual and expressive meanings: Some semantic-pragmatic aspects of grammaticalization", in: Winfred P. Lehmann & Yakov Malkiel (eds.), *Perspectives on historical linguistics*. Amsterdam: Benjamins, 245-271.
1988   "Pragmatic strengthening and grammaticalization", *BLS* 14: 406-416.
1990   "From less to more situated in language: The unidirectionality of semantic change", in: Sylvia Adamson, Vivien Law, Nigel Vincent & Susan Wright (eds.), *Papers from the 5th International Conference on English Historical Linguistics. Cambridge, 6-9 April 1987*. Amsterdam: Benjamins, 497-517.

Part I

The cognitive paradigm:
Goals, frameworks, implications

The alphabet of human thoughts

Anna Wierzbicka

1. Introduction

Over the last thirty years, linguistics has achieved glamour and prestige that it had never dreamed of before. And yet, to quote Langacker (1983: 31), there is an "amazing lack of consensus among serious scholars about the proper characterization of even the simplest or most fundamental linguistic phenomena". As he points out:

> A central reason for these shortcomings is that linguistic theory has been built on inadequate conceptual foundations. Surprisingly, little effort goes into the critical examination of deeply ingrained assumptions; into tracking down the source of apparent dilemmas, which are usually indicative of underlying conceptual confusion; or into cultivating radically new modes of thought that might enable us to break out of some of the circles we seem to keep going around in.

In view of this amazing confusion and lack of consensus it is clearly time to go back to two most basic questions: What is linguistics? And what is language?

Common sense answers to these questions are: firstly, that linguistics is the study of languages; and secondly, that language is a tool for conveying meaning (more precisely, a socially accepted system of vocal signs used for conveying meaning). It is from here that we should start our rethinking of the foundations on which we are going to build.

The hero of Nabokov's (1956) novel *Pnin*, who is a professor of linguistics, defines modern linguistics as "that ascetic fraternity of phonemes, that temple wherein earnest young people are taught not the language itself, but the method of teaching others to teach that method". Paraphrasing this definition (quoted in Haiman 1989), one might say that over the last few decades, mainstream modern linguistics has been focussing not on the study of languages, but on the methods of teaching others to study those methods.

I agree with Langacker that it is time to rethink the conceptual foundations of linguistics. But it is also time to remind ourselves that linguistics is - or should be - the study of languages, not just the study of methods of studying methods of studying languages. The rethinking should not take place in an empirical vacuum. We have to focus on studying languages; and the theoretical frameworks we propose must be assessed against the results they produce - in actually describing languages.

As Langacker (1983: 31) says, "the primary need of linguistics today ... is a conceptual framework ... which permits the unified description of the many facets of language structure that present theories insist on forcing into separate boxes". And it is particularly important (as I have argued elsewhere, cf. Wierzbicka forthcoming) that the preeminence of English in the profession does not result in a unified framework based on unconscious Anglocentric assumptions. The system of description should apply not to one language (English) but to any language.

What we need, then, is a universal framework for the description and comparison of languages; and since a language is, essentially, a tool for expressing meaning, we need a universal framework for the description and comparison of languages as different tools for expressing meaning.

This of course is not to imply that languages differ only in form and that the meanings encoded in them are the same. On the contrary, they are largely - though not entirely - language-specific. What we need, therefore, is a framework in which both the language-specific and the language-independent aspects of meaning can be adequately described.

I have been maintaining for longer than I care to remember that such a framework is available in the natural semantic metalanguage based on a hypothetical set of universal semantic primitives. This metalanguage has already proved itself, I think, as a unified descriptive framework, equally applicable to the lexicon, to morphology, to syntax, and to linguistic pragmatics; it has proved itself in wide-ranging descriptive work which has actually been done, in all these areas, with respect to languages as diverse as English, Russian, Japanese, Chinese, Pitjantjatjara and Ewe.

The crucial feature of this metalanguage is that it is (relatively, at least) language-independent and culture-free in that it is based on concepts demonstrably present in most, if not all, languages of the world.

These universal concepts, that we find in any language we direct our attention to, can be seen as linguistic reflexes of Leibniz's innate ideas, which become activated and developed by experience but which exist latently in our minds to begin with, and which are so clear to us that no explanation can make them any clearer: on the contrary, we interpret all our experience through them. It is on those basic elements that any meaningful description of language must be built. Otherwise, we will only translate unknowns into other unknowns without ever approaching, let alone reaching, any true understanding.

Leibniz (1903: 430) called those ideas with which, he believed, every human being was born, "the alphabet of human thoughts". All complex thoughts - all meanings - arise through different combinations of simple ideas, just as written sentences and written words arise through different combinations of letters from the alphabet. He wrote:

> Although the number of ideas which can be conceived is infinite, it is possible that the number of those which can be conceived by themselves is very small; because an infinite number of anything can be expressed by combining very few elements. On the contrary, it is not only possible but probable, because nature usually tends to achieve as much as possible with as little as possible, that is, to operate in the simplest manner.... The alphabet of human thoughts is the catalogue of those concepts which can be understood by themselves, and by whose combination all our other ideas are formed.

Complex meanings codified in separate words may differ from language to language because each language may choose a different combination of simple ideas to give a separate word to. But "simple ideas", on which human speech and human thought are based, are presumably the same for all people on earth.

The task of discovering the ultimate simples (the "atoms of human thought") was seen by Leibniz as difficult and time-consuming, but by no means impossible. It had to be pursued by trial and error, that is, by sustained, systematic attempts to define as many words as possible, so that one could identify on an empirical basis those concepts which serve as the building blocks from which all others are constructed. The basic guideline in this search was the requirement that the set of simple concepts should contain only those which are truly necessary for defining all the others. Whatever can be defined is conceptually complex and should be defined; whatever cannot be defined (without circularity and without going from simple to complex and from clear to obscure), should not be defined. Only in this way can the true alphabet of human thoughts be discovered. *Reducenda omnia alia ad ea quae sint absolute necessaria ad sententias animi exprimendas* ['All other (expressions) should be reduced to those which are absolutely necessary for expressing the thoughts in our minds'] (Leibniz 1903: 281). If we do not discover this alphabet of necessary concepts which cannot be made clearer by any definitions (*quae nullis definitionibus clariores reddere possunt*, 1903: 435), we can never successfully elucidate meanings conveyed in language, because without this basic tool we will only be able to translate unknowns into other unknowns.

Leibniz (1903: 430) illustrates the need for analysing all complex meanings into components which are self-explanatory with the following comparison. "Suppose I make you a gift of a large sum of money saying that you can collect it from Titius; Titius sends you to Caius; and Caius, to Maevius; if you continue to be sent like this from one person to another you will never receive anything." Definitions and other semantic formulae, which send one from one unknown to another, are like this. It is only by decomposing complex meanings into components which can be regarded as self-explanatory that any true understanding can ever be achieved.

A program similar to Leibniz's was proposed in the 1960s by Andrzej Bogusławski (1966, 1970), who saw in it a possible basis for linguistic semantics. I adopted this program in my own work, and in 1972, on the basis of empirical investigation of several semantic domains in a few European languages, I proposed in my book *Semantic primitives* a first hypothetical list of such elementary human concepts. It included fourteen elements: *I, you, someone, something, this, want, don't want, think, say, imagine, feel, part, world*, and *become*.

Since that time, semantic investigations based on the Leibnizian assumptions have been pursued on a wider empirical basis, extending to a number of non-Indo-European languages (e.g. to the African Tano-Congo language Ewe in the work of Felix Ameka, to Chinese in the work of Hilary Chappell, and to Australian Aboriginal languages in the work of Nicholas Evans, Cliff Goddard, Jean Harkins, Joyce Hudson and David Wilkins). This expansion has prompted the idea that the search for the "alphabet of human thoughts" should be linked - directly and explicitly - with the search for lexical universals, that is, for concepts which have been lexicalized (as separate words or morphemes) in all the languages of the world.

As the empirical basis of the work expanded, and as the theoretical analysis continued over the years, the list of primes originally postulated was revised and expanded. My current hypothesis is that of the fourteen primes posited in 1972 nine are truly valid: *I, you, someone, something, this, want, don't want*, (or: *no*), *say* and *think*. In addition, I would now strongly postulate as valid the following four: *say*, *know*, *where*, and *good*. Other elements which are currently being investigated as possible candidates for inclusion are: *when*, *can*, *like*, *other* (or: *the same*), *kind*, *after*, *do*, *happen*, *bad*, *all*, *because* and *two*. Four older candidates: *part*, *become*, *imagine*, and *world*, are at present regarded as problematic, but have not been definitely abandoned.

I believe that the final identification of the universal set of semantic primitives (that is, of the "alphabet of human thoughts") is an urgent task of linguistic semantics, with vital consequences not only for linguistics but also for cognitive science and for cultural anthropology, as a universal and "culture-free" analytical framework is indispensable for a rigorous analysis and comparison of meanings encoded and conveyed in language.

In 1647 a French philosopher, Père Noël, defined *light* as 'a luminary movement of luminous bodies' - a definition immortalized by Pascal, who used it to show how imperative the use of indefinables was in the study of meaning. Anyone who wants to develop a theory of meaning or a theory of human understanding while ignoring the problem of indefinables is following in the footsteps of Père Noël.

2.   Semantic primitives and lexical universals

2.1.   The search for the primitives

If there is a universal set of human concepts, is it possible to discover what they really are? And if one were faced with several alternative lists of candidates for such concepts, could one determine in a nonarbitrary way which list is most likely to be true?

The spectre of alternative lists, all equally plausible, has often been raised by students of language and thought. Curiously, however, fears of this kind are usually expressed by theorists who have never tried to engage in an empirical search for universal human concepts. Those who have engaged in such a search know that it may be easy to propose some candidates but that it is exceedingly difficult to justify them, and that the danger of several plausible lists is (at least at this stage) a myth.

The challenge consists not in proposing a list of candidates (although even this has been attempted very seldom, and by very few scholars), but in justifying it.

Chomsky (1987: 23), for example, writes: "However surprising the conclusion may be that nature has provided us with an innate stock of concepts, and that the child's task is to discover their labels, the empirical facts appear to leave open few other possibilities." This is correct, I believe: I have been trying to establish it for twenty years. But it is not clear what kind of "empirical facts" Chomsky has in mind. If his "empirical criteria" lead him to the conclusion that English words such as *table*, *chase* or *persuade* (not to mention *bureaucrat* or *carburetor*) stand for innate, universal human concepts, then - whatever those criteria are - they can hardly have much in common with those employed in my own work.

In my research, and in that of my colleagues, there are two independent avenues of empirical evidence: (1) the role a given concept plays in defining other concepts, and (2) the range of languages in which a given concept has been lexicalized. For example, the concept realized in English by the verb *say* is useful for defining, among other things, hundreds of English verbs of speech, such as *ask*, *demand*, *apologize*, *curse*, *scold*, *persuade*, *criticize*, and so on (cf. Wierzbicka 1987a). By contrast, words such as *chase* or *persuade* are not similarly useful in defining other words. Furthermore, the concept realized in English as *say* is known to have its exact semantic equivalents in hundreds of other languages, and in fact there is no known human language which does not have a word expressing this concept. By contrast, English words such as *chase* or *persuade* are highly language-specific, and it is questionable whether they have exact semantic equivalents in any other language, let alone in every other language.

The combination of these two independent criteria - defining power and universality - provides a powerful empirical check on the range of hypotheses which could be put forward on the basis of mere speculation, and gives the program of research defined in this way a strongly empirical character.

When the great seventeenth-century thinkers (above all, Descartes) first formulated the idea that there is an innate stock of human concepts, they offered two criteria for their identification: (1) these concepts must be intuitively clear and self-explanatory; and (2) they must be impossible to define. For example, it was claimed that it is impossible to define the concept of *thinking* (in particular, the concept of *cogito* 'I think'), and any attempt to do so can only lead to greater obscurity and confusion; furthermore, there is no need to define this concept, because its meaning is intuitively clear to us.

However, Descartes' two criteria have proved insufficient as operational guidelines: it is not always clear whether a concept can or cannot be further defined (without circularity and without increased obscurity) and whether a concept is, or is not, as clear and self-explanatory as any human concept can be.

Leibniz added to Descartes' two criteria a third one, which has proved much more helpful as an operational guideline: (3) the requirement that the ultimate "simples" in the alphabet of human thought should be not only clear and indefinable, but also demonstrably active as "building blocks" in the construction of other concepts. It is this third criterion which made Leibniz engage in extensive lexicographic experimentation: to see which concepts have a potential for defining other concepts, one has to try them out in vast numbers of tentative definitions.

In recent linguistic work, we have added two further criteria to the three inherited from the seventeenth century: (4) the requirement that candidates for the status of innate and universal human concepts should "prove themselves" in extensive descriptive work involving many different languages of the world (genetically and culturally distant from one another); and (5) the requirement that the concepts which have "proved themselves" as building blocks in definitions should also prove themselves as lexical universals, that is, as concepts which have their own "names" in all the languages of the world. Of the candidates considered by Leibniz, some (for example *I* and *this*) have proved themselves in this respect, while others (for example *more*) have not.

It should be noted that the criterion of "universal words" (or morphemes) is entirely independent of the criterion of "versatile building blocks", and that there are very few human concepts which can be suspected of satisfying both: in all probability, fewer than two dozen.

Humboldt claimed that all languages revolve, both in grammar and in lexicon, around a small number of universal concepts, which are determined completely *a priori*; and that these concepts "can be sought and really found". But he did not say how they can be found or how one can even start looking for them.

I believe the answer to the basic question of how to start lies in Leibniz's idea of "building blocks" which have to prove themselves in definitions. A plausible set of indefinables which can "generate" all other words (and all the grammatical meanings) of a language can be tentatively established on the basis of any human language (Latin, English, or whatever). But before accepting such a set as a likely "alphabet of human thoughts" we would first have to verify its applicability to other languages. The criterion of "universal words" quickly exposes some weak points of any tentative set of indefinables, and points to the need for revisions. This leads to an amended set of candidates, which can in turn be checked against the requirement of "universal words". The process of adjustments and readjustments may be a long one, but it is a task for decades, not centuries or millennia. Above all, it can be seen as a realistic and realizable goal, not a golden dream to be relegated to the realm of utopia.

2.2. The problem of polysemy

Unlike the search for indefinables, the search for lexical universals may seem to be a purely empirical task: laborious, to be sure, but relatively straightforward. In fact, however, the presence or absence of a word for a given concept cannot be established by any mechanical, checklist method. The search is empirical, but it also necessarily has an analytical dimension. Above all, there is the problem of polysemy. I have postulated *you* and *I* as universal semantic primitives, but what I mean by *you* is *you* SG ('thou'), rather than *you* PL or *you* SG/PL. Yet one does not have to look further than Modern English to find a language which does not seem to have a word for *thou*. To maintain the claim that *thou* is a lexical universal we would have to posit polysemy for the word *you*: (1) you SG, (2) you PL. Initially, this seems an unattractive solution, but I think there are good reasons for accepting it. Polysemy is a fact of life, and basic, everyday words are particularly likely to be polysemous (cf. Zipf 1949). For example, *say* is polysemous between the abstract sense, which ignores the physical medium of expression (e.g. *What did he say in his letter?*; *The fool said in his heart: there is no God*), and the more specific sense, which refers to oral speech only. *Know* is polysemous between the two senses which are distinguished in French as *savoir* and *connaître* or in German as *wissen* and *kennen* (cf. *I know that this is not true* vs. *I know this man*).

It goes without saying that polysemy must never be postulated lightly, and that it has always to be justified on language-internal grounds; but to reject polysemy in a dogmatic and *a priori* fashion is just as foolish as to postulate it without justification. In the case of the English word *you*, I think its polysemy can be justified on the basis of the distinction between the forms *yourself* and *yourselves*; the choice between *yourself* and *yourselves* is determined by the choice between *you* SG and *you* PL (*you must defend yourself* vs. *you must defend yourselves*).

2.3. Semantic equivalence vs. pragmatic equivalence

If there are scholars who - like the ordinary monolingual person - believe that most words in one language have exact semantic equivalents in other languages, there are also those who believe that no words in one language can have exact equivalents in many other languages, let alone in all the languages of the world. For example, they say, there are languages which have no personal pronouns, no words for *you* or *I*. Japanese is sometimes cited as an example of this. This, however, is a fallacy, not a fact. The truth of the matter is that, for cultural reasons, Japanese speakers try to avoid the use of personal pronouns (cf. Barnlund 1975). It is polite not to refer overtly to *you* and *I* in Japanese, and the language has developed a wealth of devices which allow its speakers to avoid such overt reference, without producing any misunderstandings. For example, there are certain verbs in Japanese (so-called honorific verbs) which are never used with respect to the speaker; and there are "humble", self-deprecating verbs which are never used with respect to the addressee; the use of such verbs often sufficiently identifies the person spoken about as to make an overt reference to *you* and *I* unnecessary. But the words for *you* and *I* do exist, and can be used when necessary or desired.

It is also true that many languages, especially South-East Asian languages, have developed a number of elaborate substitutes for *you* and *I*, and that in many circumstances it is more appropriate to use some such substitute than the barest, the most basic pronoun. For example, in a polite conversation in Thai, the use of the basic words for *you* and *I* would sound outrageously crude and inappropriate. Instead, various self-deprecating expressions would be used for *I* and various deferential expressions for *you*. Many of the expressions which stand for *I* refer to the speaker's hair, crown of the head, top of the head, and the like, and many of the expressions which stand for *you* refer to the addressee's feet, soles of the feet, or even to the dust underneath his feet, the idea being that the speaker is putting the most valued and respected part of his own body, the head, at the same level as the lowest, the least honorable part of the addressee's body (cf. Cooke 1968). But this does not mean that Thai has no personal pronouns, no basic words for *you* and *I*.

A language may not make a distinction which would correspond to that between the words *he* and *she*, and in fact many languages, for example Turkish, have just one word for *he* and *she*, undifferentiated for sex. But no known language fails to make a distinction between the speaker and the addressee, i.e. between *you* and *I*.

This does not mean that the range of use of the words for *you* and *I* is the same in all languages. For example, in Thai, the word *chán*, which Thai-English dictionaries gloss as 'I', has a range of use incomparably more narrow than its English equivalent. When used by women, it is restricted to intimates, and it signals a high degree of informality and closeness; when used by men, it signals superiority, rudeness, disrespect (Treerat 1986; Cooke 1968). But since there are no invariant semantic components which could be always attributed to *chán*, other than 'I', the heavy restrictions on its use must be attributed to cultural rather than semantic factors. In a society where references to oneself are in many situations expected to be accompanied by expressions of humility or inferiority, a bare *I* becomes pragmatically marked, and it must be interpreted as either very intimate or very rude. But this pragmatic markedness should not be confused with demonstrable semantic complexity.

Similarly, in Japanese there are many different words corresponding to the English word *you*, none of which has the same range of use as the English word *you*. Nonetheless I would claim that one of these words, *kimi*, can be regarded as a semantic equivalent of *you*. Originally, *kimi* meant 'ruler, sovereign', and presumably conveyed deference or respect, but in current usage no constant and identifiable attitude can be ascribed to this word. "Women use *kimi* only with intimates or those of inferior status, but men use it when speaking to strangers and in any situation" (Russell 1981: 120). This range of use is different from that of *you*, but it can make perfect sense if we assume that in terms of meaning, *kimi* is identical with *you* SG, and that in Japan women are expected to show respect to people of equal or higher status with whom they are not intimate.

The foregoing discussion notwithstanding, the search proposed here is aimed at real semantic universals, not at approximations. For example, the suggestion that the Gidabal dialect of the Bandjalang language in Australia does not have an exact semantic equivalent for the English word *this*, because the nearest Gidabal equivalent, *gaya*, implies "visibility" as well as "thisness" (Brown 1985: 287), represents potentially a serious counter-example to the claim that *this* is a lexical universal. What matters here is not so much that the Gidabal word *gaya* has a range of use somewhat different from that of the English word *this*, but that this difference in use appears to be due to a specifiable semantic difference: 'this' (in English) vs. 'this which I can see' (in Gidabal).

Closer inspection, however, suggests that this particular counter-example is more apparent than real. Crowley's (1978: 72) authoritative study of Bandjalang makes it clear that the so-called "visible" demonstrative is in fact unmarked, and that there is another, marked "invisible" demonstrative. The closest Bandjalang equivalent of *this* does not mean 'this which I can see'; it means simply 'this' (cf. also Holmer 1971).

Differences in the range of use can often be explained in terms of factors other than semantic. But the presence of a specifiable semantic difference could not be reconciled with the claim that the two lexical items have the same meaning. Experience shows, however, that reports concerning alleged semantic differences cannot always be accepted at face value.

2.4. Why aim at a minimal set of primitives?

One last aspect of the search for a plausible set of universal semantic primitives which must be touched upon concerns the size of this set. As George Miller (1978) asked, why should we necessarily pursue a minimal set of hypothetical primitives?

Miller's own answer ("the fewer items we posit, the smaller the chance of error", 1978: 76) makes sense, but I do not think it covers the most important point, namely that only a minimal set of primitives can enable us to account for all the semantic relations which give structure to the lexicon. If a single semantic "molecule" is left unanalyzed, and is allowed to pass for a semantic "atom", the relations between this "molecule" and many other lexical items will be necessarily left unexplained.

A good illustration of the disadvantages of having a large meta-lexicon is provided by Longman's (1978) ambitious *Dictionary of contemporary English*, an innovative dictionary operating with a "controlled" vocabulary of 2,000 words in terms of which all the other words included in the dictionary are defined. Because of the huge number of undefined words, the relations between words such as *request*, *demand*, *order* and *command* are not explained at all (since all these words are included in the set of 2,000). Moreover, the words outside the set of the "basic" 2,000 cannot be satisfactorily defined either, because the large semantic chunks such as *request* or *demand*, operating as indefinables, are too big to be of much use in defining words such as *urge, persuade* or *appeal* (which are not in the basic set). To capture the differences and the similarities among all such verbs we need "small", fine-grained semantic components (such as *want, think* or *say*), not bulky ones (such as *request* or *demand*).

If such fine-grained components are necessary for semantic comparisons within one language, they are ten times more necessary for semantic comparisons across language boundaries. For example, if we want to compare speech act verbs from different languages, we can do so only if we present their meanings as configurations of a small number of simple components such as *want, think* or *know*, not as configurations of a larger number of components some of which would necessarily be quite complex. The point is that relatively complex concepts are usually language-specific. Only very few and very simple concepts have any chance of belonging to the shared lexical core of all languages. For cross-linguistic semantic research we must rely on the shared concepts. The problem before us is how to find any such concepts. Only the trimmest possible set of hypothetical indefinables established within any one language may have any chance at all of having a matching set of semantic equivalents in all other languages of the earth. (I stress the word *semantic* to avoid confusion with absolute equivalents, which we cannot expect to find at all; see 3.3.)

3.   The need for a natural semantic metalanguage

Needless to say, the reader has the right to remain skeptical with respect to all the main tenets advanced here, and to say: I do not know if there are any "universal words"; and even if there are such words, I do not know if there are any indefinable words in terms of which all the other words can be defined; and even if there are such words, I do not know if they can ever be identified; furthermore, even if there is a set of indefinables and defining concepts, and even if there is a set of universal words, I do not know if the former necessarily corresponds to the latter; that is, I do not know if there is a set of concepts which meets both of these criteria at the same time.

In response to such skepticism, however, I would reply that if there were no such set, it would have to be invented: meanings cannot be rigorously described and compared without some kind of culture-free semantic metalanguage.

To explain any meanings we need a set of presumed indefinables; and to explain meanings across language and culture boundaries we need a set of presumed universals. We can understand ourselves to the extent to which we can rely on some concepts which are self-explanatory (*si nihil per se concipitur, nihil omnino concipietur*, Leibniz 1903: 430; that is, 'if nothing can be understood by itself, nothing at all can ever be understood'); and we can understand other languages and other cultures to the extent to which we can rely on shared concepts. To be able to elucidate the meanings encoded in other languages we need a "natural" semantic metalanguage which is maximally universal and maximally self-explanatory.

In the modern linguistic literature, attempts have often been made to represent meaning in terms of various artificial symbols, features, markers, and the like. I believe that such attempts are fundamentally misconceived because all artificial symbols have to be explained, and to explain them we need other symbols, and so on - until we reach the level of symbols which are self-explanatory. (It is again the story of Titius, Caius and Maevius.) Artificial languages are never self-explanatory; an artificial "Featurese" or "Markerese" can never lead us to true understanding, because, as Lewis (1970) put it, "we can know the Markerese translation of an English sentence without knowing the first thing about the meaning of the English sentence". And within natural language, there is also only a small minority of words which can plausibly be regarded as self-explanatory.

Jerry Fodor (1975: 120), one of the main promoters of the use of artificial symbols in semantic analysis, responded to Lewis' remarks in the following way:

> It is ... true that "we can know the Markerese translation of an English sentence without knowing the first thing about the meaning of the English sentence"... But, of course, this will hold for absolutely any semantic theory whatever so long as it is formulated in a symbolic system; and, of course, there is no alternative to so formulating one's theories. We're all in Sweeney's boat; we've all gotta use words when we talk. Since words are not, as it were, self-illuminating like globes on a Christmas tree, there is no way in which a semantic theory can guarantee that a given individual will find its formulae intelligible.

I believe, with Descartes and Leibniz, that there are words which are "self-illuminating like globes on a Christmas tree". But even if there were no such absolutely self-illuminating words, surely it would have to be conceded that some words are more so than others. For example, *person* is more "self-illuminating" than *animate, this* is more so than *deictic, think* more so than *cognition, do* more so than *agency, say* more so than *locutionary* and so on.

Similarly, even if there were no absolutely "universal words", there can be little doubt that some words are "more universal" than others. Whether or not words such as *person, this, think, say, want* or *do* are absolutely universal, they do have their semantic equivalents in countless languages of the world, and they do differ in this respect from words such as *animate, deictic, cognition, locutionary, deontic,* or *agency*. Whether or not we can find a set of concepts which would be truly clear, truly simple, and truly universal, if we want to be able to understand, and to explain, what people say, and what they mean, we must establish a set of words which would be maximally clear, maximally simple, and maximally universal. If we cannot discover an "alphabet of human thoughts", we should construct one.

I believe the best strategy for trying to discover such an "alphabet" (if there is one) is to try to construct one; or rather, to construct a number of successive approximations of such an alphabet and to test them in wide-ranging cross-cultural semantic analysis. The natural semantic metalanguage employed and tested in this and other works by myself and colleagues is based on this assumption.

Any postulated set of universal semantic primitives will readily attract a barrage of counter-examples. The challenge consists in continuing the search until a set is found which will not collapse under their weight. But the evidence cannot be even looked for until there is a hypothetical set of primitives to be tested.

Abstract speculation about semantic primitives can be useful in that it can help to identify some plausible candidates. But a set of plausible candidates constitutes only the starting point of the search. "In any case, a great deal of detailed lexical analysis would be required in order to determine which concepts should be taken as cognitive atoms for building all the others" (Miller 1978: 76).

This echoes Leibniz's (1903: 187) view:

> Les premiers termes indéfinibles ne se peuvent aisement reconnoistre de nous, que comme les nombres premiers: qu'on

ne sçauroit discerner jusqu'icy qu'en essayant la division (par tous les autres qui sont moindres).

[The primary terms, the indefinables, cannot be easily recognized by us except in the way that the primary numbers are: we can only recognize them as such if we try to divide them (by all the smaller ones).]

4.   The limits of translatability

I believe that the past two decades of extensive and wide-ranging lexicographic experimentation conducted by colleagues and myself confirm my initial hypothesis (Wierzbicka 1972) that the stock of elementary human concepts is very restricted, and that in all probability it comprises fewer than two dozen elements. It is possible that the set of "universal words" is somewhat larger. For example, Berlin and Kay (1969) have produced evidence suggesting that all, or nearly all, languages may have words for two basic colors: black and white (or, perhaps, dark and light); and I have argued (in Wierzbicka 1987b; see also 5 below) that all languages appear to have words for *mother* and *father*, which are not indefinable, but which still may be universal. Nonetheless, there can be little doubt that the bulk of the lexicon of any language is, to a greater or lesser degree, language-specific - despite Chomsky's (1987: 48) dogmatic assertion that "the conceptual resources of the lexicon are largely fixed by the language faculty, with only minor variation possible". If by "conceptual resources" is meant the innate "alphabet of human thoughts", then there is no evidence suggesting that there is in this area any cross-linguistic variation whatsoever; if, however, this means the vocabulary as a whole (as Chomsky apparently intends), then cross-linguistic and cross-cultural variation is not minor but colossal - as Leibniz, Humboldt, Sapir, Whorf, Weisgerber, and many other scholars of the past clearly saw, and as fresh empirical evidence constantly confirms. Furthermore, fresh empirical evidence constantly confirms the basic insight that lexical variation reflects cultural differences between different speech communities and thus provides priceless clues to the study of culture and society.

To quote Locke (1959: 480ff):

A moderate skill in different languages will easily satisfy one of the truth of this, it being so obvious to observe a great

store of words in one language which have not any that answer them in another. Which plainly shows that those of one
country, by their customs and manner of life, have found
occasion to make several complex ideas, and given names to
them, which others never collected into specific ideas. This
could not have happened if these species were the steady
workmanship of nature, and not collections made and abstracted by the mind, in order to naming, and for the convenience of communication. The terms of our law, which are
not empty sounds, will hardly find words that answer them in
the Spanish or Italian, no scanty languages; much less, I
think, could any one translate them into the Caribbee or
Westoe tongues: and the versura of the Romans, or corban
of the Jews, have no words in other languages to answer
them; the reason whereof is plain, from what has been said.
Nay, if we look a little more nearly into this matter, and
exactly compare different languages, we shall find that,
though they have words which in translations and
dictionaries are supposed to answer one another, yet there is
scarce one of ten amongst the names of complex ideas,
especially of mixed modes, that stands for the same precise
idea which the word does that in dictionaries it is rendered
by.... These are too sensible proofs to be doubted; and we
shall find this much more so in the names of more abstract
and compounded ideas, such as are the greatest part of those
which make up moral discourses: whose names, when men
come curiously to compare with those they are translated
into, in other languages, they will find very few of them
exactly to correspond in the whole extent of their
significations.

The experience of bilingual people all over the world echoes Locke's
remarks. But monolingual popular opinion often dismisses, or ignores,
the evidence of bilingual witnesses and the insight of keen observers
such as Locke, and follows speculations which are totally at variance
with empirical evidence, as a recent discussion of the concept encapsulated in the Russian word *glasnost* illustrates (*The New Yorker*, March
30, 1987, editorial comments):

> Linguists call the belief that words determine thought
> "linguistic relativism" - or the Whorfian hypothesis. ... most

linguists aren't crazy about the Whorfian hypothesis. It suffers from circular logic, since the only way we English speakers can talk about supposedly untranslatable concepts is to put them into English. The appeal of linguistic relativism in our time ... may involve what the philosopher Karl Popper calls "the myth of the framework": our desire to believe that people who differ from us are beyond the reach of rational discussion, shut off in an imprisoning framework of words and concepts utterly alien to our own.... But, fortunately, *détente*, *freedom*, and *glasnost* are concepts available to all of us. It is not the barriers of language that keep us from applying them.

This passage is conspicuous for its naivety, wishful thinking, and ethnocentrism, betraying a lack of any deep familiarity with languages and cultures other than the writer's own. Empirical study of different languages of the world shows that their lexicons are full of concepts "utterly alien to our own". For example, the Russian words *duša* (roughly 'soul') and *sud'ba* (roughly 'fate'), which I have studied in some recent work (Wierzbicka 1989, to appear) are truly alien to speakers of English. I believe the meanings of these concepts, which are essential to the understanding of Russian culture and Russian national character, can be explained in English, and in the work in question I attempt to do so. But no understanding of such crucial and culture-specific concepts will ever be achieved if it is not grasped at the outset that they are "alien to our own".

But if every language provides its own set of lexicalized concepts, every language suggests its own categorization and its own interpretation of the world; consequently, every language is indeed a different "guide to reality" (cf. Sapir 1949: 162). If most linguists seem nonetheless "not crazy about the Whorfian hypothesis", as *The New Yorker* put it, the reason is not that they have any evidence to the contrary, but that, until recently, tools were lacking which would have made possible a rigorous comparison of conceptual systems embodied in the lexicons of different languages (and, for that matter, in their grammars; cf. Wierzbicka 1988). But the availability of a natural semantic metalanguage, based on presumed lexical universals, makes such a rigorous comparison possible.

Anyone who has undertaken such comparison must conclude, I think, that the lexicons of different languages do indeed suggest different conceptual universes, and that not everything that can be said in one language can be said (without additions and/or subtractions) in another. On the other hand, there are good reasons to believe that every language has words available for the basic human concepts, and that everything that can be expressed at all can be expressed by combining those basic concepts in the right way. In this sense - but only in this sense - anything that can be said in one language can be translated, without a change of meaning, into other languages. Complex and culture-specific concepts such as those encapsulated in the Russian words *duša*, *sud'ba* or *glasnost'* can be defined in terms of the basic concepts, and the definitions can be translated into the English version of the metalanguage, as they can be translated into Japanese, Chinese, Pitjantjatjara, or Ewe versions. Each such version can be regarded as a natural semantic metalanguage, intelligible, in principle, to native speakers of the language in question. Nonetheless, each such version represents a standardized and nonidiomatic metalanguage rather than a natural language in all its richness and idiosyncraticity. This difference between a natural language and a natural semantic metalanguage derived from natural language defines the limits of precise translatability.

As pointed out by Grace (1987: 14), the modern linguistic literature tends to treat the "intertranslatability postulate" as a kind of unquestionable assumption. For example, Grace quotes Lenneberg's statement: "A basic maxim in linguistics is that anything can be expressed in any language." (Cf. also Carroll 1953: 47; Osgood & Sebeok 1954: 13; Searle 1969: 19; Katz 1976: 37.) Grace rejects this basic assumption, and argues instead that a language is shaped by culture, and that "what can be said ... may be quite different from one language-culture system to another". (Cf. also Pawley 1987.)

I agree with Grace on all of these crucial points. I think, however, that he goes too far when he claims that "what is said cannot in any satisfactory way be separated from the way in which it is said" (1987: 10), or that the worlds of meaning associated with different language-culture systems are incommensurable because there is no "common measure" (1987: 7).

The universal alphabet of human thoughts offers such a common measure, and makes different semantic universes associated with different languages commensurable.

It is true that in natural language what can be said cannot be fully separated from the way in which it is said; but in natural semantic metalanguage, the "what" can be separated from the "how". For this reason, the use of the natural semantic metalanguage enables us to compare meanings across language and culture boundaries. In particular, it enables us to show how highly culture-dependent most meanings are.

If every language, has, so to speak, some "one-element words" from the "alphabet of human thoughts", expressing those basic concepts, every language also has a vast repertoire of complex concepts ("many-element words"), which constitute culture-specific configurations of the elementary building blocks, and which provide clues to culture-specific ways of thinking.

I do not claim, needless to say, that the absence of a word in a language proves the absence of the corresponding concept, or the inability to form this concept. But the presence of a word proves the presence of the concept and, moreover, its salience in a given culture; cf. Humboldt (1903-1936, IV: 248):

> From the mess of indeterminate and, as it were, formless thought a word pulls out a certain number of features, connects them, gives them form and colour through the choice of sounds, through a connection with other related words, and through the addition of accidental secondary modifications.

Languages are the best mirror of the human mind (Leibniz 1949: 368), and it is through them, I believe, that we can identify the "alphabet of human thoughts", that is, the basic conceptual framework with which human beings operate. At the same time, languages are the best mirror of human cultures, and it is through the vocabulary, and through the grammar, of human languages that we can discover and identify the culture-specific conceptual configurations characteristic of different peoples of the world.

5. Is human thinking "fuzzy"?

The assurances of universalists notwithstanding, not everything that can be said in Russian can be said in English, or *vice versa*. (*Inye mysli na inom jazyke ne mysljatsja*, 'some thoughts cannot be thought in some languages', wrote the emigré Russian poet Tsvetaeva 1972: 151.) Everything, however, can be translated into the natural semantic metalanguage, in its Russian, English, Pitjantjatjara, or any other natural-language-based versions. The concomitant claim is, of course, that every word (other than the members of the basic "alphabet") can be defined.

The traditional assumption that words can be defined, however, has recently fallen on bad times. Many linguists, philosophers, and psychologists have come to doubt the definability of words and, moreover, are trying to present their pessimism and despair on this score as a new and superior wisdom. For example, Lyons (1981: 56) starts his discussion of the problem with the quotation from *Hamlet*:

To define true madness
What is't but to be nothing else but mad?

and then, after reflecting on the meanings of concrete words such as *table* and *chair*, he comments (1981: 56): "the whole question of definition is far more complex - and a good deal more interesting - than most people realize. Madness it may be to define not only *madness*, but any word at all."

And he concludes (1981: 73f):

we have come finally to the view that most everyday words - words denoting natural and cultural kinds - are necessarily somewhat indeterminate in meaning, and, therefore, for theoretically interesting reasons, undefinable.

The most influential example of a "fuzzy" and "indefinable" concept offered in the literature is no doubt that of *game*, first introduced by Wittgenstein (1953) in a famous passage of his *Philosophical investigations*, and endlessly repeated by other writers, linguists, philosophers, psychologists, and others. Concepts, Wittgenstein argued, are mutually related by "family resemblance". They cannot be given accurate definitions in terms of discrete semantic components; it is impossible to capture the semantic invariant of a concept such as, for example, *game*, because all that different instances share is a vague "family resemblance", not a specifiable set of components.

Wittgenstein's idea of "family resemblance" has played a colossal role in the development of what is called "prototype semantics", and has acquired the status of an almost unchallengeable dogma in the current literature on meaning (cf. e.g. Jackendoff 1983; Baker & Hacker 1980; Rosch & Mervis 1975).

The new slogan "against definitions" is now proclaimed even in the titles of some scholarly publications (cf. e.g. Fodor et al. 1980). A new climate of opinion has emerged in which anyone who tries to define anything at all runs the danger of being seen as an old-fashioned figure, out of touch with his or her times and intellectual currents. To be "with it", a semanticist is expected to talk not about definitions but about family resemblances, prototypes, and the fuzziness of human thought. (Cf. Wierzbicka in press.)

The "modern" view on the subject is, it is assumed, that words cannot be defined because the meaning encoded in human language is essentially "fuzzy", as is human thinking in general. It is sometimes acknowledged that, for "practical reasons" definitions may be necessary, but this "practical task" is regarded as pedestrian, and it is left to lexicographers.

Theoreticians, it is implied, have higher things to attend to. Remarkably, nobody seems to believe that dictionary definitions are good, but to try to improve on them, or to develop methods for doing so, is seen as being neither necessary nor possible; in any case, it is not something that theorists of language and thought should be expected to take an interest in. The task was not deemed unworthy by Leibniz, Spinoza, Hume or Sapir, but it is below the dignity of most language theorists in the second half of the twentieth century.

In this new climate of opinion even those language theorists who do not claim that human thinking is "fuzzy" nonetheless assert confidently that words cannot be adequately defined, and present this discovery as "good news", or at least as something that there is no reason to worry about. For example, Chomsky (1987: 21) writes:

> Anyone who has attempted to define a word precisely knows that this is an extremely difficult matter, involving intricate and complex properties. Ordinary dictionary definitions do not come close to characterising the meaning of words.

That much is certainly true, and uncontroversial. But Chomsky continues:

> The speed and precision of vocabulary acquisition leaves no real alternative to the conclusion that the child somehow has the concepts prior to experience with language, and is basically learning labels for concepts that are already part of his or her conceptual apparatus. This is why dictionary definitions can be sufficient for their purpose though they are so imprecise; the rough approximation suffices, because the basic principles of word meaning (whatever they are) are

known to the dictionary user, as they are to the language learner, independently of any instruction or experience.

But imagine a child (or an immigrant) trying to find out what the word *insinuate* means, and finding in a dictionary (*Webster's new school and office dictionary* 1977) the information that it means 'to hint or suggest indirectly', whereas *to hint* means 'to give a hint', a *hint* is 'a slight indication, an indirect allusion', and an *allusion* is 'an alluding'. Will this language learner - helped by his or her "conceptual apparatus" - know what the word *insinuate* means, and how to use it?

Or consider the following set of dictionary definitions (*OED* 1933):

reprove	'rebuke, deride'
rebuke	'reprove, reprimand, censure authoritatively'
reprimand	'rebuke'
censure	'blame, criticize unfavorably, rebuke'
criticize	'discuss critically, censure'

Can any language learner find out from such "definitions" (again, helped by his or her "conceptual apparatus") what the verbs in question mean, and how they differ from one another?

When it comes to key concepts in distant cultures - such as, for example, *amae* in Japanese, or *liget* in Ilongot, or *toska* in Russian (see Wierzbicka to appear) - the idea that they might be accessible to outsiders "without instruction or experience" must seem even more fanciful; and the suggestion that they do not need adequate definitions, even more unhelpful.

Of course, it may be argued that Chomsky is talking about children acquiring their first language, not about the understanding of other languages and other cultures. But children acquiring the basic vocabulary of their native language do not need dictionaries at all. It is above all second language learners who need dictionaries - and they need good ones, not bad ones.

What is most striking in Chomsky's remarks is the absence of any cross-cultural perspective whatsoever, and the complete disregard for the fact that words differ in meaning across language and culture boundaries. For any language and culture learner, a good dictionary is a tool of prime importance; and it is an odd view for a linguist to take that there is no need to try to improve on the existing dictionaries, however bad they may be, because one can always rely on one's innate conceptual apparatus!

To anyone seriously trying to learn another language and to understand another culture, the "discovery" that words cannot be defined ("for theoretically interesting reasons") can hardly be anything but very bad news. Fortunately, this "news" is not true. As Armstrong, Gleitman and Gleitman (1983: 268) point out, "the only good answer [to the question why so many doubt the validity of the definitional view] is that the definitional theory is difficult to work out in the required detail. No one has succeeded in finding the supposed simplest categories (the features)".

But very few semanticists have actually tried to find the "simplest categories": and among those who did, most looked in the wrong direction, looking indeed for features instead of looking for words. But, as I have argued earlier, what is needed is not some artificial Featurese or Markerese, but a natural semantic metalanguage, derived from natural language, and therefore intuitively intelligible. The reason why "definitions haven't been forthcoming" is that very few linguists have tried to provide them, or to develop a coherent theoretical foundation on which adequate definitions can be based.

Serious lexicographic research, based on rigorous theoretical foundations, is just beginning. The success of this research will depend (among other things) on sustained efforts to establish the basic stock of human concepts - universal semantic primitives - out of which thoughts and complex concepts are constructed and in terms of which all complex concepts, in any language, can be explained. It will also depend on a critical reexamination of the fashionable prejudice that human thinking is "fuzzy" and that meanings cannot be analyzed in an accurate and rigorous way.

It is of course entirely possible, and even likely, that in addition to a universal set of elementary concepts there are also certain universal principles of semantic structure which facilitate the acquisition of meaning. But if there are such principles, they can only be discovered through systematic lexicographical research, on a broad cross-linguistic and cross-cultural basis. This is another reason why linguists should engage in such research, instead of continuing to treat it as unnecessary or unimportant.

6.   "God's truth" and "human understanding"

It is impossible for a human being to study anything - be it cultures, language, animals, or stones - from a totally extra-cultural point of view. As scholars, we remain within a certain culture, and we are inevitably guided by certain principles and certain ideals which we know are not necessarily shared by the entire human race.

We must also rely on certain initial concepts; we cannot start our inquiry in a complete conceptual vacuum. It is important, however, that, as our inquiry proceeds, we try to distinguish what in our conceptual apparatus is determined by the specific features of the culture to which we happen to belong, and what can be justifiably regarded as simply human.

In the past, Western science and philosophy was motivated to a large extent by a desire to find the truth (objective, culture-independent truth, "God's truth"). At the same time, however, it was, and often still is, profoundly ethnocentric. For example, many psychologists (and even many anthropologists) rely uncritically on concepts such as *mind*, *anger*, *fear* or *depression*, regarding them as essential aspects of "human nature", and apparently without ever suspecting that these concepts are culture-specific.

In anthropology, concepts such as *lineal*, *collateral*, *generation*, *descending* and *ascending* are routinely used for the description of kinship vocabulary, and they are often claimed to be not only convenient descriptive tools but parts of the "meaning" intended by the Eskimos, the Tahitians, or the Zulus. Philosophers often rely uncritically on concepts such as *freedom*, *courage*, *justice* or *promise*, without even suspecting that these concepts, too, may be creations of one particular culture (their own). (Cf. e.g. Searle 1979.) Even linguists sometimes assert that certain "simple words" from their native language (e.g. *table*, *chair*, and *persuade*) stand for innate and universal human concepts.

But it is not enough to be aware of the dangers of ethnocentrism. Cultural relativism, too, presents dangers to any pursuit of truth, as well as to scholarly inquiry into language, thought, and culture. Discussing Nietzsche's cultural relativism, Alan Bloom (1987: 204) points out that:

> at the center of his [Nietzsche's] every thought was the question "how is it possible to do what I am doing?" He tried to apply to his own thought the teachings of cultural relativism. This practically nobody else does. For example, Freud says that men are motivated by desire for sex and power, but he did not apply those motives to explain his own science or his own scientific activity.

Trying to explore both the universal and the culture-specific aspects of meaning, we should beware of using concepts provided by our own culture as culture-free analytical tools, but we should also be aware that we do need some such tools. We, too, must ask ourselves: "How is it possible to do what I am doing?"

As human beings, we cannot place ourselves outside all cultures. This does not mean, however, that if we want to study cultures other than our own, all we can do is describe them through the prism of our own culture, and therefore to distort them. We can find a point of view which is universal and culture-independent; but we must look for such a point of view not outside all human cultures (because we cannot place ourselves outside them), but within our own culture, or within any other culture that we are intimately familiar with. To achieve this, we must learn to separate within a culture its idiosyncratic aspects from its universal aspects. We must learn to find "human nature" within every particular culture. This is necessary not only for the purpose of studying "human nature" but also for the purpose of studying the idiosyncratic aspects of any culture that we may be interested in. To study different cultures in their culture-specific features we need a universal perspective; and we need a culture-independent analytical framework. We can find such a framework in universal human concepts, that is in concepts which are inherent in any human language.

If we proceed in this way, we can study any human culture without the danger of distorting it by applying to it a framework alien to it; and we can aim both at describing it "truthfully" and at understanding it.

We cannot understand a distant culture "in its own terms" without understanding it at the same time in our own terms. What we need for real "human understanding" is to find terms which are both "theirs" and "ours". We need to find shared terms; that is, universal human concepts.

There is no conflict between a search for truth, "God's truth", and a search for understanding, "human understanding". The truth about "human understanding" is, I believe, that it is based on a universal, and presumably innate, "alphabet of human thoughts"; and it is this "alphabet of human thoughts" which offers us a key to the understanding of other peoples and other cultures. And also to the understanding of ourselves.

To the portrait of Leibniz

When, like a shy pupil, I delve
Into your calm reflective lines
I know you are with me! I see a stern visage
I clearly hear important precepts.

O Leibniz, o sage, creator of prophetic works
You stood above the world, like the oracles of old
Your age, while praising you, could not grasp your prophecies
And mingled flattery with insane reproach

But without cursing them, concealing yourself from people
And hiding your thoughts in symbols, you instructed them like children
You were the attentive custodian of their childish dreams

And later, a foolish age made fun of you
And for long you awaited your hour of destiny
But now you rise before us, as our Master, our Teacher.

(Valerij Brjusov; poem quoted,
in the Russian original, in Percova 1985)

References

Armstrong, Sharon Lee, Lila Gleitman & Henry Gleitman
    1983   "What some concepts might not be", *Cognition* 13: 263-308.
Baker, G.P. & P.M.S. Hacker
    1980   *Wittgenstein: Understanding and meaning*. Oxford: Blackwell.
Barnlund, Dean C.
    1975   *Public and private self in Japan and the United States: Communicative styles of two cultures*. Tokyo: Simul Press.
Berlin, Brent & Paul Kay
    1969   *Basic color terms: Their universality and evolution*. Berkeley: University of California Press.
Bloom, Alan
    1987   *The closing of the American mind*. New York: Simon and Schuster.
Boas, Franz
    1911   "Introduction". *Handbook of American Indian languages*, vol. 1. Bureau of American Ethnology, *Bulletin* 40: 583.
Bogusławski, Andrzej
    1966   *Semantyczne pojecie liczebnika*. Wrocław: Ossolineum.

1970   "On semantic primitives and meaningfulness", in: Algirdas J. Greimas, Roman Jakobson & M.R. Mayenowa (eds.), 143-152.

Brown, Cecil
1985   "Polysemy, overt marking, and function words", *Language Sciences* 7: 283-332.

Carroll, John B.
1953   *The study of language.* Cambridge: Harvard University Press.

Chomsky, Noam
1987   "Language in a psychological setting", *Sophia Linguistica* (Tokyo) 22: 173.

Concise Oxford dictionary of current English
1976   6th edn., ed. by J.B. Sykes. Oxford: Clarendon Press.

Cooke, Joseph R.
1968   *Pronominal reference in Thai, Burmese, and Vietnamese.* Berkeley: University of California Press.

Crowley, Terry
1978   *The middle Clarence dialects of Bandjalang.* Canberra: Australian Institute of Aboriginal Studies.

Fodor, Jerry A.
1975   *The language of thought.* New York: Thomas Y. Crowell.
Fodor, Jerry A., M.F. Garrett, E.C. Walker & C.H. Parkes
1980   "Against definitions", *Cognition* 8: 263-267.

Grace, George W.
1987   *The linguistic construction of reality.* London: Croom Helm.
Greimas, Algirdas J., Roman Jakobson & M.R. Mayenowa (eds.)
1970   *Sign, language, culture.* (Janua Linguarum, Series Maior, 1.) The Hague: Mouton.

Haiman, John
1989   "Alienation in grammar", *Studies in Language* 13: 129-170.
Halle, Morris, Joan Bresnan & George Miller (eds.)
1978   *Linguistic theory and psychological reality.* Cambridge: MIT Press.

Holmer, Nils M.
1971   *Notes on the Bandjalang dialect spoken at Coraki and Bungawalbin Creek, NSW.* Canberra: Australian Institute of Aboriginal Studies.

Humboldt, Carl Wilhelm von
1903-1936   *Wilhelm von Humboldts Werke,* ed. by Albert Leitzmann. 17 vols. Berlin: B. Behr.

Jackendoff, Ray
1983   *Semantics and cognition.* Cambridge: MIT Press.

Katz, Jerrold J.
1976   "A hypothesis about the uniqueness of natural language", in: Stevan Harnad, Horst Steklis & Jane Lancaster (eds.), *Origins and evolution of language and speech. Annals of the New York Academy of Sciences,* vol. 280.

Langacker, Ronald W.
1983   *Foundations of cognitive grammar.* Bloomington: Indiana University Linguistics Club.

Leibniz, Gottfried Wilhelm
1903   *Opuscules et fragments inédits de Leibniz,* ed. by Louis Couturat. Paris.
[1961]   [Reprint: Hildesheim: Georg Olms.]
1949   *New essays concerning human understanding.* La Salle: Open Court.

Lewis, D.K.
    1970   "General semantics", *Synthese* 22: 18-67.
Locke, John
    1630   *An essay concerning human understanding*, ed. by A.C. Fraser. New
                  York:
    [1954]   Dover.
Longman dictionary of contemporary English
    1978   Ed. by Paul Procter. London: Longman.
Lyons, John
    1981   *Language, meaning and context*. Bungay, Suffolk: Fontana.
Miller, George
    1978   "Semantic relations among words", in: Morris Halle, Joan Bresnan &
                  George A. Miller (eds.), 60-118.
Nabokov, Vladimir
    1956   *Pnin*. New York: Athenaum.
Osgood, Charles E. & Thomas A. Sebeok (eds.)
    1954   "Psycholinguistics: A survey of theory and research problems", *Interna-
                  tional Journal of American Linguistics*, Memoir 10.
Pawley, Andrew
    1987   "Encoding events in Kalam and English", in: Russell S. Tomlin (ed.),
                  329-360.
Percova, N.N.
    1985   *Semantika slova v lingvisticeskoj koncepcij g.v. Lejbnica*. Moscow: In-
                  stitut Russkogo Jazyka AN SSSR.
Rosch, Eleanor & Carolyn B. Mervis
    1975   "Family resemblances: Studies in the internal structure of categories",
                  Cognitive Psychology 7: 573-605.
Russell, H.
    1981   "Second person pronouns in Japanese", *Sophia Linguistica* 8/9: 116-
                  128.
Sapir, Edward
    1949   *Selected writings of Edward Sapir in language, culture and personality*,
                  ed. by David Mandelbaum. Berkeley: University of California Press.
Searle, John R.
    1969   *Speech acts*. Cambridge: Cambridge University Press.
    1979   *Expression and meaning*. Cambridge: Cambridge University Press.
Tomlin, Russell S. (ed.)
    1987   *Coherence and grounding in discourse*. Amsterdam: John Benjamins.
Treerat, Wipa
    1986   The semantics of "I" and "you" in Thai. [Unpublished MS.]
Tsvetaeva, Marina
    1972   *Neizdannye pis'ma*. Paris: Imca Press.
Webster's new school and office dictionary
    1977   New York: World Publishing Co./Crest Books.
Wierzbicka, Anna
    1987a   *English speech act verbs: A semantic dictionary*. Sydney: Academic
                  Press.
    1987b   "Kinship semantics: Lexical universals as a key to psychological real-
                  ity", *Anthropological Linguistics* 29: 131-156.
    1988   *The semantics of grammar*. Amsterdam: John Benjamins.

1989   "Soul and mind: Linguistic evidence for ethnopsychology and cultural history", *American Anthropologist* 91: 41-58.

in press   "Prototypes save: On the uses and abuses of the concept 'prototype' in current linguistics, philosophy and psychology", in: Savas L. Tsohatzidis (ed.), *Meanings and prototypes: Studies in linguistic categorization.* London: Routledge.

to appear   *Semantics, culture and cognition.*

Wittgenstein, Ludwig

1953   *Philosophical investigations.* New York: Macmillan.

Zipf, George K.

1949   *Human behavior and the principle of least effort: An introduction to human ecology.*

[1965]   [Facsimile edition. New York: Hafner.]

Cognitive semantics and the history of philosophical epistemology

Dirk Geeraerts

1. Introduction[*]

In spite of the methodological difficulties that interdisciplinary comparisons inevitably entail, enquiries into the philosophical background of Cognitive Semantics are indispensable for two reasons. First, if cognitive science is ever to become an integrated interdisciplinary enterprise, crossing disciplinary boundaries cannot be avoided. And second, Cognitive Semantics explicitly considers itself to be a general theory of categorization, i.e., a theory whose relevance is not restricted to linguistics. Such a theory cannot escape a confrontation with existing epistemological theories. Specifically, while the best-known definition of the philosophical position of Cognitive Semantics is the experientialist view of George Lakoff and Mark Johnson (Lakoff 1987, Johnson 1987, Lakoff & Johnson 1981), the history of philosophical epistemology may be treated in more detail than has so far been done in the writings of these authors.

Lakoff's discussion of the anti-objectivist epistemological position of Cognitive Semantics concentrates on two periods in the history of Western philosophy. On the one hand, the sources of objectivism are found in the classical philosophy of Aristotle. On the other hand (and much more prominently), there is a confrontation with contemporary objectivist points of view (in particular, such as they may be associated with the tradition of logical semantics). This means that the history of philosophy is only partially covered by the discussion in Lakoff (1987), but of course questions about the objectivity of knowledge have dominated the development of Western philosophy ever since the moment when Descartes began to doubt the scholastic extrapolation of Aristotelian objectivism. The basic Aristotelian point about objectivism (basic also to Lakoff's attack) is the view that cognitive categories faithfully mirror the objective structure of the world; in particular, this objective structure is taken to be a structure of essences. In scholastic philosophy, this view is mostly taken over with a theological twist: on the one hand, the world springs from the divine intellect, its creator, and on the other hand, the human intellect is created by God in His own image. The epistemological ground of our objective knowledge of the world is the fact that the world and the mind are both creations of God: God created both an intelligible universe and the human intellect - and He created them in mutual compatibility, so that the latter can know the former, and the former is knowable to the latter.

Although Descartes did perhaps question the reality of objective knowledge less than the explanatory basis it received in the scholastic extrapolation of the Aristotelian view, his dualistic answer with regard to his own question ("How can certain knowledge be obtained?") soon led to the split between empiricist and rationalist tendencies in philosophy that dominated the epistemological scene for at least three centuries. Lakoff mentions this debate only incidentally (1987: ch.11), both positions being subsumed under the general label of objectivism. From a philosophical point of view, this is unsatisfactory, if only because the nativist, mentalist offshoot of Cartesian dualism also led to extreme subjectivist positions (as in some forms of German idealism, for instance). That is to say, if the split between empiricists and nativists indeed arises from the Cartesian attempt to give knowledge a new methodological underpinning, the philosophical elucidation of the cognitive-semantic rejection of objectivism should, first, make clear how it avoids the split between nativism and empiricism, and second, confront the philosophies that tried to overcome the split in the past. In this respect, I will try to add something to the brief historical remarks in Lakoff (1987) and - more specifically - to those in Johnson (1987: xxv-xxix, xxxvii), where the link of Cognitive Semantics with Kantianism and phenomenology that I will be discussing is succinctly mentioned. At the same time, I will try to broaden the scope of the confrontation with contemporary philosophy by means of a brief discussion of Derrida's position.

Before going any deeper into the matter, two points have to be made. First, the modern philosophical debate about objective knowledge is not restricted to philosophical epistemology. The debate between nativism and empiricism has also become a question of (developmental) psychology. The question "Where does knowledge come from?" not only leads to a quest for the fundamental philosophical preconditions of knowledge, but it also calls for an investigation of the psychological processes by means of which individual cognition develops. It may be sufficient to refer to Fodor's (1981) defence of a downright mentalist nativism to make clear that the debate between empiricism and nativism is indeed still a contemporary

one within developmental psychology. Other psycholinguistic points of
view indicate the same thing. Thus, Kelley and Krueger (1984) have
argued, first, that any prototypical theory of categorization requires a
theory of abstraction, and second, that such a theory of abstraction
inevitably involves the philosophical issues of the nativist/empiricist
debate. That is to say, they suggest (as I do) that there is a link between
classical philosophical issues and current theories of categorization, and
that the point of contact precisely involves the debate between empiricism and rationalism.

Second, Lakoff's position is less simplistically anti-objectivist than
may be suggested by the introductory passage above. His position on
the matter of objectivism is put into relief by his adherence to the
"internal realism" of Putnam (1983),[1] who explicitly tries to get rid of
the post-Cartesian dichotomies such as that between subject and object.
So the point I will be trying to make is *not* that Lakoff's position, which
stresses the anti-objectivist characteristics of Cognitive Semantics,
inevitably leads to extreme subjectivism (this danger is checked by
Putnam's internal realism), but rather that the link between Cognitive
Semantics and experientialism resides in more than the former's
experientialist aspects alone.

2. The Cartesian epistemological split

In a general sense, the post-Cartesian split in philosophical epistemology opposes empiricists of the Anglo-Saxon brand (Locke, Hume,
and the like) and rationalists of the Continental kind (Leibniz, Spinoza,
and others).[2] The basic question that divides the two camps may be
traced to the Cartesian dichotomy of mind and matter. One of the few
things that we may be certain about (i.e., one of the *idées claires et
distinctes* that stand up against critical doubt and that thus form the
basis of true knowledge) is that matter has an extension, whereas the
mind is characterized by the absence of it. So how can the gap between
the two be bridged? How can the human mind, which is so fundamentally distinct from matter that it is its exact opposite, know anything
for certain about matter - to begin with, the extensionality of matter
itself? On one common reading, Descartes' own answer involves an
ironic lapse into the theological superstructure of epistemology that he
himself began to shy away from: the ultimate guarantee for the validity
of our *idées claires et distinctes* is God. Not surprisingly, the post-
Cartesian philosophers tried to push the Cartesian program to a more

consistently untheological kind of epistemology. The two main options are logical opposites: if there is a link between mind and matter to be explained, one can trace the origin of that link to either of the entities. In each case, two things are needed: some cognitive phenomenon that seems safe from an epistemological point of view, and a procedure that takes one from that foundation to less clear cases.

For the empiricists, experience is the basis of all knowledge; sense data are the locus of the interface between mind and matter - with the clear understanding that the mind is passive in its receptive function. Knowledge that is not of an immediately sensorial kind is always indirectly derived from sensory experience by a process of inductive abstraction. A well-known example is Hume's analysis of the emergence of the concept of causality in terms of repeatedly observed sequences of phenomena.

For the rationalists, the basis of knowledge is to be found in ideas that are (like Descartes' *idées claires et distinctes*) beyond doubt, and that, because of their universal character, may be considered innate. Through logical reasoning, further consequences are derived from the basic ideas. Think, for example, of the way in which Spinoza derives his metaphysical system *more geometrico* from an axiomatic basis. It should be made clear, incidentally, that the innate basis of knowledge not only includes "concepts" or "ideas" in the traditional sense (such as, for instance, Descartes' concept of extensionality), but also includes principles of thought, such as the principle of non-contradiction that guides logical reasoning.

In the same way that the epistemological positions of empiricism and rationalism mirror each other, both lead to fundamental problems that are each other's opposites. Not surprisingly, empiricism is marred by problems concerning the origin of abstract thought, whereas rationalism has difficulties ensuring the relationship between thinking and the outside world.

The structure of the empiricist problem (as identified, for instance, by Kant in connection with Hume's logic of induction, and as taken up again by Popper 1963 in the context of the methodology of science) may be rendered in the following way. Moving from sensorial experience to abstract concepts involves seeing similarities; distinct sense data are grouped together in categorial classes on the basis of their similarities. But seeing similarities presupposes a *tertium comparationis*: similar with regard to what? A sense datum x and a sense datum y are not similar as such; as such, sensory experience is just a continuum of sensations in which it would be difficult to identify distinct sense data at all if there were not already principles structuring the substance of sensation - the same principles, obviously, that allow us to see similarities between distinct sense data. Now, it is intuitively appealing to identify these "principles" with some sort of innate ideas, or at least with some sort of innate mental endowment - where else, in fact, would those principles come from, if they are not given in experience? But if an extreme empiricist position denies that there can be such principles, it clearly becomes difficult to move from the level of sensations to that of abstract, generalizing concepts.

Conversely, once it is accepted that there are at least some innate principles of thought (and experience), where is the end to them? From an epistemological point of view, there is no fundamental distinction between having one "innate idea" and having only innate ideas. If you accept that there is at least one case in which you can have certain knowledge that is not based on experience, the fundamental position of experience as the ultimate safeguard of knowledge is implicitly dropped, and the road is open to extreme forms of rationalism in which the experience of the world itself may ultimately be questioned, or at least reduced to the status of an innate idea. This subjectivist tendency is not a necessary development out of a moderate kind of nativism, but the history of philosophy testifies that it is a real danger: think, for instance, of Leibniz's "windowless monads" (isolated egos that are created by God as mirroring the world, but that do not interact directly with it or with each other), or of post-Kantian German idealism (such as Hegel's, in which the objective world is conceived of as an emanation of the Absolute Spirit - albeit an exteriorization that is necessary for the Spirit to achieve self-consciousness).

It is interesting to note that this swing of the pendulum from empiricism towards radical mentalism is not confined to philosophy. In the context of the psychology of concept acquisition, Fodor (1981) has defended a generalized nativism on the basis of an argumentation that is reminiscent of what has just been said. To begin with, he rejects an empiricist model of concept acquisition on the basis of a variant of Popper's criticism with regard to Hume's logic of induction. Empiricist concept formation, Fodor says, takes the form of a process of trial and error in which hypotheses about the content of a specific category are tested. But where do the hypotheses come from? Because deriving them from experience would entail an infinite regress, it is necessary to assume that there is at least something non-experientially given in the mind that allows the inductive process to get started at all. Fodor then argues from this restricted nativism to a generalized nativism in a less traditional way. Because it may be assumed that non-innate, acquired concepts are complex, i.e., that they are ultimately decomposable into primitive concepts (learning them is, so to speak, a process of assembling them from basic concepts), innate, unlearned concepts are typically taken to be unstructured. But psycholinguistic evidence (in particular, Fodor et al. 1980) has shown that such decomposable concepts hardly exist. So, Fodor concludes, the set of primitive, unlearned concepts that constitute the innate structure of the mind is much richer than a restricted kind of nativism assumes.[3]

Fodor's argumentation may be subjected to several kinds of criticism. It may be questioned, for instance, whether the experiments reported on by Fodor and his associates actually prove what Fodor says. The experiments do show that a number of concepts that were often cited by linguists as bona fide examples of compositionality did not exhibit compositionality effects in comprehension tasks - but does the fact that a concept is not understood compositionally mean that it is not acquired compositionally? Might it not just be the case that a category that is learned by assembly becomes so entrenched in our habits of thought that it is later understood holistically? There might be more to say about Fodor (among other things about his discussion of prototypicality), but the important point to be made at the moment is this: Fodor's argumentation illustrates how a restricted form of nativism may open the way towards more radical varieties of mentalism. (See Figure 1.)

3.   The position of Cognitive Semantics

Now where does Cognitive Semantics stand with regard to the debate between empiricists and mentalists summarized in Figure 1? For the sake of the discussion, let us summarize the empiricist position in the statement that experience determines conceptuality (through inductive abstraction, of course). Rationalism, on the other hand, implies the proposition that conceptual knowledge determines experience (for instance, by providing the principles that structure the chaotic mass of sensory data). When seen in the light of these two summary statements, Cognitive Semantics clearly links up with both of them. For one thing, Lakoff's experientialism represents a position with empiricist leanings:

thought is embodied, that is, the structures used to put together our conceptual systems grow out of bodily experience and make sense in terms of it; moreover, the core of our conceptual systems is directly grounded in perception, body movement, and experience of a physical and social character (Lakoff 1987: xiv).

	EMPIRICISM	RATIONALISM
dominating pole of the Cartesian dichotomy	matter	mind
epistemological foundation	experience	innate ideas
secondary process	induction	deduction
basic epistemological problem	whence abstraction?	whence the world?

Figure 1

For another thing, Cognitive Semantics also allows for the formative influence of existing concepts on new experiences. This is the "paradigmatic" aspect of Cognitive Semantics explored in Geeraerts (1985). The basic point here is that the structure of conceptual categories mirrors their epistemological function. In particular, the prototypical organization of semantic categories allows for instances that are more or less deviant with regard to the conceptual center to be incorporated into the category; as such, existing categories appear to function as expectational patterns into which new experiences are fitted, even if they do not conform rigidly to the existing category. The fact that slightly deviant nuances may be developed within a particular concept indicates that conceptual categories are interpretive principles for dealing with the changing conditions of the world. The structural incorporation of slightly deviant nuances under the cover of an existing conceptual model demonstrates the constitutive role of existing knowledge in the process of the acquisition and the development of knowledge. New knowledge takes on its actual form through the integration of new data with extant models. Because new experiences are interpreted in the light of old knowledge, even if they do not conform rigidly to the categories constituting the latter, knowledge works as a self-preserving system that is able to accommodate new information. The paradigmatic structure of knowledge proves that cognition transforms itself, not by merely accumulating new facts, but by incorporating new experiences into the existent cognitive complexes. New knowledge comes about through the interaction of experiences and existing conceptual systems, working as frameworks for the interpretation of those experiences (Geeraerts 1985: 153f; see also Geeraerts 1988b).

This epistemological position is called "paradigmatic", first, in accordance with the etymological meaning of *paradigm* as 'exemplar, example, model': existing concepts are guidelines, principles, indicative examples for interpretive extensions; language indeed appears to be a flexible instrument that does not work in a rigidly deductive way, but that makes use of analogy, global correspondences, vague nuances, metaphorical extensions, and so on. Second, the terminology provides a link with Thomas Kuhn's paradigmatic theory of science (1962): the structure and the epistemological role of scientific paradigms (seen as a set of theories clustered round a number of central assumptions) are similar to those of natural language categories (seen as clusters of conceptual applications concentrated round a prototypical center). Since both have a formative influence with regard to, respectively, new theories and new concepts, prototypical categories may be seen as a reflection, on the microstructural level of individual natural language concepts, of the same "paradigmatic" principles that govern the development of science on the macrostructural level of scientific theories.

Given this double experientialist and paradigmatic interpretation of the epistemological position of Cognitive Semantics, it should first be established that the two interpretations are not in opposition with each other. They need not be incompatible with each other, in fact, if it is taken into account that an individual person's cognitive system has a history: the very flexibility of natural language categories that is highlighted by prototype theory indicates that categories constantly develop. As such, one may postulate that the experientialist aspect of Cognitive Semantics is particularly important in the first stages of conceptual development (when abstract concepts are first being formed), whereas the paradigmatic aspect becomes more important once these abstract concepts are firmly established, and themselves give rise to further extensions. As a brief illustration, note that metaphorical processes may link concrete and abstract domains in both directions. Next to the classical metaphors in which an abstract domain is understood in terms of one that is more directly linked to concrete experience (cf. Lakoff & Johnson 1981 for numerous examples), there are those in which concrete things are understood in terms of abstract schemata. (Suppose x says that y is *a sexual connotation come alive*; the concrete person is then metaphorized in function of a more abstract concept. A similar thing happens in some cases of metonymy: in a case like *Your Majesty*, a concrete person is perspectivized in terms of an abstract property.)

Even more important than the insight that experientialism and paradigmatism are not incompatible is the recognition that together they seem to avoid the philosophical pitfalls of the classical post-Cartesian epistemological debate.

First, the embodiment of thought provides an answer with regard to the question where the principles come from that structure experience: these are given in our corporeal existence. Our being in the world as a living organism itself organizes our experience, and organizes it in a way that is existentially meaningful. Thus, for instance, what we perceive as salient colors is determined by physiological characteristics of the eye; similarly, when our sensory experience takes shape along an all-important vertical axis, this is not because we apply an innate concept of verticality to the raw mass of impressions that we get from the outside world, but because our body itself, being subject to gravitation, structures our visual experience. Contrary to what is suggested by the Cartesian dichotomy of mind and matter, we are not detached pure minds that either passively receive objectively structured impressions from the outside world, or that mould an unstructured mass of raw sensory data by means of innate concepts. Rather, we are primarily bodies, and it is the body that shapes our experience. There is no need for an innate set of abstract concepts if our instrument of perception, the body, itself imposes a meaningful structure upon experience (not in the sense that there is first a raw mass of impressions that is secondarily formatted, but in the sense that any experience is itself inevitably pre-formatted.) Because these experiential structuring principles have an obvious permanence, experience as such is already tinged with a certain amount of abstraction, at least if abstraction is taken to refer to those aspects of knowledge which transcend all that is immediately given.

Second, the paradigmatic flexibility that is a structural characteristic of conceptual categories checks any remaining generalizing idealist tendencies. The fact that conceptual categories continuously evolve indicates that they are not as such innately given, but rather develop through a never-ending experiential interaction with the environment. The formative influence of existing categories with regard to experience can never achieve Hegelian absoluteness, because the very structure of categories reflects a history of continuous adjustments to something outside the concept (which obviously restricts the absoluteness of the concept).[4]

If it can be accepted, then, that Cognitive Semantics is able to transcend the post-Cartesian epistemological dichotomy, it should be remarked, in the first place, that both of the points just mentioned have consequences that go against Fodor's argumentation for innateness. On the one hand, as remarked earlier, Fodor does not take into account the possibility of a developmental perspective (which might, in particular, account for the fact that what is learned compositionally need not be interpreted compositionally), whereas such a developmental perspective is intimately bound up with the paradigmatic view that categories are flexibly evolving entities. Of course, Fodor's theory of maturation introduces some kind of developmental perspective into his nativist view, but such nativist maturation seems to imply the discovery of "full-grown" concepts when the time is ripe, rather than the development of the categories themselves through continuous experiential interaction. On the other hand, as remarked by Kelley and Krueger (1984: 64), Fodor's argument rests at least partly on the assumption that all successive stages in any cognitive process involve only conceptual representations. This assumption is undermined by the recognition that the very embodiment of sensory experience forms the basis for conceptual abstraction. As mentioned before, the structured character of sensory experience introduces a degree of abstraction into experience; as such, Cognitive Semantics is able to link up with Kelley and Krueger's suggestion that abstraction might be at least in part a preconceptual process.

In general, the picture that follows from these two points, involving *abstraction as a developmental process moving from preconceptual to conceptual stages*, is similar to the genetic epistemology of Piaget: it is sufficient to reread the first pages of his *Epistémologie génétique* (1970) to be reminded that his psychogenetic developmental psychology is an explicit attempt to overcome the dualism of empiricism and nativism. This brings us, however, to a second point. The epistemological position here attributed to Cognitive Semantics is as yet only a philosophical point of view, defined against the background of the classical debate between empiricists and rationalists. It is not yet a psychological theory that describes in detail, for instance, how the process of abstraction takes place, or how corporeal predispositions have a formative influence on all aspects of sensory experience. As the focus of this paper is on the philosophical implications of Cognitive Semantics, it may suffice here to note that this philosophical analysis defines a research program for psychology. At the same time, however, note that this introduces an important degree of conditionality into the analysis proposed here. The claim that Cognitive Semantics is able to transcend the dichotomy of empiricism and nativism will ultimately be justified only to the extent that successful theories are developed that provide a psychological elaboration of the epistemological assumptions in question.

4.   The philosophical antecedents of cognitive semantics

Having argued that, epistemologically speaking, Cognitive Semantics may best be characterized as an attempt to avoid the post-Cartesian dichotomy of empiricism and rationalism, we can now address the question whether there are any existing philosophies which have tried to do the same thing and which might thus be said to embody, or at least come near to, the epistemological position of Cognitive Semantics.

The starting point of the discussion should obviously be Kant, who explicitly tried to bring together the philosophical approaches connected with two poles of Cartesian dualism. Kant's thesis that knowledge is not a passive reception of impressions, but that it is nevertheless based on experience, consists of a specific combination of rationalist and empiricist ideas. On the one hand, the basic material of knowledge consists of experiential impressions; on the other hand, knowledge goes further than these impressions, because they are immediately cognitively processed by means of the innate categories of the human mind (such as the relational categories of cause and effect, and of substance and accident). As it is impossible not to apply these categories (of which there are twelve in all), the experiences that we are consciously aware of are already categorially structured.

Against the background of the discussion of the previous paragraphs, it will be clear that Kant's restricted acceptance of nativism does not really block the road towards a generalized idealism. How can we be sure that an external reality corresponds to the experiences that we are conscious of, if these experiences are (partly) created by the action of our own categorial conceptual apparatus? Note that causality cannot be invoked to ensure the existence of an outside world; according to Kant, the categories can only be applied to the mutual relations between specific experiences (such as when causality structures the relationship between the visual experience of rain and the tactile experience of feeling wet), but not to the relationship between experience (as such and as a whole) and what is supposed to lie at the other side of experience (the real world). But if the reality of the external cause of our subjective experience may be doubted, idealism lurks around the corner. It is no surprise, then, that the 19th-century German idealist philosophies that culminate in Hegel are actually derived from an extrapolation of Kantianism.

A new attempt to transcend the Cartesian dualism was clearly called for. The phenomenological approach developed in the beginning of our century by Edmund Husserl specifically tries to overcome the one-sidedness of empiricism and rationalism. On the one hand, the rationalist thesis that the subject has an active role in the construction of knowledge is taken over, and on the other, the empiricist rejection of the autonomy of the mind is accepted. The key concept here is that of *intentionality*. Consciousness, says phenomenology, always implies an intentional relation with the world. The existence of the latter need not be proved; because consciousness is always consciousness of something, the world is given as the correlate of our consciousness of it. At the same time, the human mind is not a passive receiver of the impressions stemming from that outside reality, but has an active role in the constitution of knowledge and experience. Knowing and perceiving are intentional constructions of a cognitive relationship with the world. Contrary to the Kantian conception, the world is not a causal factor *behind* experience, but what presents itself *in* experience. Similarly, the subject is not a passive receptacle for external impressions; it actively goes out to meet the world.

But while this basic standpoint of phenomenology exhibits a fundamental correspondence with the epistemological views that I have attributed to Cognitive Semantics (at least if the concept of intentionality is given a realistic interpretation, as e.g. in De Waelhens 1959), Hussserl's original position also contains the germ of a shift towards idealism that is most markedly present in his *Cartesianische Meditationen* (1929); it induces him to "put between brackets" the objective existence of an outside reality and to maintain as indubitably real only the phenomenal consciousness as such. To put the matter as succinctly as possible, Husserl's idealism results from his attempt to construe philosophy as a "rigid" or "strict" science that might realize the Cartesian ideal of finding an absolute basis for knowledge. In order to find the required first truths, Husserl uses the criterium of "apodictic evidence": an apodictic truth is not only experienced as being true, but as being beyond possible doubt. But the existence of external reality as something that exists on its own, in absolute independence of the subject that experiences it, is not guaranteed by apodictic evidence. In fact,

> Nicht nur daß Einzelerfahrenes die Entwertung als Sinnen-schein erleiden kann, auch der jeweils ganze, einheitlich überschaubare Erfahrungszusammenhang kann sich als Schein erweisen, unter dem Titel *zusammenhängender Traum* (1929: 57).

> [Not just a single, isolated experience can be devalued as illusion, the permanently unitary, internally coherent whole of experiences as well can reveal itself as illusion, under the label of a *coherent dream*.]

But while we may have to abstain from existential statements about the objective existence of what appears in consciousness, we cannot doubt that there is such an appearance. Thus, by replacing the indubitability of the existence of the external world by the indubitability of the phenomenal appearance of the world, the existence of a transcendental consciousness is revealed. To the extent, in fact, that the phenomenal appearance of the world is always an appearance in and for consciousness, the reflecting consciousness that suspends the belief in the objectivity of the appearing world retains itself and its phenomenal contents of experiences and thoughts as a sure foundation.

The development of phenomenology after Husserl has been quite diverse; for one thing, the existentialist interpretation of intentionality in the work of Heidegger, Sartre, Marcel, and others tends to shift the focus from epistemological towards metaphysical, religious, or ethical matters. More important from our point of view is the way in which Merleau-Ponty has tried to avoid the idealistic turn of the later Husserl by a reconsideration of the notion of intentionality. Consider, to begin with, the following statement:

> Dès qu'il y a conscience, et pour qu'il y ait conscience, il faut qu'il y ait un quelque chose dont elle est conscience, un objet intentionnel, et elle ne peut se porter vers cette objet qu'autant qu'elle s'«irréalise» et se jette en lui (Merleau-Ponty 1945: 141).

> [From the moment that there is consciousness, and in order that there be consciousness, there has to be something that it is consciousness of, an intentional object. Consciousness cannot direct itself towards this object if it does not "un-realize" itself (go beyond itself) and throw itself towards it.]

Whereas the first part of the statement might still be compatible with a passive, empiricist conception of consciousness, the second part points towards an active role of the subject in the constitution of knowledge. This active part of the subject is the very essence of intentionality:

> La vie de la conscience ... est sous-tendue par un «arc intentionnel» qui projette autour de nous notre passé, notre avenir, notre milieu humain, notre situation physique, notre situation idéologique, notre situation morale, ou plutôt qui fait que nous soyons situés sous tous ces rapports (Merleau-Ponty 1945: 158).

[The life of consciousness ... is supported by an arc of intentionality that projects around us our past, our future, our
human environment, our physical situation, our ideological
situation, our moral situation, or rather, which ensures that
we occupy a particular position in the light of these perspectives.]

That is to say, consciousness does not consist of passively receiving impressions in the empiricist manner, but is an active encounter with reality in which experience takes shape by an intentional projection of the
subject. Consciousness, in fact, is the capacity "à disposer derrière le
flux des impressions un invariant qui en rende raison et à mettre en
forme la matière de l'expérience" (Merleau-Ponty 1945: 141) [to situate
behind the continuum of impressions something invariant that makes
sense of them and that shapes the substance of experience]. Consciousness, in other words, is a capacity for abstraction, an abstracting activity
that is immediately present in experience itself - just like the position
attributed to Cognitive Semantics in the previous paragraph.

Now the crucial point where Merleau-Ponty goes beyond Husserl is
his analysis of corporality. The intentional relationship between subject
and object, between the individual and the world is situated in the body,
not in the sense that the body is an instrument used by a purely spiritual, disembodied subject in his interaction with the world, but so that
consciousness itself is present in the corporeal experience of the world:
"La conscience est l'être à la chose par l'intermédiaire du corps"
(Merleau-Ponty 1945: 161). [Consciousness is being at the object
through the intermediary of the body.] In painstakingly careful analyses
of different forms and aspects of perception, Merleau-Ponty shows that
consciousness and corporality are inextricably linked in the experience
of the world; the body is "animated" and the mind is "incorporated",
and the two cannot be separated.

It is, then, precisely through his focus on the epistemological role of
the body that Merleau-Ponty tries to counter the idealist tendencies of
the later Husserl. Because our sensory consciousness of the world is
embodied, we do not have complete conscious control of it; and because we do not have complete control of it, an idealist shift towards an
absolute consciousness is out of the question. One premise of this argumentation is that the absoluteness of an idealist transcendental ego
implies a complete transparency of the perceived world (which is then
allegedly constituted entirely by consciousness): "Si ma conscience con-
stituait actuellement le monde qu'elle perçoit, il n'y aurait d'elle à lui

aucune distance et entre eux aucun décalage possible" (Merleau-Ponty 1945: 275). [If my consciousness actually constituted the world that it perceives, there would be no distance between them, no possible gap between the two.]

The other premise is that bodily perception precisely does not exhibit this transparency, in particular because it is never more than a perspective on the world. Because in an act of perception the perceived object is never exhibited in its entirety, perception is characterized by a profound "perspectivism" (1945: 85).[5] The conclusion, then, is obvious: since an idealistic transcendental consciousness would be able to dispense with the imperfect, perspectival nature of perception to begin with, the very existence of perception testifies against idealism:

> Or si le corps propre et le moi empirique ne sont que des éléments dans le système de l'expérience, objets parmi d'autres objets sous le regard du véritable Je, comment pouvons-nous jamais nous confondre avec notre corps, comment avons-nous pu croire que nous vissions de nos yeux ce que nous saisissons en vérité par une inspection de l'esprit, comment le monde n'est-il pas en face de nous parfaitement explicite, enfin comment se fait-il que nous percevions? (Merleau-Ponty 1945: 241)

> [If, in fact, our own body and our empirical ego [the locus of phenomenal appearances, as opposed to the transcendental, reflecting ego - DG] are but elements in the system of experience, objects among other objects perceived by the true Ego, how can we ever confuse ourselves with our bodies, how could we ever believe that we saw with our eyes what we actually grasped intellectually, how come the world does not present itself to us in perfect clarity, how come, finally, we do perceive at all?]

In short, if there is one existing epistemological point of view that comes close to that of Cognitive Semantics, it is probably that of Merleau-Ponty, in general because of his realistic interpretation of the phenomenological concept of intentionality, and more specifically because of the stress he puts on the epistemological role of the body. The first point corresponds with the general attempt of Cognitive Semantics to overcome the classical dualism of empiricism and rationalism, the second more specifically with the experientialist aspect of that attempt. These correspondences are important enough to recognize that the philosophical position of Cognitive Semantics is not a revolutionary novelty within the history of philosophy, but that it has respectable philosophical antecedents. At the same time, the question arises whether there are any aspects of Merleau-Ponty's philosophy that link up with the paradigmatic side of Cognitive Semantics.

It is important to note, in this respect, that while we have so far been concerned mainly with Merleau-Ponty's *Phénoménologie de la perception* of 1945, the later stages of his intellectual development witness a shift towards Saussurean linguistics (most notably in *Signes* and *La prose du monde*).[6] Whereas the early phenomenological movement was not in close contact with contemporary linguistics, Merleau-Ponty's discovery of Saussure stresses the importance of the notion of *parole* rather than *langue* as the contribution of linguistics to a phenomenology of the speaking subject. On the one hand, "structure" is seen as a mediation between subject and object:

> Présente hors de nous dans les systèmes naturels et sociaux et en nous, comme *fonction symbolique*, la structure indique un chemin hors de la corrélation sujet-objet qui domine la philosophie de Descartes à Hegel (Merleau-Ponty 1960: 154).

> [Being present outside of us in natural and social systems, and within us as a symbolical function, the structure indicates a direction away from the correlation between subject and object that dominates philosophy from Descartes to Hegel.]

On the other hand, the act of speech may dynamically change what is given in linguistic and cultural structures:

> La parole, en tant que distincte de la langue, est ce moment où l'intention de signifier encore muette et tout en acte, s'avère capable de s'incorporer à la culture ... en transformant le sens des instruments culturels (Merleau-Ponty 1960: 115).

> [*Parole*, as distinct from *langue*, is the moment when an expressive intention that is as yet merely speechless and in the

making, becomes able to incorporate itself into the culture ...
by changing the meaning of the cultural instruments.]

Together, these points may be seen as a shift towards the paradigmatic part of our analysis of Cognitive Semantics, where existing conceptualizations are seen as flexibly constitutive of experience: like Merleau-Ponty, paradigmatism accepts the mediating role of existing categorizations, and like Merleau-Ponty, these categories are not fixed and immutable structures.

But as structural linguistics stressed the Saussurean concept of *langue* rather than *parole*, the philosophical extrapolations of structuralism that became fashionable in French philosophy in the late 1950s tended to stress the epistemological importance of supra-individual structures at the expense of the active role of the subject. As Merleau-Ponty was not unaware of the danger that the static kind of structuralism that he knew (he died in 1961) presented for his original project of a phenomenology of the speaking subject, there is a tension between his epistemological position and his structuralist allegiancies. It has been suggested by Fontaine-de Visscher (1974) that the Chomskyan introduction of a subjective dynamism into structuralist thought salvages Merleau-Ponty's speaking subject from its structuralist suppression, but it is questionable whether the Chomskyan notion of creativity makes any fundamental difference from a philosophical point of view, since the creative contribution of the subject is restricted to rule-applying rather than rule-changing behavior. Rather, what seems necessary for the incorporation of linguistics into the phenomenological project of Merleau-Ponty is a concept of linguistic structure such as the one put forward by Cognitive Semantics, i.e., one in which the possible transcendence of given possibilities is part and parcel of the structure of concepts itself. (The correspondences between Cognitive Semantics and the views of Merleau-Ponty are summarized in Figure 2.)

5.   Contemporary perspectives

As mentioned in the introduction, an enquiry into the philosophical consequences of Cognitive Semantics should also survey the contemporary philosophical scene beyond analytical philosophy. Valuable though a confrontation with analytical philosophies of mind may be, there is more to contemporary philosophy than that; and specifically, there is more to the contemporary philosophical discussion about language, consciousness, and knowledge. Given that a complete coverage of the field is impossible in the context of this paper, there is at least one influential current in present-day philosophical thought that cannot pass unmentioned, viz. the post-structuralist movement most prominently connected with the name of Jacques Derrida. There are two reasons why a discussion of Derrida is suggested by our discussion of Merleau-Ponty.

	EMPIRICISM	RATIONALISM
reflection in Cognitive Semantics	experientialism	paradigmatism
reflection in the philosophy of Merleau-Ponty	Phénoménologie de la Perception: corporality of experience	Signes: flexibly mediating role of structures

Figure 2

First, the conception of language that underlies the views of Derrida is decidedly structuralist; his extrapolations and amendments of the structuralist views that became fashionable in France in the late 1950s and the first half of the 1960s (and that are perhaps most intimately connected with the anthropological thought of Lévi-Strauss) directly refer to Saussure. In spite of Derrida's denunciation of Saussure's alleged "logocentrism" (his neglect of writing in favor of speech), his own key concept rests crucially on the Saussurean view of language as a system of oppositions. The *différence* that Derrida relentlessly exposes as the origin of all signification is perhaps best thought of (to the extent that the concept can be defined at all) as a general epistemological extrapolation of the distinctiveness, the oppositionality, that is the foundation of linguistic meaning according to Saussure: because each individual member of a symbolic system gets its semantic value only through a set of distinctive oppositions with the other symbols, the existence of such a system of oppositions (and more generally, of an abstract distinctiveness as such) is the fundamental precondition of meaningfulness. But as Derrida's conception of such systems of oppositions has nothing of the static structures of earlier philosophical structuralism, the question arises whether his dynamization of earlier structuralist notions yields precisely that flexible conception of structure that would suit (as argued above) Merleau-Ponty's phenomenology of the speaking subject.

Second, Derrida starts off, just like Merleau-Ponty, with a discussion of the idealist tendencies of Husserl. Specifically, both thinkers try to avoid the idealist dangers inherent in Husserl's later development.[7] Derrida and Merleau-Ponty alike try to avoid an idealistic lapse into an absolute subject, but the course they take is radically different: whereas Merleau-Ponty relativizes the subject by focussing on its embodied nature, Derrida lets the subject evaporate into the *différence* together with its absoluteness. Merleau-Ponty merely points out that there can be no absolute subjects because of their inevitable experiential embodiment; the subject as such, however, retains an epistemological role. Derrida, on the other hand, seems to discard the subject together with its absoluteness: it is the language that talks through the individual, rather than the reverse. (Given that symbolic structures thus acquire absolute epistemological primacy, one could say that Derrida's is an idealism without subjects. Whereas classical idealism is characterized by a vigorous logocentrism (in the sense, this time, of a focus on the mind), structuralist idealism may be characterized as textuocentrism. The basic locus of knowledge is not subjects, but languages and texts.[8] If it is correct, in short, that there is a connection between Cognitive Semantics and a philosophical position à la Merleau-Ponty, it may also be surmised that Cognitive Semantics contains characteristics that go against the grain of Derrida's views.

In this respect, the following three theses may be put forward as topics for a thoroughgoing investigation into the relationship between Derrida and Cognitive Semantics.[9]

In the first place, *Cognitive Semantics rehabilitates the epistemological function of individual entities within a structure against that of the oppositional system of distinctions among those entities.* While philosophical structuralism posits that the value of individual signs within a system derives from the system of oppositions in which they partake, prototype theory will say that the set of oppositions depends on the significative content of the individual signs.[10] This relates, of course, to the paradigmatic part of Cognitive Semantics: new contents are, so to speak, attracted by existing ones; their position within the language is not determined primarily by the existing set of distinctive oppositions, but by the way in which they orbit into the sphere of existing categories. Thus, the internal structure of lexical concepts itself reveals their epistemological importance, and this paradigmatic importance of individual categories casts doubts on the structuralist primacy of distinctive structures.

In the second place, *Cognitive Semantics rehabilitates the epistemological role of the individual subject against that of the linguistic code.* The experiential side of Cognitive Semantics heralds the return of the vanishing individual into epistemology. Because Cognitive Semantics can demonstrate that linguistic meaning is experientially grounded, the subject and its individual experience reappears as an active epistemological entity: the construction of meaningfulness appears to depend on individual factors as well, and not just on the structure of the language as an abstract, supra-individual entity.

In the third place, *Cognitive Semantics rehabilitates the notion of "preferred interpretation" against the "disseminating free play of interpretations".* The potential infinity of interpretations that Derrida mentions as an argument for the primacy of the language over the communicative intentions of the language user is in practice constrained by the prototypical structure of linguistic categories. Derrida points out that language users are never in full possession of (never have full control over) the message they emit, because the semantic structure of the language always allows for interpretations other than the one intended by the sender of the message. Now, while the dynamic flexibility of prototypical categories does indeed demonstrate the interpretive potential of linguistic categories, it also constrains the set of possible interpretations, as these are required to link up with existing concepts. Interpretation does not go wild (except in deliberate efforts such as those of some of Derrida's Yale followers) because speaker and hearer share a system of preferential interpretations that also constrains the form deviant readings may take. The theoretically important point is that this restrictive preferential pattern shows up in the structure of language itself (viz. in prototypicality). It would therefore be wrong to stress only the potentially infinite set of interpretations that languages allow: the interpretive constraints that lie at the basis of mutual understanding are *also* part of the structure of language.

6. Overview

By way of a summary, let us enumerate the main propositions that have been put forward in the foregoing pages. *First*, the historical elucidation of the philosophical position implied by Cognitive Semantics can be made more detailed than is done in Lakoff (1987) or Johnson (1987). Specifically, any philosophical discussion of objectivism should include an explicit consideration of the post-Cartesian debate between empiricism and rationalism. *Second*, the epistemological position of Cognitive Semantics cannot be defined only in terms of the experientialism described in Lakoff (1987), but should also take into account the paradigmatism explored in Geeraerts (1985). While the former deals with the embodiment of language, the latter takes care of the expectational nature of natural language categories that is reflected in their prototypical characteristics. *Third*, because experientialism and paradigmatism together define a mutual cognitive determination of objective and subjective factors, Cognitive Semantics is able to transcend the post-Cartesian dichotomy of empiricism and rationalism. On the one hand, experientialism demonstrates how experiential factors shape the structure of cognition; on the other hand, paradigmatism points out how existing conceptualizations may influence the interpretation of new experiences. *Fourth*, by transcending the classical epistemological dichotomy, Cognitive Semantics links up with the phenomenological movement inaugurated by Husserl. More specifically, it finds a close philosophical antecedent in Merleau-Ponty, both because of his realistic interpretation of the phenomenological concept of intentionality and because of his highlighting of the embodied nature of consciousness. *Fifth*, Cognitive Semantics casts doubts on some of the basic assumptions of post-structuralist philosophy. Specifically, the absolute epistemological primacy of linguistic structures (seen as a set of distinctive oppositions) is difficult to maintain, given the fact that the structure of the language itself reflects the epistemological importance of individual experience and individual categories. And *sixth*, the philosophical enquiry into Cognitive Semantics attempted here should be supplemented with the development of a corresponding psychological theory. Among other things, such a psychological elaboration should contain a theory of abstraction as a process moving from preconceptual to conceptual stages.

The latter remark is, to be sure, all-important. Even apart from the fact that the succinctness of the discussion in this paper calls for a certain amount of caution, it is vital to notice that what I have offered here is merely an attempt to define the philosophical position of Cognitive Semantics against the background of continental, non-analytical philosophies of mind and knowledge. The discussion may be considered adequate, that is, to the extent that it faithfully renders the philosophical points of view under consideration, and adequately elucidates the epistemological implications of Cognitive Semantics. But that does not make it necessarily true: establishing a basic correspondence between two conceptual edifices adds to their interest, but does not necessarily *prove* the correctness of either of them. Apart from the specific methodological criteria that apply to Cognitive Semantics as a linguistic discipline, its epistemological extrapolation cannot be confined to philosophical speculation, but calls for psychological verification. I would argue, then, that there are two kinds of research to be conducted alongside the development of Cognitive Semantics as a linguistic form of investigation: one in which the philosophical consequences of the linguistic findings are explored against the background of classical and contemporary philosophical debates, and another that psychologically tests the epistemological position that may be derived from this philosophical extrapolation.

Notes

*   The present paper has taken up again the philosophical topics of Geeraerts (1985); there is a shift of emphasis with regard to my previous treatment of the matter, in the sense that the paper contains a confrontation with the experientialism of George Lakoff and Mark Johnson. For comments and suggestions with regard to an earlier version, my thanks go to Bart Geurts, George Lakoff, Kathleen Dahlgren, Chris Sinha, and Henning Andersen.

1.   In Putnam (1987), it is suggested that "pragmatic realism" might be a more appropriate name. This terminological matter is not without importance for any attempt to trace the historical background of the Cognitive Semantic position; it confirms the suggestion (made to me in personal communication by H. Andersen), that next to the pheno-menological connection explored in this paper, another line of allegiances to be studied starts with the pragmatist position of Peirce; more indirectly, the same point is made in Proni's review (1988) of Geeraerts (1985). More generally, the confrontation with the history of philosophy attempted here is not the only way in which the philo-sophical position of Cognitive Semantics might be further elucidated. Notice, for instance, that the philosophical allegiancies of the prototypical conception of categorial structure differ widely according to the various authors that have considered the question. Whereas the classical Roschian statement of the matter (Rosch 1975, Rosch &

Mervis 1975), expanded in Lakoff's experientialist position, characterizes prototype theory as basically Aristotelian and Wittgensteinian, Givón (1986) has argued that the theory is non-Wittgensteinian. But while Givón also describes prototype theory as non-Platonic (Aristotle hardly enters the picture in his paper), Wierzbicka (1985) precisely presents an explicitly Platonic version of prototype theory. This muddled situation may be attributed to two factors. On the one hand, Wierzbicka's Platonistic view derives directly from her introspective methodology, which in turn is related to the fact that she restricts her semantic descriptions to the prototypical centers of the linguistic categories she examines; as argued elsewhere (Geeraerts 1988a), the desirability of both methodological steps within a cognitive conception of semantics may be questioned. On the other hand, Givón's point of view is based on a highly restrictive conception of the kind of family resemblance structures posited by Wittgenstein and Rosch. In particular, his argument rests on the assumption that Wittgenstein only talks about linear concatenations of similar concepts, whereas Rosch, obviously, primarily means family resemblances grouped round a central application ("circular" concatenations of overlapping concepts, so to say). That is to say, while Wittgenstein is said to describe a family resemblance structure ABCDE, where A and B, B and C, C and D, D and E, but not, for instance, A and E are similar to the highest degree, Rosch is said to describe a family resemblance with C as the central member, so that A and C, B and C, D and C, and E and C (but not necessarily B and D or A and E) are maximally similar within the cluster. But even though the radial sets model, which is now one of the major elements of cognitive-semantic attempts to explain prototype results (see Lakoff 1987 and also Kleiber (1988) for the stages in the development of prototype theory), is undoubtedly able to incorporate the linear concatenations attributed to Wittgenstein by Givón, this attribution itself is doubtful. For Wittgenstein's reference to "a complicated network of similarities overlapping and criss-crossing" (1953: §§66f) can hardly be said to exclude the "circular" structures with which the allegedly Wittgensteinian linear concatenations are compared. (It may be noted that the ABCDE-example does not stem from Wittgenstein directly, but is Rosch's presentation of the Wittgensteinian view.) Moreover, Givón pays insufficient attention to the anti-essentialist position that joins Wittgenstein and Rosch against Plato (and Aristotle).

2.   The very general reconstruction of the history of philosophy attempted here can hardly do justice to the detail of the individual philosophies that will be mentioned; we shall be concerned with general developments, and such generalizing perspectives obviously do not leave enough room for a detailed exposition of individual positions.

3.   This does not mean, by the way, that all concepts are taken to be primitive, nor that all primitive concepts are considered to be immediately available to any individual. That hierarchy of acquisitional availability is the result of a process of maturation in which concepts are successively triggered by previous stages of development. It is not made clear, incidentally, exactly to what extent this process of

maturation is a pre-programmed biological one, and to what extent interaction with the environment plays a role in it.

4.   This conclusion may be further corroborated by exploring the consequences of a paradigmatic conception of cognition for the theory of self-consciousness (since an idealistic absolute consciousness is also, by definition, an absolute self-consciousness). For reasons of succinctness, we shall not pursue that line of thought here; the reader is referred to Geeraerts (1985) for further discussion.

5.   A classical example is the perception of a house: one can never see all sides at the same time.

6.   The shift has often been noted; see e.g. Chiss & Puech (1988), Schmidt (1985).

7.   See Dews (1987: ch.1), to whom I am much indebted for this passage.

8.   This position unexpectedly turns up again in Winograd & Flores's (1986) recent reconsideration of the basis of AI.

9.   Remarks on Derrida from a Cognitive Semantic point of view may also be found in Turner (1987); his rejection of the deconstructionist approach refers to the second point in my enumeration of three distinguos.

10.   The plausibility of the latter view follows, among other things, from a consideration of the question: where does the locus of semantic change lie? The characteristics of actual semantic changes demonstrate that the locus of semantic change is the individual category rather than the system. Though this need not always be so (think of generalized metaphors), the most common mechanisms of semantic change that we know of (such as metaphor and metonymy) are mechanisms that involve individual categories. It may perhaps be noted in this respect that there is a difference of emphasis in the two main lines of thought that have so far characterized Cognitive Semantics. On the one hand, prototype-based studies tend to stress the importance of the individual concept, whereas work on general conceptual metaphors tends to stress supralexical factors. The imminent tension between the two approaches has not yet received explicit treatment in the literature.

References

Chiss, Jean-Louis & Christian Puech
      1988   *Fondations de la linguistique: Etudes d'histoire et d'épistémologie.* Brux-
                   elles: De Boeck.
De Waelhens, Alphonse
      1959   "L'idée phénoménologique d'intentionnalité', in: Herman van Breda &
                   Jacques   Taminiaux   (eds.),   *Husserl   et   la   pensée   moderne.*
                   (Phaenomenologica 2.) Den Haag: Nijhoff, 115-129.
Dews, Peter
      1987   *Logics of disintegration: Post-structuralist thought and the claims of*
                   critical theory. London: Verso.
Fodor, Jerry A.
      1981   *Representations: Philosophical essays on the foundations of cognitive*
                   science. Cambridge: MIT Press.

Fodor, Jerry A., Merrill Garrett, Edward Walker & C. Parkes
1980   "Against definitions", *Cognition* 8: 263-367.
Fontaine-de Visscher, Lucie
1974   *Phénomène ou structure? Essai sur le langage chez Merleau-Ponty*.
            Bruxelles: Facultés Universitaires St.-Louis.
Geeraerts, Dirk
1985   *Paradigm and paradox: Explorations into a paradigmatic theory of
            meaning and its epistemological background*. Leuven: Universitaire
            Pers.
1988a   "Review of Anna Wierzbicka, *Lexicography and conceptual analysis*",
            Language in Society 17: 449-455.
1988b   "Where does prototypicality come from?", in: Brygida Rudzka-Ostyn
            (ed.), *Topics in cognitive linguistics*. Amsterdam: Benjamins, 207-229.
Givón, Talmy
1986   "Prototypes: Between Plato and Wittgenstein", in: Colette Craig (ed.),
            Noun classes and categorization. Amsterdam: Benjamins, 77-102.
Husserl, Edmund
1929   *Cartesianische Meditationen und Pariser Vorträge*. Den Haag: Nijhoff
            (1950, ed. Stephan Strasser).
Johnson, Mark
1987   *The body in the mind: The bodily basis of meaning, imagination, and
            reason.*. Chicago: Chicago University Press.
Kelley, David & Janet Krueger
1984   "The psychology of abstraction", *Journal for the Theory of Social Be-
            haviour* 14: 43-67.
Kleiber, Georges
1988   "Prototype, stéréotype: Un air de famille?", *DRLAV. Revue de
            Linguistique* 38: 1-61.
Kuhn, Thomas
1962   *The structure of scientific revolutions*. Chicago: University of Chicago
            Press.
Lakoff, George
1987   *Women, fire, and dangerous things: What categories reveal about the
            mind*. Chicago: Chicago University Press.
Lakoff, George & Mark Johnson
1981   *Metaphors we live by*. Chicago: Chicago University Press.
Merleau-Ponty, Maurice
1945   *Phénoménologie de la perception*. Paris: Gallimard.
1960   *Signes*. Paris: Gallimard.
Piaget, Jean
1970   *Epistémologie génétique*. Paris: Presses Universitaires de France.
Popper, Karl
1963   *Conjectures and refutations*. London: Routledge and Kegan Paul.
Proni, Giampaolo
1988   "Circularity and pragmatism", *Semiotica* 68: 145-154.
Putnam, Hilary
1983   *Realism and reason: Philosophical papers 3*. Cambridge: Cambridge
            University Press.
1987   *The many faces of realism*. LaSalle: Open Court.

Rosch, Eleanor
     1975   "Cognitive representations of semantic categories", *Journal of Experimental Psychology. General* 104: 192-233.
Rosch, Eleanor & Carolyn B. Mervis
     1975   "Family resemblances: Studies in the internal structure of categories", *Cognitive Psychology* 7: 573-605.
Schmidt, James
     1985   *Maurice Merleau-Ponty: Between phenomenology and structuralism.* New York: St.Martin's Press.
Turner, Mark
     1987   *Death is the mother of beauty: Mind, metaphor, criticism.* Chicago: Chicago University Press.
Wierzbicka, Anna
     1985   *Lexicography and conceptual analysis.* Ann Arbor: Karoma.
Winograd, Terry & Fernando Flores
     1986   *Understanding computers and cognition: A new foundation for design.* Norwood N.J.: Ablex.
Wittgenstein, Ludwig
     1953   *Philosophical investigations.* Oxford: Basil Blackwell.
Zwicky, Arnold & Jerry Sadock
     1975   "Ambiguity tests and how to fail them", in: John Kimball (ed.), *Syntax and semantics IV.* New York: Academic Press, 1-36.

From meaning to message in two theories: Cognitive and Saussurean views of the Modern Dutch demonstratives

Robert S. Kirsner

1. Introduction*

The purpose of the present paper is to compare two analyses of the Dutch demonstrative adjectives: one undertaken within the framework of Cognitive Grammar, the other within the framework of the Columbia School, a largely Saussurean approach to linguistics. The comparison is useful for two reasons. First, Cognitive Grammar and the Columbia School have much in common (cf. Langacker 1987: 4). Like Cognitive Grammar, the Columbia School has long recognized the impact of human abilities and interests in determining both language structure and language use (cf. Contini-Morava 1989: 173f, 179; Diver 1979; Reid 1979: 66f).

A second reason is that the two approaches have different and to some extent complementary views of the way in which speakers infer messages from meanings.[1] In a nutshell (but at the risk of oversimplification), Cognitive Grammar tends to emphasize a "bleaching" view of communication in which meanings can be used metaphorically where they are literally inappropriate. The hearer is viewed as ignoring those details of meaning which are irrelevant to the intended message, so that ultimately chains of conventionalized metaphorical extensions are established. Adopting a "maximalist" attitude (Langacker 1988b: 131), Cognitive Grammar views these individual metaphorical "uses" as the basic units with which speakers actually operate. It remains an open question whether speakers derive more abstract "schematic" units expressing the semantic commonality over such uses (Langacker 1988b: 133).

The Columbia School, in contrast, emphasizes a "fill-in" view of communication stressing the distinction between the relatively imprecise information communicated by a linguistic sign - its *meaning* - and the multiplicity of rich, concrete *messages* which can be communicated by signaling that meaning in different linguistic and extralinguistic contexts. The "gap" between meaning and message is bridged by inference (cf. Contini-Morava 1989: 42-44). Adopting a relatively "minimalist" attitude and what Ruhl (1989: 4) has called the "Monosemic Bias", the Columbia School views linguistic meanings not as little semantic "building blocks" and not as abstractions over "uses" but rather as imprecise hints at messages (cf. Diver 1975: 5-15, 23-25). The hearer is viewed as inferring - "filling in" - all sorts of details of the message on the basis of extralinguistic knowledge, psychological biases, and also knowledge of what other signal-meaning relationships could have been used in the situation at hand, but were not (cf. Kirsner & Thompson 1976: 200-204).

From the point of view of each approach, the other approach misses something crucial. A comparison, therefore, can serve the useful function of putting issues on the table which must be dealt with if we are to determine how language actually works.

At the same time, it must be noted that the present paper can only sketch the theories and the analyses. A full treatment of demonstratives in any language and in any theory would require at least a monograph.

2.   Data

Traditional grammar recognizes a proximate demonstrative adjective *deze* (with the allomorph *dit* modifying neuter singular nouns) and a distal demonstrative adjective *die* (with the allomorph *dat* modifying neuter singular nouns). Both forms contrast with the definite article *de* (with the corresponding allomorph *het*) in indicating that the noun's referent still has to be attended to, that its identity cannot be taken entirely for granted, that in some sense it has to be "picked out" from other, competing referents. For example, if one conjoins noun phrases to refer to two distinct referents, as in (1) below, *deze* and *die* will both be acceptable in identical noun phrases, but *de* will not be (cf. Kirsner 1990b: 197):[2]

(1)   a.   *Deze jongen en deze jongen waren stout.*
             'This boy and this boy were naughty.'
       b.   *Die jongen en die jongen waren stout.*
             'That boy and that boy were naughty.'
       c.   **De jongen en de jongen waren stout.*
             'The boy and the boy were naughty.'

That is, *de* - indicating that, for all practical purposes, the intended referent has already been picked out - is less useful than *deze* or *die* when the referent is still being zeroed in upon.

Further, each demonstrative has associated with it a number of distinct uses. For present purposes, we may informally distinguish the following. The classification is not airtight, but will serve to indicate what a semantic analysis of the demonstratives must explain:

General Local use:
Deze indicates objects near the speaker in space, *die* objects far from the speaker: *Deze man ziet die boom* 'This man sees that tree'.

Specifically Proximate use:
Deze and *die* are both used to indicate objects near the speaker in space, but *deze* suggests more of a contrast with other competing objects, as in *Vindt u dat deze das bij het jasje past?* 'Do you think that this particular tie goes with the jacket?' versus *Vindt u dat die das bij het jasje past?* 'Do you think that this tie goes with the jacket?' Cf. also the example from the Dutch author Hermans cited in Kirsner (1979a: 356), where *deze straat* is translated into British English as 'this street' and *die straten* as 'these bloody streets', using *these* rather than *those*. A third example is the aside of a television talk-show host to the audience about the guest that the host is interviewing: *Let u maar niet op die oen naast me* 'Don't pay any attention to that idiot next to me' (where *die* is sometimes said to communicate a pejorative flavor reminiscent of Latin *iste*).

Temporal use:
Deze indicates current time, *die* remote time. *Deze zomer* 'this summer' versus *die zomer* 'that summer'.

Information Status use:
With nouns unmodified by a "referent establishing clause" (cf. Hawkins 1978: 130f), *deze* indicates a "new" referent in discourse and *die* an "old" one; cf. *Ik wil nu deze opmerking maken* 'I now want to make this - previously unmentioned - remark' versus *Ik wil nu die opmerking maken* 'I now want to make that - previously mentioned - remark'.

Anaphoric use:
In written discourse, *die* tends to be used to repeat reference to a previously mentioned entity (a) over relatively short distances (typically with-

in the sentence) and (b) often with the identical noun used earlier to refer to that referent, while *deze* is used (c) over longer distances (across sentence and paragraph boundaries) to (d) reinterpret or "rechunk" reference to earlier material (cf. Kirsner 1987: 91-108; Kirsner & van Heuven 1988: 214-231).

Emphatic use:
Die but not *deze* is used as an emphatic version of the definite article: *Die enkele keer dat ik naar de kerk ga...* [that rare time that I to the church go... 'Those few occasions when I go to church...'.

Imprecise use:
Die but not *deze* is used in a reduplicated construction to indicate some specific but not further identified referent: *Als getuige moet je een eed afleggen dat je aanwezig was op die en die plaats en op dat en dat tijdstip* 'As a witness you must swear an oath that you were present in such and such a place and at such and such a time'.[3]

Salutatory use:
Die but not *deze* is used in face-to-face greetings, or to comment immediately afterwards on someone's remarks or behavior: *Ha die Bob!* 'Here's good ol' Bob again!; There goes Bob again!'

It will be noted that while the Dutch demonstratives are grossly similar to the English ones, there are also striking differences. For example, the following text, from the back cover of a book of essays (van Oorschot 1983), cannot be translated literally; in its Anaphoric use, *die* can appear where English *that* would be contradictory and unacceptable:

> *Dit boekje gaat uit van de werkelijkheid. Die werkelijkheid is het wereldwijde conflict tussen democratie en dictatuur.*
> *De schrijvers aanvaarden* dit conflict *en kiezen in* dat conflict *zelfs onvoorwaardelijk partij: zij verkiezen een in vele opzichten onvolkomen democratie boven de totalitaire dictatuur.*
> [This little book is based upon reality. That reality is the worldwide conflict between democracy and dictatorship.
> The authors accept *this conflict* and even unconditionally take sides in *that conflict*: they prefer a democracy which in many respects is imperfect to a totalitarian dictatorship.]

The other side of the coin is that there is no "new-this" use of Dutch *deze* as a nascent indefinite article the way there is in English (cf. Wald 1983: 94-114). The proper translation of (2a) is not (2b) but (2c), with the genuine indefinite article *een* (cf. Aarts & Wekker 1987: 152):

(2) a. *I'm standing at the bar
         and this little man comes up to me...*
     b. **Ik   sta   bij   de   bar   en   dit   kleine*
         I   stand   by   the   bar   and   this   small
         mannetje   komt   naar   me   toe...
         man-DIMINUTIVE   comes   towards   me   to
     c. *Ik   sta   bij   de   bar   en   dan   komt   er*
         I   stand   by   the   bar   and   then   comes   there
         zo   'n   klein   mannetje   naar   me   toe.
         such   a   small   man-DIMINUTIVE   towards   me   to.

The challenge for any semantic analysis is to make sense out of these various uses, to integrate them in a principled way. It stands to reason that the two linguistic schools under discussion, operating with different assumptions, will arrive at different integrations, different choices of which uses of the demonstratives to foreground at the expense of which other uses. Insofar as Saussurean linguistics in general and the Columbia School in particular antedate Cognitive Grammar, it may be appropriate to consider the Columbia analysis first.[4]

3. A Columbia School analysis

3.1. Theoretical preliminaries

The Columbia School is a sign-oriented approach which attempts to ground both its theoretical constructs and its analytic methodology on the obvious fact that language is (a) an instrument of communication used (b) by human beings.[5] Its Saussurean orientation leads to the working hypothesis that the basic units of language will not be rules but signs: invariant signals of invariant meaning used by intelligent speakers and hearers to hint at and to infer messages. The "human factor" orientation leads one to expect that both the structure and the use of signs will reflect such human influences as finite memory, egocentricity, and the avoidance of inferential complexity.

Because human beings are capable of drawing inferences and making inductive leaps, the meaning signaled by a form can be far less precise than the concrete, detailed messages which can be inferred from the use of the form in specific linguistic and extralinguistic contexts. The analytical problem is to determine precisely what is in the linguistic system itself, i.e. *langue*, and what can be attributed to the language-independent properties and knowledge of the speakers. In a successful analysis, one does not build into the description of *langue*, as a communicative tool, properties which are really a general part of human nature and human behavior (cf. Kirsner 1979a: 372f). In practice, this analytical attitude has resulted in relatively minimalistic analyses proposing that the actual meaning indicated by a signal (namely, its "information", its invariant contribution to all communications effected through its use) is far less precise, much more abstract, than is usually assumed, even by those linguists who are willing to entertain the notion of "pragmatic inference".

Additional working hypotheses are (i) that grammatical systems, in contrast to lexical items, subclassify semantic domains exhaustively, and (ii) that these semantic domains are homogeneous, concerned with such topics as the time of an event, the degree of responsibility for it of the various participants, the degree to which the occurrence of the event is taken for granted or is questioned, etc.[6]

Furthermore, there is the hypothesis (iii) that language users develop conventionalized strategies for the communicative exploitation of meanings. This last point can be viewed as an extension of the famous Saussurean analogy between language and chess. The invariant meaning signaled by a form is considered similar to the definition of the way a chess piece moves; it is the generalization that is consistent with all individual uses. The strategies, in contrast, are considered similar to the development of such patterns of play as openings, tactics for the middle game, endings, and also even "schools" of chess. The meanings (definitions) make possible the strategies (openings, tactics, schools) but do not mechanically determine them (cf. Kirsner 1989: 163f). Conversely, the existence of particular strategies (openings, etc.) restricts the actual observed usage of signals; the meanings (pieces) are not used in all the possible ways in which they theoretically could be, given their general, abstract (or rather: imprecise) character. Meanings relate to conventionalized strategies very roughly in the way, in Cognitive Grammar, a superschema relates to schemata.

Analyses undertaken within the Columbia framework exhibit three interesting characteristics. First, the distinction between meaning and message is drawn more consistently than most readers of traditional grammars are accustomed to; traditional "uses" of a form are not automatically considered to be "meanings". Second, there is a constant weighing of the Saussurean notions of substance and value, with the consequence that there has been a willingness to experiment with meanings defined relationally (cf. Diver 1982: 19-27). Third, because meanings are viewed as abstract hints to messages, one is free to conceive of them as instructions as well as descriptions. A meaning might well comment on the degree or kind of problem-solving which the hearer must perform in order to "match" the message which the speaker is trying to communicate.

3.2. The analysis

The particular analysis of the Dutch demonstrative adjectives sketched here was first presented in Kirsner (1979: 358-373); refinements, critical comments, and more detailed exposition are found in Kirsner (1987: 95-110; 1989: 165-173), and Kirsner & van Heuven (1988: 231-240). This is not the only analysis of the Dutch demonstratives possible within the Columbia School framework, but its decidedly non-traditional flavor does have the merit of exemplifying the three characteristics discussed above with maximum clarity.

3.2.1.   Inadequacies of NEAR vs. FAR

The first claim of the analysis is that the traditional view of *deze* as signaling a meaning NEAR and *die* a meaning FAR is inadequate. There are five arguments: First of all, the Specifically Proximate use of *die* and the Emphatic use of *die* suggests that *die* does not signal 'far' but is simply neutral to location, i.e. unmarked. Second, the observations that *deze* (a) cannot be used in greetings even when the person being greeted is near (*Ha deze Bob!* is unacceptable) and (b) can be inappropriate in non-contrastive reference to near things (cf. Kirsner 1979a: 357) suggest that nearness is not the essence of *deze*. A third argument, borrowed from Wierzbicka (1980: 37 fn. 20), is that a sentence such as *Deze tand doet pijn!* 'This tooth hurts!' (said, for example, to one's dentist, as one points extralinguistically to the tooth) cannot be reasonably paraphrased by anything like *De tand die het dichtst bij me is, doet pijn!* 'The tooth which is nearest to me hurts!' A fourth argument is that, in genuine locative use, *deze* and *die* often have to be reinforced with the adverbs *hier* 'here' and *daar* 'there'. If *deze* and *die* were still synchronic locatives, this should not be necessary. Finally, claiming that *deze* signals NEAR and *die* FAR provides no straightforward way of understanding the fact that *deze* tends to refer backwards in texts over greater distances than *die*; cf. Kirsner & van Heuven (1988: 214-231) and the example from the book cover (van Oorschot 1983) in section 2, above, where *dit conflict* refers backwards to *het wereldwijde conflict tussen democratie en dictatuur* over both a sentence boundary and paragraph boundary, while *dat conflict* refers backwards within its own sentence to *dit conflict*. On the contrary, this contrast in use between *deze* and *die* seems to conflict directly with any "common-sense" interpretation of NEAR versus FAR.

3.2.2.   The system of Deixis

It is argued that synchronically the meanings signaled by *deze* and *die* are no longer descriptive, no longer spatio-temporal, but are rather instructions concerned with directing the hearer's attention to the particular referent of the noun which the speaker has in mind. The substance, or semantic domain of the system, is termed Deixis, defined specifically as 'instruction to the hearer to seek out and attend to the noun's referent'. *Deze* is said to signal the meaning HIGH DEIXIS 'Greater urging to the hearer to seek out and attend to the noun's referent' and *die* is said to signal the meaning LOW DEIXIS 'Lesser urging to the hearer to seek out and attend to the noun's referent'. The system may be diagrammed as in Figure 1.

There are several things to be noted here. First, this is an analysis not of messages but of the *meanings* signaled by *deze* and *die* in *langue*, the abstract system of language as a communicative instrument. The *messages* of proximity, emphasis, and so forth communicated with the forms *deze* and *die* are here viewed as precisely that: messages, i.e. *inferences* from the "real" meanings HIGH DEIXIS and LOW DEIXIS.

Note, second, that the meanings postulated are clearly both relative and instructional. A third point is that since both HIGH DEIXIS and LOW DEIXIS subcategorize the semantic domain of attention, the system is homogeneous. Fourth, in this Saussurean analysis, there is, again at the level of *langue*, no polysemy. Finally, this analysis claims in effect that the Dutch demonstratives have completed the process of subjectivization discussed by Traugott (1986: 540). That is, they are now concerned more with the discourse situation than with the objective situation.

deze = HIGH DEIXIS

' Greater urging to the hearer to seek out and attend to the noun's referent [i.e., a more forceful instruction]'

Deixis
'Instruction to the hearer to seek out and attend to the noun's referent'

die = LOW DEIXIS

'Lesser urging to the hearer to seek out and attend to the noun's referent [i.e., a less forceful instruction]'

Figure 1

3.3.   Discourse exploitations

The present analysis explains the discourse distribution of the demonstratives straightforwardly. The basic claim is that the speaker selects HIGH DEIXIS and LOW DEIXIS to hint to the hearer how much the hearer will have to attend to the referent of the noun.

For example, if it is true, as Chafe (1987: 31f) suggests, that totally new information (not already in the hearer's awareness) is more difficult to process than old information, one can argue that the hearer's attention has to be drawn more forcibly, more strongly to the former than the latter. One can then understand why, all other things being equal, *deze* would be used for new referents (e.g. *Ik wil nu deze opmerking maken* 'I now want to make this remark') and *die* for old ones, rather than the reverse; cf. the Information Status use in section 2 above.

Now with respect to the Anaphoric use, it can be argued (cf. Kirsner & van Heuven 1988: 228-231) that both the greater referential distance and the greater frequency of reinterpretation associated with noun phrases containing *deze* rather than *die* reflect the use of the demonstratives to distinguish between more important and less important referents in a text. It makes eminent sense that the speaker would use HIGH DEIXIS to direct more attention to the referents which are crucial to his or her purpose and LOW DEIXIS to direct less attention to the entities which play only supporting roles. It also makes sense that, as shown in Kirsner (1987: 102-107), the more salient an entity becomes in discourse, through discussion, exemplification, or definition, the more likely it is to be designated with *deze* as more worthy of the hearer's attention.

3.4.   The inference of 'proximity'

Given the abstractness of the present analysis, the grammarian must argue that many uses of the demonstratives reflect and are partially determined by psychological and pragmatic factors. Consider, first, the association of *deze* and *die* with messages of proximity and distance. If 'near' and 'far' are not considered meanings of the forms (and in the present analysis, they are not), these message components must be viewed as inferences. In this particular case, the inferential process can be viewed as influenced by (i) the speaker's and the hearer's own natural egocentricity, coupled with (ii) the pragmatics of pointing out entities in space.

Granted that both speakers and hearers are egocentric, each will view what is near himself or herself as most important. If it is most important and the speaker wants to talk about it, the speaker will urge the hearer to attend to it strongly rather than weakly. Accordingly, he or she will employ the HIGH DEIXIS meaning of *deze* to communicate the message of 'nearness to speaker' even though this is not, according to the analysis, what *deze* itself, in *langue*, actually signals. Conversely, LOW DEIXIS, lesser urging, will be used for what is not near the speaker.

Consider now the pragmatics of locating entities in space. If the speaker, in using *deze*, is urging the hearer very strongly to attend to the noun's referent, the most reasonable first conclusion for the hearer to draw is that there is in fact a particular referent to attend to and that it is located somewhere. Otherwise there would be no communicative point to all the urging. Hence, use of *deze* suggests more strongly than *die* that the hearer must actually look for the referent.

Note, secondly, that it is the speaker who is urging the hearer to attend to the referent and that speakers can point out objects extralinguistically more precisely if the objects are near (preferably within reach, hence physically manipulable) rather than far. This fact is reflected in English by the behavior of the intensifier *right* and in Dutch by the behavior of *pal* (cf. Kirsner 1987: 87), which are more coherent with references to near locations than reference to far ones:

(3)   a.   *Hij woont naast me.*
           'He lives near me.'
      b.   *Hij   woont   een   heel   eind   weg.*
           he   lives   a   whole   distance away
           'He lives very far away.'
      c.   *Hij woont pal naast me.*
           'He lives right near me.'
      d.   **Hij   woont   pal   een   heel   eind   weg.*
           *he   lives   right a   whole   distance away
           *He lives right very far away.'

Accordingly, if *deze* suggests more than *die* that the hearer must actually look for the referent, then (i) the precise location of the referent is an issue and (ii) the best conclusion for the hearer to leap to is that the referent is near the speaker, where it can be pointed out precisely. The inference of 'near speaker' is more congruent with the greater degree of insistence to attend than 'far from speaker'.

A third point is that, in the absence of any other clues, the hearer can in fact locate the entity far more precisely if it is near the speaker. If one imagines the speaker to be inside a series of concentric circles, there are fewer possible locations inside the innermost circle than outside it. Again, the message of 'near speaker' is highly congruent with the forceful instruction to attend signaled by the choice of *deze* over *die*. The hearer can locate the entity and therefore comply with the speaker's instruction to attend more easily if the object is near the speaker.

Finally, since it is the speaker who is urging the hearer to attend, it is reasonable that the hearer would turn toward rather than away from the speaker for any extralinguistic clues that he would need to find the referent. It is thus in principle possible to explain the General Local use of the demonstratives without assuming that synchronically the forms necessarily have to signal locative meanings.

3.5.   *Other uses*

The analysis also provides a framework for understanding the other specific uses of demonstratives, each of which would be considered a particular strategy of exploitation of the meaning in question; cf. the chess analogy in section 3.1. Because of space limitations, the discussion here will be brief; the general theme is that the HIGH DEIXIS meaning of *deze* is used to alert the hearer to attend more strongly to the noun's referent or to otherwise put forth more inferential effort with respect to that referent than would be communicated by the LOW DEIXIS meaning of *die*.

For example, one can argue that it takes more effort for the hearer to distinguish an intended referent when there is a field of competing identical referents than when the referent is unique or alone. Accordingly, it is understandable that *deze* rather than *die* should be used to alert the hearer to such a task. We thus have a basis for explaining the contrastive sense of *deze* 'this particular X' in the Specifically Proximate use as well as the fact that *die* but not *deze* has a purely Emphatic use, an Imprecise use, and a Salutatory use, none of which is contrastive. Given, for example, that in the Imprecise use a specific referent is not being fully picked out, it makes sense that it is the LOW DEIXIS meaning of *die* which is exploited here rather than the HIGH DEIXIS meaning of *deze*. Furthermore, the pejorative flavor sometimes associated with *die* (particularly in combination with negative lexical items such as *oen* 'idiot') makes sense if one considers that it is reasonable to focus attention on what is agreeable and to withdraw attention from what is disagreeable. Finally, the Temporal use of *deze* and *die* would reflect the fact that time periods and events which are directly experienceable, hence relatively salient, would be worthy of greater attention than those which are not; cf. Kirsner (1987: 88f).

4.   A Cognitive Grammar analysis

The general theoretical framework of Cognitive Grammar will be familiar to the audience of this volume. The following analysis necessarily reflects my own interpretation of that framework, based primarily on the recent books by Lakoff, Langacker, and Rudzka-Ostyn.

4.1.   The locative prototype

The use of the Dutch demonstrative adjectives to direct attention to entities in space is fundamental in the experience of both the adult user of the language and the child acquiring it. Accordingly, one may view the various exploitations of the Dutch demonstratives as forming a chain of metaphorical extensions from a basic locative oppositional model (cf. Lakoff 1987: 103). The prototypical situation is pictured in Figure 2 below. If one imagines a speaker facing forward, all entities which he or she can manipulate or touch directly without moving or turning around are candidates for *deze*; all points outside of this region (including touchable objects outside the speaker's field of vision) are candidates for *die*.

The further semantic analysis of the demonstratives, on the basis of this locative prototype, confronts us with two separate issues. The first is the problem posed by the "directive" nature of both demonstratives in contrast to the definite article *de*; cf. the discussion of example (1) in section 2 above. Do the two demonstratives signal some general "class meaning", aside from their locative information, which sets them apart from *de*? The second issue is the precise nature of that locative information, specifically the character of the opposition between *deze* and *die*.

die

die

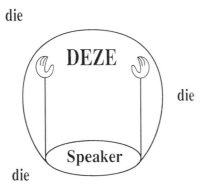

die

die

die

Figure 2

4.2.   The problem of "imperative force"

With respect to the question of the "class meaning" of the demonstratives, two answers are possible: "yes" and "no". One way of answering
"yes" would be to postulate that both *deze* and *die* signal an explicit instruction to the hearer to attend to some referent or other; i.e. a general
meaning DEIXIS, more or less as defined above in the Columbia School
treatment (but without differentiating between a stronger HIGH DEIXIS
and a weaker LOW DEIXIS). Remarks by Eco (1979: 118), Peirce
(Buchler 1940: 107-111), and Wierzbicka (1980: 37 fn. 20) on the
"imperative-like character" of the English demonstratives apply equally
well to the Dutch ones. Consider examples such as (4), which can be interpreted as demonstrating that the directive force of demonstratives
cannot be derived solely from locative information:

(4)   a.   *De auto's hier zijn groter dan de auto's daar.*
           'The cars here are bigger than the cars there.'
      b.   *Deze auto's zijn groter dan die auto's.*
           'These cars are bigger than those cars.'

Whereas (4a) could be used in a general discussion of the differences
between life in the United States and life in the Netherlands (with *hier*
and *daar* referring, respectively, to the two countries), sentence (4b) is
most appropriate on the premises of a car dealership, with the speaker
physically pointing out - on the scene - the contrasting groups of cars in
question, and preferably standing close enough to a large car to be able
to touch it. The locative information communicated with the demonstratives is somehow much more "immediate" than it is in the putative
paraphrases. Accordingly, for both *deze* and *die*, one could postulate an
explicit component of meaning DEIXIS, informally paraphrasable as
'speaker actively directs hearer's attention'.

   The second approach, the "no" answer which I shall adopt here, also
recognizes the "imperative force" of the demonstratives but regards it
not as basic but as derived. It would be considered the result of iconic
factors, namely as a consequence of the simultaneous signaling of both
'definiteness' (to be defined below) and locative information in a single
unit, i.e. within a single word, one standing in a de facto opposition to
both the definite article, on the one hand, and the looser multi-word
paraphrases with article and locative adverb, on the other.

   In other words, the observation that *deze X* 'this X' packs more of a
"directive impact" than *de X hier* 'the X here' would, in this second

approach, be seen as a consequence of the signaling of location as an integral part of the determiner unit itself rather than as something optional tacked on analytically with a separate adverb; cf. Haiman (1983: 783-788, 796). The general claim would then be that *deze X* relates to *de X hier* roughly as the single lexical item *kill*, communicating a maximally direct kind of killing, relates to its indirect paraphrases *cause to die* and *cause to become not alive*.[7]

The derivation of the demonstratives' "imperative force" from their status as single units may be outlined as follows: Let us assume that the above-mentioned component of 'definiteness' (which *deze* and *die* share with the traditional definite article *de*) may be adequately paraphrased as an assertion that, as far as the speaker is concerned, 'the particular referent of the noun which the speaker has in mind both (a) needs to be and (b) has been adequately differentiated, picked out, from all other potential referents of the noun'; cf. Kirsner (1979b: 47-66), where the meaning of *de* is stated as DIFFERENTIATION REQUIRED AND MADE. Now if - in addition to this assertion - *deze* and *die* also signal the referent's location (however imprecisely), then the most reasonable inference the hearer can make is that location is relevant to differentiation (for otherwise the speaker could have just used *de*). Even stronger: the hearer can assume from the speaker's choice of the single-unit "package" that it is only by virtue of the locative information signaled together with DIFFERENTIATION REQUIRED AND MADE that the speaker can claim that DIFFERENTIATION is, in fact, *made*. Signaling location directs the hearer's attention towards the referent, while signaling DIFFERENTIATION MADE indicates that he or she need look no further, that the task of finding the referent is complete. The linguistic fusion (or at least integrity) in the single units *deze* and *die* signals a conceptual fusion (cf. the citation of Haiman in Givón (1985: 216 fn. 12)), while the linguistic independence of *de...hier* and *de...daar* signals conceptual independence, and, hence, an uncoupling of the DIFFERENTIATION process from location. The "directive force" of the demonstratives is, then, a consequence of the dependence of differentiation on location which is indicated iconically by the status of *deze* and *die* as single units rather than collocations. Just as the single lexical item *kill* communicates the spatiotemporal contiguity of the event of causing and the event of dying (in contrast to the multiword paraphrases *cause to die* and *cause to become not alive*), *deze* and *die* communicate an "epistemic contiguity" of identification and location, in comparison to the multi-word paraphrases *de...hier* and *de...daar*.[8]

4.3.   The locative opposition

Assuming, then, that *deze* and *die* signal, in addition to DIFFERENTIA-
TION REQUIRED AND MADE, only locative information, and not an
added meaning DEIXIS, let us now determine precisely what that locative information is.

Returning to the discussion in section 4.1. on the locative prototype, I
postulate for *deze* a component NEAR, here defined with reference to
Figure 2 as 'within the speaker's active domain', i.e. that area which the
speaker can touch and which he or she is looking at. Evidence for this
position is provided by sentences (5) and (6):

(5) a. *Hoe vind je   dit   schilderij   achter   me?*
         how find you   this   painting   behind   me
         'What do you think of this painting behind me?'
     b. *Hoe vind je   dat   schilderij   achter   me?*
         how find you   that   painting   behind   me
         'What do you think of that painting behind me?'

(6) a. **Kijk   eens   naar   deze   boom*
         look   PARTICLE   at   this   tree
         in   de   verte.   Hij   is   zo   ver   weg   dat
         in   the   distance. It   is   so   far   away   that
         je   ernaar   moet   turen om   hem
         you   there-towards   must   peer   in-order   it
         te   kunnen   zien.
         to   can   see
         'Look at this tree in the distance. It is so far away that you
         have to squint to be able to see it.'
     b. *Kijk eens naar die boom in de verte. Hij is zo ver weg dat*
         je ernaar moet turen om hem te kunnen zien.
         'Look at that tree in the distance. It is so far away
         that you have to squint to be able to see it.'

Sentence (5a) is most coherent when the speaker is within a yard of the
painting and turns around to look at it; (5b), in contrast, can be used
when at least one of these conditions does not hold. Sentences (6) show
that *deze* is appropriate only when the referent is near; cf also **Kijk eens
naar deze vliegtuigen aan de horizon! Zijn het Duitsers?* 'Look at these
planes on the horizon! Are they Germans?' versus the normal *Kijk eens
naar die vliegtuigen aan de horizon!* 'Look at those planes on the
horizon!' The starred sentence could be used perhaps only when the

speaker is pointing out airplanes on a photograph, so that their image would physically be within his or her active domain.

What component of meaning should one then postulate for *die*? Paardekooper (1971: 227f) has suggested that, in comparison to *deze*, *die* is actually unspecified for location, i.e. that instead of saying FAR, it says nothing. However, there are two problems with treating *die* as unmarked: one theoretical, the other empirical.

The theoretical problem is that if all *die* signaled were DIFFERENTIA-TION REQUIRED AND MADE, and not, in addition, something like FAR, it should be synonymous with the definite article *de*, which is definitely not the case. To account for the fact that *die* often occurs as a more emphatic form of *de*, we would then have to adopt the first alternative discussed (and rejected) in section 4.2. and attribute a meaning DEIXIS to both *deze* and *die*. Accordingly, we would then analyze *deze* as signaling DEIXIS: NEAR, *die* as signaling just DEIXIS, and *de* as signaling DIFFERENTIATION REQUIRED AND MADE. In this fashion, the meanings of both *deze* and *die* would be clearly demarcated from that of the less forceful article *de* and the alleged markedness relationship between *deze* and *die* would be accounted for. The disadvantage of this solution (with respect to the notion of Ockham's razor) is that the "imperative-like" character of the demonstratives would have to be accounted for with something "extra", a meaning DEIXIS, and would no longer be an automatic consequence of the status of *deze* and *die* as single words.

The empirical problem (which may render the theoretical one irrele-vant) is that *die* does not behave consistently the way it should if it were unmarked. Many native speakers of Dutch repeatedly testify that it is strange to use *die* to refer to entities within the speaker's own private manipulable region, which is what one would expect to be possible if *die* were entirely neutral to location. Consider the following judgments of several consultants; the sentences all concern items of clothing which the speaker is actually wearing:

(7) a. *Vind je dat deze/?die hoed bij het jasje past?*
         'Do you think this/?that hat goes with the jacket?'
     b. *Vind je dat deze/?die das bij het jasje past?*
         'Do you think this/?that tie goes with the jacket?'
     c. *Vind je dat deze/?die trui bij het jasje past?*
         'Do you think this/?that sweater goes with the jacket?'
     d. *Vind je dat deze/?die broek bij het jasje past?*
         'Do you think these/?those pants go with the jacket?'

e.   *Vind je dat deze/die schoenen bij het jasje passen?*
'Do you think these/those shoes go with the jacket?'

Only in (7e) is *die* considered to be as normal as *deze*, but (as was pointed out by the consultants) objects on one's feet are in fact more distant, more peripheral than a tie, sweater, or pair of pants worn on one's torso.[9] One can touch shoes one is wearing only if one bends one's knees. Consider further (8) and (9):

(8)   a.   *Kijk eens naar deze affiche op de muur achter me. Weet je soms wie hem geschilderd heeft? Mondriaan!*
'Look at this poster on the wall behind me. Do you happen to know who painted it? Mondriaan!'
    b.   *Kijk eens naar die affiche op de muur achter me...*
'Look at that poster on the wall behind me...'
    c.   *Kijk eens naar deze affiche op de muur pal achter me...*
'Look at this poster on the wall right behind me...'
    d.   *?Kijk eens naar die affiche op de muur pal achter me...*
'Look at that poster on the wall right behind me...'

(9)   a.   *Kijk eens naar deze boom naast me.*
'Look at this tree next to me.'
    b.   *?Kijk eens naar die boom naast me.*
'Look at that tree next to me.'
    c.   *Kijk eens naar deze boom pal naast me.*
'Look at this tree right next to me.'
    d.   *??Kijk eens naar die boom pal naast me.*
'Look at that tree right next to me.'

The message communicated with (8a) is that the speaker is turning around to look at and point at the poster; the message with (8b) is that this is not the case. The message communicated with (8c) is the same as with (8a), except that the poster is characterized with *pal* as being maximally near the speaker. Sentence (8d), however, is strange. The reinforcement of proximity with *pal* clashes with the use of *die*, given that *deze* is available. Example (9) is parallel to (8), except that *naast me* 'next to me' brings the tree more directly into the speaker's visual field than *achter me* 'behind me', so that the inappropriateness of *die* is accentuated and the clash with *pal* is somewhat greater.[10]

Faced with these facts, the most reasonable conclusion would seem to be that *die* is not unspecified for location; it is opposed to *deze* directly, signaling NOT NEAR as opposed to NEAR, i.e. 'not within the speaker's active domain'.

Observe further that stating the opposition in these terms, as a negative, allows the analyst to have his cake and eat it, too. If *die* claims that the referent is both picked out (DIFFERENTIATION REQUIRED AND MADE) and not within the speaker's active domain, it can of course be used to communicate that the referent is at a distance. But *die* can also be used, like other negative expressions, to deny the assertability of NEAR on the metalinguistic level (Sweetser (1986: 529); for example (i) when the referent is not maximally localized, as in the Imprecise use mentioned in section 2, or (ii) when its particular location is not as issue, as in the Emphatic use (cf. section 4.4.4. below).

To summarize, then, in the basic locative model, *deze* and *die* both signal DIFFERENTIATION REQUIRED AND MADE, with *deze* signaling an extra component NEAR, indicating that the entity in question is inside the speaker's active domain, and *die* signaling an extra component NOT NEAR.[11]

4.4. Metaphorical extensions

4.4.1.   Temporal use

The Temporal use of *deze* and *die* may be viewed as a metaphorical extension of the basic locative model in several different ways. First, one can observe the parallelism between temporal and locative expressions, such as the prepositional phrases in *Op dit ogenblik is Jan op kantoor* 'At this moment John is at the office', and assert, in the manner of Lakoff and Johnson, that there is a general ontological metaphor that TIME IS A LOCATION. One can also claim that, just as the physical area defined by *deze* is the region in which the speaker can act, so is the temporal area defined by *deze* the region in which one can act, i.e. the present moment.

4.4.2.   Anaphoric use

The use of *deze* and *die* to refer, respectively, to more important and less important given referents in discourse can be rationalized in at least two ways. First, one could note that the division of space into what is inside the speaker's active domain and what is outside sets up an opposition between, from the speaker's point of view, central and peripheral. One could then simply assert that there is a general metaphor to the effect that MORE IMPORTANT IS CENTRAL, LESS IMPORTANT IS PERIPHERIAL; cf. expressions like *marginale jongeren* 'marginal young people, i.e. unimportant young people on the edge of society', and, in English, *Harry is central to our purpose, Sam is a marginal scholar*, and *He presents only peripheral criticisms*. One would then claim that there has been an image mapping from the basic locative situation (section 4.1. above) onto the abstract region defined by the discourse, cf. Lakoff & Johnson (1980: 92).

4.4.3.   Information Status use

The use of *deze* to introduce new referents into discourse and *die* to repeat mention of old ones can likewise be rationalized in at least two ways. One could view it as a special case of the use of the demonstratives to differentiate between more important and less important referents.

A second way would be to note that new information is entirely "owned" by the speaker introducing it and, hence, is more appropriately viewed as within rather than outside the speaker's active domain, with the concept of "domain" now extended metaphorically to include the discourse itself.

4.4.4.   Other uses

The Imprecise use of *die* makes sense given the well-known fact that objects which are close to the speaker, within his or her active domain, are more vivid, can be seen and heard more clearly than those which are not; cf. the discussion of CLOSENESS IS STRENGTH OF EFFECT in Lakoff & Johnson (1980: 128). The ultimate explanation comes from physics; the closer an object is, the larger is the image it forms on the retina; cf. Gregory (1978: 152). One could then invoke the metaphor that UNDERSTANDING IS SEEING; cf. Lakoff & Johnson (1980: 48) on *clear argument* and *murky discussion*. Referents which are vague cannot be understood, i.e. be "seen" or visualized, as well as referents which are sharply defined. One might then claim that, within the conceptual domain of epistemic distance (cf. Langacker 1978: 872-880), vague referents are more distant than sharp ones.

The Emphatic and Salutatory uses of *die* make sense given that *die*, unlike *deze*, does not assign the referent to a highly restricted region around the speaker. The message of 'emphasis' in the former case would presumably be a consequence of the fact that, unlike use of the definite article *de*, which says nothing about the referent's location, use of *die*, asserting NOT NEAR and hence suggesting a division of possible locations, claims that localizability, in a general sense, is at least "at issue", at least relevant to the speaker's intended message. If localizability is relevant, then the referent cannot be regarded as already completely pinned down the way it would be if location were claimed to be irrelevant (and the speaker had simply chosen *de*). It follows that the use of *die* tells the hearer that he or she cannot take the identity of the noun's referent entirely for granted; it will have to be searched for or attended to more intently than would have been communicated by *de*. Furthermore, since the negation NOT NEAR can be interpreted metalinguistically as well as linguistically, namely as raising the possibility of specifying a precise location, but then denying it (cf. the reference to Sweetser in section 4.3.), *die* can communicate that the referent's specific physical location (as within versus outside the speaker's active zone) is not germane to the message.[12] When the hearer is told that localizability is important but that the specific issue of "nearness versus farness" is irrelevant, what remains is the extra searching for and extra attention to the referent. It is this which is interpreted as the emphasis communicated with *die* as opposed to *de*.

The Salutatory use of *die*, as in *Ha die Bob!* 'Here's good ol' Bob again!', makes sense insofar as someone being greeted is not already in the speaker's own private region in the way that a "new" referent may be considered to be in the Information Status use discussed above in 4.4.3. In fact, the meaning postulated for *die* (namely DIFFERENTIATION REQUIRED AND MADE, NOT NEAR) seems quite appropriate when one considers that, in contrast to *Ha Bob!*, which merely greets Bob, *Ha die Bob!* communicates an additional modicum of surprise either at Bob himself or what he has just said.[13] This surprise or unexpectedness seems maximally congruent with NOT NEAR (interpreted perhaps "epistemically" as a lack of familiarity) as opposed to the NEAR of *deze* or the total absence of locative information signaled by *de*.

4.5.   The resultant network

The first thing to notice is that the opposition between *deze* and *die* is preserved in the mappings onto various domains. *Deze* may be conceived of as constantly associated with greater magnitude of the relevant dimension, as in Figure 3:

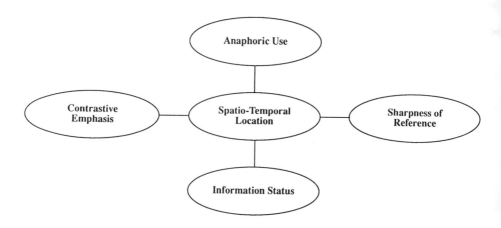

Figure 3

We may also observe that, insofar as the metaphorical extensions have been discussed independently, without any one extension seen as the basis for a further one, the cognitive domains appear to be linked radially, perhaps as in Figure 4:

	Spatiotemporal location	Sharpness of definition	Importance of referent	Novelty in discourse	Contrastive Emphasis
deze	NEAR	VIVID	GREATER	GREATER	MORE
die	NOT NEAR	DULL	LESSER	LESSER	LESS

Figure 4

5. Comparison

5.1. Deficits of the Columbia School treatment

From the viewpoint of Cognitive Grammar, one can object to the Columbia School analysis of the Dutch demonstratives in three ways.

First, one can question the adequacy of the meanings. The postulation of purely directive, instructional meanings seems to be dictated more by the internal dialectic of Columbia School theory than by empirical observation. Granted that if (i) *die* seems to be unmarked with respect to location and if (ii) systems must not mix semantic substances, then it follows (iii) that *deze* cannot be specified for proximity but must (iv) share properties with *die*, in which case the present solution in terms of stronger and weaker "demonstrativity" is justified. But one can ask if these meanings actually account for the data. If all *deze* really signaled was the meaning HIGH DEIXIS, with no synchronic trace of locative meaning whatsoever, one would expect that the strategy of using *deze* to refer to near objects could in fact occasionally be overridden, since that is the key distinction between strategy and meaning; cf. García (1975: 117). One would then expect that *deze* could in exceptional circumstances be used to draw particularly strong attention to distant objects. But this, as we have seen above, does not happen; sentences like *Kijk eens naar deze vliegtuigen aan de horizon!* 'Look at these planes on the horizon!' remain strange.[14] The only way left of explaining this ironclad association of *deze* with proximity is then to consider it a conventionalized strategy (Kirsner 1979a: 370f), which is consistent with the Columbia School approach but nonetheless appears ad hoc. Methodologically it seems ill-advised to claim that the overwhelming association of *deze* with NEAR, to which all native Dutch speakers attest, is merely a phantom deriving from a less precise meaning. Besides, there are arguments against considering *die* unmarked; see 4.3. above. And if *die* must be considered as signaling NOT NEAR, then the motivation is destroyed for considering *deze* as free of locative information.

Our second point concerns the status of strategies. In the Columbia School analysis, speakers are viewed as learning the meanings HIGH DEIXIS and LOW DEIXIS, together with various conventionalized strategies: the association of *deze* with messages of proximity, importance in discourse, etc., and the association of *die* with messages of distance, unimportance in discourse, and brute emphasis, etc. These strategies are all taken as things done with the meanings. But, from the hearer's point of view, is not the connection between signal and conventionalized strategy basically analogous to the arbitrary, i.e. conventionalized, connection between signal and meaning in a Saussurean analysis? If it is, why should it be described any differently? Why, instead of speaking of strategies, can one not speak of "sub-signs"? Why can the difference between signs and sub-signs not be one of degree rather than kind?

This brings us to the issue of polysemy. Kirsner (1979a: 372 fn. 11) suggested a parallel between the analysis of the Dutch demonstratives and the analysis of the English modal verbs, stating that if one wishes to avoid postulating synchronic homonyms, one should pick the less precise use as basic (the epistemic rather than the deontic sense of the modals, the discourse rather than the purely locative use of the demonstratives). However, the *if* can be challenged. Sweetser (1986) presents evidence that the English modals should be considered neither monosemous nor homonymous but rather polysemous; the same arguments seem applicable to the Dutch demonstratives.

The conclusion one can draw is that, on balance, an analysis in terms of polysemy is preferable. Such an analysis can meet the objections listed in section 3.2.1.

5.2. Deficits of the Cognitive Grammar treatment

From the viewpoint of the Columbia School, the Cognitive Grammar analysis of the Dutch demonstratives sketched here suffers from three flaws:

1.   The appeal to metaphor, at least in the style of Lakoff & Johnson (1980), seems uncontrolled. Does one want to rationalize the use of *deze* to introduce new referents by claiming (a) that they are important, hence central, and that CENTRAL IS IMPORTANT, or by claiming (b) that a new referent such as 'remark' in *Ik wil deze opmerking maken* 'I want to make this remark', still belongs to the future, that THE FUTURE IS AHEAD OF US, so that the speaker, facing it as it comes toward him (Lakoff & Johnson 1980: 44), has to use *deze* rather than *die* as it moves into his active domain? How does one decide? And does it make any empirical difference?

2.   Not enough attention is paid to the inferential mechanisms, the pragmatic and discourse mechanisms, underlying both the communicative use of meanings and their metaphorical extensions. New cognitive domains seem to be declared by fiat. But this begs a crucial question: When does one have a new cognitive domain?

3.   As a consequence of (2): analyses in the framework seem to exhibit considerable non-uniqueness. For example, if it is the case that the use of *deze* to introduce new referents in discourse and *die* to refer to old ones is a special case of the use of *deze* to refer to important referents and *die* to unimportant ones, then the Information Status node in Figure 4 could be viewed as (i) emerging from the Anaphoric use node or (ii) entirely absorbed within it. There are thus at least three ways of drawing Figure 4, and it is not at all clear whether the three different diagrams would make different empirical predictions about the actual use of the language or what speakers actually learn.

This is not all; the Information Status node could also be viewed as emerging from the Sharpness of Reference node. Consider:

Following the discussion of metaphor in Sperber & Wilson (1986: 233-237), we might view the basic mechanism behind the metaphorical extension of the Dutch demonstratives as follows: The speaker claims that entities are in or not in the speaker's active domain when the entities cannot actually be taken as localizable in space. The speaker's purpose in doing so is to communicate something about the entity which *would be true if it were in fact a localizable physical object*. For the communication to be successful, hearers must be willing to infer and appreciate the relevance of that something to the intended message and to ignore or disregard those features of meaning which are literally untrue. But examples of such disregarding are legion in human problem solving; cf. De Bono (1971: 86,174).

Recall now our earlier point in section 4.4.4. that objects which are close to the speaker, within his or her active domain, are more vivid, can be seen and heard more clearly than those which are not. It then follows (assuming a Sperber-Wilson type of mechanism) that if one wishes to communicate that some discourse referent, some entity (e.g. an idea, a theory) is vivid or sharply defined even when it is not localizable in space, one could do so by asserting, through the use of *deze*, that it is in one's active domain. Although the entity is not really in the speaker's active domain, it would be vivid if it were there, and this is what the speaker wishes to communicate. Conversely, if the speaker wants to communicate that the entity is poorly defined or dull, he can do so by claiming with *die* that it is not in his active domain. We have now moved from the central Spatio-Temporal Location node to the Sharpness of Reference node in Figure 4.

The next step in the metaphorical extension is to observe that entities which are vivid typically attract attention, are somehow automatically "worthy" of scrutiny. Accordingly, if the speaker wants the hearer to attend to the entity, he can claim, through the choice of *deze*, that the entity is vivid even if it is not. Although the entity is not actually vivid, it would attract attention if it were, and this is the speaker's ultimate message. Conversely, if the speaker wants to communicate that the entity is not worthy of attention, he can claim, by selecting *die*, that it is not vivid but dull. In this manner, we arrive at the directive function of the demonstratives, in which *deze* communicates a forceful instruction to the hearer to attend to the referent and *die* a weak one. One special case of this directive function use would be the Anaphoric use of *deze* and *die* to refer to more versus less important previously mentioned referents. Another would be the Information Status use of *deze* and *die* to differentiate new referents from the previously mentioned ones; cf. the argument in Kirsner & van Heuven (1988: 234).

Accordingly, we now have the choice of (i) linking the Sharpness of Reference node directly to the Information Status and the Anaphoric use nodes, or (ii) through some intermediate "abstract" node labelled Directive Function. Again, by what principled (non-arbitrary) criteria does one decide what the individual cognitive domains are and how they relate to one another?

In response to these questions, one could suggest that it is a strength of Cognitive Grammar that it does not force the analyst to seek a unique description of a conceptual network when alternative ones are in fact possible: cf. recent work by Barsalou, Brooks, and Medin & Wattenmaker suggesting that the same conceptual domain can be categorized in different ways. Nevertheless, if it is to reflect the learnability of language, a linguistic analysis must be finite in some sense. Not all arrangements of "uses" in a network will be realistic. Besides, cognitive grammarians themselves have seen the necessity of rejecting some analyses within their framework: cf. Taylor (1988: 313f) on how his analysis of *over* differs from Brugman's.

6.   The central issue

The Columbia School achieves analytical control by invoking the concept of the Saussurean sign (Reid 1974: 33) and various working hypotheses. The danger is that the speakers of the language may not be as consistent, thorough, and rigorous as the Saussurean linguist. Rather than relating all uses to single imprecise meanings, they may instead make do, perhaps exclusively, with intermediate-sized units lying halfway in between the classic sign and the individual messages.

Cognitive Grammar, on the other hand, achieves analytical control by invoking a kind of "common-sense realism", sticking close to the uses (which one needs to describe anyway) and recognizing that the imprecise Saussurean-style meanings which could be proposed might lack psychological reality; cf. Langacker (1987: 381). The danger here seems to be that, having jettisoned the "upper bound" of the Saussurean concept of sign, cognitive grammarians will miss real generalizations and arrive at essentially arbitrary analyses with arbitrary cut-off points. Consider, as a cautionary tale, García's report (1975: 1) that Spanish traditional grammarians typically postulate from two to eleven different "kinds" of the pronoun *se*. Even if these different uses were treated within Cognitive Grammar not as independent homonyms but as "structured polysemy", there would still be ample room for indeterminacy in both the postulation and the arrangement of cognitive domains. García's hypothesis of a single meaning for *se*, entering into various oppositional relations with the other Spanish pronouns, at least indicates where the analysis should stop.

The analytical challenge posed by the Dutch demonstratives resides in the fact that it is not immediately absurd to entertain the hypothesis that their various uses are exploitations of single meanings related in a single opposition. The case is not parallel to Fillmore's fable or caricature (1977: 67), in which Roman Jakobson allegedly claims that all senses of the English noun *bachelor*, a lexical item, can be derived from the meaning 'unfulfilled in a typical male role'. Furthermore, the possibility that the association of *deze* with 'near' is due to a strategy rather than a synchronic meaning cannot be rejected out of hand; cf. Diver (1979) on the "invisibility" of all linguistic units. But the other side of the coin is that, even within the Columbia School, there is the possibility of claiming that the same morphological "chunk" is utilized in *different systems*; cf. the discussion of Dutch *zou* 'should' as a signal of both PAST HYPOTHETICAL and NONPAST HYPOTHETICAL LESS LIKELY referred to in Kirsner (1979b: 36). It would thus be an analytical option within the Columbia school to set up two systems containing *deze* and *die*, one concerned strictly with spatiotemporal location, the other - used when the context indicates that location is not at issue - with relative deictic force. This new analysis, which would perhaps be analogous to unpublished analyses by Diver in which Greek case morphology participates both in a place system and a participant system, might meet the objection that the single-meaning approach is "too abstract".

Perhaps the only way out of the dilemma is to shift our goal from achieving analytical control on paper (on the basis of some esthetic or philosophical principle) to that of discovering - by means we have not yet developed - what the units are that speakers *really* operate with. In this respect, and in view of Langacker's comment (1988a: 4) that biology rather than mathematics is the more appropriate model for linguistic research, the following remarks by a Nobel Prize winning molecular biologist point to the path we may have to follow if linguistics is to achieve scientific maturity (Crick 1988: 141f):

> The basic trouble is that nature is so complex that many quite different theories can go some way to explaining the results. If elegance and simplicity are, in biology, dangerous guides to the correct answer, what constraints can be used as a guide through the jungle of possible theories? It seems to me that the only really useful constraints are contained in the experimental evidence... One should ask: What is the essence of the type of theory I have constructed and how can that be tested? even if it requires some new experimental method to do so.

Notes

*   This research was supported by grant 2964 from the Academic Senate of the University of California, Los Angeles. I would like to thank Jeanine Deen, Ad Foolen, Nel Keijsper, Justine Pardoen, and Martine van der Vlugt for discussing various Dutch examples with me. I would also like to thank Brygida Rudzka-Ostyn, Gary D. Prideaux, William R. LaFleur, and an anonymous referee for critical comments on earlier drafts. Michael E. Cohen of the UCLA Humanities Computer Facility provided invaluable assistance with word-processing programs; Jolanta U. Balikowska, also of UCLA-HCF, produced the illustrations.

1.   In this paper, I shall use the plural term *speakers* to indicate language users, encompassing speakers, hearers, readers and writers. Elsewhere, I shall use the singular terms *speaker* and *hearer* to refer respectively to writers as well as speakers and readers as well as listeners.

2.   Given that Dutch is closely related to English, word-for-word glosses will be provided only when strictly necessary. Note that for examples (1a) and (1b) to be intelligible, the speaker must be physically pointing out each individual boy. But no amount of physical pointing will render (1c) coherent.

3.   That *die en die* is semantically definite rather than indefinite is shown by its non-occurrence in presentative sentences containing the adverbial pronoun *er*. Just as one has *Hij moet weg* 'He must leave' and not **Er moet hij weg* [There must he leave], we have *Die en die mensen moeten weg* 'Such and such people must leave', and not **Er moeten die en die mensen weg*. Compare *Er moet iemand weg* [there must someone away] 'Someone must leave'. I thank an anonymous referee for this point. The imprecise reference of *die en die* thus seems to be similar to the imprecise use of such definite pronouns as *je* 'you' and *ze* 'they'.

4.   Historically, the Cognitive approach arose in part in response to perceived problems with Saussurean linguistics, but discussions of these problems in print (e.g. in Janda's thesis) have focussed only on the Jakobsonian school. The Columbia School notion of *strategy* (García 1975: 49f, 193-273) seems to meet some of the objections one can have to Jakobsonian analyses.

5.   Monographs outlining the approach are García (1975) and Kirsner (1979b). Tobin (1987) contrasts it with the Guillaumean and the Jakobsonian schools, to which it bears superficial similarities. See further Reid (in press) and Tobin (1990).

6.   There are superficial similarities between these working hypotheses and some proposed in Talmy (1988: 166-173). For additional discussion, see Kirsner (1990a: section 2).

7.   Compare also Bolinger's discussion (1975: 443) of the contrast between the fused form *c'mere* and the full expression *come here*; the former can only be used when the hearer is in the immediate environment of the speaker and the distance to the speaker is easily traversed. (*C'mere* would be out of place in suggesting that the hearer undertake a cross-country trip to reach the speaker). Perhaps recognition of the iconic impact of packaging meaning in single units rather than collocations of units would force a reappraisal of Wierzbicka's example *This tooth*

hurts! (1980: 37 fn. 20) and her argument, based upon it, that demonstratives do not signal location.

8.   The conceptual separateness of location and identification in the multi-word paraphrases as opposed to the demonstratives may be illustrated in two additional ways. First, any attempt to systematically paraphrase *deze* and *die* with *de...hier* and *de...daar* fails when confronted with such expressions as *deze boom hier* 'this tree here', for *deze* would then have no "equivalent": cf. **de boom hier hier*. The use of *hier* as a reinforcing locative in *deze boom hier* demonstrates the difference between the *subjective* character of locative information in the demonstrative, where it is part of the speaker's "construal mechanism" (cf. Langacker 1989: 1f, 12), versus its more objective and "profile-able" use in the paraphrase. Second, the paraphrase obviously fails when demonstratives are used non-locatively, e.g. temporally or emphatically/pejoratively. *Dit jaar* 'this year' and *die smeerlap!* 'that bastard!' cannot be paraphrased as *het jaar hier* [the year here] or *de smeerlap daar!* [the bastard there!].

9.   Note that judgments can apparently differ here. The native speaker originally consulted on what is here printed as sentence (7b), namely sentences (10) in Kirsner (1979a: 360), accepted *die* and said that it communicated a less contrastive message than *deze* would; cf. the paragraph on the Specifically Proximate use in section 2, above. If this judgment is accepted as data and if one does not want to argue that the lack of contrast shows that *die* contains less information than *deze* (i.e. is unmarked), one could perhaps derive it from the meaning NOT NEAR (see below) by arguing that, in terms of pragmatics, there are more entities farther from the speaker than nearer to him. Categorizing a tie as not near rather than near picks it out less strongly, thereby suggesting that forceful, contrastive pointing out of the tie was less necessary, and, hence, that there was less competition. (This would be the mirror-image of the third argument presented in section 3.4.).

10.   The contrast of the questionable sentence (9b) with the acceptable but parallel sentence *Let u maar niet op die oen naast me* 'Don't pay any attention to that idiot next to me' (considered above in section 2) will ultimately find its explanation in the difference between literal versus metaphorical interpretations of distance. Sentence (9b) is incoherent because the only way to interpret the distance suggested by *die* is as physical distance, which is contradicted by *naast me*. In the *oen*-sentence, however, the pejorative lexical meaning of *oen* permits the hearer to take distance as psychological rather than physical: *die oen* is something which Ego (speaker) does not want to identify himself/herself with, i.e. 'be close to'.

11.   The present analysis differs from that in Kirsner & van Heuven (1988: 234f) in suggesting that *die* and *deze* form an equipollent rather than a privative opposition.

12.   Compare Lyons's example (1977: 772), *The present King of France is not bald: there is no King of France.* By analogy, *die*, signaling NOT NEAR, could be used to deny the assertion of nearness (because specific location is not relevant to the speaker's purpose) as well as asserting non-nearness.

13.   I owe this observation to Ad Foolen.

14.   An anonymous referee has observed, in further support of this point,
        that in contrast to the combinations *deze...hier, die...hier* and *die ...daar*,
        the combination **deze... daar* is ungrammatical.

References

Aaronson, Doris & Robert W. Rieber (eds.)
    1979   *Psycholinguistic research: Implications and applications*. Hillsdale,
                N.Y.: Lawrence Erlbaum.
Aarts, F.G.A.M. & H. Chr. Wekker
    1987   *A contrastive grammar of English and Dutch: Contrastieve grammatica
                Engels/Nederlands*. Leiden: Martinus Nijhoff.
Amacker, René & Rudolf Engler (eds.)
    1990   *Présence de Saussure: Actes du colloque internationale de Genève (21-
                23 mars 1988)*. (Publications du Cercle Ferdinand de Saussure 1)
                Geneva: Librairie Droz.
Barsalou, Lawrence W.
    1987   "The instability of graded structure: Implications for the nature of con-
                cepts", in: Ulric Neisser (ed.), 101-140.
Bluhme, Hermann & Göran Hammarström (eds.)
    1987   *Descriptio linguistica: Proceedings of the first conference on descriptive
                and structural linguistics, Antwerp, 9-10 September 1985*. Tübingen:
                Gunter Narr.
Bolinger, Dwight
    1975   *Aspects of language*. (2nd edition). New York: Harcourt Brace Jo-
                vanovich.
Brooks, Lee R.
    1987   "Decentralized control of categorization: The role of prior processing
                episodes", in: Ulric Neisser (ed.), 141-174.
Buchler, Justus (ed.)
    1940   *The philosophy of Peirce: Selected writings*. New York: Harcourt, Brace
                and Company.
Casad, Eugene H. & Ronald W. Langacker
    1985   "'Inside' and 'outside' in Cora grammar", *International Journal of
                American Linguistics* 51: 247-281.
Chafe, Wallace
    1987   "Cognitive constraints on information flow", in: Russell S. Tomlin
                (ed.), 21-51.
Contini-Morava, Ellen
    1989   *Discourse pragmatics and semantic categorization: The case of negation
                and tense-aspect with special reference to Swahili*. Berlin: Mouton de
                Gruyter.
Crick, Francis
    1988   *What mad pursuit: A personal view of scientific discovery*. New York:
                Basic Books.
De Bono, Edward
    1976   *Practical thinking*. Harmondsworth: Penguin.

112   Robert S. Kirsner

Diver, William
1975   "Introduction", *Columbia University Working Papers in Linguistics* 2: 1-25.
1979   "Phonology as human behavior", in: Doris Aaronson & Robert W. Rieber (eds.), 161-182.
1982   "The focus-control interlock in Latin", *Columbia University Working Papers in Linguistics* 7: 13-31.
Eco, Umberto
1979   *A theory of semiotics*. Bloomington: Indiana University Press.
Fillmore, Charles J.
1977   "Scenes-and-frames semantics", in: Antonio Zampolli (ed.), 55-81.
García, Erica C.
1975   *The role of theory in linguistic analysis: The Spanish pronoun system.* Amsterdam: North-Holland.
Givón, Talmy
1985   "Iconicity, isomorphism, and non-arbitrary coding in syntax", in: John Haiman (ed.), 187-219.
Givón, Talmy (ed.)
1979   *Discourse and syntax.* (Syntax and Semantics 12) New York: Academic Press.
Gregory, R. L.
1978   *Eye and brain: The psychology of seeing.* New York: McGraw-Hill.
Haiman, John
1983   "Iconic and economic motivation", *Language* 59: 781-819.
Haiman, John (ed.)
1985   *Iconicity in syntax: Proceedings of a symposium on iconicity in syntax, Stanford, June 24-6, 1983.* Amsterdam: Benjamins.
Hawkins, John A.
1978   *Definiteness and indefiniteness: A study in reference and grammaticality prediction.* London: Croom Helm.
Janda, Laura A.
1984   A semantic analysis of the Russian verbal prefixes *ZA-, PERE-, DO-,* and *OT-*. [Unpubl. Ph.D. Dissertation, University of California at Los Angeles].
Kirsner, Robert S.
1979a   "Deixis in discourse: An exploratory quantitative study of the Modern Dutch demonstrative adjectives", in: Talmy Givón (ed.), 355-375.
1979b   *The problem of presentative sentences in Modern Dutch.* Amsterdam: North-Holland.
1987   "What it takes to show whether an analysis 'fits'", in: Hermann Bluhme & Göran Hammarström (eds.), 76-113.
1989   "Does sign-oriented linguistics have a future? On the falsifiability of theoretical constructs", in: Yishai Tobin (ed.), 161-178.
1990a   Review article of Brygida Rudzka-Ostyn (ed.), *Topics in cognitive linguistics.* [To appear in *Studies in Language*].
1990b   "Grappling with the ill-defined: Problems of theory and data in synchronic grammatical description", in: René Amacker & Rudolf Engler (eds.), 187-201.
Kirsner, Robert S. & Sandra A. Thompson
1976   "The role of pragmatic inference in semantics: A study of sensory verb complements in English", *Glossa* 10: 200-240.

Kirsner, Robert S. & Vincent J. van Heuven
1988   "The significance of demonstrative position in Modern Dutch", *Lingua* 76: 209-248.
Klein-Andreu, Flora (ed.)
1983   *Discourse perspectives on syntax*. New York: Academic Press.
Lakoff, George
1987   *Women, fire, and dangerous things: What categories reveal about the mind*. Chicago: University of Chicago Press.
Lakoff, George & Mark Johnson
1980   *Metaphors we live by*. Chicago: University of Chicago Press.
Langacker, Ronald W.
1978   "The form and meaning of the English auxiliary", *Language* 54: 853-882.
1987   *Foundations of cognitive grammar I: Theoretical prerequisites*. Stanford: Stanford University Press.
1988a   "An overview of cognitive grammar", in: Brygida Rudzka-Ostyn (ed.), 3-48.
1988b   "A usage-based model", in: Brygida Rudzka-Ostyn (ed.), 127-161.
1989   "Subjectification". Linguistic Agency University of Duisburg: Series A. Paper No. 262. [Revised version in: *Cognitive Linguistics* 1 (1990): 5-38.]
Lyons, John
1977   *Semantics*. Volume 2. Cambridge: Cambridge University Press.
Medin, Douglas L. & William D. Wattenmaker
1987   "Category cohesiveness, theories, and cognitive archeology", in: Ulric Neisser (ed.), 25-62.
Neisser, Ulric (ed.)
1987   *Concepts and conceptual development: Ecological and intellectual factors in categorization*. Cambridge: Cambridge University Press.
Nikiforidou, Vassiliki (ed.)
1986   *Proceedings of the Twelfth Annual Meeting of the Berkeley Linguistics Society, February 15-17, 1986*. Berkeley: Berkeley Linguistics Society.
Oorschot, G. A. van (ed.)
1983   *Te beginnen bij Nederland: Opstellen over oorlog en vrede*. [To begin with the Netherlands: Essays on war and peace] Amsterdam: G. A. van Oorschot.
Paardekooper, P.C.
1971   *Beknopte ABN-syntaksis* [Concise Standard Dutch syntax]. Den Bosch: L.C.G. Malmberg.
Reid, Wallis
1974   "The Saussurean sign as a control in linguistic analysis", *Semiotext[e]* 1: 31-53.
1979   The human factor in linguistic analysis: The *passé simple* and the *imparfait*. [Unpubl. Ph.D. dissertation, Columbia University.]
in press   *Verb number in English: A functional explanation*. London: Longman.
Rudzka-Ostyn, Brygida (ed.)
1988   *Topics in cognitive linguistics*. Amsterdam: Benjamins.
Ruhl, Charles
1989   *On monosemy: A study in linguistic semantics*. Albany: State University of New York Press.

Sperber, Dan & Deirdre Wilson.
1986   *Relevance: Communication and cognition.* Oxford: Basil Blackwell.
Sweetser, Eve E.
1986   "Polysemy vs. abstraction: Mutually exclusive or complementary?", in:
            V. Nikiforidou (ed.), 528-538.
Talmy, Leonard
1988   "The relation of grammar to cognition", in: Brygida Rudzka-Ostyn
            (ed.), 165-205.
Taylor, John R.
1988   "Contrasting prepositional categories: English and Italian", in: Brygida
            Rudzka-Ostyn (ed.), 299-326.
Tobin, Yishai
1987   "Three sign-oriented theories: A contrastive approach", in: Hermann
            Bluhme & Göran Hammarström (eds.), 51-75.
1990   *Semiotics and linguistics.* London: Longman.
Tobin, Yishai (ed.)
1989   *From sign to text: A semiotic view of communication.* Amsterdam:
            Benjamins.
Tomlin, Russell S. (ed.)
1987   *Coherence and grounding in discourse.* Amsterdam: Benjamins.
Traugott, Elizabeth Closs
1986   "From polysemy to internal semantic reconstruction", in: Nikiforidou
            (ed.), 539-550.
Wald, Benji
1983   "Referents and topic within and across discourse units: Observations
            from current vernacular English", in: Flora Klein-Andreu (ed.), 91-116.
Wierzbicka, Anna
1980   *Lingua mentalis: The semantics of natural language.* New York:
            Academic Press.
Zampolli, Antonio (ed.)
1977   *Linguistic structures processing.* Amsterdam: North Holland.

A functional view on prototypes

Hansjakob Seiler

1. Introduction

The human mind may produce prototypization within virtually any realm of cognition and behavior. A comparative prototype-typology might prove to be an interesting field of study - perhaps a new subfield of semiotics. This, however, would presuppose a clear view on the samenesses and differences of prototypization in these various fields. It seems more realistic for the time being for the linguist to confine himself to describing prototypization within the realm of language proper.

The literature on prototypes has steadily grown in the past ten years or so. I will confine myself to mentioning the volume on *Noun classes and categorization* (Craig 1986), which contains a wealth of factual information on the subject, along with some theoretical vistas. By and large, however, linguistic prototype research is still basically in a taxonomic stage - the precondition for moving beyond. The procedure is largely *per ostensionem*, and by accumulating examples of prototypes. We still lack a comprehensive prototype theory.

The following pages are intended, not to provide such a theory, but to take the first steps in this direction. Section 2 will feature some of the elements of a functional theory of prototypes. They have been developed by the author within the framework of the UNITYP model of research on language universals and typology. Section 3 will provide a discussion of prototypization with regard to selected phenomena from a wide range of levels of analysis: phonology, morphosyntax, speech acts, and the lexicon. Prototypization will finally be studied within one of the universal dimensions, that of *apprehension* - the linguistic representation of the concepts of objects - as proposed by Seiler (1986).

2. Elements of a functional theory of prototypes

1. The notion of prototype with its content, parametric optimization with regard to a given function, belongs to the basic premises of

any speech activity. It does not in any strict and direct way derive from empirical research. There are, of course, empirical correlates that may serve as heuristics in the search for prototypes. For example, the prototype of a category is most wide-spread cross-linguistically; it is first learned by children; it may be substituted for non-prototypical instances, etc.

2.   A prototype is the result of operations that go on in the minds of participants in language communication. The primary goal of the analyst must be to reconstruct these operations. Emphasis is therefore laid not on the result, the "thing", the "prototype", but on the operations, which we shall subsume under "prototypization".

3.   Prototypization characterizes a particular instantiation of the relation between a *repraesentandum* (that which is to be represented) and a *repraesentans* (that which represents) in the process of representation of a conceptual content by a linguistic expression. The relation between a *repraesentandum* and a *repraesentans* is called function.

4.   Prototypization is the optimization of a function, resulting in high saliency.

5.   Prototypization implies parametrization.

6.   Prototypization results from optimal choices made by speakers/hearers from a plurality of options on a plurality of parameters.

7.   Prototypization can only be understood and adequately described in full cognizance of the entire spectrum of options for a given function, including the non-prototypical or marginal ones.

8.   Prototypes are the epitome of categories.

9.   A category is constituted by a bundle of properties/features (intension), and by the set of its members (extension).

10. A property/feature is a *principium comparationis* and is instantiated by a parameter. The parameter is a scalar ordering of options and represents the range of variation. It is embraced by an invariant.

11. Variation on the parameters is characterized by markedness relationships: either bi-polar, i.e. marked-unmarked; or continuous, i.e. increasing/decreasing markedness, with two extreme poles.

12. There are dependency relations among the properties/features constituting a category.

13. Prototypization involves a hierarchy of levels of categorization and of parametrization. There are basically three levels: (1) superordinate, (2) basic, (3) subordinate.

14. The conceptual side of a category (the *repraesentandum*) is discrete and can be defined by a finite number of properties. The linguistic side of a category (the *repraesentans*) shows prototypical and non-prototypical (marginal) instantiations in a gradient transition.

3.   Domains of prototypization

The tenets under section 2 may be substantiated within different domains and on different levels of linguistic analysis. A more detailed and extensive treatment will be given to one of the universal dimensions of language, viz. that of *apprehension* (the linguistic representation of objects), as presented by Seiler (1986). Here the overall function of the dimension as well as the functions of the techniques and of the subdimensions have been worked out and definitions are available. The internal structure of the defining parameters (continua) is brought to the fore. A sufficient body of data is also presented.

Before embarking on this enterprise, however, let us briefly look at some selected phenomena pertaining to such levels as phonology, morphosyntax, the speech acts, and the lexicon.

3.1. Phonology

The superordinate category is that of speech sounds. Vowels vs. consonants are basic categories. Different subclasses of vowels and of consonants are subordinate. It appears that prototypization is prominent on the basic level, i.e. in the class of consonants and in the class of vowels. These major classes along with the two intermediate classes of liquids and glides have been exhaustively defined by a finite number of features in their appropriate marked vs. unmarked specifications as bundles of the following form:

True Consonant	Vowel	Liquid	Glide
+ cons - voc	- cons + voc	+ cons + voc	- cons - voc
e.g. /p/	/a/	/l/	/y/

(Jakobson & Halle 1956: 29f). Problems with these features were pointed out by Chomsky and Halle (1968: 354), and different feature specifications were proposed. For our present purpose we will disregard these differences and retain the fact that basic classes of speech sounds have been defined as bundles of features.

When phonologists speak of "optimal" or prototypical vowels vs. consonants, the respective function of these classes comes into play:

> Syllables are the fundamental divisions of any sequence, and in all languages they follow a clearcut constructional model which consists of a nucleus ... and margins. Vowels function in languages as the only or at least as the most usual carriers of the syllabic nuclei, whereas the margins of syllables are occupied chiefly or solely by consonants (Jakobson & Waugh 1979: 85f).

An optimization of these two contrasting functions is obtained respectively by an appropriate bundling and specification of distinctive features. The need for sonority of a syllable nucleus is met by the closer connection of the sonority (or chromaticity) axis with vocalism, whereas syllable margins favor the closer connection of the tonality axis with consonantism. Correspondingly, the compact-diffuse relation is the fundamental axis of the vocalic system, and the optimal and thus unmarked vowel is the pole of compactness (/a/). Conversely, the compact-diffuse relation is accessory in respect to consonantism, and the pole of compactness shows a marked consonant (/k/). On the other hand, the optimal unmarked consonant is highly diffuse and minimally compact (/p/). "Primarily, optimal vowel phonemes are voiced, in contradistinction to the optimal voiceless consonants; secondarily, optimal vowel phonemes are tense and therefore particularly distinct, in contrast to the optimal, lax consonants" (Jakobson & Waugh 1979: 135ff). Although the justification for what are the primary and the secondary feature specifications is not always clear, it remains that there is a certain amount of dependency and hierarchization in the constitution of these respective sound classes. We must keep in mind that the distinctive features are *principia comparationis* instantiated by parameters with two poles, one carrying the mark, the other lacking it. The parameters constituting the categories of the levels above the phonemic are also bi-polar, but normally show intermediate stations. In spite of this difference it is precisely the similarity in the processes of prototypization which suggests that both kinds of parameter should be subsumed under a common invariant.

3.2. Morphosyntax: the noun/verb [N/V] distinction

First a general note on the nature of grammatical categories and on the problem of their universality. We are indebted to the clarifying views of Coseriu (e.g. 1974: 49ff). When linguists examine the distinction between N and V in a language L_x they consciously or unconsciously start from certain assumptions or expectations about Ns and Vs and their defining properties. In other words they apply certain conceptualizations about Ns and Vs, and they apply them in principle to any language in order to see how these conceptualizations are materialized, e.g., in L_x, L_y, etc. In this sense, the categories of N and V - and any other grammatical categories as applied by linguists - are universal and their definition must be universal. Such definitions constitute the necessary *tertium comparationis* that enables linguists to speak of Ns and Vs in different languages L_x, L_y, etc. and thus write grammars that can be compared with one another. Categories are thus defined as possibilities for languages, with no claim implied about their being materialized in all the languages of the world (Coseriu 1974). This should end the eternal quibble about whether or not Ns and Vs are found "in every language". In fact, they need not be, and in some languages the distinction is minimized to a point where one might prefer to posit a single category of "content words" instead.

The past few years have seen the appearance of a number of important contributions to the topic of N/V distinction: Walter (1981); Hopper & Thompson (1984); Langacker (1987); Broschart (1987). The works of Walter and Broschart are based on the UNITYP model.

For UNITYP the N/V distinction is one of the techniques within the dimension of participation (Seiler 1984). A systematic discussion of this technique will be presented in a comprehensive treatment of participation (Seiler in press). Only the following points shall be highlighted in the present context of prototypization:

1. *Function*. The overall function of participation consists in the representation of a relation, the relation between participants and a participatum ("that which is participated in"). The participatum is that term of the relation which - partly or totally - includes reference to the relation as a whole, and hence also to the participant(s) (inherent relation). The technique of N/V distinction is close to the indicative pole of the dimension, which means that inherence of the relation is more or less taken for granted, while in a more predicative technique such as complex sentences the relationship is made much more explicit. While N/V distinction is low in predicativity, it is correspondingly high in indicativity, and this includes an essential association with pragmatic factors of discourse and context. This is basically in accordance with the findings of Hopper and Thompson (1984). The function corresponding to N/V distinction is optimally served when participatum and participant(s) are respectively represented by terms of high formal and semantic saliency in paradigmatic contrast, without the addition of further syntagmatic material.

2. *Correlativity*. This point deserves particular attention: nouns and verbs are correlative categories. It does not make any sense to speak of nouns without at the same time considering verbs, and vice versa - just as the category of vowels cannot be adequately described without reference to the consonants. And just as the distinction of these two basic classes of speech sounds is described in terms of parameters common to both, we also need a set of parameters where some are common to both N and V in order to account adequately for the prototypization of these two correlative categories.

3. *Defining parameters*. (1) The parameter of relationality: relational vs. absolute. The optimal V is highly relational, which means involving participants, and is minimally absolute. In many languages the participant(s) is/are inherent in the verb, either with or even without an incorporated agreeing element, and no further specification of nominals is needed for a clause to be complete. The optimal N is highly absolute and minimally relational. (2) The identity parameter: referential vs. non-referential. Optimal Ns are highly referential, definite and specific. Optimal Vs are non-referential, but highly general. (3) The stability parameter: time-stable vs. time-unstable. Optimal Ns are highly time-stable, i.e. do not admit differentiation with regard to the time axis. Optimal Vs show the opposite characteristics.

I do not claim that these necessary parameters are also sufficient to exhaustively define the N/V distinction. However, I hope we are now in a position to show what it means to say that prototypes are optimal bundlings of defining parameters. The optimal bundling of parameters (1) to (3) would be: highly relational/highly general/highly time-unstable for Vs, and highly absolute/highly referential/highly time-stable for Ns. Now, optimality and prototypicality is an option among others. As we lower optimality on one or several of the parameters we gradually move away from prototypicality. In our particular case this means that the N/V distinction is weakened. This process can be observed both within a single language and in cross-language comparison. Relevant exemplification can be found in all four works cited above, with regard to parameters especially in Broschart (1987). When non-optimality is reached on all defining parameters "we end up with basically one class of general property words which class-internally may show certain preferences of contextual use, but only a handful of absolute restrictions" (Broschart 1987: 80).

A final word on markedness: Variation on the parameters is characterized by markedness relationships. At first sight one would assume that in a parameter relational vs. absolute the former is marked, the latter unmarked, once and forever. However, in parameters such as this one which correlatively accomodate both Ns and Vs it is the case that one extreme, relational, has the mark for Ns and is unmarked for Vs, while the other extreme, absolute, has the mark for Vs and is unmarked for Ns.

3.3. Speech acts

In his enlightening contribution to the problem of prototypes Givón has successfully counteracted the still widespread tendency of looking only at the prototype peaks while neglecting the other, non-prototypical or atypical manifestations (Givón 1986: 94ff). The four speech acts generally recognized in any language and syntactically coded as, respectively, (a) declarative, (b) imperative, (c) interrogative (i) WH-question, (ii) YES/NO question, he correlates with one another under the common denominator of a cluster of "socio-psychological" parameters which span a continuum leading from the prototypical syntax of one speech act to the prototypical syntax of its correlate. Here is one of his examples (with its original numbering):

(20)   *From imperative to yes/no question*:

[most prototypical imperative]
(a) Pass the salt!
(b) Please pass the salt.
(c) Pass the salt, would you please?
(d) Would you please pass the salt?
(e) Could you please pass the salt?
(f) Can you please pass the salt?
(g) Do you see the salt?
(h) Is there any salt around?
[most prototypical interrogative]

The two extremes on the scale, (20a) and (20h), correspond most closely to their respective speech-act prototypes both semantically/functionally and syntactically. In contrast, the two most clear intermediate points on the semantic continuum, (20c) and (20d), also show intermediate syntactic properties (Givón 1986: 95).

The parameters or dimensions which comprise the semantic/functional space along which syntactic codings of speech acts receive a natural ordering are provisionally determined as follows:

(21)   a.   The *power/authority gradient* between speaker and hearer
        b.   The speaker's *urgency* in eliciting *action*
        c.   The speaker's *ignorance* in eliciting verbal response

At the top of scale (20) - (20a) - the value of (21b) is highest, (21c) lowest and the power gradient (21a) tips toward the speaker. At the bottom of the scale - (20h) - the value of (21b) is lowest, the value of (21c) is highest and the power gradient in (21a) tips toward the hearer (Givón 1986: 96).

In a similar way Givón (1986: 96ff) presents us with continua "from imperative to declarative", and "from declarative to yes/no question", each with its appropriate "socio-psychological" parameter(s). The prototypical syntactic representation of the imperative, e.g. would result as a cluster of the syntactic optima within each of the dimensions where imperative appears as one of the correlates.

In summing up the results from section 3 thus far, the following analogies between classes of speech sounds, basic grammatical categories, and classes of speech acts can be stated:

1. Categories or classes are constituted by a number of parameters, each comprising a number of options ordered on the basis of markedness relations in a continuum with two poles and possibly intermediate steps.
2. The parameters which constitute a category interact with one another. "Bundling" was the expression used for such interaction in phonology (Bloomfield 1933: 79; Jakobson & Waugh 1979: 19f). This metaphor can now be replaced by a more precise notion. The decisive point of "bundling" or "meeting" of the constitutive parameters is "the prototype", i.e. that instantiation of the category where all the parameter options are optimal for the given function of the category.
3. As the choice of options on one or several of the parameters moves away from optimality, the categorial representation of the given function moves toward marginality.
4. Irrespective of absolute markedness values within each parameter, it is the superordinated function of the category that determines that the optimal value is always unmarked. This may involve a reversal of markedness.
5. As there is correlativity among categories, such as vowel/consonant, N/V, imperative/interrogative, or, generally speaking, A/A', at least some of the constituting parameters are common to both correlates, where the optimal, unmarked value for category A is the least optimal, marked one for category A', and vice versa.

3.4. The lexicon

We shall confine ourselves here to a few general remarks.

In the wake of Rosch's seminal work on human cognition and categorization (Rosch 1977, 1978 for references), many linguists insist that human categorization in general and linguistic categorization in particular - the lexicon has received particular attention - lack well-defined boundaries (Lakoff 1973: 458ff; 1986: 43ff). *Fuzziness* is the magic word. Even upon cursory reflection it should be clear that a statement of fuzziness, no matter whether true or false, necessarily presupposes knowledge of a basis of comparison which in itself is not fuzzy, thus which does have well-defined boundaries. There is something in human, particularly lexical, categorization which does have well-defined boundaries, and something which is fuzzy.

How can this paradox be resolved? Let us try it with an example, the much discussed "meaning of *bird*" (Rosch 1975: 193; Lakoff 1973: 458; Wierzbicka 1985: 180, in press: example 4). What the participants in the debate seem to have in common is that they can reasonably argue about the inclusion or exclusion of a particular animal in the category. There may be disagreement, not only about inclusion but even about the pertinent criteria; nevertheless, well-defined boundaries and criteria are the necessary background of such discussion.

It is actually possible to define the concept underlying the English word *bird*, or at least to reasonably argue about such a definition, e.g. whether flying is an essential part of it, alongside components referring to feathers, beaks, eggs, and nests (cf. Wierzbicka 1985: 180, and in press). One would certainly agree with Wierzbicka (to appear) that bats "are no more birds than cows are, but ostriches and emus - which do not fly - ARE birds". One would also agree with Lakoff (1986: 33) that "robins and sparrows are typical birds". Such statements and discussions relate to the concept underlying the English word *bird*. Defining concepts is, after all, a fundamental activity of the human mind, where the scientific, in our case the zoological definition, is only a special case of such activity. It is also possible to define the concept underlying the word for *bird* in such other languages as, e.g. the Australian Nunggubuyu (Wierzbicka to appear: Note 2), where bats as well as grasshoppers are included. The gist of our argument is that the result of such activities, i.e. the concepts defined, may be subject to debate and to eventual revision, whereas the mental operations involved in defining a concept aim at discreteness and at well-defined borders. The character of such operations is, in principle, an onomasiological one; it is furthermore abductive, proceeding, that is, by advancing hypotheses and by subsequent testing.

Now, defining a concept underlying the English word *bird* should be carefully distinguished from describing the meaning of that English word. The relevant operations here are semasiological, and are of an inductive character, proceeding by way of generalization and eventually arriving at a common denominator. Unfortunately, the difference between defining the concept underlying a word and describing its meaning is still widely ignored. The most incisive formulation of this difference under the respective terms of *Bezeichnung* vs. *Bedeutung* has been worked out by Coseriu in several of his earlier and more recent publications (see, e.g. Coseriu 1973: 1ff, 1987: 1ff).

Describing the meaning of *bird* involves, above all, noticing its contextual variants and bringing them into an order. Here the masses of texts and contextual uses within a language, in our case English, are the *primum datum*. An overview can be gained from the respective dictionary article. We find that some of the parameters of the proposed conceptual definitions of *bird* are over-extended, such as when *bird* is applied to humans - e.g. for 'girl' (slang), or as in *birds of a feather* 'people of like character'; or when parameters show up that were neglected in the hitherto proposed definitions, such as the bird's vocal productions - e.g. in *a little bird* for 'source of information not to be disclosed' or in *get/give the bird* for 'disapproval by hissing, booing', etc. In sum, describing the meaning of *bird* brings to light metaphorical and other over-extensions, over-emphasis of certain components at the detriment of others, fuzzy boundaries - a considerable range of variation.

Now, variation is unthinkable without admitting a common denominator. In fact, it is possible, by way of generalization, to arrive at such an invariant - for *bird* as well as for any other word. The resolution of the above formulated paradox lies in the fact that conceptual definition and description of a meaning invariant are not disparate operations; there is an interface between them. The clearest manifestation of such an interface appears when we compare the English word *bird* with its variational range of meanings with the word for 'bird' in Nunggubuyu with its different range of meanings - an activity which is at the basis of any translation.

4.   Universal dimensions and prototypization

4.1.   Generalities

The title refers to functional dimensions as proposed by the UNITYP research group. They embrace phenomena that may differ from one another both in form and in meaning, phenomena that relate to all levels of linguistic analyis. The phenomena are dimensionally ordered, and the order holds both for any particular language and cross-linguistically. The superordinated functional denominators constitute the names of the following dimensions proposed thus far: *apprehension* - the linguistic representation of the concepts of objects (Seiler 1986); *possession*

(Seiler 1983); *determination* (Seiler 1978, 1985); *nomination* - formerly *descriptivity* (Seiler 1975); *participation* (Seiler 1984).

Our exemplification here will be drawn from the dimension of *apprehension*. The ordering of the linguistic data follows two converse functional principles: *indicativity* vs. *predicativity*. Applied to the dimension of *apprehension* indicativity means the following. The object is apprehended by pointing it out; to indicate means to point (deixis). The object pointed out is an individualized object. Predicativity means that the object is apprehended by predicating about it, its properties, manifestations, and the like. Predicativity is syntactically manifested as relationality. A relation is general, not individual. The predicated object is a generalized object. The co-presence of the two functional principles, indicativity vs. predicativity, in the linguistic - and cognitive - apprehension of objects is reflected in Aristotle's appraisal that a "thing" is at the same time a "such" and a "this" (citations in Seiler 1986: 17).

The dimension represents an overall parameter or continuum. The UNITYP dimensional model features parametrization in three hierarchical levels: (1) dimensions (superordinate), (2) techniques (basic), (3) subdimensions (subordinate). Prototypization seems to preferably occur on the basic level of techniques. With this situation one may compare Rosch's and Tversky's findings about a basic level of categorization in human cognition (Rosch 1978; Tversky 1986). Each of the techniques has its particular function and is constituted by a bundle of parameters (subdimensions), the bundling being commanded by the convergence point of the optima of the parameters - in other words, by the prototype. Within each technique both functional principles are active, but at different degrees of dominance. Predicativity predominates at the leftmost pole of the dimension, viz. within the technique of *abstraction* - however, with indicativity not being totally absent. Indicativity predominates at the rightmost pole, viz. within the technique of *namegiving* - however, with predicativity not being totally absent. For further details the reader is referred to Seiler (1986).

The so-called classificatory techniques that we shall now inspect more closely occupy a medial space within the dimension.

4.2.   Numeral classification and other classificatory techniques

4.2.1.   Generalities

Classification occurs as a component of several techniques pertaining to several different functional dimensions: *apprehension* - the linguistic representation of the concepts of objects - is one (Seiler 1986); *possession* - the linguistic representation of the relation of appurtenance - is another (Seiler 1983); *aspectual classification and argument structure* (our dimension of *participation*) is a third (Silverstein 1986). A true insight into the workings of classification in each of these cases can only come from an understanding of their respective functional context.

Within the dimension of *apprehension*, I have distinguished the following classificatory techniques in the following order: classification by verbs, classification by articles, numeral classification. Their ordering is determined by a decrease in predicativity and an increase in indicativity. The technique adjacent to numeral classification, viz. agreement in gender and number, also shows a classificatory aspect, although here classification is subservient to agreement which fulfills the function of indexing and reference. Again, within each of the techniques mentioned classification has a somewhat different role, and we expect that prototypization of class membership is different, too.

4.2.2.   Numeral classification

This technique is spread over a vast geographical area - roughly circum-Pacific - and is encountered in a great number of languages of quite diversified structure. Nevertheless it is possible to formulate a common functional denominator for all of the numeral classifier constructions. It is determined by the ratio between the two functional principles, i.e. between a predicative/generalized vs. an indicative/individualized representation of objects. These languages show an extended area of neutrality where an unclassified noun does not represent any object at all, but a species or concept. This is why an isolated noun in these languages cannot be directly combined with a quantifier (numeral), since only individuals, not concepts, can be counted. The primary function of classifier constructions is individualization. The task is fulfilled by the operation of classification whereby the N is subsumed under a property concept as represented by the classifier (CLF), and is thus made countable.

Like all the other techniques of *apprehension*, numeral classification is multi-factorial. I have posited five parameters defining this technique (Seiler 1986: 98f):

1. Neutrality. Unclassified nouns, i.e. nouns appearing outside of numeral or related contexts are transnumeral, i.e. neutral with regard to distinctions between singular, dual, and plural. Most classifier languages do not show grammatical number distinctions. This accounts for the impossibility in these languages of any direct collocation of quantifier-noun (Q-N).
2. The context is basically that of numeration (counting), where CLF is obligatory. Other possible contexts are: demonstrative (optional), and qualifier (infrequent).
3. The constituent structure is such that, irrespective of variations in word order, Q and CLF are never separated. This shows that quantification and classification are intimately linked with one another.
4. Classification. This is an operation, an operation of subsumption, such that the unclassified N falls under a concept X. It is not an operation of qualification - in contradistinction to attribution; nor is it an operation of indexing - in contradistinction to the technique of gender agreement.
5. Solidarity between CLF and the classified N. In principle the relation between CLF and N is one-many; i.e. one given N takes one CLF, but one and the same CLF classifies many Ns. Solidarity means that the classification is based on some property that essentially has to do with properties of the object as represented by the N. The rationale of this connection of properties may vary from one N to another. This is turn means that the criteria for classification are subject to variation.

There are, of course, dependency relations among these parameters. The primary one seems to be neutrality, on which the others depend. Specifically, it represents the problem to be solved, while classification and solidarity represent the answer. As they interact with one another, a certain conflict is preprogrammed: In parameter 4 the classification regards the N, i.e. the word representing the object, not the object itself. The operation thus seems to be a predominantly metalinguistic one. In parameter 5 the solidarity between CLF and N is based on properties of the represented object. This then points to object-linguistic operations. As parameters 4 and 5 are equally constitutive for the solution of the problem, we predict that prototypization within the technique of numeral classification will come out with a mean midway between the two; in other words, it will show classes that are mildly, but not overly, heterogeneous with regard to properties of the objects as represented by the Ns.

Extreme, non-prototypical realisations of Numeral Classification we obtain when either parameter 4 or parameter 5 is overextended or stretched. First, three examples for overextension of the metalinguistic aspect:

1. For Garo, a Tibeto-Burmese language of Western Assam, Adams and Conklin (1973: 2) report the following situation: "... *stone, ball, eye, coin,* and *fruit* are all included in one class based on their roundedness. This class also includes *banana,* although it is not round (like oranges, mangos, etc.), because all other fruits are in this class".

    Does this mean that the Garo show a peculiar, exotic indifference vis-à-vis the shape distinction between round vs. oblong objects? In other words, would they be unable to classify bananas among the long, not among the round objects? Certainly not. What happened in their linguistic classifier system is a shift of criterion from roundness to fruitness. Given the overall context as described by the authors, the shift makes perfect sense, it is well motivated. Lakoff (1986: 18ff) is right in putting emphasis on the distinction "between giving principles that *motivate,* or *make sense of,* a system, and giving principles that *generate,* or *predict,* a system". But he errs when he concludes that "categories on the whole need not be defined by common properties" (Lakoff 1986: 17). How else could they be defined, if not by common properties? The technique of numeral classification can be defined, as we have shown, by a set of properties embodied in five interacting parameters. The parameters show that it is not the purpose of this technique to simply classify the objects out there (object-linguistically). Rather, the purpose is to classify Ns (metalinguistically) in a solidarity relation between CLF and N based on properties of the object represented by N - which allows for changing motivations and eventually results, if one looks only at the objects, in apparently heterogenous classes.

2. Still more extreme seems to be a case in Vietnamese as reported by Weidert (in press): CLF *thó-t* is used with Ns for 'elephant', 'garden', and 'raft'; CLF *tâ'm* is used with Ns for 'bolt of cloth', 'board' or 'plank', 'hide', 'photograph', 'ticket', 'mirror', 'heart', 'example'.

3. The metalinguistic aspect of numeral classification appears patently in the so-called repeater constructions where the N and the CLF are represented by one and the same lexeme, and which is thus plainly tautological, as e.g. in Thai:

Thai
(1) *prathêet   săam   prathêet*
     country   three   CLF:country
     'three countries'

No information about properties of the *object out there* is supplied by the CLF.

Now an example for an overextension of parameter 5, which results in the opposite extreme: CLFs are highly informative about properties of the object and fairly homogeneous classes of objects. The so-called temporary classification is attested in Middle and South American Indian languages, and especially well in Tzeltal, a Mayan language, where it has been studied in detail (Berlin 1968; Serzisko 1980 and 1982). An instructive example, taken from Berlin's book on Tzeltal numeral classifiers (1968: 39) is this:

Tzeltal
(2) *ho   -b'ehč'   laso*
     five   -CLF1   rope
     'laso in the state of five sequential wraps around a long non-flexible object'

Tzeltal
(3) *ho   -hiht'   laso*
     five   -CLF2   rope
     'laso in five lash loops around two pieces of long non-flexible object at 90° angles to one another, as in fence making'

Here, classifiers CLF1 and CLF2 do add a great deal of information about the object out there; in fact all that is contained in the glosses beside the numeral and the word for rope. In view of this, it has even been proposed (Berlin & Romney 1964: 79) that the classifier ought to be considered rather as a nominal qualifier like an adjective. However, I think Serzisko (1980 and 1982) is right in considering the examples as manifestations of classifier constructions on the grounds (a) that they belong to the same substitution class, and (b) that they cannot occur together with inherent classifiers. After all, classifiers CLF1 and CLF2 above do and, apparently, must occur in counting contexts, and they constitute a class of nouns which, beside *laso*, includes the word for 'cord', 'vine', 'grass', and 'belt', thus 'slender flexible objects' (Berlin 1968: 37). The relation between N and CLF is one of solidarity, where a classifier and a classified noun and their meanings reciprocally condition each other. Tzeltal shows an exceedingly high number of classifiers - over 500 - with noun classes that are small in number and that correspond well with properties of the represented objects.

As all these extreme cases of numeral classification show, it would not do to define the technique, and the resulting category, solely on the basis of its prototypical manifestations, because this would mean that the Garo, Vietnamese, and Tzeltal cases would have to be excluded, which, however, would run against the remainder of available morphosyntactic and semantic evidence. The entire range of variation must be covered by the definition of a category.

As noted before, the prototype of numeral classification must lie somewhere between these extremes. To determine its exact location we need to look at the entire range of the superordinated dimension of *apprehension* and compare the technique with its immediate and its more distant neighbors, in the direction of both greater predicativity and greater indicativity. Such comparative work should now be possible along the lines laid down in my work on *apprehension* (Seiler 1986). In the framework of the present paper a few glimpses will have to suffice.

4.2.3.   Numeral classification and mass and measure

Measuring is a kind of interaction between humans and objects, more specifically, continuous objects or masses. There are different kinds of masses, and we interact differently with them. When we want to measure liquids we put them into cups or gallons or pints, grain into sacks, etc. We expect the function of the linguistic representation of such activities to include particular attention to the properties of the represented objects.

In the technique of "mass and measure" we have two directionalities of the operation. In the dissociative measure construction an object is represented as a mass, a *quale*, by the very fact that a certain portion or *quantum* is being dissociated from it. In the associative container construction a *quantum* is represented as having boundaries and shape and other qualities, and thus the object appears again as a mass. The qualitative (predicative) aspect prevails. This makes it understandable that the qualities in the linguistic representation of the objects match the qualities of the real world.

As Greenberg (1972) has shown, classifier constructions and mass/measure constructions show comparable or identical structures in many languages. Thus, in Thai:

> Thai
>
> (4) *rôm*   *săam*   *khan*
>   umbrella   three   CLF: long, handled object
>   'three umbrellas'

is a classifier construction, as compared with

> Thai
>
> (5) *phâafâaj sâam   pháp*
>   cotton   three   MENS:roll
>   'three rolls of cotton',

a measure construction. Examples and interpretation are from Hundius & Kölver (1983: 166f). As Kölver has convincingly shown in several of her publications (e.g. 1982: 162ff), classifier constructions, as in (4), are both formally and semantically distinct from measure constructions, as in (5). For one thing, measure terms (mensuratives, MENS) express "some notion of quantity which is *extrinsic* to the lexical content of the head noun; they provide additional information" (Hundius & Kölver 1983: 168). Thus, in the Thai example (Hundius & Kölver 1983: 170)

> Thai
>
> (6) *náamtaan   săam   kiloo/   thûaj/   kɔ̆n*
>   sugar   three   kg   cup   lump

the mensuratives are relatively extrinsic to the lexical content of 'sugar' (on restrictive "relatively" see below), and they add the new information of differing quantities. Numeral classifiers, such as *khan* 'long handled object' in (4), "reflect *intrinsic* semantic properties of nouns that they are systematically related to" (Hundius & Kölver 1983: 169). Thus, in principle, they do not add new information about the object, i.e. they are low in predicativity.

A comparison between (6) and the following measure construction of Thai (Hundius & Kölver 1983: 170) shows that the above statements about extrinsic and intrinsic need to be relativized:

(7)   Thai
       klûaj   sǎam   kiloo/   takrâa/   wǐi
       banana   three   kg/   basket/   hand

Apparently, bananas and sugar may either both take *kg* as a mensurative, or they take different mensuratives such as "cup", "lump" for sugar vs. "basket", "hand" for bananas. And this doubtlessly has to do with the semantic difference between the two head nouns - and with the properties of the objects they represent. There is a classificatory aspect in this, but it is much more in accordance with the properties of the things measured than is classification in numeral classification. From all this we learn that classification is an operation that works differently according to the purposive function served by the respective techniques. Prototypization differs accordingly.

4.2.4.   Numeral classification and agreement in gender and number

For a detailed treatment of this technique the reader is again referred to Seiler (1986: 110ff).

Agreement serves a predominantly indexical function. It signals constancy of reference; it conveys the idea that - within the discourse or context - I am still talking about the same object. The object is thus apprehended by signalling its constancy.

Again, the technique, and the resulting category, is constituted by a bundle of parameters:

1.   The basis of gender is agreement.
2.   Gender involves a classification. But the classification is subservient to agreement.
3.   Gender is always linked up with number. The noun as characterized by the gender-number amalgam is always individualizable.
4.   Semanticity:
4.1.   Gender classification is exhaustive. This means that each N must be a member of a particular class.
4.2.   Gender classification stands in a relation to biological sex.

4.3.   Only a small percentage of the objects denoted by nouns of a particular gender are in fact sexually differentiated.

5.   Pragmaticity: This involves discourse functions (constancy of reference) and metalinguistic operations (reflections on gender assignment).

If we take the aforementioned definitory parameters together - especially 4 with its subcomponents - we reach the conclusion that, given the overwhelming majority of nouns viz. the inanimate ones, it is not the purposive function of this technique to convey the idea that N_1 is a man, and N_2 is a woman, and N_3 is neither a man nor a woman. Rather, we are faced with a highly grammaticalized technique, where semanticity/predicativity is correspondingly low, i.e. says little or nothing about properties of the represented objects. The respective classes of masculine, feminine, neuter are in this sense heterogeneous, and 4.1. - 4.3. even lead us to expect that heterogeneity prevails. This is widely confirmed by the facts of languages with gender/number agreement.

Lakoff in his treatment of classifiers (1986: 13ff; 1987: 92-102) has offered his interpretation and "some speculations" (1986: 20) regarding the classifier system of Dyirbal. Dixon's discussion of Dyirbal (1986: 105ff) - see also the description in his grammar (1972: 44ff) - suggests that classification in this language is intimately linked with referentiality and indexicality: "A noun is normally accompanied by a *noun marker* that shows its class" (four classes distinguished), "agrees with it in case, and also yields information on the location of the referent of that occurence of the noun" (Dixon 1972: 45). In several of his publications on the subject, Dixon has quite rightly insisted on the distinction between "the grammatical category of *noun classes* (including most types of gender system) and the lexico-syntactic phenomenon of *noun classification* (including numeral classifiers)" (Dixon 1986: 45). Dyirbal shows "a full-blown grammatical noun class system" (Dixon 1972: 110) and as such it is close to gender agreement.

With regard to properties of the objects out there denoted by the nouns, the four classes are patently heterogeneous. I do not deny that good motivations for shifting criteria for the inclusion of this or that noun entity designating this or that disparate object into the class can be adduced (Lakoff 1986: 15ff). But I think it is altogether unnecessary to speculate on the coherence of classes including "women, fire, and dangerous things" (Lakoff 1986: 13; 1987), because, in the first place, they are not classes of things, but classes of nouns.

"Classifiers as a reflection of mind" is another of Lakoff's suggestive titles (1986: 13), and an entire edifice called "the ecological aspect of mind" (Lakoff 1986: 49) is construed along these lines. Surely, classifiers are a reflection of mind, but in the almost trivial sense in which all of language is a reflection of mind. It is also a near-truism that the reflection is not a direct one. Numeral classifiers cannot be taken at their face value in that they would tell us how the Thai or the Vietnamese classify the objects of the "real world". They tell us how the language classifies nouns for the purpose of making them accessible to quantification - and that is a quite different matter. As we have seen, classification within the technique of "mass and measure" has a different function, and within agreement of gender/number the function of classification is again a different one.

The prototype of this last-mentioned technique features a small sub-class of nouns - humans, and, to a lesser degree, animals - where gender distinction reflects properties of the designated objects; and an over-whelming majority of nouns where the gender distinction does not re-flect any coherent classification of objects, or only rudimentary so (see Zubin & Köpcke 1986: 139ff).

Yet overextensions in semanticity of the classificatory parameter do occur. It was said above that metalinguistic activities with regard to gender assignment are part of the defining parameters of this tech-nique. Now, it is precisely in the situation of experiments that overex-tensions appear. Jakobson (1959 [1971]: 265) reports that a test in the Moscow Psychological Institute (1915) showed that Russians, prone to personify the weekdays, consistently represented Monday, Tuesday, and Thursday as males, and Wednesday, Friday, and Saturday as females, without realizing that this distribution was due to the masculine gender of the first three names (*ponedeln'ik, vtornik, cetverg*) as against the feminine gender of the others (*sreda, pjatnica, subbota*).

When the frame conditions of the experiment are set up in such a way that weekdays are persons, then the correspondence between their sex and nominal gender comes as no surprise. (For an analogous re-mark regarding a Roschian experiment see Wierzbicka to appear: example 4.) This shows overextension in the classificatory parameter of gender agreement. But it is nevertheless part of the facts of language and can and must be accommodated by the definition of that particular technique.

5.   Concluding remarks

The reader is invited to return to our "elements of a functional prototype theory" and to compare them with the foregoing.

The most important points shall be highlighted here. The inclusion
of prototypization into the dimensional model of UNITYP opens up new
vistas which ultimately should lead us to a coherent treatment of the
relation between conceptualizations and meanings, as well as of
categories and of their defining parameters on all levels of linguistic
analysis, including the phonological.

1.   Categories are constituted by interacting parameters of variation.
2.   The reference or meeting point of such interaction is the prototype
      of the category, determined by the convergence of the optimal val-
      ues of the parameters with regard to a given function. Morphologi-
      cal categories represent the kernels of the prototypes.
3.   Cognizance of the full variational range of all constitutive parame-
      ters is necessary for an adequate definition of a category. Defining
      by its prototype manifestations alone would not do.
4.   Our work throughout is characterized by combining two ap-
      proaches and respective results that should be neatly distinguished,
      although not separated, from one another:
      a.   The onomasiological approach. It consists in positing con-
            cepts and in defining them by a set of properties. They are
            not derived in any direct way from empirical observation.
            The move is *abductive*, i.e. by hypothesis and subsequent
            testing. These concepts are universal in the sense that they
            are applied in grammatical research to any language. They
            are the *repraesentandum*. Categories on all levels,
            grammatical, syntactic, semantic - even the notion of
            prototype itself - have such an aprioristic aspect.
      b.   The semasiological approach. It consists in assembling data
            within the framework of the posited categories; in ordering
            them into scalar parameters (continua), and, by way of
            inductive generalization, in arriving at a common denomina-
            tor of meaning. These meanings are not universal; they are
            language-specific. Their boundaries are fuzzy. They are the
            repraesentantia.
5.   Function is the central notion that allows conceptualizations and
      common denominators of meaning to be brought together. It is the
      superordinated instance that commands prototypization. It can do

this because of its Janus-like nature, combining the abductive and the inductive aspects. To do nothing but posit a function would result in mere speculation. In a second move it must be subjected to tests pertaining to inductive generalization, and, in this context the construction of parameter/continuum is a particularly powerful tool. The moves need to be in constant alternation, up and down, and, as Heraclitus would have it: "The upward and the downward path are one and the same. Removing one, you remove both."

References

Adams, Karen L. & Nancy F. Conklin
1973   "Toward a theory of natural classification", *Papers from the Ninth Regional Meeting, Chicago Linguistic Society* 9: 1-10.
Berlin, Brent
1968   *Tzeltal numeral classifiers: A study in ethnographic semantics.* (Janua Linguarum, Series Practica 70). The Hague: Mouton.
Berlin, Brent & A. Kimball Romney
1964   "Descriptive semantics of Tzeltal numeral classifiers", *American Anthropologist Special Publication* 66, No.3, Part 2: 79-98.
Bloomfield, Leonard
1933   *Language.* New York: Henry Holt.
Broschart, Jürgen
1987   *Noun, verb, and PARTICIPATION. (Arbeiten des Kölner Universalien-Projekts* 67.) Köln: Institut für Sprachwissenschaft.
Chomsky, Noam & Morris Halle
1968   *The sound pattern of English.* New York: Harper & Row.
Coseriu, Eugenio
1973   *Probleme der strukturellen Semantik.* Vorlesung gehalten im Wintersemester 1965/66 an der Universität Tübingen. Autorisierte und bearbeitete Nachschrift von Dieter Kastovsky. (Tübinger Beiträge zur Linguistik 40). Tübingen: Narr.
1974   "Les universaux linguistiques (et les autres)", in: Luigi Heilmann (ed.), *Proceedings of the Eleventh International Congress of Linguists, Bologna 1973.* Bologna: Mulino, vol. I, 47-73.
1987   "Bedeutung, Bezeichnung und sprachliche Kategorien", *Sprachwissenschaft* 12: 1-23.
Craig, Colette (ed.)
1986   *Noun classes and categorization: Proceedings of a symposium on categorization and noun classification, Eugene, Oregon, October 1983.* Amsterdam: Benjamins.
Dixon, R. M. W.
1972   *The Dyirbal language of North Queensland.* Cambridge: Cambridge University Press.
1986   "Noun classes and noun classification in typological perspective", in: Colette Craig (ed.), 105-112.

Givón, Talmy
1986   "Prototypes: Between Plato and Wittgenstein", in: Colette Craig (ed.), 78-102.
Greenberg, Joseph
1972   "Numeral classifiers and substantival number: Problems in the genesis of a linguistic type", *Working Papers on Language Universals* 9: 1-39.
Hopper, Paul & Sandra A. Thompson
1984   "The discourse basis for lexical categories in universal grammar", *Language* 60: 703-752.
Hundius, Harald & Ulrike Kölver
1983   "Syntax and semantics of numeral classifiers in Thai", *Studies in Language* 7: 165-214.
Jakobson, Roman
1959   "On linguistic aspects of translation", in: Roman Jakobson, *Selected writings*
[1971]   *II. Word and language*. The Hague: Mouton, 260-266.
Jakobson, Roman & Morris Halle
1956   *Fundamentals of language*. S'Gravenhage: Mouton.
Jakobson, Roman & Linda R. Waugh
1979   *The sound shape of language*. Bloomington: Indiana University Press.
Kölver, Ulrike
1982   "Klassifikatorkonstruktionen in Thai, Vietnamesisch und Chinesisch: Ein Beitrag zur Dimension der Apprehension", in: Hansjakob Seiler & Christian Lehmann (eds.), *Apprehension. Das sprachliche Erfassen von Gegenständen. Teil I. Bereich und Ordnung der Phänomene.* (Language Universals Series, 1/I.) Tübingen: Narr, 160-185.
Lakoff, George
1973   "Hedges: A study in meaning criteria and the logic of fuzzy concepts", *Journal of Philosophical Logic* 2: 458-508.
1986   "Classifiers as a reflection of mind", in: Colette Craig (ed.), 13-51.
1987   *Women, fire, and dangerous things: What categories reveal about the mind*. Chicago: Chicago University Press.
Langacker, Ronald W.
1987   "Nouns and verbs", *Language* 63: 52-94.
Rosch, Eleanor
1975   "Cognitive representations of semantic categories", *Journal of Experimental Psychology: General* 104: 192-233.
1977   "Human categorization", in: Neil Warren (ed.), *Studies in cross-cultural psychology*. London: Academic Press, 1-49.
1978   "Principles of categorization", in: Eleanor Rosch & Barbara B. Lloyd (eds.), *Cognition and categorization*. Hillsdale, N.J.: Lawrence Erlbaum, 27-48.
Seiler, Hansjakob
1975   "Die Prinzipien der deskriptiven und der etikettierenden Benennung", in: Hansjakob Seiler (ed.), *Linguistic Workshop III: Arbeiten des Kölner Universalienprojekts*. München: Wilhelm Fink, 2-57.
1978   "Determination: A functional dimension for interlanguage comparison", in: Hansjakob Seiler (ed.), *Language universals. Papers from the conference held at Gummersbach / Cologne, Germany, October 3-8, 1976.* (Tübinger Beiträge zur Linguistik 111). Tübingen: Narr, 301-328.

1983   *POSSESSION as an operational dimension of language.* (Language
            Universal Series 2). Tübingen: Narr.
1984   *Die Dimension der* PARTIZIPATION. Vorlesung Wintersemester
            1983/84. Bearbeitet von Michael Kurzidim und Thomas Müller-
            Bardey. [Manuskript]. Köln: Institut für Sprachwissenschaft.
1985   "Kategorien als fokale Instanzen von Kontinua: gezeigt am Beispiel
            der nominalen Determination", in: Bernfried Schlerath & Veronica
            Rittner (eds.), *Grammatische Kategorien. Funktion und Geschichte:
            Akten der VII. Fachtagung der Indogermanischen Gesellschaft, Berlin,
            20.-25. Februar 1983.* Wiesbaden: Dr. Ludwig Reichert Verlag, 435-448.
1986   *Apprehension: Language, object, and order.* Part III. *The universal
            dimension of apprehension.* (Language Universals Series 1/III).
            Tübingen: Narr.
in press   *The universal dimension of participation.* (Language Universals Series
            7). Tübingen: Narr.
Serzisko, Fritz
1980   *Sprachen mit Zahlklassifikatoren: Analyse und Vergleich.* (Arbeiten des
            Kölner Universalien Projekts 37.) Köln: Institut für Sprachwis-
            senschaft.
1982   "Temporäre Klassifikation: Ihre Variationsbreite in Sprachen mit
            Zahlklassifikatoren", in: Hansjakob Seiler & Christian Lehmann
            (eds.), *Apprehension: Das sprachliche Erfassen von Gegenständen. Teil
            I: Bereich und Ordnung der Phänomene.* (Language Universals Series
            1/I). Tübingen: Gunter Narr Verlag, 147-159.
Silverstein, Michael
1986   "Classifiers, verb classifiers, and verbal categories", *Proceedings of the
            Annual Meeting of the Berkeley Linguistic Society* 12: 497-514.
Tversky, Barbara
1986   "Components and categorization", in: Colette Craig (ed.), 63-76.
Walter, Heribert
1981   *Studien zur Nomen-Verb-Distinktion aus typologischer Sicht.* (Structura
            13). München: Wilhelm Fink.
Weidert, Alfons K.
in press   "The classifier construction and its historical southeast Asian back-
            ground". To appear in *Kailas.* Kathmandu.
Wierzbicka, Anna
1985   *Lexicography and conceptual analysis.* Ann Arbor: Karoma.
to appear   "Prototypes save: On the uses and abuses of the concept 'prototype' in
            current linguistics, philosophy and psychology".
Zubin, David & Klaus Michael Köpcke
1986   "Gender and folk taxonomy: The indexical relation between
            grammatical and lexical categorization", in: Colette Craig (ed.), 139-
            180.

Process linguistics: A cognitive-scientific approach to natural language understanding

Geert Adriaens

... the first order of business for linguistic theory is the construction of tentative models of linguistic performance. It is a matter of indifference, really, who does the work, though I suspect that the best approach would be for linguists and psychologists to collaborate on the problem (Derwing 1973: 281).

1. Introduction

The motto of this article was Derwing's conclusion at the end of an extensive critique of the foundations of generative grammar. The reason why I have chosen it is that it will serve as a good starting point for the presentation of *process linguistics* (henceforth: *PL*). For one thing, *PL* is also partly inspired by a dissatisfaction with mainstream (generative) linguistics. This dissatisfaction is closely related to the competence-performance distinction, whose reinterpretation is a central issue for *PL* (see 3.1.). For another, *PL* puts itself in a broader *cognitive-science* context, and somehow Derwing's conclusion is a call for cognitive-scientific research *avant-la-lettre*, when he suggests that the best approach would be a collaboration of linguists and psychologists. (He failed to mention the researchers in artificial intelligence, but the field of AI was not that well known to linguists at the time.) As we will see below, the need for interdisciplinarity is crucial to the cognitive-science enterprise.

Before I begin the presentation of *process linguistics* via a short introduction to cognitive science, a brief note about its exact nature is in order. I want to stress that *PL* is NOT a linguistic theory as it stands, but rather a framework of principles and notions within which a (growing) number of existing (especially computational) approaches to natural language can be accommodated. Several other researchers have expressed the same ideas in different ways, especially Winograd (1977, 1983), when he introduced the "computational paradigm" for the study of language. If bringing these principles and notions together can be a stimulus for other researchers to work along the same lines, then the main aim of this presentation will have been reached.

2.   Cognitive science

2.1.   A new paradigm

Cognitive science[1] is a contemporary scientific paradigm that is attempting to bring together a number of existing fields (artificial intelligence, psychology, neuroscience, philosophy, linguistics and anthropology) in a concerted effort to study the complex domain of cognition/intelligence in its broadest sense (including, for example, problems of knowledge representation, language processing, learning, reasoning and problem solving). To reach this goal it uses the research tools recently developed in its participating sciences. Its most important tools come from artificial intelligence (computer simulation of theories, using a wide variety of computer languages and formalisms) and cognitive psychology (rigorous experimentation and disciplined introspection (see Simon & Ericsson 1984)). So a full-scale cognitive-scientific study of natural language processing should fulfill the requirements of *computational realizability* and *psychological reality:* a model/theory should be accompanied by a computer program simulating its workings, and embedded within corroborating research findings from psycholinguistic experiments. I will consider both requirements in closer detail, concentrating most of the discussion within the subsection about psychological reality (2.3.).

2.2.   Computational realizability

The requirement to show that a model or theory can be complemented with a computer program illustrating its principles is an interesting one because it forces researchers to formalize their theories as explicitly and completely as possible. For AI researchers working in the area of natural language processing,[2] presenting programs that support their theories has always been a methodological must. For linguistics, it is a relatively new development of the last decade to show that linguistic theories can be implemented in programs that learn, analyze or produce language;[3] computational linguistics (including the study of the complexity of algorithms, see e.g. Barton, Berwick & Ristad 1987), has become a very active area of research.

As a methodological requirement, computational realizability in itself seems to be a healthy and relatively unproblematic one for linguists to consider when developing their theories (but see e.g. Herskovits 1988 for a skeptical view on the computational realizability of the complex models of cognitive linguistics). Problems *do* arise, though, when the issue of psychological reality is brought in as well.

2.3. Psychological reality

To demonstrate that bringing in psychological considerations into the study of natural language and its processing is indeed a moot point, the following quote from Gazdar et al. (1985: 5) is illustrative:

> In view of the fact that the packaging and public relations of much recent linguistic theory involves constant reference to questions of psychology, it is appropriate for us to make a few remarks about the connections between the claims we make and issues in the psychology of language. We make no claims, naturally enough, that our grammatical theory is eo ipso a psychological theory... Thus we feel it is possible, and arguably proper, for a linguist (qua linguist) to ignore matters of psychology.

So, for researchers like Gazdar et al. (who accept the requirement of computational realizability - different implementations of the theory of GPSG exist),[4] the issue of psychological reality is one they would rather not consider at all. Others, however, (like Bresnan 1982) *do* attach importance to the psychological reality of the computational models they present with their linguistic theories. Reasoning from the theory or the computational model to psychological reality is, however, a precarious enterprise, as is very lucidly discussed by Clark and Malt (1984), specifically within the context of methods and tactics in cognitive science. I will try to summarize the problems here, because they form the background for the introduction of the notion of *processing competence*, central to *PL*.

2.3.1.   Competence and performance

The relationship between linguistic theory and language use has - at least in the generative tradition - usually been approached through the well-known and much-debated[5] competence-performance distinction. The rules or principles of a generative grammar constitute the knowledge a speaker-hearer has of his language; this knowledge is his competence, and it is the object of study of generative linguistics. The *competence hypothesis* (Bresnan & Kaplan 1982: xvii) forms the link between competence or grammar and performance or language use: a model of the latter must incorporate the former as a central component. It has often been deplored that generative linguists have done little to show the validity of this claim, but recently several attempts have been made to *realize* generative grammars in models of (human) language processing.[6] Notice that this is different from merely showing the computational realizability of a theory: one can devise computer algorithms that deal with rules or principles of a theory, without ever making any claims about psychological reality. Here, claims are made that relate the theory and/or the computational model to characteristics of the human language user. Still, on closer inspection, it becomes clear that in fact the models do *not* go beyond showing the computational realizability of the theory, and have little to say about what really goes on in the language user, hence, have little psychological reality.

Clark and Malt's (1984) discussion of weak and strong psychological constraints on language and its use is particularly illuminating in this context. Very generally, they show that the psychological constraints posited by most linguists are only *weak* constraints. This means among other things that they (1) are motivated only by considerations internal to the linguistic theory itself (facts about the structure of language, not facts about processes in language use), and (2) are not based on firm psychological evidence.[7] The dangers of (1) are particularly great, because in a context of trying to *explain* facts of language by so-called psychological constraints, they give rise to circular reasonings that do nothing but reformulate the theory or redescribe the same facts.

If one really wants to explain the characteristics of language by referring to psychological constraints or processes (i.e. if one aspires to psychological reality of one's theory or computational model), one has to make sure the constraints/processes are independent of the structure of language and are grounded on firm psychological evidence. In short, truly cognitive-scientific research in language and its processing requires that one take a closer look at what psychologists have to say about this processing (see 3.1).

2.3.2.   Structure and process

A distinction that is closely related to the competence-performance distinction is the structure-process distinction. In the generative tradition, concentrating on competence has been synonymous with concentrating on syntactic structure solely, pushing off semantics and pragmatics (the things that really matter in language use) till "later". Yet when one looks at some of the studies of semantics and (especially) pragmatics that are being carried out,[8] there is more reference to cognitive processes that drive language processing than there is to structure.

When studying syntax, researchers seem to adhere to the *anteriority of structure* principle, when going beyond syntax, the *anteriority of process* principle reigns (cf. the distinction between "Chomsky's wager" and "Wundt's wager" made by Clark and Malt (1984: 211)). In 2.3.1., the discussion of psychological reality pointed towards the dangers of the *anteriority of structure* principle. Processes get grafted onto syntax that prove to be purely motivated by the linguistic theory itself, or by formal considerations of computer algorithms, so that explanations of phenomena in terms of what goes on in the human language user can hardly be given. If one starts out by looking at cognitive processes in the first place (adhering to the *anteriority of process* principle), it seems likely that one can avoid the pitfalls of a purely structural-syntactic approach, and head towards truly cognitive-scientific research with strong explanatory power. Let me hasten to add that this does not imply that one cannot look at language structure in an attempt to hypothesize psychological constraints or processes that explain its nature. After all, weak constraints may be an interesting starting point for psychological research which may eventually turn them into strong ones. Moreover, as e.g. Jackendoff (1987) stresses (see also 3.2.1.), structure is much more tangible than process, so we have concrete material to start from if we look at structure in the first place.

However, structure is also deceptive, in that it may start to lead its own life, away from the processes that deal with it. Studying structure, we often forget that in real language use it is never there in the a-dynamic, timeless *post-process* form of linguistic description, but evolves in time, being produced or understood incrementally. For adherents of the *anteriority of process* principle, there is a strong belief that these processes not only deploy structures, but determine how they look as well as why they are the way they are. Moreover, as we will see below, it is no longer the case that hardly anything can be said about what is really going on in the language user, so we should also take into account what we know about processes in a full-scale cognitive-scientific approach to language.

3.   Process linguistics

From the discussion in section 2, it is clear that an approach aspiring not only to computational realizability but also psychological reality cannot accept a narrow definition of competence as knowledge about linguistic structure, because reasoning from this structure to the processes at work in linguistic performance is problematic and fallacious. Hence, the central notion of *process linguistics*: if we want to stick to some distinction between competence and performance, competence has to be redefined as *processing competence*. Only then does it become possible to smoothly reason from this competence to the way it manifests itself during performance.

3.1.   *Processing competence*

3.1.1.   General definition

Processing competence is defined as a set of *processing universals*, strong (see 2.3.) cognitive constraints on and characteristics of processes active during language *understanding*, *producing* and *learning*. These processes draw from a set of knowledge sources, of which linguistic knowledge is only one (see 3.1.2.). Since the three modalities of language use are mentioned here, I want to add that in what follows I will concentrate mostly on the process of understanding, my main area of interest (see the models briefly presented in 3.2.). As to the other modalities: for production, I refer to e.g. Kempen and Hoenkamp's "incremental procedural grammar" (1982, 1987) as a model compatible with PL; for language learning (a major issue in generative linguistics), a little more must be said.

Regarding the acquisition process, a number of researchers have proposed an alternative to the Chomskyan view of acquisition (Slobin 1966, 1984; Putnam 1975b; Derwing 1973). The Chomskyan view, called the "content" view of acquisition, holds that a child is born with the entire set of linguistic universals (plus evaluation procedures) and that he somehow uses this set as a grid through which the particular language he is exposed to is filtered (cf. Derwing 1973: 53). The alternative view is called the "process" (!) view, according to which "the child is born not with a set of linguistic categories but with some sort of process mechanism - a set of procedures and inference rules, if you will - that he uses to process linguistic data" (Derwing 1973: 53). Under such an interpretation as this, then, any linguistic universal would be "the result of an innate cognitive competence rather than the content of such a competence" (Slobin 1966: 87). Needless to add, this is the view of the acquisition process adhered to in *PL*, though I will not go into it any further here.

3.1.2.   Normal mode and metamode

When considering the link to performance (which is now simply processing competence at work in actual behavior), I distinguish two modes in which processing competence can operate. The two modes also show the role of linguistic knowledge (the contents of the Chomskyan competence notion) in performance. In the normal mode the processing universals are at work and there is no awareness of linguistic knowledge being accessed (this mode corresponds to non-conscious performance); in the other mode (less often at work), which I call the *metamode*, awareness of the linguistic knowledge accessed is required (this mode corresponds to conscious performance). Whereas the normal mode of processing competence involves just the (innate) processing universals, the metamode also depends on acquired skills and knowledge, e.g. a capacity for word play, education in language(s), knowledge of linguistic theories. Note that in performance involving the metamode (as in that involving the normal mode) there is no awareness of the processes themselves, but merely of structural characteristics of their output, language. This awareness can take the form of rules about structure, rules that can sometimes help solve problems occurring in normal mode but that are not in any way "used" in this normal mode. Hence, normal mode and metamode can interact, but the metamode is secondary and less often appealed to.

A final note about performance: phenomena like hesitations, errors, shifts of attention (performance matters of no importance to Chomskyan competence) are considered indications of processing mechanisms at work (or in trouble) and may be very important in an attempt at studying the underlying competence (both its normal and its metamode). (For instance, many "uh's" of spoken language are examples of hesitations in the normal mode (we are not aware of all the "uh's"); on the other hand, elaborate self-corrections after completing a sentence are instances of metamode processing interrupting (viz. monitoring) normal processing.)

3.1.3.   Limited working memory capacity

A widely accepted and empirically supported[9] cognitive constraint on language processing is that of the limited capacity of working memory. Already in the earliest attempts at realizing the Chomskyan competence model into a performance model (Miller & Chomsky 1963), the constraint received a lot of attention. In recent models in the generative tradition (Bresnan 1982), it figures again as an important constraint. In AI research into natural language processing (especially the Yale school), the characteristics of human memory have always been an obvious factor to take into account.

To illustrate that it is not always easy to link a psychological constraint to language and the way it is processed, it is interesting to take a brief look at how the constraint is handled in the generative tradition.

In the early days (Chomsky 1963, Miller & Chomsky 1963), the treatment was pretty rough. There was no room for limited memory capacity within the competence-as-generative-grammar notion, so it was seen as a pure performance phenomenon (along with distractions, hesitations, errors, etc.). Since the theory of grammar made crucial reference to the notion of recursion (needed to account for the infinite set of sentences a grammar must be able to generate with finite means (lexicon and rules)), the ideal speaker-hearer was simply endowed with an unlimited memory capacity, and that was it. In other words, limited memory capacity was not allowed to constrain the form of the grammar. Bresnan and Kaplan's (1982) account of limited memory capacity in a generative context is more subtle, but is also related to the formal theory-internal notion of recursion. Their argument is that if grammars generate infinite sets of sentences (the "creativity" of language, another would-be psychological constraint), and use finite means, then language has to be recursive. As Clark and Malt (1984: 202f) point out, it is the contents of the theory that determines how the (weak) constraint is used (cf. the *anteriority of structure* principle). They go on to suggest that one can interpret the constraint in a completely different way: rather than having it constrain the set of lexical items and grammatical relations of a language, one can just as well have it constrain recursion itself! If one starts by looking at true linguistic performance rather than at the linguistic theory, it seems that one is even forced to do so.

Human beings can hardly deal with typical products of recursive rule application like *The dog the cat the mouse hates likes went out*, and it is perfectly plausible that this is due to limited working memory capacity, which is then interpreted as constraining depth of recursion - if one retains the notion at all. At the same time, one can stress the infinite expandability of the lexicon (rather than positing that it is finite), and consider this as part of the true creativity of language, rather than the capacity of a grammar to generate an infinite set of sentences through recursion. It is important to note, of course, that psycholinguistic research[10] has indeed shown that multiple nesting makes a sentence incomprehensible, and casts doubts on the need of the notion of recursion (the need of it has, to my knowledge, never been shown by psycholinguistic research). If limited working memory capacity is to be a strong psychological constraint (meaning that it should be motivated by independent psycholinguistic considerations or research - the *anteriority of process* principle), it seems that Bresnan and Kaplan's interpretation of the constraint is not satisfactory. It will be clear that within the framework of *process linguistics*, limited memory capacity is precisely an indication of the fact that recursion is *not* an essential characteristic of language, which may have consequences for the construction of a computational model of language understanding. But of course, "no recursion" is not the most interesting characteristic to relate to the memory constraint. A much more interesting one is that of *interactive incremental processing* (see especially Kempen & Hoenkamp 1987 or Briscoe 1987 for a detailed discussion of this constraint in relation to language production and understanding, respectively).

3.1.4.   Interactive incremental processing

If the human being is faced both with a limited working memory capacity and transitory (spoken) language he wants to understand, he cannot afford to just store incoming input and postpone understanding until a complete sentence has come in. Through introspection, anyone can see that there is no postponing at all: input is interpreted as it comes in, on a word-by-word basis, and all knowledge sources that aid understanding are appealed to. A representation of the incoming input is gradually built up as more words are processed. From a processing point of view, it is not hard to accept this view; for linguists used to dealing with complete sentences as static objects, however, it is slightly discomforting. Moreover, it has serious consequences for the cognitive-scientific validity of a processing account of language use. If someone proposes a model that needs a complete sentence before it can do anything interesting with it, the constraint of incremental processing is not satisfied.

The issue of incremental processing is closely related to a general distinction between two types of processing models proposed by psychologists: the *autonomous component model* and the *interactive model*. In the *autonomous component model* (see especially Forster 1979) the language processor consists of a linear chain of three separate and autonomous processing systems: a lexical processor locating the input elements in the lexicon, a syntactic processor assigning syntactic structures to the input and a semantic processor (called "message processor") building conceptual structures. (Note the correspondence between levels of processing and levels of linguistic description.) Thus, the input enters the lexical processor, whose output enters the syntactic processor, whose output in turn enters the message processor; no other communication among the processors is allowed. All three processors have access to a "language-oriented data storage", the lexicon.

The alternative model (Marslen-Wilson & Tyler 1980 for spoken language; Just & Carpenter 1980 for written language) is the *interactive model*. Rather than viewing language processing as organized in neatly separated processors, it stresses the purposeful integration of knowledge of all kinds in the understanding process (implying multiple interactions of knowledge sources). Marslen-Wilson and Tyler's model of spoken language understanding (partly a critique of Forster's model) starts from the claim that a listener tries to fully interpret the input as he hears it, on a word-by-word basis. The processing (recognition) of the words is directly influenced by the contextual environment in which they occur; this implies that lexical, structural (syntactic) and interpretative knowledge sources communicate and interact freely in an optimally efficient and accurate way during language comprehension, without any delays in availability of information.

The same view of the comprehension process is held by Just and Carpenter in their model of written language understanding: their "immediacy assumption" posits that all knowledge sources in working and long-term memory aid undelayed interpretation of the words of a textual fragment as they are read. Both interactive models also stress that the words themselves are the primary information sources the language user has; thus, bottom-up (data-driven) processes triggered by the words are more important than the top-down (hypothesis-driven) ones that further aid interpretation (see 3.1.5. for a discussion of the lexical nature of language processing). Introspection and the experimental research done in the context of the interactive model[11] reveal that the *autonomous component model* is incorrect. Hence, the interactive nature of linguistic processing is one of the essential characteristics of processing competence.

There is one consequence of the adherence to the interactive model that I would like to stress in concluding this discussion. Among researchers in natural language processing (linguists, psychologists, AI researchers), a controversial point has always been: how much syntactic information do we need in a model of language understanding? Can we afford to postpone semantic/pragmatic analysis until a full syntactic analysis of constituents or clauses is found? It looks as though the interactive model will allow us to settle the dispute and point in the direction of what is really important. Any type of knowledge, be it syntactic or semantic, can be helpful to interpret linguistic input. Even the adherents of "purely semantic" models of understanding (from the AI community) must admit that they *do* use syntactic information, be it in covert ways. On the other hand, linguists who keep pushing off semantic or pragmatic considerations until some far-off integration phase of separate components is finally fully developed are stuck within the syntactic level of linguistic description and also ignore many of the interfacing problems of "neat" modules. In the context of the interactive model, it is no longer a question of what comes first and what after, or how much of this and how much of that, but a question of what gets used *when* and *how*, a question of the exact nature of the interactions.

The interactive nature of linguistic processing also fits in with the importance of exhaustive lexical information retrieval and the robustness of processing discussed in the next sections.

3.1.5.   Exhaustive retrieval of lexical information

The reality of the word as a basic unit for (spoken and written) language understanding is an important aspect of the interactive models mentioned in 3.1.4. Intuitively, it is easy to see that if a language user needs to extract as much information as possible from linguistic input as it comes in word-by-word, access of knowledge stored with these words has to proceed without delay. Recent psycholinguistic research into the nature of lexical access and idiom processing[12] has indeed pointed in the direction of the importance of lexically stored information and the automatic, exhaustive nature of the retrieval process.[13] It was found that *all meanings* of a word are initially retrieved (regardless of the preceding context!), and context filters out the appropriate one later. The lexical retrieval process is a strong, autonomous, exhaustive phenomenon insensitive to preceding context. For models of language and its use, this means that lexically stored information plays a crucial role, and that processing models have to account for the way appropriate meaning gets chosen through interaction of a word with its context. To my knowledge, few approaches try to account for contextual disambiguation (mainly because most models - especially those inspired by linguistic theories - hardly go beyond syntactic processing); in 3.2.2. below, one approach that considers full contextual understanding through disambiguation as the driving force of the understanding process is briefly presented.

3.1.6.   Robustness

As human beings, we are very well capable of dealing with input that is noisy, incomplete, grammatically incorrect, or otherwise defective. Any model of language processing should be able to account for this aspect of human processing competence. Traditionally, only "grammatical" sentences are dealt with in models of language understanding in the linguistic tradition (again, because they are mainly motivated by syntactic concerns), whereas these sentences form only the tip of the iceberg. Not only is spoken language far from grammatical, but also the real-life written language that serious understanding systems should be able to handle is not usually conceived by linguists.

This requirement implies that semantic and pragmatic knowledge sources must be deployed in models of natural language understanding. A syntactic parser that receives input not fitting any of its rules will not "gracefully degrade"; it will crash. It seems reasonable to relate robustness to lexical access as an independent, automatic and exhaustive aspect of understanding leading to retrieval of all meanings of a word (see 3.1.5.). When the input degrades and contextual clues are poor, a language user will have accessed all the knowledge attached to the words he did pick up, enabling him to fill in many of the gaps.

Moreover, words not only carry semantic/pragmatic content, but also project expectations about the linguistic nature of what can follow them.

Robustness seems guaranteed by the very nature of the understanding process itself, guided as it is by principles of exhaustive access and interaction through "feedforward" (expectation projection) and feedback. All information is retrieved, a number of expectations are projected to potential subsequent input, and contextual feedback takes care of narrowing down this *abundance* and *redundance* of information to a unique interpretation of the input, where all knowledge sources that aid the disambiguation process can be deployed interactively, in parallel. If subsequent input is noisy or distorted, it is the exhaustive retrieval (abundance) and interactive expectation-feedback cycles (redundance) that help fill in the gaps.

3.1.7. Summarizing remarks

To summarize the story so far: I have sketched what I believe a cognitive-scientific approach to language and its use should look like ideally. The stress has been on the harmonious realization of both *computational realizability* and *psychological reality*. Especially the need for a serious commitment to the latter requirement has led to the stress on the *anteriority of process (over structure)* thesis, and a redefinition of "competence" as *processing competence*. This redefinition allows for a smooth integration with "performance", *processing competence* at work in reality. I have tried to show that this notion of competence is not a vague black box, but that research into the nature of human language processing allows us to start positing some processing universals constraining language and its use. This also refutes an argument that is often adduced to defend the competence-as-structure versus performance-as-process view against attempts to redefine the dichotomy, viz. that of the necessity of idealization in scientific research.

Letting processes into the competence-notion would mean that one loses this desirable quality of research. On the one hand, many non-generative linguists, psychologists and AI researchers have expressed their doubts about the honesty of the idealization argument if it leads to abstracting away all the essential characteristics of one's supposed object of study, or if it is meant to restrict the evidence that can be brought in to support or refute a model.[14] On the other hand, redefining competence as processing competence allows one to "abstract away" from performance in a more realistic way: processing competence deals with general, universal processing mechanisms that are the essence of performance itself.

If we want to study performance seriously, a quest for these mechanisms seems like a sound enterprise. And there will still be enough to abstract away from, but in a more justifiable way (e.g. fatigue, absent-mindedness in the hearer/reader, bad articulation in the speaker, noise in the channel, etc.). In this section about processing competence, I have tried to show that it is possible to start building a general theory of linguistic performance by fitting together strong constraints on it.

Of course, much remains to be done, and even more is left untouched here. For one thing, we are only starting to explore the nature of *interaction,* a notion that creates such a degree of complexity that it is understandable if many scientists refrain from considering it, especially when they aim at building "neat" theories allowing for precise predictions. Still, interaction and parallelism have become major topics in cognitive-scientific research,[15] so that hopefully we will no longer just be groping in the dark when dealing with these issues. For another, a question that has been left untouched is that of the structure of knowledge. Processes receive all attention here, and little is said about the structure of the knowledge sources they deploy or the structure of the representations they incrementally build up. All these matters of structure need to be studied as well (*process linguistics* does not aim to be an all-process, no-structure approach), but in the light of the contents of processing competence. Processes should not be grafted post-hoc onto independently motivated structures, but the structures must be considered in a way that allows them to be easily integrated with the view of language as an interactive process. A far-reaching implication of this is that it is considered to be a wrong-headed enterprise to build e.g. a completely independent syntactic knowledge module without considering its interactions with semantic and/or pragmatic knowledge. It may be better to start with toy systems that consider all knowledge sources right away (but only limited aspects of them), and to look for ways to model interactive understanding on a small scale.

I conclude this section about processing competence and its implications by stressing that a lot of recent knowledge-structure related work in cognitive semantics and pragmatics exists that fits in with the views expressed here and that is needed to come to an encompassing theory of language and its processing. Some examples of relevant topics in cognitive semantics, for instance, are: the conceptual processes related to the delineation of word meanings (cf. 3.2.2); the structure of these meanings and their relation to "cognitive domains", etc. (see e.g. Langacker 1986, Gorayska 1985). In pragmatics, discourse phenomena are also being studied in relation to cognitive processes. Crombie's "Perceptual Process Model", for instance, looks at how semantic relationships like agent-action or reason-result exemplify general perceptual processes such as that of cause and effect (Crombie 1985). Sperber and Wilson's (1986) theory of relevance stresses the principle of maximization of relevance as an important cognitive process driving language understanding.

In the last section of this presentation, I will briefly discuss three existing interactive models of language understanding that to various degrees can be said to fit in with the framework of *process linguistics*. It is a happy coincidence that there is a model from each of the three disciplines central to the cognitive-scientific study of language: the first stems from cognitive psychology, the second from artificial intelligence, and the third from linguistics. I hasten to add that it is not my intention to force other people's work into a framework that they may want to dissociate from completely, but rather to show that interactive models are starting to appear, all of them situated within the broader context of cognitive-scientific research into the nature of human intelligence.

3.2.   Existing interactive models of understanding

3.2.1.   Jackendoff 1987

With an oversimplification, one can say that whereas *process linguistics* is an attempt to break through the structure-bias in mainstream linguistics, Jackendoff's *Consciousness and the computational mind* can be seen as an attempt to break through the process-bias in psychology and computer science/artificial intelligence. Jackendoff presents his "intermediate-level theory of consciousness" in an exploration of the way in which "the character of experience can be explained in terms of the forms of information in the mind and the processes this information undergoes" (1987: xi); or, to put it differently, in an exploration of the way in which the phenomenological mind can be explained in terms of the computational mind (made up of structure - information - and processes handling this information). Although this exploration has many fascinating aspects, I will limit the discussion to the aspects that are directly related to my presentation here. Jackendoff strongly expresses and defends his adherence to the *anteriority of structure* thesis (1987: ch. 4), and to the traditional division of modules of linguistic description (phonological, syntactic and semantic structure, all of which are presented in great detail). Still, since an account of the computational mind requires that both structure and process be considered, he also presents a theory of language processing (both perception and production).

In keeping with the *anteriority of structure* thesis, Jackendoff starts with the premise that the modular organization of linguistic structure has to be respected by the processes working with it. Concretely, for understanding, it means that these processes have to always take into account phonological, syntactic and semantic information in such a way that the adjacency of the components is respected. All components must always be considered, plus the additional constraint that non-adjacent ones cannot be linked directly (viz. phonological and semantic information; linkage must pass through syntax). Jackendoff calls this constraint the *logical structure of language processing (LSLP)*. He then goes on to look for a processing model that respects *LSLP* and is in keeping with our intuitions about language understanding and with psychological research. This search will lead him to gradually reduce the size of processing components, and increase the amount of interaction among them.

Jackendoff starts by considering the autonomous processing component model as sketched in 3.1.4., where "each linguistic level is derived in its entirety from the next lower level before proceeding to the derivation of the next higher level. (Bottom-up sequential)" (1987: 92), and rejects it on the basis of the intuition that "we do not wait until the end of an utterance before starting to interpret the intended meaning" (1987: 93). The next step is to look at the input as being divided up into smaller units, and to allow parallel treatment of these units while still respecting the three levels of structure and processing for each unit: "In speech understanding each part of each linguistic level is derived from information of the next lower level. (Bottom-up parallel)" (1987: 94).

This view is also rejected, after some detailed considerations of two dichotomies: localistic versus holistic perception (related to *intralevel* effects) and bottom-up versus top-down perception (related to *interlevel* effects). The first dichotomy has to be understood as follows: localistic processing allows no intralevel effects (e.g. between a large syntactic unit and a small one), whereas holistic processing does allow intralevel effects. The second dichotomy has to do with interlevel effects: bottom-up processes only allow effects starting from the lowest level up, whereas top-down ones only allow effects starting from the highest level down.

The second view Jackendoff discusses would only allow localistic and bottom-up effects, but is contradicted by intuition and by experimental research. The perception process must allow both localistic and holistic effects, as well as bottom-up and top-down ones. (As to the latter distinction, Jackendoff supports the view that bottom-up effects predominate over top-down ones in understanding; cf. 3.1.4.) So, finally, Jackendoff arrives at a view of the understanding process that allows both interlevel and intralevel interaction, where the interlevel interactions must still respect the adjacency of linguistic levels (no direct interaction between phonological and semantic processes). "In speech understanding, each part of each level of representation from phonology up is derived by virtue of correspondences with neighboring levels. (Interactive parallel)" (1987: 101). Jackendoff interprets this view as a reconciliation of the autonomous component model (Forster 1979) and the interactive model (Marslen-Wilson & Tyler 1980), but to this end it looks as if he is only willing to retain the stress on autonomous syntactic processing in Forster's model, and not the overall processing view (1987: 102). Jackendoff concludes his discussion by showing that the view is in keeping with lexical access research and a view of memory components as active devices.

Although in a process-linguistic account of language understanding the starting point would not be the premise of the modular organization of linguistic structure, the modularization of knowledge components is certainly a necessity on any account, whether the knowledge gets carved up along traditional linguistic lines, or is organized differently (see also 3.2.2.). Yet by adhering to *LSLP*, Jackendoff has to restrict the interactions to adjacent components, whereas there is evidence from psychological research that this is not the case. Marslen-Wilson and Welsh (1978) present examples of interactions between word recognition (the phonological level) and semantic analysis. So one could say that Jackendoff did not go far enough in allowing interactions among components. Although his processing theory is certainly valid, and the modularization of knowledge, too, the question is whether *LSLP* can be allowed to constrain the nature of the interactions. In the two models that are discussed next, it is not.

A final note about Jackendoff's model: I repeat that it is only a minor part of a much broader cognitive-scientific enterprise which does not stand or fall with the account of linguistic processing. A major difference with respect to the two models discussed next is also that it was not Jackendoff's intention to show the computational realizability of his processing theory (no computer model is given that realizes his views, though it would certainly be interesting to try to develop one!); only the aspect of psychological reality is given attention.

3.2.2.   WEP (Small 1980 and others)

The second interactive model to be presented is the *Word Expert Parser,* an understanding program in the AI tradition of semantic parsing. It was first developed by Small (1980), and later attempts were made to improve the model and use it in different contexts (Adriaens 1986, Hahn 1987 and 1989, Devos, Adriaens & Willems 1988). Small (1980: 26) situates his model in a cognitive-scientific perspective, which also expresses the adherence to the *anteriority of process* thesis:

> The WEP approach was originally motivated by observations about human language processing, on the one hand, and computational efforts to engineer and/or model the process, on the other. Certain phenomena of human language use have particularly influenced this perspective, such as the relative ease with which people understand idioms and collocations, organize and select appropriate word senses, and perform reference. An important computational influence has been the difficulty of incorporating such mechanisms into computer programs organized along traditional (rule-based) lines. Viewing language comprehension from the perspective of individual words demystifies many classical semantic complexities and suggests an entirely different set of language analysis mechanisms based on distributed lexical control.

In contrast to most approaches considering words as static containers of information to be retrieved by a syntactic processor, WEP considers the words themselves as active agents (word-experts) triggering processes that idiosyncratically control the whole parsing process. This process involves continuous interaction of a word with a number of knowledge sources in memory: the words in their immediate context, the concepts processed so far or expected locally, knowledge of the overall process state, of the discourse, and real-world knowledge. These knowledge sources are not invoked uniformly by a general interpreter, but are accessible at all times by the word-expert processes throughout the overall process of sense discrimination. As such, they enable the experts to eventually agree on a context-specific semantic interpretation of a fragment of text. It will be clear from this description that parsing is not just the assignment of a syntactic structure to a sentence, but full understanding of language in context. As a side-effect of the overall understanding process, WEP builds a semantic/conceptual structure. In short, understanding is seen as a highly interactive data-driven (word-by-word) process.

Sense discrimination through interaction is seen as a driving force in understanding (cf. 3.2.3. below), and dynamically interpreted lexical elements get to play an unusually important role in the model. The different meanings of a word are organized in a discrimination network consisting of nodes of context-probing questions and arcs corresponding to the range of possible answers; each of the leaves of the network represents a specific contextual meaning of the word in question reached after network traversal (word-expert execution) during sentence processing.

Small (1980) contained the (complex and not always well-documented) computational realization of this view, and subsequent work (Small & Lucas 1983, Adriaens & Small 1988) has dealt with the psychological reality of it, in which the lexical access research (cf. 3.1.5. and 3.2.1.) again figures as an important area of research relevant to cognitive-scientific linguistic approaches.[16]

A number of drawbacks of the system have been pointed out by several people, and subsequent models (Hahn 1987, Devos, Adriaens & Willems 1988) have tried to remedy these.

First, from a linguistic point of view, the model overstressed the sole reality of the word as an important unit. The only experts allowed were the word-experts, and, moreover, each of them was completely idiosyncratically defined, without generalizations across experts. Syntactic information was (covertly) encoded into the experts along with semantic and pragmatic information. In the subsequent models, the basic idea of lexically distributed interaction has been retained, but higher-level experts have been introduced, as well as various ways to modularize the processes and knowledge sources (among others by the introduction of prototypic experts). It should be stressed, though, that by concentrating all knowledge and processing in the words, Small's approach suggests ways of organizing knowledge different from the classical division into large components. Maybe human knowledge can be viewed as a huge conceptual network to which the words of a language form the entry points. For *WEP* and its successors, this knowledge representation bottleneck is still an important area of research, where insights from cognitive semantics and pragmatics will certainly be useful.

A second drawback of the fully integrated interactive *WEP* model (see also 3.2.3. below) has been the obscureness and complexity of its computational realization. The mixture of sequentiality and intended parallelism during the multiple interactions has made it difficult to see what was really going on during processing. A descendant of *WEP* (*PEP*, the Parallel Expert Parser (Devos, Adriaens & Willems 1988)) has tried to constrain the interactions and make the model truly parallel.

I wish to conclude this brief presentation of *WEP* and its descendants by pointing out the fact that up till now (to my knowledge, at least) no other system has attempted to model a completely integrated inter-active semantic/pragmatic approach. It is my conviction, though, that this is the model we will eventually have to end up with; in spite of our limited capacity to grasp all the complexities involved, it remains a viable approach to explore further.

3.2.3.   LEXICAT (Briscoe 1987)

The last interactive model compatible with many of the ideas expressed here is to my knowledge the most encompassing cognitive-scientific (in the sense sketched in 2.) approach to language understanding to date. Briscoe explicitly puts his work in a multidisciplinary cognitive-science context, and is equally concerned about psychological reality and the computational realizability of his model of speech understanding. His starting point is the *anteriority of process* thesis, which he also opposes to the reigning views in generative linguistics: "much of the motivation of this study comes from the belief that insight into language will come from research into the information processing tasks that underlie language use" (1987: 2). In contrast to *process linguistics,* Briscoe does not go so far as to reject the existing competence-performance distinction, be it that it is only retained as a "useful methodological distinction between knowledge and its deployment during processing" (1987: 10). Still, the stress is on performance, and the way aspects of language use determine language. One could say that Briscoe espouses the same views as *PL,* but that he situates both processing competence and performance on the performance side; *PL,* on the other hand, situates both the universal processing constraints and the knowledge sources they deploy within human processing competence.

Starting from four psychological constraints (cf. 3.1.), viz. modularity, working memory limitations, incremental interpretation and graceful degradation (robustness), Briscoe develops his interactive deterministic parsing model, called *LEXICAT*. A computational realization is presented, and the predictions of the model are tested in a series of psychological experiments. Finally, he also discusses the explanatory value of the model (in the "good" sense discussed in 2.3.2.) in relation to, among others, parsing theory, grammatical universals, and the organization of grammar.

More concretely, Briscoe argues that a "satisfactory model of human parsing must proceed with no or little delay and must be capable of resolving ambiguities correctly as they arise" (1987: 2). To realize this, an interactive deterministic model is needed: ambiguities are not carried along during analysis, but are resolved right away (deterministically) through interactions among different processing components.[17] In contrast to *WEP*, however, Briscoe concentrates on the morphosyntactic component of his understanding model, and at the same time restricts the types of interaction that help solve morphosyntactic ambiguities. All interaction is initiated by the morphosyntactic analyzer through a limited number of communication channels with the phonological analyzer and the semantic/pragmatic analyzer (1987: 150). This restriction is motivated mainly for (understandable) methodological reasons: fully integrated models can be obscure in their workings, and do not allow clear predictions. Still, the restriction is also unfortunate, because the system gives the impression that the syntactic processor is the heart of the model, directing the whole understanding process. Briscoe admits that a full account would have to consider more than just the interactions flowing into the morphosyntactic parser, but prefers to stay on the methodologically safe side.[18] As to the choice of syntactic theory, it is interesting to note that the requirement of incremental interpretation is one of the elements that forces Briscoe to choose a lexically-based theory, viz. Generalized Categorial Grammar (hence the name *LEXICAT*). This points again to the importance of the lexicon (cf. 3.1.4. and 3.1.5.; Briscoe does not consider lexical access research, though), even though for the syntactic processor only syntactic information associated with words is considered (whereas for *WEP* and its variants, a much richer lexical representation is sought).

As was done in Adriaens & Small (1988) for *WEP*, Briscoe also devotes a whole chapter (1987: ch. 7) to the presentation of experimental research that supports the interactive deterministic view of understanding. Whereas the *WEP* account had difficulties in linking the research to exact *WEP*-specific characteristics (partly due to the choice of an unconstrained integrated model), Briscoe is able to link the research more directly and more convincingly to his approach. For reasons of limited space, I cannot go into details here, and have to refer the reader to Briscoe's book.

A final word is in order about the attempt to show the explanatory value of the model of speech comprehension in relation to language, since that is after all the main advantage of choosing an approach that looks for independently motivated constraints in performance (in this case, processing competence). A few of Briscoe's considerations are highlighted here. First, there is a strong claim in relation to parsing theory: "If the parsing model which follows naturally from the IDH [incremental determinism hypothesis, G.A.] is correct, then this suggests that 'worst case' ambiguities are irrelevant to an assessment of the parsability of a particular syntactic theory. The size of the syntactic search space can only be relevant if that space is searched during parsing. A parser operating deterministically will never do this" (1987: 211). This claim implies that it is not sufficient and even wrong-headed to look at considerations that are important in formal computational theories of complexity and draw conclusions from them in relation to the human parsing process. Once again, the danger of staying within a formal approach, and extrapolating from it to human performance without really considering this performance is stressed. Next, Briscoe considers some language universals (e.g. related to word order) and tentatively suggests explanations in terms of the pressures of memory limitations and the need for incremental interpretation during speech comprehension.[19] Finally, he discusses the implications of the model for the organization of grammar in linguistic theory. As was done in 3.2.1. in relation to Jackendoff's *logical structure of language processing*, it is stressed that linguistic models not allowing direct influences between phonological and semantic (logical) form are at least incomplete, if not incorrect, in the face of interactive processing models. Further, as far as the relationship between prosody and syntax is concerned, Briscoe's verdict after a detailed discussion is again very strong.

The structuralist/generative accounts of the relationship between PF [phonological form, G.A.] and morphosyntax appear to have swung from a too restrictive morphosyntactic determination of PF to a too loose and unrevealing one-to-many mapping. By relating aspects of PF to morphosyntactic *ambiguity* rather than morphosyntactic *structure* and grounding a theory of interaction in a precise and detailed account of language use, the IDH succeeds in predicting more successfully when some types of phonological phrasing will be obligatory (1987: 223).

4. Conclusion

In this presentation I have tried to bring together a set of notions and views that form a broad framework (termed *process linguistics*) within which a growing number of cognitive-scientific approaches to language and its use can be accommodated. That they are cognitive-scientific means that multidisciplinarity involving the fields of linguistics, psychology and artificial intelligence is necessary. At the same time, the computational realizability and psychological reality of the approaches are essential. Together, they lead to the *anteriority of process* thesis, which states that process deploys and determines structure. In this light the much-debated competence-performance distinction is redefined, with competence becoming *processing competence,* a set of processing universals, strong psychological constraints using and creating knowledge structures without being determined by them. This set of constraints defines language processing (viz. understanding) as a robust, incremental, lexically-driven, semantic/pragmatic interactive process. Modelling this process in a cognitive-scientific perspective has proved not only possible, but also rich in potential explanatory power. To end with a quote from Briscoe's (1987: 227) conclusion that stresses this aspect:

> A more detailed understanding of the psychological processes and mechanisms which underlie language acquisition, production, and comprehension offers the possibility of considerably increasing our understanding of language, both by bringing to light new facts (such as correlations between prosody, parsing strategies and ambiguity) and by offering insightful explanation for such facts.

Notes

1.   See Collins (1977), Norman (1981), Kintsch et al. (1984), Gardner (1985) for similar definitions of *Cognitive Science*.

2.   See e.g. Winograd (1983 and passim), Schank & Riesbeck (1981), Marcus (1980) for examples of AI research in the area of natural language processing.
3.   See e.g. Bresnan (1982), Berwick & Weinberg (1984), Naumann (1988) or any issue of *Proceedings of the Association for Computational Linguistics (ACL)*, or of the *International Conference on Computational Linguistics (COLING)*.
4.   See Naumann (1988) and references therein for several approaches to the implementation of GPSG.
5.   See e.g. Levelt (1974: III), Winograd (1977), Tyler (1980), Moore & Carling (1982), Kintsch (1984), Langacker (1988).
6.   Especially Bresnan (1982) for LFG theory, and Berwick & Weinberg (1984) for GB theory.
7.   Within the limited scope of this article, it is impossible to repeat the full discussion of psychological constraints by Clark and Malt, so I have to refer to their article for the details. See also Givón (1979), Sampson (1983) or Adriaens (1986: ch. 2) for similar discussions.
8.   See e.g. Allan (1987: parts II and III, and especially pp. 428f) for the issue at hand, Crombie (1985), Sperber & Wilson (1986). It must be stressed, though, that a lot of other work in semantics and pragmatics concentrates on structure as well (see e.g. Lehrer 1974, Cruse 1986, and many others). The point here is that the notion of process (like that of performance) has rarely found its way into the study of syntax, whereas with the study of semantics and pragmatics, processing can no longer be "swept under the rug".
9.   See e.g. Baddeley (1976) for an overview of experiments related to limited working memory capacity.
10.   See Levelt (1972: III, 71) for references to early psycholinguistic research that showed the incomprehensibility of sentences with multiple nesting.
11.   Marslen-Wilson & Welsh (1978), Marslen-Wilson & Tyler (1980) or Just & Carpenter (1980) contain examples of experiments showing that knowledge of different levels is deployed interactively without delays.
12.   See e.g. Swinney (1979), Tanenhaus et al. (1979), Seidenberg et al. (1982 and 1984); related research into the nature of idiom processing also points out the importance of lexical storage and exhaustive access of linguistic information (see e.g. Swinney & Cutler 1979, Estill & Kemper 1982, Glass 1983).
13.   In linguistics in general the importance of the lexicon (sometimes at the cost of syntax) is also becoming more and more acknowledged. See e.g. Bresnan (1982), Chomsky (1981), Berwick & Weinberg (1984), Diehl (1981), Ades & Steedman (1982), Proudian & Pollard (1985) for generative approaches attaching great importance to the lexicon; examples of non-generative approaches are Gross (1979, 1984), Lehrer (1974), Starosta (1988), Hudson (1984), Cruse (1986), Geeraerts (1985, 1986); Haiman (1980) and Langacker (1983, 1986, 1988) also deal with issues of the nature of the lexicon.
14.   See e.g. Derwing (1973), Gross (1979), Bresnan & Kaplan (1982: xxiii), Winograd (1977), Schank & Riesbeck (1981).

15. See e.g. Cottrell & Small (1983), Cottrell (1985), Hinton & Anderson (1981), McClelland & Rumelhart (1981, 1982, 1986), Rumelhart & McClellan (1986), Adriaens & Hahn (in press).

16. In Adriaens (1986: ch. 5), the *Word Expert Parser* is also confronted with neurolinguistic research into aphasia: it is shown that a completely lexically-based model like *WEP* can straightforwardly be "lesioned" to exhibit aphasic behavior.

17. As an aside in relation to the determinism hypothesis (first expressed most firmly in Marcus 1980), it is interesting to note that Briscoe rejects Marcus' way of realizing determinism in his Parsifal parser, viz. by allowing the parser to look ahead a number of constituents. Briscoe's approach (like Small's) realizes determinism by interaction.

18. In this respect, the critique uttered against a fully integrated interactive model like *WEP* that it is "scruffy" is not completely fair: on Briscoe's account the exact nature of the interactions and their implementation do not receive the attention they deserve (the simple statement in the algorithm p. 143, "If checking is ambiguous, then resolve by interaction", is more easily made than realized). In *WEP,* the complexities of a fully integrated interactive system were considered and implemented right away, be it indeed in unclear and certainly improvable ways (see 3.2.2.).

19. Although I cannot go into this important issue, the exact *linkage* of a constraint to a language universal (an important characteristic of strong psychological constraints discussed by Clark and Malt 1984: 198) still remains problematic, even in Briscoe's account.

References

Ades, Anthony E. & Mark J. Steedman
    1982   "On the order of words", *Linguistics & Philosophy* 4: 517-558.
Adriaens, Geert
    1986   Process linguistics: The theory and practice of a cognitive-scientific approach to natural language understanding. [Unpubl. Ph.D. Dissertation, University of Leuven].
Adriaens, Geert & Udo Hahn (eds.)
    in press   *Parallel natural language processing.* Norwood, N.J.: Ablex.
Adriaens, Geert & Steve L. Small
    1988   "Word expert parsing revisited in a cognitive science perspective", in: Steve L. Small, Gary W. Cottrell & Michael K. Tanenhaus (eds.), 13-43.
Allen, James
    1987   *Natural language understanding.* Menlo Park, CA: Benjamin/ Cummings.
Baddeley, Alan D.
    1976   *The psychology of memory.* New York: Harper & Row.
Barton, G. Edward, Robert C. Berwick & Eric S. Ristad
    1987   *Computational complexity and natural language.* Cambridge: MIT Press.

Berwick, Robert C. & Amy S. Weinberg
1984   *The grammatical basis of linguistic performance: Language use and ac-quisition*. Cambridge: MIT Press.
Bever, Thomas G., John M. Carroll & Lance A. Miller (eds.)
1984   *Talking minds: The study of language in cognitive science*. Cambridge: MIT Press.
Bresnan, Joan (ed.)
1982   *The mental representation of grammatical relations*. Cambridge: MIT Press.
Bresnan, Joan & Ronald M. Kaplan
1982/1984   "Grammars as mental representations of language". Introduction to Bresnan 1982: xvii-lii. Reprinted in: Walter Kintsch, James R. Miller & Peter G. Polson (eds.), 103-135.
Briscoe, Edward J.
1987   *Modelling human speech comprehension: A computational approach*. Chichester: Ellis Horwood.
Chomsky, Noam
1963   "Formal properties of grammars", in: Robert Luce, R. R. Bush & Eugene Galanter (eds.), 323-418.
Clark, Herbert C. & Barbara C. Malt
1984   "Psychological constraints on language: A commentary on Bresnan and Kaplan and on Givón", in: Walter Kintsch, James R. Miller & Peter G. Polson (eds.), 191-214.
Collins, Alan
1977   "Why cognitive science?", Editorial of *Cognitive Science* 1: 1-2.
Cooper, William E. & Edward C.T. Walker (eds.)
1979   *Sentence processing: Psycholinguistic studies presented to Merrill Garrett*. Hillsdale, N.J.: Erlbaum.
Cottrell, Gary W.
1985   A connectionist approach to word sense disambiguation. [Unpublished Ph.D. Dissertation, University of Rochester.]
Cottrell, Gary W. & Steve L. Small
1983   "A connectionist scheme for modelling word sense disambiguation", *Cognition and Brain Theory* 6: 89-120.
Crombie, Winifred
1985   *Process and relation in discourse and language learning*. Oxford: Oxford University Press.
Cruse, D. Alan
1986   *Lexical semantics*. Cambridge: Cambridge University Press.
Derwing, Bruce L.
1973   *Transformational grammar as a theory of language acquisition: A study of the empirical, conceptual and methodological foundations of contemporary linguistics*. Cambridge: Cambridge University Press.
Devos, Mark, Geert Adriaens & Yves D. Willems
1988   "The parallel expert parser (PEP): A thoroughly revised descendant of the word expert parser (WEP)", *Proceedings of the 12th International Conference on Computational Linguistics (Budapest, August 1988)*. Volume I, 142-147.
Diehl, Lon G.
1981   Lexical-generative grammar: Toward a lexical conception of linguistic structure. [Unpublished Ph.D. Dissertation, Indiana University.]

Estill, Robert B. & Susan Kemper
    1982   "Interpreting idioms", *Journal of Psycholinguistic Research* 11: 559-568.
Forster, Kenneth I.
    1979   "Levels of processing and the structure of the language processor", in:
                William E. Cooper & Edward C.T. Walker (eds.), 27-85.
Gardner, Howard
    1985   *The mind's new science: A history of the cognitive revolution.* New York:
                Basic Books.
Gazdar, Gerald et al.
    1985   *Generalized phrase structure grammar.* Cambridge: Harvard University
                Press.
Geeraerts, Dirk
    1985   *Paradigm and paradox: Explorations into a paradigmatic theory of
                meaning and its epistemological background.* Leuven: Leuven University
                Press.
    1986   *Woordbetekenis: Een overzicht van de lexicale semantiek.* Leuven: Acco.
Givón, Talmy
    1979   *On understanding grammar.* New York: Academic Press.
Glass, Arnold L.
    1983   "The comprehension of idioms", *Journal of Psycholinguistic Research*
                12: 429-442.
Gorayska, Barbara
    1985   Semantics and pragmatics of English and Polish with reference to
                aspect. [Unpubl. Ph.D. dissertation, University College London.]
Gross, Maurice
    1979   "On the failure of generative grammar", *Language* 55: 859-885.
    1984   "Lexicon-grammar and the syntactic analysis of French", *Proceedings
                COLING*, 275-282.
Hahn, Udo
    1987   Lexikalisch   verteiltes   Text-Parsing: Eine   objekt-orientierte
                Spezifikation eines Wortexpertensystems auf der Grundlage des
                Aktorenmodells. [Unpublished Ph.D. Dissertation, University of
                Konstanz.]
    1989   "Making understanders out of parsers: Semantically driven parsing as
                a key concept for realistic text understanding applications",
                International Journal of Intelligent Systems 4: 345-393.
Haiman, John
    1980   "Dictionaries and encyclopedias", *Lingua* 50: 329-357.
Herskovits, Annette
    1988   "Spatial expressions and the plasticity of meaning", in: Brygida
                Rudzka-Ostyn (ed.), 271-297.
Hinton, Geoffrey E. & James A. Anderson (eds.)
    1981   *Parallel models of associative memory.* Hillsdale, N.J.: Erlbaum.
Hudson, Richard
    1984   *Word grammar.* New York: Basil Blackwell.
Jackendoff, Ray
    1987   *Consciousness and the computational mind.* Cambridge: Bradford
                Books, MIT Press.
Just, Marcel A. & Patricia A. Carpenter
    1980   "A theory of reading: From eye fixations to comprehension", *Psy-
                chological Review* 87,4: 329-354.

Kempen, Gerard & Edward Hoenkamp
    1982   "Incremental sentence generation: Implications for the structure of a syntactic processor", *Proceedings COLING*, 151 - 156.
    1987   "An incremental procedural grammar for sentence formulation", *Cognitive Science* 11: 201-258.
King, Margaret (ed.)
    1983   *Parsing natural language*. London: Academic Press.
Kintsch, Walter
    1984   "Approaches to the study of the psychology of language", in: Thomas G. Bever, John M. Carroll & Lance A. Miller (eds.), 111-145.
Kintsch, Walter, James R. Miller & Peter G. Polson (eds.)
    1984   *Methods and tactics in cognitive science*. Hillsdale, N.J.: Lawrence Erlbaum.
Langacker, Ronald W.
    1986   "An introduction to cognitive grammar", *Cognitive Science* 10: 1-41.
    1987   *Foundations of cognitive grammar*. Vol. 1: *Theoretical prerequisites*. Stanford: Stanford University Press.
    1988   "A usage-based model", in: Brygida Rudzka-Ostyn (ed.), 127-161.
Lehrer, Adrienne
    1974   *Semantic fields and lexical structure*. (North-Holland Linguistic Series 11.) Amsterdam: North-Holland.
Levelt, Willem J.M.
    1974   *Formal grammars in linguistics and psycholinguistics*. Vol I: *An introduction to the theory of formal languages and automata*. Vol II: *Applications in linguistic theory*. Vol III: *Psycholinguistic applications*. (Janua Linguarum Series Minor 192/1-3.) The Hague: Mouton.
Luce, Robert, R. R. Bush & Eugene Galanter (eds.)
    1966   *Handbook of mathematical psychology*. Vol II. New York: Wiley.
McClelland, James L. & David E. Rumelhart
    1981   "An interactive activation model of context effects in letter perception: Part 1. An account of basic findings", *Psychological Review* 88: 375-407.
    1982   "An interactive activation model of context effects in letter perception: Part 2. The contextual enhancement effect and some tests and extensions of the model", *Psychological Review* 89: 60-94.
    1986   *Parallel distributed processing: Explorations in the microstructure of cognition*. Volume 2: *Psychological and biological models*. Cambridge: MIT Press.
Marcus, Mitchell P.
    1980   *A theory of syntactic recognition for natural language*. Cambridge: MIT Press.
Marslen-Wilson, William D. & Lorraine K. Tyler
    1980   "The temporal structure of spoken language understanding", *Cognition* 8: 1-71.
Marslen-Wilson, William D. & A. Welsh
    1978   "Parsing interactions and lexical access during word recognition in continuous speech", *Cognitive Psychology* 10: 29-63.
Miller, George A. & Noam Chomsky
    1963   "Finitary models of language users", in: Robert Luce, R. R. Bush & Eugene Galanter (eds.), 419-491.

Moore, Terence & Christine Carling
    1982   *Language understanding: Towards a post-Chomskyan linguistics*. New York: St. Martin's Press.

Naumann, Sven
    1988   *Generalisierte Phrasenstrukturgrammatik: Parsingstrategien, Regelorganisation und Unifikation*. Tübingen: Niemeyer.

Norman, Donald A. (ed.)
    1981   *Perspectives on cognitive science*. Norwood, N.J.: Ablex.

Proudian, D. & Carl Pollard
    1985   "Parsing head-driven phrase structure grammar", *Proceedings of the 23rd Annual Meeting of the ACL*, 167-171.

Putnam, Hilary
    1975a   *Mind, language and reality: Philosophical papers*. Vol. 2. Cambridge: Cambridge University Press.
    1975b   "The 'innateness hypothesis' and explanatory models in linguistics", in: Hilary Putnam 1975a, 107-116.

Rudzka-Ostyn, Brygida (ed.)
    1988   *Topics in cognitive linguistics*. (Current issues in linguistic theory 50.) Amsterdam: Benjamins.

Rumelhart, David E. & James L. McClellan
    1986   *Parallel distributed processing: Explorations in the microstructure of cognition*. Vol. 1: *Foundations*. Cambridge: MIT Press.

Sampson, Geoffrey R.
    1983   "Deterministic parsing", in: Margaret King (ed.), 91-116.

Schank, Roger C. & Christopher K. Riesbeck (eds.)
    1981   *Inside computer understanding: Five programs plus miniatures*. Hillsdale, N.J.: Erlbaum.

Seidenberg, Mark S., Michael K. Tanenhaus, James M. Leiman & Marie Bienkowski
    1982   "Automatic access of the meanings of ambiguous words in context: Some limitations of knowledge-based processing", *Cognitive Psychology* 14: 489-537.

Simon, Herbert A. & K.A. Ericsson
    1984   *Protocol analysis*. Cambridge: Bradford Books, MIT Press.

Slobin, Dan I.
    1966   "Comments on developmental psycholinguistics", in: Frank Smith & George A. Miller (eds.), 85-91.
    1984   *The crosslinguistic study of language acquisition*. Hillsdale, N.J.: Erlbaum.

Small, Steve L.
    1980   Word expert parsing: A theory of distributed word-based natural language understanding. [Unpubl. Ph.D. dissertation, University of Maryland.]

Small, Steve L., Gary W. Cottrell & Michael K. Tanenhaus (eds.)
    1988   *Lexical ambiguity resolution: Perspectives from psycholinguistics, neuropsychology, and artificial intelligence*. San Mateo: Morgan Kaufmann.

Small, Steve L. & Margery M. Lucas
    1983   *Word expert parsing: A computer model of sentence comprehension*. University of Rochester Cognitive Science TR-1.

Smith, Frank & George A. Miller (eds.)
    1966   *The genesis of language: A psycholinguistic approach*. Cambridge: MIT Press.

Sperber, Daniel & Deirdre Wilson
1986   *Relevance*. Oxford: Blackwell.
Starosta, Stanley
1988   *The case for lexicase: An outline of lexicase grammatical theory*.
            London: Pinter.
Swinney, David A.
1979   "Lexical access during sentence comprehension: (Re)consideration of
            context effects", *Journal of Verbal Learning and Verbal Behavior* 18:
            645-659.
Swinney, David A. & Anne Cutler
1979   "The access and processing of idiomatic expressions", *Journal of
            Verbal Learning and Verbal Behavior* 18: 523-534.
Tanenhaus, Michael K., James M. Leiman & Mark S. Seidenberg
1979   "Evidence for multiple stages in the processing of ambiguous words in
            syntactic contexts", *Journal of Verbal Learning and Verbal Behavior* 18:
            427-440.
Tyler, Lorraine K.
1980   *Serial and interactive parallel theories of syntactic processing*. MIT
            Center for Cognitive Studies Occasional paper No. 8.
Winograd, Terry
1977   "On some contested suppositions of generative linguistics about the
            scientific study of language: A response to Dresher and Hornstein's
            'On some supposed contributions of artificial intelligence to the
            scientific study of language'", *Cognition* 5: 151-179.
1983   *Language as a cognitive process*. Volume I: *Syntax*. Reading: Addison-
            Wesley.

Requirements for a computational lexicon: a cognitive approach

Wolf Paprotté

0. Introduction

The lexicon, its organization, and the lexical processes involved have been drawing substantial interest in recent years. This seems to be a direct result of developments in the cognitive sciences and in theoretical and computational linguistics. In addition, this lexical perspective is based on requirements of natural language processing systems and on developments in database theory. Furthermore, the language industries are showing a resurgent interest in lexicography and lexicology: The "parvenue concept of a lexicon" (Henderson 1989: 358) now enjoys a position of central importance in linguistics (Flickinger 1987), and "perhaps the most striking point of agreement among contemporary grammatical theorists is the centrality of the lexicon as a repository of information about sentence structure" (CSLI Annual Report 1987, Stanford University).

Lexicon is intended to denote an abstract repository of information about words and their sentential contexts. This repository has a fourfold realization: as the mental lexicon of a human speaker, as a module of a grammatical theory or a description, as a module of systems for natural language processing, and as a traditional dictionary.

As an object of study, the lexicon appears to be relevant to two classes of "informavores" or "cognizers": human beings and computer systems. Representations are the basis of the behavior of both classes (Pylyshyn 1986: xii). Lexical representations, for example, enable human beings to act linguistically (to lexicalize intended meanings or to identify incoming acoustic-phonetic signals and their signified meanings). Lexical representations are physically instantiated as cognitive codes which allow operations to be carried out on them, and cause observable linguistic acts. As computers also function on the basis of some physically instantiated internal representation, Pylyshyn claims that cognition is a type of computation. He assumes the widely accepted opinion, that with certain strict constraints, a computer program may be viewed as a literal model, not a metaphor, of human cognition (Pylyshyn 1986: xiii; 26).

The purpose of this paper has little to do with Pylyshyn's perspective.[1] Its main objective is to look into the consequences of a reversal of this perspective for the organization of the lexicon in natural language and information processing and to ask what can be learned from the mental lexicon for the design of a computational one.

1.   The issues

The cognitive sciences share the view that it is legitimate and necessary to posit mental and computational rule systems and representations to explain human behavior and machine performance. Pylyshyn (1986) argues for a three-level distinction. The predictive generalizations of cognitive science covering behavioral acts, he assumes, occur at the biological/physical level, at the symbolic/syntactic level and at the semantic/knowledge level. Biological factors interact with the symbolic level to produce the computational resources for realizing cognitive representational processes, the functional architecture of a system. Representational or semantically expressed processes are realized by symbol systems, that is by computation.

The picture of cognitive processing that emerges is one of the mind as operating upon symbolic representations or codes, that is upon data structures that bear information, have a format of representation, and an organization. The semantic contents, the knowledge, goals, inferences, intentions of resulting mental states are encoded by properties of the brain; similarly, semantic contents of the computer's representations are encoded by physically instantiated structures.[2] Thus, the lexicon is part of the knowledge level and subject to processes operating at this level.

I shall ignore questions relating to the functional architecture and neural encoding of the mental lexicon and shall not discuss questions such as von Neumann machine vs. parallel distributed processing and the connectionist framework and its modelling potential (Elman 1989: 231).

Secondly, I shall reduce the issue of possible relations and morphisms between the instantiations of an abstract lexicon to the basic assumption of this paper that a computational lexicon may be devised as a functional model of the mental lexicon. I assume that the computational lexicon may be designed so as to resemble the performance characteristics of the mental lexicon. As a functional model it need not exhibit similarity of physical (neural) architecture or of representational format but should display a basic similarity in operation and procedural properties to mental processes and the content of the lexical representation. The question of whether we can better understand and explain the mental lexicon because of a well-functioning computational model will not concern me here.

I shall not discuss similarities and differences of content and representation between dictionaries and lexical components in a linguistic theory, or the influence of theory-dependent notions on the conceptual schema of a lexicon or a dictionary (Lang 1983: 76). The decision as to where to delimit lexical and grammatical information and what to include in a lexicon is highly theory dependent and reflects much of the history of linguistic thinking in this century (Steinitz 1984).

In an attempt to reverse the standard assumption that a successful computational lexical model will explain the mental lexicon, I shall outline some properties of the mental lexicon (complexity; learnability; textuality; context sensitivity; active (early) selection) and argue for the necessity of including these properties in the list of specifications and performance requirements for a computational lexicon. Thus, I assume that a computational lexicon should be modelled according to our present knowledge of the mental lexicon and simulate its functional achievements. For example, in human speech comprehension, the mental lexicon provides the basis for an on-line projection of the speech signal onto the mental representations of word forms and thus guarantees the syntactic and semantic interpretation of the incoming message. Marslen-Wilson distinguishes *form-based functions and processes* from *content-based functions and processes* of the mental lexicon and notes: "The specific and immediate puzzle is to understand how the system is able to solve this problem - to project sound onto meaning - with the speed and the seamless continuity that is evidenced by our subjective experience and by experimental research" (Marslen-Wilson 1989: 4).

Furthermore, this paper assumes that lexical representations in linguistic theory are more complex and detailed now than they were envisaged some years ago. They contain pragmatic information and, in the form of lexical redundancy rules, paradigms and a sorted hierarchy of lexical types. Much of what formerly was considered part of the syntactic component is now in the lexicon. The borderline between common sense and encyclopedic knowledge, and semantic information in the lexicon needs to be redrawn. In general, an increase in lexical information per entry is called for (Dahlgren 1988; Hobbs 1987).

A final assumption of this paper concerns the macrostructure of the lexicon. I shall argue that the lexicon displays textual structure, i.e. it is not a set of discrete entries but rather a structure with coherence where cohesive, associative, lexical and encyclopedic functions relate different entries. The notion of coherence relations among lexical entries is not well defined. Intuitively, it is a notion of non-linear semantic connectedness which is at the base of our capacity to navigate in the mental lexicon.

2. Lexical information from the point of view of grammatical theory

As a first approximation, a lexicon specifies acoustic or visual signal properties (phonological and graphemic form) of a lexical item paired with a representation of its meaning and combinatorial potential, i.e. syntactic category and subcategorisation features (Flickinger 1987; Pollard & Sag 1987; Bierwisch 1986). With a slight extension of Saussure's notion, linguistic signs are thus lexically characterized by phonological, syntactic and semantic information; and the set of all lexical entries could simply be considered the lexical component of a grammatical theory. This is an oversimplification:

1. the content per lexical entry seems unduly restricted;
2. the notion of "entry in a lexicon" needs to be refined;
3. different kinds of linguistic information pertaining to predictable, regular, rule-governed properties versus idiosyncratic properties need to be (formally) specified;
4. interface structures mediating between the different levels of lexical representation and kinds of lexical expressions need to be considered;[3]
5. links and connections relating individual lexical entries and creating a lexical macrostructure must be accounted for.

Ad 1: Restriction of lexical information per entry: It is amazing that most of the linguistic and computational literature on the lexicon omits pragmatic information in lexical entries, thus missing a distinction which was already drawn by Morris. He defined pragmatics as "the study of the relation of signs to interpreters" (1938: 6); and noted that "pragmatics ... deals with the origin, uses and effects of signs within the behavior in which they occur" (1946: 219).

The distinction between semantics and pragmatics was intensively discussed and elaborated in the fifties by Carnap and Bar-Hillel who saw pragmatics as including descriptive semantics of natural languages. Gazdar (1979) even formalized some basic pragmatic notions. Omitting pragmatic information means neglecting those facets of a linguistic sign which relate to the situation of use, to its use by speaker and hearer in a specific linguistic context, or to what has been termed *common ground, mutual knowledge* (Clark & Marshall 1982; Clark, Schreuder & Buttrick (1983) or *discourse relevant mutual knowledge* (Paprotté & Sinha 1987). Here, common sense or naive theories supplement semantic readings of lexical items; in fact, the latter seem to be nothing but shorthand notions of beliefs, assumptions, knowledge and generalizations of daily practice and canonical relations in a linguistic community (Hobbs 1987).

Traditional dictionaries have always included pragmatic information, e.g. information pertaining to discourse domains, social and regional usage and variants of linguistic items, to register and stylistic level, and frequently common sense knowledge as part of the semantic explication of an item. Dictionaries thus codify part of the pragmatic and encyclopedic knowledge of native speakers.

An exception to the omission of pragmatic information in computational lexicons can be found in the work by Pollard and Sag: in the attribute value matrices format of linguistic description, lexical signs have a path of attributes SYNSEM|LOC|CONTEXT whose values BACKGROUND and CONTEXTUAL-INDICES contain context-dependent information belonging to the rubrics presupposition, and conventional implicature, also to indexical coordinates such as SPEAKER, ADDRESSEE, indices of spatio-temporal location (utterance time, reference time, event time) etc. (Pollard & Sag in press: chap. 1). Common sense notions may apparently be included as values of the BACKGROUND feature.

Ad 2 and 3: An extended notion of lexical entry: With Jackendoff's (1975) "full entry" hypothesis, the concept of a lexicon as a list of fully specified word types has gained ground. The lexicon is thus neither a morpheme or root-entry nor a word-form lexicon and strives to attain a subtle balance between idiosyncratic and predictable, generalized information. For Chomsky (1965) and Bloomfield the lexicon by definition contains only linguistic information that cannot be derived by rule. A hypothetical position at the other extreme would consider all linguistic information, even redundant specifications, as belonging essentially in the lexicon.

Redundancy elimination as achieved in lexicons containing only root entries does not seem to be the concern of those arguing for a full listing hypothesis (cf. Henderson 1989; Hankamer 1989), although it is clearly necessary to avoid redundancy to some extent. Arguing from evidence in agglutinative languages like Turkish, Hankamer allows full listings only for some morphologically complex forms which involve both derivational and inflectional processes. He notes that for morphological parsing involved in lexical access in these languages, roots and suffix formatives will by necessity have to be represented in the lexicon. It remains possible that in languages with prefixation and inflectional affixation different factors are at work; however, the correct "universal" model is probably closer to a mixed model in which some morphologically complex forms are listed while lexical formative entries are included as well as elements necessary for processes of morphological analysis, e.g. in the recognition of innovative input.

To avoid redundancy, a maximum of generalized information should be specified in the lexicon; to minimize storage requirements, the lexicon should contain a minimum of idiosyncratic information. The available instruments with respect to morphological and syntactic information are lexical redundancy rules, and inflectional paradigms, both well known from traditional lexicography. Idiosyncratic lexical entries will be marked for membership in a class of items exhibiting some kind of "regular, predictable" linguistic behavior, e.g. inflectional pattern, derivational variation, passivization, etc. which is formalized in a lexical rule. Inflectional paradigms and lexical rules thus also qualify as lexical entries. However, in the computational context, strategies for achieving an economical representation of lexical information and for minimizing storage requirements may raise access time in retrieval so that, depending on the specific tasks, an optimal balance between storage requirements and access time will have to be found. Furthermore, as Henderson (1989: 366f) argues, default rules which apply unless blocked in the individual entry may not always be feasible or at least may lead to problems; e.g. a mere listing of root-affix combinations does not in itself adequately specify the position of affixes in derivations with multiple suffixes. The order of application of affixes to the root needs to be specified.

Complex lexical information (phonetic, phonological, morphological syntactic, semantic, pragmatic) is necessary for semantic disambiguation and a variety of decoding tasks in natural language processing of human and machine processors. A lexicon, serving the double function of production and generation will have to put differential emphasis on the different informational dimensions, unless two kinds of lexicons are assumed to exist. In comprehension, in order to deal with innovations and possible, but not actual words of a language, word-formation rules must be represented in the lexicon. On the other hand, to avoid overgeneration in production, derived words will have to be fully listed as separate entries (*Unglücklosigkeit; *manifestationalize; *defortify). For a number of reasons, the notion of a word-type lexicon with fully specified entries is therefore not sufficient; the mixed model lexicon must contain words, (idiomatic) phrases, and formatives (affixes, stems, morphs, parts of compounds) and rules. Abstract entities such as CAUSE, underlying forms such as ostrac- for ostracise or elements of the lexicographic metalanguage normally will not be contained in the lexicon - unless they are also part of the object language and unless the linguistic or computational lexicon is made to simulate the basic reflexive and self-monitoring capacity of a human speaker.

I thus consider a lexicon an open, ordered set of sets of LEXICAL EXPRESSIONS:

(1)   Lexicon = {{LEx}}

A lexical expression is either: a LEXICAL ENTRY (LEn) for a word type, an (idiomatic) phrasal sign, or a formative; or a GENERIC FRAME (GF) specifying predictable values for syntactic category and/or subcategorization features of classes of word types or formatives; or a LEXICAL (REDUNDANCY) RULE (LR) systematically relating lexical entries; or a PARADIGM (PA) specifying predictable information on inflectional characteristics of classes of word types:

(2)   LEx = LEn v GF v PA v LR.
        {{LEx}} = {{LEn}, {GF}, {PA}, {LR}}.
        LEn = word LEn v phrasal LEn v formative LEn.

(3)   LEn = < lemmaname, lexical sign properties >

A LEXICAL ENTRY (LEn) is a pair < lemma-name, lexical sign properties > where lemma-name is a string and lexical sign properties its associated phonetic/graphemic, morphological, syntactic, semantic and pragmatic characteristics represented in the format of attribute value matrices (cf. Calder 1989; Flickinger 1987).

Predictable properties of an individual entry which result from its membership in a lexeme or formative type can be filtered out of the individual entry and be represented in a GENERIC FRAME (GF). A GF is an attribute value matrix which is typed to an element of the lexical sorts (word LEn, phrasal LEn, formative LEn), or to an element of the hierarchy of lexical types (major or minor lexical sign; head element; nominal, verbal, adjectival or prepositional head; main verb, auxiliary verb, verb form finite etc.) or to an element of the hierarchy of subcategorization types (strict intransitive, intransitive-raising, intransitive-equi, transitive, ditransitive etc.) (Pollard & Sag 1987). GFs filter out those properties of their subtypes that are shared with the class of similar signs; the attributes and restrictions appropriate for any type of GF are thus also appropriate for any subtype of that GF and inherited by the subtype. It is possible to indicate attribute sharing by marking in each LEn its membership in a number of GFs:

(4)   GF =   [   ] ^{V} [   ] ^{V} [   ]
            lexsort   lextyp   subcattyp

A LEXICAL RULE (LR) is a triple <name, input entry characteristics, output entry characteristics>. All properties of the rule's input entries which are not mentioned remain unchanged (Calder 1989). LRs thus systematically relate well-formed LEns, or LEns and GFs. Output entries of such rules must be considered entries generated on demand; they have no stable representation.

In order to include derivational rules in the set of lexical redundancy rules, one may want to view an LR as a function of E in L, where L is the set of lexical entries {LEn}, while E is the set of all well-formed expressions in the language under consideration (Hoeksema 1984: 16f):

(5)   LR = <name, input LEn characteristics, output
            representation characteristics>.

Finally, a PARADIGM (PA) is a quadruple <name, input entry form specification, [lexical rule$_1$ ... lexical rule$_n$], [output string$_1$ ... output string$_n$]> which relates a formally specified lexical input entry to a derived output string(s) via a (set of) lexical rule(s) (Calder 1989):

(6)   PA = <name, input LEn forms, {LR$_1$ ...LR$_n$},
            {output string$_1$ ....output string$_n$}>.

Ad 4: Lexicon internal interface structures. It is here impossible to do justice to the set of problems which have to do with correlating syntactic and semantic relations of and among lexical entries, and with correlating semantic and pragmatic/encyclopedic information. Typically, interface structures within a lexical entry involve mappings of syntactic categories or constituents onto syntactic functions and, depending on the theoretical orientation, mappings of both onto semantic cases, theta roles etc.

The discussion of lexicon internal interface structures cannot be dissociated from the notion of valence, i.e. the idea that the lexical selection and realization of specific constituents (especially of verbs) has direct consequences for their syntactic environment. The discussion, therefore, hinges on the lexical representation of valence or subcategorization information and on the assumption that both syntactic and semantic phenomena determine the valence dimensions of lexemes; valence is a multidimensional concept. Jacobs (1987; 1989) distinguishes seven distinct and independent realizations of valence; Langacker (1987: 277ff) lists the four factors *correspondence, profile determinacy, conceptual autonomy and dependence*, and *constituency*. Valence minimally embodies two syntactic and two semantic relations between constituents of a sentence. The syntactic aspects include (1) the necessary/obligatory occurrence of complements of a head lexeme and (2) the (formal) morphosyntactic or syntactic positional specification of the functional syntactic properties of the elements depending on the valence bearing (head) element. The semantic relations concern (1) content-specific relations (selectional restrictions) between head constituent and complements, and (2) functor-argument relations which may be mapped onto semantic cases.

Some of the problems of the lexical representation of valence phenomena relate to attempts to map the semantic valence of an item onto its syntactic valence and to distinguish (semantically) incorporated arguments from syntactically expressed ones. As a rule, *semantic arity* (*Wertigkeit*) is said to be larger than or at least equal to *syntactic valence* (*Stelligkeit*; Wotjak 1989). Thus,

(7)   *pfeffern*, v 'someone (AGENT) spices something
       (PATIENT) with pepper (INSTRUMENT/MEANS)'

requires in its basic proposition three arguments, but takes syntactically only two obligatory ones and is said to incorporate an INSTRUMENT/MEANS:

(8)   *Hans pfeffert den Salat.*
       *Hans pfeffert den Salat mit Pfeffer.

(Wotjak 1989: 325). This analysis is dependent on a number of assumptions as to the nature of the underlying predicate argument structure and raises some problems of a general nature. Thus consider the basic structure of logically obligatory argument in (9):

(9)   *lie* 'someone does not tell the truth about
       something to someone else (and knows it)'

Semantically obligatory arguments can be omitted in some utterances depending on structural context (10a), common ground or focussing mechanisms (10b), stylistic register as in (10c) or situational factors as in (10d, 10e):

(10) a.   *Peter rasiert sich/den alten Mann.*
            'Peter shaves himself/the old man.'
            Peter kann rasieren.
            'Peter can shave.'
(10) b.   *Peter lied.*
            Peter lied to Mary.
            Peter lied to Mary about his evening out.
(10) c.   *Das habe ich ihm gesagt.*
            'I told him that.'
            Hab ich ihm gesagt.
            'I told him.'
(10) d.   *Er betritt den Raum.*
            'He enters the room.'
            Zutritt verboten!
            'No entry!'
(10) e.   *Otto als Vorsitzender? Unmöglich!*
            'Otto as chairman? Impossible!'

Thus, in (10b) *Peter lied* the argument roles addressee and content of the lie are not realized. Does this mean that *lie* should have several homonymous lexical entries differing in their subcategorization potential? Does it mean that *lie* can be specified disjunctively by several possible subcategorization (predicate) frames, or will *lie* allow empty argument positions in its lexical representation? It seems possible to solve some of these problems by including a type of lexical redundancy rule which will specify argument reduction of different word forms (e.g. if verb form is imperative then subject position is not filled). The difficulties of formulating rules for the admissibility of argument reduction in the case of stylistically and situationally induced changes (10c, d) point to the necessity of further research into the variation of lexical valence information due to diverse pragmatic factors; it raises serious doubts about whether the assumption of constant subcategorization potentials of lexical entries can be maintained.

Lie seems to differ from *pfeffern* inasmuch as the instrument/means argument of *pfeffern* can not be realized whereas all semantically deep arguments of *lie* can. But clearly this is not true: "incorporated" arguments can also surface due to contextual, pragmatic, stylistic, etc. factors:

(11)   *Man pfeffert mit Pfeffer, man salzt mit Salz*
        und zuviel schmeckt man immer mit der Zunge.

The German verbs *lügen* (intransitive) and *belügen* (transitive) share argument types and number in the abstract predicate argument structure or predicate frame. However, with *belügen* the addressee of the lie is obligatorily realized (normally) as a direct object; with *lügen* the addressee may not be realized (cf. Steinitz 1984 for some further problems). Does *lügen*, therefore, incorporate two inherent argument roles? In cases such as *würzen* 'spice' (the superordinate of *pfeffern*) or *walk* neither the means/instrument role of the specific spice used in the act of *würzen* need be realized nor the legs one walks with as an argument of *walk*, nor the spatio-temporal substrate implicit in every act of walking.

Arguing for incorporations misses the point that every verb is a shorthand expression for a situation with entities and relations in which only some participants in the situation are syntactically realized as complements and adjuncts. The *Cobuild* definition 19 of *lie*, "If someone lies or is lying, they are telling a lie on a particular occasion. You also say that someone lies when they tell lies often or habitually" and definition 20, "If you say that something lies, you mean that it does not indicate or express the truth or the whole truth" *(Collins Cobuild English language dictionary* 1987) confirm this. Not only do the definitions indicate aspectual or *Aktionsart* marking ("particular occasion"; "often", "habitually") which could be interpreted as obligatory temporal complements, incorporated adjuncts or even subclasses of complements in subject position. They also specify a part-whole relation between two complements (truth - whole truth) but use the distinction between human and non-human subject complements as the basis for a new subarticle.

Like most other valence-oriented theories, the theory of incorporation lacks clearcut criteria for distinguishing obligatory, optional and free arguments (adjuncts) on the semantic, propositional, as well as on the syntactic level, and seems to rest on the freedom of a speaker to view the verb and its satellites, as is shown by the *Collins* examples.

To account for the phenomena of argument or valence reduction, addition, and incorporation, it may be assumed that the predicate argument structure of every verb is "ontologically" incremented in a prototypical description of the verbal situation. This amounts to supplanting the semantic description by common sense knowledge of the situation or scene. This description spells out all the predicate argument roles that are involved in the situation and gives the predicate's semantic arity or *Wertigkeit*.

In some cases, an argument role is obligatorily realized, e.g. where the predicate is a more neutral superordinate term (*cut, move*); in other cases, often more specific predicates, an argument role is syntactically blocked (*saw, walk, pfeffern*). This and similar phenomena will account for the fact that syntactic arity (*Stelligkeit*), lexically represented under the SUBCAT attribute, strictly defines the mimimum number of necessary obligatory complements under normalized, canonical, default conditions of use (e.g. simple, active, affirmative, declarative sentence) while the predicate's semantic arity always characterizes a larger number of arguments.

All ontological arguments, obligatory and optional ones, adjuncts, and incorporated argument roles may have a surface realization or be omitted, given specific conditions of use, of stylistic level, of membership in a paradigmatic relation to the head element, of redundancy, emphasis, focussing, and common ground. The situation/scene or *Wertigkeit* of a verb then describes and spells out obvious, inherent and inferred partners in the situation and its possible modifications in terms of a zero common ground value for the communicating systems. Argument reduction rules relate the ontological (semantic and pragmatic) arity (*Wertigkeit*) to the syntactic arity (*Stelligkeit*) as a variation-in-use of the lexical subcategorization frame. Topicalization, backgrounding and foregrounding seem to be the most important factors determining the *Stelligkeit* to *Wertigkeit* reduction rules.

In this scheme, obligatory head complement structures obtain only under normalized syntactic conditions; optional complements and adjuncts are treated on a par and distinguished from obligatory complements by *Wertigkeit* to *Stelligkeit* rules, reduction or addition functions which can be represented by specific kinds of lexical mapping rules.

Ad 5: The lexicon and textuality. In distinguishing the lexicon as a virtual system from the actual representation of lexical facts in acts of processing, one may note that the virtual system is characterized by a large degree of stability and continuity. Furthermore, elements of structure provide the lexicon or its subcomponents with conceptual connectivity (coherence) and sequential connectivity (a low degree of cohesion).

To facilitate lexical access in language understanding, some kind of sequential connectivity of lexical entries must exist; to facilitate conceptual planning, encoding, but also to increase depth of interpretation of input, a lexicon has to provide recoverable conceptual links between lexical entries. These include (1) associative links, often based on collocation, logical relations such as causality, temporal or spatial proximity, temporal precedence, instrumentality; (2) equivalence relations based on synonymy, compatibility, semantic congruence and field structures; but also on antonymy, semantic opposition, and incompatibility; (3) hierarchical ordering of hyponyms and superordinates and part-whole relations (Cruse 1986), (4) encyclopedic links between events, actions, objects and situations which are mostly thought to be represented in terms of lexical functions (Mel'cuk 1988; Beaugrande 1980). There is an unavoidable overlap between (1) and (4), and an obvious link between the notion of textuality and the notion of a thesaurus.

In the textuality perspective, the lexicon can also be constructed as a collection of text fragments corresponding to the semantic representations of lexical entries which function as nodes in a complex structure of a network of links. The activation of specific links may depend on considerations of relevance. The semantic representations thus have "active cross-reference" in a manner reminiscent of the notion of hypertext. The textuality characteristics of lexical representations are part of a yet to be developed coherent theory of semantic representations.

3.   Some psycholinguistic insights into the mental lexicon

3.1.   Lexical processing

One of the main psycholinguistic research perspectives on words is concerned with lexical access and retrieval, with how, when, and to what extent lexical information is activated in lexical processing.

Levelt and Schriefers (1987) point to the impressive capability of
quick access and retrieval of a human language user, his ability to
access the right word and to select it from his mental lexicon at a rate of
roughly three words per second, or one word every 400 msec. The
effortless efficiency and rapidity of lexical processing occurs despite the
size of the lexicon (estimates range from 60,000 to 250,000 words;
Aitchison 1987: 7), despite the imperfections of input (noise; intra- and
inter-speaker variation of speech signals; variable local phonetic
environments, and co-articulation), despite the segmentation problem
of continuous speech, and despite the short duration of the signal.
Speech is continuously interpreted and immediately understood as
heard; there is evidence for a hearer's identification of spoken words in
an utterance context even before sufficient acoustic-phonetic
information for correct recognition of the word in isolation has been
accumulated. Efficiency of processing seems due to our recognition of
words on the basis of partial information; we also seem to utilize
context information such as prosody, paralinguistic information and
system-internal knowledge of situational and linguistic context.

In the processing of the incoming signal, the mental lexicon mediates
between an acoustic-phonetic analysis of the sensory input *(access function)* and the syntactic and semantic interpretation of the message being
communicated *(integration function)* (Marslen-Wilson 1989: chap.1). In
the form-based access function and processes, the speech signal is
mapped onto the mental representation of word forms; in the integration function and processes recognized word forms are mapped onto
the representation of their syntactic and semantic properties.

In language understanding, the how and when of lexical processing
can be explained through basically two kinds of models: a model of autonomous lexical processing in which contextual factors interfere only
post-lexically; and an interactive model in which sensory input, context
information, and other processing factors (e.g. modality, spoken or written; word length and word structure; frequency; syntactic category; semantic properties of the word) interact in lexical processing, and make

the information associated with the retrieved entry available to the tasks of syntactic parsing and further stages of processing.[4]

Experimental methods include studies of naming tasks, word recognition (under noise), lexical decision tasks, speech shadowing, gating tasks and detection tasks. The main parameters include (1) stimulus quality, (2) context type, (3) parameters of word structure (length, syntactic category, semantic properties, ambiguity, polysemy), and (4) word frequency (Blutner 1986; Cutler 1986).

Interesting results emerged from Marslen-Wilson's shadowing tasks. Subjects proved capable of repeating a spoken input target word even before the auditive presentation had been completed. Close shadowers accessed the target word with 250 msec delay; distant shadowers with a delay of 650 msec. Assuming that the subject's articulatory organization takes roughly 75 msec, close shadowers achieved lexical access after 175 msec, that is roughly after the presentation of the first two to three phonemes of the target word (Marslen-Wilson & Welsh 1978; Marslen-Wilson 1989).

These findings suggest that speakers achieve lexical access on the basis of partial sensory information because they actively fill the informational gaps and utilize available contextual information. Context effects were also found in the case of incorrect input; almost half of all subjects were not aware of having "corrected" the input stimulus. A semantically strong context correlated with an increase in "subconscious" corrections of faulty target words. Marslen-Wilson & Welsh (1978) report a dependence of strength of context effects on the position of the faulty phoneme in the word. The differences in the number of corrections between a weak and a strong context were noticeably fewer when the faulty phoneme occured early in the word.

An autonomous model of lexical access with postlexical context effects can probably be ruled out. Morton's Logogen Model (Morton 1968; 1979) allows only passive direct access. A logogen fires once a specific frequency dependent threshold level is reached and then releases its information. Faulty input cannot be dealt with. What is needed then is a model of the lexicon and of lexical access in speech with an active selection mechanism. Marslen-Wilson's Cohort Model (Marslen-Wilson & Welsh 1978; Marslen-Wilson 1989) assumes that in terms of "sequential" connectivity, lexical representations consist of strings of phonemes or feature structures. Form-based processing on the basis of sensory input depends on sensory and contextual constraints. Sensory constraints concern the goodness of acoustic fit between input and phonological representation, while contextual constraints concern the goodness of fit to content, context and situation. Together, these constraints define a unique intercept and the single correct path between sound and meaning (Marslen-Wilson 1989: chap.1). Contextual information is thus used to dispose of potential candidates for access, a cohort, by an active selection mechanism. Lexical access is achieved in three steps: (1) An autonomous stage with multiple activation of the words matching onset characteristics of the sensory input. A cohort is set up specifying an initial consonant cluster plus vowel. (2) An interactive stage with active multiple assessment selection by sorting out inappropriate cohort members on the basis of sensory and context properties. (3) The selection stage: With further input matching against the remaining cohort members, a point of uniqueness is reached, and the appropriate candidate is chosen for lexical access.

As Cutler (1986) points out, gating tasks confirm the point of uniqueness and supporting evidence can be found for cross modal priming and semantic priming by cohort members. Recognition of non-words can also be explained in this model: if the active selection mechanism of the cohort empties it completely, the input is a non-word.

The Cohort Model with its emphasis on correct initial input segments has been criticized (Blutner 1986) for mainly two reasons: (1) Fluent speech does not provide the necessary reliable information about word onsets so that difficulties emerge for setting up the initial cohort. (2) It is the total amount of overlap between input and lexical representation rather than directionality of mapping which is important. Marslen-Wilson (1989) points to impressive evidence that (a) partial word-initial overlap is sufficient to activate lexical representations; (b) the total amount of overlap which may be large as in cases of rhymes is ineffective in priming their targets; a rhyme is never treated as if it were the original word. Strong directionality is, therefore, assumed in the access process.

As words are recognized in context even before sufficient sensory information for correct recognition on the sensory basis has accumulated, better empirical evidence for contextual effects in on-line lexical processing is needed. Although multiple activation of different meanings associated with a homophone has been shown, Marslen-Wilson (1989) assumes that sentential context does not function to override perceptual hypotheses. Context seems to have an inhibitory or facilitatory effects amplifying the results of perceptual analysis. This confirms an informed common sense opinion.

With respect to design features of the lexicon, the preceding outline of lexical processing points to interpretive mechanisms in the lexicon. They simultaneously activate different kinds of information and context representations, and integrate diverse information into the segmentation, classification and mapping of the incoming, continuous speech signal onto lexical representations. Efficient retrieval is achieved by an active selection mechanism which utilizes contextual information. This would seem to support a pragmatically enriched lexical semantics but furthermore points to a mental system with multiple access to lexical forms and information, and with multiple assessment of the contextual appropriateness of the lexical information associated with the lexical forms.

3.2. The acquisition of lexical information

There are estimates that children build up their lexicon at the rate of roughly 10 to 15 entries per day; they learn to master large parts of the vocabulary of their language in a relatively short time under both informal and formal learning conditions and will have acquired on the average 60,000 lexemes by the age of 18 to 20 (Aitchison 1987). Lexical acquisition by a human is a lifelong process. Similarly, lexicographers reckon that every 10 years 10% to 15% of the entries of a dictionary have become obsolete. Besides acquisition, there is also a lifelong process of lexical maintenance and updating by speakers and lexicographers who adapt to the dynamics of lexical change.

Besides the phonetic and graphemic signal characteristics of linguistic signs, their semantic content and syntactic properties such as syntactic category and valence or subcategorization (of head categories) must be learned and represented. The valence/subcategorization information consists of several layers of information, e.g. quantitative information (number of arguments); information about the syntactic categories the arguments belong to (e.g. NP_{NOM}; NP_{ACC} etc.); information about the syntactic functions the arguments participate in (SUBJ; DOBJ; IDOBJ; OBL), about the morphological specification of the complements; information about thematic roles of the arguments (AGENT, GOAL, INSTRUMENT, LOCATION etc), about the number and kind of argument roles in a scene representation, and information about selectional restrictions on possible lexical realizations of the arguments etc. In addition, argument reduction rules and information relating to the use of the specific sign as well as links between semantic content and world knowledge, and relations to other meanings etc. have to be acquired and represented.

For reasons of efficiency of storage, we assume that the mental lexicon is no full word form lexicon but contains "canonicized" words (lexemes) which are also marked for the morphological property of belonging to a certain inflectional paradigm, and for being a possible candidate for the application of specific lexical (redundancy) rules.

Pinker (1984) proposes four learning mechanisms for the acquisition, maintenance and updating of fully specified lexical entries:

1.   Direct learning from positive evidence. The learner accepts linguistic input, processes it lexically, parses it, and encodes new lexical entries in his mental lexicon by appropriately representing the kind of lexical information which has been extracted from the input string. Learning from positive evidence presupposes an existing lexical representation which is enriched and made more complex by a continuing stream of confirming material; it also presupposes a monitoring mechanism which is capable of marking something as "positive" evidence.

2.   A canonical mapping process for the inscription of canonical predicates. Pinker (1984: 300) assumes that canonical predicates display "near universal regularities in lexical subcategorization" under normalized conditions of simple, active, affirmative, declarative, minimally presuppositional and pragmatically neutral sentences, and allow a "canonical mapping between a predicate's thematic roles and canonical grammatical functions corresponding to them" (ibid. p. 297). This clearly is an easy way out of the problem because it does not explain how, when and for whom normalized conditions obtain, why they should obtain especially for children, and how the acquisition of the variety of thematic realizations of syntactic functions is achieved. If there were canonical subcategorization frames in the mental lexicon and mappings of functions onto thematic roles, as Pinker assumes, children could start with a variety of syntactic structures and would not have to work their way into two and three word utterances with the small amount of syntactic structure they possess. Paprotté (1985) assumes that one and two word utterances can be taken to denote full situations in the child's world with the complete inventory of participating individuals and relations but children do not yet express them linguistically because they lack *inter alia* the means of calculating the DRMK.

3./4. Learning by application of lexical rules and noncanonical mappings. These mechanisms either lead into a circle in that the abovementioned mappings between functions and roles are to a large extent presupposed in lexical redundancy rules or else may only be used to explain updating and maintenance activities of adult learners. A problem not accounted for is the acquisition of lexical constraints on productivity: How does the child learn or acquire the information that lexical items for the most part are constrained in their membership in lexical redundancy rules (e.g. dative movement applies to *show, tell, give, send* but not to *demonstrate, inform, donate, transfer*; subject raising to *is likely* but not to *is probable*; etc.)? It seems reasonable to assume that the mechanisms at work are the same as in paradigm formation and paradigm splitting (Pinker 1984: 322).

Two points emerge: first, the notion of the mental lexicon as a dynamic representation which takes time to build up, which has to be updated and maintained and corrected; second, lexical learning involves learning in general and may be based on a process of acquiring representations of scenes in which functors and their arguments represent real world circumstances mediated and accompanied by the context of utterances. Building up a fully specified lexical representation would then involve processes of abstracting structure from scene representations and learning how to encode lexical and syntactic functors/head elements and their arguments/complements, possible modifications, etc. Learning about the world, about language and the conventions of use contributes towards a complex, dynamic, active mental lexicon.

4.   The lexicon as a component of NLP systems

Currently, there is no NLP system that provides a reasonably broad coverage based on a comprehensive cognitive and linguistic theory (Obermeier 1989); worse still is the situation for the lexical component of such systems. In Whitelock et al. (1987: 233), as part of a discussion, Shieber notes the scarcity of lexical resources and estimates the average size of the lexical components at roughly 1,500 entries. Since then, the situation has not really changed. The lack of versatility of NLP systems is to a large extent due to the small lexicons they are supplied with.

Three problems figure prominently in a discussion of computational lexicology: the problem of acquisition, the problem of theoretical orientation and format, and the problem of lexical semantics.

4.1. Acquisition of lexical components of NLP systems

Developing large lexicons for formal systems is an expensive and time consuming task if undertaken by traditional lexicographic methods. At present, mainly two methods are being used to develop large scale lexicons, overcoming time and cost factors. In a number of projects, machine readable dictionary sources (i.e. the printing tapes of traditional dictionaries) serve as bases for automatic extraction of lexical information and for reformatting (Boguraev & Briscoe 1989; Evens 1988; Wilks et al. 1987, 1988; Klavans 1988). If these attempts are successful, large scale lexicons in the form of lexical databases will be available within a short time. However, traditional dictionaries are geared to human users and rely heavily on their intuitive understanding and on bridging assumptions to make up for inconsistencies. Klavans (1988) investigated the subcategorization features of the LDOCE Box codes in relation to the examples given and found numerous inconsistencies. She concluded that the Box Codes in LDOCE had to be carefully re-evaluated before they could be used (p. 820). Human post-editing is apparently necessary to achieve consistent results from automatic reformatting experiments of lexical data from printing tapes, quite apart from the effort necessary for correcting mistakes of the source and for updating the MRD lexicon.

Another problem concerns the usability and extractability of the semantic information provided in a machine-readable dictionary (MRD). Any system capable of automatic analysis of available lexical resources is itself in need of a lexical subcomponent. The semantic information of an MRD or of printing tapes can therefore not be extracted in a form that is usable in NLP systems. What can be achieved is a kind of net of co-occurrence relations between *definiendum* and *definiens* in lexical entries as a rough representation of semantic relations obtaining in the lexicon. Carroll and Grover (1985: 125) conclude

> that fully automatic processing of LDOCE in order to derive the type of lexical entries required by the analysis system is not feasible. (Indeed we believe that no existing MRD provides a complete, consistent and totally accurate source of lexical information.) In the light of this, the solution we have

adopted is a semi-automatic system, a "Lexicon Development Environment" (LDE), interacting with a linguist or lexicographer.

The second method of lexical acquisition is based on authentic text materials (text corpora) as a type of machine-readable data which are readily available today. Text corpora are "naturally occurring" materials (not invented for the sake of proving a point of linguistic argumentation), and they are mass data which NLP systems eventually will have to cope with. An analysis system, "a lexicographic expert", automatically derives lexical information, ideally lexical entries from the text corpus, and interacts with a linguist or lexicographer in order to inscribe the lexicographic information into a lexical database (Paprotté, Lemnitzer & Barkey 1989). (The idea is rather similar to Carroll and Grover's LDE.) The two advantages of this approach are (1) the higher degree of descriptive adequacy that can be achieved and (2) the fact that it will allow easy updating and maintenance of the lexical database. The disadvantage is that it requires a high amount of linguistic expert knowledge to be built into the system, and that it requires a bootstrap lexicon with which to start the analytical processes. This system may thus be slightly slower and more complex than the first approach but is in the long run more efficient and certainly less expensive.

In a narrow sense of "learning", such a system has the ability to learn in that it can utilize successfully extracted and interactively confirmed lexical information which has been inscribed into its lexical database for re-runs and increasingly more accurate parses of textual input. The system under development thus aims at modeling learnability in a weak notion of learning.

4.2. Lexical formats and theoretical orientation

The problem of the format of lexical data arises because lexical descriptions rest on theoretical orientations. Each lexical metalanguage shares assumptions, axioms, theoretical entities and constructs with a specific linguistic theory. In order to avoid costly re-accumulation of data, lexical items should be represented in a theoretically uncommitted way or at least in a fashion which is appropriate for a family of grammatical theories. For example, the family of unification grammars, especially the head grammars (Categorial Grammar; GPSG; HPSG; LFG; FUG etc.), can be said to utilize only slightly different formats of a lexicon. Present work, therefore, should aim at developing lexical databases, a precise, formal and consistent descriptive language and a set of mapping or conversion rules with which to configure lexical data and information to the specific needs of an NLP-system or a formalism, and convert data and information into expressions of the language used by the particular formalism or theory.

It may be worth looking at some design choices shared by the above mentioned grammatical formalisms, by Hudson's Word Grammar (1984) and Starosta's Lexicase framework (1988). These formalisms are

- underivational, monostratal and surface based, i.e. grammatical descriptions directly characterize the surface order of elements of a sentence and thus define admissible structures;
- informational in the sense that the lexicon is the major informational domain and the central grammatical component;[5]
- head driven, i.e. basic assumptions of dependency or valency grammar are valid (cf. Tesnière 1959; Helbig & Schenkel 1969; Helbig & Buscha 1972; Anderson's dependency case grammar 1971). One consequence being that word classes separate along the line of major head word classes which subcategorize for something (roughly: N, V, ADJ, PREP) and those that do not, the minor ones.
- "untransformational"; there is no level of transformations in such a model of lexicon grammar; strings and informational structures are related (paired) in terms of permissible associations (pairings), not in terms of how strings are computed;
- feature based; the informational elements are represented in structures of features associated with values taken from a well-defined, empirically motivated domain (feature value matrices);
- lexicalist ("panlexicalist", Starosta 1988: 1) in the sense that the word is the main unit bearing information, and that systematic relations between word types and word form types are accounted for by lexical redundancy rules.

4.3. Semantic representations: semantic ambiguity

Except for the work done by Wilks and colleagues, there is no general and coherent view of the semantic structure of the entire lexicon. Neither is there a consistent theory of the interaction and interdependence of lexical semantics and other linguistic levels of theory.

Attempts at treating polysemy and lexical ambiguity and at giving an empirical foundation to decisions about different senses of polysemous words (Small, Cottrell & Tanenhaus 1988; Wilks et al. 1988) show that it is necessary to distinguish different senses on the basis of syntactic environments, and on the basis of semantic rules.

For example, *bake* can have a 'change of state' sense as in *bake the potato* or a 'create' sense as in *bake a cake*. Pustejovsky (1989) treats these and similar cases of systematic ambiguity (e.g. of verbs allowing resultative constructions *wipe the table* vs. *wipe the table clean*, of shifts of aspectual type) as cases of logical polysemy. That is, he tries to account for them by rules and principles of semantic composition. This includes considering properties of the nominal arguments of verbs:

> In explaining the behavior of the systematic ambiguity above, I made reference to properties of the noun phrase that are not typical semantic properties for nouns in linguistics; e.g. artefact, natural kind ... I call this the Qualia Structure (Pustejovsky 1989: xxi).

His notion of qualia structure allows dealing with semantic indeterminacy of cases discussed in Nunberg (1979). It can also be used to deal with metonymy where a subpart or related part of an object "stands" for the object itself, as in *Eiche, Kirsche, Kastanie* which denote both 'tree' and specific 'kind of wood'; *Kirsche* and *Kastanie* also denote the fruit of the tree. If the qualia structure, as he deems "reasonable to assume" (p. xxii), specifies what artefacts are used for, that trees supply wood and bear fruit, the problem of lexical ambiguity disappears in the richer and more complex semantic representation which is essentially encyclopedic in nature; Pustejovsky's proposal thus confirms the necessity of extending semantic representations into common sense theories (Hobbs 1987) or world knowledge.

In lexical semantics, there is no agreement on whether the semantic structure embodies a representation of world knowledge as is claimed by Wilks et al. (1988) and Guo (1988).[6] Motivated by shortcomings of text understanding systems of the present, Dahlgren (1988) has developed an interesting proposal. It consists of representing common sense knowledge as naive, probabilistic theories on the level of what is linguistically interesting and shared by members of a linguistic community (subculture). A naive theory is not a scientific theory but rather a set of related beliefs that form a construct which is employed in understanding natural language. For example, a lexical representation of *shirt* is made to contain the following information:

> if something is a shirt it probably has buttons, 1 collar, 1 front, 1 back, 2 armholes, 1 neck, 2 sleeves, 1 cuff, pockets, is white, is experienced as warm and soft, and inherently its function is for a person to wear it and to cover the person, and it is made out of cloth. Conversely, if something has these features, it's probably a shirt (Dahlgren 1988: 31f).

Regardless of the problem of delimitation of such information (shirts sometimes lose buttons, need washing and ironing etc.), the accessibility of such information to an NLP system is important and can be guaranteed due to the syntactically regimented structure of the representation. Dahlgren's proposal expands a narrow semantic representation and directly links the lexicon to encyclopedic knowledge structures. Thus, even in formally precise and explicit representations of computational lexicons it is possible to enrich the semantic component and to provide it with textuality. This may also be achieved by using pseudo-texts (Wilks' preference semantics), sense frames from collative semantics (Fass 1986) or integrated semantic units (Guo 1988).

Langacker (1987: 154) holds that the distinction between semantics and extralinguistic knowledge is largely artefactual "and the only viable conception of linguistic semantics is one that avoids such false dichotomies and is consequently *encyclopedic* in nature". This position allows to account for facts of language acquisition, of language use, comprehension and of semantic indeterminacies (Paprotté 1985), and permits a natural and unified account of valence relations. Furthermore, it integrates Langacker's (1987: 159) notion of *centrality*, i.e. the degree of relevance, frequency and generality of facets of encyclopedic knowledge connected with a linguistic item. With respect to the computational lexicon, it simply points to the huge task of devising a suitable means of knowledge acquisition and a complex structure of knowledge representation.

5. Conclusion

By drawing on linguistic theory, certain experimental psycholinguistic results, a short assessment of the practical problems of lexical acquisition and the needs of NLP systems, I have argued for a notion of "lexicon" that is empirically motivated: for a lexicon that is capable of learning and extending itself, that is essentially encyclopedic in its knowledge and integrates "common sense" theories; for a lexicon that displays a rich texture of meaningful links between its entries, and is complex both with respect to the types of lexical expressions and the amount of grammatical information it contains.

Notes

1. It is clearly a question of belief to deny or grant that computers will achieve intelligence. However this may be, computers are still a long way away from being intelligent. To become so, a conceptual barrier will have to be broken and a qualitative jump will be necessary: we need a program that is capable of learning and becoming more intelligent than the programmer. At present, computers can only handle things that are mathematically computable whereas the brain deals with things that are noncomputable in the mathematical sense.

2. Similarly, Marr (1982) distinguishes three distinct but systematically interrelated levels of explanation. The computational level identifies what the system is doing. It explains the structure of mental representations and the operations that apply to them in terms of what is computed. It thus provides an abstract formulation of the information processing task which defines a given psychological task (competence) together with a specification of the constraints involved. The algorithmic level gives an account of how the representations are processed. It specifies the psychological processes utilized in the performance of the task. At the third level, the realization of the computation by "hardware", by neural mechanisms, is explained (cf. Boden 1988: 48ff). The crucial point is that we cannot understand the mental lexicon without recourse to these three levels.

3. The question of interfaces to lexicon-external components of a grammar will not concern me here. An answer would depend on the specific linguistic theory chosen so that with regard to an abstract lexicon as an isolated component a greater amount of independence from specific linguistic theories would seem to be called for.

4. Clear representational differences exist between lexical access and syntactic parsing: sentences cannot but, in general, words must be permanently stored. However, there are not only multi-word lexical entries such as phrasal lexemes, idioms, and proverbs but also problems of identity and length of words in languages like Turkish. There is also enormous variability in the physical shape of words to account for; derivational rules, necessary for the production and understanding of innovations are included in the lexicon. In general, then, the lexicon must be thought of as a dynamic rule-engulfing component.

5. "This means that a lexicon by itself generates the set of grammatically well-formed sentences in a language: each word is marked with

contextual features which can be seen as well-formedness conditions on trees, and a well-formed sentence is any configuration of words for which all of these well-formedness conditions are satisfied. ... Consequently a fully specified lexicon is itself a grammar, even if it is not associated with a single grammatical rule" (Starosta 1988: 1).
A lexicon in this sense is a grammar of words which includes generalizations about the internal composition of lexical entries, about their cooccurrence potential and distribution. Some few rules for generating and modifying trees are not part of the lexicon. These substitute for PS-rules and appear in the ID/LP rule format of HPSG and GPSG. Regular patterns of correspondence between word forms, phrases or sentences are stated in terms of lexical rules integrated into the lexicon.

6. "However, we do not intend to mark computational semantics off from knowledge realms and their formal expression: on the contrary, the position we take in this chapter is that knowledge of language and of 'the world' are not ultimately separable, just as they are not ultimately separable into data bases called, respectively, dictionaries and encyclopaedias." (Wilks et al. 1988 in Boguraev & Briscoe 1989: 194).

References

Aitchison, Jean
      1987   *Words in the mind: An introduction to the mental lexicon.* Oxford: Basil
                    Blackwell.
Anderson, John M.
      1971   *The grammar of case: Towards a localistic theory.* (Cambridge Studies
                    in Linguistics 4.) Cambridge: Cambridge University Press.
Bar-Hillel, Yehoshua
      1964   *Language and information.* Reading, Mass.: Addison-Wesley.
Beaugrande, Robert de
      1980   *Text, discourse and process.* London: Longman.
Bierwisch, Manfred
      1986   "Some aspects of lexical knowledge", *Linguistische Studien Reihe A*
                    153: 142-156.
Blutner, Reinhard
      1986   "Lexikalischer Zugriff: Experimentelle Paradigmen und Erklärungsan-
                    sätze", *Linguistische Studien Reihe A* 153: 1-23.
Boden, Margaret A.
      1988   *Computer models of mind: Computational approaches in theoretical
                    psychology.* Cambridge: Cambridge University Press.
Boguraev, Bran & Ted Briscoe
      1989   *Computational lexicography for natural language processing.* London:
                    Longman.
Calder, Jo
      1989   "Paradigmatic morphology", *Proceedings of the 4th Conference of the
                    European Chapter of the Association for Computational Linguistics,
                    Manchester:* 58-65.
Carnap, Rudolf
      1955   "On some concepts of pragmatics", *Philosophical Studies* 6: 89-91.

Carnap, Rudolf
    1955   "On some concepts of pragmatics", *Philosophical Studies* 6: 89-91.
Carroll, John & Claire Grover
    1989   "The derivation of a large computational lexicon for English from LDOCE", in: Bran Boguraev & Ted Briscoe (eds.), 117-134.
Chomsky, Noam
    1965   *Aspects of the theory of syntax*. Cambridge: MIT Press.
Clark, Herbert H. & Catherine R. Marshall
    1982   "Definite reference and mutual knowledge", in: Aravind K. Joshi, Ivan Sag & Bonnie Webber (eds.), *Elements of discourse understanding*. Cambridge: Cambridge University Press.
Clark, Herbert H., Robert Schreuder & Samuel Buttrick
    1983   "Common ground and the understanding of demonstrative reference", *Journal of Verbal Learning and Verbal Behavior* 22: 245-258.
Cruse, D. Alan
    1986   *Lexical semantics*. Cambridge: Cambridge University Press.
Cutler, Ann
    1986   "Phonological structure in speech recognition", *Phonology Yearbook* 3: 161-178.
Dahlgren, Kathleen
    1988   *Naive semantics for natural language understanding*. Boston: Kluwer.
Elman, Jeffrey L.
    1989   "Connectionist approaches to acoustic/phonetic processing", in: William D. Marslen-Wilson (ed.), 227-260.
Evens, Martha W. (ed.)
    1988   *Relational models of the lexicon: Representing knowledge in semantic networks*. Cambridge: Cambridge University Press.
Fass, Dan C.
    1986   "Collative semantics: An approach to coherence", *Memorandum MCCS-86-56*, Computing Research Laboratory, New Mexico State University.
Flickinger, Dan
    1987   Lexical rules in the hierachical lexicon. [Unpubl. Ph.D. dissertation, Stanford University.]
Gazdar, Gerald
    1979   *Pragmatics: Implicature, presupposition, and logical form*. London: Academic Press.
Günther, Hartmut
    1988   "Experimentelle Morphologieforschung", in: Hartmut Günther (ed.), *Experimentelle Studien zur deutschen Flexionsmorphologie*. Hamburg: Buske.
Guo, Cheng-ming
    1988   "Knowledge acquisition with a machine lexicon", *Report MCCS-88-131*. Computing Research Laboratory, New Mexico State University.
Hankamer, Jorge
    1989   "Morphological parsing and the lexicon", in: William D. Marslen-Wilson (ed.), 392-408.
Helbig, Gerhard & Joachim Buscha
    1972   *Deutsche Grammatik*. Leipzig: VEB Enzyklopädie.

Helbig, Gerhard & Wolfgang Schenkel
    1969   *Wörterbuch zur Valenz und Distribution deutscher Verben*. Leipzig: VEB
            Bibliographisches Institut.
Henderson, Leslie
    1989   "On mental representation of morphology and its diagnosis by
            measures of visual access speed", in: William D. Marslen-Wilson (ed.),
            357-391.
Hobbs, Jerry
    1987   "World knowledge and word meaning", *Theoretical Issues in Natural
            Language Processing (TINLAP)* 3: 20-27.
Hoeksema, Jacob
    1984   Categorial morphology. [Unpubl. Ph.D. dissertation, Rijksuniversiteit
            te Groningen.]
Hudson, Richard
    1984   *Word grammar*. Oxford: Blackwell.
Jackendoff, Ray
    1975   "Morphological and semantic regularities in the lexicon", *Language* 51:
            639- 671.
Jacobs, Joachim
    1987   Kontra Valenz. [Unpubl. MS.]
    1989   Was ist Valenz? [Unpubl. MS.]
Klavans, Judith
    1988   "COMPLEX: A computational lexicon for natural language systems",
            *Proceedings of the 12th International Conference on Computational
            Linguistics (COLING)*. Budapest, Vol II: 815-823.
Lang, Ewald
    1983   "Lexikon   als   Modellkomponente   und   Wörterbuch   als
            lexikographisches Produkt: Ein Vergleich als Orientierungshilfe",
            Linguistische Studien. Reihe A, Arbeitsberichte 109: 76-91. Hrsg. von
            Joachim Schildt & Dieter Viehweger, Akademie der Wissenschaften
            der DDR, Zentralinstitut für Sprachwissenschaft, Berlin.
Langacker, Ronald W.
    1987   *Foundations of cognitive grammar*. Vol 1: *Theoretical prerequisites.*
            Stanford: Stanford University Press.
Levelt, Willem J.M. & Herbert Schriefers
    1987   "Stages of lexical access", in: Gerard Kempen (ed.), *Natural language
            generation*. Dordrecht: Martinus Nijhoff.
Marr, David
    1982   *Vision: A computational investigation into the human representation and
            processing of visual information.* San Francisco: Freeman.
Marslen-Wilson, William D. & Alan Welsh
    1978   "Processing interactions and lexical access during word recognition in
            continuous speech", *Cognitive Psychology* 10: 29-63.
Marslen-Wilson, William D. (ed.)
    1989   *Lexical representation and process*. Cambridge: MIT Press.
Mel'cuk, Igor
    1988   "Semantic description of lexical units in an explanatory combinatorial
            dictionary: Basic principles and heuristic criteria", *International Journal
            of Lexicography* 1: 165-188.
Morris, Charles W.
    1938   "Foundations of theory of signs", in: Charles Morris (1971).

1946   *Signs, language and behavior.* Englewood Cliffs, N.J.: Prentice Hall.
1971   *Writings on the general theory of signs.* The Hague: Mouton.
Morton, John
1968   "Interaction of information in word recognition", *Psychological Review*
            76: 165-178.
1979   "Facilitation in word recognition: Experiments causing change in the
            Logogen model", in: Paul A. Kolers, Merald Wrolstad & Herman
            Bouma (eds.), *Processing of visible language.* Vol 1. New York: Plenum
            Publ.
Nunberg, Geoffrey
1979   "The non-uniqueness of semantic solutions: Polysemy", *Linguistics and
            Philosophy* 3: 145-184.
Obermeier, Klaus K.
1989   *Natural language processing technologies in artificial intelligence: The
            science and industry perspective.* Chichester: Ellis Horwood.
Paprotté, Wolf
1985   "Metaphor and the first words", in: Wolf Paprotté & René Dirven
            (eds.), *The ubiquity of metaphor.* Amsterdam: Benjamins.
Paprotté, Wolf, Lothar Lemnitzer & Reinhild Barkey
1989   "Zur Entwicklung eines lexikographischen Werkzeugs", *Sprache und
            Datenverarbeitung* 13:3-24.
Paprotté, Wolf & Chris Sinha
1987   "Functional sentence perspective in discourse and language
            acqusition", in: René Dirven & Vilem Fried (eds.), *Functionalism in
            linguistics.* Amsterdam: Benjamins.
Pinker, Steven
1984   *Language learnability and language development.* Cambridge: Harvard
            University Press.
Pisoni, David B. & Paul A. Luce
1987   "Acoustic-phonetic representations in word recognition", *Cognition* 25:
            21 -52.
Pollard, Carl & Ivan A. Sag
1987   *Information based syntax and semantics.* Vol. 1. *Fundamentals.*
            Stanford: CSLI Lecture Notes 12.
in press   *Information based syntax and semantics.* Vol. 2: *Topics in binding and
            control.* Stanford: CSLI.
Pustejovsky, James
1989   "Current issues in computational lexical semantics", *Proceedings of the
            4th Conference of the European Chapter of the Association for
            Computational Linguistics, Manchester:* xvii-xxv.
Pylyshyn, Zenon W.
1986   *Computation and cognition.* Cambridge: MIT Press.
Seidenberg, Mark S.
1989   "Reading complex words", in: Gregory N. Carlson & Michael K.
            Tanenhaus (eds.), *Linguistic structure in language processing.* Boston:
            Kluwer.
Shieber, Stuart
1987   quoted from one of his contributions to a discussion, in: Whitelock et
            al. (eds.), 1987.
Small, Steven I., Garrison W. Cottrell & Michael K. Tanenhaus (eds.)
1988   *Lexical ambiguity resolution.* San Mateo, Calif: Morgan Kaufmann.

Starosta, Stanley
1988   *The case for lexicase: An outline of lexicase grammatical theory.*
            London: Pinter.
Steinitz, Renate
1984   "Lexikalisches Wissen und die Struktur von Lexikoneinträgen",
            Linguistische Studien, Reihe A 116: 1- 88.
Tanenhaus, Michael K. & Margery M. Lucas
1987   *Context effects in lexical processing.* Boston: Kluwer.
Tesnière, Lucien
1959   *Eléments de syntaxe structurale.* Paris: Klincksieck.
Whitelock, Peter, Mary McGee Wood, Harold Somers, Rod Johnson & Paul Bennett
(eds.)
1987   *Linguistic theory and computer applications.* London: Academic Press.
Wilks, Yorick, Dan C. Fass, Cheng-Ming Guo, James E. McDonald, Tony Plate &
Brian Slator
1987   "A tractable machine dictionary as a resource for computational
            semantics", *Memorandum in Computer and Cognitive Science, MCCS-
            86-105,* Computing Research Laboratory, New Mexico State
            University.
1988   "Machine tractable dictionaries as tools and resources for natural
            language processing", *Proceedings of the 12th International Conference
            on Computational Linguistics. COLING.* Budapest. Vol. 2: 750-755.
Wotjak, Barbara
1989   "Inkorporierungen und Valenztheorie", *Deutsch als Fremdsprache* 6:
            323-329.

Some pedagogical implications of cognitive linguistics

John R. Taylor

0. Introduction[1]

Any major innovation in linguistic theory is bound, sooner or later, to have an impact on the foreign language teaching profession. No doubt - and this is true especially if one takes a wide-angle view of the history of linguistics - the innovative character of cognitive linguistics is less dramatic than some of its current exponents would have us believe. Even so, there is little doubt that the recent work of Lakoff, Langacker, Talmy and many others does represent a major break with the trans-formational-generative paradigm which has dominated mainstream academic linguistics during the past 30 years or so. In this paper I intend to evaluate the possibility of exploiting the insights of cognitive linguistics in the teaching of grammar in foreign language pedagogy. The background to the paper is a proposed pedagogical grammar of English on cognitive principles, to be co-authored with René Dirven. Work on this *Cognitive Grammar of English* - CGE for short - is still in its early stages. For this reason, the present paper is more a statement of principle than a full-fledged progress report. In the first section of the paper, I will give a brief characterization of the nature of pedagogical grammar, and then go on to discuss a number of salient aspects of cognitive linguistics, focusing on the potential relevance of these aspects to a pedagogical presentation of the grammar of a foreign language. The discussion will be illustrated by reference to the manner in which certain topics of English grammar are to be presented in CGE.

1. Pedagogical grammar

A pedagogical grammar may be characterized as a description of a language which is aimed at the foreign language learner and/or teacher, and whose purpose is to promote insight into, and thereby to facilitate the acquisition of, the foreign language.[2]

It needs to be stressed from the outset that a pedagogical grammar differs fundamentally from a descriptive, or linguistic, grammar (Dirven 1985). Linguistic grammars (or grammar fragments) are written by linguists, for fellow linguists, and are evaluated against the demands of linguistic theory. On the other hand, a pedagogical grammar, as we have said, is written to meet the needs of the language learner and/or teacher, and is evaluated by its success in promoting insight into, and acquisition of, the foreign language.

In accordance with its purpose, a pedagogical grammar will differ from a linguistic grammar with regard to both content and presentation. Obviously, to reach its intended audience, a pedagogical grammar will make use only of concepts and terminology that are easily accessible to the linguistically naive reader. But a pedagogical grammar is not simply a linguistic grammar whose terminology has been simplified. Chomsky (1986: 6) observes that the concerns of linguistic and pedagogical grammar are "in a certain sense, complementary". A pedagogical grammar will focus of necessity on learning problems, i.e. in the main on what is "idiosyncratic" in a language, rather than on those aspects of general cross-linguistic validity. Yet a pedagogical grammar need not reduce to a statement of prescriptive rules, supplemented by lists of ad hoc exceptions. On the contrary. A pedagogical grammar will strive to present even the idiosyncratic and language-particular as coherent and systematic. This is to be achieved, firstly, through the judicious ordering of the different components of the grammar, and through the highlighting of interrelationships among the various subsystems. Of no less importance is the need to offer explanations - explanations that are at once succinct, readily comprehensible, and intuitively plausible - as to why the foreign language should be as it is. Explanations constitute a powerful promoter of insight, and without insight, learning can scarcely progress beyond rote memorization.

Against this broad characterization of a pedagogical grammar, we may draw some further distinctions, according to the proposed context of use of the grammar (Greenbaum 1987). A pedagogical grammar might be aimed primarily at the teacher trainee, at the practising teacher, or at the course or syllabus writer. Alternatively, a pedagogical grammar might have as intended audience the learners themselves, i.e. the grammar might be an intrinsic component of a set of teaching materials, or it might serve as a reference work for the intermediate to advanced student. *A Cognitive Grammar of English* is aimed at the more advanced student of English (at secondary and tertiary levels), and at trainee teachers of English. It will serve not only as a reference work, to be consulted on specific problems, but also as a text for extended perusal and study.

2. The need for pedagogical grammar

Motivating the present project is the belief that a pedagogical grammar can make a vital contribution to the process of "consciousness raising", in the sense in which Sharwood Smith (1981) and Rutherford (1987) have used the term. It would exceed the scope of this paper to present a detailed model of foreign language acquisition, and to outline the role of pedagogical grammar within such an acquisition model. Instead, I will address some of the arguments that are often heard against the need for pedagogical grammar. Doubts come from many quarters. These may be dealt with in the context of the theory of language acquisition proposed by Stephen Krashen in numerous publications (e.g. Krashen 1981, 1982; Dulay, Burt & Krashen 1982; Krashen & Terrell 1983).

Fundamental to Krashen's theory is a distinction between conscious "learning" and unconscious "acquisition". Acquisition, it is claimed, takes place under conditions of communicative language activity, and is driven by the operation of the "Language Acquisition Device", with which both adults and children are said to be endowed. A further claim is that the course of acquisition is relatively constant across individuals, the only barrier to the attainment of full mastery being the "affective filter", which for various reasons can block the "intake" of relevant aspects of language "input". In this scheme of things, conscious learning has only a very limited role to play. In fact, conscious learning will only come to fruition in those rare circumstances in which a learner has the time and the incentive to "focus on form". Crucially, it is claimed that the conscious application of a learned rule cannot cause learning to "turn into" acquisition. Consequently, the main, indeed the only, duty of the language teacher is to set up conditions which will promote acquisition. If the teacher is successful, the need for learning falls away. So too does the need for pedagogical grammar, since the raison d'être of a pedagogical grammar is to raise the learner's consciousness of the structures of the target language.

Krashen's theory needs to be evaluated with circumspection. Certain aspects are surely uncontroversial. No one, presumably, would query the notion that a good deal of language learning is unconscious, that affective barriers hinder learning, that a necessary (although not perhaps sufficient) precondition for learning is comprehensible input, and that important duties of a language teacher are to provide that input and to reduce affective barriers. But many of Krashen's assumptions and theoretical constructs have not gone unchallenged (Munsell & Carr 1981; Gregg 1984). Consider the hypothesis that learning does not "turn into" acquisition. If true, this hypothesis would leave no room for the conscious study of grammatical structure (or, for that matter, for the conscious study of *anything* in a language, not even word meanings). It certainly happens - as Krashen notes in support of his hypothesis - that learners often continue to make errors in spite of conscious knowledge of the rules they are violating. Yet, equally, learners sometimes *do* achieve errorfree mastery of a form subsequent to conscious study and practice. Even adult native speakers extend their competence in this way - by looking up unknown words in a dictionary! One could, no doubt, argue that in such cases acquisition has taken place *in spite of* conscious learning. Yet such a rejoinder merely renders Krashen's hypothesis unfalsifiable, and therefore vacuous. And even if we were to accept the general thrust of Krashen's position, it is by no means clear why the output of conscious rule applications, as well as the interrelationships highlighted by a pedagogical grammar and the arrays of illustrative examples with which grammar rules are explicated, should not themselves count as "comprehensible input" to the Language Acquisition Device. This kind of concentrated input is likely to be at a premium precisely in those situations where the learner has only limited access to foreign language data, e.g. in the foreign language classroom.

Krashen's distinction between "learning" and "acquisition" thus turns out to be anything but clear-cut. Equally suspect is the distinction between two kinds of learner activity, viz. "form-focused" activities and "meaning-focused" (or "content-focused") activities, whereby focus on form typifies the conscious application of learned rules, while focus on content characterizes the spontaneous, interactive, communicative use of language. The very fact that Krashen (and his sympathizers) can invoke such a dichotomy would appear to rest, not just on the postulated learning/acquisition distinction, but also on a highly impoverished understanding of what constitutes "grammar". To judge from the repeated citing of "morpheme studies" (i.e. studies of the acquisition of 3rd person singular verb inflection, and the like) and the (by their own admission "excruciatingly boring") form-focused exercises reviewed in Krashen & Terrell (1983: 142ff), grammar, for Krashen, would seem to comprise little other than inflectional morphology and the formation of negative and interrogative sentences. Few linguists - least of all cognitive linguists - would subscribe to such a narrow view.

The cognitive linguist would fully endorse the following remarks in Gregg's critique of Krashen: "focusing on form *is* focusing on meaning"; and: "focus on form ... boils down to trying to say what one means to say" (Gregg 1984: 83). The import of these remarks to the cognitive linguistic program will become clear in Section 3 of this paper, where we examine some of the basic theses of cognitive grammar.

3.   Cognitive grammar

According to Anna Wierzbicka (1988: 491), a dominant characteristic of linguistics in the last quarter of the 20th century has been "a new emphasis on the non-arbitrariness of grammar". By "the non-arbitrariness of grammar" is meant, above all, the thesis that syntax is motivated by semantics. Among the exponents of this thesis are, in addition to Wierzbicka herself, such linguists as Dwight Bolinger, John Haiman, and Robert Dixon. Bolinger (1977) argues that different wordings always correlate with semantic differences; for Haiman (1985) the surface form of a sentence iconically "diagrams" its semantics; while Dixon (1982: 8) states that his own work has been informed by "the assumption that the syntactic properties of a lexical item can largely be predicted from its semantic description". Cognitive Grammar, as developed by Ronald Langacker (1987a), George Lakoff (1987), and others (see e.g. the contributions in Rudzka-Ostyn 1988), needs to be seen in this context. Thus, Langacker (1987a: 12) writes that "grammar is simply the structuring and symbolization of semantic content", while for Lakoff (1987: 491) one objective of the cognitive program is to "show how aspects of form can follow from aspects of meaning".

The thesis of the non-arbitrariness of syntax is, of course, in polemical opposition to some major assumptions of Chomskyan linguistics, as well as to post-Bloomfieldian structuralism, out of which Chomskyan linguistics developed. The Chomskyan paradigm is built on the twin assumptions of modularity and autonomy. The "language faculty" is construed as a module of the mind independent of (though interacting with) other mental modules, e.g. conceptual knowledge and pragmatic competence. Thus, language competence is autonomous of a person's other cognitive abilities and social skills. Further, knowledge of language is itself viewed as a system of autonomous modules. Thus, in the *Aspects* model (Chomsky 1965), syntax is autonomous of semantics and phonology, in the sense that syntactic rules operate on strings of symbols which lack phonological and semantic content. In recent years there has, it is true, been a considerable shift of emphasis in Chomsky's thought. Now, it seems, syntax is the product of the "projection" of properties of lexical items (Chomsky 1986: 84ff). At first sight, the projection principle might be seen as a move towards the position espoused by Dixon. But this rapprochement is only apparent. Consider, as a case in point, some facts of verb complementation. (1a) is grammatical, while (1b) is ungrammatical:

(1)   a.   *I believe that I am right.*
       b.   **I believe to be right.*

Within the Chomskyan paradigm, these grammaticality judgments follow from the fact that the lexical item *believe* is subcategorized as in (2a), not as in (2b):

(2)   a.   *believe*   [that S]
       b.   *believe*   [PRO to VP]

   Cook (1988: 10), in a recent introduction to Government and Binding theory, stresses that subcategorization frames constitute *arbitrary* syntactic facts about lexical items. In contrast, the thesis of the non-arbitrariness of syntax demands a semantic explanation for the data in (1). To this end, we would need to offer a semantic characterization, firstly, of the verb *believe*, and secondly, of a subjectless infinitival complement, such that we can derive the ungrammaticality of (1b) from the semantic incompatibility of the verb and its complement. Analogously, from the semantic characterization of a *that*-clause we want to be able to infer that a *that*-complement *is* compatible with the meaning of *believe*. Similar arguments apply, *mutatis mutandis*, to the status of, e.g. *furniture* and *information* as mass nouns in English. Do we simply subcategorize these nouns as [-COUNT], and be done with it? Or do we relate the syntactic behavior of the nouns to their semantic properties?
   These two opposing approaches to syntactic phenomena have their counterparts in pedagogical presentations of grammar. The autonomous syntax position would lead to an exhaustive listing of verbal predicates according to their subcategorization patterns (verbs that take a *to*-infinitive, an accusative object plus *to*-infinitive, a gerund, a *that*-clause, etc.). Similarly, membership in the categories [COUNT NOUN]

and [MASS NOUN] would be stated by a listing of the respective classes. These classes and their membership would constitute arbitrary facts about the language, which would "just have to be learned". The semantics-based approach, on the other hand, would attempt to provide a semantic characterization of the various categories, such that learners would be in a position to predict the syntactic distribution of each element from their understanding of its semantics.

Over and above the obvious pedagogical advantage of the second approach, certain facts of language use lend support to the need to offer semantic explanations of syntactic facts. For it is not the case that each and every noun in English may be categorized as either [+COUNT] or [-COUNT]. Most nouns can in fact be used both as count nouns and as mass nouns. Similarly, the vast majority of complement-taking verbs are compatible with more than one complement type. The choice of one complement type rather than another goes with sometimes very subtle semantic differences in the resulting sentences. Compare:

(3)   a.   *I propose to leave tonight.*
      b.   *I propose leaving tonight.*

In (3a) it is the speaker himself who intends to leave, while in (3b) it is not clear who is to leave (perhaps it is the speaker, perhaps other people); the speaker is only proposing the activity of leaving. A mere listing of predicates according to the complements that they take would be unable to accommodate facts of this nature.

Having positioned cognitive linguistics within the context of some recent trends in linguistic theory, I shall now in the remaining part of this paper examine some specific claims of cognitive linguistics, drawing attention to their relevance to pedagogical issues.

3.1.   Symbolic units

The basic construct in cognitive grammar - just as it was for Saussure - is the linguistic sign, or "symbolic unit". For Saussure, the linguistic sign was the association of a "concept" with an "acoustic image"; similarly, for Langacker (1987a: 11), the symbolic unit "associates a semantic representation of some kind with a phonological representation". In fact, for Langacker, a language is nothing other than an open-ended yet structured inventory of symbolic units.

We need to elaborate on several details of the above claim. First, what counts as a symbolic unit? Saussure himself had explicated his notion of linguistic sign on the example of the lexical item *arbre* 'tree'. And indeed, the Saussurian sign is often popularly identified with the morphemes and words of a language.[3] Langacker proposes to extend the inventory of symbolic units to comprise, not only the morphemic and lexical resources of a language, but also:

(i)   morphosyntactic categories, i.e. [PAST TENSE], [PLURAL], etc.
(ii)   lexical categories, i.e. [NOUN], [COUNT NOUN], [VERB], etc.
(iii)   syntactic constructions of varying sizes and complexity, e.g.
         [TRANSITIVE SENTENCE], [*that*-CLAUSE], [NOUN PHRASE], etc.
(iv)   instances of syntactic constructions, i.e. actual noun phrases,
         that-clauses, etc.
(v)   idioms and formulaic phrases, of varying degrees of internal
         complexity and productivity.

Symbolic units differ with respect to their abstractness, or, in Langacker's terminology, their "schematicity". A schema is described as

> an abstract characterization that is fully compatible with all
> the members of the category it defines...; it is an integrated
> structure that embodies the commonality of its members,
> which are conceptions of greater specificity and detail that
> elaborate the schema in contrasting ways (Langacker 1987a:
> 371).

Thus, the symbolic unit [TREE] is an instance of the symbolic unit [COUNT NOUN]; conversely, [COUNT NOUN] is schematic for the symbolic unit [TREE] (as it is for all other count nouns in the lexicon). Similarly, the symbolic unit [NOUN] is schematic for both [COUNT NOUN] and [MASS NOUN], while these latter instantiate the more abstract unit [NOUN]. Very importantly, grammatical constructions are regarded as schemas for integrating two or more simpler units into a more complex, composite unit. For example, the expression *the tree* instantiates the schema [DET N], which in turn is an instantiation of the symbolic unit [NOUN PHRASE]. [DET N] has the status of a noun-phrase construction, which provides a pattern for the syntagmatic combination of component signs to form a more elaborate structure. Schematicity is one important principle according to which the inventory of symbolic units of a language is structured. The inventory is open-ended as a consequence of the fact that grammatical constructions are "productive", i.e. their instantiations do not have to be learned individually (although they may be, as in the case of certain frequently used expressions), but can be created from a knowledge of the construction schema and of the symbolic units that can serve as its constituents.

It follows from the above account that a study of the forms of a language cannot legitimately be divorced from a study of the meanings symbolized by the forms. For if we extend the notion of linguistic sign to comprise, not only the words and morphemes of a language, but also lexical categories and syntactic constructions, we are under the obligation to provide characterizations of the semantic content of these signs. Obviously, the semantic content of these highly schematic units will itself be highly schematic. Consider again the examples mentioned in the previous section. *Furniture* is a mass noun in English, which is to say that *furniture* instantiates the symbolic unit [MASS NOUN], and so, at its semantic pole, elaborates with greater specificity the semantic content of [MASS NOUN]. Obviously, the account would be incomplete without a statement of the semantic content of [MASS NOUN]. Similarly, the inability of *believe*, as used in (1), to take a subjectless *to*-infinitive needs to be explained in terms of the semantic incompatibility of *believe* with this kind of complement structure. Again, this account places us under the obligation to spell out the semantic content of a *to*-infinitive, in contrast to, say, a gerund or a bare infinitive.

3.2. Schemas and prototypes

Alongside the relationship of schematicity, Langacker also recognizes the role of prototypes in the structuring of the symbolic units of a language. Whereas a schema is an abstract characterization that is fully compatible with all its instances, a prototype is a typical instance, and other elements get assimilated to a category in virtue of some kind of similarity to its prototype (Langacker 1987a: 371). Categorization by prototype and categorization by schema are not in principle incompatible. For instance, a prototype and its more peripheral exemplars might still be compatible with an abstract, schematic representation (Langacker 1987a: 136f). More complex categories (e.g. the "radial categories" discussed at length by Lakoff 1987 and Taylor 1989), however, will typically be structured by relationships of both schematicity and prototypicality. The mental representation of the prototype will itself be schematic to some degree, while an element associated, through similarity, with the prototype could itself function as a prototype to which further elements get associated. Alternatively, an element peripheral to the central prototype could have the status of a "sub-schema" vis-à-vis its more specific instantiations.

Both schematic and prototype characterizations have their place in a pedagogical grammar. The virtue of a schematic characterization lies in the fact that it makes possible a concise statement of the conceptual unity of a category. We may illustrate on the example of the *to*-infinitive (cf. Dirven, in press a). The schematic meaning of a *to*-infinitive is to denote an instance, or series of instances, of a situation, in contrast with a gerundial complement, which denotes merely a kind of situation. These schematic characterizations make possible an explanation of

(a)   the use of the infinitive after various kinds of predicates, e.g. predicates which denote a desire to bring about a new situation (*want, intend, mean*, etc.), predicates which denote an effort leading to an accomplishment (*manage, try, strive*), and predicates of influence and indirect causation (*persuade, ask, get*)

(b)   the inappropriateness of a *to*-infinitive with other kinds of predicate, e.g. those which denote a psychological experience (such as *enjoy*), or an attitude to a proposition (such as *believe*)

(c)   the semantic contrast between a *to*-infinitive and a gerund after certain predicates. Consider the following examples with *propose, like* and *be afraid*:

(4)   a.   *I propose to go there tomorrow.*
              (a specific event is proposed)
       b.   *I propose going there tomorrow.*
              (a kind of event is proposed)
(5)   a.   *I like to go to the cinema on Saturday evenings.*
              (an indefinite number of events)
       b.   *I like going to the cinema on Saturday evenings.*
              (a kind of event)
(6)   a.   *I'm afraid to go there alone.*
              (on this particular occasion)
       b.   *I'm afraid of going there alone.*
              (in general)

In other cases, an overarching schematic characterization is of more limited pedagogical value. Consider the case of mass nouns and count nouns. Langacker (1987b) has proposed schematic characterizations of

[MASS NOUN] and [COUNT NOUN]: a count noun designates a "bounded region in a domain" while a mass noun designates an "unbounded region in a domain".[4] These characterizations are of limited pedagogical value for two reasons. Firstly, the characterizations appeal to a technical concept ("region in a domain") which can only be understood within the context of Langacker's more general semantic theory, and are thus not likely to be transparent to the intended user of a pedagogical grammar. More seriously, perhaps, is the fact that the characterizations do not provide a basis for predicting membership in the two categories (Taylor, in press). Langacker's schemas for [COUNT NOUN] and [MASS NOUN] would probably be valid, with little or no modification, for the large number of languages of the world which make a grammatical distinction between count and mass nouns. Yet membership in the categories varies considerably from language to language. For example, the translation equivalent of *information* in many languages is a count noun, a consequence of this fact being that errors such as *an information* are highly "fossilized" (Selinker 1972) elements in the speech even of quite proficient learners of English. To account for the idiosyncratic specifics of category membership, we need to appeal to categorization by prototype. CGE proposes, as the prototypes of [COUNT NOUN] and [MASS NOUN], a three-dimensional, concrete "thing" and an internally homogeneous, divisible "substance". The schema of a concrete "thing" then gets projected onto entities in other domains, such as units of time (*minute, year*), products of mental and creative activity (*idea, poem, symphony*), events (*earthquake, football match*), etc. The schema for a completely homogenous "substance" is likewise projected onto more abstract domains, such as emotional states (*anger, love*) and activities (*dancing, research*).

The above account of the mass/count noun distinction needs to be extended by the postulation of additional sub-schemas for mass nouns. In the first place, there are a number of mass nouns (examples include *furniture, fruit, traffic, luggage*, etc.) which do not designate a homogeneous "substance", but which rather have the status of superordinate terms which focus on some common property of different kinds of things. Secondly, there is the group of what are called in CGE "plural mass nouns". Examples include *groceries, left-overs, clothes, dishes* (as in *wash the dishes*), *contents*, etc. These nouns, like the preceding group, are superordinate terms for things of different kinds. What distinguishes them is the fact that they denote different kinds of things which are found together in a single place, or which have been brought together for a specific purpose (cf. Wierzbicka 1988).

3.3. Conventionalized conceptualizations

The semantic representations which constitute the semantic pole of a linguistic sign are not to be understood in terms of truth conditions on the possibility of successful reference. Rather, semantic representations are equated with "conventionalized conceptualizations", of varying degrees of schematicity (Langacker 1988: 94). By "conceptualization" is meant mental experience, in the broadest sense. Lakoff (1987) - developing ideas in Lakoff & Johnson (1980) - has emphasized the role of bodily perceptions and of experiential gestalts in cognition, and the importance of metaphor and metonymy in people's attempts to understand their experiences. Langacker (1987a) has appealed more to the contribution of general aspects of cognitive processing to the manner in which a person "construes" a state of affairs: scanning, profiling, level of specificity, focal adjustment, perspective, figure-ground imagery, and so on. Indeed, Langacker goes so far as to state that a full description of a language would presuppose (and might even be partly co-extensive with) "a full description of human cognition" (Langacker 1987a: 64).

If the meanings of linguistic forms are equated with conceptualizations, it has to be remembered that these conceptualizations are nevertheless "conventionalized", i.e. the conceptualizations are made available to speakers of a language by the language system that they have learned. For its linguistic expression, mental experience must first be organized in such a way as to conform with the conceptual structures symbolized by the available symbolic units. This position has important consequences for foreign language pedagogy (as well as for the contrastive study of languages),[5] viz. that formal differences between languages are symptomatic of differences in conceptualization. Thus, learning a foreign language will involve not only learning the forms of the language but simultaneously learning the conceptual structures associated with these forms. Not infrequently, the conceptualizations symbolized by the forms of the foreign language will not be isomorphic with those of the learner's native language. Now this point is readily accepted with regard to the lexical resources of a foreign language. Anyone learning English not only has to learn the phonological form associated with the word *tall*, he also has to learn the highly idiosyncratic and language-specific categorization of vertical space symbolized by this word (cf. Dirven & Taylor 1988). The distinctive contribution of cognitive grammar is to approach other symbolic units - including lexical categories and syntactic structures - in the same way in which words are approached, i.e. not as forms whose distribution is governed by an autonomous syntax, but as forms which symbolize meanings.

3.4. Languages in contrast

The nature and purpose of a pedagogical grammar requires that it focus on learning problems. In the final analysis, the identification of learning problems is a matter for empirical enquiry, and practising teachers are usually very adept at anticipating the kinds of difficulties that their students will experience. A concern of applied linguistics, however, has been a search for principles which will predict learning problems. One explanation that has enjoyed considerable currency over the years is the contrastive hypothesis, according to which the structures of the foreign language will be difficult to learn to the extent that they are non-isomorphic with the structures of the language(s) already known to the learner (Lado 1957). The failure of contrastive analysis to predict a learner's errors led a number of investigators to appeal to another kind of mechanism, viz. unrestrained rule-generalization on the part of the learner (Richards 1972). Recent work within the Chomskyan paradigm suggests a third possibility, i.e. that target language structures will constitute learning difficulties to the extent that they diverge from the principles of "Universal Grammar" (Rutherford 1987; Cook 1988).

Cognitive grammar suggests an alternative approach. Given the symbolic nature of syntax, we could expect that target language structures will be difficult to learn to the extent that they symbolize "idiosyncratic" conceptualizations, i.e. conceptual categories which are not found in the learner's mother tongue, or which are not completely isomorphous with those of the learner's mother tongue. The position, it will be noted, is similar to that of the contrastive hypothesis à la Lado - with the difference that the focus is now not on the distribution of formal elements per se, but on the meanings symbolized by these units. It follows that a pedagogical grammar will need to be inherently contrastive. CGE is not overtly contrastive, that is to say there are no explicit comparisons between English and any other language. It is, however, covertly contrastive, in that the treatment of the issues is informed throughout by an awareness of the idiosyncrasies of English vis-à-vis certain other languages. Obviously, this contrastive aspect of CGE is limited by the range of languages known to the authors (mainly, the Germanic and Romance languages of Western Europe and the Bantu languages of Southern Africa). To what extent the treatment accorded to the different topics would be valid from the perspective of speakers of e.g. Asian languages is an open question.

On the other hand, one could speculate on the possibility of a universal metric of conceptual idiosyncrasy. This is a position which would have certain affinities with the distinction between "core grammar" and "the periphery" in Chomsky's recent work, again with a focus on semantic content rather than on merely formal entities. Thus, one might hypothesize that certain conceptualizations display a high degree of cognitive "naturalness"; one would expect these conceptualizations to be symbolized in very many languages of the world, and they would be easily learnable by speakers of any language, as well as by children acquiring their mother tongue. Cognitive naturalness would presumably be a function of universal processes of concept formation, universal features of the human environment, and so on. Other categories, on the other hand, might be cognitively "marked"; one would not expect them to be symbolized in language after language (they might even be attested in only a single language), and their learning would require considerable cognitive effort. Such a possibility is suggested by Berlin and Kay's work on color terminology. Berlin and Kay (1969), in their investigation of the color terminology of some 98 languages, found that the category "red" was present in practically all the languages of their sample. This category presumably enjoys the highest degree of cognitive naturalness. Others, like "grey", "brown" and "pink", were attested only in languages with more elaborate color terminologies. For the domain of color at least, it does seem plausible to establish a hierarchy of cognitive markedness. Dirven and Taylor (1988) likewise argued for the marked status of the category symbolized by English *tall*, adding that it would be highly remarkable if another language were to have an exact translation equivalent of *tall*, which categorized the dimension of vertical space in precisely the same way as the English word.

For the import of the above remarks, consider again the categories of mass noun and count noun in English. Presumably, the status of *chair* and *water* as, respectively, count and mass nouns is highly "natural". But what about the three nouns *information*, *advice* and *news*? Prima facie, one would expect them to be count nouns. *To inform* (*someone of something*), *to advise* (*someone to do something*), *to report* (*something to someone*) denote events. (Only on a habitual reading would *He advised me what to do* be taken to refer to an activity.) Consequently, what is conveyed by an act of informing, of advising or of reporting could plausibly be conceptualized as so many discrete "things", and not as a divisible, replicable, and internally homogeneous "substance".

And yet the English conceptualization is not without its own logic. The nouns *information, advice* and *news* all invoke the conceptual domain of verbal communication. *Information, advice* and *news* denote some of the different kinds of things that can be communicated from one person to another by means of language. Reddy (1979) has documented in great detail the "conduit metaphor" which underlies much of our talk, in English at any rate, about verbal communication. According to the metaphor, the mind is construed as a container. Communication involves sending the contents of the mind - suitably packaged in containers of another kind, i.e. words - from one mind to another along a conduit, i.e. a communication channel.

Now a container - a box or a bucket, for example - may be filled either with things (*The box is full of books*) or with a substance (*The bucket is full of water*). We find the same possibilities with regard to the metaphorical containers which are words and the mind. These containers may be filled with non-individuated "substances", e.g. states and qualities like *knowledge, learning, experience, wisdom, imagination*. The metaphorical containers may also be filled with individuated "things". These include *facts, ideas, thoughts, hints* and *suggestions*. Most languages construe information, advice and news as "things"; English categorizes these contents of communicative acts,[6] somewhat idiosyncratically perhaps, as "substances", analogous to knowledge, wisdom and learning. As noted earlier, even highly proficient non-native speakers of English occasionally make errors, in spontaneous speech, on the three words in question. Possibly, the persistence of these and other "fossilizations" is symptomatic of precisely this low degree of naturalness of the grammatical phenomena in question.[7] If this speculation is valid, the need for a pedagogical grammar which motivates syntactic phenomena, by focusing attention on idiosyncratic conceptualizations conventionalized in the grammatical system of a language, becomes even more pressing.

3.5. *Imagery*

It is well known that learning is enhanced if reinforced by visual input. Since imagery plays an important role in cognitive accounts of meaning, it is not surprising that cognitive linguistics is rich in insights for pedagogical exploitation.

There are several dimensions of imagery. Firstly, the term has to do with specifically visual images. These may involve the construing of a spatial situation, or the metaphorical construing of a non-spatial situation in spatial terms. Langacker also uses the term in a more abstract sense still, to denote the way a speaker "manipulates" the elements of a conceived situation.

Consider, to begin with, those elements of language that have to do with the conceptualization of spatial relations between entities, in particular the prepositions. The spatial meanings of the prepositions are most directly explicated, not by verbal description, but by schematic drawings, of the kind used by Brugman (1981) in her study of the polysemy of *over*. The pedagogical possibilities of this technique have been systematically explored by Dirven (1989). But alongside their spatial meanings, prepositions also have a vast range of non-spatial uses. To account for these, cognitive grammar appeals in particular to processes of metaphor, whereby non-spatial domains are understood in spatial terms. On this perspective, "idiomatic" uses of prepositions turn out to be subject to a high degree of semantic motivation. *Over*, in one of its spatial uses, designates the surmounting of an obstacle on a path (*He jumped over the wall*). Given that life itself is often conceptualized, metaphorically, as a journey along a path, it comes as no surprise that difficult episodes in one's life can be conceptualized as "obstacles" which one tries to "get over".

As an illustration of a more abstract understanding of imagery, consider the contrast between a partitive expression of the kind *three of the boys*, and a quantifier-plus-noun expression like *three boys*. The principal semantic difference between the two expressions has to do with the set of boys from whom the three exemplars are to be selected. *Three boys* invites the hearer to create a set of individuals, by selecting, randomly, any three members of the category "boys". *Three of the boys*, in contrast, presupposes a set of particular boys, from which three are to be selected. More subtle is the contrast between *both boys* and *both of the boys*. Both expressions presuppose a set of two known individuals, with the consequence that the two expressions might appear at first sight to be semantically equivalent. The same goes for *each boy* and *each of the boys*, both of which likewise presuppose a fairly small set of particular individuals. Nevertheless, the syntax of the expressions does suggest different "imagings" (in Langacker's sense) of the situation. *Both boys* merely invokes the two members of a given group of boys. *Both of the boys*, on the other hand, explicitly instructs the hearer to select from the given set of two boys.

3.6. Rules

Like all pedagogical grammars before it, CGE will continue to offer the learner "rules" for correct usage. But these rules are not the categorial devices of formal linguistics, defining all and only the grammatical sentences of a language. A rule of grammar merely states a conventionalized pairing of semantic content with a formal structure. As a consequence, the ungrammaticality of a sentence is to be explained in terms of the oddness, incongruity, or other kind of ill-formedness of the meaning that the sentence has, or would have, and not in terms of the violation of some arbitrary rule of syntax.

The facts of verb complementation provide many illustrations of this principle (Dirven to appear a). Sentence (7):

(7)   *I enjoyed that he played the piano.*

is ungrammatical. The ungrammaticality results from the incompatibility of *enjoy* and a clausal complement. *Enjoy* denotes a psychological experience of a situation, while a *that*-clause denotes not a situation or the experience of a situation but a proposition, i.e. a mental representation (an "idea", "thought", or "knowledge") of a situation. Thus, while one can *enjoy listening* to someone play the piano, one cannot *enjoy the fact* that he plays the piano.

Consider next the oddity of (8a) in contrast with (8b) and (8c):

(8)   a.   *?I hope I'll leave tonight.*
       b.   *I hope to leave tonight.*
       c.   *I hope I'll be able to leave tonight.*

The acceptability of (8c) shows that we cannot account for the oddity of (8a) by means of some rule stating that, in case the subject of the complement sentence is identical with that of the main clause predicate, *hope* must take a *to*-infinitive rather than a clausal complement. But if we examine the meanings of the two kinds of complement - and the different meanings that *hope* acquires in the different contexts - then the oddity of (8a) ceases to be a mystery. *Hope* with an infinitive belongs to that class of predicates which denote an intention to bring about a new situation. In this case, it is assumed that the person who hopes has some control over the future situation. Alternatively, *hope* can denote a mental attitude towards the idea of some possible future situation. Here, there is no suggestion that the person is able to control the future. Thus

(8c) may be roughly paraphrased: "I hope that circumstances over which I have no control will be such that I'll be able to leave". (8a) is odd precisely because it presents a future act of the speaker as one over which he has no control.

While CGE strives to offer semantic explanations for grammatical rules, the learner's attention also needs to be drawn to the possibility of "breaking" rules, just in case a special, unusual, or even bizarre conceptualization is called for. To state that *cat* is a count noun does not exclude its use as a mass noun, e.g. in the sentence *After the accident, there was cat all over the road*. Consider also certain uses of the progressive in English. It is frequently noted that the progressive cannot be used with stative predicates, like *cost*. An explanation that is often offered for this restriction is along the lines that a state, by definition, continues through time; it is therefore redundant to mark continuity by means of the progressive aspect. This kind of explanation - to which even Langacker (1987b) appears to subscribe - can hardly be correct. Multiple redundancy - the conveying of information by more than one means - is endemic in human language, and while redundancy might in some cases be censured on the grounds of stylistic infelicity, it is inconceivable that redundantly conveyed information could result in such a strong constraint on grammaticality as the one under discussion. Rather, the explanation must lie with the semantic incompatibility of progressivity and stativity. CGE develops the view that progressivity is only compatible with situations that are (a) incomplete and (b) changing, i.e. in the main, with activities. Yet, in apparent contradiction to this principle, the progressive can be used with stative predicates, just in case the stative predicate has some connotations of change. For instance, the stative situation may be one of quite short duration, or of recent beginning (*Meat is costing a lot these days*).

One question that inevitably arises in the context of this discussion is: How far can and should one go in offering semantic explanations for syntax? Dixon, it will be recalled, claimed that "syntactic properties ... can largely be predicted from semantic description". Interestingly, Dixon found it necessary to hedge his statement with the word *largely*. This suggests that *some* syntactic properties are not predictable from semantics, i.e. that there will always exist a certain residue of arbitrariness. Wierzbicka (1988), in contrast, appears to adopt an uncompromisingly "maximalist" position, according to which a residue of arbitrary syntactic phenomena would merely betray the linguist's failure to come up with the appropriate semantic generalization.

The present writer sympathizes with Wierzbicka's position. That all syntactic phenomena are subject to a semantic explanation should at least constitute the researcher's null hypothesis, to be modified only in the face of intractable evidence to the contrary. But a pedagogical grammar imposes its own constraints, including the constraint of ready accessibility to the unsophisticated reader, not to mention publishers' constraints on volume length and submission dates! For practical reasons, therefore, it will often be necessary to accept an arbitrary residue.

Consider, as an example, the attributive use of nouns. Clearly, there is a generalization to be drawn, viz. that attributive nouns are uninflected for number: *a pet owner*, not **a pets owner*. An explanation might be sought along the lines that the attributive noun merely denotes a category of entity, rather than individual instance(s) of the category. The generalization even holds for the attributive use of plural mass nouns: *a grocery store*, not **a groceries store*. But there are numerous "exceptions". In *a savings account*, the attributive noun does have the plural inflection. Possibly, some of the exceptions can be explained by the need to avoid ambiguity. We need the plural inflection in *a goods train* to avoid confusion with *a good train*. Likewise with *a means test* (cf. *a mean test*.) But the contrast between *an accounts clerk* and *a book-keeper* and between *a clothes cupboard* and *a grocery store* does suggest the existence of two different patterns for the attributive use of plural mass nouns, the application of the one rather than the other being largely a matter of idiom, and lacking a semantic motivation.

4.   Conclusion

The function of a pedagogical grammar is to promote the learner's insight into the foreign language system. In essence, promoting insight means reducing the perceived arbitrariness of the foreign language system. A person perceives something as arbitrary if he can see no reason why it should be as it is. For this reason, it is not enough to merely inform the learner that a particular element belongs to a given formal category and not to another, and thus behaves in this way rather than that, or to state that such-and-such an expression is grammatically correct while other wordings are grammatically incorrect. Rather, we need to explain to the learner why the foreign language should be as it is.

The CGE project is motivated by the belief that the insights of Cognitive Grammar - presented in a suitable pedagogical format - can contribute substantially to the attainment of this objective. If the basic assumptions of the cognitive program are correct, it should be possible to realize the objective by bringing to the learner's consciousness the conceptualizations conventionally associated with the structures of the foreign language. In order to be able to use the word *tall* correctly, the learner needs to grasp the meaning of *tall*, i.e. the language-specific conceptualization of the vertical dimension conventionally symbolized by *tall*. Likewise, in order to be able to handle the aspect system of English, or verb complementation, the learner needs to know the meaning of the progressive, and the meaning of a *to*-infinitive and of a gerund, etc. The challenge of applying cognitive linguistic insights to a pedagogical grammar lies precisely in searching for descriptively adequate, intuitively acceptable, and easily accessible formulations of these meanings.

Notes

1. The financial assistance of the Institute for Research Development of the Human Sciences Research Council towards this research is hereby acknowledged. Opinions expressed in this publication and conclusions arrived at are those of the author and do not necessarily represent the views of the Institute for Research Development or the Human Sciences Research Council.
2. I shall use the term *foreign language learner* to include certain kinds of second language learner. For a review of the very extensive literature on pedagogical grammar, see Dirven (to appear b).
3. This popular view is not in strict accordance with Saussure's thought, as recorded in the *Cours* (Taylor in press). Thus it is stated, in connection with the issue discussed here, that "ce qui est dit des mots s'applique à n'importe quel terme de la langue, par exemple aux entités grammaticales" ('what is said of words is true of any other element of language, for example, grammatical entities') (Saussure 1964: 161). The brief remarks on syntax in the *Cours* suggest a view of the syntagmatic combination of signs which is highly compatible with Langacker's more elaborate discussion of the issue.
4. [MASS NOUN] and [COUNT NOUN] are instances of the still more schematic category [NOUN], whose semantic content is stated to be "region in a domain". In proposing a semantic characterization of [NOUN] - and of other lexical categories - Langacker is departing from the received doctrine of the arbitrariness of lexical categories. Thus Jackendoff - whose recent work adopts a perspective which is in some respects compatible with that of Cognitive Grammar - dogmatically states "it is well known that ... the grammatical category *noun* cannot be identified with any coherent semantic category" (Jackendoff 1983: 14).
5. For a contrastive study undertaken within a cognitive linguistic framework, see Taylor (1988).

6.   And not only these. Note the mass noun status of *council* (as in *to give someone council*) and *intelligence* (as in *military intelligence*), *nonsense*, and *old hat* (*What he said was nothing but old hat*).
The existence of two alternative "paradigms" for the conceptualization of what is conveyed through acts of communication - we might call these the "*fact*-paradigm" and the "*knowledge*-paradigm" - is brought into focus by the fluctuating use of the word *data*. Some speakers, aware of the status of this Latin borrowing in the donor language, use *data* as a plural noun, i.e. the word is assimilated to the *fact*-paradigm. On the other hand, data is also used as a singular mass noun, i.e. it is assimilated to the *knowledge*-paradigm.

7.   Another highly "fossilized" error concerns the choice of tense after certain temporal conjunctions, e.g. *When I know* (**will know*), *I will tell you*. Again, the learner's error lies in the use of a form which is arguably more "natural" than the one conventionalized in English.

References

Berlin, Brent & Paul Kay
    1969   *Basic color terms: Their universality and evolution*. Berkeley: University of California Press.
Bolinger, Dwight
    1977   *Meaning and form*. London: Longman.
Brugman, Claudia
    1981   Story of *over*. [Unpublished M.A. Thesis, University of California, Berkeley].
Chomsky, Noam
    1965   *Aspects of the theory of syntax*. Cambridge: MIT Press.
    1986   *Knowledge of language: Its nature, origin, and use*. New York: Praeger.
Cook, V[ivian] J.
    1988   *Chomsky's universal grammar: An introduction*. Oxford: Blackwell.
Dirven, René
    1985   "Definition of a pedagogical grammar", *I.T.L. Review of Applied Linguistics* 67-68: 43-67.
    1989   "Space prepositions", in: René Dirven (ed.), *A user's grammar of English*. Frankfurt: Lang, 519-550.
    to appear a   "A cognitive perspective on complementation".
    to appear b   "Pedagogical grammar: The state of the art", *Language teaching: The international abstracting journal for language teachers and applied linguists*.
Dirven, René & John R. Taylor
    1988   "The conceptualization of vertical space in English: The case of *tall*", in: Rudzka-Ostyn (ed.), 379-402.
Dixon, R. M. W.
    1982   *Where have all the adjectives gone?* Berlin: Walter de Gruyter.
Dulay, Heidi, Marina Burt & Stephen Krashen
    1982   *Language two*. Oxford: Oxford University Press.

Greenbaum, Sidney
1987   "Reference grammars and pedagogical grammars", *World Englishes* 6:
            191-197.
Gregg, K.
1984   "Krashen's monitor and Occam's razor", *Applied Linguistics* 5: 79-100.
Haiman, John
1985   *Natural syntax*. Cambridge: Cambridge University Press.
Jackendoff, Ray
1983   *Semantics and cognition*. Cambridge: MIT Press.
Krashen, Stephen
1981   *Second language acquisition and second language learning*. Oxford:
            Pergamon.
1982   *Principles and practice in second language acquisition*. Oxford: Perg-
            amon Press.
Krashen, Stephen & Tracy Terrell
1983   *The natural approach: Language acquisition in the classroom*. Oxford:
            Pergamon.
Lado, Robert
1957   *Linguistics across cultures*. Ann Arbor: University of Michigan Press.
Lakoff, George
1987   *Women, fire, and dangerous things: What categories reveal about the
            mind*. Chicago: Chicago University Press.
Lakoff, George & Mark Johnson
1980   *Metaphors we live by*. Chicago: Chicago University Press.
Langacker, Ronald W.
1987a   *Foundations of cognitive grammar*. Vol. 1. *Theoretical prerequisites*.
            Stanford: Stanford University Press.
1987b   "Nouns and verbs", *Language* 63: 53-94.
1988   "The nature of grammatical valence", in: Brygida Rudzka-Ostyn (ed.),
            91-125.
Munsell, P. & T. Carr
1981   "Monitoring the monitor: Review of second language acquisition and
            second language learning", *Language Learning* 31: 493-502.
Reddy, Michael
1979   "The conduit metaphor - A case of frame conflict in our language
            about language", in: Andrew Ortony (ed.), *Metaphor and thought*.
            Cambridge: Cambridge University Press, 284-324.
Richards, Jack
1972   "Error analysis and second language strategies", *Language Sciences* 17:
            12-22.
Rudzka-Ostyn, Brygida (ed.)
1988   *Topics in cognitive linguistics*. Amsterdam: John Benjamins.
Rutherford, William E.
1987   *Second language grammar: Learning and teaching*. London: Longman.
de Saussure, Ferdinand
1964   *Cours de linguistique générale*. Paris: Payot. [First published 1916).]
Selinker, Larry
1972   "Interlanguage", *IRAL* 10: 209-231.
Sharwood Smith, Michael
1981   "Consciousness-raising and the second language learner", *Applied
            Linguistics* 2: 159-168.

Taylor, John
    1988   "Contrasting prepositional categories: English and Italian", in: Brygida Rudzka-Ostyn (ed.), 299-326.
    1989   *Linguistic categorization: Prototypes in linguistic theory*. Oxford: Oxford University Press.
    in press   "Schemas, prototypes, and models: In search of the unity of the sign", in: Savas L. Tsohatzidis (ed.), *Meanings and prototypes: Studies in linguistic categorization*. London: Routledge.

Wierzbicka, Anna
    1988   *The semantics of grammar*. Amsterdam: John Benjamins.

Part II

Meaning and meaning extension

On representing and referring

Chris Sinha

1. Introduction

Some years ago, Johnson-Laird (1980) remarked that, if cognitive science did not exist, it would be necessary to invent it, and no doubt the same could be said of its "sub-interdiscipline" cognitive linguistics.

This volume is itself a testimony to the value which many linguists now attach to an interdisciplinary orientation to language, communication and cognitive processes. As a nonprofessional in linguistics, I share the current enthusiasm both for interdisciplinarity in general, and for the particular forms it has taken in the work of Langacker (1987) and Lakoff and Johnson (1980), among others. I wish to suggest, however, that such enthusiasm needs to be tempered by a recognition that the very qualifier - "cognitive" - which is employed to denote the inter-disciplinarity of the "new" linguistics, is itself a potential source of ambiguity and confusion. This confusion stems from assumptions embedded in the "classical" program of "cognitive science" itself; which should, in my view, be recognized as resting on a fundamentally mistaken conception of "mental representation", which has brought in its train an intensification, rather than a resolution, of the crisis currently affecting not only linguistics, but all the human sciences.

1.1. Meaning and the human sciences

In using the term *human sciences*, I am already signalling a particular point of view: that the interdisciplinary study of language and cognitive processes, in order to make progress, necessitates the recognition that we are engaged in a very particular kind of scientific enterprise, characterized by a very particular dimension of complexity which is simply not present in sciences of other domains. That dimension is *meaning*, which structures, organizes and is implicated in all aspects of human behavior, human cognition and human language which are the object of studies in the human sciences.

Two brief points are in order here. First, there are doubtless processes which are necessary for human cognition, language, etc. which can, in principle, be studied independently of the dimension of meaning, using the methodologies of the natural sciences (physiology, spectrography, etc.). But, as the great Viennese psycholinguist Karl Bühler put it, such sciences must be considered as "auxiliary" to linguistics (and other human sciences), inasmuch as the latter are guided by the "fundamental principle of the sign character of language" (Bühler 1933; transl. in Innis 1982: 103).

Second, both the natural sciences and the human sciences are subject (in various degrees) to the methodological requirement of *formalization*. Linguistics is indisputably the discipline within the human sciences where the requirement for formalization plays the most important role, and has for this reason frequently (and not, perhaps, always usefully) been viewed (like physics in the natural sciences) as the paradigm case for theory building in the human sciences.

Necessary, however, as formalization may be, it is neither the sole goal and imperative for the human sciences, nor does it of itself provide solutions to the fundamental epistemological problems which beset the human sciences. Indeed, I would claim that the virtually exclusive preoccupation with formalization in recent years, in linguistics and in "classical" cognitive science, has been a source of weakness rather than strength, and has led to widespread underestimation, if not outright denial, of the depth of the "crisis in the theory of meaning" identified by Johnson (1987). Formalization, unconstrained by attention to the specifically semiotic dimension of human language and human cognition, perpetuates the scientistic myth that the methodologies of the natural sciences, without supplementation or qualification, provide a necessary and sufficient epistemological basis for the human sciences.

Against the contemporary manifestations of scientism - that is, formalism and cognitivism - I wish to assert the following:

1.1.1.   Cognitive linguistics is (or should be) the linguistic "moment" of an interdisciplinary enterprise focussed on human natural language, cognition and communication, situated within the human sciences.

1.1.2.   The defining characteristic of the "objects" of the human sciences, and hence of their methodologies, is the *semiotic dimension*.

1.1.3.   The resolution of the "crisis in the theory of meaning" requires the reformulation of the concept of *representation*, and the acceptance of the following principles:

(i)   "mental representation" is first and foremost *inter*-subjective, and the cognitive and linguistic capacities of individuals derive from their appropriation of socially constituted, discursive representations (the principle of the intersubjectivity of representation);

(ii)   discursive and conceptual representations depend upon "embodied" or "material" structures and practices (the principle of the materiality of representation);

(iii)   anything having the character of a sign may be employed for the purposes of representation, and all representation employs signs, but not all signs are representations (the Principle of the Asymmetry of representation and signification).

I expand on these proposals below. Right now, I wish simply to emphasize that the perspective on cognitive linguistics which I am advocating situates it in a particular "semiotic" tradition, most notably developed by Prague School linguistics, which attempts to relate formal analyses both to communicative functions and to wider issues in the theory of meaning, and in language, culture and society. The point of view I advocate is thus consonant with the view of Dirven, Geiger & Rudzka-Ostyn (1988) that "cognitive description is complementary to ... the 'functional' analysis of language", but I wish to strengthen this conception of "complementarity" by suggesting that "functionality" (including intentionality) is also a crucial aspect of cognitive description.

2.   Reference and representation

The problem of representation is, as we all know, inextricably intertwined with the problem of meaning and reference. The ancient debate between supporters of "nominalism" and "realism" (or what I shall, for consistency, henceforth refer to as "conventionalism" and "naturalism") has never adequately been resolved, and indeed finds a contemporary expression in the arguments of, on the one hand, the post-structuralists such as Derrida (1973, 1976, 1981), and, on the other hand, the "new naturalists" ranging from Kripke (1980) and Putnam (1975) to Rosch (1973, 1978). We might say that, ever since Aristotle rejected the naive conception of a direct relation of word and thing, and posited "representation" ("affections of the soul") as a mediating "third order" between language and the world, representation itself has (inevitably) been the battleground of the conflicting claims of sign and referent. If, as Frege (1892) considered he had demonstrated, representation (sense) *grounds* reference and the very possibility of truth, then what grounds representation - the nature of the referent or the relational and "disseminative" system of signifiers? Few contemporary linguists or philosophers (though see Katz 1981) would be content to follow Frege in positing a Platonic realm of objective, eternal, but immaterial, non-extensive "senses" waiting to be "grasped" or "intuited"; if only because such a solution seems merely to postpone the problem: what enables the subject to carry out this mental act, if not mental representation? (See Putnam 1981: 27.)

I argue below for what amounts to a principled compromise which attempts to save the most important insights of both naturalism and conventionalism. I have elsewhere (Sinha 1988, 1989) called the general position I am adopting "socio-naturalistic"; and I shall outline here the particular form the position takes with respect to the problem of reference. I cannot hope to present a conclusive argument in this paper, and indeed I doubt whether any such conclusive argument is attainable.

What I can do, more modestly, is to show how the account that I advance resolves a number of troublesome issues in the theory of reference, without necessitating either an untenable "objectivist" theory of meaning such as criticized by Lakoff (1987) and Johnson (1987), nor a "conceptualism" or "psychologism" such as has been criticized by writers from Frege (1892) to Wittgenstein (1953, 1980). First, however, I shall try to show how two previous attempts to reconcile naturalism and conventionalism, through the simple expedient of allowing each to hold in separate linguistic and ontological domains, are unsatisfactory.

2.1. Natural and other kinds

To begin with, let me recapitulate very briefly the "standard modern" naturalist account. This hinges on a rejection of the (until recently dominant) conventionalist view of concepts and categorization, which latter may be summarized (paraphrasing Gardner 1987: 341f) as involving the three claims that: (1) categories are arbitrary and linguistically determined; (2) categories have defining or criterial attributes; and (3) the intension determines the extension of a category. The modern naturalist theorists reject all three of these universal claims, arguing that (1) some domains (e.g. color) are structured not according to the contingencies of particular lexicons, but according to principles of the organization of the human nervous system, which are reflected in lexical facts; (2) some categories are psychologically structured around prototypes or best exemplars, not criterial attributes; (3) some categories (in particular natural kinds) are like proper names, inasmuch as they possess extensions but no intensions: their names are designators, inherited through an ostensive chain, of a class which is defined by the identity of essential (but not necessarily known) properties shared with a (notional) aboriginal sample (prototype or stereotype).

Now, as many commentators have pointed out, the (psychological) measurement of differences in the accessibility, codability, goodness rating etc. of different category members does not provide unequivocal evidence regarding the nature of linguistic meaning or representation: some instances of such categories as "odd number" or "bachelor" may be judged as "better" exemplars than others, but this provides, in itself, no compelling reason to reject a "classical" or "intensional" - or indeed "analytic" - account of the meaning of the terms *odd number* or *bachelor* (Armstrong, Gleitman & Gleitman 1983; Lakoff 1987; Vandeloise 1989).

That is to say, empirical evidence regarding disputed points (1) and (2) above cannot alone decide disputed point (3), which is the kernel of the issue as far the fundamentals of linguistic theory are concerned. For if the naturalist claim (3) is correct, then it follows that (as Putnam has argued) *meaning* - at least the meaning of natural kind terms - is in the fullest possible sense a language-world relation, rooted in the biological and historical circumstances in which human beings engage in transactions with the material world. And if that is so, then the notion of any kind of autonomous linguistic meaning, or pure intra-linguistic semantics - again, at least of natural kind terms - is untenable.

Meanings (of natural kind terms) are, on this view, not only not "in the head", but they are not "in language" either, if one believes that "linguistic knowledge" is "mental representation of language".[1]

Now I have not attempted to reproduce Putnam's arguments to his conclusions, for reasons of space; but let me assume for current purposes that his reasoning is correct for natural kind terms, independently of the plausibility lent to it by the psycholinguistic investigations of

Rosch and others. There remains, still, a large number (in fact a majority) of lexical items - non-natural kind terms - to which it does not, in the original formulation, apply. A plausible-seeming story might then be as follows. A naturalist theory of meaning is required for natural kind terms, but a conventionalist theory of meaning is required for other lexical items which do not denote natural kinds (leaving proper names aside). While the meanings of natural kind terms are grounded in "essences" or "underlying traits" proper to the class to which they refer, the meanings of other terms are "nominal" in nature, agreed by convention, and not grounded in anything essential to their referents.

Such an account has been advanced independently by Schwartz (1979) and Johnson-Laird (1983). Schwartz distinguishes (p. 311) between strict natural kind terms, such as *gold*, which "lack a meaning dimension" (i.e. do not possess intensions), and "nominal kind" terms, such as *bachelor*, whose extensions are fixed by their intensions, and whose meanings are rooted in linguistic convention. He suggests that terms for "kinds of artifacts ... distinctions of rank, relations of people, legal terms, ceremonial terms [etc.]" are nominal kind terms.[2] Schwartz concedes the existence of "mixed" terms, or what he calls "non-strict natural kind terms", such as *vixen*: "*Fox* is a strict natural kind term and its extension is gathered by an underlying trait. Vixens are a subclass of the things that have this trait, the ones that satisfy a certain description, namely, being female."

A similar account is proposed by Johnson-Laird (1983: 195f), who employs a different terminology to construct a tripartite classification of nouns:

> Some nouns are "analytic" in that their meaning comprises a set of essential conditions that support necessary truths ... Other nouns such as *apple*, *silver* and *yeti* are indeed natural kind terms. Their true intensions are unknown, and their mental representations consist of schemata specified by default values that correspond to simple theories of their designata. Still other nouns like *home*, *chair*, and *melody*, have what I shall call a "constructive" semantics. The intensions of these words are mental constructions, imposed on the world, and although they designate entities in the world those entities do not possess an underlying structure that determines their membership of the extension. Constructive terms have no objective correlates in reality; their meaning is a matter of convention and is open to social negotiation, par-

ticularly in the case of dubious exemplars. The names of artifacts are also constructive, because what is central to their
specification is their intended function rather than their intrinsic structure ... There is no need for tests known only to
experts and no fixing of extensions by the ostensive use of
samples.

Unlike Schwartz, Johnson-Laird does address the isssue of non-nominal
terms (i.e. non-nouns), such as spatial prepositions, which he takes to
exemplify a constructive semantics.

Both Schwartz's and Johnson-Laird's analyses capture important insights about the nature of language and the nature of categorization,
but I would suggest that they do so at the price of a considerable degree
of incoherence and/or inconsistency. Schwartz's analysis, for example, is
open to a classical Saussurean objection: that what is a "strict" natural
kind term in one language may be translated by a "non-strict" natural
kind term in another language. Saussure's own example of *mouton* and
sheep in fact exemplifies this problem, the first being a "non-strict" and
the second a "strict" natural kind term, on Schwartz's analysis. This
problem is compounded by the further problem (which Johnson-Laird
also notes in relation to the "myth" of ostensive chains) of comparative
language change (e.g. Dutch *dier* 'animal', *hert*[N] 'deer', Eng. *deer*[N], *hart*;
where superscript N denotes "strict Natural kind term"). Far from
solving the problem of the relations between language, culture and society, classically exemplified in semiotic analyses by oppositions such as
that of "raw" vs. "cooked", Schwartz's analysis leads straight back to it
(Lévi-Strauss 1970; Saussure 1966).

Johnson-Laird's account is considerably more consistent, since it divides the lexicon according to putative sign-referent relations, and not
according to epistemological considerations relating to the referent "in
itself"; but the consistency is bought here at the price, ultimately, of the
naturalist thesis itself.

Roughly speaking, Johnson-Laird maintains that there is a kind of
scale of "intensionality of meaning". At one end, we find terms for
which the intension is definitional, analytic and therefore intra-linguistic; at the other end we find natural kind terms with no intension, whose
meanings are fixed extra-linguistically. In between, there is an area of
contextually variable "prototypic" intensions, whose descriptions are
not wholly structured by language, and which are open to social negotiation.[3]

Intuitively however, there is already, to say the least, something peculiar about an analysis in which the meaning of a term for an artefact such as *cup*, or a spatial preposition denoting a relationship of containment (*in*), is understood to be "constructive", which roughly glosses as "conceptual and intersubjective", whereas the meaning of a term for an imaginary being, such as *unicorn*, is understood to be "fixed" by its referent (designatum).

The problem here is that the argument is self-defeating, because essentially circular in a meta-linguistic sense. According to Johnson-Laird, if I (as a typical speaker) *stipulate*, using language, that (for example) unicorns are such and such a beast, then my stipulation entails that the relation holding between sign and referent is one which exemplifies natural kinds, and it will henceforth simply *be understood* that a unicorn is a natural kind (albeit an imaginary one). If we understand Johnson-Laird's argument in this way, then the meaning of natural kind terms is one which involves an *interpretation* of the term in a particular kind of way (i.e. as a relationship of designation), and that interpretation rests upon a convention. My claim, then, is that Johnson-Laird's account is one which, in the end, leads us back, via a circular route, to conventionalism. This does not of course mean that his argument is wrong, but it does show how extremely difficult it is to accommodate any kind of naturalistic thesis in a theory which is, on its own account, fundamentally grounded in the notion that meaning is a species of mental representation.

3.   The conditions on representation

In what follows, I attempt a re-analysis of the concept of representation, which draws upon the insight shared by all proponents of naturalist semantic theories, that meaning is intimately related to the cognitive procedures involved in the recognition of instances of categories, but which does not assume that linguistic meaning is reducible to such procedures. The re-analysis of representation thus involves the re-analysis of precisely what it is that speakers intend and enable listeners to recognize when they utter a linguistic expression. My starting point is a modified Gricean (Grice 1968) definition of representation, as a communicative act having particular conditions of fulfilment. These I call *the conditions on representation*, which I define, for a canonical case of representation, as follows:

3.0.1.   To represent something - a scene, an event, an object, an interest, etc. - is to cause something else to stand for it, in such a way that both the relationship of "standing for", and that which is intended to be represented, can be recognized.

It is important to note that the intention underlying representation is a *double* one. To qualify as a representation, a sign must not only be intended to represent something, but must also be intended to be recognizable, in the first place as a representation (not a simple object, and not a non-representational vocalization or pattern); and in the second place as a representation of whatever it is specifically intended to represent.

Sperber and Wilson (1986) have offered an analysis of communicative acts which is similar in some respects to the analysis of representation that I have suggested.[4] They suggest that communication involves:

3.0.2.   An Informative intention:
          to inform the audience of something;
3.0.3.   A Communicative intention:
          to inform the audience of one's informative intention
          (Sperber & Wilson 1986: 29).

They later redefine these as follows:

3.0.4.   Informative intention:
          to make manifest or more manifest to the audience a set of assumptions;
3.0.5.   Communicative intention:
          to make it mutually manifest to audience and communicator that the communicator has this informative intention (Sperber & Wilson 1986: 59ff).

It is not necessary to expand on Sperber and Wilson's terminology to examine the similarities between their analysis and the present one. What I shall suggest is that Sperber and Wilson's analysis is complementary to the definition of the conditions on representation that I have offered, and which for convenience is repeated here in shortened form:

3.0.6.   To represent something is to cause something else to stand
               for it, in such a way that both the relationship of "standing
               for", and that which is intended to be represented, can be
               recognized.

Sperber and Wilson's "Communicative intention" seems to correspond to the condition on representation that the relationship of
"standing for" should be recognizable - that is, that it should be
"manifest" both to the interpreter and also to the producer of the
representation. Their "Informative intention" seems, on the other hand,
to correspond to the condition on representation that whatever is
intended to be represented should also be recognizable, or manifest.
Such manifestness, or recognizability, need in neither case be a property
of a single sign-unit in isolation. In linguistic communication, it is
usually unnecessary to render the "Communicative intention" explicitly
and independently of the "Informative intention", although such formulaic expressions as *by the way* can serve such a function - as in: *By the
way, John is coming to dinner.*

It should also be apparent that representation, as I have defined it,
depends upon a sign-function (signification, or the relationship of
"standing for"), but is not *reducible* to this sign-function. Signification,
as has long been recognized (as witness the classical example *smoke
signifies fire*) need not involve the intentions of a producer, whereas
representation always involves the double intentionality of a producer
(i) to recognizably be intending to represent something and (ii) to make
whatever is intended to be represented recognizable. There can, however, be no representation without signification, since only through the
medium of a sign can a representation attain the material and
"graspable" character which enables the intention to represent to be
apprehended by another subject. In short, the analysis of the conditions
on representation, and the distinction which flows from it between
representation and signification, together exemplify the claims I made
in Section 1.1.3., that:

(i)   "mental representation" is first and foremost inter-sub-
               jective, and the cognitive and linguistic capacities of in-
               dividuals derive from their appropriation of socially-consti-
               tuted, discursive representations (the Principle of the In-
               tersubjectivity of representation);

(ii)   discursive and conceptual representations depend upon "embodied" or "material" structures and practices (the Principle of the Materiality of representation);

(iii)   anything having the character of a sign may be employed for the purposes of representation, and all representation employs signs, but not all signs are representations (the Principle of the Asymmetry of representation and signification).

3.1. Language and context

I now wish to show, using one of Sperber and Wilson's examples, how the distinction between representation and signification can clarify the relationship between language and context, and thus contribute to the construction of a theory of meaning. The example is as follows:

> Mary wants Peter to mend her broken hair dryer, but does not want to ask him openly. What she does is begin to take her hair dryer to pieces and leave the pieces lying around as if she were in the process of mending it. She does not intend Peter to be taken in by this staging; in fact, if he really believed that she was in the process of mending her hair dryer herself, he would probably not interfere. She does expect him to be clever enough to work out that this is a staging intended to inform him of the fact that she needs some help with her hair dryer. However, she does not expect him to be clever enough to work out that she expected him to reason along just these lines. Since she is not really asking, if Peter fails to help, it will not really count as a refusal either (Sperber & Wilson 1986: 30).

Sperber and Wilson comment:

> Mary does intend Peter to be informed of her need by recognizing her intention to inform him of it. Yet there is an intuitive reluctance to say that Mary *meant* that she wanted Peter's help, or that she was *communicating* with Peter in the sense we are trying to characterise.

But, of course, it all depends on what we mean by *mean*. What we can say is that Mary has contrived a situation which does precisely "mean" that she wants Peter's help, inasmuch as it signifies a request. The request is not, however, represented as being such - and so Mary can honestly say that she has not made or "meant" a request. In this case, although the signifying structure has been intentionally produced, it has not been produced in such a way that it can be read as a representation of that intention - the signification, and hence the meaning, is real enough, but it is opaque to any reading of it which would allow Mary's intention to be attributed to her.

This again illustrates the proposition that signification encompasses a wider field of phenomena than representation, both in principle and in everyday interactions. Thus, most "paralinguistic" devices contribute to meaning by way of signification, rather than representation. Facial expression and intonation, for example, may convey (signify) the speaker's *attitude* to what is being represented, without affecting *what* is intended to be recognized as being represented in the utterance; though it should be noted, too, that they may also be used to explicitly represent the purpose of the utterance, by enabling the listener to identify whether the speaker is making an assertion, asking a question etc.

Furthermore, what is signified may be outside the deliberate control of the producer. Features of accent and dialect, for example, may affect listeners' evaluations of speakers and messages (Giles 1973). To that extent, they are "significant" features of language, contributing to the speaker's meaning for the listener in a sociolinguistic context. Most semantic (and many pragmatic) theories would not, however, incorporate such features in their accounts, because they do not fall within the purview of either truth-based or intentionality-based views of meaning.

Given this analysis, it would be wrong to identify "meaning" exclusively with either representation or signification. It is clear not only that natural signifiers (i.e. those which do not depend on human agency) can be interpreted as meaningful, but also that non-representational motifs can also signify without involving any Informative intention beyond the informing of the interpreter of the Communicative intention (as in the case of what Malinowski (1930) called "phatic communion"). It would be arbitrary to exclude these phenomena from the realm of meaning, and furthermore would conflict with the intuition that intended, represented meaning is linked in some fundamental way with the "meanings" in the world in which we perceive and act, as well as communicate. For this reason, I suggest that "meaning" is a general property of sign-systems and sign-usage, and that it embraces both *representational meaning*, defined in terms of the conditions on representation, and *contextual meaning*, which translates as "all non-representational aspects of a signifying situation".

In this sense a picture, as well as an utterance in language, can both represent, and signify, and both of these are equally aspects of meaning. The distinction between representation and signification therefore also assists us in clarifying the confusion which surrounds the frequent (and erroneous) dichotomy between "meaning" and "representation", as exemplified in the following quotation from Gombrich (1985: 20):

> Only in the discussion of language can we distinguish between statements that have a meaning and strings of words that are devoid of meaning ... A painting of a moonlit landscape does not "mean" a moonlit landscape, it represents one.

To use Gombrich's example, a representation of a moonlit landscape may, depending upon how it is depicted, signify an attitude of enchantment by natural beauty, or desolation, loneliness and fear. While the signification (or significance) of a visual image may in part be determined by representations which are intended as conventionally symbolic (such as an apple "standing for" forbidden knowledge), the response evoked by a painting reaches beyond representation, whether literal or symbolic, to non-represented (contextual) aspects of meaning, simply by virtue of the fact that a painting is a signifying structure as well as (or even without being) a representation. At least in this limited sense, it is also possible to speak of a "language" or "languages" of art, and of artistic effect as being achieved (or read) through signifying structures.

By the same token, any rule-governed use of a signifying system, including natural language, will tend to be "read" as significant, even when there is no apparent representational content. This can be seen in examples such as Lewis Carroll's nonsense poem "Jabberwocky", or even Chomsky's celebrated "meaningless" sentence *Colorless green ideas sleep furiously*. The "contextual meaning" which lends "significance" to such strings is nothing other than the structure of the signifying system itself.

It is important to add here that "contextual meaning" is not independent of representational meaning - "context" is not something added to representation which enables the interpreter to "fill in" what is not represented. Rather, there is a dialectical relationship between representa-

tional and contextual meaning, in which each conditions the signification of the other.

A closer look at the example I have already borrowed from Sperber
and Wilson helps to make this clear. Let us suppose that, Peter, perceiving the dismembered hair dryer, says *Would you like me to mend
that?*, and Mary replies *Oh thank you, Peter, I was hoping you'd do that.*
Peter's utterance demonstrates that he has read the signifying situation
as Mary hoped he would, and Mary's utterance re-contextualizes the
signifying situation by representing it as a request-offer-acceptance
sequence. The contextual meaning initially produced (but not represented) by Mary has thus become a part of (mutually - thus successfully)
represented meaning, and the politeness routines associated with such a
representation may be engaged in, without Mary having to have formulated (represented) an initial request.

Although representational meaning is by definition intentional, the
difference between meaning as signification, and meaning as representation, does not correspond to a simple dichotomy between "intentional" and "non-intentional". As the example of Mary's hair dryer shows,
signification may be intentional without being representational. Nor is it
simply a matter of "meaning from the producer's point of view" versus
"meaning from the interpreter's point of view". Rather, representation
involves, canonically, a relationship of *identity* between what the producer intends to be represented, and what the interpreter understands
the producer to have intended to be represented. It is thus a matter of
the *mutual recognition* by producer and interpreter, both of the
representational intention of the producer, and of the object under
representation. Although such mutuality is definitional of the canonical
case of representation, it may equally be seen as a goal of representation (and communication), and as a regulative principle underlying
the social negotiation of meaning.

Signification, on the other hand, is more than merely the means by
which the identification of what is to be represented is achieved, since it
involves all of contextual meaning. Signification is not only a necessary
condition for representation, but it also tends continually to defeat the
ideal transparency to which representation aspires. Where representation attempts to render an object (situation, scene, etc.) in its specificity,
signification ceaselessly reduplicates the represented, multiplying
meanings and resituating the represented in a network (or vortex) of
signifiers. Because representation can only proceed by signification, it is
continually subverted, each new appropriation of the sign forcing into

existence a spectral world of virtual meanings, the skeletons of previous appropriations and the ghosts of choices unmade.

If representation struggles to reproduce the "signified" in a manageable, negotiable and mutually-manifest intersubjectivity, signification opens representations to what post-structuralist philosophers call the "dissemination" of meaning: the subterranean operations of the signifier through which, even as we appropriate language to our own ends, language "speaks us", and meaning evades determinacy.

4. A sketch of a theory of meaning

The notion of "dissemination" may be seen as perhaps the most extreme possible version of a "conventionalist" theory of meaning, in which conventionality itself is undermined by the indeterminacy of meaning entailed by the very use of language and other signifying systems. Is it remotely possible to reconcile such a view with the naturalist theories I discussed in Section 2? I wish to argue here that a degree of reconciliation is both possible, and indeed necessary, if we are to develop an adequate and general theory of meaning. The sketch of a theory of meaning that I offer below is based upon a re-working of Frege's sense-reference distinction on the basis of the analysis of representation I gave above. In this sketch I attempt to specify in what precise way recognitory procedures for recognizing instances of classes - the central focus of naturalistic accounts - enters into linguistic meaning. I do not have the space here to reproduce the argument that I originally employed in introducing this account (see Sinha 1988), but it should at least be clear how it relates to the analysis in the preceding section.

The sketch of a theory of meaning is as follows:

4.0.1.   Sense
          The sense of a term is its content as a discursive concept, and is that which enables it to fulfil, in discourse, the conditions on representation. The sense of a term (or expression) is thus its representational meaning, as defined above.

4.0.2.   Semantic value
          The semantic value, or lexical meaning, of a term is that aspect of its sense which relates it to other senses (discursive concepts) within a language, and governs the lexico-grammatical distribution of the term (in the classical formulation,

in terms of the paradigmatic and syntagmatic relations which the term contracts with other terms).

4.0.3.   Denotation

The denotation of a term is that aspect of its sense which relates it to the recognitory procedures associated with what is definitionally, canonically or prototypically represented by the term. In the theoretical position which I am advocating, denotation is a language-to-world relation, independently of whether the term is, in traditional parlance, analytic or non-analytic.

4.0.4.   Reference

The reference of a term, for an interpreter on a given occasion of discourse, is that which is identified by the term by virtue of the fulfilment of the conditions on representation.

4.0.5.   Signification

The signification of a term, for an interpreter on a given occasion of discourse, is the representational meaning of the term plus its contextual meaning.

5.   Concluding remarks

The account sketched above does not assign primacy to either the semantic value or the denotation of a term in the determination of its sense, or representational meaning. It is assumed that all terms, including natural kind terms, function in the same way in discourse: that is, all discursive concepts have the same essential *duality of structure* as far as their "content" is concerned. The case of terms for imaginary entities, such as *unicorn*, is solved by supposing, not that they lack denotations (since there are, indeed, recognitory procedures associated even with imaginary entities), nor that (as in Johnson-Laird's account) their semantic values are determined by their denotation, but by postulating that their denotations are qualified as "imaginary" and "nonexistent".

Equally, the (standard) recognitory procedures associated with natural kind terms such as *gold* may be directed towards properties which are, as Kripke (1980) proposed, "epistemically uncertain but necessary if true"; and they may also be, as Putnam (1975) proposed, only known by experts. Again, however, this does not mean that such terms lack "sense", even for lay speakers, since they possess semantic values which are (in principle) available to be acquired by all speakers, even those with a merely cursory knowledge of the detailed procedures entailed by a full specification of the denotation of the term.

As for terms for artefacts, such as *cup*, or spatial prepositions, such as *in*, the fact that, as Johnson-Laird pointed out, their denotations cannot be determinately fixed by reference to their semantic values does not distinguish them in any way from other non-analytic terms (including natural kind terms). In any case, one might wish to argue that "analyticity" is best understood as a (contestable) meta-linguistic convention, by means of which, in certain cases and in certain discourse contexts, speakers or communities stipulate that semantic value determines denotation. The fact that the denotations of terms like *in* cannot, either, be fixed by reference to "underlying natural traits" does not, however, warrant the conclusion that these denotations are merely "constructions of the human mind", as Johnson-Laird claims. On the contrary, containment, for example, is a real relationship, embodied in physical objects, although it is not only a physical relationship, but also a relationship embodying human practices and intentionality (of both discursive and non-discursive kinds).

The "embodiment" or materiality of representation encompasses more, though, than simply the socio-natural materiality of the signified which "grounds" the denotational aspects of sense. It extends also to the real, though non-physical, structure of the signifying system, which "grounds" (and disseminates) semantic value. In the account which I have offered, representational meaning and contextual meaning are not independent, but interact, in actual discourse; and what is "meant" by the use of a conventional sign is (in part) a dynamic product of selection processes operating over fields of semantic values which are "virtually" co-present simply by virtue of the selection of a particular signifier.

This is, in essence, what I take the notion of "dissemination" to mean. Indeterminacy is an inevitable concomitant of all representation, since all representation employs signs.

Indeterminacy is not the same, however, as the kind of wilful arbitrariness which is celebrated and propounded in some versions of post-structuralist theory, nor is it the same as a view in which meanings are "mental representations" of the sort favored by many cognitive scientists. Individual mental representations, in the account which I have offered, are derivative from discursive representations, and discursive representations are articulated upon the world, and not just upon our "ideas" of the world.

The theory of meaning which I have sketched above preserves the "realist" Fregean doctrine of the primacy of "sense" over "reference": i.e. reference is accomplished by virtue of the recognition by the interpreter of the sense of an expression. It departs from the Fregean analysis, however, inasmuch as the analysis of both sense and reference is based upon the completion of conditions upon successful intersubjective action in a discursive context, rather than upon the truth conditions attaching to isolated expressions.

Within the socio-naturalistic perspective, truth is only intelligible as a relationship between *representans* and *representandum* within a particular universe of discourse, defined in terms of relations between foreground propositions and background presuppositions. Propositional truth is thus a species of adequacy, and only in certain specialized discourse contexts is it possible to isolate it from other (discourse pragmatic) aspects of adequacy. Exclusive resort to models based upon such contexts does not provide a satisfactory basis for an interdisciplinary approach to cognitive linguistics, within the human sciences. In place of the univocal and de-contextualized concept of "truth" presumed by "objectivist" theories of meaning, the socio-naturalistic account stresses the perspectival and co-constructive nature not only of representational adequacy, but of cognitive and communicative processes in general.

Notes

1. This argument is highly condensed, and represents an extension of Putnam's own argument; but it follows logically from Putnam's general position that "concepts cannot be identical with mental objects of any kind" (Putnam 1981: 21).
2. Presumably, on Schwartz's view, performative verbs share properties with nominal kind terms, but he does not address the general issue of non-nominal meanings.
3. Johnson-Laird prefers the more general term "procedural" to "prototypic".
4. It should be emphasized that the notion of representation employed here is quite different from that employed by Sperber and Wilson; see Sperber & Wilson (1986: 226ff).

References

Armstrong, Sharon L., Lila R. Gleitman & Henry Gleitman
    1983   "What some concepts might not be", *Cognition* 13: 263-308.
Bühler, Karl
    1933   "The axiomatization of the language sciences", in: Robert Innis, 91-164.
Derrida, Jacques
    1973   *Speech and phenomena*. Evanston: Northwestern University Press.
    1976   *Of grammatology*. Baltimore: Johns Hopkins University Press.
    1981   *Dissemination*. London: Athlone Press.
Dirven, René, Richard A. Geiger & Brygida Rudzka-Ostyn
    1988   "Brief statement on cognitive linguistics", Paper for L.A.U.D. Symposium "Cognitive Linguistics".
Frege, Gottlob
    1892   "Über Sinn und Bedeutung", *Zeitschrift für Philosophie und Philosophische Kritik* 100: 25-50.
Gardner, Howard
    1987   The mind's new science: A history of the cognitive revolution. (2nd edition). New York: Basic Books.
Giles, Howard
    1973   "Accent mobility: A model and some data", *Anthropological Linguistics* 15: 87-105.
Gombrich, Ernst
    1985   "Scenes in a golden age: Masters of seventeenth century Dutch genre painting", *New York Review* Vol. XXXII No. 10: 20-22.
Grice, Paul H.
    1968   "Utterer's meaning, sentence meaning and word meaning", *Foundations of Language* 4: 225-242.
Innis, Robert
    1982   *Karl Bühler: Semiotic foundations of language theory*. New York: Plenum.
Johnson, Mark
    1987   *The body in the mind*. Chicago: University of Chicago Press.
Johnson-Laird, Philip N.
    1980   "Mental models in cognitive science", *Cognitive Science* 4: 71-115.
    1983   *Mental models*. Cambridge: Cambridge University Press.
Katz, Jerrold
    1981   *Language and other abstract objects*. Oxford: Blackwell.
Kripke, Saul A.
    1980   *Naming and necessity*. Oxford: Blackwell.
Lakoff, George
    1987   *Women, fire and dangerous things: What categories reveal about the mind*. Chicago: University of Chicago Press.
Lakoff, George & Mark Johnson
    1980   *Metaphors we live by*. Chicago: University of Chicago Press.
Langacker, Ronald W.
    1987   *Foundations of cognitive grammar*. Vol.1: *Theoretical prerequisites*. Stanford: Stanford University Press.

Levi-Strauss, Claude
  1970   *The raw and the cooked: Introduction to a science of mythology.*
                London: Jonathan Cape.
Malinowski, Bronisław
  1930   "The problem of meaning in primitive languages", in: Charles K.
                Ogden & I.A. Richards (eds.) *The meaning of meaning.* (2nd edition).
                London: Routledge & Kegan Paul.
Putnam, Hilary
  1975   *Mind, language, and reality: Philosophical papers,* Vol. 1. Cambridge:
                Cambridge University Press.
  1981   *Reason, truth and history.* Cambridge: Cambridge University Press.
Rosch, Eleanor
  1973   "Natural categories", *Cognitive Psychology* 4: 328-50.
  1978   "Principles of categorization", in: Eleanor Rosch & Barbara B. Lloyd
                (eds.), *Cognition and categorization.* Hillsdale, N.J.: Lawrence
                Erlbaum, 27-48.
Saussure, Ferdinand de
  1966   *Cours de linguistique générale.* New York: McGraw-Hill.
Schwartz, Stephen
  1979   "Natural kind terms", *Cognition* 7: 301-315.
Sinha, Chris
  1988   *Language and representation: A socio-naturalistic approach to human
                development.* London: Harvester-Wheatsheaf.
  1989   "Naturalism or reductionism? A rejoinder to Paul Churchland",
                Cultural Dynamics 1: 438-452.
Sperber, Dan & Deirdre Wilson
  1986   *Relevance: Communication and cognition.* Oxford: Blackwell.
Vandeloise, Claude
  1989   "Representation, prototypes and centrality", Duisburg: L.A.U.D.
                Paper
                A 211.
Wittgenstein, Ludwig
  1953   *Philosophical investigations.* Oxford: Blackwell.
  1980   *Remarks on the philosophy of psychology.* 2 vols. Oxford: Blackwell.

Minimal and full definitions of meaning

Zoltán Kövecses

1. Introduction

I have a modest goal in this paper. The essence of what I have to say
can be summarized in two sentences. The first is that, contrary to the
teachings of some mainstream views in semantics, I no longer believe
that sense is a more important aspect of meaning than reference in the
study of meaning in language. The second is that I no longer believe,
again contrary to an age-old doctrine in word semantics, that it is possible and useful to separate core meaning from residual meaning and to
consider the core as more important. These are conclusions that I have
come to in the light of what I have learned from recent work in cognitive semantics. These may not be very interesting conclusions. However,
they bring with them a shift in our thinking about word meaning: they
force us to leave behind the notion of minimal definitions of meaning
and recognize the possibility, reality, and importance of what can be
called "full definitions". Full definitions, in turn, enable us to make the
relationship between language and the world outside language an
object of study within linguistic semantics.

I wish to raise and attempt to answer the following question: How
does the emergence of certain new ideas in cognitive semantics lead us
to reappraise basic assumptions in lexical semantics? These assumptions have to do with two fundamental distinctions that are commonly
made. First, it is a widely accepted practice in lexical semantic studies to
take sense, rather than reference, as the proper subject matter of lexical
semantics. This assumption is predicated on the distinction between
sense and *reference* (or *intension* and *extension*). Second, sense is seen as
representing the *core* of the meaning of a word. The core is contrasted
with *connotation* (residual or peripheral meaning) which is usually held
to be a less important aspect of meaning. Sense is thus viewed as an
aspect of meaning whose privileged status in linguistic semantics seems
to be doubly motivated: both in its relation to reference (in that sense
should have priority over reference in the study of linguistic meaning)
and in its relation to connotation (in that core meaning is a more
important aspect of meaning than connotation). The relationship

between the two assumptions is that core meaning (identified with sense) is seen as determining reference, i.e. the relationship between language and the world outside language.

By contrast, I will try to argue that none of these views is correct. In particular, I will suggest that neither the primacy of sense over reference, nor the primacy of sense (i.e. the core) over connotation can be justified. Instead, I will show that there is a position within cognitive semantics which enables us to eliminate the sense (core) vs. connotation distinction and which, as a result, enables us to give a more accurate account of the referential function of language which was unavailable for those working within the framework of the traditional theory.

2.   Arguments for the primacy of sense over reference

Several arguments are provided for the view that sense is a more important aspect of meaning, and hence of our semantic competence, than reference. Let us examine these in turn.

2.1.   The autonomy of semantics

The first is that if semantics is to become an autonomous field it must find its subject matter inside rather than outside language. This claim can be seen as a reaction to those linguists who saw the study of meaning as essentially the study of the relationship between language and the world outside language (e.g. Bloomfield 1933). Since the study of the relationship between language and the outside world presupposes the study not only of language but also of the outside world, the linguist's task, the argument goes, is to study language and not the real world, which is studied by physicists, biologists, psychologists, metallurgists, etc.

2.2.   Properties and relations within the language

Some linguists, especially those in the generative tradition, find it sufficient to characterize semantic competence in terms of properties and relations within the language. That is, they ignore reference as a necessary part of semantic competence. The question that these linguists ask is: "What kind of knowledge do we need to understand and produce sentences?" Among the kinds of knowledge most often cited are such semantic properties and relations as ambiguity (of which a special case is polysemy), paraphrase (or synonymy), entailment, anomaly, etc. The overall result then is a complete neglect of, or in some cases a lack of interest in, the relationship between language and the world.

2.3.   Sense can account for semantic competence

Given this self-restriction on the scope of what a semantic theory must embrace, it is not surprising that sense is seen by many as having a privileged status. It is a further aspect of the above view that these various properties and relations can be accounted for in terms of "meaning as sense". That is, the claim is that if it is possible to account for semantic competence by means of sense alone, this renders reference an aspect of meaning in linguistic semantics which can be ignored by semanticists and can be handed over to philosophers for investigation. "Meaning as sense" is defined by componential formulas that utilize such features or components of meaning as HUMAN, MALE, CAUSE, ALIVE, EGO etc. To see how various semantic phenomena can be accounted for by these and similar sense components, we can take the issue of polysemy first. The polysemy of, say, the word *man* as exemplified by the sentences *The men were bowling and the women were knitting*, on the one hand, and *All men are equal*, on the other, can be accounted for by saying that the two senses would receive different componential definitions. The sense exemplified in the first sentence could be characterized by the componential formula [+HUMAN, +ADULT, +MALE] and the sense in the second sentence by the componential definition [+HUMAN]. Furthermore, anomaly which results from a violation of selection restrictions is explained along the same lines. It is proposed that the issue of selection restrictions, or collocation, can be adequately handled by matching the sense components in one item with those in another. As a final example, the notion of lexical fields is also based on the idea that what links a number of lexical items together can be explained by attending to the sense components associated with these items. In short, componential definitions (of meaning as sense) are seen as providing the basis of explanations for most, if not all, semantic phenomena and thus sense is taken to be the linguistically crucial aspect of meaning.

3. Arguments for the priority of core over periphery

In the subsections below we will survey the arguments most commonly offered for the claim that linguistic semantics should be limited to the study of core meaning - to the exclusion of residual meaning, or connotation, the periphery.

3.1. Essential properties

The idea of the primacy of core meaning over residual meaning receives support from the view that sense components capture what is essential about categories, while nonessential properties become the features that constitute residual meaning (or connotation). This idea goes back to the Aristotelian notion of essential and incidental properties. The core is regarded as being constituted by properties that are essential to things and events, whereas the periphery is viewed as a set of properties whose presence or absence does not contribute to making the thing or event what it is. The properties constituting the core must always be present to make the thing or event what it is, since they provide its essential nature. If an essential property is absent, the thing or event is not the category that it would be taken to be were the property present. Nonessential properties do not affect categorization in this manner. Consequently, essential properties are considered more important than nonessential properties in the study of word meaning.

Within componential analysis two general directions can be distinguished. In one, essential properties appear in the form of abstract concepts, like HUMAN, MALE, ADULT, etc. That is to say, these are features that do not correspond directly to attributes of referents, but can be regarded as generalizations of them. For example, the abstract feature HUMAN can be seen as an abstraction from such referential attributes as "being erect", "being two-footed", "being able to talk", etc. In the other, essential properties do not assume the form of abstract concepts. Instead, just like nonessential properties, they are plain referential attributes. For example, one of the definitions of the word *man* is that man is a "featherless biped", a definition which uses two referential attributes. It thus follows that in the first approach (which is perhaps the dominant one) the essential properties making up the core are abstract features and all referential attributes are considered nonessential properties that make up the periphery, or connotation (for example, Leech 1982). In the second approach, however, since no abstract features are employed, both the core and the periphery are constituted by referential attributes, but some referential attributes are essential and some are not. In both approaches, the core (composed of essential properties) is viewed as having a distinctive status in relation to the periphery, or residual meaning, or connotation (composed of nonessential properties).

3.2. The economy of core definitions

Those who favor the separation of the core from the periphery find further support in the *kind* of meaning definitions they can offer. They claim that their definitions of meaning are as economical as these definitions can be. This means that to define core meaning one needs only a minimal number of sense components. For example, the word *woman* can be defined as [+HUMAN, +ADULT, -MALE]. Thus this definition provides the difference between, for example, *woman* and *man* in terms of the contrasting feature [-MALE] and [+MALE]. Regardless of any other differences between the referents of these words, it is only (the abstract idea of) maleness which serves as the basis for making a conceptual distinction between their meanings. It is such systematic conceptual distinctions that make up core meaning. That is, core meaning is made up of a minimal number of sense components. This means that sense components are just enough to distinguish each meaning from every other meaning in the language. The economy of the statement of core meaning is favorably contrasted with the indeterminate character of residual meaning. The implication is that only core meaning is regarded as suitable for a scientific study of word meaning.

It has to be noted here that it is also suggested that sense (the core) consists of a fixed number of conceptual components (i.e., singly necessary and jointly sufficient components). That is, not only do we have a minimal number of components but the number of these is also fixed; they are all present in every case when the category is used appropriately. This follows from the claim that categories are defined by certain essential properties. Essential properties must always be present.

3.3. The indeterminacy of the periphery

A still further reason for the claim that core meaning needs to be separated from peripheral meaning and that the former is a more important aspect of meaning than the latter is closely related to the claim that semantics as an autonomous field must find its subject matter inside language, a claim which is used to support the primacy of sense over reference. It is feared that the adoption of a view of meaning that focuses on connotative meaning would commit us to the "impossibly vast study of everything that is to be known about the universe in which we live" (Leech 1982: 8). The claim is that there is no natural stopping point in accumulating knowledge about (the nonessential properties of) the referents of linguistic expressions (i.e. about residual meaning), and so we would have to characterize (kinds of) referents by means of infinitely long lists of attributes. That is to say, connotative, or residual, meaning is vague and indeterminate and hence cannot be the proper domain of study for semanticists.

3.4. Sense is objective meaning

Yet another reason, formulated either explicitly or implicitly, for the separation of core meaning from connotation and the primacy of the former over the latter is that sense components (i.e. the essential properties that make up the core) are objectively real while the nonessential attributes of referents (i.e. the elements of connotative meaning) are merely subjective. The subjective nature of connotation is seen as arising from various sources. It may come from our expectations about the world, from a certain viewpoint we have adopted, and from the individual views of a person. For example, people may think of women as "emotional", "cowardly", "talkative", etc. These would then be some of the nonessential attributes of the referent of the word *woman*, but they would not be a part of the sense (or core meaning) of the word, which, as we have seen, is constituted by the formula [+HUMAN, +ADULT, -MALE]. These sense components are objectively real in the sense that they apply to women independently of how we *conceive of* women. That is, women *are* human, adult and female independently of our expectations, viewpoints or individual biases. Thus these essential characteristics of women have a status very different from such nonessential attributes as "emotional", "cowardly", etc., which are a matter of our subjectivity. In sum, the constituents of core meaning and hence core meaning itself are assigned a privileged status due to their supposed objective nature.

3.5. Sense is structured

It is also characteristic of mainstream approaches to word meaning that most of them regard sense (the core) as having a great deal of structure while connotation is assumed to lack any comparable structure. For example, even Palmer, who otherwise also disagrees with the view that sense should have a distinctive status, apparently believes that sense (the core) is more systematic than reference (connotation). He writes:

> Sadly, one is tempted to conclude that when scholars have concentrated on sense to the exclusion of reference (in its widest sense), they have done so because it is easy to describe. It has structure and can be accurately and precisely determined (Palmer 1976: 33).

This structure is seen as arising from several sources. To begin with, as we have seen above, one source is the utmost economy of meaning (sense) definitions, which consist of a minimal number of conceptual components. Furthermore, it is assumed that there is a system of conceptual components, where each component stands in opposition to another component. The oppositions are mostly binary contrasts, but other kinds of opposition are also recognized. The sense components that are necessary for the definition of the meaning (sense) of particular lexical items are taken from this system of sense components. In addition, the sense components entail a number of other sense components. These are called "redundancy rules" (Leech 1982). These rules state that an item which is marked by, for example, the component HUMAN is also ANIMATE. However, this latter component does not need to be explicitly stated since it follows from the component HUMAN. This aspect of the structure of sense is especially utilized in the statement of selection restrictions. A possible further source is that according to some linguists componential definitions are not just random lists of sense components but are best viewed as ordered sets of components. For example, the sense components of the verb *kill* can be shown to have the hierarchical structure (*cause*(*to become*(*not*(*alive*)))), instead of a simple collection of conjoined components. Finally, it is believed by some linguists that there is a universal system of sense components from which each language uses a subset in the definition of meanings. In sum, all these various assumed characteristics of sense have the combined effect of presenting sense as a highly structured area of meaning, a property which is presumed to be missing from connotative meaning.

3.6. Sense can be studied systematically

It is proposed, as is also suggested by the quotation from Palmer, that not only does sense (the core) have a structure unavailable for connotation but that the conceptual components that make up sense can be arrived at in a systematic and principled way which is not available for obtaining the components of connotative meaning. Let us consider the words *man* and *woman* again. We can say that *man* is to *woman* as *boy* is to *girl* and *gander* is to *goose*, etc. This procedure gives us a way of extracting some common factors in these words. *Man*, *boy*, and *gander* share the conceptual component MALE, while *woman*, *girl*, and *goose* have in common [-MALE]. In a similar way, we can isolate the feature [+ADULT] and [-ADULT] in these words. This simple but principled methodology enables us to identify conceptual components in a systematic way. By contrast, it is suggested that it is not possible to study connotative meaning in this manner. There does not seem to exist any such simple mechanism with which we could systematically describe the nonessential properties of categories.

4.   Counterarguments to the priority of sense

In this section, we will be concerned with some possible counterarguments that have emerged in cognitive semantics to considering sense as a more important aspect of meaning than reference.

4.1.   Can semantics be autonomous?

As we have seen above, the first reason given for the priority of sense over reference was that if semantics is to become an autonomous science it should have its subject matter inside rather than outside language, the latter being studied by experts other than linguists. Some recent results in cognitive semantics have made us aware that this argument cannot be accepted. First of all, it has turned out that in a large number of cases the determinants of meaning lie outside language as narrowly conceived by most scholars working in mainstream semantics. In particular, it has been found that meaning is very often a function of conceptual systems (in the sense of systems of motivated knowledge representation), contextual information, cultural influences, and the neural and biological makeup of human beings. If these are all determinants of meaning, it is unreasonable to talk about the autonomy of semantics. Furthermore, it no longer seems to be true that the only alternative to the study of meaning inside language is the study of the world outside language. In at least one version of cognitive semantics we have come to realize and accept the fact that the world and language are mediated by what is called human understanding. And in linguistic semantics we search for what the world is like not in and of itself but as it is understood by us. In other words, in the study of meaning at least some cognitive semanticists go beyond language, but they do not go as far as the world outside language. Finally, it is no longer believed that, as regards the students of meaning in language, the only choice is between "straight" linguists (who study meaning inside language) and experts like biologists, psychologists, metallurgists, etc. (who can supposedly provide us with a picture of what things really are like in the outside world). There is a new brand of scholar on the rise who studies language and the way the world is conceptualized and understood in terms of, or through, language. Of course, through this conceptualization of the world they also deal in an indirect way with the world outside language, but this does not mean that they have to be, say, biologists or physicists.

4.2. Is there a strict language vs. reality distinction?

A further argument is that it is sufficient to characterize semantic competence in terms of properties and relations within the language. By contrast, in the light of cognitive semantics it is found to be an intuitively unsatisfactory linguistic approach to lexical meaning which is not concerned with the relationship between language and the world. If there is anything one would expect a semantic theory and a semanticist to do, it is that they should provide an account of how we can pick out certain aspects of the world (i.e. things, events, states of affairs) by means of language. The delimitation of the scope of semantic competence to intra-language properties and relations is based on the mistaken idea that language and the external world can be viewed as constituting two independent domains. However, as has been pointed out above, in at least one version of cognitive semantics there is a conceptual system which represents the *world as understood*. Language has as one of its integral parts the *world as understood*, and the *world as understood* is our only guide to the *world as it is*. In this way, the world is inseparable from language and meaning. The separation cannot be made for an additional reason. As Kay (1983) has pointed out, people conceive of (knowledge of) a language as a part of (their knowledge of) the world. This is especially obvious in the way we use hedges.

4.3.   Can meaning as sense account for semantic competence?

Finally, it is claimed that all properties and relations of semantic competence can be accounted for in terms of sense as core meaning. We have seen that the core is defined by minimal componential definitions. If the claim were true, it would render the referential aspect of meaning secondary to sense. However, in recent years several scholars have found that one of the key aspects of our semantic competence, polysemy, cannot be given an account in terms of sense as a fixed and minimal number of components. It has also been shown that metaphorical and metonymical meaning cannot be adequately explained in terms of meaning as sense either. In addition, it has been argued that sense cannot serve as a basis for an account of collocation and semantic fields. If correct, these findings suggest that large portions of our semantic competence cannot be adequately handled in terms of sense as minimally defined core meaning. It would then follow that the connotative aspect of meaning must also play a role in these phenomena, which would considerably weaken the claim for the privileged status given to sense in linguistic semantics.

5.   Counterarguments to the separation of core from periphery

The following is an attempt to discuss briefly some of the possible counterarguments to the view that meaning has a core and that this core has to be separated from residual meaning.

5.1. Can we isolate a core?

We have observed above that the division of meaning into core and residual meaning (i.e. connotation) goes back to the Aristotelian distinction between essential and nonessential properties. It has been assumed ever since that all categories are *defined* in terms of essential properties; that is, essential properties are also defining properties, and thus nonessential properties do not play a role in the definition of categories and meaning. This is the basis of the argument for the separation of core meaning (identified with sense) from residual meaning (connotation). Thus the notion of core meaning is based on the idea that all categories are defined by essential properties. Indeed, there are categories that are defined by essential properties. For example, the category of square can only be defined as (1) closed figure, (2) four sides, (3) sides equal, and (4) angles equal. These are all features that are individually necessary and jointly sufficient for something to be a square. But, as research since Wittgenstein has revealed, the majority of our categories are not like this. The categories of *game* (Wittgenstein 1953), *cup* (Labov 1973), *climb* (Fillmore 1982), *mother* (Lakoff 1987), *anger, pride* and *love* (Kövecses 1986), to name just a few, are all categories that do not seem to have a fixed set of properties. This means that these and a large number of other categories cannot be defined by a set of essential properties. And if we cannot identify essential properties in so many cases, the very basis for the separation of essential from nonessential properties is called into question. In short, in the majority of cases no core can be isolated in the study of word meaning and thus the separation of a core from a periphery becomes an impossible task.

5.2. Prototypes are not embodied by minimal knowledge

The notion of meaning as a fixed and minimal set of conceptual components has received a major blow from prototype research initiated by Berlin and Kay, and Rosch and her associates. Theories of meaning based on necessary and sufficient conditions are called "checklist theories" of meaning. Research has demonstrated that meaning is not to be construed as a minimal list of (abstract, logical) conditions which have to be met in order for us to use categories appropriately. Instead, meaning often has an analog, rather than a digital, nature. In many cases it is best viewed as or can be defined in terms of a cognitive prototype, an idealization (which is not necessarily visual)

from which deviations of all kinds are possible. The description of prototypes requires the activation of a full amount of knowledge
corresponding to the idealized case in question. Thus, the prototype
view brings with it the notions (1) that meanings are not sets of abstract,
logical conditions on the use of categories and (2) that meaning cannot
be defined in terms of a *minimal amount* of knowledge. What is
particularly relevant in the present connection is the notion of minimal
knowledge. If meaning cannot be defined as minimal knowledge associated with categories, then the economy of minimal knowledge cannot
be used as an argument either. In other words, if there is no core construed as minimal knowledge, it cannot be argued on the grounds of
economy that the core is superior to residual meaning, or connotation.

5.3. Minimal vs. infinite knowledge: a false choice

The necessity of the separation of core from connotative meaning is
based on a further erroneous assumption. Specifically, it is claimed that
the only alternative to minimal (and hence economical) definitions of
meaning is the total (and hence uneconomical) knowledge of the world.
It is suggested that if we allow in the characterization of meaning such
nonessential properties as, for example, "cowardly" in the case of the
word *woman*, we open the gate to infinitely many such properties. Thus
we would end up with unmanageable lists of properties, and the neat
and simple structure of sense based, as we have seen among other
things, on minimal sense components would be gone. But, again in the
light of recent work in cognitive semantics, these two extremes - infinitely long lists of properties on the one hand and minimal sense components on the other - are not the only alternatives we have. There
seems to be a level between the two where concepts are characterized
by features that are neither too numerous nor minimal. The conceptual
tool that has evolved in cognitive semantics to capture this middle-
ground of knowledge is the notion of frame. According to the most accepted definition, frames are coherent organizations of experience
shared by (at least some members of) a speech community. Frames
have both a qualitative and a quantitative aspect. As regards the quantitative aspect, it is perhaps one of the major characteristics of frames
that they are human-sized, which means that they are specified by not
more and not fewer features than ordinary people use for the understanding of a given area of experience. According to the way I conceptualize frames, this number is neither minimal nor infinite, but occupies

a region between the two (of course closer to the minimal end). If frames do indeed embody this medium-sized, or human-sized amount of knowledge, then the choice offered between minimal and infinite knowledge in the conceptualization of meaning is a false one, and hence it cannot be used as an argument to justify the separation of a core from a periphery.

Now of course, the question arises: how can we find out exactly how many features are used by ordinary people for the comprehension of an aspect of the world? This issue will be taken up when we discuss the methodology with which frames, or cognitive models, can be investigated.

5.4.   To what extent is meaning objective?

Let us now turn to the qualitative aspect of frames. This is important because it bears on the claim that the components that make up the core are objectively real while the nonessential properties arise from our subjectivity. The study of the nature of frames provides three types of evidence against this claim. The first type of evidence has to do with interactional properties. In a large number of cases, at least some of the features in terms of which frames can be characterized are ones that arise from various aspects of human beings; they are based on human physiology, human biology, and general human functioning. These are features that are not inherent characteristics of some objective reality. Features of this kind are also pervasive among what we would otherwise consider the core and not just among what we would regard as nonessential properties. For example, according to the classical view, the core meaning (sense) of the word *chair* contains the feature "allows us to sit". However, this would not be an objective feature of chairs; it would be a feature that has to do with what human beings do with respect to a chair.

The second type of evidence concerns metaphor and metonymy. Some recent research suggests that the features that make up frames are often metaphorical and metonymical in nature. This is typical of abstract concepts like emotion concepts. What is particularly interesting about these cases is that even the components of the core can be metaphorical or metonymical. Let us take a metaphorical example, as provided by the meaning of the word *pride* in one of its senses. This sense can be classically defined in terms of a minimal number of sense components as "valuing oneself highly as a result of an achievement". It has been argued that the core component "valuing oneself" in the meaning of *pride* is not an objectively real part of the meaning (sense) in question but arises via the PEOPLE ARE COMMODITIES metaphor. Since metaphors are processes that involve human imaginative capabilities, it follows that some core components are the products of human thought processes, rather than being objectively real.

The third type of evidence has to do with folk models. The frames that are of the greatest relevance for a study of meaning in ordinary language are also folk models. Folk models represent the way in which ordinary people think of things and events in the course of and for the purposes of their everyday lives. Folk models, and thus many frames, incorporate knowledge that is not an internal representation of an externally existing objective reality, but knowledge that is the product of a subjectively constructed reality. Let us take an example from Taylor (1989: 81ff.). The feature [+ANIMAL] is a part of the core meaning of *dog* and (if anyone elaborated it) it would also have to be a part of the frame (folk model) associated with that category. The difference in the status of this feature in the two meaning representations (classical core meaning vs. folk model) would be that whereas in the classical core meaning definition [+ANIMAL] is regarded as an objective property, in the folk model it would not be regarded as such. The reason is that if it turned out that dogs were robots that are controlled and manipulated from outer space, the classical definition of *dog* would have to drop the feature [+ANIMAL] as an essential property. No matter how deeply entrenched the belief is that dogs are animals, it does not follow that [+ANIMAL] should be regarded as an objectively real property of dogs. This example suggests that often (classical) definitions of the core strive to achieve objectivity in the sense of being scientific, for scientific definitions also classify dogs as animals. This tendency is shown by the fact that both the core meaning definition and possible scientific definitions operate with the feature [+ANIMAL]. In this case, as in many other cases, the definition of core meaning is supported by scientific definitions. The corresponding folk model has the same feature but the feature has a different status in it. Now there are cases where folk models do not contain features that are present in the core. This typically occurs when the core is defined scientifically. If, for example, the word *salt* is defined as "NaCl" (as it was by Bloomfield), this is not likely to be a part of our everyday conception, or folk model, of salt.

In summary, we have seen that frames are different from core meaning definitions in several important ways; they contain features that are not objective in the sense that they are based on human physiology and biology, that they are the products of human imaginative capabilities, and that they reflect the way in which human beings understand their world. We have seen furthermore that often the features of the core are also included in frames and folk models, but in the frames and folk models they have a different - a nonobjective - status. Since these are features common to both classical core definitions and frames (and folk models) and since these are all features that arise from human subjectivity and not from an objective reality, it cannot be claimed that the core is more important than the periphery because it represents objective meaning. It seems that there are many subjective elements in the core as well, and not only in the periphery.

5.5. Is the core the only structured domain of meaning?

The qualitative aspect of frames has an additional characteristic. This concerns the issue of structure. It will be remembered that the claim here is that the core has a great deal of structure, whereas the periphery does not, and consequently the core is the more important aspect of meaning. However, the findings of the cognitivist studies cited above indicate that what we have viewed as the periphery so far can have just as much structure, though of a different kind, as the core. Many of the features previously viewed as referential attributes have been found to be parts of frames, or cognitive models (either prototypical or nonprototypical), and frames, or cognitive models, have been shown to have a great deal of structure. This structure arises from a variety of sources. The source that is perhaps the most relevant as regards features (either core or peripheral) is ontology. Ontologies are constituted by a system of entities and predicates (i.e. properties and relations). (It is the predicates that correspond to features as normally understood.) The entities and predicates combine into propositions which constitute (propositional) cognitive models, or frames. Thus entities and predicates are ingredients of frames that are responsible for some of the structure found in frames. A further aspect of the structure of frames is that the propositions are arranged in some order, which can be causal, temporal, etc., or it can simply be the order defined by the degree of their prototypicality. In addition, within a frame the propositions can be arranged along certain dimensions of experience, like function, purpose, motor activity, etc. in the case of object categories.

These are not the only sources for the structure of frames, or cognitive models. Moreover, abstract concepts seem to be different from concrete concepts as regards structure in that they are often structured metaphorically and metonymically. But this is not the issue just now. The point that needs to be stressed is that frames are every bit as clearly structured as classical core definitions, although their structure is of a different kind. The implication of this in the present connection is that the "core as the only structured aspect of meaning" argument cannot be used to support the claim that the core should be given a distinctive status in the study of meaning. Frames incorporate, among other things, what can be considered both core and periphery features, and they are clearly structured configurations of human cognition.

5.6.   Can only the core be studied systematically?

The final counterargument is concerned with the issue of methodology. The assumption here is that only the core can be studied in a systematic way. The properties of residual meaning, since they are haphazard and arise from our subjectivity, are elusive and hard to arrive at. In view of the work done in cognitive semantics so far, we disagree with this assumption. Roughly, two general approaches can be distinguished in this line of research. One is more characteristic of psychologists and is a more direct method, while the other more of (linguistic) anthropologists and can be viewed as a less direct one. In their effort to obtain the features in terms of which prototypes are represented, psychologists typically begin their work by asking subjects directly to list those features that they think characterize the things or events under investigation. As a second step, they employ a variety of tests to make sure that the features listed are indeed prototypical. Among the tests they use we find tasks that have to do with memory, ease of learning, ease of identification, sentence construction and rejection, etc. All of these take the form of controlled experiments. Linguists and anthropologists, on the other hand, typically employ a different strategy. Their approach is less direct in that they begin their work with the collection of (possibly) all the conventionalized linguistic expressions in a given language that have to do with the area of experience they wish to study. (By conventionalized linguistic expressions are meant more or less fixed linguistic expressions that convey pieces of our folk understanding of a given aspect of the world.) That is, they are interested in the language people use to talk about (the various aspects of) their experience. Assuming a relationship between language and conceptual systems, they try to arrive at features (and entities) on the basis of this conventionalized language. Illustrating this with an example from Taylor (1989: 89) again, we can take the concept *elephant*. Since the sentence *Elephants never forget* represents a piece of conventionalized language (in that it is more or less fixed and expresses a belief about elephants), it is likely that it constitutes a feature in the frame associated with elephants. We have of course a large amount of other knowledge in connection with elephants. However, it is not the case that every piece of this knowledge will also be a part of the prototypical frame associated with elephants. We know, for example, that elephants are an endangered species, but, since this knowledge is not conveyed in the form of conventionalized language we use to talk about elephants, this knowledge will not be a part of the (prototypical) frame. It is along these lines that it is possible to specify which pieces of knowledge are and which ones are not contained in (prototypical) frames - an issue we have raised above. Just as in the case of the other approach, there is a way to test our results for prototypicality in this one. The linguistic test that is commonly used for this purpose is the *but*-test, as elaborated, for example, by Cruse (1986). The methodology is richer and more complicated in the case of abstract concepts.

To conclude, we seem to have two ways of arriving at the constituents of frames. Both methods are systematic. Admittedly, their systematicity is different from what we are used to in componential analysis. But this is only to be expected. The investigation of a different type of meaning requires a different methodology. However, this is not the major conclusion. What is really significant for our purposes here is that it seems that not only the core can be studied in systematic ways. If this is correct, the final argument given for the separation of a core from a periphery loses its force.

6. What determines reference?

According to Fregean theory, it is the core (sense) that determines reference. However, it should be obvious from the discussion above that this cannot be the case. If no core (either in the form of abstract features or in the form of referential attributes) can be isolated in all cases and if the identification of certain properties as constituting the core cannot be justified in all cases, it follows that no entity like a core (sense) can be used to determine reference in all cases.

Some scholars like Smith and his associates, even among those who maintain the core-periphery distinction, have come to the same conclusion. They claim that the core is used in determining the relations of a concept to other concepts and the properties of the periphery function as what they call "identification procedures" in recognition, that is, in determining reference. While I am in agreement with these scholars that reference cannot be achieved through the core (sense), I disagree with their claim that it is achieved through the properties in the periphery (i.e. through referential attributes). As it should be clear by now, the basis for this disagreement is that I have come to believe that no "core", i.e. no fixed and minimal set of properties (either in the form of abstract features or in the form of referential attributes), can be separated from a "periphery". Just as importantly, it cannot be maintained, as apparently these authors would want to maintain, that *all* frames are mere collections of referential attributes.

Many frames, or cognitive models, are composed of configurations of propositions, which are in turn composed of entities and predicates (properties and relations). In most cases, there are no properties that can be said to form the (traditionally conceived) core of a frame. Frames are cognitive structures where the division of features into essential and nonessential simply does not exist. Thus neither essential nor nonessential features can determine reference. If it is meaning that determines reference (i.e. if we go by the reference-via-meaning doctrine), then it is the meaning embodied by frames that does it.

7.   Conclusions

We have examined a number of arguments for two claims: (1) that in linguistic semantics the study of sense should have priority over the study of reference, and (2) that there is a core meaning and a residual meaning, and that the two have to be kept clearly distinct. The counterarguments provided by recent research in cognitive semantics suggest that neither of the claims can be maintained. I have been led to conclude that the study of reference should be an equally important part of the semanticists' enterprise. Linguistic semantics cannot be complete without studying the relationship between language and the world. As regards the second claim, the counterarguments make it clear that the separation of a core from a periphery of meaning is neither possible nor justified. What has emerged in cognitive semantics in place of core and residual meaning is the notion of prototypical frame, or idealized cognitive model. The conclusion that core and residual meaning cannot be separated has a bearing on the issue of what determines reference. Given that sense is equated with core meaning and that the notion of frame subsumes both core and residual meaning (and more), it seems reasonable to believe that the relationship between language and the world outside language is established via the notion of frame. Finally, since frames incorporate much more knowledge than minimal definitions (but not an infinite amount), we seem to have overwhelming evidence for the view that, in many cases at least, the notion of minimal meaning has to be replaced by what we have called full meaning, embodied by frames, or cognitive models.

References

Berlin, Brent & Paul Kay
    1969   *Basic color terms: Their universality and evolution*. Berkeley: University of California Press.
Bierwisch, Manfred
    1970   "Semantics", in: John Lyons (ed.), *New horizons in linguistics*. Harmondsworth: Penguin, 166-184.
Bloomfield, Leonard
    1933   *Language*. New York: Holt, Rinehart, & Winston.
Brugman, Claudia
    1981   Story of *over*. [Unpubl. M.A. thesis, University of California, Berkeley.]
Cruse, D. A.
    1986   *Lexical semantics*. Cambridge: Cambridge University Press.
Fillmore, Charles J.
    1975   "An alternative to checklist theories of meaning", *Proceedings of the First Annual Meeting of the Berkeley Linguistic Society*, 123-131.
    1982   "Frame semantics", in: Linguistic Society of Korea (ed.), *Linguistics in the morning calm*. Seoul: Hanshin, 111-138.
    1985   "Frames and the semantics of understanding", *Quaderni di Semantica* 6: 222-253.
Fodor, Janet D.
    1980   *Semantics: Theories of meaning in generative grammar*. Cambridge: Harvard University Press.
Johnson, Mark
    1987   *The body in the mind: The bodily basis of reason and imagination*. Chicago: University of Chicago Press.
Katz, Jerrold
    1972   *Semantic theory*. New York: Harper & Row.
Katz, Jerrold & Jerry A. Fodor
    1963   "The structure of a semantic theory", *Language* 39: 170-210.
Kay, Paul
    1983   "Linguistic competence and folk theories of language: Two English hedges", *Proceedings of the Ninth Annual Meeting of the Berkeley Linguistics Society*, 128-137.
Kövecses, Zoltán
    1986   *Metaphors of anger, pride, and love: A lexical approach to the structure of concepts*. Amsterdam: Benjamins.

1988   *The language of love: The semantics of passion in conversational English*. Lewisburg, PA: Bucknell University Press.
Labov, William
1973   "The boundaries of words and their meanings", in: Joshua Fishman (ed.), *New ways of analyzing variation in English*. Washington, D.C.: Georgetown University Press, 340-373.
Lakoff, George
1987   *Women, fire, and dangerous things: What categories reveal about the mind*. Chicago: University of Chicago Press.
Lakoff, George & Mark Johnson
1980   *Metaphors we live by*. Chicago: University of Chicago Press.
Leech, Geoffrey
1982   *Semantics*. (Revised edition). Harmondsworth: Penguin.
Lindner, Susan
1981   A lexico-semantic analysis of verb-particle constructions with *up* and *out*. [Unpubl. Ph.D. dissertation, University of California, San Diego.]
Osherson, Daniel & Edward Smith
1981   "On the adequacy of prototype theory as a theory of concepts", *Cognition* 9: 35-58.
Palmer, F. R.
1976   *Semantics*. Cambridge: Cambridge University Press.
Rosch, Eleanor
1973   "Natural categories", *Cognitive Psychology* 4: 328-350.
1978   "Principles of categorization", in: Eleanor Rosch & Barbara B. Lloyd (eds.), *Cognition and categorization*. Hillsdale, N.J.: Lawrence Erlbaum Associates, 27-48.
Rosch, Eleanor & Carolyn Mervis
1975   "Family resemblances: Studies in the internal structure of categories", *Cognitive Psychology* 7: 573-605.
Smith, Edward E. & Douglas E. Medin
1981   *Concepts and categories*. Cambridge: Harvard University Press.
Taylor, John
1989   *Linguistic categorization: Prototypes in linguistic theory*. Oxford: Clarendon.
Wittgenstein, Ludwig
1953   *Philosophical investigations*. New York: Macmillan.

Metacognitive aspects of reference: Assessing referential correctness and success

Richard A. Geiger

"Hey, you've got GARMENTS *all over your back!"*
"Oh, get them off of me!"

1. Introduction

Two circumstances led me to write this paper. First, the present state of reference research is characterized by an inflation of approaches, terminologies and unsystematized evaluation criteria, while the literature on reference, already vast, continues to grow at a fast rate (cf. Geiger 1991). As a result, there is, in my opinion, an ever greater need for the establishment of a unified framework for research on reference-related phenomena with a simplified but adequate technical terminology. Within the limits of a publication of this length, I will attempt to outline what such a framework might initially look like in the area of reference evaluation. The framework might then later be extended to encompass other reference-related phenomena.

Second, many philosophers of language express, with seemingly great self-assurance, opinions about the nature of linguistic reference based on their own intuitions. In particular, their opinions about referential effectiveness and appropriateness often seem to me unduly dogmatic, *ad hoc* and unsubstantiated by convincing evidence or arguments. Taking a different approach, I will discuss the evaluations of reference made most often by philosophers, *successful/unsuccessful* and *correct/incorrect*, in the light of assessments made by other cognitive scientists on empirical grounds.

As they are usually stated, questions about reference success and correctness generally reflect the view (often expressed only implicitly) in the bulk of the literature that referential assessments are an "either/or" affair. Such binary and unilevel approaches, however, have proved to be patently unsuitable for doing justice to the complex evaluative processing of reference in ordinary communication. In the answers

I propose to these questions, several sorts of analytical parameters are involved, of which I will discuss the following.

First, referential assessments are made by all individuals who are direct or indirect participants in a verbal exchange (viz. as speakers, addressees and others). Thus, *perspective* is one parameter. Second, referential assessments are often not merely "simple", a person's own direct evaluation of reference, but rather "reflexive" in addition (involving "metaperspectives"). That is, in taking into account other participants' (assumed) evaluations of reference, a person's assessments vary as to *degree of recursiveness*. And third, scalar, rather than polar, assessments are the rule (in spite of the fact that cognitive simplifications tend to occur frequently). Thus, the parameter of *gradation* is also involved in metacognitive referential activity.

1.1. Cognition vs. metacognition

A great deal of human cognitive activity - above all perhaps in the formation of beliefs - obviously involves making assessments, for example judgments that some beliefs which people hold are well-grounded while others are not. Referring, of course, reflects cognition, because in mentioning something to someone in order to be able to talk about it, we implicitly, and at times even explicitly, communicate certain aspects of our beliefs about that something. Furthermore, while selecting the means to refer to things, we automatically take into account what we assume to be the relevant beliefs of the persons we are speaking to. Thus, linguistic reference has long been thought of as a species of cognitive activity par excellence and accordingly been a popular topic of study in all of the disciplines concerned with human cognition, most prominently in philosophy.

Most of the assessing of ongoing referential talk in human communication takes place automatically and below the level of consciousness. I call this assessing *metacognitive* in full awareness that there exists as yet no recognizable consensus about the exact nature of the differences between cognition and metacognition (cf. Forrest-Pressley & Waller 1984: 120). Generally, however, psychologists interested in studying the two do so by measuring cognition as a person's ability to accomplish assigned tasks which require thinking, and by measuring metacognition as a person's ability to reflect on that cognition.

Usually considered typical of metacognition are several types of awareness (cf. Forrest-Pressley & Waller 1984: 36), among which are, first, the awareness that the same problems can often be solved in various ways (that is, awareness of the multiplicity of possible responses to problems); second, the awareness that different approaches to problem-solving yield variable results (awareness of the multiplicity of outcomes); and third, the awareness that people evaluate particular approaches to problems nonhomogeneously with respect to their appropriateness and effectiveness relative to the circumstances (awareness of the multiplicity of perspectives). It is above all this third type of awareness - involving evaluations of reference - with which I will be concerned here.

Again, because I view referential assessing as a process which parasitically depends on the referential process, I think of it as a metacognitive activity. Still, there have been warnings about confounding metacognition and metaprocess, on the grounds that the *meta-* in *metacognition* "usually implies conscious, verbal explanation" (Karmiloff-Smith 1978: 198). When I use the term *metacognition* in conjunction with referential assessments, however, I am not trying to prejudice the issue one way or the other, because no doubt most of our referential assessments do occur, as I have said, subconsciously. Many of the examples I mention hereafter will indeed reflect subconscious processing.[1]

Nevertheless, there are good reasons, I believe, for considering such assessing a kind of metacognition. First of all, whenever there arise problems in communication we usually reflect and often speak metacommunicatively about them in order to solve them as well as to avoid repetitions of the same problems in the future. This is as true of referential talk as it is of other aspects of communication.

Second, the experience both of having made and having witnessed mistakes in judgments in the past leads us to realize that our own and others' beliefs are not always correct. This "realization" is of course in itself a belief about beliefs, a metabelief which directly involves reference. As Langford (1986: 25) points out in this connection, we not only have words like *see, believe, think* and so on to speak about "our epistemic relations with the world" but also words like *evidence, justified* and *true,* "the function of which is to assess the adequacy of that relation [sic]".

Finally and most importantly, our thinking about our own and other people's thinking, which we revealingly call "reflection", is an essential part of our social awareness (e.g. of "how others see us"). We very obviously conceive of the mind, therefore, both as a CONTAINER (cf. Lakoff 1987: 450) and as a MIRROR (cf. Antaki & Lewis 1986a; Johnson 1987) which enables us to see the contents of our own minds and the contents of other minds as well. And included among the contents of other minds are of course their conceptions of the contents of our minds. Metaphorical mind-mind "reflections", like their nonmetaphorical mirror-mirror counterparts, are available to our perception and cognition in practice only to a very limited extent. We have no trouble, that is, imagining an object and assessing ways of referring to it. For example,[2] with respect to the deictic center/ego ground, (1) reveals my image of the USA from my own deictic center:

(1)   *I'm probably* going *to the USA next year.*

We can picture someone else's picture of an object and that person's assessment of ways to refer to it, too. Example (2) reveals my image of your image of the USA from your deictic center:

(2)   *I'm probably* coming *to the USA next year.*

We can possibly even imagine someone's image of our image and perhaps assess how that person might assess our assessment of it.[3] Soon after this, however, metacognitive assessment becomes very difficult (even "mind-boggling") for most of us as the thrice-reflected image in the mind's mirror quickly grows dim, and it is precisely this dimming which is responsible for at least some of the "opacity" of language discussed by philosophers and linguists. I will return to this point further down.

1.2.   The metacognition of reference

The foregoing was a justification of my use of the term *metacognition* in connection with reference. Why make a study, however, of metacognitive aspects of reference? To answer this question, let us take a very brief look at the history of reference research.

As long as language was studied as a low- or no-context, idealized phenomenon, reference research was conducted almost exclusively by philosophers of language hoping to discover semantic principles that could be stated as truth conditions on propositions (not utterances) about things in the so-called Real World. In the late Middle Ages, truth was defined by Thomas Aquinas as *adaequatio intellectus et rei,* the agreement between the world, or reality, and cognition, one's view of the world. Since that time, the philosophical concept of truth for many philosphers has represented the relationship between human thinking, then, and the universe. Since human minds are not external to, but on the contrary very much a part of that universe, the philosophical study of truth has therefore been, to a great extent, the very complicated activity of minds reflecting (about) themselves.

One of the very noteworthy characteristics of philosophical inquiry is that it has traditionally demonstrated a fascination with linguistic topics. Yet not language per se but language (and especially written language) as a reflection of abstract thought seeking universal validity was perhaps what philosophers found so attractive that they have tended to reify it - and thereby to lose sight of its quite limited and feeble human origins. Thus, the study of truth shifted to the presumably "more objective" study of the relationship between the world and language about the world, or, in the popular formulation, between words and things (cf. Geeraerts 1985).

There has been a growing dissatisfaction with that particular research paradigm during the second half of this century, perhaps brought about by the combination of a weakening of beliefs in transcendental, universal truth in general and a need felt more strongly for better understanding of human thinking and communication. In any case, a small part of the story is that we have witnessed during our own times - along with the rise of pragmatics - a growing desire to understand the mind-mind relationship and the mind-language relationship as they are manifested in verbal and nonverbal communication. Absolute truth (in the mind-universe version as well as in its offspring, the language-universe version) has lost much of its fascination for scholars and has been replaced by an interest in relative, that is, contextualized, "truths". (This is especially the case with cognitive linguists; cf. e.g. Johnson 1987; Lakoff 1987.)

In short, language was studied for a very long time as the reified object of human cognition, and reference was correspondingly defined as the quasi-timeless relation between words and things. In recent years, along with the use of language in communicative contexts becoming a respectable subject of research, there has been a concomitant greater readiness among linguists and other cognitive scientists to study reference to what is now known as "mental objects". Stimulated especially by Roger Brown's early work, for example, on addressing behavior (cf. Brown & Gilman 1960, Brown & Ford 1961), reference has been studied by many people (e.g. Geiger 1979) as the cognitive processing in an individual which takes place when one person speaks to another. More and more, it is being situated in a larger interactive context in which two or more "minds" collaborate with each other in the establishment and maintenance of discourse grounding (cf. Geiger 1988).

2.   Reference evaluation

One of the most noticeable aspects of research on reference is the richness of the vocabulary used to talk about it. This applies especially to terms of referential assessment, and within this area especially to negative evaluations. Thus, one finds, for example, on the positive side the term *paradigmatic reference* (Martinich 1984), along with *fully consummated reference* and *successful reference* (Searle 1969) and *valid reference* (Martin 1981); then in the middle of the spectrum *potential* and *purported reference* (Boguslawski 1982) as well as *putative reference* (Nunberg 1977); and at the negative end terms ranging from *ungrounded* (Martin 1979), *defective* (Martinich 1984), *non-effective reference* (Over 1983) all the way down to *misreference* (Marslen-Wilson, Levy & Tyler 1982) and *reference failure* (Parsons 1980). This list of idiosyncratic evaluative terms is by no means exhaustive nor limited to the authors named. For the most part, the terms are not defined systematically in relation to one another and for this reason remain unsatisfactory elements in an overall theory of reference.

2.1.   Reference vs. non-reference

The first step in setting up a typology of reference evaluation is to distinguish between reference and non-reference, because in order to be evaluated, reference must previously have occurred. But already here, above all here, expert opinions diverge widely, mainly as a result of the different approaches to reference taken. It is, however, no doubt safe to say for those working within a pragmatic, rather than a traditionally semantic, framework that the primary criterion used in making the distinction between reference and non-reference is the presence or absence of a referential intention on the part of a person speaking.

Yet referential intention itself is of course not a sufficient condition for reference. Leech (1983: 207) has, for example, pointed out that an utterance like:

(3)   *I* tried to ... refer *to the driver.*

implicates that an intended referential act has failed because something has gone awry in the speaker's encoding process, that he has "failed to find a suitable verbal representation...." The speaker's failure in attempting "to speak his mind" may be merely a momentary tip-of-the-tongue linguistic (lexical) malperformance, or it may be due to some indecisiveness concerning the best way to formulate a referential concept for an intended audience adequately or appropriately. In other words, without a referential expression of some kind (including nonverbal) there can be no reference, despite intentions to the contrary.

In contrast to Leech, I do not believe, however, that (3) necessarily suggests that the speaker was unable to encode a reference but rather that he or she was not able to fulfill an intention to refer, for whatever reason. For example, (3) might be continued with the words ... *but you weren't listening* or ... *but they gagged me so I couldn't*. Thus, I take "non-reference" to mean the non-occurrence of reference because no linguistic expression is being or has been uttered by a speaker with the intention of referring to something.

One way philosophers speak about non-reference is by means of the expression *failure to refer,* as in Linsky's (1967: 122) well-known tongue-in-cheek example:

(4)   *In your article you may* fail to refer *to my article.*

Unfortunately, the term *reference failure* has usually been used in a different sense. In the older philosophical tradition (e.g. Russell 1905), reference failure was said to occur whenever the referent of a nominal expression either does not exist or is not unique, as in the sentences:

(5)   The square circle *is an impossibility.*
        (a case of contradiction, and therefore of non-existence)
(6)   The whale *is a mammal.*
        (a case of so-called generic reference, and therefore of
        non-uniqueness)

In other words, the assessment as a reference "failure" in such cases is based solely on the lack of a correspondence between the "semantic facts" (that is, the meanings) of a given linguistic expression, and appropriate "ontological facts", that is, the existence of a unique referent in the extra-linguistic world. This time it is not a speaker but rather a linguistic expression which is said to "fail to refer". Speaker intention is not taken into consideration at all in such assessments.

In some of the newer pragmatic approaches to reference, one also finds talk of "radical" (i.e. complete) "failures" of reference. I am thinking here especially of certain uses of nominals in utterances like the following, which Donnellan (1978: 50f) has called "attributive":

(7)   The strongest man in the world *(can lift at least 450 pounds)*.

The term *attributive* is meant to indicate that a person using such an expression may not be thinking of a specific individual at all nor even necessarily believe that there exists a unique individual who will fit the description. But it is noteworthy that nothing about the expression itself would cause reference failure, given the right speaker intention at the time of its utterance.

2.2.   *Successful vs. unsuccessful reference*

Once reference can be taken as established in a pragmatic sense, it can be evaluated in terms of its communicative success. Searle (1969: 89) deserves recognition for pointing out the fact that there are degrees of reference success; many writers still, however, continue to evaluate reference in this respect (and others) in a binary fashion, as completely successful or completely unsuccessful.

The main evaluative criterion in the case of reference success is a hearer's "understanding" of an intended reference. For the cases in which a hearer realizes that a specific reference has been made but is unable to identify the speaker's referent at all or at best only vaguely, Searle speaks of "referential success". For completely successful reference (total identification), he speaks rather solemnly of "fully consummated reference" (Searle 1969: 89).

Empirical work in conversational and discourse analysis has provided us with evidence that referential success is far from being limited to the hearer's (un)certainty, however. Speakers, too, are regularly unsure about the success of their references, as Sacks and Schlegloff pointed out in the 1970s. They introduced the term *try-marker* for referring expressions uttered with rising (i.e. question) intonation and followed by a brief pause such as the following, which they found in their analysis of ongoing conversation (Sacks & Schegloff 1979: 19):

(8)   A: ... *well I was the only one other than* the
              Fords? Mrs. Holmes Ford? *You know*// the cellist?
       B: // *Oh yes.*
              She's the cellist.
       A: *Yes, well she and her husband were there.*

              (simplified; // indicates the beginning of
              simultaneous speaking)

Speakers indicate their insecurity that there will be referential success by means of the rising intonation and then pause just long enough
to give hearers the chance to signal recognition or non-recognition.

Among others, Schiffrin has pursued the same line of research. In
one of her earlier articles entitled "Meta-talk" (1980) she identified
three types of language which can be used to "talk about itself". In addition to "meta-linguistic referents", such as *the former* and *the latter*,
which others had already reported on before her, and "meta-linguistic
verbs", like *say, tell* and *clarify*, she described "meta-linguistic opera-
tors", like *true* and *false* (p. 201), which I would prefer to call
metacognitive indicators because they are not used primarily to talk
about talk itself but rather to give one's evaluations of someone's
beliefs. Schiffrin pointed out that meta-talk can be used both for
organizational purposes and to form what she called "evaluative
brackets" (p. 218) which are assessments of a speaker's own or someone
else's speech.

In subsequent publications she has concentrated on other discourse
markers, of which the word *well* is particularly enlightening for anyone
interested in finding out how people evaluate reference success in everyday conversation. Let us look at a (simplified) example from her
data (Schiffrin 1985: 657):

(9)   Zelda: *Do you know* where the cemetery is,
                 where Smithville Inn is?
       Debby: *Yeh.*
       Zelda: Well, *when you get to the cemetery,*
                 you make a right.

Her interpretation of the use of *well* here is that it demonstrates "the
successful completion of an exchange of information on which the directions are dependent", that, in other words, the speaker is responding

"to a referent which is in itself composed of an embedded referent/response pair".

In the following (slightly modified) example of talk about taxicabs which I have taken from Schegloff (1980: 133), it becomes clear that *well* is only one of a series of metacognitive referential markers that both sides in conversation can and do use for explicit confirmations of their common knowledge at a given point in conversation:

(10)   A: *You are aware of how that light works on top, aren't you,*
        B: Well, *I know that it says "off duty" when they're off duty*
        A: Well,   *// did you al-*
        B: *// And I know it's lit up when they are available*
        A: *When they're empty.* Right.
        B: Correct.

Viewed in such immediate juxtaposition with the words *right* and *correct,* which have a related function, it seems strange that Schiffrin more than once stresses that the word *"well* has no inherent semantic ... properties..." (1985: 642). Surely, it belongs to the same group of words as *real* and *true* which, as Brugman (1984: 33) has noted, "all deal with rectitudes either of real-world behavior or of linguistic behavior..." This is obviously at least the beginning of a semantic description.

Schegloff (1980), in his paper entitled "Preliminaries to preliminaries", brought our attention to reference preparation. Since successful reference is a vital prerequisite for the success of the communicatively more important act of predicating, speakers often feel the need to extract reference for prior separate processing in order to ensure its success. Consider the following (modified) example he gives (1980: 112f; similar examples can be found in Dirven & Geiger 1989):

(11)   R: *Remember* the blouse you made a couple of weeks ago?
        L: *Ya.*
        R: Well *I want to wear it this weekend to Vegas but my mom's buttonholer is broken.*

This is only one of several types of "referent foregrounding" (as it has been called by Ochs Keenan & Schieffelin 1983, and others) which has been studied - for primarily syntactic reasons - under the name of "left dislocation" at least since the 1960s. But in conversational and discourse analysis and more recently in psycholinguistics, it has been cited as evidence for the thesis that reference is by nature a collaborative process, in which expressed or tacit feedback is a constant necessity (cf. Clark & Wilkes-Gibbs 1986; Geluykens 1988, and this volume).

Geluykens (1988: 152) gives an interesting example which demonstrates another way that referential success can go awry, or we might better say, be thwarted:

(12) A: *and* that table tennis room of mine -
      B: *oh just shut up -- I couldn't care less --*
      A: *ahm -- well -- as I was saying...*

It is too bad the example breaks off where it does. As it is, without knowing how A will next attempt to refer (with a repetition of the noun phrase or with an anaphoric expression instead), we cannot be sure whether the foregrounding actually appeared to A as unsuccessful as B obviously intended it to be. A's response, however, seems to indicate otherwise, that s/he feels s/he has referred "well" - that is, successfully - in spite of B's rudeness.

2.3. *Correct vs. incorrect reference*

Far more so than the problem of reference success, the problem of reference correctness has long occupied philosophers of language, though not many linguists. It has been a problem for philosophers and logicians because of its close connection with their central concern, truth.

Linsky (1967: 118f) once pointed out that it is one thing to refer to an object and something else entirely to refer to it correctly. Ordinary talk is of course full of explicit evaluations of reference correctness such as:

(13) A: *Where did you get* that frisbee?
      B: It's not a frisbee; it's an aerobie.

Interruptions like this made in order to indicate opinions about incorrect references and to repair them are every bit as frequent in everyday conversation as the metacognitive discourse we have seen in the case of reference success. Harmony, of course, is not always achieved, as is well documented, for example, by the widespread debate over whether certain kinds of abortion are "murder" or not. The important question here, as in all such evaluations, concerns the criteria used to evaluate correctness.

Traditionally, philosophers assessed referential correctness ontologically, on the basis of the truth value of the statements involved. What this means, to put it somewhat differently, is that for a reference to be correct, the referring expression involved must "conventionally denote" its referent in the Real World. Put less formally, if the meaning of the expression is a true description of the thing it indicates, then the expression refers correctly. (Note the use of the "timeless" present tense of the verb *refers;* it indicates the universal validity intended.) The hitch here was and for many still is the ontological status of the referent. In Russell's view, statements like the following are false:

(14)   George Bush *is bald.*
(15)   The present king of France *is bald.*

both when an assertion (like *is bald)* is objectively false of an existing referent (the George Bush you and I know has hair on his head) and also false when a potential referring expression *(the present king of France)* is "vacuous", that is, when there is no referent in existence which is correctly described by the expression *the present king of France.* (As we have seen, Russell called this "reference failure".)

Other philosophers (like Strawson) were of a different opinion; they felt that sentences such as (15) are not false but rather have no truth value at all. Questions arose in connection with the easily imaginable cases in which a person believes, for whatever reason, that the referential use of an expression like *the present king of France* is not incorrect. How was one to treat such cases? Even the most traditionally thinking philosopher was now forced to take language out of a timeless and spaceless platonic realm and put it back into the minds of human beings - or at the very least to look for newer and better arguments for his position.

The issue of "incorrect reference" was taken up (though not under this designation) in the 1960s and quickly became a topic of much serious and often heated debate among philosophers, debate which, incidentally, brought with it a distinction between the terms *reference* and *referring.* The issue was perhaps formulated most succinctly by Donnellan (1978: 47) in the opening words of one of his papers, in which he declared: "People refer and expressions refer. Let us call these phenomena SPEAKER REFERENCE and SEMANTIC REFERENCE, respectively."[4] By the end of the 1970s it had thus become clear that at least some philosophers of language were convinced that not one but two kinds of (meta-) referential objects were involved in their debate and that clarity demanded a careful distinction between the two.

In the mid-1960s some philosophers had come to accept as an "obvious principle of reference" (Linsky 1967: 9) "that what is true of something is true of it whatever expression we may use to refer to the thing in stating that truth". They no longer recognized "semantic facts" as the criterion for judging reference correctness but rather (pragmatic) speaker beliefs and intentions instead. The possibilities, of course, for "correctly" referring to persons and things outside of the Real World, such as all of the fictional Tarzans and mythical Easter rabbits we talk about, have thereby become for all intents and purposes infinite, and the corresponding philosophical discussion pro and contra of "reference without referents" (cf. Droste 1978), reference to "nonexistent objects" (cf. Parsons 1980) and the like shows no signs yet of diminishing.

Meanwhile, neighboring cognitive disciplines have been affected by the discussion of reference in philosophy. And while the overwhelming tendency in the others has been to take the more recent pragmatic view of reference and even enhance it by upgrading the perspectives of interacting persons other than just the speaker, as we have seen, the older semantic view of reference is still held by a number of people. In her review of Fauconnier's (1985) book, *Mental Spaces,* for instance, McConnell-Ginet (1987: 146) recently declared that "an adequate theory of linguistic communication must pay attention both to reference, i.e. connections between language and the world, and to representation, i.e. connections between language and mental structures" and that "in the absence of reliable connections [by which she no doubt means "true" or "correct" connections] between language and something extra-mental, comprehension is incomprehensible".

I am apparently not the only one who disagrees with that thinking. Wright and Givón (1987: 1f), for example, cite sentences like:

(16)   a.   *I once had*   a unicorn   *who loved to eat lettuce.*
        b.   *I once had*   a horse   *who loved to eat lettuce.*

to demonstrate that the same grammatical devices are used to talk about "really existing" referents as to talk about "nonexistent" ones. This is proof, they feel, that "reference in human language is not a mapping from linguistic terms to individuals existing in the Real World, but rather to individuals established verbally ... in the Universe of Discourse. ... when the two worlds do not overlap, the grammar of reference cheerfully disregards Real-World denotation, abiding instead by denotation in the universe of discourse." Droste (1978: 44) goes even further when he writes: "Every form of reference is reference to an illusion..." by which he means an entity in our cognitive domain.[5]

What kind of linguistic evidence can be offered for the metacognition of reference correctness? Brugman, whose work I have already mentioned in connection with reference success, studied a set of words which are used with the "metalinguistic" function of indicating what she calls "precise reference". One of her examples (Brugman 1984: 24) is the following:

(17)   *In presenting her analysis she used Chomsky's* very *words.*

about which she says: "What *very* is doing here is signaling that there is a unique referent of the noun phrase and that it has been picked out precisely." Translated into my terminology, *very* indicates a speaker evaluation of the use of a referential expression as "correct to a high degree", and is only one out of the set of metacognitive lexical items consisting of *real, identical, exact, just* and others which Brugman and others have reported on.

An example of a corresponding negative speaker evaluation is the following sentence (Lakoff 1987: 124):

(18)   *The general is president of* a so-called democracy.

Here, the expression *so-called,* one of a number of linguistic "hedges" studied by Lakoff and Kay, indicates that, in the speaker's opinion, the term *democracy* is not a good term to use to refer (correctly) to the entity involved.

3.   Folk models vs. philosophical theories of reference

We have seen that the conflicting reference evaluations presented by philosophers differ in several respects from those made by cognitive linguists, so the question arises as to how this difference can be accounted for. Fortunately, there is an account. Kay (1983; cf. also Lakoff 1987: 121ff) has offered an attractive hypothesis which explains the origin and tenacious quality of the conflicting philosophical theories of reference, on the one hand, and (implicitly) why linguists' evaluations of reference are different from them.

In his renewed attention to the hedges *loosely speaking, strictly speaking, technically,* etc. that had been studied earlier by Lakoff, Kay discovered that people have different grounds for the metacognitive statements they make using such hedges. Consider the following examples which I have invented to illustrate them:

(19)   A: *Could you hand me my tuxedo from those chairs?*
        B: Loosely speaking, *that suit is a tuxedo, but*
              strictly speaking, *only the jacket of it is a tuxedo.*
(20)   A: *Did you hear that threat? Next he'll be assaulting*
              us, I guess.
        B: Technically, *his threat already was an assault.*

In (19) speaker B is indicating that the word *tuxedo* has one and only one inherent or "real" meaning, even though people (like A) are not always careful to use the word referentially correctly. In (20) B is indicating that the word *assault,* though often used "incorrectly" by ordinary people (like A), has a more precise meaning for specialists like lawyers and judges. As Kay (1983: 131) says, one of the ways people can speak "loosely" is by "the use of a coherent but wrong description in an act of reference"; in my terms this is a case of a reference judged by a speaker to be incorrect to some unspecified degree.

One may not agree with all of the details of Kay's analysis - e.g., strictly speaking, or better, technically, not all of his examples are examples of reference per se - but there is no question in my mind that it does give us a method of explaining the discrepancies already mentioned which, until now, have remained remarkably unexplained.

Kay's hypothesis is this. The layman's referential evaluations are based on the same two different "commonsense" or "folk" models that form the basis of the philosopher's abstract theories of reference. The one model/theory takes for granted that words have inherent meanings, which are the things in the world they refer to. The other takes for granted that only "experts" know (and can thus stipulate) what the meanings of certain words are and therefore how they should be used in reference. Common to both is, first, an objective view of the world and of language and, second, the view that there are purely objective criteria for determining when words are used legitimately or correctly.

4.   Perspectives vs. metaperspectives

I have already noted that there are referential evaluations by speakers of their own speech as well as of the speech of someone else. Primarily I was talking about verbally explicit evaluations. Naturally, speakers also evaluate references like everything else without always doing so overtly. And in the same way, speakers assume that addressees and other members of their audiences are doing so likewise. In short, reference analysed as a subjective notion is evaluated from as many viewpoints as there are people interpreting the given communication.

The perspective on which evaluations are based in many of the studies on reference in the older philosophical tradition (e.g. Frege, Russell), the tradition which understands reference as an objective phenomenon, however, is implicitly that of an "omniscient," "divine" or "Olympian" observer, as critics of this approach have recently been calling it (cf. Shadbolt 1983: 71; Harnish 1984: 37; Beaugrande 1987: 155). Martinich (1984: 191) puts it ironically: "Mortals, communicating with other mortals ... do not and cannot have the Olympian view - only God (always) and philosophers (sometimes) - have it..."

In some of the more recent philosophical research (especially following Putnam and Kripke), the perspective has shifted to that of some sort of expert observer. Neither of the two groups of objectivists seem to be particularly bothered by the fact that human communicators are never privy to the truth presumably held by an omniscient observer nor by the equally obvious fact that "experts", even if they could be consulted in a given communication problem, might also very well disagree in their own evaluations.

In addition, it has apparently not been noticed by the objectivists that evaluations tend to vary over time and place and whenever metaperspectives are involved. The recent cognitive science literature is full of very complicated examples of the latter (cf. e.g. Perrault & Cohen 1981: 222ff). In this connection, Wright and Givón (1987: 3) have pointed out that referential opacity can be explained as increased perspective complexity. Consider the increasing difficulty of hearer assessment in the following (invented) utterances by Tom to Dick:

(21)   *The woman you see there at the door is Mary Smith.*
(22)   *Harry wants to meet Mary/the woman at the door.*
(23)   *Bill is aware that Harry wants to meet Mary/his wife/the woman at the door.*

In the case of (21), Dick processes the utterance from (his own view of) Tom's perspective only. However, in (22) and (23) Dick might well realize that the person Harry wants to meet is not known to Harry as being Mary Smith, Bill Smith's wife or the woman at the door and that, in addition, Bill may or may not be aware of that fact. In other words, by adding other perspectives (other minds) to an utterance in intensional contexts of this kind, a speaker no longer projects his or her own perspective alone: because the beliefs of the speaker may differ from those of the additional minds involved, the utterance becomes "opaque" for the hearer.

I believe that the recursiveness of referential perspective can possibly be used to help explain a lot of other "opaque" phenomena cognitive scientists have been wondering about, including at least some of the uses of discourse markers like *well, OK* and perhaps even *oh,* and some of the evaluation problems involved in the metaphorical uses of expressions like *putting a muzzle on someone* (cf. Pauwels & Simon-Vandenbergen, this volume) as well. Kuno, who has been working toward incorporating various types of perspective into a theory of grammar, is also of this opinion. He stresses that what he calls the empathy perspective "will continue to play a crucial role in providing natural explanations for a wide range of otherwise mysterious linguistic phenomena" (Kuno 1987: 270).

5. Conclusion

The approach outlined on the foregoing pages is intended as an initial step toward systematizing from a cognitive perspective the previously unsystematic theories of reference assessment in philosophical and linguistic studies. The three metacognitive parameters of perspective, degree of recursiveness and gradation were introduced and discussed and taken together form the basis of a unified framework for all reference-related phenomena. The framework, once expanded, will encompass the many other facets of the problem of reference such as, for example, its ecological aspects, including above all a treatment of the acquisition of reference, in order to avoid the previous idiosyncratic and unrelated treatments of referential processing.

The approach involved, first, making explicit the nature of reference and what constitutes it, pointing out that at least three concepts of reference are in competition at present. It rejected the prescriptive traditional notion of semantic reference as the "objective" relationship between words and things independent of contextualized human cognition in favor of the more recent pragmatic notion of collaborating-speaker reference as a subjective relationship between minds using language or some other semiotic system. It rejected, in addition, the equally prescriptive recourse to "omniscient" viewpoints in favor of limited mortal viewpoints in referential assessments.

Second, it analytically separated the dimensions of referential correctness and success, demonstrating that correctness is concerned with the "fit" or appropriateness involved in the particular use of a referring expression relative to the perspective of a communicating person, including his or her assumptions concerning the perspectives of others, notably those of the persons to whom the reference is being addressed. Referential success was shown to be the degree of effectiv₁ ıess of the referential act as prerequisite to the communicative act of predicating. As we have seen, the two assessments can be dealt with separately in a theory of reference; in practice, however, reference-processing individuals probably make both sorts of assessment concurrently and to a great extent subconsciously.

I would like to close now with a personal anecdote which shows very clearly how much work still remains to be done toward systematizing referential evaluation. The anecdote is expressed in language that I remember hearing and using as a child in a southern variety of American English. Its point rests upon the phonetic similarity between the word *garments* 'clothes' (which was unfamiliar to many of the younger children where I lived) and the word *varmints* (which all of the children knew), a dialectal variant of *vermin* meaning 'disgusting and poisonous little animals or insects'. The similarity was regularly exploited by older children in order to terrify younger children on the school playground.

I invite readers so inclined to undertake an exact analysis of the degrees of referential effectiveness and appropriateness of the word *garments* from the various recursive perspectives (speaker, addressee, expert and nonexpert observers) outlined in the above approach which are imaginable in the following exchange:

(24)   Older child speaking with an excited voice to younger child:
        Hey, you've got GARMENTS all over your back!
        Younger child horrified:
        Oh, get them off of me!

In view of examples such as this, it seems safe (despite Jaworski 1983: 170) to assume that referential effectiveness does not necessarily depend on referential appropriateness - at least not always or from everybody's perspective.

Notes

1. Cf. also the distinction made by Adriaens (this volume) between the two modes, "normal mode" and "metamode", in which processing competence operates. Obviously, there is yet a lot of work to be done on the conscious/subconscious processing of language before we can begin to make more definitive statements about it.

2. In examples (1) and (2) the speaker must be imagined in Germany and the addressee in the USA. For suggesting these examples and other ways of improving an earlier version of this paper I am greatly indebted to Bruce Hawkins.

3. Compare the difference in the reflexive evaluations expressed by (the conjunction of) the verbs *know* and *believe* in the sentences (with apologies to Lewis Carroll):

   (a) The Mad Gardener believes I know that the banker's clerk is a hippopotamus.
   (b) The Mad Gardener knows I believe that the banker's clerk is a hippopotamus.

4. On the polysemy of the verb *refer,* see Geiger (1988).

5. As one of several valuable critical comments aimed toward improving this paper, which I would like to acknowledge here very gratefully, Brygida Rudzka-Ostyn has reminded me that referential uses of language have an ecological basis, as well as a purely intellectual one (cf. Neisser 1987). While this is unquestionably true, it might be the case that our experience with language in and of the Real World is only one of the major factors in the formation of the intellectual basis of language use, and that the latter, once established, perhaps more or less supercedes the original ecological basis.

References

Antaki, Charles & Alan Lewis
  1986a   "Mental mirrors: Metacognition in social knowledge and communication", in: Charles Antaki & Alan Lewis (eds.), 1-10.
Antaki, Charles & Alan Lewis (eds.)
  1986b   *Mental mirrors: Metacognition in social knowledge and communication.* London: Sage.
Beaugrande, Robert de
  1987   "Determining distributions in complex systems: Science, linguistics, language, life", *Zeitschrift für Phonetik, Sprachwissenschaft und Kommunikationsforschung* 40: 147-190.

Bogusławski, Andrzej
   1982   "Semantic and pragmatic aspects of reference: Selected problems", in:
               Frantisek Daneš & Dieter Viehweger (Hg.), *Pragmatische
               Komponenten der Satzbedeutung*. (Linguistische Studien Reihe A:
               Arbeitsberichte 91/1.) Berlin (Ost): Akademie der Wissenschaften der
               DDR, 1-111.
Brown, Roger W. & Marguerite Ford
   1961   "Address in American English", *Journal of Abnormal and Social
               Psychology* 62: 375-385.
Brown, Roger W. & Albert Gilman
   1960   "The pronouns of power and solidarity", in: Thomas A. Sebeok (ed.),
               Style in language. Cambridge: MIT Press, 253-276.
Brugman, Claudia M.
   1984   "The *very* idea: A case study in polysemy and cross lexical
               generalizations", in: David Testen, Veena Mishra & Joseph Drogo
               (eds.), *Papers from the parasession on lexical semantics*. Chicago:
               Chicago Linguistics Society, 21-38.
Clark, Herbert H. & Deanna Wilkes-Gibbs
   1986   "Referring as a collaborative process", *Cognition* 22: 1-39.
Cole, Peter
   1978a   "On the origins of referential opacity", in: Peter Cole (ed.), 1-22.
Cole, Peter (ed.)
   1978b   *Pragmatics*. (Syntax and Semantics 9.) New York: Academic Press.
Dirven, René & Richard A. Geiger
   1989   "Reference: Determiners and pronouns", in: René Dirven & Richard
               A. Geiger (eds.), *The structure of sentences,* Part B of: René Dirven
               (ed.), *A user's grammar of English*. (Duisburg Papers on Research in
               Language and Culture 2.) Frankfurt: Lang, 355-396.
Donnellan, Keith S.
   1978   "Speaker reference, descriptions and anaphora", in: Peter Cole (ed.),
               47-68.
Droste, Flip G.
   1978   "Reference without referents", in: Wolfgang U. Dressler & Wolfgang
               Meid (eds.), *Proceedings of the Twelfth International Congress of
               Linguists (Vienna 1977)*. Innsbruck: Institut für Sprachwissenschaft,
               178-181.
Dougherty, Janet W.D. (ed.)
   1985   *Directions in cognitive anthropology*. New York: Academic Press.
Forrest-Pressley, Donna-Lynn & T. Gary Waller
   1984   *Cognition, metacognition, and reading*. (Springer Series in Language
               and Communication 18.) New York: Springer.
Geeraerts, Dirk
   1985   *Paradigm and paradox: Explorations into a paradigmatic theory of
               meaning and its epistemological background*. (Symbolae Facultatis
               Litterarum et Philosophiae Lovaniensis, series A, 14.) Leuven: Leuven
               University Press.
Geiger, Richard A.
   1979   "Third-person reference in German", *Papers in Linguistics* 12: 535-552.

1988   "The problem of reference and the indeterminacy of *refer*", in: Werner
            Hüllen & Rainer Schulze (eds.), *Understanding the lexicon: Meaning,
            sense and world knowledge in lexical semantics.* (Linguistische Arbeiten
            210.) Tübingen: Niemeyer, 85-96.
Geiger, Richard A.
1991   *References to REFERENCE and related phenomena: A multidisciplinary
            bibliography (2nd extended version 1991).* (Series A, Paper no. 289.)
            Duisburg: Linguistic Agency University of Duisburg.
Geluykens, Ronald
1988   "The interactional nature of referent-introduction", in: Lynn Macleod,
            Gary Larson & Diana Brentari (eds.), *Papers from the general session
            of the 24th annual meeting of the Chicago linguistic society.* Chicago:
            CLS, 141-154.
Harnish, Robert M.
1984   "Communicative reference: An inferential model", *Conceptus* 18/44:
            20-41.
Jaworski, Adam
1983   "Referring: A sociolinguistic perspective", *Studia Anglica Posnaniensia*
            16: 161-171.
Johnson, Mark
1987   *The body in the mind: The bodily basis of meaning, imagination, and
            reason.* Chicago: University of Chicago Press.
Karmiloff-Smith, Annette
1979   *A functional approach to child language: A study of determiners and
            reference.* (Cambridge Studies in Linguistics 24.) Cambridge:
            Cambridge University Press.
Kay, Paul
1983   "Linguistic competence and folk theories of language: Two English
            hedges", in: *Proceedings of the Ninth Annual Meeting of the Berkeley
            Linguistics Society.* Berkeley: BLS, 128-137. Reprinted in: Dorothy
            Holland & Naomi Quinn (eds.), *Cultural models in language and
            thought.* Cambridge: Cambridge University Press, 1987, 67-77.
Kuno, Susumu
1987   *Functional syntax: Anaphora, discourse and empathy.* Chicago:
            University of Chicago Press.
Lakoff, George
1987   *Women, fire, and dangerous things: What categories reveal about the
            mind.* Chicago: University of Chicago Press.
Lakoff, George & Mark Johnson
1980   *Metaphors we live by.* Chicago: University of Chicago Press.
Langford, Glenn
1986   "The philosophical basis of cognition and metacognition", in: Charles
            Antaki & Alan Lewis (eds.), 11-26.
Leech, Geoffrey N.
1983   *Principles of pragmatics.* London: Longman.
Lehman, F.K.
1985   "Cognition and computation: On being sufficiently abstract", in: Janet
            W.D. Dougherty (ed.), 19-48.
Linsky, Leonard
1967   *Referring.* London: Routledge & Kegan Paul.

Marslen-Wilson, William D., Elena Levy & Lorraine K. Tyler
1982   "Producing interpretable discourse: The establishment and maintenance of reference", in: Robert J. Jarvella & Wolfgang Klein (eds.), *Speech, place, and action: Studies in deixis and related topics.* New York: Wiley, 339-378.
Martin, Graham D.
1981   *The architecture of experience: A discussion of the role of language and literature in the construction of the world.* Edinburgh: Edinburgh University Press.
Martin, Richard M.
1979   *Pragmatics, truth, and language.* (Boston Studies in the Philosophy of Science 38.) Dordrecht: Reidel.
Martinich, Aloysius P.
1984   *Communication and reference.* Berlin: de Gruyter.
McConnell-Ginet, Sally
1987   Review of Gilles R. Fauconnier, *Mental spaces: Aspects of meaning construction in natural language.* (Cambridge: Cambridge University Press, 1985), *Language* 63: 142-146.
Neisser, Ulric (ed.)
1987   *Concepts and conceptual development: Ecological and intellectual factors in categorization.* Cambridge: Cambridge University Press.
Nunberg, Geoffrey D.
1977   The pragmatics of reference. [Unpublished Ph.D. dissertation, City University of New York.] Circulated by: Bloomington: Indiana University Linguistics Club, 1978.
Ochs Keenan, Elinor & Bambi B. Schieffelin
1983   "Fore-grounding referents: A reconsideration of left dislocation in discourse", in: Elinor Ochs & Bambi B. Schieffelin (eds.), *Acquiring conversational competence.* London: Routledge & Kegan Paul, 158-174.
Over, D.E.
1983   "Effective and non-effective reference", *Analysis* 43: 85-91.
Parsons, Terence
1980   *Nonexistent objects.* New Haven: Yale University Press.
Perrault, C. Raymond & Philip R. Cohen
1981   "It's for your own good: A note on inaccurate reference", in: Aravind K. Joshi, Bonnie L. Webber & Ivan A. Sag (eds.), *Elements of discourse understanding.* Cambridge: Cambridge University Press, 217-230.
Russell, Bertrand
1905   "On referring", *Mind* 14: 479-493.
Sacks, Harvey & Emanuel A. Schegloff
1979   "Two preferences in the organization of reference to persons in conversation and their interaction", in: George Psathas (ed.), *Everyday language: Studies in ethnomethodology.* New York: Irvington, 15-21.
Schegloff, Emanuel A.
1980   "Preliminaries to preliminaries: Can I ask you a question?", in: Don H. Zimmerman & Candace West (eds.), 104-152.
Schiffrin, Deborah
1980   "Meta-talk: Organizational and evaluative brackets in discourse", in: Don H. Zimmerman & Candace West (eds.), 199-236.
1985   "Conversational coherence: The role of *well*", *Language* 61: 640-667.

Searle, John R.
1969   *Speech acts: An essay in the philosophy of language.* Cambridge:
            Cambridge University Press.
Shadbolt, Nigel
1983   "Processing reference", *Journal of Semantics* 2: 63-98.
Wright, S. & T. Givón
1987   "The pragmatics of indefinite reference: Quantified text-based
            studies", *Studies in Language* 11: 1-33.
Zadeh, Lotfi A.
1977   "Fuzzy sets", in: Jack Belzer, Albert G. Holzman & Allen Kent (eds.),
            Encyclopedia of computer science and technology. New York: Marcel
            Dekker, VIII, 325-363.
Zimmerman, Don H. & Candace West (eds.)
1980   *Language and social interaction.* Special issue of *Sociological Inquiry*
            50.3/4.

An image-schematic constraint on metaphor

Mark Turner

A general constraint on conceptual metaphor is presented: In metaphoric mapping, for those components of the source and target domains determined to be involved in the mapping, preserve the image-schematic structure of the target, and import as much image-schematic structure from the source as is consistent with that preservation.

1. The nature and scope of the constraint

In a conceptual metaphor, we map a source domain onto a target domain. But that mapping cannot be arbitrary. What constrains such a metaphoric mapping?

According to Lakoff and Johnson (1980), a basic metaphor, however flexible in its periphery or its instantiations, has a centrally fixed mapping that carries a fixed source domain onto a fixed target domain. To know the conceptual metaphor is to know its mapping, and we are constrained to preserve that mapping exactly unless we wish to be taken as challenging the conceptual metaphor.

Such metaphors are conventionalized specific-level conceptual metaphors. But according to Turner (1987) and Lakoff and Turner (1989), there are in addition to these basic metaphors certain conventionalized generic-level conceptual metaphors such as EVENTS ARE ACTIONS (as in *Events conspired against us*) and CAUSATION IS PROGENERATION (as in *Fear is the father of cruelty*). These conceptual metaphors do not have fixed mappings. Instead of fixed mappings, they have generic-level constraints on possible mappings.

Here I hypothesize a general constraint that governs all conceptual metaphor, including basic, specific-level, generic-level, and novel conceptual metaphor. George Lakoff and I implicitly presented this constraint in Lakoff & Turner (1989). We now call it "the Invariance Hypothesis". The core of the constraint is that in conceptual metaphor we are constrained not to violate the image-schematic structure of the target domain.

2.   Traditional work on constraints

Aristotle originally noticed that a metaphor is constrained not to violate various things in the target domain. He expressed this by saying that the source must fit the target in certain ways, including what appear to be conceptual ways.[1]

Considering that the problem of fitness was raised by Aristotle and that the theory of metaphor in thought and language has in many ways been a series of responses to and developments of Aristotle's few comments on metaphor, it is odd how little inquiry has been made into the actual details of what makes a metaphor conceptually fit. This topic has been overshadowed by other topics in the theory of metaphor. There has been voluminous work on what constitutes metaphor and how metaphoric language is demarked from other forms of language, on how it is that a metaphor can mean, and on whether or not metaphor can have truth-value, but relatively little work, at least until very recently, on the conceptual details of metaphor.[2]

To be sure, there have been blanket general characterizations of the conceptual process of metaphor, such as Aristotle's apparent characterization of the invention of metaphor as the perception of similarity in dissimilar things (*Poetics*, 1459a), Max Black's characterization of metaphor as the interaction of two different entire systems of implications,[3] Nelson Goodman's characterization of metaphor as "a transfer of a schema" (1974: 73), or as concerned with "withdrawing a term or rather a schema of terms from an initial literal application and applying it in a new way to effect a new sorting either of the same or of a different realm" (1979: 178), and Paul Ricoeur's (1977) elaborate characterization of metaphor, quite difficult to summarize, as novel attribution that creates semantic tension (because of its deviance from the literal) that results in new meaning (all at various levels, from the word to the sentence to the text). At the opposite pole, there have been multitudinous specific analyses of how specific linguistic metaphors can be read. But there has been very little work at a level between these blanket characterizations and these self-contained case studies. There has been little mid-level work that would tell us about the general constraints on conceptual fit between source domain and target domain in a conceptual metaphor.[4] In this article, I hypothesize such a general constraint.

3.   Some specific evidence of constraints on metaphoric mapping

Let us begin to work up to this general constraint by looking at a particular conceptual metaphor, LIFE IS A JOURNEY, and at what appear to be certain specific constraints on its operation.

The basic metaphor LIFE IS A JOURNEY is conventionalized in a multitude of expressions, such as "He's *getting nowhere* in life", "She's *on the right track*", and "He *arrived* at a new stage in life". Such a conceptual metaphor maps a source conceptual schema (JOURNEY) onto a target conceptual schema (LIFE). Here we notice the first evidence of a constraint on the mapping: it appears that such metaphors are constrained against mapping two distinct senses in the source onto one sense in the target. To map two distinct senses in the source onto one sense in the target would be to destroy the identity of that one sense in the target. The conventionalized conceptual metaphor automatically satisfies that constraint by virtue of its one-to-one fixed mapping. For example, the traveler corresponds to the person leading the life, and the destination corresponds to one of his or her goals; distinct senses in the source are mapped onto distinct senses in the target. If we look at an extension of the conventional metaphoric understanding of life as a journey, we find that the constraint against violating identity in the target still applies. For example, if we say, extending the conventional metaphoric understanding of life as a journey, that *I am a traveler through life and I am the destination*, then we find ourselves constrained to take the first and second *I* as pointing to two different senses in the target (such as the knowing self and the self to be known) so that two different senses in the source (traveler and destination) do not map onto one sense in the target.

We can see a different specific constraint on LIFE IS A JOURNEY by looking at order relations in the target. We conventionally conceive of the moments of life as being temporally ordered:[5] for any two moments in life, one must precede the other; no moment precedes itself; and precedence is transitive. We conventionally conceive of the points on a path, such as the path of a journey, as spatially ordered: for any two spatial points on the path, one must precede the other; no point precedes itself; and precedence is transitive. We also conventionally conceive of a traveler on a journey as encountering the spatial points on the path in the order of their physical succession. Here we observe a specific constraint on the mapping in LIFE IS A JOURNEY: when we understand life metaphorically as a journey, we are constrained not to violate the order of moments in our concept of life. We cannot without provoking remark say, for example, *First I was getting somewhere in life and then I got off to a good start,* because we take this as asking us to violate the original temporal order of two moments in the target: the *prior* moment in the target (*First I was*) is forced to correspond to the *later* moment in the source (*getting somewhere*) and the *later* moment in the target (*and then I*) is forced to correspond to the *prior* moment in the source (*got off to a good start*). This reverses the order of moments in the our schema of life - which is the target - and disturbs us badly.

Many utterances simply express basic metaphors whose satisfaction of such constraints is pre-fabricated in their fixed mappings. But there are utterances that ask for originality in satisfying these constraints. In the Farewell Discourse (chapters thirteen through seventeen) of the Fourth Gospel, Jesus speaks to the Apostles (John 13: 36 - 14: 6):

> "Set your troubled hearts at rest. Trust in God always; trust also in me. There are many dwelling-places in my Father's house; if it were not so I should have told you; for I am going on purpose to prepare a place for you. And if I go and prepare a place for you, I shall come again and receive you to myself, so that where I am you may be also; and my way there is known to you." Thomas said, "Lord, we do not know where you are going, so how can we know the way?" Jesus replied, "I am the way; I am the truth and I am the life; no one comes to the Father except by me". *(The New English Bible)*

Jesus will take a journey and then return, he implies, to take the Apostles on the same journey to the same destination. This may be read literally or metaphorically or both. The metaphoric reading calls upon the conventional metaphoric understanding of life experiences as a journey, and its conventional extension to the metaphoric understanding of death as a departure (see further Lakoff & Turner 1989). To this point, there is no felt violation of the target. The metaphoric reading simply inherits from basic metaphors pre-fabricated satisfactions of constraints.

At this point Thomas asks a perfectly sensible question that makes sense either literally or metaphorically. It concerns the state of knowledge of the person being told about the journey. The first reading of his question is the literal: How can we know the physical path to a destination whose location is unknown to us? The second reading is metaphoric: How can we know the "way" that will "lead us" to a goal when the goal is unknown to us? This is a question about conceptual structure, and applies equally to the literal and the metaphoric reading.

When Jesus answers that he is the way, both the literal and the metaphoric readings fall apart. Literally, his statement violates our schema of a journey because a person cannot be a way, much less both a traveler *and* a way. Metaphorically, his statement asks us to map two senses in the source, namely both the traveler and the way, onto one sense in the target, Jesus. We feel this construal to be a flagrant violation of protected structure in the target.

It is this dissonance that signals to us that we must perform some original work to arrive at a different construal that satisfies constraints. One strategy is to attribute to the passage a double reading: Jesus is taking one journey, whether literal or metaphoric, in which he is the literal or metaphoric traveler; and we, or the Apostles, are to take another journey, a metaphoric journey, in which we, or the Apostles, are the metaphoric travelers and Jesus is the metaphoric way, the metaphoric conduit to some state of being that is metaphorically both a location and the destination of this particular journey.

There are other ways to attempt to satisfy constraints. We might observe that divinity in the Fourth Gospel is marked not by iconographic attributes or miracle stories but rather by discourse that violates what we take to be reliable conceptions. In this text, divinity talks like this. The divine, unlike the mortal or the everyday, can be a traveler and a way, an agent and a path. The divine can violate identity, as when, in trinitarian doctrine, we are told that three are one.[6]

4.   The general constraint

We have seen a few specific manifestations of what may be a general constraint on metaphor, and demonstrations of the unoriginal and original exploitations of that general constraint. Let us now try to articulate that general constraint.

4.1. Image-schemas

This constraint has to do with the forms of our experience, and how those forms structure our thoughts. We experience images in various modalities: a visual image of a road, an auditory image of a scream, a kinesthetic image of a pinch, an olfactory image of the smell of roses, and so on. Each rich image is not wholly unique; rather, it shares skeletal structure with other images. We have a skeletal image of a scream that inheres within our rich images of particular screams. We have a skeletal image of a flat bounded planar space that inheres within our rich images of individual tables, individual floors, individual plateaus. We have a skeletal image of verticality that inheres within our rich images of individual trees, individual buildings, individual people. Following Mark Johnson, I will use the technical term *image schema* for such skeletal forms that structure our images.[7]

As I conceive of them, image-schemas are extremely skeletal images which we use in cognitive operations. We have many such image-schemas: of bounded space, of a path, of contact, and of orientations such as up-down, front-back, and center-periphery. We have many image-schemas of part-whole relational structure. We also have dynamic image-schemas, such as the image-schema for a rising motion, or a dip, or an expansion, and so on. When we understand a scene, we naturally structure it in terms of such elementary image-schemas.

4.2. The mapping of an image onto an image

Let us turn to a first approximation of the general constraint on metaphor by taking up just images. It appears to be the case that when we map one image metaphorically onto another, we are constrained not to violate the schematic structure of the target image. For example, a verticality schema in the target cannot have mapped onto it its inverse; a bounded interior in the target cannot have mapped onto it both bits of an interior and bits of an exterior; and so on.

Consider, for example, Auden's lines from "1929": "But thinking so I came at once/ Where solitary man sat weeping on a bench,/ Hanging his head down, with his mouth distorted/ Helpless and ugly as an embryo chicken." The hanging head of the solitary man is a bounded interior, with an exterior; it has an internal up-down structure (for example, the top of the head and the bottom of the head); its direction is roughly down (looking down); its open mouth is a concavity in the boundary; its parts (mouth, eyes, top of head, and so on) have relational structure such as adjacency. Although our rich image of the hanging head may include all sorts of detail, that detail is structured by such image-schemas. I refer to this structure as the *image-schematic structure* of the image. We are constrained not to violate it when we map the image of the embryo chicken onto it: the interior of the chicken head maps to the interior of the human head; the boundary to the boundary; the verticality to the verticality; and so on. A similar example might be Blake's personification of a sunflower, in which the image of a human body is mapped onto the image of a sunflower, preserving the part-whole relations and the orientation of the sunflower. The schematic structure of the target image is not violated.

4.3.   Image-schematic structure in non-images

The next consideration to bring to bear in formulating the general constraint is that many things other than images appear to be structured by image-schemas. Our concepts of time, of events in time, and of causal relations seem to be structured by these image-schemas. We conventionally conceive of time, which has no shape, as having a shape, such as linear or circular, and of that shape as having skeletal structure. We conventionally conceive of events in time, which have no shape, as having shape, such as continuity, extension, discreteness, completion, open-endedness, circularity, part-whole relations, and other aspectual attributes. We conventionally conceive of causal relations as having skeletal shapes such as links and paths. These shapes, these image-schemas, need not be static. We have a dynamic image-schema of one thing coming out of another, and we use it to structure one of our concepts of causation. And all these conventional conceptualizations are productive in ordinary speech.

4.4.   The general constraint and commentary

With this addition we can reformulate the core of the general unoriginal constraint on metaphoric invention thus: *In metaphor, we are constrained not to violate the image-schematic structure of the target; this entails that we are constrained not to violate whatever image-schematic structure may be possessed by non-image components of the target.*

The formulation of this constraint requires many clarifications and comments. First, the constraint says nothing about what can or cannot or should or should not be mapped from the source to the target, nothing about what components of the target can or should be involved in the metaphoric invention, nothing whatever about strategies of mapping or of reconception that might be used in the service of satisfying the constraint.

Second, the constraint is not inviolable; however, if it is violated, the violation is to be taken as a carrier of significance. Usually, we assume that violations are to be avoided as we construct a meaning for the utterance. The constraint thus guides our understanding by blocking certain possibilities. But when we conclude that the utterance is to be taken as violating the constraint, then we must look for some significance in the violation. For example, we can take such a violation as asking us to re-conceive the target through exactly and specifically that violation at the expense of our previous conception. The violation is then specific and aggressive. But we assume that a violation of the constraint is never insignificant or to be ignored. If ultimately we find no significance in the violation, we will find the metaphoric invention either faulty or beyond our powers of understanding. Typically, it is only in novel metaphors that the constraint is violated. Systematically conventionalized metaphors and their linguistic expressions obey the constraint.

Third, this formulation is summary, and does no more than hint at the complexity of the subject. I have nothing approaching a definition or taxonomy of image-schemas, a theory of how they arise and work, or an explanation of their role in structuring concepts. Finding a fair characterization of these phenomena would require a theory of image-schemas, of their relation to images, of their origin, of their relation across modalities (as when we talk of a *screaming red* or a *sharp tartness*), of their use in structuring concepts, and, beyond all this, a larger theory that could account for why they seem to have privilege in metaphor.

4.5.   *An illustration of the general constraint*

Let us illustrate the general image-schematic constraint by looking at the opening sentence from a travel article in a Sunday newspaper: *Trees climb the hills toward the Golan and descend to test their resolve near the desert.* Here, a static configuration appears to be understood metaphorically as a dynamic movement, and the agent-less event of dynamic movement appears to be understood metaphorically as an action by an intentional agent. We are not bothered that dynamism is apparently mapped onto stasis, that an action is mapped onto an event, and that intentional animate agents are mapped onto plants. Why are we not bothered by these violations? An answer to this question may be provided by the image-schematic constraint on metaphor.

We can understand the form of the line of trees as the trace (or "summary scan") of a movement: the trace of a climb that crests and then descends has the same image-schematic structure as the line of the trees. Consequently, when one is mapped onto the other, there is no violation of the image-schematic structure of the target. So much for the images. Now consider the events and actions in this passage. The target is an event that involves the trees and the desert: the trees occupy a position (a literal position) and are opposed in their occupation of that position by desert forces that may dislodge them from that position. The source for understanding this target event metaphorically is an action: testing one's resolve. Such testing has an event shape: we occupy a position (metaphoric or literal) and are opposed in that occupation by some force that would (metaphorically or literally) dislodge us; if we abandon that position, we say our resolve failed. The event shape of the source corresponds to the event shape of the target. Both are structured as a positioned entity that has been moved to that position by one force exerted upon it, and that encounters in that position countervailing force. The outcome is the stasis or movement of that entity, and this outcome is determined by the size of the vector forces. Again, the image-schematic structure of the target (here the image-schematic structure of the event shape) is not violated. So much for the events and actions. Finally, consider the causal structure of the target: there is a causal link between the desert and the endpoint of the line of trees in the target; there is a causal link between the desert and the intentional holding or abandoning of the occupied literal or metaphoric position in the source. Mapping one onto the other does not violate the causal structure of the target: a link is mapped onto a link.

5.   Other current conjectures and the maximal version of the constraint

There have been before now random observations that specific metaphoric mappings are unacceptable because they go awry in some way. For example, Eva Kittay and Adrienne Lehrer (Kittay 1987: 273, Kittay & Lehrer 1981: 47) note that when we attempt to make sense of Donn's "The Bait", in which courtship is presented metaphorically in terms of fishing, there is one mapping that we might try out but that is unacceptable because it "does not work. The 'beloved' cannot at once be the prey and herself the means of catching the prey." That observation is true, even obviously true, but no account is given of why that specific metaphoric mapping is constrained in that way, and no general constraint is given.

There are, however, two current proposals for general constraints on metaphoric mapping, one by Dedre Gentner, the other by George Lakoff. Gentner's hypothesis pre-dates the one I offer. Lakoff's is a development of work Lakoff and I did jointly in writing *More than cool reason* (Lakoff & Turner 1989).

The image-schematic constraint hypothesized here bears a complicated relationship to Gentner's structure-mapping theory of analogy (Gentner 1983 and 1986). Gentner writes:

> The central idea in structure-mapping is that an analogy is a mapping of knowledge from one domain (the base) into another (the target) which conveys that a system of relations that holds among the base objects also holds among the target objects. Thus an analogy is a way of focusing on relational commonalities independently of the objects in which those relations are embedded. In interpreting an analogy, people seek to put the objects of the base in one-to-one correspondence with the objects in the target so as to obtain the maximum structural match. Objects are placed in correspondence by virtue of their like roles in the common relational structure; there does not need to be any resemblance between the target objects and their corresponding base objects. Central to the mapping process is the principle of systematicity: people prefer to map connected *systems of relations* governed by higher-order relations with inferential import, rather than isolated predicates (Gentner 1986: 3f.).

Gentner here hypothesizes a heuristic used in analogical understanding. Let us explore its relationship to the image-schematic constraint on metaphor I propose. If relational structure is image-schematic, as it would seem to be, then the constraint I propose entails that we are constrained not to violate the relational structure of the target. This corollary to the image-schematic constraint is compatible with Gentner's heuristic just in those cases of metaphor where the relational structure of the target is not violated and is also maximally involved in the mapping: such a case satisfies both the image-schematic constraint and Gentner's heuristic.

In one way, the relational corollary to the image-schematic constraint on metaphor is stronger than Gentner's heuristic because Gentner's heuristic of seeking maximal structural match does not imply a constraint against violating relational structure in the target; indeed, Gentner's heuristic apparently would allow us to violate some relational structure in the target if doing so enabled us to involve more of the relational structure in an analogical match than otherwise would be possible. Violating some relational structure in the target should be welcomed on Gentner's heuristic if it permits greater final structural match.

In another way, the relational corollary to the image-schematic constraint on metaphor is weaker than Gentner's heuristic because it is merely a constraint against violating image-schematic structure in the target, and says nothing about what should be involved in the mapping, whereas Gentner's heuristic concerns exactly that.

Although the image-schematic constraint and Gentner's heuristic can in some cases be compatible, the image-schematic constraint concerns many aspects of metaphor that Gentner's heuristic apparently does not. The full image-schematic constraint itself concerns all image-schematic structure, including many things (like *slowness* as part of an event shape) that are crucial to metaphor but that do not appear to fall under what Gentner would describe as relational structure. (See further Turner 1988.)

The rudiments of the image-schematic constraint conjectured here are presented implicitly but not analyzed in *More than cool reason* (Lakoff & Turner 1989). George Lakoff, in his paper "The invariance hypothesis: Do metaphors preserve cognitive topology?", phrased our hypothesis as "Metaphorical mappings preserve the cognitive topology (this is the image-schema structure) of the source domain". But this strong version of the Invariance Hypothesis was potentially misleading in two ways. The first way is trivial. Many components of image-schematic structure in the source are simply not involved in the mapping. For example, when we understand our boss as a crab, the image of the crab, and consequently its image-schematic structure, are simply not part of the mapping. Consequently, that image-schematic structure in the source is not preserved by the mapping; it is not carried over to the target. Lakoff and I implicitly explain this in chapter four of *More than cool reason* when we discuss how the Maxim of Quantity guides us to exclude various components of the source and target from the mapping. The second way in which the strong version is too strong is substantive: components of the source that are indeed involved in the mapping often have image-schematic structure that is not mapped onto the target. Consider LIFE IS A JOURNEY. There is a path in the source domain, and it is mapped onto the target. That path in the source has image-schematic structure. But much of this image-schematic structure is simply not mapped onto the target. For example, it is part of the image-schematic structure of the path that the path is fixed. It is independent of our traversal of it. Traversing the path does not create or destroy the path. Consequently, we can meet a fork in the path, choose one fork, take a step, change our mind, step back, and take the other fork. Metaphorically, meeting a fork corresponds to coming upon alternatives. But the fixity of the fork does not map over onto the fixity of the alternatives. Many of our decisions are irrevocable. Shall we boil this egg or scramble it? Shall we marry Tom or Harry? In these cases, the rejected alternative disappears the moment we engage in the chosen alternative. If we boil the egg, we cannot then scramble it, and if we scramble it, we cannot then decide to boil it. Metaphorically, one of the forks is destroyed the moment we step down the other. We cannot take a step back and be again at the metaphoric fork in the road, *because the fork doesn't exist anymore.* The metaphoric path, unlike the source path, changes as a result of being traversed. The fixity of the path in the source, its independence of our traversing it, is not mapped over onto the target. The reason it cannot be mapped onto the target in these cases is that to do so would violate the image-schematic structure of the target. In the source, there is preservation, which is image-schematic structure. In the target, there is destruction, which is image-schematic structure. To map the source preservation over onto the target destruction would be to violate the image-schematic structure of the target, and so we do not map that part of the image-schematic structure of the source. We see from this example that the strongest version of the constraint and the one I propose above are incompatible for a range of cases. For these cases, obeying the strong version of the constraint violates the weaker version, and obeying the weaker version of the constraint violates the stronger version. It appears that the strongest acceptable version of the constraint is: *In metaphoric mapping, for those components of the source and target domains determined to be involved in the mapping, preserve the image-schematic structure of the target, and import as much image-schematic structure from the source as is consistent with that preservation.* This is the Invariance Hypothesis.[8]

6. Conclusion

There is a system to conceptual metaphor and to its conventionalized linguistic expression. Conceptual metaphor is not a matter of arbitrary fixity. Individual basic metaphors and even generic-level metaphors are not isolated: if the hypothesis in this article is correct, then there is a higher unity to metaphor that governs not only all basic and generic-level metaphor, but all novel metaphor as well. That image-schematic unity further connects metaphor as a conceptual and linguistic phenomenon to other non-metaphoric phenomena at the basis of cognitive linguistics.

Notes

1.   Aristotle writes in the *Rhetoric*, book 3, chapter 2, "Metaphors, like epithets, must be fitting, which means that they must fairly correspond to the thing signified: failing this, their inappropriateness will be conspicuous: the want of harmony between two things is emphasized by their being placed side by side" (Tr. W. Rhys Robert).

    There are many grounds on which a metaphor might be judged fitting or unfitting. As Booth (1979) points out, any rhetoric text from Aristotle to Whately would comment that a metaphor might be judged appropriate or inappropriate in its grandeur or triviality to what is being presented, in its contribution to the ethos the speaker desires to establish, in its level of difficulty or interest for the audience, in the style of its expression, and so on. I am concerned not with these forms of fitness, but rather with the conceptual fitness of a metaphor.

2.   For a survey of such work, see Cooper (1987). Recent work on the conceptual details of metaphor includes most prominently Gentner (1983), which I will discuss toward the end of this article. Older work on the conceptual details of metaphor centers around the chestnut that metaphors are conceptually constrained not to be "mixed", but this claim is in general false; often mixed metaphors do not bother us, and often different metaphors can cohere (see Lakoff & Turner 1989: 70f., "Composing", and 86-89, "Coherence among metaphors"). Booth (1979: 50) gives the following example of a "mixed" metaphor that does not disturb us at all, and that may be all the stronger for being mixed. A lawyer expresses the struggle between a large utility company and a small utility company in a figure: "So now we see what it is. They [the large utility company] got us [the small utility company] where

they want us. They holding us up with one hand, their good sharp fishin' knife in the other, and they sayin', 'you *jes* set still, little catfish, we're jes going to *gut* ya.'" Booth observes later in the article that consistency would require that the catfish be told to "hang still" rather than "set still", but that this conceptual inconsistency does not bother us. I suspect that we would be rather bothered indeed if the metaphor were instead "You jes vanish, little catfish, we're jes going to gut ya" or "You jes jump back in the water, little catfish, we're jes going to gut ya" or "You jes digest, little catfish, we're jes going to gut ya" or "You jes grow older, little catfish, we're jes going to gut ya," although these metaphors are not mixed, and that we would be equally bothered if the metaphor were "You jes hold a board meeting, little catfish, we're jes going to gut ya," which is mixed. In all these cases, we hear the conceptual gears of the metaphor grind. We feel that something at the conceptual level does not fit. Something at the conceptual level has gone awry.

3.   See Black (1979: 28): "The metaphorical utterance works by 'projecting upon' the primary subject a set of 'associated implications', comprised in the implicative complex, that are predicable of the secondary subject".

4.   Goodman (1974: 74f.) implies that such constraints exist, but gives only hints about what they might be, as in: "A schema may be transported almost anywhere. The choice of territory for invasion is arbitrary; but the operation within that territory is almost never completely so. We may at will apply temperature-predicates to sounds or hues or personalities or to degrees of nearness to a correct answer; but which elements in the chosen realm are warm, or are warmer than others, is then very largely determinate. Even where a schema is imposed upon a most unlikely and uncongenial realm, antecedent practice channels the application of the labels. When a label has not only literal but prior metaphorical uses, these too may serve as part of the precedent for a later metaphorical application; perhaps, for instance, the way we apply 'high' to sounds was guided by the earlier metaphorical application to numbers (via number of vibrations per second) rather than directly by the literal application according to altitude". What is missing from this enticing passage is any account of why certain choices are determinate, how antecedent practice channels the application of labels, or how prior uses serve as part of the precedent for later metaphorical application.

5.   Technically, a relation < on a set A is called an order relation (or a simple order, or a linear order) if it has the properties of comparability (for every x and y in A for which x does not equal y, either $x<y$ or $y<x$), nonreflexivity (for no x in A does the relation $x<x$ hold), and transitivity (if $x<y$ and $y<z$, then $x<z$).

6.   We have an image-schema for *one* and a different image-schema for *three*. In quotidian experience and in our metaphoric conception of a target, three cannot be one. The divine is marked as transcending such constraints.

7.   *Image-schema* is Mark Johnson's term. An image-schema, according to Johnson, "is a recurring, dynamic pattern of our perceptual interactions and motor programs that gives coherence and structure to

our experience. The VERTICALITY schema, for instance, emerges from our tendency to employ an UP-DOWN orientation in picking out meaningful structures of our experience. We grasp this structure of verticality repeatedly in thousands of perceptions and activities we experience every day, such as perceiving a tree, our felt sense of standing upright, the activity of climbing stairs, forming a mental image of a flagpole, measuring our children's heights, and experiencing the level of water rising in the bathtub" (Johnson 1987: xiv.)

The notion that we use image-schemas to structure our perceptions and conceptions is implicit in Palermo (1987, 1988a, 1988b). Langacker (1986, 1988a, 1988b) has since 1974 been articulating the ways in which semantic structure is based on what he calls *images*, which resemble Johnson's image-schemata. Technically, Langacker views Johnson's "image-schemata" as a subset of Langacker's "images" (personal communication, 1988).

8.   Claudia Brugman (personal communication) is at work on a much more elaborate survey of possible formulations of the hypothesis.

References

Black, Max
       1979   "More about metaphor", in: Andrew Ortony (ed.), 19-43.
Booth, Wayne
       1979   "Metaphor as rhetoric", in: Sheldon Sacks (ed.), 47-70.
Cooper, David E.
       1987   *Metaphor*. (Aristotelian Society Series 5). Oxford: Blackwell.
Gentner, Dedre
       1983   "Structure-mapping: A theoretical framework for analogy", *Cognitive Science* 7: 155-170.
       1986   "The mechanisms of analogical learning". [Paper presented at the ARI Conference on Analogical Similarity, appeared in: Sella Vosniadou & Andrew Ortony (eds.), *Similarity and analogical reasoning*. Cambridge: Cambridge University Press, 1989, 199-241.]
Goodman, Nelson
       1974   *Languages of art*. Indianapolis: Hackett Publishing Company.
       1979   "Metaphor as moonlighting", in: Sheldon Sacks (ed.), 175-180.
Johnson, Mark.
       1987   *The body in the mind*. Chicago: University of Chicago Press.
Kittay, Eva
       1987   *Metaphor: Its cognitive force and linguistic srtucture*. Oxford: Clarendon.
Kittay, Eva & Adrienne Lehrer
       1981   "Semantic fields and the structure of metaphor", *Studies in Language* 5, 31-63.
Lakoff, George
       1989   "The invariance hypothesis: Do metaphors preserve cognitive topology?" [Paper presented at the International Symposium on Cognitive Linguistics, University of Duisburg. Available from the Linguistic Agency University of Duisburg.]

Lakoff, George & Mark Johnson
    1980   *Metaphors we live by*. Chicago: University of Chicago Press.
Lakoff, George & Mark Turner
    1989   *More than cool reason: A field guide to poetic metaphor*. Chicago:
                University of Chicago Press.
Langacker, Ronald.
    1986   *Foundations of cognitive grammar*, vol. 1. Stanford: Stanford University
                Press.
    1988a   "An overview of cognitive grammar", in: Brygida Rudzka-Ostyn (ed.),
                3-48.
    1988b   "A view of linguistic semantics", in: Brygida Rudzka-Ostyn (ed.), 49-
                90.
Ortony, Andrew (ed.)
    1979   *Metaphor and thought*. Cambridge: Cambridge University Press.
Palermo, David
    1987   "The transfer dilemma: From cross-modal perception to metaphor".
                [Paper presented at the Third International Conference on Thinking,
                Honolulu, Hawaii.]
    1988a   "Metaphor: A portal for viewing the child's mind", in: L. P. Lipsitt et
                al., (eds.), *Essays and experiments in honor of Charles C. Spiker*.
                Hillsdale, NJ: Lawrence Erlbaum Associates.
    1988b   "Knowledge and the child's developing theory of the world", in: H.W.
                Reese (ed.), *Advances in child development and behavior*, vol. 22. New
                York: Academic Press.
Ricoeur, Paul
    1977   *The rule of metaphor: Multi-disciplinary studies of the creation of
                meaning in language*. Toronto: University of Toronto Press. A
                translation by Robert Czerny of *La metaphore vive*.
Rudzka-Ostyn, Brygida (ed.)
    1988   *Topics in cognitive linguistics*. Amsterdam: John Benjamins.
Sacks, Sheldon (ed.)
    1979   *On metaphor*. Chicago: University of Chicago Press.
Turner, Mark
    1987   *Death is the mother of beauty: Mind, metaphor, criticism*. Chicago:
                University of Chicago Press.
    1988   "Categories and analogies", in: David H. Helman (ed.), *Analogical
                reasoning: Perspectives of Artificial Intelligence, Cognitive Science, and
                Philosophy*. Dordrecht: Kluwer Academic Publishers, 3-24.

The axiological parameter
in preconceptional image schemata

Tomasz P. Krzeszowski

0. Introduction

One of the most striking tenets of cognitive linguistics involves the obliteration of various traditionally recognized and, for many years unchallenged distinctions, for example between competence and performance, synchrony and diachrony, semantics and pragmatics, etc. (see Langacker 1983, and, especially with regard to the semantics/pragmatics opposition, Jackendoff 1983). Also the distinction between denotation and connotation (including various "emotive" aspects of meaning) has been suggested to be superfluous. So far, however, no extensive study pursuing this line of thinking within the context of cognitive linguistics has been conducted. The present paper constitutes a small fragment of a larger study of meaning, conducted within the framework of cognitive linguistics, and specifically employing the concept of idealized cognitive models (henceforth ICMs) as described by Lakoff (1987: 68ff). Lakoff's ICMs are used as a starting point for the development of a general theory of values as necessary components in the description of all aspects of human language, including various simple and complex forms at all levels of language functioning. The study of values with reference to the meaning of various linguistic expressions constitutes the scope of what might be called *axiological semantics*, whose task is to describe those values and the ways in which they determine both the structure and the functioning of human language as manifested in communication.

A major consequence of the adopted framework is the abandonment of the traditional myth of objectivism in approaches to linguistic semantics and the adoption of the experiential myth (for discussion and details see Lakoff & Johnson 1980: 185ff, Lakoff 1987: 196ff). One of the secondary consequences of adopting this framework is the obliteration of the distinction referred to above. More specifically, the adoption of the concept of ICMs renders it unnecessary to distinguish between denotation and connotation, without, however, ignoring any relevant linguistic facts and without losing any of the possible insights that this distinction might lead to.

The superfluity of this distinction in any description of meaning which resorts to ICMs should become obvious if one considers the following: since meanings of all words are defined relative to ICMs (Lakoff 1987: 790ff), denotationally identical words with different connotations will have to be defined relative to different ICMs, containing clusters of properties ideally characterizing meanings of those words. Such words as *cat*, *pussy*, *kitten*, *tom-cat*, and *mouser*, which, according to the traditional distinctions, differ with regard to their connotations but, presumably, have identical denotations, will be defined relative to different ICMs. This is best seen when a cartoonist is asked to draw pictures representing each variant of "a well-known carnivorous quadruped which has long been domesticated, being kept to destroy mice and as a house pet" (*The Oxford English dictionary*). Considerably different images will be obtained, each expressing the specific features constituting the corresponding ICM. In the light of this, the claim that these words are denotationally identical is also hard to defend. Although each picture will depict the animal called *cat*, this does not necessarily mean that the obvious differences between the particular pictures ought to be attributed to their different connotations. It seems that the relevant distinction involves the *level* at which the concepts <cat> and <pussy> are categorized. Specifically, <cat> is a *basic level* concept, while <pussy> is a concept formed at the *subordinate level* of categorization. It is difficult to see, though, how these differences in the level of categorization could be brought to bear on the possible distinctions between denotation and connotation, which in the framework of ICMs do not seem to have any relevance. Whatever properties characterize the "emotive" or "denotational" aspects of words must necessarily be present in the gestalt ICMs relative to which these words are defined. It is, morever, clear that just as in all other instances these ICMs define prototypical examples of particular categories at whatever level of categorization. Therefore, a prototypical cat may be different from a prototypical pussy, but the corresponding words will be defined relative to their specific ICMs. The respective ICMs must contain clusters of features (of whatever nature) which best describe the concepts of the respective animals as these concepts emerge through human sensory, motor, interactional and emotional experience. It is important to emphasize, however, that there is no reason why human emotional experience, necessarily present in the process of concept forming and eventually reflected in the resulting ICMs, should be separated from other sorts of experiences underlying the process of concept forming. Every kind of experience has its share in the process, and is somehow reflected in the resulting ICMs of those concepts.

In what follows I intend to investigate the aspect of ICMs which has traditionally fallen within the domain of connotation and "emotive" meaning and which has to do with the human experience of values. The study will trace values to their experiential grounding, which, as will be demonstrated, is rooted in a modified version of preconceptual image schemata as originally described in the works of Johnson (1987) and Lakoff (1987).

1. Preconceptual image schemata

Cognitive Linguistics approaches meaning experientially rather than objectively (see Lakoff 1982, 1987; Johnson 1987). Briefly speaking, this means that, whereas in objectivist approaches meaning is defined in abstraction from the nature and experience of human beings, in experientialist approaches meaning is *embodied* (Lakoff & Johnson 1980: 197ff; Lakoff 1987: 12ff). According to this view, meaning is structured partly in terms of "preconceptual" experience, which is itself structured and which gives rise to "conceptual" structure (Lakoff 1987: 267). Preconceptual bodily experiences give rise, on the one hand, to directly formed physical concepts, and, on the other hand, through metaphorical extensions, to abstract concepts formed indirectly but ultimately also grounded in and motivated by our bodily experience.

Johnson and Lakoff distinguish two kinds of structures defining preconceptual experiences:

(a)   Basic level structure
(b)   Kinaesthetic image schematic structure (Lakoff 1987: 267; Johnson 1987: 208ff)

(a)   Basic level structure is associated with basic level categories (cf. Rosch 1973, 1978) which are defined by human "gestalt" perception, capacity for bodily movement and ability to form "rich mental images". This latter concept is sharply distinguished from (b), i.e. from "image schemata", which are relatively simple structures constantly recurring in our everyday bodily experience. Basic level structures give rise to abstract concepts through projection to superordinate (and subordinate?) categories. We shall not concern ourselves with these projections in the present paper.

(b)   Kinaesthetic image schemata give rise to abstract concepts through *metaphorical projections* from physical to abstract domains. Among these schemata are CONTAINERS, PATHS, LINKS, FORCES, BALANCE as well as such orientations and relations as UP-DOWN, FRONT-BACK, PART-WHOLE, CENTER-PERIPHERY, and quite a few more. As a matter of fact, the number of various image schemata may not be fixed (cf. Johnson 1987: 126).

The basic claim put forward in this paper is that all preconceptual image schemata proposed by Johnson and Lakoff must incorporate an additional parameter which we would like to call PLUS-MINUS. Furthermore, we wish to suggest that this parameter is directly responsible for the dynamism of the metaphorization processes inherent in the formation of concepts based on the relevant schemata. Among these concepts are the abstract concepts of <good> and <bad>, <beauty> and <ugliness>, <truth> and <falsehood> as well as other concepts of varying degrees of abstraction and of varying degrees of axiological load. Before we elaborate this suggestion and provide some factual evidence, let us take a closer look at the very conceptual image schemata.

Johnson describe preconceptual image schemata as recurring patterns involved in "human bodily movement, manipulation of objects, and perceptual interactions"; without these patterns "our experience would be chaotic and incomprehensible" (Johnson 1987: xxxvi). On the one hand, he emphasizes the fact that these image schemata are not propositional in the sense used in objectivist semantics, but rather they have analog nature. On the other hand, image schemata cannot be identified with rich, concrete images or mental pictures as psychic reflections of the elements of the real world or as elements of some imagined world.

In what follows, I wish to show that each image schema is activated by the fundamental dynamism PLUS-MINUS, as a vector built into each schema. Considering several examples, I shall try to show how in each case the fundamental PLUS-MINUS dynamism present in a particular image schema is manifested in conventional as well as unconventional (creative) linguistic expressions grounded in that schema and how the dynamism is reinforced by corresponding metaphorical projections (see also Krzeszowski in press).

Among many other schemata Lakoff (1987) and Johnson (1987) distinguish the following kinaesthetic image schemata:

2.   The PART - WHOLE schema

This schema is connected with the experience of our own bodies as organized WHOLES consisting of PARTS. We experience WHOLE as *positive*, and consequently, on a more abstract level as *good*. The most fundamental experience of WHOLE is being in ONE PIECE, when nothing is missing of the canonical shape of one's body. The human *hand* is also experienced as a *whole* consisting of structurally and functionally interrelated *parts*: fingers, the thumb, joints, nails, etc. The human hand as the most rudimentary tool and weapon is also a realization of a unitary structure and is experienced as such rather than as disparate parts. Losing a limb or an organ is experienced as a LACK, hence as *negative* and ultimately as *bad*.

Consistent with this fundamental axiology are such conventional linguistic expressions as: positive: *to keep body and soul together* 'to stay alive', *to come back in one piece, to be whole and sound*; negative: *to fall apart, to fall to pieces, to desintegrate*, etc.

It is also interesting to note that the words *health* and *whole* derive from the same Old English root, viz. *hāl*, meaning 'whole', whereas such notoriously negatively charged words as *devil* and *idiot* are derived from Greek words meaning 'set at variance' and 'separate, isolated', respectively.

Certain reinforcing, secondary experiences are consistent with this basic axiology. Putting things together in order to *construct a whole*, for example, building a house, writing a poem, ie. putting words *together* when *com-posing* it, is experienced as good. Conversely *de-struction* typically involves ruining the organized whole and depriving it of its canonical shape. Therefore, ruining a thing, destroying an organized structure, disintegrating a system are experienced as bad. These negative and positive experiences are reflected in various conventional and unconventional linguistic forms, all of which undergo metaphorical extensions, which intensify the axiological load in accordance with the axiological principle (Krzeszowski in press). Thus there exist such positive concepts, relating to things and processes (cf. Langacker 1983, II: 96ff, 157ff), as *totality, integrity, ensemble, collectiveness, unity, completeness, integration, render complete, fill, charge, load, replenish, make up, supply deficiencies, fill up, perfect and complete, unabridged*, and many others. Conversely, there exists a host of negative concepts based on the minus pole of the schema, such as *decomposition, decay, rot, putrefaction, decompose, disembody, break up, break down, distintegrate, disperse, crumble into dust, disjoined, come off, fall off, fall to pieces, get loose, detach, unfasten, separate, cut off, segregate, set/keep apart, insulate, isolate,* etc. Many of these negative concepts refer to the process and/or the result of depriving things of their canonical shape.

There are other schemata which are also grounded in the experience of our bodies as structures and which are endowed with analogous axiological vectors. The most productive are the CENTER - PERIPHERY schema and the LINK schema.

3.   The CENTER - PERIPHERY schema

This schema, like the previous one, is also primarily grounded in our experience of the human body and its various parts, some of which are central while others are increasingly peripheral. The most central parts are the trunk and various internal organs; ther peripheral parts include fingers, toes, fingernails, hair, and to a certain extent various limbs. The basic axiology which emerges from this schema can be summarized as "the more peripheral, the less good". Thus, too long hair, too long fingernails require cutting and trimming. Cutting off involves separating excessively long peripheries - it will be recalled that the word *evil* is related to the concept of excess. Thus, the axiology of the CENTER - PERIPHERY schema interacts with the axiology of the BALANCE schema (see below) and is consistent with the basic principles of axiology which we shall return to in a subsequent section. At this point, let us only note that in the context of the CENTER-PERIPHERY schema this logic is consistent with the positive value of expressions such as *cut off*, which in terms of other schemata assume negative values.

The schema provides experiential grounding for the concept of < good > in the sense 'just right', 'not too big and not too small', 'fitting'. It also provides experiential grounding for the original sense of the word *evil* as 'excessive'.

The CENTER - PERIPHERY schema is further reinforced by such secondary experiences as pruning trees, trimming hedges, cutting hair and nail, and by such conventions as placing important things and persons in the center. It is in this position that chairs for chairpersons, monarchs and other priviledged persons are situated. By contrast, less important things and persons are conventionally placed less centrally. Thus, the schema motivates various linguistic and non-linguistic conventions which, in turn, provide secondary reinforcement for the experiences in which this schema is inherent.

Among linguistic expressions consistent with this schema we find such positively loaded ones as *he is in the middle of things, he occupies the central position in our cultural life, center-piece,* etc. and such negative ones as *this is of peripheral/marginal importance, social margin, he comes from the margin of society, their activities are of marginal importance,* etc.

4.   The LINK schema

The primary bodily experience of the LINK schema involves the umbilical cord. Being linked to one's mother provides not only security but also means of acquiring energy and hence life from a source to which one is linked. This fundamentally positive value of the original link is later projected to other kinds of human links, including the act of copulation as transmission of life, as well as to various social links such as marriage, community, peer groups, etc. Therefore, human beings have a deep-rooted tendency to form links. Being alone is considered pathological in most societies. Having no connections in professional life is usually detrimental to one's progress and advancement. The LINK schema (together with the PART-WHOLE schema) underlies such positive concepts as *unity* and its negative counterpart *lack of unity*. This basic axiology is manifested in such positive expressions as *the common interest that unites our countries, let us unite in fighting poverty and disease, united means joined in spirit by love and sympathy, they form a perfectly united family, they live in a perfect union,* and many others. The ideas expressed in the formation of the *United* States, the *United* Nations and various other political unions originally also involve highly positive values. On the contrary <lack of unity> and various related concepts are inevitably negative. Among them are *disunion, divergence, disagreement, difference, incongruity, discord,* and many others.

Various words associated with the LINK schema collocate naturally with other positive concepts, possibly based on other image schemata. For example, in the sentence:

(1)   *The boy* connected *the garden hose to the water faucet.*

the positive value of the PART - WHOLE schema combines with the positive value of the LINK schema. *Connecting* the hose to the faucet enables the hose to operate usefully by creating a functional WHOLE consisting of interrelated parts: garden-hose, water-faucet, water. Notice the contrast present in such expressions as (2) and (3):

(2)   *In order to make it useful, the boy* connected *the hose*
         to the water faucet.
(3)   *?In order to make it useful, the boy* disconnected *the hose*
         from the water faucet.

Whereas (2) as an "out-of-the-blue sentence" contains nothing that
calls for an additional explanation, (3) sounds odd and requires
reorientation of values to achieve its communicative goal. This
reorientation somehow has to be overtly expressed if communication is
to be successfully sustained. Briefly speaking, in the case of (3), the
reorientation would involve attributing to the normally negative word
useless some positive value relative to some specific hierarchy of values
subscribed to by the speaker either temporarily or permanently, but
different from the hierarchy conventionally expected in this situation.
Hence one can expect a sentence like *I don't quite understand what you*
mean as a reaction to (3), whereupon its speaker is obliged to offer
some explanation, for example, *Oh, yes! He's going to use it as a towing-*
line; his car has broken down and we haven't got any rope around here. In
this case the reorientation of values is temporary and involves change in
the funtional utility of a garden hose; on this particular occasion it can
serve usefully only if disconnected from the faucet. Whatever happens,
the axiological clash possibly present in (3) turns out to be only
apparent. If no additional explanation is offered, communication breaks
down. No such possibility is imminent in (2).

The axiology grounded in the LINK schema is closely connected with
the CONTAINER schema, and particularly with its BODY-IN-THE
CONTAINER version. Therefore, we shall discuss some of the ensuing
problems jointly in the section devoted to the CONTAINER schema
inasmuch as the experience of being born is associated both with cutting
the umbilical cord and with emerging from a container. Both these
experiences provide experiential grounding for such abstract concepts
as <freedom> and <bondage>.

5.   The CONTAINER schema

We experience our bodies both as containers and as things *in* containers
(Lakoff 1987: 271ff, Johnson 1987: 21ff). Therefore, the CONTAINER
schema has two variants based on those two kinds of experience. We
shall respectively refer to them as the BODY-AS-A-CONTAINER schema

and the BODY-IN-A-CONTAINER schema. Since the axiologies emerging from these two variants partially overlap, but are to some extent different, we shall describe the two variants separately.

The fundamental experiences associated with the BODY-AS-A-CONTAINER schema are *breathing* and *eating*. Both air, which we breathe IN, and food, which we take IN, are indispensable as sources of life-sustaining energy. Therefore, the orientation INTO associated with these experiences is necessarily positive. In its canonical shape the human body contains only things which are necessary and which contribute to its well-being, i.e. to its health. We, moreover, tend to introduce into our bodies only things which we consider as contributions to our well-being, while we tend to reject and get rid of things which we consider as harmful; such things are discharged or thrown OUT. Breathing out and excretion as experiences opposite to those of breathing in and eating are necessarily associated with negative values grounded in the orientation OUT. However, since the CONTAINER schema has two variants, the related axiology is not always directly connected with just these two orientations. Moreover, the CONTAINER schemata often enter into complex relations with other schemata. Therefore, we shall refrain from providing linguistic examples illustrating this axiology until we have presented and discussed the other variant and some possible combinations of the CONTAINER schemata with other schemata.

The BODY-IN-THE-CONTAINER variant of the CONTAINER schema is associated with a less straightforward axiology inasmuch as it provides experiential grounding for the fundamental dialectics of values which extends to what might be called *axiological dynamism*. As Johnson (1987: 30f) and Lakoff (1987: 271ff) rightly point out, we constantly experience our bodies as objects *in* containers or objects going *into* containers and coming *out* of containers. However, the primary experience associated with the container schema is that of being in our mother's womb, which is the first container that we ever find ourselves in. Birth is primarily experienced as *getting out* of that container. The axiological dialectics is grounded in the contradictory values attributed to and associated with being in and getting out of this original container. On the one hand, we experience getting out of the container as being born and as gaining freedom, becoming independent, etc. On the other hand, getting out of the original container may be experienced as leaving the security of the protective confines of a SHELTER and being exposed to various external dangers. Therefore, we often long to *return* to some protective container. Consequently, the PLUS - MINUS parameter in this version of the CONTAINER schema is not systematically correlated with the two orientations IN - OUT. The changing values of the two poles in this orientation promote the continual dialectical struggle of good and evil, which also constitutes one of our basic experiences. This sort of dialectics is additionally reinforced by the axiological status of the LINK schema. When we are born, we get OUT of the original CONTAINER, and at the same time the umbilical cord, our first LINK, is broken. In this way, both getting out of our mother's womb and severing the umbilical cord constitute primary experiences of acquiring freedom. The concept of <freedom> is therefore ultimately grounded in the experience of being born.

However, the LINK is only physically broken. On the social level it continues to exist as we still very much depend on our parents for both food and protection within the bounds of the family, which we begin to conceive metaphorically as a SHELTER. We live by the metaphor FAMILY IS A SHELTER or perhaps even FAMILY IS A WOMB. Further in life, we form new links and enter new containers: friendships, peer groups, marriage, our own family, etc., and our freedom is constrained by new links and new containers. Thus, the dialectical struggle grounded in this primary axiological experience continues within us: on the one hand, we wish to be free, and we consider freedom to be among the most outstanding positive values, while, on the other hand, we willingly impose constraints on our freedom to obtain security and protection.

This oscillating axiology is reflected in certain language conventions: we use such negatively loaded words as *break* (*breaking the umbilical cord*) and *leave* (*leaving the womb*) to refer to the definitely positive event of birth. All the same, the negative aspect clearly inherent in leaving the secure shelter of our mother's womb can easily be detected in our unconscious lifelong struggle for the "paradise lost" which we somehow feel we have been *ex*pelled from and to which we hope to return either in this life or in some future existence. The archetype of "paradise lost" present in many mythologies and religions must somehow be grounded in these basic experiences of birth as leaving a CONTAINER. This is why we continually strive for something better, which we somehow feel we have lost and which we wish to regain. Therefore, being IN is ultimately experienced as good as long as it refers to natural, canonical situations, which are by their very nature good. For the same reason, *returning* is usually positively charged. The archetype of return is realized in such myths and biblical stories as Ulysses' return to Ithaca, the return of the prodigal son, and the Christian concept of the return to Eden as a metaphor of salvation, which are all instantiations of the same RETURN schema with the positively loaded IN orientation. The conventional association of IN with the positive value and of OUT with the negative one is reflected in numerous contrasting linguistic expressions, such as *in business - out of business*; *in work - out of work*; *in favor - out of favor*; *in one's (right) mind - out of mind; within reach - out of reach; within having - out of having; coffee is in - we are out of coffee*; *in sight - out of sight*; *the Democrats are in - the Republicans are out*; *you are in (the game) - you are out*; also *out!* (arch. exclamation of indignation and reproach); *fire is out* (if canonical fire under human control is meant).

Briefly speaking, the axiology which emerges from the BODY-AS-A-CONTAINER versions of the schema is generally stable and straightforward, being well motivated in our experience of the orientation IN as positive and OUT as negative. The axiology stemming from the BODY-IN-THE-CONTAINER version is less stable inasmuch as the assignment of values in this version of the schema may depend on a number of factors, such as other schemata which may interact with the CONTAINER schema as well as the value of the container itself; if the container, for example home, is positively charged, being IN it is also positively charged; if the container, for example prison, is negatively charged, being IN it is also negatively charged. (Various details, examples, apparent exceptions and certain principles of axiology are discussed at length in Krzeszowski, forthcoming.)

6.   The SOURCE-PATH-GOAL schema

This schema is connected with the concept of oriented motion, i.e. changing position in space from an initial place called SOURCE to a destination called GOAL along a PATH. The schema underlies the abstract metaphorical positively valued concept of <purpose>, which is grounded in our experience of reaching a goal. The schema also involves a number of implications which have axiological relevance. Since oriented motion is a necessary condition of reaching a goal, purposeful motion is also positively valued, while motionlessness is negatively valued. Both these evaluations are manifested in various more or less conventional expressions such as *Actions speak louder than words, we poets are the movers and shakers of the world* (A.W.E. O'Shaughnessy). On the other hand, *being out of action* is usually described in negative terms. For example, *The world book encyclopedia dictionary* describes *out of action* as 'not operating or working, especially because of *damage* [emphasis my own]' and *idle* as 'useless, worthless: without any *good* [emphasis my own] reason, cause, or foundation'. Furthermore, the same dictionary describes one of the senses of the word *goal*, inherently connected with purposeful motion, as 'a thing for which effort is made: thing wanted'. *The Random House dictionary of the English language* describes *aim* as 'something intended or desired to be attained by one's efforts: purpose'. These descriptions are remarkable for the resemblance they bear to the definition of the word *good* in one of its senses: 'such as should be desired or approved'. Thus, it turns out that in certain senses *goal* and *good* are nearly synonymous, which shows the fundamentally positive charge of the concept <goal>.

In view of this, it is not surprising that the word *goal* and its synomyms, without special qualifications to the contrary, tend to appear in the contexts of words with a high positive charge, for example: *The goal of his ambition was to be a great doctor* (*The world book encyclopedia dictionary*). *Their paintings have a freshness and vitality - above all a consistency of purpose* (*New Yorker*). While GOAL and, consequently, its various linguistic exponents usually receive positive value (unless specifically and explicitly marked otherwise), PATH can receive both positive and negative value depending on additional conditions. Since reaching a GOAL involves oriented motion along a PATH, and since GOAL is valued positively, it follows that in most situations the PATH which is the shortest is the best inasmuch as it most expediently allows one to reach the desired goal. Therefore a *straight* path is valued more highly than a *twisted* one. Expectedly, the concept <straight> and the word *straight* with its synonyms grounded in the S-P-G schema have a high positive charge. Consequently, we have such positive words and expressions as *direct, undeviating, unswerving, straightforward, even, right, true, in a line, unbent, undistorted, straight as an arrow*, etc. We also have such negatively charged words and expressions as *curved, devious, bowed, vaulted, crooked, oblique, twisted, warped, diverted, aberration, drift, zig-zag, detour, wandering, vagrancy, swerve, deflect, divert from its course, divagate, meander, go astray, go adrift*, and many others.

7. The BALANCE schema

Maintaining the balance of the body in action constitutes such a funda-mental experience that we are normally unaware of balance until we lose it and strive to restore it. We directly experience balance when we walk on a narrow pavement, when we cycle, or when we try to juggle. Walking on a rope is a limiting case in the experience of balance, when our sense of equilibrium is tested and we become sharply aware of both its quality and its importance. We also experience other things as being "out of balance", whenever there is "too much" or "not enough" in comparison with what we feel to be the normal, canonical organization of forces, processes and elements (cf. Johnson 1987: 75). Our bodily response to such imbalance involves adding heat to our hands, moistening our mouth, draining the bladder, breathing more rapidly, drinking liquids when we are thirsty, etc. until we restore balance. The sense of balance is not something that can be described in terms of rules; therefore, the meaning of balance emerges only through acts of balancing and through the experience associated with these acts.[1]

Through bodily experience, the BALANCE schema is related to the UP-DOWN schema and to the SOURCE-PATH-GOAL schema: when we LOSE BALANCE we fall DOWN and are unable to move FORWARD and reach the GOAL, while MAINTAINING BALANCE allows us to retain the UPWARD vertical position and continue FORWARD towards the GOAL. Therefore, expectedly, BALANCE and all the associated concepts receive positive axiological charge, while IMBALANCE is evaluated negatively.[2]

The BALANCE schema permeates our experience of the world and is present in all walks of our physical and spiritual life. Johnson distinguishes various kinds of balance, including systemic balance, psychological balance and mathematical balance (equality). Thus the balance schema appears to be the central schema providing grounds for various ethical and aesthetic concepts. Among others, it directly motivates that sense of *good* which can be spelled out as 'having the right or desired qualities', which in fact means 'balanced with regard to the relevant properties, not excessive in any direction'. This fundamental sense of the word *good*, related to the BALANCE schema, is manifested in the form *not too...* meaning 'just right', when referring to values at the sensory level (see Krzeszowski in press). Thus, at that level, coffee may be good if it is not too sweet, a bed is good if it is not too hard or too soft, and soup is usually good if it is neither too cold nor too hot. In those cases the word *too* is a linguistic exponent of negative values and expresses axiological reorientation of otherwise positively charged adjectives. It must be noted that concepts at higher levels of the hierarchy of values are less prone to deterioration expressed by *too*. Therefore, in such collocations as *too happy, too honest, too loving,* or *too good* the word *too* brings about a different effect. Such collocations often appear in conventional phrases, for example, *too good to be true*. In any event, they evoke a lower level of the hierarchy of values, as in *he is too honest to survive in this world, she was too happy to notice the frown on his face, his wife is too good to him*. Without changing the positive axiological load of the corresponding adjective, *too* suggests some lower level of values, optionally specified by the infinitival phrase, compared to which the qualities expressed by the adjective are evaluated as excessive; though in absolute terms, one cannot talk about excess of happiness, honesty, love or goodness. Thus, in collocation with adjectives expressing higher, spiritual values, *too* acquires roughly the meaning 'in excess for a particular purpose with some negative aspect either overtly expressed or hidden'. For example, *survival in this world* (positive at the level of vital values) requires some dishonesty, while *frown* (negative value) expresses unpleasant emotions, etc.

There are a number of conventional expressions associated with the concept of <balance> with a high degree of axiological charge. For example, one of the figurative senses in which the word *balance* is used is conventionally connected with the metaphor BALANCE IS A VALU-ABLE OBJECT realized by such expressions as *his mental balance was remarkable, she is a very well-balanced person, to strike a balance between*. In all these contexts the word *balance* denotes 'mental steadiness, poise'. Other senses of the word *balance* are consistent with this positive axiology, as in *a balanced composition* denoting a harmonious and orderly composition in contrast to the negatively valued messy and disorderly one; *a balanced diet* denotes correct amounts of all kinds of food necessary for *good health*. The word *symmetry* is consistently defined as '*pleasing* proportions between the parts of a whole, *well*-balanced arrangement of parts'.

Consistently, *imbalance* and its synonyms are inevitably negatively valued, which is manifested in various conventional expressions such as *lose one's balance*, described as being synonymous with *fall to the ground, stick in the mud, run aground, break down, be upset, lose poise*, etc.

8.   The ORIENTATIONAL schemata

Orientational schemata are directly related to the structure and functioning of the human body in its canonical form, i.e. the shape in which it presents itself at its best and can function most effectively. The basic orientations are defined by the way in which human bodies are oriented in the three dimensional and temporal world.

9.   The UP-DOWN orientation

The canonical form best represents our membership in the human species. In its canonical shape the human body is directed *upwards*. This is how man is depicted in anatomical atlases, this is how he stands in front of recruiting boards, and this is how he stands at attention. Man also *grows* upwards. *Growing upwards* appears to be our primary positive experience associated with the orientation UP. Naturally enough, there is also an abundance of supporting socio-cultural experience: when we are healthy, when we feel well, we stand erect with our heads *lifted* and our faces *up*turned. We greet friends with *up*lifted hands. Our thumb directed *up*wards is a sign that everything is fine. Last but not least, through our mouths, situated in the upper part of our bodies, we take in nourishment which sustains our life. In this way the UP orientation is reinforced in its positive value with the IN orientation of the CONTAINER schema. A smile as an expression of joy and happiness involves *upward* curving of the corners of the mouth.

Conversely, when we are ill and when we die, we *stoop* to the ground, where we rest after death. We defecate through the hole situated in the *lower* part of our body, disposing of *harmful* and/or *useless* substances. Expectedly, the orientation DOWN is charged with negative values and, thus, the direction *downwards* signifies evil; our thumb pointing downwards means that things have assumed a bad turn; when our head sinks down we are sad, we feel defeated and miserable. Grimaces and crying as expressions of pain and sorrow involve *downward* curving of the lips.

Innumerable linguistic expressions illustrate the two opposing poles of this axiology. We have such positively charged expressions as *he has risen to the top, you're in high spirits, you've grown in my eyes, this is a heart-lifting moment, it was a top performance*, etc. By contrast, we associate what is negative and bad with the orientation DOWN: *He is depressed, he fell into a depression, he fell ill, he came down with flu, he dropped dead, he fell into the abyss of depravity*, and many more.

Consequently, various metaphorical concepts, such as <joy> and <love> are understood in terms of the orientation UP, and they necessarily assume positive values, while such concepts as <sorrow>

and <hatred>, understood through the orientation DOWN, assume negative values.

10.   The FRONT-BACK orientation

Because of the structure of the human body, the FRONT-BACK schema is related to the UP-DOWN schema. Due to evolutionary processes, at some stage of his development, man assumed the erect position as a result of which what was originally FRONT (the head) became also UP without actually ceasing to be FRONT (human face). Similarly, what was BACK became DOWN without ceasing to be BACK. Actually, in many languages, the *lower, rear* part of the human body is referred to by means of various words related to the concept <back> (cf. Pol. *tyłek, zadek*, Cz. *zadnica*, Fr. *derrière*, and English both *backside* and *bottom*). This anatomical affinitiy of UP and FRONT and of BACK and DOWN is well seen in both the parallel axiology of these orientations and in the linguistic convention whereby UP and FRONT, on the one hand, as well as BACK and DOWN, on the other, jointly embrace the same orientation, for example, in *Will you please move up front?* and *Come up here to the front.*

FRONT has a defintely positive value due to the fact that the fundamental experience connected with this orientation is the experience of the human face, the most representative part of the human body. As Lakoff and Johnson (1980: 37) point out, we often metonymically identify human face with entire person in photographs, portraits, etc. We have a natural tendency to present ourselves at our best, and, since our face metonymically represents our entire selves, all concepts associated with this part of our body naturally assume positive values.

The orientation FRONT is based on yet another fundamental experience, entailing a whole cluster of concepts with positive associations which further reinforce the basic axiology of the orientation FRONT. When we move along a PATH towards a GOAL (positive), we canonically move FORWARD (positive) in the direction of our line of vision (positive).

These two fundamental experiences of the FRONT orientation are supported by a number of socio-cultural conventions reinforcing the positive axiology of this orientation; front portions of buildings are usually finer and more decorative as opposed to their back sides. The front sides are better exposed and often illuminated. Models of new cars are usually presented from the front or side but never to display their rears. The front seats in theaters are considered to be the best. The front position in various racing events is considered the best both at the start and, most certainly, at the goal. There are countless other situations in which the front position is deemed the most privileged and the most important. Among many senses of the word *front* we find two metaphorical senses in which the positive value is increased in accordance with the axiological principle (Krzeszowski in press): 1. 'an outward appearance of *wealth, importance,* etc.' 2. 'a person appointed to add respectability or prestige to an enterprise' (*The world book encyclopedia dictionary*).

The negative value attributed to the BACK orientation is equally well motivated in our fundamental experience. The back parts of our bodies are certainly less representative of us as human beings. Our rear parts provide ample reference for various derogatory or plainly filthy terms in various languages. Unless we are nudists, our lower and back parts are usually covered and hidden from sight. Showing one's rear to another person is an expression of utmost contempt. In many languages various words referring to those parts of the body are metonymically used to designate persons with definitely negative qualities.

A large number of conventional linguistic expressions with distinctly negative axiological charge are motivated by our experience of the BACK orientation. Among them we find: *to talk behind one's back, to be on one's back* 'to be sick and helpless', *to make one's back up, to turn one's back on somebody, backcountry, backdoor, backset, backwards, backwash,* etc.

11.   The RIGHT-LEFT orientation

Most people are right-handed, which means that they use their right hand to work, fight, write and perform countless other activities. The right hand is usually the more dexterous and stronger one. The predominance of the right hand in performing these activities constitutes the primary experience connected with the orientation RIGHT. This primary experience motivates the fundamentally positive axiology associated with the orientation RIGHT.

As in the case of other schemata, there is also ample secondary, socio-cultural experience supporting this axiology. By social convention, we hold out our right hand to greet other people and to shake hands with them, and if we are Christians, we cross ourselves with our right hand. Many dictionaries define the word *right* with reference to the right hand. For example, *The concise Oxford dictionary* defines *right* as 'having relation to front & back that equinoctical sunrise has to north & south, on or towards that side of human body of which the hand is *normally more used* [emphasis is my own], on or towards that part of an object which is analogous to person's [right] side or (with opposite sense) which is nearer to the spectator's [right] hand'. Interestingly enough, the same dictionary defines *right hand* as 'the better hand'.

The most fundamental positive experience connected with the right hand is that of *providing*: most people work and eat using their right hand. Primeval man killed game with his right hand, worked on the tools with his right hand and introduced food into his mouth with his right hand. Through eating, the orientation RIGHT is naturally linked with the orientations IN, UP and FRONT, as a result of which the positive axiology associated with these orientations is remarkably coherent and consistent, being grounded in fundamental human bodily experience. Consequently, the word *right* embraces a number of highly positive senses such as 'morally good', 'required by law or duty', 'true', 'correct', 'satisfactory', etc.[3]

The word *right* has a strong tendency to appear in expressions carrying a very high positive axiological load. Note that in many of these examples the positive axiology of the orientation RIGHT is consistent with the positive axiology of the orientations FRONT, UP and BALANCE which are often combined in a single linguistic expression: *right arm/hand* 'one's most reliable helper', *the right man in the right place*, *Mr./Miss Right* 'destined husband or wife', *the right side of the fabric* 'that meant for show or use', with the co-occurring orientation FRONT, *right side up* (with the co-occuring orientation UP), *to be in one's right mind*, *to right oneself* 'to recover BALANCE', and many others.

In comparison with English, in many languages, including Polish, this tendency is much more conspicuously present in the linguistic convention. For details see Krzeszowski (in press). However, it is interesting to observe that the central, early sense of *left* was 'weak, worthless', even if the ultimate origins of the word are unknown. In Modern English, too, the word often appears in negatively loaded expressions such as *over the left shoulder* 'what is said is to be interpreted by contraries', or *left-handed compliment* 'a compliment of doubtful sincerity'.

The figurative senses of the expression *left-handed*, as listed in *The concise Oxford dictionary*, include 'awkward, clumsy, ambiguous, double-edged, ill-omened, sinister, of doubtful sincerity or validity' (esp. *left compliment*). *Left marriage* means 'fictitious marriage'. Note, too, that the words *dexterous* and *sinister* are derived from Latin words denoting right and left, respectively.

12.   Some preconceptual axiological principles

The preconceptual image schemata enriched by the axiological vectors introduced above are associated with the following preconceptual axiological principles:

1. Image schemata are bi-polar, i.e. they have a plus pole and a minus pole.
2. Being is plus, not being is minus; negation is fundamentally experienced as LACK.
3. WHOLE, CENTER, LINK, IN, GOAL, UP, FRONT, RIGHT are plus; PART, PERIPHERY, NO LINK, OUT, NO GOAL, DOWN, BACK, LEFT are minus.
4. BALANCE is plus, IMBALANCE is minus.
5. In their canonical form all things are plus, because they are in the state of BALANCE.
6. When OFF BALANCE everything tends to RESTORE BALANCE.
7. When IN BALANCE everything is prone to LOSE BALANCE.
8. 6 and 7 underlie the dialectical struggle between plus and minus, positive and negative, and, on the conceptual level between <good> and <bad>, as basic axiological concepts.

13.   Some basic axiological concepts

Axiological concepts emerge from the axiological poles of preconceptual image schemata through metaphorical extensions. Concepts with a positive and negative axiological load emerge, respectively, from the plus and minus poles of the schemata. Thus, such basic axiological concepts as <good>, <beautiful>, <true>, <bad>, <ugly>, <false> emerge from preconceptual image schemata in accordance with the principles outlined above. Although positive concepts are all grounded in the plus poles of preconceptual image schemata, they are based on different clusters of experiences, highlighting different schemata as experiential foundation for different concepts. The concepts of <good> and <bad> appear to be the most general of all axiological concepts inasmuch as, on the one hand, they are least context-sensitive and have the largest scope of application, and, on the other hand, they can emerge from practically all preconceptual image schemata and refer to values at all levels of the axiological hierarchy. However, the two concepts are by no means parallel. It follows from Principle 1 above that <bad> can be defined relative to <good>, but not vice versa; since the experience of <bad> is grounded in the experience of <lack>, things can be "bad" only to the extent to which they are "not good". This relation between the two concepts provides strong motivation for various linguistic conventions, whereby negatively charged concepts are much more likely to be linguistically expressed by means of derived forms, involving the addition of various exponents of negation to bases with a positive axiological charge. Therefore, we have regular and highly productive word formation processes yielding such forms as *un*happy, *dis*satisfied, *im*moral, *in*justice, or *dis*pleasure. The opposite direction is extremely rare if at all encountered, while parallel independent forms such as *good - bad*, *life - death*, or *health - illness* are highly unpredictable and certainly non-productive.[4]

Appendix

All of the image schemata discussed above and their associated axiologies can be summarized as follows:

WHOLE-PART

Basic positive experience: integrity of human body, integrity of human hand
Basic negative experience: losing a limb or an organ
Supporting positive experience: building houses, constructing machines, writing poems
Supporting negative experience: ruining houses, dismantling machines, burning books, etc.
Connection with other schemata: LINK as inherently present in PARTS forming a WHOLE

CENTER-PERIPHERY

Basic positive experience: central parts of human body (vital)
Basic negative experience: peripheral parts of human body (less vital or not vital)
Supporting positive experience: priviledged places, thrones, chairs situated centrally
Supporting negative experience: cutting nails, hair; less privileged places situated more peripherally

LINK - NO LINK

Basic positive experience: the umbilical cord
Basic negative experience: abortion, beheading (?)
Supporting positive experience: copulation, marriage, family, society, human communication
Supporting negative experience: loneliness, isolation, lack of connections, lack of communication
Connection with other schemata: BODY-IN-THE-CONTAINER, WHOLE-PART.

CONTAINER

a) BODY-AS-A-CONTAINER

Basic positive experience: breathing in, eating
Basic negative experience: breathing out, excretion
Supporting positive experience: ?
Supporting negative experience: ?
Connection with other schemata: IN-OUT, LINK, WHOLE-PART

b) BODY-IN-A-CONTAINER

Basic positive experience: being in mother's womb, being born
Basic negative experience: leaving mother's womb
Supporting positive experience: being in a shelter, at home, etc.
Supporting negative experience: being in prison, in a cage, etc.
Connection with other schemata: IN-OUT, LINK, WHOLE-PART

BALANCE - IMBALANCE

Basic positive experience: various physiological processes involved in metabolism, walking, running, riding, as well as mental balance manifested in orderly behavior
Basic negative experience: disorders of metabolism, falling down, as well as mental imbalance manifested in *disorderly* behavior.
Supporting positive experience: beauty
Supporting negative experience: ugliness
Connection with other schemata: UP-DOWN

ORIENTATIONS

a) UP-DOWN

Basic positive experience: growing, being alive and well
Basic negative experience: being ill, dying, being buried
Supporting positive experience: head uplifted, greetings, triumphant gestures, thumb upwards, smile

Supporting negative experience: head sinking, gestures of defeat, thumb downwards, grimace
Connection with other schemata: FRONT-BACK

b) FRONT-BACK

Basic positive experience: human face, movement forward
Basic negative experience: human back
Supporting positive experience: fronts of things more representative (prettier, cleaner, etc.) than their backs
Supporting negative experience: back parts of things less representative (sloppier, dirtier, etc.) than their fronts, exhaust pipes usually situated at backs of engines, etc.
Connection with other schemata: UP-DOWN, IN-OUT

c) RIGHT-LEFT

Basic positive experience: right hand more dexterous and more active
Basic negative experience: left hand less dexterous and less active
Supporting positive experience: providing, work
Supporting negative experience: left hand often used for "filthy" actions
Connection with other schemata: BALANCE, UP and IN through the concept of PROVIDING.

Notes

1.   For details concerning particular versions of the BALANCE schema see Johnson (1987: 85ff).
2.   In the present paper we do not elaborate the relationship between the BALANCE schema and the metaphorical concept of <beauty> grounded in this schema, but see Krzeszowski (forthcoming).
3.   We have no room to discuss motivations underlying the labels *left* and *right* as they refer to political orientations and the often conflicting axiologies inherent in various ICMs relative to which these orientations are defined. More is said on this issue in Krzeszowski (to appear).
4.   For more details and more examples see Krzeszowski (in press).

References

Johnson, Mark
    1987   *The body in the mind: The bodily basis of meaning, imagination, and reason*. Chicago: University of Chicago Press.
Jackendoff, Ray
    1983   *Semantics and cognition*. Cambridge: MIT Press.
Krzeszowski, Tomasz P.
    in press   "The axiological aspect of idealized cognitive models". To appear in: Jerzy Tomaszczyk & Barbara Lewandowska-Tomaszczyk (eds.).

Krzeszowski, Tomasz P.
  to appear   *Elements of axiological semantics*.
Lakoff, George
  1982   "Categories and cognitive models". Linguistic Agency University of
               Trier, Series A, No. 96.
  1987   *Women, fire, and dangerous things: What categories reveal about the
               mind*. Chicago: University of Chicago Press.
Lakoff, George & Mark Johnson
  1980   *Metaphors we live by*. Chicago: University of Chicago Press.
Langacker, Ronald W.
  1983   *Foundations of cognitive grammar*, parts I+II. Linguistic Agency
               University of Trier, Series A, Nos. 99-100.
Rosch, Eleanor
  1973   "Natural categories", *Cognitive Psychology* 4: 328-350.
  1978   "Principles of categorization", in: Eleanor Rosch & Barbara B. Lloyd
               (eds.), *Cognition and categorization*. Hillsdale, N.J.: Lawrence
               Erlbaum, 27-48.
Tomaszczyk, Jerzy & Barbara Lewandowska-Tomaszczyk (eds.)
  in press   *Meaning and lexicography*. Amsterdam: John Benjamins.

Value judgment in the metaphorization of linguistic action

Paul Pauwels
Anne-Marie Simon-Vandenbergen

0. Preliminaries

0.1. Scope: background and corpus

This paper has its origin in an inter-university research project sponsored by the Belgian Scientific Fund.[1] The aim of the project is to study the metaphorization of linguistic action, using a corpus of some 2,000 metaphorical expressions drawn from the *Longman dictionary of contemporary English* (1982). (For a description of the corpus, see Vanparys forthc.) We here wish to concentrate on one small portion of the corpus, viz. on those metaphors which originate in the conceptual domain of "body parts". These are metaphors which either contain explicit names of parts of the body or refer to processes in which body parts are implicit but play a central role. The restricted corpus consists of 177 items.

0.2. Aims

The view of metaphor we subscribe to has been outlined in Lakoff & Johnson (1980) and Johnson (1987). Metaphor is not merely another non-congruent way of referring to phenomena (processes and participants), but rather an important mode of understanding and a way of structuring experience. The concepts used in metaphorization are "concepts for natural kinds of experience and objects [which] are structured clearly enough and with enough of the right kind of internal structure to do the job of defining other concepts [which] are less concrete or less clearly delineated in their own terms" (Lakoff & Johnson 1980: 118). One important function of metaphor is then to structure abstract domains by means of projections from more concrete domains.[2] The domain of body parts and bodily functions is one such structured concrete domain. The study of metaphors of linguistic action which refer to parts of the body and their functioning may thus contribute to a clearer understanding of how physical experience is projected onto linguistic action. More specifically, the aims of this study are the following.

First, we wish to examine which aspects of linguistic action are grasped through metaphorical projection from the physical domain. This involves looking at ways in which the linguistic action domain is structured by means of various concrete domains all involving the use of body parts. We shall also look at the way a number of basic schemata (in the sense of Johnson 1987: 29) form the experiential grounding of the body part metaphors.

In the second part of the paper we shall look at the way in which the metaphors of the corpus express value judgments in the domain of linguistic action. The hypothesis is that value judgments are an important motivating factor in the creation of metaphors (see also Rudzka-Ostyn 1988: 524). In reporting someone else's speech act, a reporter may express value judgments about any aspect of the primary speech act situation.[3] This paper aims to discover which aspects of the components of the speech situation are valued positively and which negatively, and how these judgments correlate with donor domains.

1.   Structuring the LA domain: use of the body

1.1.   Donor domains

Through linguistic action (henceforth LA) human beings interact both with one another and with their environment. However, LA is only one type of action and interaction, and other types are more concrete; they involve the body more "tangibly". It is therefore logical according to our view on metaphor that these types of interaction should be used as donor domains for the metaphorization of LA.

In the following we will present a survey of the different types of donor domains involving body parts and outline how they give structure to the LA domain.

1.1.1.   Donor domains involving other uses of articulators [4]

A first set of metaphors involves body parts which function in speaking but which are put to a different use. Such donor domains are, for instance, *eating* and *breathing*. We want to emphasize from the start that not all domains are so specific in nature, and that vaguer domains like *use of the mouth/tongue/throat* should also be recognized. Some examples may clarify the picture.

Eating

This donor domain is used to structure the LA in different ways. Metaphors like *feed* and *force/ram/thrust something down someone's throat* describe the interaction between two persons; the speaker transfers something to the hearer, and the eating stands for listening. The ground for the metaphor is not the use of the mouth, common to both the activities of eating and of speaking, but the aspect of interiorization found in both eating and listening.

A second subset describes speaking in terms of eating (or part of the eating process). In *chew the rag* and *chew the fat* (meaning either 'complain' or 'chat' (L))[5] the focus is on the duration of the action - both *rag* and *fat* are substances one can chew on a long time - and the fact that not much is going to come out of it. The LA is described as of long duration and pointless. The object of the chewing can also be seen as describing the subject/content of the LA as old, leftover or of poor quality (cf. the definition 'discuss, esp. old grievances' (H)). The metaphor *eat one's words* 'admit one has said something wrong' (L) provides another kind of structure for the act of speaking. It uses the directionality of eating (ingesting) as contrasted to that of speaking (exteriorizing). The act is an undoing of a previous LA; the offensive utterance is destroyed by making it go back to where it came from: once inside the speaker it becomes invisible and cannot have an effect on the audience any more. *Eat one's heart out*, which describes silence, is similar, but here we find a combination with the donor domain of *violence*, more specifically *torture*, which will be discussed later on. *Regurgitate* does have the same directionality as speaking. It describes the utterance as something which has been ingested, but not digested. Nothing has happened to it before it is exteriorized again; it is not a proper treatment of food (or of information in this context). The substance has not been inside the speaker long enough to be treated/processed, and the speaker does not control himself or his utterance sufficiently.

Breathing

The structure of this donor domain differs from that of the previous one in one important respect, and that is directionality. In this case there is no inherent opposition to the directionality of speaking, since breathing involves both interiorizing and exteriorizing. Moreover, there is a much closer, metonymic link with the LA, since one uses one's breath in speech.

In the structuring of the LA domain, there are certain parallels to the contribution of the domain of eating. There are metaphors describing speech (*breathe, puff (out), waste one's breath*), metaphors describing uncontrolled speech (*cough (up)*), and a metaphor describing controlled silence (*choke back*). In several of these the domain of breathing interacts with another domain. In *waste one's breath*, it is the domain of valuable objects and substances. The metaphor stresses the importance of breathing for the functioning of the body, and advocates an economical use of one's resources. The LA is described as useless because it does not have an effect; it does not pay off. In *cough (up)*, the secondary donor domain is that of illness, while in *choke back*, there is an interaction with the domain of eating.

Two metaphors focus on silence that is beyond the control of the speaker. *Stick in one's throat* 'be hard to say' (L) focuses on an accidental blockage of the breathing channel. In this case there is an interaction with the domain of eating, as the prime candidate for causing the blockage is obviously food. *Take someone's breath away* 'make unable to speak' (L) attributes the inability to an external agent.

Use of articulators

The metaphor *drool* 'talk foolishly' (L) describes a natural reflex which human beings should have learned to control. The metaphor brings in three elements: the speaker's behavior is described as uncontrolled, the substance involved is characterized as valueless, and the action as a whole as distasteful for the beholder and socially unacceptable. The value of the substance (whether it be food or phlegm) and the unacceptability of the action are also involved in the metaphor *spit out* 'say or express with effort, force or anger' (L).

A number of examples focus on the movement of the visible speech organs, and clearly have a metonymic basis:[6] *keep one's mouth shut, open one's lips, and close-lipped* describe presence or absence of speech, while *lip*, *chinwag* and *jaw* describe a type of LA, and are more clearly metaphorical. These three metaphors, like *tongue in cheek* and *lie in one's teeth/throat*, seem to rely exclusively on the body part domain, although the value of the body parts derives in part from the LA domain. This stands in contrast to the majority of instances in our corpus, where the body part domain only plays a secondary role in the metaphorization, either by providing a metonymic link, or by being the chief instrument in other kinds of interaction. Also metaphors like *turn a deaf ear to*, *go in one ear and out the other* and *have a word in someone's ear* belong here.

1.1.2. Domains involving other body parts

These metaphors are based on the use of the body in other types of (inter)action. Closest to the domain of LA, one finds the domains of *nonverbal communication* and *sensory perception* (seeing, touching, smelling). Apart from these, *fighting, physical punishment, the manipulation of objects* and *walking* are also used as donors.

Nonverbal communication

With quite a few of these metaphors, there is a metonymic link with the LA domain, since the verbal and nonverbal actions frequently co-occur. This is the case for expressions like *pat on the back, bow/bend the knee/neck to, tip someone the wink, put the finger on*. Since the actions do not need to co-occur, the value of these expressions is also metaphorical. For instance, *tip someone the wink* 'let someone know quietly or secretly, so that they can take immediate action' (C) is a kind of communication which does not attract attention in comparison with full, explicit linguistic action. The secrecy is a feature in the donor domain, which is used to structure the LA.

Some of the metaphors stand out because they involve a kind of nonverbal communication which is somewhat out of the ordinary. In *pat oneself on the back* the focus is on the ridiculousness, as much as on the far more abstract unacceptability, of self-praise. The metaphor combines two donor domains: nonverbal communication and body movement. In *blow one's own trumpet* - which has more or less the same meaning - the LA is described as a way of attracting attention to oneself. The deviation from normal behavior (normally, important persons are heralded by someone else) is also significant since it heightens the impression of inappropriateness.

One other metaphor merits our attention, because it concerns animal behavior to which a communicative value is attached. In *snarl* 'speak, say in an angry, bad-tempered way' (L) the transfer to the LA domain is quite straightforward. The fact that we are dealing with a particular kind of animal behavior as contrasted with human behavior may add a relevant aspect to the metaphorization: a negative value judgment.

Sensory perception

Of this domain we only found a limited set of examples in our corpus. They stand out, however, in that they structure the LA domain in an unexpected way: instead of describing the act of hearing, they are used to focus on a relevant aspect of the act of speaking. This curious reversal is accounted for in different ways.

The metaphor *sniff* 'say something in a proud, complaining way' (L) is based on the fact that this act of perception is combined with a production of noise. The noise of sniffing, moreover, has a communicative value, since the audience is made aware of the fact that the agent smells something. This value is strengthened because the action is usually performed when the smell is objectionable in one way or another. The metaphor could also be classified in the domain of nonverbal communication.

Poke one's nose into something describes an action which is preparatory to sensory perception. Perception is here used to describe the act of eliciting information. There are two possible donor contexts: the intruder in the kitchen who goes around lifting the lids of pots and sniffing at the contents, or the picture of a dog or cat investigating dustbins. In both cases, what they are investigating belongs to other people, which is another salient aspect in the metaphorization.

Two metaphors rely on the interaction with the *animal* domain. *Prick up one's ears* describes the act of hearing, while *put out feelers* again describes the use of language to elicit information. In the last instance, there is an added focus on the care taken in the process.

Violent actions

A first subdomain is that of *boxing*, with examples like *spar, pull one's punches, beat someone to the punch, punchline*. Here we are dealing with an organized, rule-governed activity. The violence is acceptable within this context, so that the focus of the metaphor is primarily on another aspect of the interaction. The common factor lies of course in the description of the LA as involving two opponents. In *spar*, for instance, the main focus is on the preparatory character and the playful nature of the argument: 'argue, but not in an unpleasant or serious way' (C). *Pull one's punches* focuses on the directness and straightforwardness of the LA, as does the metaphor *throw dust in someone's eyes*. They both describe unfair behavior in fighting or arguing. In *pull one's punches* the speaker is described as being soft on the hearer; he does not "attack" him as strongly as he could or should. *Throw dust in someone's eyes* describes a speaker who hides his actions from the hearer by making him unable to see. Metaphors like *tongue twister* and *jawbreaker* also belong here. In these cases, a word or phrase is given the status of a fighter, who succeeds in incapacitating his opponent - the speaker. The focus is on the autonomy of words and phrases, and their control over (*tongue twister*) or destruction of (*jawbreaker*) the body parts involved in the LA.

A second subset has *punishment* for a donor domain. There is punishment as of schoolboys (*rap someone over the knuckles, burn someone's ears, browbeat*), in a military context (*tear someone off a strip*), as torture (*excoriate*) or as atonement (*bite one's tongue off*). The focus is on the experiencer of the painful sensation. The first three metaphors describe the act of scolding as causing someone pain. There is probably a metonymic basis since the physical actions are often accompanied by scolding or reprimanding. *Excoriate* 'express a very bad opinion of (a book, play, performance etc.)' (L) adds an element of destruction to the above, which is also common with other metaphorizations of the act of criticizing (see below). *Bite one's tongue off* describes silence as causing grave discomfort to the agent: the non-expression of certain feelings is seen as having a devastating effect. The same applies to *eat one's heart out*, which moreover relies on the domain of eating. The domain of punishment extends into the domain of human-animal interaction with metaphors like *muzzle* and *rub someone's nose in the dirt*.

By far the largest subgroup involves the description of *violent actions* pure and simple. In metaphors like *boot out, kick someone around, tear apart, choke off*, the relationship between agent and experiencer is transferred onto the LA domain. The relationship is asymmetrical, in that the experiencer is clearly in no position to fight back. In the first two cases, the asymmetry is expressed through the use of the foot - the experiencer is literally in an inferior position. Both describe an LA which is an assertion of authority. The metaphors *tear apart* and *choke off* focus mainly on the effect, which is destruction: the extreme nature of the violence transfers onto the LA domain, where the actions of scolding or making someone shut up may involve loudness and harsh words. The addressee is subjected to an assertion of authority.

In actions like *kick, kick up a row/rumpus/stink/shindy*, the violence is not directed at any experiencer. This aimlessness plays an important role in the metaphors: the violence is useless, the LA is described in the same way. Again this set of metaphors involves use of the foot; indeed, people often start kicking at things to express their anger. In *kick against the pricks* 'complain uselessly about something that cannot be changed' (L), the donor domain is the use of the legs by cattle to kick against the goad. Here also the meaning of useless violent action derives from a physical action by means of which the animals only hurt themselves.

Most of these metaphors describe violent actions performed by animals: *make the fur fly, backbite, bite* (N), *snap, snap at, snappish, snap someone's head off, bite someone's head off* (and maybe also *talk/shout someone's head off* and *tear apart*) focus on the violent interaction between animals. The violence is often extreme, and in the metaphorization the focus is, in most cases, on the unmotivated nature of the action. The LA is described as disproportionately hostile under the circumstances. The agent is overreacting, not controlling himself. *Backbite* and *bite* form the exceptions. In these, the action is described as intentional. *Backbite* describes an LA in which the subject is defenseless because of his absence. *Bite* merely describes the effect of the LA on the hearer in terms of a painful sensation.

It may be noted that *preparation for combat* seems to be a salient subdomain. *Spar* (from the domain of boxing) and *kick around ideas* (football) describe such preparatory actions. They describe an LA as preparatory in nature, with a focus on the non-serious nature of the argument/fight and the exercise- or test-value, respectively.

Restricted movement

This domain gives rise to five metaphors: *tonguetied, muzzle, bridle one's tongue* and *guard one's tongue* are clearcut cases; *watch one's words* is marginal.[7] The first metaphor describes inability of speaking, the second one the imposing of silence, while the other three describe self-control. In two cases the donor domain is clearly that of *animal control*, while in the remainder the donor is less specific. All metaphors describe silence or carefully controlled speech. The movement of the tongue as an articulator is a prominent element in three of the metaphors. It is described as something which may be controlled by others.

Manipulating objects

This last major donor domain contains two kinds of scene. In the first type the hands are used to manipulate objects or substances; in the second type the manipulator also uses an instrument. The aspects in focus are the skill, or lack of skill, of the manipulator (*fumble, get one's tongue round, shoot one's mouth off*), his physical capacities (*heavy-handed, a left-handed compliment*), and the value of the instrument (*silver-tongued*).

From the examples it is clear that the metaphor *fumble* has three slightly different uses:

(1)   *He often has to fumble for the right word. (L)*
(2)   *[we] are made to feel inferior if we fumble an unusual word. (W)*
(3)   *What I'm fumbling to say is that I felt different about you. (C)*
(4)   *He fumbled in answering and made them suspicious. (W)*

In (1) the act is clearly one of looking for an object. The metaphor says that the speaker is unable to produce a word, and this inability is put down to word-finding difficulty. Words are conceived as objects, which are stored away and have to be produced quickly if needed. In (2) the situation is different. The focus is in this case on the maltreatment of the object. The word is produced, but as a result of clumsiness, it comes out wrong. The descriptions in (3) and (4) pay attention to the clumsiness of the speaker, rather than to the manipulation of the objects. This clumsiness is of course the common ground in all these examples, but the first two stand out in that they allow a more specific transfer from the donor domain to the LA domain.

The metaphor *shoot one's mouth off* is still more specific. The mouth is described as a gun in its function of being able to cause harm by emitting something. In this particular instance, the harm is caused because of careless or unskillful handling of the instrument. In shooting off a gun, one wastes a bullet and one attracts attention; one might also hurt someone.

Pick a quarrel and *split hairs* are instances of skill used wrongly, in the first case because of the domain of application, in the second because of the excess.

Pick someone's brains and *brainwash* can also be classified here. Here, too, the value of these metaphors relies on far more specific sub-domains: in the first case, the corresponding metaphor *pick someone's pocket* is brought into play, and in the second the incompatibility of our conceptualization of the act of washing and our conceptualization of the brain (see also 2.4.2.).

Walking

These metaphors describe the LA as a movement of the speaker. Again, different metaphors focus on different elements. Still, the element of skill seems to play a role in all of them. In *backtrack* the elements in focus are the direction of the movement, and the fact that this is the consequence of a mistake. The LA is shown as a correction of an error, which involves a movement opposite to the normal direction of speech. In *put one's foot in it, slip of the tongue*, and *never put a foot wrong*, the focus is mainly on the skilful handling of the body. In the first metaphor there is also the aspect of stepping into some substance which is obviously to be avoided.

1.1.3. Miscellaneous

Some 20-odd metaphors escape classification in the domains mentioned above. A first set of metaphors focuses on body contents (*heart to heart, heartwarming, shit, unbosom, rattlebrained, red-blooded, full-blooded, hearty, bare one's heart/soul*). A second set concerns the position of the interactants (*talk over someone's head, tête-à-tête, hear/get it straight from the horse's mouth*), a third describes the state of a body (part) (*bald, pregnant, bellyache*). Metaphors like *mouthpiece, profile* and *rub in* stand isolated as far as donor domains are concerned - at least in our corpus, in which the presence of a body part has been the criterion for selection.

1.2. The basis for the metaphors: an image-schematic approach

1.2.1. Introduction

Following Johnson's (1987) approach, we will now describe the metaphors from another angle. According to Johnson, metaphors are based on our abstract bodily experience of the world, which we translate into basic schemata. He defines a schema as "a recurrent pattern, shape, and regularity in, or of, [our] ongoing ordering activities. These patterns emerge as meaningful structures for us chiefly at the level of our bodily movements through space, our manipulation of objects and our perceptual interactions" (Johnson 1987: 29). Johnson distinguishes several such basic schemata, and he provides a list (1987: 126) which is said to be highly selective, but still contains those schemata he thinks most pervasive. We have included the list here, and will refer to it in the discussion:

container	balance	compulsion
blockage	counterforce	restraint removal
enablement	attraction	mass - count
path	link	center - periphery
cycle	near - far	scale
part - whole	merging	splitting
full - empty	matching	superimposition
iteration	contact	process
surface	object	collection

Certain of these schemata are further specifications of a more general experience: compulsion, blockage, counterforce, restraint removal, enablement and attraction all specify the force schema. Schemata also interact, as in the case of the container schema and the full-empty schema, or the compulsion and the path schema. The schemata can be further analysed in several component elements. For the path schema these would be the source, the goal, and a sequence of locations in between; the schema is usually given a directionality which relates to the prototypical movement along a path.

In what follows, an attempt will be made to generalize over the interaction between the different donor domains and the LA domain; the focus will be on the experiential grounding of the metaphor. To exemplify the different types of interaction, we will mainly rely on those metaphors which we did not classify in specific donor domains. It can be argued that these metaphors rely most heavily on the image-schematic relationship. The similarity between donor domain and LA is less obvious than was the case in e.g. metaphors from the domain of eating (use of articulators), nonverbal communication (communication) or physical violence (interaction between human beings).

At the same time, however, we will also pay attention to those metaphors partly explainable in terms of the notion of donor domain. We will try to show that the image-schematic basis can also make a specific contribution in these cases.

First, a number of metaphors will be described which rely on the *container* schema. It appears that this schema interacts with a number of others, which we will have to include in the discussion. In the remainder of our account we will exemplify some basic uses of other schemata - notably *force, balance, path, contact* and *control* - but we will not treat them exhaustively.

1.2.2. The container schema

This schema is used to describe different elements of the linguistic action. Among the metaphors describing the speaker's actions, there are a number which describe his body as a container for language. The lips and mouth are described as the place where the container can be opened or closed (*open one's lips, shut one's mouth, close-lipped*). When the container is opened, there is LA, when it is closed, there is silence. In *bite one's lips*, the closing is combined with the use of force. The force in this case is not linear, and does not fit any of the schemata distinguished by Johnson. It comes closest to *counterforce*, but the forces do not meet head on; rather, the force is used to install a blockage (which is not the same as the blockage schema for Johnson (1987: 45)).

In *unbosom*, 'tell the secret feelings, esp. troubles and worries of oneself' (L), the container schema is combined with a *path* schema. The metaphor describes language as originating inside the bosom (which is a container within a container), and moving out. The schema which contrasts center and periphery is used implicitly. The bosom lies further away from the periphery along the path of speaking. As a central (vs. marginal) body part it is also of greater importance. The container is seen as a hiding-place: things inside are invisible and secret and become visible, perceptible in the exteriorization. This metaphor is one which relies on the combination of image-schemata, rather than on any distinct donor domain; there is no act of unbosoming outside the LA domain. Another aspect which plays a role here is the folk theory which conceives of the bosom as the seat of emotions. However, the role of folk theory with respect to metaphorization is beyond the scope of this paper.

Also in *lie in one's teeth/throat* the container is seen as a hiding place, but a defective one, because of its being on the periphery, and because, in these cases, the container is far from a prototypical container.

For the metaphor *shit* 'worthless talk' (L) the container image also provides the grounding - it is something which has been removed from the body. This basis for the metaphor, however, is not at all in focus in this case; the quality and the social judgment of the substance are what matters.

None of the metaphors we have considered so far pay attention to the experiencer in their description of the LA.[8] In the following, the container schema is used to describe the hearer, while the speaker's action is described as the exertion of some kind of *force* on the container. There are two basic situation types: the first describes the speaker as forcing entry; the second describes him as using force to keep it closed. The emphasis differs from metaphor to metaphor. In *cast/throw something in someone's face/teeth*, the intensity of the force is focused on; in *have a word in someone's ear*, the actual entry is in focus; *get an earful* pays attention to the lack of control on the part of the experiencer, while *feed, rub in, force/thrust/ram something down someone's throat, shut someone's mouth* describe all three aspects.

It may be noted that the metaphors describing entry are not just restricted to the normal way of entry in LA (the ears), but also use the mouth as an entrance, which links up with the donor domain of eating, or in this case force-feeding. *Tear into* and *rub in* stand apart in this respect. *Tear into* 'criticize very strongly' (C) does not describe the way of entry; it simply focuses on the destructive violence involved in effecting entrance. In *rub in*, the nature of the force - not extreme, but repeated - is at stake. The definitions in different dictionaries stress different aspects: 'say repeatedly' (L), 'force a lesson into someone's mind' (H), 'remind someone of something he does not want to be reminded of, usu. because it is embarrassing' (C). The *Longman* definition focuses on the repetitiveness of the rubbing, the *Hornby* definition combines the force used in the process with the description of the intended effect (lesson), while the *Cobuild* definition refers to the side effect on the hearer (embarrassment). It is indeed relevant that the act, though painful, is for the benefit of the experiencer.

The extent of entry into the container may vary, as can be seen from *put words into someone's mouth* and *force/ram/thrust something down someone's throat*. The extent of entry here correlates inversely with the subtlety of the agent's action. In this case of course there is also another contrast: whereas the second metaphor is prototypical of *forced entry* in that it describes an LA in which the speaker controls the effect on the hearer, the first metaphor draws attention to the hearer as speaker in another LA which either follows ('to tell someone what to say') or preceded ('to claim (falsely) that someone has said a certain thing') (L). The focus is on the control of someone else's speech.

Yet another use of the container image describes the LA as the removal of something from a container: *pick someone's brains, brainwash, take the words out of someone's mouth, take one's breath away*. The actions violate the self control of the affected person. His words, ideas or capacity to speak/act are influenced by an outsider. In *pick someone's brains* the interaction described is that of eliciting information. The LA is conceived as an act of stealing, but because of the skillfulness the experiencer does not notice this (cf. picking someone's pocket). The information, ideas, etc. stored in the brain are looked upon as valuable possessions, which should not be interfered with (cf. *brainwash*).[9]

A final use of the container schema is found in *poke one's nose into something* and *horn in*; here an ongoing process is described as a container, and the LA as an unacceptable attempt at entering - because it is construed as a violation of private territory. In *horn in*, this violation is combined with the use of force.

To conclude this section, let us survey the role of the body parts in these metaphors. They function as parts of the container (esp. exit and entry: lips, mouth, teeth, skin), as contents (heart, breath), as containers (brain, mouth, bosom, cheek, throat, teeth) and as instruments used in the exertion of force (hands, implicitly in most cases, and horns).

1.2.3. Force

According to Johnson (1987: 42), this schema is necessarily involved in our interaction with the environment. Our body exerts and/or undergoes force in any kind of (inter)action. In normal circumstances, however, our awareness of these forces is very low, because we take them for granted. Still, Johnson (1987: 42) remarks that "we do notice such forces when they are extraordinarily strong, or when they are not balanced off by other forces."

Such experiences of force, in other words, have the required salience to be used in metaphorization. It is therefore not accidental that such a large group of instances in the corpus actually have *violent actions* or *fighting* as a donor domain. In these cases force is clearly in focus, either because of its extreme nature, or because of the opposition of forces from different sources. The elements of the force schema which are most salient in that context are the degree of force and/or the interactional character. Still, the force schema is usually further specified in different ways through the combination with other image schemata such as *path, container*, and *balance*. Compare the following:

(5)   *He had studied very little and has no reason to kick about low grades. (W)*
(6)   *He is always kicking against the system. (C)*
(7)   *He kicks his children around a good deal. (W)*

In the first two examples, the metaphor *kick* is shown to rely exclusively on the force schema. The stress is different: in (5) the intensity of the force is at stake, in (6) there is specification of a target as well. Example (7) combines the force schema with the path schema. The movement of the experiencer becomes a relevant element.

An example of the combination with the container and balance schemata can be found in:

(8)   *The widow sat fuming and blowing off steam. (OED)*

Here, the force schema plays a secondary role. The focus is clearly on the act of restoring balance by relieving pressure.

The different types of force schema can be found back in the corpus. Example (7) above illustrates the *compulsion* schema, as is clear from the combination with the path schema. The experiencer becomes subject to the force and loses control of his movement. The same explanation would apply to a metaphor like *boot out*. Examples of *blockage* can be found most clearly in combination with the container schema. Here, the force is used to either exit from (*spit out*) or enter the container (*force/ram/thrust something down someone's throat*). Clear examples of *counterforce* were not found in this corpus, although *muzzle* could be explained in those terms (cf. *bite one's lips*). An example of *removal of restraint* is found in *bang out*. The image of force is again combined with the container schema.

1.2.4. Path

A number of metaphors from various concrete donor domains can be explained in terms of this schema. From the domain of walking comes the metaphor *backtrack* which focuses on the directionality of the movement along the path. In some metaphors from the domain of eating, the path becomes relevant because of the opposition between the directionality inherent in eating and that inherent in speaking. Examples are found in metaphors like *eat one's words* and *eat crow*, which are instantiations of a more general image of "taking back one's words".

Earlier on we discussed some other combinations of the container and path schemata, where the path referred to the movement in the container (*bite back, force/ram/thrust something down someone's throat*). In these, as in *digest* and *regurgitate*, the image schema of center-periphery also plays a role. In *bite back*, the path is cut off at the periphery, with *force/ram/thrust something down someone's throat* an attempt is made to reach beyond the periphery (oral cavity); *regurgitate* describes how the substance did not succeed in reaching the center or in staying there long enough; and *digest* says that it did.

Finally, the concept of removal, which operated in some of the cases discussed under the container schema also involves a path schema (*pick someone's brains, take the words out of someone's mouth*). In a number of other metaphors, the schema plays a similar role, but the container schema is absent. *Tear a strip off someone* combines path and force, as does *get something off one's chest*. These exemplify several types of removal, however. In the former case it violates the control of someone over his property or domain. In the latter instance, removal involves a reassertion by the agent of his self-control. Johnson (1987) would describe the second metaphor as an example of balance, more specifically of freedom from external pressure.

1.2.5. Balance, or control?

Johnson (1987: 85) describes the balance schema as "consisting of force vectors ... and some point or axis or plane in relation to which those forces are distributed. ... Balance involves a symmetrical or proportional arrangement of forces around a point or axis". The schema is closely linked to the exertion of force. In *get something off one's chest*, force is used to remove a blockage, which caused an imbalance. The agent was subject to a certain oppressive force, which he now succeeds in removing. In doing so, he restores his sense of well-being, his sense of being in control again. Other examples are *blow off steam, cough* and *cough up*.

It seems, then, that the balance schema would correlate with the absence of force. Johnson indeed implicitly suggests this when he defines force (1987: 42), adding that we only notice forces "when they are not *balanced off* by other forces" (our emphasis). This, according to us, raises some questions as to the status of the balance schema. We do not wish to suggest that the experience of balance does not exist; Johnson has clearly demonstrated that it does. What we do claim is that it could be reinterpreted in terms of another bodily experience which perhaps has greater explanatory value. The schema we are suggesting could be called *control*.

In our view this schema is basic, in the sense Johnson gives to the word. *Control* is a schema which operates both in its presence and its absence. It basically functions on the level of human interaction with the environment or with other human beings. A metaphor like *slip of the tongue* may be explained as loss of control over one's body, *drool* as lack of control, while *muzzle* involves the control of one actor over another. A human being tries to control himself and his environment in several ways, and this is a precondition for being able to make use of that environment. In *fumble*, for instance, there is a clear absence of control over the object which the agent tries to manipulate.

The control schema of course very often interacts with the force schema where the control of other agents is involved. Going back through the corpus, a lot of other metaphors can be explained from this angle: *pick someone's brain, brainwash, take the words out of someone's mouth, put words into someone's mouth* all violate the self-control of the experiencer, *talk over someone's head* can be construed as language passing the hearer by out of reach, beyond his controlled environment. In one of its interpretations, the metaphor *mouthpiece* relies on the lack of control of the speaker over the content of his utterances. He is just the channel through which the information passes, but he does not do anything with it (see also 2.3.2.).

Also the prototypical instantiations of the balance schema can be reinterpreted in terms of *self-control*. Metaphors like *get something off one's chest* and *blow off steam* describe the reassertion of self-control after an experience of outside or inside pressure. A metaphor like *cough (up)* describes an uncontrollable action, a temporary loss of self-control. Since *coughing* can also be interpreted as having a liberating effect, as taking away internal pressure, it can also be a restoration of self-control. The context will decide which interpretation is called for.

1.2.6. Contact

The final schema we would like to include in our discussion is also at work in a wide range of metaphorical expressions. In a number of metaphors it is of secondary importance; it is implicit, as in *muzzle* or *kick*, or explicit, as in *kick against the pricks*, which however focuses on another element.

In those metaphors where the schema is basic, it is used to describe two different aspects of the LA. In *in/out of touch, catch someone's ear, have someone's ear*, the schema is used to describe the relationship between two speakers, while in *touch, touch on* and *fumble* it describes the relationship between speaker and LA. The type of contact, its intensity, duration and the effort (force) involved also play a role in the metaphor.

Touch and *in/out of touch (with)* are fairly neutral in this respect; they simply use the presence/absence of contact to describe the presence/absence of a relationship between speakers or between the speaker and his subject. With *touch on* and *fumble* the contact with the object is not extensive, not firm - the metaphors rely on the contrast between mere contact and control. Absence of firm, extensive contact leads to absence of control. In *have someone's ear* and *catch someone's ear* the contact is with a body part obviously involved in listening. Of course, in this case there is also a metonymical component. *Have someone's ear* involves both contact and control, or control in terms of contact, and stresses the permanent nature of the communicative channel. *Catch someone's ear* focuses on the effort involved in establishing such a channel, which results in achieving contact and control.

1.2.7. Image schemata and LA

In retrospect, it is obvious that several image schemata should be at work together in any metaphorization of LA. LA has a complex structure involving several entities in different relationships. The schemata can hope to account for only part of this, since it is their nature to be basic and salient elements of bodily experience, which are automatically less complex.

The explanatory value of schemata for the metaphorization of LA depends on their complexity. The container schema, with the implications of contents, inside-outside orientation, central and peripheral elements, the containing structure, the possibility of things moving in and out, the possibility of quantifying the contents (full-empty) is obviously better placed in this respect than the contact schema, which is a lot simpler in structure. Still, we hope to have demonstrated that this schema also goes a long way towards explaining some of our metaphors.

We also hope to have shown the necessity of complementing the donor-domain approach with the image-schematic approach, since the first does not succeed in explaining all of our metaphors. Even with those it can explain, image-schematic notions may clarify the case, as in e.g. *eat crow*, where the opposition between the directionality of speech and the directionality of eating has a significant contribution. On the whole, the image-schematic approach explains why a similarity is perceived between the donor domain and the LA domain.

If we look at metaphor as a case of "conceiving-as", we should be aware that this process may take place at different levels of abstraction. In comparing a metaphor like *spar* with *bare one's heart/soul*, the former relies on a more concrete experience of similarity than the latter; the former can be explained on the basis of a donor domain situation, whereas for the latter this would cause problems, since a situation of this kind is just not available. It is there that the image-schematic approach is most rewarding, or, to put it differently, has a greater explanatory value. The role of folk theory in this respect needs further investigation, but, as stated before, this is beyond the scope of our paper.

2. Value judgments

2.1. Value judgment in the LA scene

When describing linguistic action, a speaker may at the same time express a judgment or give an evaluation of that LA or of any component of that LA. In looking at the LA scene, it is clear that the value judgment should be located at the level of the secondary speech act, the describing act, and that it refers to aspects of the primary speech act. The speaker's intentions and behavior, the linguistic form, manner of presentation, hearer's attitude, etc. and the relations between these components all come in for evaluation (see Verschueren 1984 and Rudzka-Ostyn 1988).

2.2.   The basis of value judgments: donor concepts and scales

In the metaphors examined, two types of criteria are used for evaluating LA: more concrete ones and more abstract ones.

The more concrete criteria are based on donor concepts; within the donor domains, certain types of behavior are approved or disapproved of on various grounds. *Social (un)acceptability* for instance is a criterion for disapproval in the domain of eating. Hence *spit out* expresses a negative value judgment. In the domain of fighting, *unfair behavior and tactics* are disapproved of, as in *throw dust in someone's eyes*. A final example is *skillfulness*, which is valued positively in the domain of manipulating objects. Hence, *fumble*, implying a lack of skillfulness, expresses a negative evaluation.

Apart from the criteria provided by concepts in the donor domains, there are more abstract criteria based on a number of value scales. A particular LA may for instance be judged as very slow, which means it has a low value on the scale of speed. The scales which we found to be relevant are the following: *intensity, frequency, duration, quantity* and *speed*. These scales correlate with the important image schemata of force, control, container, path and contact.

2.2.1.   Donor concepts

When we say that a particular metaphor contains a value judgment, this means that the reporter (or speaker in the secondary speech situation, henceforth S2), in using the metaphor, expresses a judgment of some aspect of the primary speech situation. In other words, he evaluates some aspect of the linguistic action referred to as positive or negative. A few examples may illustrate this.

The adjective *silver-tongued* expresses a positive value judgment of the manner of speaking. As pointed out in 1.1.2. above, the donor domain of manipulating objects here structures the linguistic action metonymically as the manipulation of an instrument, more specifically of the articulator "tongue". The positive evaluation is carried over from the donor domain, in the sense that silver, as a precious metal, has positive connotations in our society.[10]

The verb *backbite*, on the other hand, carries a negative evaluation of the linguistic action. Coming from the domain of violent actions performed by animals, it expresses a strong disapproval by S2. The negative features which are carried over from the donor domain are *aggression*, *pain inflicted on the victim*, and the cowardly aspect of *attacking some-one from the back*, i.e. when he is defenseless. The link between donor domain and recipient domain is that the mental harm and pain are viewed as similar to physical harm and injury.

2.2.2. Scales

Intensity

As pointed out in 1.2.3. above, the image schema of force is particularly salient in the metaphors with violent actions or fighting as donor do-mains. Force can be measured, so that an LA can be evaluated in terms of having stronger or weaker intensity. One may compare *kick someone when he's down* and *rap someone over the knuckles* in this respect. The former metaphor involves more force and refers to more violent action than the latter. The value judgment is also more negative in the former, because of the use of the feet to kick someone who is already de-fenseless. The feature "aggression" combines with the feature "unfair", and with the high degree of force being exerted. The intensity scale is also salient in a metaphor such as *pull one's punches*, where the speaker is restraining his force. Here a weak degree of force expresses less vio-lent linguistic action than might be possible in the circumstances.

The intensity scale is however not only relevant in the violent action metaphors. It is also present in metaphors such as *shut one's mouth*. Here the mouth as a container is shut, implying a sudden forceful clos-ing action. The force structure operating here is that of installing a blockage: the closing of the mouth raises a barrier to LA. The degree of force exerted is clearly stronger than in the non-metaphorical expres-sion *speak no longer*. The same applies to *keep one's mouth shut*, which involves more deliberate force than e.g. *not speak*, or *remain silent*. However, whether strong force in such examples is evaluated positively or negatively is not so clear, and will depend on the context in which they are used.

Similarly there may be different degrees of intensity in the making of a speech act. As Johnson says (1987: 59): "The difference lies in the force with which the sentence-container is thrust upon the hearer." For instance, a warning may be mild or strong. A strong warning is made more forcefully. This, as Johnson says, is mainly a question of emphasis. In a number of metaphors in the corpus, such degrees of force of the speech act are particularly salient. Good examples are *applaud* and *raise one's eyebrows*, which both have nonverbal communication as a donor domain. The meaning of *applaud* can be paraphrased as 'express strong agreement with' (L). Whether the nonverbal act accompanies the linguistic action or not, it is clear that the latter is judged by S2 to be a forceful form of approval, agreement, support etc. In contrast, the metaphor *raise one's eyebrows* means 'express surprise, doubt, displeasure by or as if moving the eyebrows upwards' (L). The speech act must here be a "mild" one, as can be judged from the fact that it would be inappropriate in a context where S1 starts shouting, crying etc. to express feelings of displeasure.

In conclusion, strong and weak force, measured on the intensity scale, are not positive or negative on their own. Degrees of force may however combine with other concepts and thus acquire a positive or a negative value. When force combines with violent behavior for instance, a negative value judgment will be strengthened.

The bodily experience of *control* was suggested in 1.2.5. above as a way of correlating the schemata of force and balance. In general, there are three types of control: (i) control over oneself, which is typically evaluated positively, (ii) control over others, which is typically evaluated negatively, and (iii) control over the environment, which is also typically valued positively. Hence, what is typically focused on is simple presence or absence of control. A metaphor in which control is salient is *flounder*. The donor domain of this metaphor is walking, and its literal meaning is 'move about with great difficulty'. Non-fluent speech is referred to in terms of lack of control of one's movements. The value judgment is hence clearly negative. In *muzzle*, the presence of control is valued negatively, because it is exerted over others. The donor domain of controlling animals adds a strong negative value judgment to the expression, since a strong form of control of humans over other humans in the way one normally deals with animals is disapproved of. Finally, instances such as *shoot one's mouth off* illustrate salience of the third type of control. The donor domain is the manipulation of objects, here a gun. One should be in control of objects, and not shoot off a gun when it is not appropriate to do so. In the metaphor, which refers to 'talking foolishly about something one should not talk about' (L), lack of control is valued negatively.

Where control involves force it may also be graded in terms of force and hence entail an evaluation on the intensity scale. For instance, *rub something in* involves less force, and hence a weaker form of control than *force something down someone's throat*. Similarly, where control links up with the contact schema, it can be measured on the duration scale.

Quantity

The relevance of quantity may be exemplified by *full-blooded (argument, style, etc.)*. In this metaphor, the donor domain is *blood*, as the source of life and energy, and the positive value judgment of a forceful manner of speaking/writing is related to the quantitative scale.

The scale of quantity is salient in a number of metaphors (all based on the container schema), though there is once again not a one-to-one relationship between much/little on the one hand and positive/negative on the other. Clearly, when "too much" is the meaning, the value judgment is negative, since "too" means *lack of balance*. An instance of this is *loudmouth*. This metonymy expresses a negative evaluation of someone who talks too much. High degree of loudness (phonetic aspect) here expresses a form of "obtrusive", hence disturbing linguistic action.

In other cases, such as *pour from/out*, the value judgment is not clear. In such utterances as (9-11), the focus is on amount and speed, combined with the physical schema of a container. Whether s2 evaluates this as positive or negative depends on other factors:

(9)   *Curses poured from his lips.*
(10)   *Words poured out of her.*
(11)   *Pour out one's thoughts, feelings, etc.*

Frequency

As with the other scales, when extremes are focused on, this is valued negatively. Examples are *rattle-brained, rub something in* and *brainwash*. In all three, repeated talking is disapproved of. In *rattle-brained*, the brain is compared to an instrument making a lot of quick little noises which, however, do not mean anything. The adjective is used metonymically of a speaker who talks all the time. The verbal *rub something in* refers, in its donor domain, to a repetitive movement of the hands applying an ointment to the skin, until it is absorbed. It is based on the container and contact schemata. The frequency of the movement is required for effect. In the same way, repeated LA leads to "absorption" of the message. It is valued negatively because the experiencer/listener loses control. *Brainwash* is very similar: again repeated LA is valued negatively because it forces the listener to absorb the speaker's ideas.

Speed

LA may be perceived by S2 as being quick or slow. In such cases as *pour out*, quantity and speed go together, but are not particularly approved or disapproved of. Speed may however combine with a value judgment. *Snap* provides a clear example. In the sense of 'say quickly, in an angry way' (L) it expresses a negative evaluation of the LA, both through the feature "violence" (from the animal donor domain) and through the feature "quickness": the unexpectedness and quickness make the victim defenseless. Speed adds to the aggression in this case.

In other cases, speed may imply fluency and hence be valued positively, while slow speech is often associated with non-fluency and awkwardness. The positive value judgment is apparent in *have a ready tongue* (*ready* here meaning 'quick'), while the negative evaluation is clear in instances such as *falter, flounder, fumble*.

Duration

Duration interacts with force, to the extent that the exertion of force may be of long or short duration. An instance is *chew the fat*, which has a high value on the duration scale. It may also relate to contact, as in *touch on*, where the contact is brief.

Further, as suggested above, the schema of control may interact with the schema of contact. In such metaphors, control may be graded in terms of duration. For instance, *have someone's ear* involves permanent control and contact (see 1.2.6.). In contrast, *go in at one ear and out the other* implies a very brief contact and hence almost total absence of control.

In conclusion, the scales of intensity, quantity, frequency, speed, and duration may interact both with one another, and with the positive-negative value judgment. A value judgment in terms of positive/negative is, however, not a necessary corollary, and there is certainly no one-to-one relationship between, say, a high or low value on one of the scales and a positive or negative value judgment.

2.3. Role of context

Metaphors expressing value judgments can be grouped into two main classes, viz. those cases where the value judgment is context-independent, i.e. inherent in the metaphor, and those where it is context-dependent.

2.3.1. Context-independent value judgments

Context-independent value judgments are always either positive or negative, no matter in what type of context the metaphor is used. *Fumble* may serve as an example. In all contexts, this metaphor expresses a negative value judgment of the manner of speaking. In the donor domain the verb refers to awkward movements with the hands, hence inefficiency, and this evaluation is carried over into the LA domain to refer to clumsiness in speech.

Another instance of context-free value judgment is found in *drool*. The meaning of the verb in the donor domain, viz. 'letting liquid flow from the mouth' (C) gives the metaphor its negative value judgment of 'talking nonsense, talking foolishly' (L). The action in the donor domain is indeed associated with imbecility, i.e. lack of control over one's own body, and therefore meets with social disapproval. In the LA domain this negative evaluation is always present.

2.3.2. Context-dependent value judgments

There are different types of context dependency to be distinguished.

In one type, the metaphor displays ambiguity, in the sense that it has two clearly distinct meanings, a positive and a negative one. The context in which the metaphor is used will make it clear which interpretation is the appropriate one. This is, for instance, the case with the noun *jaw*. This metaphor has two meanings, viz. a positive one ('chat', as in (12)), and a negative one ('impudent talk', as in (13)):

(12)   *I had a good jaw with Sally yesterday afternoon. (C)*
(13)   *...don't have to take any of his jaw. (W)*

In the donor domain, the jaw as an articulator has no value judgment. In the metaphor, the focus is on one aspect of LA, viz. the peripheral aspect of the visible movement of the jaws in speech. By reducing LA to visible articulation only, the reporter implicitly expresses that the content of the message is not important. Absence of importance of subject-matter may be valued positively, because it is part of informal conversation, the contact function of language. On the other hand, this metonymical expression may imply disapproval by focusing on manner (viz. strong movement of the jaws, perhaps due to the loudness of speech) rather than on content.

It is interesting that both meanings are separately present in two other metonymic expressions, viz. *lip* and *chinwag*. The noun *lip* means 'impudent talk' as in (14), while *chinwag* means 'an enjoyable conversation' as in (15):

(14)   *I'll have none of your lip. (W)*
(15)   *I had a good chinwag with my sister yesterday. (C)*

A second type of metaphor in this category is neutral in some contexts and value-laden in other contexts. An example is *mouthpiece*. This metaphor may be neutral, simply denoting a person who publicly states the opinions, policies etc. of another person or organization. In sentences like (16), there is no positive or negative evaluation:

(16)   *He became the official mouthpiece of the moderate leadership. (C)*

However, the metaphor is frequently derogatory. The negative value judgment comes from the fact that the speaker is compared to an instrument used by someone else. Thus, whereas the metaphor may be used in a neutral way, the negative evaluation is clear in other contexts.

A third type of metaphor combines a positive with a negative value judgment. The type may be illustrated by means of *blow off steam*. As explained in 1.2.5. above, the image schemata of force and balance are particularly salient in this metaphor. The restoration of balance is valued positively: by expressing one's feelings one restores mental balance. On the other hand, the comparison of a human being with a steam engine may express a certain amount of scorn, contempt, etc. Compare example (17):

(17)   *They can let off steam in pubs where nobody knows them. (C)*

This type is different from the type illustrated by *jaw*: whereas *jaw* is a case of ambiguity, *blow off steam* is a case of merger. The two value judgments are present at the same time, and the context may strengthen the positive or the negative side of the coin.

Another example of the merger type is *find one's tongue*. Finding an object which one needs for a certain purpose is a positive experience. Hence, the ability to speak again (after the removal of psychological barriers) is valued positively. However, finding implies previous loss, which is valued negatively. Example (18) implies annoyance of the speaker, which may also be present in (19):

(18)   *Lost your tongue?*
(19)   *Oh, you found your tongue, have you? (C)*

In (19), contextual factors reinforce the negative value judgment; the expression of scorn is salient.

Before concluding this discussion of the role of context, we need to make two remarks. First, it should be emphasized that pragmatic factors may always reverse the prototypical value judgments. In utterances such as (20), the metaphor which negatively refers to excessive control over someone acquires a positive meaning because of the ideology of the speaker:

(20)   *Fortunately, we managed to brainwash him.*

However, such factors do not detract from the inherently negative value judgment present in the metaphor.

Second, the semantic-syntactic contexts in which the metaphors frequently or typically occur may contribute to the value judgment. For instance, *pull punches* and *put a foot wrong* nearly always occur in the negative, as in (21) and (22):

(21)   *I didn't pull any punches.*
(22)   *He never puts a foot wrong.*

Although the former is inherently positive, and the latter inherently negative, their most usual contexts, i.e. negatives, reverse the value judgment of the LA. Another example is the metaphor *spit out*. The imperative (23) gives a positive value judgment to the LA referred to (though the expected message still qualifies as 'difficult', 'possibly unwelcome'), as contrasted with an utterance like (24), in which the value is negative. Mood thus also contributes to value judgment:

(23) *Spit it out. (L)*
(24) *She spat out the hateful word. (W)*

2.4. Types of transfer

There are two types of interaction between value judgments in donor domains and the recipient domain of LA: the value judgment may be directly transferred, or it may be new.

2.4.1. Direct transfer

This means that the value judgments in donor domain and recipient domain are both positive or negative. In other words, the value judgment expressed by the metaphor can be explained from the value judgment in the donor domain. In *make a clean breast of something*, for example, *clean* has a positive meaning in the donor domain, and is associated with openness and virtue. The folk vision of sin, lies, etc. as weighing on someone's breast, and thus disturbing one's balance is also salient here. By telling the truth, the dirt and weight are removed, and one's balance is restored.

In *throw dust in someone's eyes*, the value judgment of aggression, in this case a form of fighting in which one prevents one's opponent from seeing and thus from defending himself, is negative. This evaluation is carried over to the recipient domain, where verbal deception is seen as preventing someone from understanding (or seeing). Direct transfer is the most frequent type.

2.4.2. New value judgment

In this case the expression is neutral in the donor domain but acquires positive or negative connotations in the recipient domain. Some examples may illustrate this.

The donor domain of *chew someone out* is eating. In the donor domain, *chew* as an action performed on food is neutral with respect to value judgment. When applied to LA, however, the destruction of a person by verbal means acquires a negative value judgment.

The donor domain of *beat one's breast* is nonverbal communication. The gesture expresses sorrow. In the LA domain, the focus on the visual aspect (nonverbal communication is visible) may suggest dishonesty: what is visible may be in contradiction with one's intentions. Hence, exaggerated display of emotions - the metaphor has a high value on the intensity scale - is suspect.

A final example is *hand out (advice)*. In the donor domain, the verb is neutral in such contexts as (25):

(25)   *He handed out the books to the pupils.*

In the LA domain, however, *handing out advice* implies a superior attitude on the part of the speaker, because the advice, being given freely, may not have been asked for by the recipient, as in (26):

(26)   *I don't need you handing me out that sort of advice. (L)*

It may be noted that no instances of reversed value judgment were found in the corpus. A metaphor like *brainwash*, which at first sight looked like an example (because *wash* in its sense of 'removing dirt', and thus 'making something clean' is evaluated positively), was on second thought not classified as a case of reversed value judgment. The negative value judgment must indeed be ascribed to the incompatibility of *brain* and *wash*.

2.5.   *Links between the most important donor domains, image schemata, and value judgments*

2.5.1.   Eating

As pointed out above, the donor domain of eating may structure the LA in different ways.

One aspect focused on is eating as "taking in" or "incorporating" food. The relevant body parts are then the mouth, the oesophagus, the stomach. In the same way, LA may be seen as taking in information. Shared schemata are: the body as container, and the directionality of movement along a path. In both domains, the movement is one from outside the container into the container. Two metaphors which focus on LA as transfer of information are based on these schemata, viz. *feed information to someone* and *force/thrust/ram something down someone's throat*. In both, the speaker has control over the listener, but in the former metaphor the degree of force is obviously much weaker than in the latter. Because of the high degree of force used in the latter, the value judgment is negative. A different type of metaphor which is however based on the same structures is *regurgitate*. The movement from within the container to outside it presupposes a previous taking in of food, information or ideas. Here, the reverse directionality is focused on, entailing the negative evaluation of a disturbance of the normal process: undigested food is compared to ideas which have not been understood.

Another aspect of eating is taste. The experience of good and bad food is valued positively and negatively, respectively. An example of a neutral metaphor is *flavor*. A story may have a romantic, macabre, etc. flavor. The value judgment will thus depend on the context, but the basic motivating factor is the amount. (The focus is on "little".) The adjective *mealy mouthed*, on the other hand, is clearly negative. This is an interesting example in that the negative experience overrides the structure in the following way. *Mealy* is a negative property of certain kinds of fruit: peaches, pears, etc. are mealy when the flesh is powdery. Hence, the formal nature of the substance is the primary donor domain. The negative experience of eating such kinds of fruit is the second donor domain, and the link between eating and LA is explicit in the second part of the expression, viz. *mouthed*. However, the directionality is reversed in the metaphor, since 'unclear, ambiguous language' comes out of the mouth instead of going into it, as food does. The aspects focused on are the lack of clear boundaries (hence ambiguous, etc.) and the negative experience of tasting bad food.

Thirdly, eating involves the destruction of food. In the same way, LA may lead to the destruction of someone. In such metaphors, strong force exerted on a person is valued negatively. An example is *chew someone out*.

Finally, eating may be focused on as an activity with a certain duration. This can be valued positively (focus on the social aspect) or negatively (focus on duration without much result). Both evaluations may be expressed in *chew the rag/fat*, meaning 'have a conversation together' (positive) or 'complain together' (negative).

2.5.2. Breathing

The link between breathing and LA is that breath of air is an essential component of speech. In *take someone's breath away* and *waste one's breath* the value judgment is negative, through the negative evaluation of removing or wasting an essential object. Again, the schema of control may play an important role. In *cough (up)*, the lack of control over one's own body is focused on, while in *choke back* the speaker is seen as being in control. Hence, the latter carries a positive value judgment: control over one's emotions is felt to be necessary in certain contexts.

2.5.3. Nonverbal communication

The most important scale on this donor domain is that of intensity. Depending on how much physical force is involved in the gesture, and on the extent to which the gesture is salient, the speech act will be denoted as forceful or weak. Weak intensity is salient in *raise one's eyebrows*, while strong intensity is inherent in such metaphors as *fall on one's knees, applaud, bow the neck, put one's foot down*, etc. In some, though not in all cases, strong intensity may imply exaggeration when applied to LA. This seems to be the case in *beat one's breast* and *fall on one's knees*. The explanation for the negative value judgment in such cases is then that focus on visibility may imply dishonesty. (Compare also: *give someone the glad hand*). Another relevant schema here, apart from force, is center-periphery: what is visible is "outer", and may be different from what is "inner" (cf. Johnson 1987: 124ff). It may be noted in passing that the center-periphery schema is also particularly salient in metaphors referring to the expression of feelings in which the heart is seen as the center of our inner feelings: *bare one's heart, unbosom, hearty, heartwarming*.

2.5.4. Violent actions

LA seen as aggressive behavior may be referred to by metaphors which either have animal behavior or human fighting as donor domains.

In either case, the schema of control exerted over someone else is salient. The degree of force, inversely correlating with the degree of self-control of the victim, is responsible for the extent to which the activity is experienced as aggressive, and hence valued negatively. For example, *rap someone over the knuckles* is less violent than *kick someone when he's down*. Similarly, restraining one's force is valued positively, as in *pull one's punches* and *spar*. Most frequently referred to in these metaphors are the speech acts of criticizing, scolding and blaming someone.

Another type of metaphor is that where human treatment of animals is donor domain, as in *muzzle*. Here again, excessive control over another person is valued negatively.

2.5.5. Manipulating objects

One aspect focused on in these metaphors is awkwardness, inefficient movement. The negative evaluation may relate to manner of speaking, i.e. non-fluency, as in *fumble (for the right word)* (see above 2.3.1.), or to LA as obeying social norms. Violation of social norms is salient in e.g. *heavy-handed*.

Secondly, hands are used for giving something, i.e. transferring an object from one person to another one, as in *hand it to someone, hand out (advice), hand down (information)*. These metaphors are neutral, except for *hand out advice* where control is again exerted: unrequested advice is forced upon one.

2.5.6. Walking

LA as compared with movement along a path, is valued negatively in the following two cases.

First, awkward movement is related to the schemata of control and balance. Lack of self-control is negative. Again, as with the *hands* metaphors, the evaluation may relate to the manner of speaking (non-fluency) or to social norms. Examples are: *slip of the tongue, falter, flounder, never put a foot wrong, put one's foot in it*.

Second, the movement back along a path one has just covered, is seen as purposeless: the previous activity has been useless. This schema is present in *backtrack* and *backpedal*.

3.   Summary, discussion and further perspectives

In this final section we shall summarize the main findings of our research and point out which aspects need further exploration.

Although the main principle underlying the collection of our corpus was the explicit or implicit reliance on the metaphors on the functioning of the body, it is clear that there are also important differences cutting across the expressions composing the material.

One distinction, mentioned in 1.1. above, is that between metaphors based on (a) those body parts used in both speaking and some other activity, and (b) those body parts not used in LA, such as feet, hands, etc. Within each of these classes, further distinctions can be made. In class (a), a distinction can be drawn between metaphors where another domain is clearly relevant (e.g. eating, breathing) and those where no such other domain seems to be involved. An instance of the latter type is *open one's lips*. However, this type is, in our view, not merely metonymical, because at a higher level transfer does indeed take place. In the case of *open one's lips*, for instance, the body is seen as a container for language. The focus on language as coming out of a container (the speaker's body) and going into one (the listener's body) links a large number of at first sight unrelated expressions. At this higher level, such expressions as *open one's lips, shut up, pour out, rub it in, have a word in someone's ear*, etc. can all be shown to be related conceptually. In class (b) above, a further distinction can be made between those expressions where body parts are used in nonverbal communication and those where body parts are used in some type of non-linguistic (inter)action (e.g. fighting, walking, etc.).

A second major distinction can be drawn between expressions also used to refer to non-linguistic action (e.g. *muzzle a dog* vs. *muzzle a person*) and expressions which can only refer to LA (e.g. *backbite, catch someone's ear*). The fact that the latter type of items can only refer to LA does again not mean that they are not metaphorical: they can only be understood with reference to a more general metaphor, such as "LA is violent behavior" (for *backbite*), or "LA is physical contact between speaker and listener"; "catching someone is contact and control" (for *catch someone's ear*).

A third major distinction which has appeared from the corpus is that between those metaphors which can be explained from very specific donor domains and those having less specific donor domains. However, this is not a clearcut distinction but rather a case of variation on a scale: metaphors can be situated on a scale from more general to more specific donor domains. For the most specific ones, encyclopedic knowledge is essential. Examples of such expressions are: *get it straight from the horse's mouth* (encyclopedic knowledge of customs in the horse trading business is required), *kick against the pricks* (cattle breeding context), *tear someone off a strip* (military context). In such metaphors the body part domain is only marginally important. What is interesting about them is that, although in terms of specific donor domains they may at first sight look like isolated expressions, they actually fit into more general ways of conceptualizing LA, viz. "exchange of information understood in terms of path" (*get it straight from the horse's mouth*), "LA as force" (*kick against the pricks*), and "LA as force and control" (*tear someone off a strip*).

In comparison, expressions such as *eat one's words* or *kick someone around* have donor domains which are less specific: both eating and fighting are, as shown, frequently drawn upon as sources of metaphorization of LA. These expressions can be understood, without encyclopedic knowledge, with reference to the general conceptual metaphors "LA is eating" and "LA is violence".

Still further away from the specific context extreme are expressions such as *get something off one's chest, unbosom, bare one's heart*. These cannot be related to a specific donor domain. They are understood with reference to general folk models of the location of feelings and their effect on one's body (see e.g. Kövecses 1986 and Lakoff 1987). Because there is no specific donor domain, the image schemata become more directly relevant: balance, path, control, container, center/periphery.

Finally, expressions such as *put words into someone's mouth, take the words out of someone's mouth* have no donor domains except the most general ones of image schemata: the body as a container, and control.

The conclusion we draw from these types of expressions is that the image-schematic approach to metaphorization is essential, both for establishing links between metaphorical expressions originating within a particular domain and for generalizing over domains. However, some metaphors seem to work only on this most general level, while others, though ultimately also based on image schemata, depend more directly on very specific domains of experience. It follows that the relevance of these different levels of abstraction may vary from expression to expression, depending on its position on the scale. The exact relationship between domains and image schemata needs further investigation.

Value judgments are among the most important factors that facilitate metaphorical transfer. As pointed out, they may either simply be explained from more specific donor domains or they may, in addition or exclusively, be based on a number of scales. In other words, donor-based judgments also involve scales but there are judgments which seem to be based on scales only. Since *too* is negative, talking too much, too slowly, too long, too frequently, etc. is valued negatively: e.g. *rub something in* derives its negative value judgment from "too frequently". It was further emphasized that scales may be relevant without involving a value judgment: in *touch on* the brevity of the contact is relevant in the metaphorization, but the expression is not inherently positive or negative.

In conclusion, only when we show how all the factors mentioned (i.e. image schemata, domains, scales, value judgments) interact, can we capture the intricacies of metaphorization.

It is suggested in this paper that the schematic framework proposed by Johnson (1987) may have to be modified and refined. One such refinement involves the introduction of the control schema. Presence or absence of control and the type of control indeed appear to be important variables determining the value judgment. Its exact status in terms of links with the other schemata still needs to be examined, but so does, in our view, the status of Johnson's schemata. It seems possible, for instance, that some schemata are more basic than others, or, in other words, that there may be a hierarchy of schemata.

Finally, the notion of value judgment itself needs closer examination. In the first place, stricter criteria will have to be set up for distinguishing between value judgment introduced in the metaphorization process and value judgment pronounced on the primary speech act, independent of the metaphor. This involves, for instance, distinguishing between the negative connotation of *scold someone* and that of *rap someone over the knuckles*. Secondly, it would be interesting to integrate value judgments in a larger pragmatic framework, relating them to factors such as politeness and cultural or sub-cultural values.

Notes

1. We wish to thank Louis Goossens, George Lakoff, Brygida Rudzka-Ostyn and Johan Vanparys for their valuable and stimulating comments on an earlier draft of this paper.
2. The notion of domain is used here as in Rudzka-Ostyn (1988: 509).
3. Rudzka-Ostyn (1988: 512) uses this terminology to distinguish between the describing act - secondary speech act - and described - primary speech act.
4. The term "articulator" is used in the widest sense here, to include all the body parts involved in speaking: teeth, mouth, tongue, lips, throat, lungs, etc.
5. Apart from the *Longman dictionary of contemporary English* (1982) (L), a number of other dictionaries were used for the clarification of definitions and for examples, where Longman did not provide them. They are: *The Oxford English dictionary* (1933, 1972-1986) (OED), Hornby's *Oxford advanced learner's dictionary* (1974, 3rd ed.) (H), *Collins Cobuild English language dictionary* (1987) (C) and *Webster's third new international dictionary of the English language* (1971) (W).

6.   Goossens (1990) provides a more thorough explanation of the interac-
        tion between the metonymical and the metaphorical in these expres-
        sions, on the basis of a similar corpus of examples.
7.   *Guard one's tongue, tonguetied* and *bridle one's tongue* have been clas-
        sified here, rather than under 1.1., since the tongue only provides the
        link with the LA domain, while the main metaphorical element is
        clearly the absence of movement/speech.
8.   Note that *experiencer* is here used as a cover term for listener, ad-
        dressee and patient.
9.   Another possible interpretation for this metaphor was suggested by
        Louis Goossens. Birds of prey also *pick the brains* of their prey. The
        container schema is still salient in this interpretation, force becomes
        more salient, while the weakness of the undergoer and the total control
        by the agent are stressed. The evaluation of the agent is clearly socially
        determined.
10.   Cutlery is such an example where the silver instrument gets a positive
        evaluation as a marker of "class".

References

Burchfield, R.W.(ed.)
    1972-1986   *A supplement to the Oxford English dictionary*. 4 vols. Oxford: Oxford
                 University Press.
Goossens, Louis
    1990   "Metaphtonymy: The interaction of metaphor and metonymy in
                 expressions for linguistic action", in: *Cognitive Linguistics* 1: 323-340.
Gove, Philip B. (ed.)
    1971   *Webster's third new international dictionary of the English language*.
                 Chicago: G&C Merriam Co.
Hornby, A.S. (ed.)
    1974   *Oxford advanced learner's dictionary of current English*. 3rd ed. Oxford:
                 Oxford University Press.
Johnson, Mark
    1987   *The body in the mind: The bodily basis of meaning, imagination and
                 reason*. Chicago: University of Chicago Press.
Kövecses, Zoltán
    1986   *Metaphors of anger, pride and love*. Amsterdam: Benjamins.
Lakoff, George
    1987   *Women, fire and dangerous things: What categories reveal about the
                 mind*. Chicago: University of Chicago Press.
Lakoff, George & Mark Johnson
    1980   *Metaphors we live by*. Chicago: University of Chicago Press.
Murray, James A.H. et al. (eds.)
    [1933]   *The Oxford English dictionary*. Oxford: Oxford University Press.
Procter, Paul (ed.)
    1978   *Longman dictionary of contemporary English*. London: Longman.
Rudzka-Ostyn, Brygida
    1988a   "Semantic extensions into the domain of verbal communication", in:
                 Brygida Rudzka-Ostyn (ed.), 507-553.

Rudzka-Ostyn, Brygida (ed.)
  1988b   *Topics in cognitive linguistics*. Amsterdam: Benjamins.
Sinclair, John (ed.)
  1987   *Collins Cobuild English language dictionary*. London: Collins.
Vanparys, Johan
  to appear   *A corpus of metapragmatic metaphors*.
Verschueren, Jef
  1984   *Basic linguistic action verbs: A questionnaire*. (Antwerp Papers in
                Linguistics, 37). Antwerp: Universitaire Instelling Antwerpen.

Part III

Lexico-syntactic phenomena

Schematic values of the Japanese nominal particles <u>wa</u> and <u>ga</u>

Haruko Minegishi Cook

0. Introduction

The Japanese nominal particles *wa* and *ga* have puzzled a number of linguists. In this paper I will propose schematic values for *wa* and *ga* and the relation between *wa* and *ga*, which will embrace the different uses of *wa* and *ga* on the sentence level and further account for why a certain entity is chosen to be marked with *wa* or *ga* in unmarked cases. My basic assumption in this paper is that linguistic categorizations and conceptual categorizations are not in principle independent (Langacker 1987). In discussing *wa* and *ga*, my concern is not which grammatical relations are marked by these particles but rather the various uses of them described by Kuno (1973) and other linguists. Further, the goal of this paper is not to argue against the previous analyses of *wa* and *ga* but to demonstrate that it is possible that certain abstract values are schematic for the diverse instantiations of these particles.

1. Kuno's description of <u>wa</u> and <u>ga</u>

Although a number of linguists have proposed analyses of *wa* and *ga*, perhaps Kuno's (1972, 1973) work is the most important in the sense that it has influenced almost all subsequent studies of *wa* and *ga* (e.g. Hinds, Maynard & Iwasaki 1987). Here I will outline Kuno's analysis of *wa* and *ga*.

Consider the pairs of sentences in (1) and (2). The (a) and (b) sentences differ only with respect to the particle that marks the subject. The (a) sentences take *wa* and the (b) sentences *ga*:

(1)   a.   *John wa   gakusei   desu.*
                       student   COP
          'As for John he is a student.'

b.   *John ga*   *gakusei*   *desu.*
                   student   COP
          'John (and only John) is a student.'

(2)   a.   *Ame ga*   *futte*   *imasu.*
                  rain   falling   is
           'It is raining.'

b.   *Ame wa*   *futte*   *imasu.*
                  rain   falling   is
           'It is raining (but not snowing).'

Kuno (1973) refers to the use of *wa* in (1a) as "thematic *wa*". Kuno (1976) states that the "theme" is what the sentence is about. Sentence (1a) is about John. In contrast, (1b) is a statement which asserts that it is John who is a student. It singles out an individual, John, from others. Kuno calls the use of *ga* in (1b) "exhaustive listing". (2a) is a simple description of raining, whereas (2b) contrasts raining with snowing, for example. Kuno refers to the use of *ga* in (2a) as "neutral description" and to the use of *wa* in (2b) as "contrastive". Thus, Kuno identifies two uses of *wa*, namely thematic *wa* and contrastive *wa*, and two uses of *ga*, neutral descriptive *ga* and exhaustive listing *ga*.

Kuno states that the distinction between a theme and a contrastive element is that the theme of a sentence must be either generic or anaphoric. Thus, according to him, any *wa* marking non-anaphoric/non-generic NPs must be contrastive. According to Kuno, *ame* 'rain' in (2b) is non-anaphoric/non-generic and hence *wa* is contrastive in this context. Nevertheless, the distinction between themes and contrastive elements is not always clear-cut. Kuno himself notes that since both the thematic *wa* and the contrastive *wa* mark a generic or an anaphoric NP, sentences containing a generic or an anaphoric NP marked with *wa* are ambiguous. As I discuss in section 4, it seems that distinctions between thematic and contrastive *wa* are in part interpretations derived from contextual factors.

According to Kuno, the difference between the two functions of *ga* comes from a difference in verb types. He states that when the predicate of a clause is an adjective or a nominal of a more or less permanent state, an exhaustive listing interpretation results. Since (1b) concerns John's state, *ga* is interpreted as exhaustive listing. In contrast, when the predicate of a clause is an action verb, existential verb or adjective or nominal of changing state, sentences with *ga* marking their subjects can be interpreted not only as exhaustive listing but also as neutral description. Thus, *ga* in (2a), which involves an action, is interpreted as neutral description as well as exhaustive listing, and *ga* in (1b) is interpreted as only exhaustive listing.

Kuno does not offer an explanation as to why these different interpretations occur. The present proposal, which unifies these separate functions of *wa* and *ga* with abstract schemas, attempts to offer such an explanation.

2.   Schemas for <u>wa</u> and <u>ga</u> and the relation between the two

In this section I propose that there are abstract schemas for the uses of *wa* and *ga* and for the relation between these two particles. I will start by discussing the schema for the *wa-ga* relation because it will be easier to understand the individual schemas of *wa* and *ga* if we first understand the relation that exists when the two are used together.

2.1.   A schema for the <u>wa</u> - <u>ga</u> relation

The particles *wa* and *ga* may co-occur in a single sentence. In such instances, there is a relation between the *wa*-marked NP and *ga*-marked NP. A clear example of the *wa-ga* relation is the part-whole relation. Consider sentence (3):

(3)   *John wa   hana ga   hikui.*
                            nose   low
         'As for John his nose is flat.'

In (3) the relation between the *wa*-marked NP and the *ga*-marked NP is that of a whole-part relation.[1] In this relation the part must be included in the whole. In sentence (3) the part is marked with *ga* and the whole is marked with *wa*. Schematically, the part-whole relation can be represented as in Figure 1:

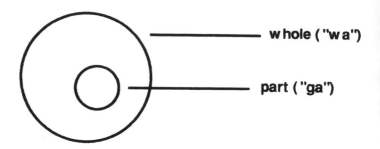

Figure 1: Part-whole relation

In the unmarked case, the part is marked with *ga* and the whole is marked with *wa*. Thus, in (3) it is natural to mark *John* with *wa* and *hana* 'nose' with *ga*. Sentences (4) through (6) offer further examples of this point:

(4)   *John wa   sei ga   takai.*
                  height   tall
       As for John, (his) height is high. (literal trans.)
       'John is tall.'
(5)   *John wa   kodomo ga   chiisai.*
                  child   small
       'As for John, (his) child is small.'
(6)   *John wa   uchi ga   ookii.*
                  house   big
       'As for John, (his) house is big.'
(7)   *Kono   ki wa   eda ga   sukunai.*
       this   tree   branch   few
       'As for this tree, its branches are few.'

As I show below, the uses of *wa* and *ga* are not limited to the part-whole relation. I hypothesize that the abstract schema, an instantiation of which is the part-whole relation, is present in any sentence containing both *wa* and *ga*. (Henceforth, I will refer to such a sentence as a "*wa-ga* sentence".) Figure 2 illustrates the abstract schema for the *wa-ga* relation:

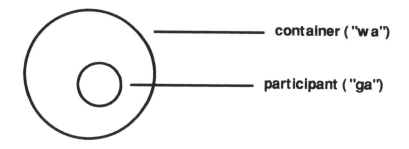

Figure 2: Abstract schema for the *wa* - *ga* relation

As shown in Figure 2, *wa* marks a container or, more specifically, the outer limitation of a container and *ga* marks a participant in the container.[2] I will refer to the schema in Figure 2 as the container-participant schema. As shown below, this schema is general enough to embrace various semantic relations.

The metaphor of taking a photograph illustrates what I mean by "container". When we look through a camera lens, our vision is limited by the periphery of the camera lens. Let us refer to exactly that which we are allowed to see through the lens as "the field of vision". Metaphorically speaking, the field of vision is a container. In taking a photograph, we normally focus on a participant contained within this field of vision (e.g. a tree in a field). With respect to the particles in question, this focussed participant is marked with *ga* and the container (=field of vision) is marked with *wa*. When we take such a picture, we are well aware of the fact that what we see through the lens (i.e. the field of vision) is a limited portion of a larger scene. The field of vision is demarcated. By "demarcated" I mean that a certain portion is separated from the rest of the scene. In sum, my proposal concerning the *wa-ga* relation is that the particle *wa* marks a container and demarcates a certain portion of a scene from the rest (cf. Iwasaki 1987); the particle *ga* marks a participant in the container.[3] In this sense, the *ga*-marked entity is a containee of the container. Below I will attempt to show that this generalization holds for various types of *wa-ga* sentences.

The particles *wa* and *ga* respectively mark a set and a singled-out member of that set. This is illustrated in (8):

(8)   *Sakana wa   tai ga   ii.*
       fish   red snapper   good
       'As for fish, red snapper is good.'

In (8) *wa* functions as a set demarcator and *ga* marks a singled-out member of the given set. We see in Figure 3 that a set and its singled-out member is an instantiation of the schema of the container and its participant:

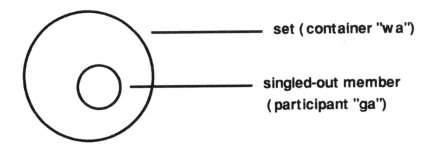

Figure 3: A set and its singled-out member

This analysis of *wa* and *ga* can account for the fact that normally only *ga* can follow a WH phrase.[4] Consider the following sentences. In asking "who came?" and answering this question, the subject is marked with *ga* but not with *wa*:

(9)   *John   to   Tom   to   Bill   no naka de wa*
                 and   and   among
       dare ga kimashita   ka?
       who   came   QUE
       'Among John, Tom and Bill, who came?'
       John ga   kimashita.
                    came
       'John came.'

(10)   **John   to   Tom   to   Bill   no naka de wa*
                     and   and   among
        dare wa   kimashita ka?
        who   came   QUE
        Among John, Tom and Bill, who came?
        *John wa   kimashita.
                        came
        John came.

In the unmarked case, a WH phrase elicits a member of a set, and because it is used to single out a member of a set, it is marked with *ga* and not with *wa* (cf. Miyagawa 1987).

The part-whole relation and the member-set relation are instantiations of the abstract schema presented in Figure 2. Another instantiation of the abstract schema is a setting and a participant. Consider the following sentence:

(11)   *Koko   ni wa   inu ga   imasu.*
        this place   LOC   dog   exist
        'In this place there is a dog.'

In (11) *koko* 'this place' is a physical location, which serves as a setting, and *inu* 'dog' is a participant of the setting. The setting and participant relation can be illustrated as in Figure 4.

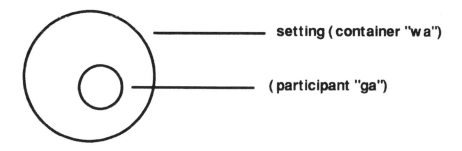

Figure 4: A setting and its participant

We see in the abstract schema in Figure 4 that the setting can serve as a container. Therefore it can be marked with *wa*. The participant of this setting is marked with *ga*.

The basic location setting exemplified in (11) has extensions into five other domains: domains of possession, cognition, perception, desire and ability.

Let us consider (12) and (13). In (12) *okane* 'money' belongs to *John*.[5] If we can think of a possessor as a setting in which a possessed item exists, then *John* serves as a setting for the money in (12). Similarly, in (13), *John* serves as a setting for the *kodomo* 'child' that he possesses. In both (12) and (13) *John* is a possessor setting, and whatever is possessed is construed as a participant in this setting:

(12)   *John   ni wa   okane ga   arimasu.*
                 LOC   money   exist
        'John has money.'
(13)   *John   ni wa   kodomo ga   imasu.*
                 LOC   child   exist (animate)
        'John has a child.'

In (14) *John* is a cognizer setting in the sense that the understanding of English takes place within *John*. Langacker (1987: 392) has also proposed that *John* in (14) is construed as the setting for a mental experience. *Eigo* 'English', which is marked with *ga*, is a participant in this cognizer setting:

(14)   *John   ni wa   Eigo ga   wakarimasu.*
                 LOC   English   understand
        'John understands English.'

In (15) and (16), *John* is a perceiver setting. Similar to the case of the cognizer setting, the involuntary hearing and seeing in (15) and (16) take place within *John*:

(15)   *John   ni wa   sono   uta ga   kikoemasu.*
                 LOC   that   song   hear
        John (involuntarily) hears that song.
        'That song is audible to John.'

(16)   *John   ni wa   sore ga   miemasu.*
        LOC   that   see
John (involuntarily) sees that.
'That is visible to John.'

In contrast with the cases above, the experiencers of predicates such as *-tai* 'want to' and *suki* 'like' do not take the locative particle *ni*. Consider (17) and (18):

(17)   *Watakushi wa   hon ga   yomitai   desu.*
        I   book   want to read   COP
'I want to read the book.'
(18)   *John wa   Mary ga   suki   desu.*
                           like   COP
'John likes Mary.'

Although these sentences do not take the locative particle *ni*, *watakushi* 'I' in (17) and *John* in (18) serve as desirer settings in the sense that a desire exists within the bounds of *watakushi* 'I' in (17) and *John* in (18). The *ga*-marked entity is a participant of this inner experience. Similarly, if we can think of an ability as residing in an individual, *John* in (19) can be conceived of as a locus of ability:

(19)   *John wa   Nihongo ga   joozu   desu.*[6]
                Japanese   good at   COP
'John is good at Japanese.'

These extensions of the physical setting and its participant can all be seen as instantiations of the abstract schema of a container and a participant.

In sum, the abstract schema is utilized to express various semantic relations such as part-whole, member-set, participant-physical setting, and participant-experiencer setting. In each of these instantiations the container is marked with *wa* and the participant (i.e. the containee) is marked with *ga*. Figure 5 summarizes the abstract schema and its instantiations:

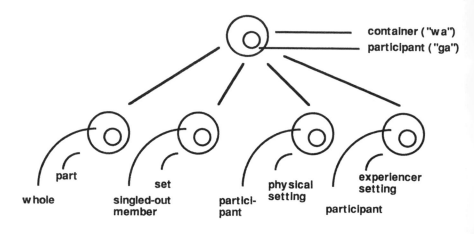

Figure 5: The abstract schema and its instantiations

2.2. *Further comments on wa*

As proposed in the foregoing discussion, the abstract schema for *wa* is a container which demarcates a certain portion of a scene. Let us now contrast this proposal with a few previous analyses of *wa*.

Chafe (1976: 50) proposes the notion of "topic, Chinese style". He mentions that "the topic sets a spatial, temporal, or individual framework within which the main predication holds". Chafe's characterization of "topic, Chinese style" is similar to the present proposal of *wa* in that a topic is a framework in which some event takes place. Iwasaki (1987), based on an experiment in which he had native speakers describe the floor plans of their residences, proposes that the main function of *wa* is scope-setting and that other functions such as thematic or contrastive functions are derivative of this general function. Iwasaki (1987: 130) states, "The particle *wa* sets a scope (or demarcates a domain) to which a predication or predications are supplied." The present proposal of *wa* is consistent with Iwasaki's claim in that in the present proposal, *wa* demarcates a certain portion of a scene. However, it differs from Chafe's "topic, Chinese style" and Iwasaki's "scope" in that the notion of a container (in the unmarked case) entails a containee, i.e. a participant. On the other hand, the notions of "topic, Chinese style" and "scope" do not necessarily entail a participant. The present proposal is also in line with that of Aoyama (1983), who claims that *wa* excludes or singles out an element whereas *ga* compares or selects an element out of a set.[7]

My notion of "container" may also be equivalent to Langacker's notion of "scope". Langacker (1987) defines "scope" of predication as "those portions of a scene that the scope of predication specifically includes".[8] According to Langacker, a concept cannot be characterized without making reference to some relevant domain. For example, a hand cannot be characterized without making reference to an arm. In this example, an arm is the scope, which is required in the characterization of a hand. Langacker's examples of scope of predication all involve nominals. Since my "container" examples are on a clausal level, it is not clear whether my notion of "container" is equivalent to Langacker's "scope of predication".

2.3. A schema for *ga*

There are participants which are not contained in containers. Therefore, the characterization of *ga* cannot be derived solely from that of the *wa-ga* relation. An entity may be a participant in an unspecified place without containment by the particle *wa*. As a result, *ga* can occur in a sentence without *wa*. The particular absence of a *wa* phrase that I am referring to is not a case of zero-pronominalization.[9] When a *wa* phrase is absent, there is no container and the construal is not that of a container and a participant but rather that of a participant in some unspecified space and time (other than the time encoded by the verb). Consider (20) through (22), all of which mark the subject with *ga* in the unmarked case:

(20)   *Inu ga   imasu.*
       dog   exist
       'There is a dog.'
(21)   *Okane ga   arimasu.*
       money   exist
       'There is money.'
(22)   *John ga   hashitte   imashita.*
                    running   was
       'John was running.'

When something or someone exists, it is assumed that it exists in some space and time. Similarly, when something or someone moves, it is assumed that it moves in some space and time. Such space and time may not necessarily be encoded with adverbial phrases, nor do they serve as containers. A container specifies and demarcates the outer limit of a particular portion of the scene. Space and time implied by the existence or movement of some entity are not necessarily specified and demarcated. Sentences (20), (21) and (22) are examples which do not encode time or space with adverbial phrases. The point is that time and space are implied by the entity's existence or movement. Therefore, in the unmarked case, our construal for an existential sentence and for a sentence involving movement is that of a participant within some unspecified time and space. Thus, *inu* 'dog' in (20), *okane* 'money' in (21) and *John* in (22) can be construed as participants in such time and space, and are marked with *ga*. If an adverbial phrase specifies a particular time or space, then it can be marked with *wa* as shown in (23), (24) and (25):

(23)　*Koko　ni wa　inu ga　imasu.*
　　　　here　LOC　dog　exist
　　　　'There is a dog here.'

(24)　*Ginkoo　ni wa　okane ga　arimasu.*
　　　　bank　LOC　money　exist
　　　　'There is money in the bank.'

(25)　*Kinoo wa　John ga　hashitte　imashita.*
　　　　yesterday　　　　running　was
　　　　'John was running yesterday.'

Now consider sentence (26). This is another case in which the subject of the sentence is construed as a participant:

(26)　*Dare ga　kimashita　ka?*
　　　　who　came　QUE
　　　　'Who came?'
　　　　John ga　kimashita.
　　　　　　　　came
　　　　'John came.'

In (26) a WH phrase elicits a chosen member out of an unspecified and undemarcated set. From the nature of a WH question, it is understood that there are a number of individuals who might have come. In (26) such unspecified individuals can be construed as a set even though the set is not encoded. They are not construed as a container (no *wa* phrase is encoded or understood). The WH phrase elicits a member of this unspecified set, and the member, in this case, happens to be John.

While *wa*, the container marker, implies *ga*, the participant marker, the converse is not true. The particle *ga* has a life of its own. The particle *ga* is a marker of a participant of some sort. It does not have to be a participant in a container. When *ga* occurs with *wa* in a sentence, *ga* happens to be a participant in a container.

In sum, I have proposed that *wa* marks a container, *ga* marks a participant of some sort, and the combination of *wa* and *ga* marks a container (*wa*) and a participant (*ga*) that it contains.

3.   Theme, exhaustive listing, and neutral description

In this section I will attempt to show that Kuno's (1973) theme, exhaustive listing and neutral description interpretations also follow from the abstract schemas that I proposed in the above sections. Reconsider sentences (1a), (1b) and (2a):

(1)   a.   *John wa   gakusei   desu.*   [theme]
                     student   COP
          'As for John he is a student.'
      b.   *John ga   gakusei   desu.*   [exhaustive listing]
                     student   COP
          'John (and only John) is a student.'
(2)   a.   *Ame ga   futte   imasu.*   [neutral description]
          rain   falling   is
          'It is raining.'

As mentioned above, Kuno (1973) calls *wa* in (1a) thematic *wa, ga* in (1b) exhaustive listing *ga*, and *ga* in (2a) neutral description *ga*.

Let us first consider (1b). When no action is involved in the predicate, the sentence does not even imply unspecified time and space. Further, such a sentence is only natural if it is an answer to a WH question (e.g. (27)), which elicits a member of a set. If it occurs in isolation, it sounds awkward. Hence, in the unmarked case, a sentence like (1b) gives rise to the exhaustive listing interpretation:

(27)   *Dare ga   gakusei   desu   ka?*
        who   student   COP   QUE
        'Who is a student?'
        John ga   gakusei   desu.
                    student   COP
        'John is a student.'

When the predicate involves some action such as in (2a) and (28), *ga* can be interpreted as a neutral description *ga* as well as an exhaustive listing *ga*:

(28)   *John ga   kimashita.*   [neutral description] or
                    came   [exhaustive listing]
        'John came.'

This last fact can be accounted for in the present analysis in the following way. On the exhaustive listing reading, the *ga*-marked NP is construed as a member of a set. On the neutral description reading, the *ga*-marked NP is a participant moving about in some time and space.

Miyagawa (1987) explains that the two uses of *ga* (i.e. exhaustive listing and neutral description) differ with respect to presuppositional information. He states (1987: 210): "If the knowledge of the existence of the property is shared in the immediate discourse between the speaker and the hearer, the *ga* phrase receives the 'exhaustive listing' interpretation, but if no such shared knowledge exists, it receives the 'descriptive' interpretation." His reasoning is that exhaustive listing sentences require a WH question which solicits a particular individual, whereas neutral description sentences do not require a prior utterance. Therefore, exhaustive listing sentences presuppose knowledge of the existence of the entity but neutral description sentences lack such a presupposition. However, contrary to Miyagawa's explanation, neutral description sentences can entail such a presupposition. Consider the following example. Two people are waiting for a bus at a bus stop. Both see the bus approaching the bus stop. One person utters the sentence *Basu ga kimashita* 'The bus has come.' In this case, the knowledge of the existence of the entity (the bus) is shared in the immediate discourse between the speaker and the hearer; however, in this context this sentence is interpreted as neutral description and not as exhaustive listing. Interpretation of *ga*, thus, does not depend on presuppositions.

In the last section we saw that *wa* marks off certain facets of a scene. This mechanism of containment can be applied to another domain. *Wa* can place an outer limit on a discourse as well. Consider (1a) again:

(1)   a.   *John wa   gakusei   desu.*   [theme]
                     student   COP
             'As for John he is a student.'

In (1a) the predicate describes an attribute of the subject *John*. If the predicate describes an attribute of an entity (i.e. if the predicate does not involve an action), in the unmarked case, the entity itself is chosen as the container. Attributes exist independently of space and time. Thus, when attributes are asserted, space and time elements are not involved in the description, and hence not chosen as containers. This is in opposition to the description of an activity or the assertion of existence. An activity entails a space and time in which it occurs, and if an entity exists, it necessarily exists in some space and time. Similarly, the singling out of a member of a set entails the other members of the set which, metaphorically speaking, surround the singled-out member; hence more than the singled-out member has to be included. The attribute is contained in the participant. In this sense, the participant, which has the attribute in question, serves as the container. Thus, the entity itself is marked with *wa*. Figure 6 illustrates this. This use of *wa* is typical of what Kuno (1973) calls thematic *wa*:

Figure 6: Attribute of an entity

I would like to add that whether a particular verbal is construed as an action or attribute does not depend on categorical classification of verbals. Rather it depends on how they are used. Consider (29):

(29)   *Ame wa   sora   kara   furimasu.*
        rain   sky   from   fall
        'Speaking of the rain (in general), it falls from the sky.'

Although the verb in (29) is *furimasu* 'fall (in the sense of precipitate)', an action verb, in this sentence it is used to describe an attribute of rain. The raining in (29) is an abstraction of what rain does and not an account of a specific instance of rain. Therefore, in (29) *ame* 'rain' is coded as a container rather than as a participant.

In sum, Kuno's thematic *wa*, exhaustive listing *ga* and neutral description *ga* follow from the abstract schemas of *wa* and *ga*. When the entity is a member of a set, the entity is construed as a singled-out participant of a set. Therefore, it is marked with *ga*. When the predicate involves an action, in the unmarked case, the actor is construed as a participant in some time and space. Therefore, it is marked with *ga*. When the predicate describes an attribute of an entity, the attribute is contained in the entity, and in the unmarked case, the entity itself is construed as the container. Hence, the entity is marked with *wa*.

4.   Contrastiveness

Kuno (1972, 1973) has suggested that there are two functions of *wa*, namely thematic *wa* and contrastive *wa*. Based on examples such as (30), he further claims that thematic *wa* must mark an anaphoric or generic NP, but contrastive *wa* does not have such a constraint. Let us assume that the *wa* in (30a) is thematic and that *wa* in (30b) is contrastive. Further, the NP marked by *wa* in both cases is necessarily non-anaphoric/non-generic because of the quantifier *oozei*:

(30) a.   **Oozei no   hito wa   party   ni   kimashita.*
            many   people   to   came
            Speaking of many people, they came to the party.

     b.   *Oozei   no   hito wa   party   ni   kimashita   ga*
            many   people   to   came   but
            omoshiroi   hito wa   hitori   mo
            interesting   people   one person   even
            imasen   deshita.
            was   not
            'Many people came to the party indeed, but there was nobody who was interesting.'

According to Kuno, (30a) is ungrammatical because the NP marked by a thematic *wa* is neither generic nor anaphoric, whereas (30b) is grammatical because the non-generic and non-anaphoric NPs are marked by a contrastive *wa*. However, Kuno (1973: 46) also states that the NP *no* Quantifier construction can enter into the theme freely giving examples such as (31). Unlike (30a) the *wa* in (31) can be interpreted both as thematic and contrastive:

(31) *Ooku   no   gakusei wa   dokushin   desu.*
      many   student   single   are
      'Many students are single.'

Apparently, Kuno's formulation that thematic *wa* must mark an anaphoric or generic NP but contrastive *wa* does not have such a constraint cannot account for (31). The question is why the *wa* in (31) can be readily interpreted as thematic and the *wa* in (30a) cannot when the *wa*-marked NPs in these sentences are both non-generic/non-anaphoric. The present analysis can account for this. We can account for (30a) by saying that since the verb involves an action, in the unmarked (non-contrastive) case, the subject NP is construed as a participant in some time and space. Hence it is marked with *ga* but not with *wa*. Therefore, (30a) sounds awkward: since it is non-contrastive, *ga* rather than *wa* would be expected. On the other hand, the verb in (31) does not involve action but describes an attribute of the subject NP. As I discussed above, if the predicate describes an attribute of an entity, in the unmarked case, the entity itself is chosen as the container. The contrastive interpretation of (30b) and (31), as I will discuss below, comes from a marked choice of container.

A number of linguists have argued that the contrastive uses of *wa* are identified by a contrastive stress on the *wa* phrase. However, for the following reasons, I do not consider such a stress pattern here: (1) To my native ear, a *wa* phrase can indicate contrastiveness without contrastive stress. (2) Clancy and Downing (1987) report that they did not clearly identify a contrastive stress on the contrastive uses of *wa* in the oral narratives by 27 native speaker subjects.

Recently a number of researchers have pointed out that in many cases whether *wa* is thematic or contrastive is not easy to distinguish (e.g. Clancy & Downing 1987), or they have proposed that the distinction of thematic *wa* and contrastive *wa* is derived from a more general function of *wa* (e.g. Iwasaki 1987; Miyagawa 1987).

I have mentioned above that the function of *wa* is to contain a certain portion of a scene relevant to a participant and demarcate that portion from the rest of the scene. Demarcation, which sets off a certain portion of a scene from the rest, implies a contrast. Compare the following pair:

(32) a. *Koko   ni wa   neko ga   imasu.*
          this place   LOC   cat   exist
          'In this place there is a cat.'
      b. *Koko   ni   neko ga   imasu.*
          this place   LOC   cat   exist
          'In this place there is a cat.'

We see that in (32a) *koko ni* 'in this place' is marked with *wa* and in (32b) it is not marked with *wa*. While (32a) can be used to contrast *koko* 'this place' with *soko* 'that place', for example, (32b) cannot be used to make such a contrast. Apparently *wa* is required in order to create contrast. This contrast probably derives from the demarcating function of *wa*. The awkwardness of (34) further indicates that contrastiveness comes from *wa*'s function of demarcation rather than from a juxtaposition of two contrastive words. Compare (33) and (34):

(33)   *Koko   ni wa   inu ga   imasu ga,*
        this place   LOC   dog   exist   but
        soko   ni wa   neko ga   imasu.
        that place   LOC   cat   exist
        'In this place there is a dog but in that place there is a cat.'
(34)   ??*Koko   ni   inu ga   imasu   ga,*
        this place   LOC   dog   exist   but
        soko   ni   neko ga   imasu.
        that place   LOC   cat   exist
        'In this place there is a dog but in that place there is a cat.'

In (33) both *koko* 'this place' and *soko* 'that place' are marked with *wa* and contrasted. On the other hand, in (34) these contrasted words, *koko* 'this place' and *soko* 'that place' are juxtaposed, but the sentence does not give rise to a contrastive interpretation. This is why (34) is odd. Since (33) is identical to (34) except for the presence of *wa*, we can conclude that the contrastive effect of (33) derives from the particle *wa*. A contrastive interpretation does not merely come from mentioning two or more elements; they must be marked with the demarcating particle *wa*.

Both Clancy and Downing (1987) and Iwasaki (1987) suggest that the effect of contrastiveness follows from *wa*'s function of demarcation. That is, demarcating some entity pragmatically implies contrasting it with others. Thus, the thematic and contrastive uses of *wa* are not radically different; they can both be seen as cases of demarcation.

This view has the interesting implication that any use of *wa* is potentially contrastive.[10] The use of *wa* in (1a), which Kuno (1973) describes as thematic, can be given a contrastive reading. Contextual factors contribute to the contrastive interpretation. For example, if (1a) is followed by a statement that Mary is a teacher, (1a) is interpreted as contrastive:

(1)   a.   *John wa   gakusei   desu.*
                      student   COP
          'As for John he is a student.'

Although any use of *wa* is potentially contrastive, there are different degrees of contrastiveness in sentences in isolation. Compare sentences (1a) and (2b) again:

(1)   a.   *John wa   gakusei   desu.*
                      student   COP
          'As for John he is a student.'
(2)   b.   *Ame wa   futte   imasu.*
           rain   falling   is
          'It is raining (but not snowing).'

Between (1a) and (2b), (2b) is judged to be more strongly contrastive. Perhaps on the basis of such native speaker's intuition, Kuno (1973) refers to the use of *wa* in (1a) as thematic and that of *wa* in (2b) as contrastive. The present analysis explains that the stronger effect of contrastiveness derives from the marked choice of the container. As I mentioned above, in the unmarked case, since (1a) describes an attribute of John, *John* is chosen as a container. On the other hand, since (2b) describes an action, *ame* 'rain' is construed as a participant in some time and space but not as a container (again in the unmarked case). To choose *ame* 'rain' in (2b) as a container is a marked choice. Such a choice is likely to be made if a contrast is being made with other entities. Therefore, this marked choice involves contrastiveness. Another motivation for choosing a marked particle comes from the discourse level. For example, if the discourse topic is rain, we may produce (2b) instead of using the particle *ga*. However, since the discourse level is beyond the scope of this paper, I will not further consider the choice between the particles *wa* and *ga* on the discourse level.

As I mentioned above, normally a WH word is not followed by *wa*. However, under certain conditions, *wa* can attach to a WH word. Miyagawa (1987: 188) proposes two conditions that have to be met in order for *wa* to follow a WH word. These two conditions are:

1. The speaker and the hearer share the knowledge of the existence of an identifiable set of individuals in the immediate conversational context.
2. Every member of this set must be exhaustively represented in the WH *wa* question.

Sentence (35) in isolation does not meet the above conditions, while (36) does:

(35)   *Dare wa   kimashita   ka?
        who   came   QUE
        Who came?

(36)   John   mo   Mary   mo   paatii ni
                   also   also   party to
        kuru   to   itte   imashita   ga,
        come   that   saying   was   but
        hitori   shika   konakatta   soo desu ne.
        one person   only   came not   HEARSAY right
        'Both John and Mary said that they would come to the party, but I heard that only one person came.'
        Dare wa   kite,   dare wa   kimasen
        who   came   and   who   came not
        deshita   ka?
        COP   QUE
        'Who came and who did not come?'

Miyagawa's conditions do not explain why this occurs. The present analysis can account for why *wa* can attach to a WH word when each member is represented. In (36) the construal is not that of choosing one member out of a set of many individuals. Rather, it is that of identifying the individuals with two contrasted acts (i.e. coming to the party and not coming to the party). As I mentioned above, contrast motivates the speaker to choose to mark what would be otherwise construed as a participant as a container. Thus, in matching contrasted elements with their respective predicates, *wa* can be used with a WH question.

In sum, the contrastive effect of *wa* derives from the function of *wa* as a demarcator and from the marked choice of a participant as container.

5.   Multiple instantiations of the schema

So far I have discussed single instantiations of the abstract schemas. A schema is not limited to a single instantiation. A schema may be construed multiply. In some instances, more than one entity may be chosen as a participant. Consider sentence (37):

(37)   *John ga   hana ga   hikui   desu.*
                       nose   low   COP
         'John's nose is flat.'

This sentence sounds awkward in isolation but when it is the answer to a WH question, it sounds appropriate:

(38)   *Dare ga   hana ga   hikui   desu   ka?*
         who   nose   low   COP   QUE
         'Whose nose is flat?'
         John ga   hana ga   hikui   desu.
                       nose   low   COP
         'John's nose is flat.'

Dare 'who' elicits a member of a set of individuals. Our construal includes a set, which is unidentifiable in this case, and the participant *John*. *Hana* 'nose' is construed as a participant of *John*. In other words, *John*, construed as a participant of a set of individuals, in turn serves as a container for *hana* 'nose'. When a participant is both contained and a container, the participant marking (*ga*) overrides the container marking (*wa*). Figure 7 illustrates this:

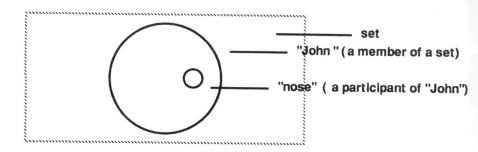

Figure 7: Multiple Instantiation of the participant

In other instances, more than one entity may be chosen as a container, as in (39):

(39)   *John wa   hana wa   hikui   desu   ga,*
               nose   low   COP   but
    me wa   ookii   desu.
    eye   big   COP
    'As for John, his nose is flat but his eyes are big.'

Both *hana* 'nose' and *me* 'eyes' are part of a person. Thus, in the unmarked case, *hana* 'nose' and *me* 'eyes' are construed as participants of a person. However, in (39) *hana* 'nose' and *me* 'eyes' are contrasted with each other. Whereas a flat nose is looked down upon, big eyes are appreciated. Such a contrast leads to the marked choice of a participant as a container. That is, what would otherwise be a participant is now chosen as a container. The latter part of (39) may be omitted as in (40):

(40)   *John wa   hana wa   hikui   desu.*
               nose   low   COP
    'As for John the nose is flat.'

(40) states that John's nose is flat (exhibits a negative characteristic) but it implies that something else (e.g. eyes, mouth, etc.) exhibit a positive characteristic. The existence of a contrasted element makes the speaker encode what would otherwise be a participant as a container. The case of multiple containers is illustrated in Figure 8:

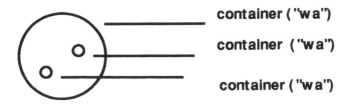

Figure 8: Multiple containers

6. Summary and conclusion

In this paper I have proposed abstract schemas for *wa* and *ga* and the relation between *wa* and *ga*. *Wa* marks a container and it demarcates a certain portion of a scene relevant to a participant. *Ga* marks a participant in some portion of a scene but does not necessarily have to be a participant in a container. When *wa* and *ga* co-occur in a single sentence, *wa* marks a container and *ga* marks a participant contained in that container. My claim is that any use of *wa* and/or *ga* on the sentence level is an instantiation of these schemas. I have shown that various semantic relations held between *wa*-marked NPs and *ga*-marked NPs can be subsumed under this analysis. These are the relations of whole-part, set-member, physical setting-participant and experiencer setting-participant. A contribution of the present analysis of *wa* and *ga* is that it can give semantic explanations to Kuno's (1973) categorizations of theme, contrastiveness, neutral description and exhaustive listing.

The scope of this paper has been limited to uses of *wa* and *ga* at the sentence level. Recently, some researchers have moved the focus of the study of *wa* from the sentence level to the discourse level (Hinds 1987; Hamada 1983; Maynard 1980, 1987; Iwasaki 1987; Clancy & Downing 1987; Watanabe 1989). The findings of the discourse investigations concerning *wa* differ depending on the types of discourse studied. Those who studied written discourse (Maynard 1980, 1987; Hamada 1983; Hinds 1987) claim that *wa* marks a discourse topic. In contrast, those who investigated spoken narratives of cartoons, films, etc. found that *wa* marks locally contrastive elements in discourse (Clancy & Downing

1987). Moreover, Watanabe (1989) argues that *wa* marks the deictic center of a discourse. My suspicion is that the uses of *wa* and *ga* in discourse can be related to the schema analysis that I have proposed here; however, I will leave that matter for future research.

Notes

1.   The normal English expression is "part-whole relation", but I will use both the normal expression and "whole-part relation" in order to keep the elements in the order of discussion.

Shibatani (1978) recognizes the use of *wa* and *ga* in asserting whole-part relations. He assumes that the whole is a topic and that part of the topic must be included in the comment in the underlying structure. He gives the following sentences:

(i)   a.   *Zoo wa   hana ga   nagai.*
            elephant   nose SUB   long
            'An elephant's nose is long.'

       b.   *Zoo wa   [zoo   no   hana   ga   nagai.]*
            elephant   *elephant's   nose*   SUB   long
            WHOLE   PART
            'An elephant's nose is long.'

(ii)   a.   *Jisho wa   ii.*
            dictionary   good
            'The dictionary is good.'

       b.   *Jisho wa   [jisho wa   ii.]*
            dictionary   *dictionary*   good
            WHOLE   WHOLE
            'The dictionary is good.'

Shibatani derives the surface structures (ia) and (iia) from the underlying structures (ib) and (iib), respectively. The whole-part relation must hold in the underlying structure. In (ib) such a relation holds but in (iib) that is not the case. In (iib) the two nominals (i.e. *jisho* 'dictionary') are both wholes. This leads Shibatani to say that all sentences with topic *wa* cannot be derived from the whole-part relation in the underlying structure.

2.   Lakoff and Johnson (1980) discuss a container metaphor with respect to arguments. My analysis is interested in the function word *wa* rather than a content word, for example, *argument*. However, one could very well say that I am proposing that we can understand the particle *wa* in terms of a container metaphor. It was suggested by Ikegami at the Duisburg symposium "Cognitive Linguistics" that the notion of "container" might not be native to the Japanese culture. To this I would respond that there are commonly used native Japanese words that indicate the notion of container. These words include *hako* 'box', *utsuwa* 'container' and *kakoi* 'enclosure'. This fact indicates that the notion of container is not foreign to Japanese culture. Therefore, this notion is not inappropriate for describing the phenomenon of *wa*.

3.   *Ga* is not limited to marking participants in a container. As we will see below, *ga* also marks participants that are not restricted to containers.

4.   In a very limited case, *wa* can be attached to a WH phrase (cf. Miyagawa 1987). I will discuss this point in section 4.

5.   The idea "John has money" can also be expressed with the verb *motte imasu* 'to have' as shown in (i):

   (i)   *John wa*   *okane o*   *motte imasu.*
                         money OBJ   have
         'John has money.'

   With the verb *motte imasu* 'have' the particle marking *okane* 'money' is the object marker *o* and not *ga*. This is because the *motte imasu* construction has a different construal from the *x ga arimasu* construction. In the *motte imasu* construction, the *o*-marked NP is a direct object, and it is not construed within the possessor.

6.   It is not clear to me why the nominal predicate *joozu* 'good at' does not take the locative marker *ni* when the verb *dekimasu* 'can do' does:

   (i)   *John ni wa*   *sore ga*   *dekimasu.*
                LOC   that   can do
         'John can see that.'

7.   I, however, do not agree with Aoyama's (1983) terms, *high* and *low* focus. By "focus", he means concentration of attention. He claims that *wa* is a high focus marker and *ga* is a low focus marker. The notions of high and low focus cannot account for the occurrences of *wa* in Iwasaki's (1987) experiment and those of *ga* in my recent experiment. In his experiment, Iwasaki had native speakers describe their houses. In these expository narratives, most rooms of a house are marked with *wa*. In contrast, in my recent experiment, in which native speakers were asked to fill in the ellipted *wa* or *ga* in transcripts of a swimming race radio broadcast, swimmers are marked with *ga* in most instances and *wa* rarely occurs. Why are rooms marked with *wa* and swimmers marked with *ga*? Since swimmers move around, don't we need more concentration of attention in describing swimmers than rooms? The present proposal can explain these results. The rooms of a house are perceived as containers. Therefore, they are marked with *wa*. In contrast, swimmers are perceived as participants in a swimming pool. Therefore, they are marked with *ga*.

8.   Langacker (1987) uses the term *predication* to mean the semantic pole of a linguistic expression.

9.   When a *wa* phrase is anaphoric in the discourse, it may be zero-pronominalized as shown in speaker B's utterance in the following discourse:

   Speaker A: *Koko*   *ni wa*   *nani ga*   *imasu*   *ka?*
                this place   LOC   what   exist   QUE
                'What's here?'

   Speaker B: *Inu ga*   *imasu.*
                dog   exist
                'A dog is (here).'

10. Inoue (1982) mentions that *wa* has an inherent sense of contrast and claims that in *wa* a contrastive sense is basic.

References

Aoyama, Takashi
    1983   "The free-floating focus system in Japanese: Form-content analysis of *wa* and *ga*", *Gengo kenkyu* [Language research] 83: 41-60.

Chafe, Wallace L.
    1976   "Givenness, contrastiveness, definiteness, subject and topic", in: Charles N. Li (ed.), 27-55.

Clancy, Patricia M. & Pamela Downing
    1987   "The use of *wa* as a cohesion marker in Japanese oral narratives", in: John Hinds, Senko Maynard & Shoichi Iwasaki (eds.), 3-56.

Hamada, Morio
    1983   Referential choices in theme, subject and ellipsis in written narrative discourse: A case study of Japanese folktales. [Unpublished M.A. thesis, Cornell University.]

Hinds, John
    1987   "Thematization, assumed familiarity, staging and syntactic binding in Japanese", in: John Hinds, Senko Maynard & Shoichi Iwasaki (eds.), 83-106.

Hinds, John, Senko Maynard & Shoichi Iwasaki (eds.)
    1987   *Perspective on topicalization: The case of Japanese wa.* Amsterdam: Benjamins.

Inoue, Kazuko
    1982   "An interface of syntax, semantics, and discourse structures", *Lingua* 57: 259-300.

Iwasaki, Shoichi
    1987   "Identifiability, scope-setting, and the particle *wa*: A study of Japanese spoken expository discourse", in: John Hinds, Senko Maynard & Shoichi Iwasaki (eds.), 107-41.

Kuno, Susumu
    1972   *Nihongo bunpoo kenkyuu* [Studies of Japanese grammar]. Tokyo: Taishukan Shoten.
    1973   *The structure of the Japanese language.* Cambridge: MIT Press.
    1976   "Subject, theme and the speaker's empathy: A reexamination of relativization phenomena", in: Charles N. Li (ed.), 417-44.

Lakoff, George & Mark Johnson
    1980   *Metaphors we live by.* Chicago: University of Chicago Press.

Langacker, Ronald W.
    1987   *Foundations of cognitive grammar.* Stanford: Stanford University Press.

Li, Charles N. (ed.)
    1976   *Subject and topic.* New York: Academic Press.

Maynard, Senko K.
    1980   Discourse functions of the Japanese theme marker *wa*. [Unpublished Ph.D. dissertation, Northwestern University.]
    1987   "Thematization is a staging device in the Japanese narrative", in: John Hinds, Senko Maynard & Shoichi Iwasaki (eds.), 57-82.

Mikami, Akira
    1963   *Nihongo no ronri* [The logic of the Japanese language]. Tokyo: Kuroshio Shuppan.

Miyagawa, Shigeru
    1987   *"Wa* and the WH phrase", in: John Hinds, Senko Maynard & Shoichi
                  Iwasaki (eds.), 185-220.
Shibatani, Masayoshi
    1978   *Nihongo no bunseki* [An analysis of Japanese]. Tokyo: Taishukan.
Watanabe, Noriko
    1989   *"Wa* and *ga*: From the perspective of the deictic center in narrative",
                  Paper presented at the Southern California Japanese/Korean
                  Linguistics Conference. August 4-6.

The meaning of (a)round:
A study of an English preposition

Rainer Schulze

0. Introduction

0.1. General assumptions

The main thesis of current linguistic theory is that the grammatical organization and structure of a text (spoken or written) is motivated by
properties of the human cognitive system (Wierzbicka 1988), an
interpretative system that above all monitors perceptual input and
"generates" thought and language in a human being. This system, it can
be assumed, is partly innate and partly learned by the individual. The
grammatical or syntactic component of language, as is claimed in our
paper, is not a separate and isolated module within language or within
general cognition. More emphatically, syntactic constructions and
grammatical relations are neither wholly innate nor are they linguistic
primitives; moreover, they are not simply context-neutral markers of
position or relation, but are quite meaningful in their own right (cf.
Schmid (1986: 95f), for example, for a different view). As has already
been shown for the meaning of certain words and word classes (cf.
Lindner (1981) on verb particles, Brugman (1981) on the preposition
over or Sweetser (1984) on conjunctions), many grammatical elements
are very rich in meaning and, additionally, most have a multitude of
meanings. Yet these meanings are not unrelated and for most such
grammatical words in English, e.g. *(a)round*, polysemy is rampant, and
furthermore, there are systematic correspondences between many if not
most of their senses.[1]

0.2. Particle, preposition, adverb

(A)round may be seen as a representative of different grammatical
classes. Thus, *(a)round* may be used as a preposition in *Ruth drove
round the corner*, as an adverb particle in *Jan came round* or as an adverbial particle as part of a more complex construction (phrasal verb or

two-word verb or multi-word verb or verb-particle construction) in *Eve managed to talk Michael round*. The major defect of this attempt at classification is that classificatory criteria which should be kept distinct are very often confused, i.e. (*a*)*round* is simultaneously classified on syntactic grounds, on historical grounds and on semantic grounds. It is very often maintained that the notion of preposition can properly be approached by the enumeration of the syntactic properties of the prepositions, thus claiming that the preposition is either followed by a complement realized by a noun phrase or by a *wh*-clause, an *-ing* participial clause or another prepositional phrase (Quirk et al. 1985), but that in English a preposition cannot be followed by a *that*-clause or a *to*-infinitive. The Extended Standard Theory (Chomsky 1981) takes account of these formal linguistic criteria and posits at least three different subclasses, i.e. the three classes are referred to as *syntactic prepositions* (the occurrence of these depends on the syntactic configuration of the sentence), *subcategorized prepositions* (prepositions which are selected by the verb) and *lexical prepositions* (prepositions which have a lexical content of their own). Three different rules within the EST-model are applied at different stages: All three types are inserted before *Move alpha* operates; the insertion of lexical items (including lexical and subcategorized prepositions), however, must precede the insertion of grammatical formatives (syntactic prepositions) (Bennis, Prins & Vermeulen 1983, Fries 1988).

As can be seen from the discussion so far, the description of a lexical item and the assignment of this item to a particular grammatical class is largely governed by syntactic criteria. This approach is closely linked to a grammatical theory which seeks to uncover the language user's latent knowledge about his/her grammar.

In our view all this is insightful and true, but it does not seem to be sufficient to convey any idea of what lies at the bottom of the language user's verbal products. If we are to look for the concepts which underlie language production, we have to start from a purely semantic viewpoint and equate (grammatical) meaning with conceptualization (or mental experience) (Langacker 1988: 6). Taking this as a viable alternative to Chomsky's approach, it becomes more than obvious that instances of (*a*)*round* as a preposition, as an adverb, as an adverbial particle and as part of a prepositional verb share more common semantic properties than syntacticians might be ready to admit. Thus, different grammatical instances of (*a*)*round* form a homogeneous group, and different grammatical realizations of (*a*)*round* are nothing but a reflex of diverse ways of denoting distinct event patterns (Lutzeier 1988: 367, Givón 1989: 59).

Or to put it briefly: "'Surface differences' point to differences in meaning. Differences in grammatical form are not arbitrary, but signal differences in meaning" (Wierzbicka 1988: 14); they are, we are tempted to add, reflections of semantic and functional shifts.

Starting from these assumptions we feel justified in suggesting the following terminology: We will use the cover term *preposition* whenever we identify *(a)round* in its general, unspecified sense; we refer to *prepositional* or *adverbial* whenever the lexical item is examined in its particular occurrences (collocations).

0.3. Image-schemata and use types

In the ensuing investigation we will use the notion of a prototype (paradigm case) in order to characterize the structure of the overall concept of the preposition *(a)round*. We assume that the paradigmatic use of *(a)round* corresponds to a holistic concept in the language user. This concept will be identified as an object-independent, prototypical core meaning (prototypical image-schema) which specifies the configurational properties of *(a)round* (Hottenroth 1986: 107ff). This explication parallels Lakoff's "minimal specification interpretation" (1987: 420). All semantic elaborations and extensions from the superordinate schema confirm the polysemous character of the preposition. The locative meaning of *(a)round* will be assumed as the prototypical image-schema; elaborations from the core meaning extend the prototype to non-locative concepts which can then serve as the basis for alternative image-schemata. To conclude these theoretical prerequisites: The prototypical core meaning may be identified as the schema at the highest level of abstraction; less prototypical meanings may be located at a lower level.

0.4. Aim of the paper

In this paper we present a semantic analysis (heavily relying on previous investigations in Cognitive Grammar) of the prototypical and less prototypical usages of *(a)round*, describing the usages in some detail, and setting forth schematic structures which embody the generalizations obtaining among them and point out their relatedness. Both the spatial and the non-spatial senses of *(a)round* (and thus extending Hawkins' (1985) analysis of the spatial senses of *(a)round*) will be under investigation, i.e. the literal and the metaphorical (elaborated and extended) usages of (a)round.[2]

1.   The cognitive approach to the description of prepositions

The framework we will use is that of Cognitive Grammar, which assumes an ideational or conceptual view of meaning. A complete description of the theory would be impossible here, but the basic ideas and assumptions can be formulated rather succinctly and will serve our purposes. It is claimed in Cognitive Grammar that all grammatical constructs have conceptual import: There are no meaningless morphemes nor abstract structures void of semantic content. Grammatical items resemble lexical items in that they are polysemous. The alternative values of a grammatical construct such as (a)round form a network of more or less closely linked senses around a prototype. In general, one (general abstract) value in the network will be schematic in that its characterization will hold for all instantiations of the construct. The meaning of any grammatical or lexical item is referred to as *predication*. Predications are characterized in terms of cognitive domains which, to simplify matters, are equivalent to Fillmore's frames and Lakoff's idealized cognitive models. Any conceptualization or knowledge system can function as a cognitive domain. Predications are either nominal or relational. Relational predications profile (or designate) the interconnections among different facets of a conceived situation. They designate either atemporal relations or processes and correspond to the traditional categories of verbs, adjectives and prepositions. Relational predications (or predicates) single out one entity involved in a profiled relationship and make it the most prominent entity within the profile. This entity is referred to as the *figure* (= F) within the relational profile, the less salient entity is referred to as the *ground* (= G). It is typically the case that G provides a point of reference in a predication with respect to which F moves or is located. Cognitive Grammar recognizes only two levels of structure in language, i.e. the semantic pole (which is at issue in our investigation) and the phonological one. No separate level of autonomous syntax is claimed to be necessary for an adequate linguistic description of (a)round (cf. Hawkins (1985: 63ff) for the additional descriptive inventory (i.e. base, domain, profile, etc.) for the description of prepositional predicates, which we will use throughout the paper).[3]

2.   The English data: A representative sample

In the standard descriptions and grammars of English, accounts of the semantics of *(a)round* are essentially unenlightening. Some authors, such as Bennett, are mainly interested in how well-formed semantic structures are generated and mapped onto lexemic representations (surface structures) within the framework of stratificational grammar. Rather than being interested in exhaustive explanations of the semantics of *(a)round*, Bennett's (1975: 84ff) major aim is to characterize the overall semantic structure of the item. Though Lindkvist (1976: 133ff) in his detailed descriptivist approach to prepositional meanings provides us with examples from a plethora of literary sources, we prefer to have recourse to three different types of corpora: (a) the Lancaster-Oslo/Bergen (LOB) corpus, containing a number of written texts (all of them published in 1961) dealing with different subjects and being of different styles as indicated by the headings of the categories (press: reportage; press: editorial; press: reviews; religion; skills, trades, and hobbies; belles lettres, essay; learned and scientific writings; general fiction; romance and love stories, etc.); (b) the *Oxford dictionary of current idiomatic English* (ODCIE). Volume 1: *Verbs with prepositions & particles* comprising contemporary sources, mainly written, but also spoken (works of fiction, biography, history, etc.); (c) the *Collins Cobuild English language dictionary* (COBUILD) basing its entries on a 20-million word database (words taken from books, magazines, newspapers, pamphlets, leaflets, conversations, radio, and television broadcasts, etc.). While this range of text corpora does not exhaustively cover the data relevant to fully characterizing the semantics of *(a)round* we will nevertheless take it as representative of the whole because of space limitations.

3.   The (a)round-structure

Figure 1 contains the network of prototypical and less prototypical image-schemata with the preposition *(a)round*, including all the relevant use types as indicators of various classes of usages distinguished by different F/G-configurations. The submeanings of *(a)round* given under each image-schema should not be interpreted as semantic attributes, but rather should facilitate the identification of the numerous *(a)round*-instances. Image-schema I serves as the first object-independent, prototypical core meaning at the highest level of abstraction, from which all other image-schemata and use types in this network may be derived. Figure 1 also supplies information on the difference between categorization by prototypical use type or by image-schema. In the former case, less typical use types can be thought of as extensions from the prototype, while in the latter, individual use types represent elaborations of the schema. The two ways of categorization are similar; the schema, however, must fully sanction all members of the category while the prototypical use type allows for partial sanction (Langacker 1988: 51f).

3.1.   Image-schema I: The prototypical core meaning of (a)round

(*A*)*round* evokes an F/G-configuration in which the circular movement of F (*a*)*round* G is of prime importance. The path (covered by F) ideally and continuously runs in circles with F partially or completely surrounding G. The movement of F is typically conceptualized as self-initiated (see Figure 1).

3.1.1.   Use type: "Circular movement about a central point outside F"

The conceptualization of entities in motion is one of the cornerstones of human experience. Apart from the conceptualization of linear movement, the idea of circular movement may be grasped as a subtype, which can be detected in numerous conceptual schemata. The prototypical instance of (*a*)*round* includes F as a punctiform or dimensionless entity in (very often supposedly) self-initiated movement and G as an additional dimensionless entity as stationary reference point; F's circular movement is grasped as a constant movement. This type of movement should be interpreted as "oriented", though the language user's attention does not focus on the starting-point and goal of the movement. This "imperfective" type of (forward?) motion is opposed to the "terminative" type which suggests the conception of enclosure. (*A*)*round* profiles a relation against a base containing the cognitive domain of oriented physical space. This interpretation includes event patterns which are verbalized as follows:

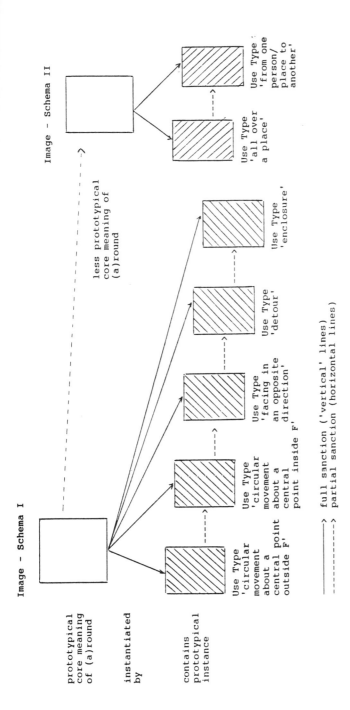

Figure 1: The semantic structure of (a)round

(1)   *We knew from the number of vultures circling round that some liv-*
       ing creature - whether an animal or a human being - was nearing
       its end below (ODCIE)
(2)   *tongue went in deeper and touched his own, gliding round it, pulling*
       (LOB)

F typically stands for (pro-)nouns which denote animate beings, capable of self-initiated movement. But F may also represent (pro-) nouns which denote select parts of the body to which some agentive function may be assigned. The latter possibility is guaranteed by the process of ontological metaphorization (Lakoff & Johnson 1980: 25ff) where entities are further specified as animate so that we have the opportunity to express a diversity of experiences with non-human entities in terms of human activities and characteristics. Furthermore, the prototypical (*a*)*round*-instance entails the particular distribution of the grammatical roles of F and G, thus assigning the function of sentential subject to F and presenting G as a part of an optional prepositional phrase. The place for G is then typically filled by (pro-)nouns such as *world, earth, sun, moon, bowl* or others indicating animate beings that may act as an axis of rotation.

The idea of F's constant rotation about a real or imaginary axis is also present in all those samples which are marked for F's other-initiated motion. The conceptualization of this event pattern is reflected in a particular grammatical pattern, in which F takes the function of a sentential object or a grammatical subject in passive constructions:

(3)   *chases her round the kitchen table* (LOB)
(4)   *The brambles were twined around the garden fence*
       (ODCIE)

In addition to the specifics of the F/G-relationship mentioned above, some more attributes have to be adduced for this (*a*)*round*-instance: F is represented by (pro-)nouns which stand for entities in their elongated extension, thus comprising nouns such as *sash,* (*a piece of*) *wool,* (*piece of*) *wire,* (*length of*) *thread,* (*strip of*) *bandage* or *rag*. If G is lexicalized (e.g. as *waist, finger, ankle*), it denotes entities which allow their "wrapping up". Whereas in the prototypical (*a*)*round*-instance G is marked for its non-supportive function with regard to F, we now have to assume a contiguity relation between F and G since some part of F coincides with some part of G:

(5)   *The mayor had a tricolour sash wrapped round his waist* (ODCIE)
(6)   *The wire was coiled round the cylinder, and then the current was turned on* (ODCIE)

This subschema is responsible for the generating of additional semantic extensions:

(7)   *He put his arms round her* (COBUILD)
(8)   *The cat coiled round his legs* (COBUILD)

and evokes the cognitive domain "warmth" or "sympathy". Note that it is not the idea of constant motion which is central here, but a conceptual schema which is closely linked to the idea of enclosure, while still showing some major differences to the latter with regard to a particular type of motion.

Another semantic extension traces its origin from this contiguity relationship of F and G and its scope of usage is restricted to all those F/G-relationships in which F is represented by (pro-)nouns for human beings and/or their proper names, and G stands for *finger* as in:

(9)   *I believe, if she wanted to, she could twist anyone round her little finger* (ODCIE)

This contiguity relationship profiles relations against a base ("influencing control") containing the domain "intersociability". Due to the limited choice of real-world entities for F and G and due to the historically-motivated pctrification of the construction, this relation should be seen as an optimum semantic extension. If we take into account the syntactic-semantic features of this construction, we are justified in classifying it as a phraseological unit (Gläser 1988: 265).

More semantic extensions are discernible if F and G or their (pro-)nouns (respectively) do not denote real-world objects or beings, but entities of a more abstract nature. This type of extension again reflects the possibilities of ontological metaphorization: Actions or events now take on a more "substantial" character and are meant to show, by analogy with the prototypical *(a)round*-instance, either an agentive function (as a sentential subject) or an axis function (as a noun in the prepositional phrase) in:

(10)   *whose hobby revolves round a doll's house* (LOB)

(11)   *The grazing and silage-making programme revolves round Italian ryegrass* (LOB)
(12)   *The discussion revolved round three topics* (COBUILD)

F stands, as is partly shown, for (pro-)nouns such as *life, argument, debate, discussion, dispute, struggle,* etc. All the nouns mentioned are not parts of a strictly limited semantic field, i.e. a group of words which are interrelated and organized into particular areas (Trier 1968: 10f). Rather they form parts of an inventory which can be conceived of as a result through a process of holistic conceptualization - *Hypostasierung* (Leisi 1961: 24) - and whose entities may be metalinguistically referred to in everyday discourse. F then exclusively appears as sentential subject and with G profiles relations against a base ("metadiscourse") containing the cognitive domain "communication".

3.1.2.   Use type: "Circular movement about a central point inside F"

Starting from the assumption that the prepositional usage of (*a*)*round* is indicative of its prototypical instance, we then regard the following examples as samples of the less prototypical instances of (*a*)*round*:

(13)   *Finally, never, never pull a drill around by its power lead* (LOB)
(14)   *the wine glass, turning it round in her fingers* (LOB)
(15)   *turning the brim round in his hands* (LOB)

As can be shown, F follows a circular course, the movement itself being of the other-initiated type. The reference point (G) for F's movement is not an external one, but part of F itself; G is not lexicalized and has to be inferred by the language user. F as a sentential object stands for (pro-)nouns such as *earpieces, brim, drill, wine glass, wheel,* etc. and denotes entities which can be characterized by attributes such as "roundness" or "sphericity" and which allow a twisting movement about their own axis. This conception is the central one for this use type; especially if we bear in mind that the twisting motion of a wheel is closely linked to one of the primary cognitive and visual experiences of small children with regard to this event pattern. Apart, for example, from balls which may be conceptualized as round entities from every vantage point, other objects such as wheels or glasses allow a particular perspectivization, which only then conveys the idea of roundness. These "preferred" perspectives dominate others, dependent on the context and the formation of schemata; (drinking) glasses, for example, may also yield a vertically organized concept which, moreover, is intrinsically marked. The language user's cognitive faculty for abstraction, i.e. his/her preference for particular perspectives or the suppression of others, is again reflected in all those samples in which "non-round" objects change their gestalt and, put conceptually, become "round" ones:

(16)   *The leaves whirled round as they fell to the ground*
(17)   *The room seemed to whirl around* (LOB)

Samples of this type (at least in the LOB corpus) are rare and we should inquire into the causes of this fact. Though we do not have a definite answer to this problem, we assume that the limited number of objects and/or beings for F (with regard to the domain of oriented physical space) finds its counterpart in a very limited number of processes of holistic conceptualization, so that the degree of the predictability of possible F/G-configurations in more abstract domains is fairly low.

3.1.3.   Use type: "Facing in an opposite direction"

Here the idea of a conceptual unit of F and G is picked up again. The conceptual difference to the schemata mentioned before is due to the fact that F is not in constant and circular movement, but, at most, in semicircular movement. F, incorporating G, is typically exemplified by (pro-)nouns which denote human beings. It is an F/G-relationship which is profiled against a base containing the domain of oriented physical space:

(18)   *He turned around to find a policeman eying him suspiciously* (ODCIE)
(19)   *I twisted round, so that I* (LOB)
(20)   *Then, abruptly, she turned round. "Oh* (LOB)

While G is apparently not lexicalized, F appears exclusively as sentential subject, so that *(a)round*, in grammatical terms, is used adverbially. The distance covered by F in semicircular movement is not imperfective any longer: Rather, the schematic representation of F's movement focuses on the point of departure and the goal of F's movement which, as is shown above, is marked by its abrupt and unexpected coming to a standstill. Moreover, we are able to assign a particular functional quality to this standstill: F turns round in order to take a look at something very special, in order to devote himself/herself to another activity or in order to get in touch with somebody else. It is not the attribute "abruptness" which is responsible for the generation of additional semantic extensions, but the attribute "purposefulness" which is expressed in the following samples:

(21)   *Won't the child turn round and blame the school* (COBUILD)
(22)   *Then the owner turned round and said we couldn't have the house after all, because he'd promised it to a friend* (ODCIE)

Even though F as sentential subject stands for (pro-)nouns which denote human beings, we are faced with an F/G-configuration which profiles a relation against a base not containing the domain of oriented physical space; instead, this F/G-configuration carries a more negative connotation as the equation "change of place corresponds to change of mind" may be enriched by the attributes "ingratitude" or "self-complacency".

The discussion of various (*a*)*round*-instances has revealed so far that all the human beings or their respective bodies denoted by F are intrinsically marked; i.e. human beings or their bodies are conceptualized as entities with inherent backs and fronts. Semantic extensions within this use type take up this conceptual subschema and incorporate in their corresponding F/G-relations entities to which an agentive function and intrinsic structure may be ascribed. Such a process of ontological metaphorization results in samples such as:

(23)   *The American market turned round very sharply about a week ago* (ODCIE)

where F is verbalized by nouns such as *money market, stock market, economy, sterling, the dollar*, etc. Apart from the cognitive domain "financial world" there are further domains in which other F/G-relations are constituted correspondingly. The domain "navigation", for example, is evoked in:

(24)   *One of the factors in the profitability of passenger ships is how quickly they can be turned round* (ODCIE)

where F takes nouns such as *ship, liner, tanker* as examples. These mostly passive constructions profile an F/G-relation which incorporates the attributes "disembarkation" and "unloading".[4]

This raises the question of whether different nouns such as *bus, taxi* or *train*, thus showing an intrinsic structure, may equally well occur as F. A plausible explanation might be that the latter objects also serve for the conveyance of passengers; they are, however, conceptualized as easily steered vehicles, their "about-turns" being less difficult and less costly. Our assumption may be corroborated by the fact that F, in grammatical terms, cannot take a position in the sentence exhibiting agentive function.

The schema discussed so far is a very productive one, generating additional F/G-configurations with, for example, the cognitive domain "weather" in:

(25) *The breeze had swung round, so that now instead of fighting against it we were being borne along with it* (ODCIE)

Whether a noun such as *public opinion* may be conceptualized as an entity with back and front or not cannot be settled here. If we take, however, the unpredictability of changes of wind direction for granted, then the following sample should be allowed as a semantic extension of our schema:

(26) *Since the last election public opinion has swung round completely on the question of allowing heavy traffic into the centre of cities* (ODCIE)

Thus, *public opinion, electorate,* etc. are nouns for F in an F/G-relation evoking the domain "politics".

Similarly, other examples show that F's local semicircular movement may be equated with a change of function. This assumption is based on the idea that the "local" movement finds its conceptual counterpart in a temporal dimension; metaphorically speaking, the change of place, i.e. from l_1 to l_2, involves some change of time, so that $t_1 < t_2$, and F is supposed to change his/her functional quality (gestalt). F as sentential subject occurs in:

(27) *After a certain number of points, the players changed round so that neither could benefit unduly from the wind or the position of the sun* (ODCIE)

(28)   *"Perhaps you and Brown had better change round: you need more experience of office routine"* (ODCIE)

The agentive schema is also constitutive for all those constructions in which F is seen as being in other-initiated movement and in which F occurs as sentential object. Again, the intrinsic structure of F is decisive and F's abrupt change of direction in some of the above examples is now replaced by the idea of a forcefully caused action with F as patient:

(29)   *Esmond turned me round, pushed the hair from* (LOB)
(30)   *You're going to turn that caravan around and head back out of here* (LOB)

But not only the domain of oriented physical space is evoked; the domain "change of mind" is also focused on in:

(31)   *I'll talk them round. They* (LOB)
(32)   *He didn't really want to go to France, but I managed to talk him round* (COBUILD)

What is common in all these samples is that *(a)round* is exclusively used in adverbial function.

The agentive schema with F in semicircular movement also incorporates *(a)round*-instances which may be labelled "causative". What we have in mind are F/G-configurations in which F is represented by a noun that denotes the head of the body; this metonymic extension finds its local and especially causative counterpart in a kernel paraphrase such as X SENDS HIS/HER HEAD ROUND (Ikegami 1984: 56), which leaves, in deep semantics terminology, F in the position of a "sentential" object. The *(a)round*-instance involved is seen as derived from the schema with the entire body in motion. Our assumption is supported by the fact that *look round* requires a range of F/G-relations very similar to that of *turn round*, as becomes obvious in the following:

(33)   *I made a rustling sound and the lady looked round angrily* (ODCIE)
(34)   *Her head snapped violently around and sideways* (LOB)

This local variant is also paralleled by a more abstract one. The look ahead thus corresponds to the glimpse of the future, the look back to the glimpse of the past, and both opposite fields of "vision" again take up the idea of the intrinsic structure of the human body. F and G here profile relations against a base ("self-contemplation") containing the domain "emotion":

(35)   *She looked around her. Part of her life was ending* (LOB)
(36)   *She sang in clubs and in concerts, until she looked around one day and asked herself* (LOB)

Again, *(a)round* occurs exclusively as an adverbial.

3.1.4.   Use type: "Detour"

The idea of F's straight-line movement incorporates the idea of covering a particular distance in the shortest possible time. If this is not the case, then F's change of place is seen as the deviation from the ideal direction of motion and a deviant schema is generated. The F/G-configuration involved profiles a relation against a base ("detour") containing the domain of oriented physical space. F is typically represented by nouns which denote (human) beings in self-initiated movement; G is part of an optional prepositional phrase containing a noun which denotes (human) beings or objects as obstacles on F's way:

(37)   *Round the first bend* (LOB)
(38)   *who had just disappeared round the corner* (LOB)
(39)   *He went round the deal table* (LOB)

Thus, possible candidates for obstacles are entities such as headlands, promontories (including their proper names), bends, corners, but also tables or persons which prevent F from following a direct course. Although the "motional" schema is constitutive for this type, some few examples invite the language user to infer the dynamic element from his/her personal experience:

(40)   *One is hungry; food is around the corner* (LOB)

The dynamic schema in general takes up two different types of movement verbs which are responsible for the deictic character of this schema: If F moves round an obstacle, then F may either enter or leave the visual range (field) of an imaginary observer:

(41)   *all armed with rifles. As the nearest of them came round the shack,*
       his rifle at the ready, I saw that it was Nick (LOB)

Again, we are able to discern a syntactic-semantic pattern which is
equivalent to a subschema as semantic extension. F as sentential object
in:

(42)   *sent him round to the back* (LOB)
(43)   *He made her walk round to the garage* (LOB)

or as conceptually "materialized" entity in:

(44)   *She looked cautiously round the edge* (LOB)

have already been exhaustively presented. A very similar interpretation
applies to a type of metonymic extension where a central part of the
body represents the body in its entirety, as in:

(45)   *a child of about fifteen put her head round it* (LOB)

All the F/G-configurations mentioned so far profile relations against
various bases, but all of them containing the domain of oriented physical space. Derived from the local domain is a construction, where F as
sentential object (and in other-initiated movement) is prevented from
straight-line movement; the prevention is subsequently identified with
deviant behavior on the part of F and realized as:

(46)   *The job drove me round the bend* (COBUILD)
(47)   *You two will drive me round the bend soon* (ODCIE)

The domain "social relationship" is evoked in all those cases where F is
represented by (pro-)nouns for human beings; all (*a*)*round*-instances
occur as adverbials, and G is not lexicalized. F as sentential subject occurs in:

(48)   *If you come round to my house at 4.30* (LOB)
(49)   *Nip round to Sammy and give him this* (LOB)

or as sentential object in:

(50)   *Do bring your wife around one evening. We're longing to meet her*
       (ODCIE)

The non-straight-line movement of F is directed to an imaginary observer, so that the schema of at least two meeting entities is evoked.
This schema is typically realized by verbs such as *bring* or *come*, not by
take or *go*. These take account of the fact that F's reaching his/her goal
goes together with a change in gestalt quality, since F's arrival at the
imaginary observer turns him/her from an invisible human being into a
visible one. This change of gestalt quality becomes apparent in additional *(a)round*-instances which are more abstract in nature. Again, G
remains non-lexicalized, and F is realized by (pro-)nouns for events as
conceptually materialized entities which then, metaphorically speaking,
may follow a course. The nouns under discussion are *Christmas, Easter,
payday, birthday, conference*, etc., and they are parts of F/G-configura-
tions which profile relations against the base "occurrence of an event"
containing non-local domains. F takes the role of a sentential subject
and suggests agentive function in (supposedly) self-initiated movement.
The dynamic element which is inherent in this subschema is responsible
for the conception of events being placed out of human beings' reach,
but still being expectable:

(51)   *Labour movement was coming round in support of his views* (LOB)
(52)   *when lunch came round again it* (LOB)
(53)   *She'll be a jolly tough candidate to beat when the election comes
       round* (COBUILD)

Closely linked to this schema and also deictically motivated are again
those F/G-relations in which F denotes human beings, as in:

(54)   *spent the morning fainting and coming round over and over again*
       (LOB)
(55)   *Nobody was making any attempt to bring her round* (COBUILD)

These constructions profile relations against the base "recovery of consciousness" with F either as sentential subject or object. F follows a
course, metaphorically speaking, this event being equivalent to the effort to turn F from one gestalt quality into another. Attributes which
play a major role here are "unconsciousness" vs. "consciousness",
"darkness" vs. "brightness" or "non-visibility" vs. "visibility". This

motional schema is deictically motivated in that F's change of gestalt quality is directed towards the imaginary observer.

Another subschema is discernible with an F/G-configuration which profiles relations against the base "change of mind". The deictic and motional concept is realized by *come* or *bring*, depending on F's occurrence as sentential subject or object:

(56)   *We did our best to bring him round to our point of view* (COBUILD)
(57)   *Mother came round to my way of thinking, thus making life a lot easier* (ODCIE)

Non-deictic instances of (*a*)*round* do not basically focus on the end-point of F's movement, but rather take account of the fact that F "... frequently deviating from a straight line" (Cresswell 1978: 15f) moves round an obstacle. Here F and G evoke an optional prepositional phrase. This schema finds its extensions in all those samples where abstract entities turn into "obstructionable" entities by hypostatization. Nouns such as *law*, *regulation* or *rule* are possible candidates for G (if lexicalized):

(58)   *The lawyer was well known for his skill at getting round the law, usually on technical points* (ODCIE)
(59)   *She knew the ways to get round the rules* (COBUILD)

F and G profile relations against the base "legislation", which is part of a non-local domain. The base "solution of a problem" is profiled as soon as nouns such as *problem*, *obstacle*, *difficulty*, *subject*, etc. occur as examples for G. Again, these nouns represent "obstructionable" entities which are subject to the similar process of hypostatization; they present, however, a "more" open-ended list of possible candidates:

(60)   *"Let's not skirt round the awkward questions - let's try and answer them"* (ODCIE)
(61)   *"It says here that an applicant should have three years' experience, but I think we can scrub round that"* (ODCIE)

These (*a*)*round*-instances are comparable to instances in which (*a*)*round* does not occur as a preposition, but exclusively as an adverb; G is a covert element in the corresponding constructions so that no explicit mention is made of the obstructing element on F's straight path.

The attribute "effort" which characterizes F's non-rectilinear movement comes to the fore in samples such as:

(62)   *Perhaps we would get around to letters later* (LOB)
(63)   *I didn't get round to taking the examination* (COBUILD)

and thus profiles relations to a base which belongs to a non-local base.

3.1.5.   Use type: "Enclosure"

While in all the use types we have discussed so far the conceptualization of F's movement (self- or other-initiated) was of prime importance, it now dwindles into insignificance. We admit that the ensuing *(a)round*-instances do not profile F/G-configurations which are static in nature, but the question of where the movement of F originates is irrelevant. The local domain here is evoked by F/G-configurations which profile relations with F as a (pro-)noun for a group of persons and G (if lexicalized) as a (pro-)noun for a single person:

(64)   *The boys crowded round him* (COBUILD)
(65)   *Reporters clustered around the distinguished visitor*
       (ODCIE)

Here F takes the role of the sentential subject whereas G is part of an optional prepositional phrase. What distinguishes this configuration from others is not only the close link between F and G produced by the semantic construction, but the close link is also reflected by our personal (*"lebensweltlich"*) experience: In a group of people with a hierarchical structure persons of prime importance within this group form the center around which all other inferior members of the group gather.

This assumption holds both for teacher/pupil-relations or superior/subordinate-relations or paterfamilias/family member-relations, and the schema established by *(a)round* is such a prolific schema that it generates semantic extensions in which the concept of F's (supposedly) self-initiated movement is suppressed in favor of a concept of movement which is felt to be initiated from the outside towards the center:

(66)   *The barker managed to gather a small group of curious passers-by*
       round the platform (ODCIE)

(67)   *Passengers in the dining car were clustered round a radio*
(COBUILD)

Another aspect is important in this connection: Since not all entities can be grouped round a singular one, we have to assume that this fact is mirrored in the grammatical realizations of the corresponding event patterns; that is to say that F occurs as a pluralized constituent against G as non-pluralized constituent, as in:

(68)   *they settled round the fire while* (LOB)
(69)   *men round the billiard table, pockets* (LOB)

Extensions of this pattern comprise F/G-configurations which profile relations against the base "negotiation" with "interpersonal relation" as cognitive domain:

(70)   *What the strikers want is that the dismissed men should get rein-stated. Until they are, they say they won't get round the table with anybody - employers or arbitrators* (ODCIE)

Pluralized entities may also be encoded by partitive constructions for F (Quirk et al. 1985: 249f) in which aspects of quality and quantity are foregrounded:

(71)   *A shower of sparks sprayed around the chimney* (LOB)
(72)   *I threw a sprinkle of small grit around them* (LOB)

In all these configurations we are faced with large numbers of entities which center around all those in small numbers, and it is precisely this schema we have to keep in mind when we refer to additional (*a*)*round*-instances. Here, G, if lexicalized, is represented by (pro-)nouns or preferably persons; (pro-)nouns, however, which stand for F as abstract nouns denote characteristics, events, states or ideas. These, grammatically speaking, "look" singular, but refer, conceptually interpreted, to a multiplicity of entities:

(73)   *all the familiar life around them is* (LOB)
(74)   *as if it were a kind of darkness around him* (LOB)
(75)   *The silence was tight around them all* (LOB)

Again, we are faced with a very close link between F and G, but here emphasis is placed on F, the existence of which G cannot escape. F stands for "materialized" entities which are not, grammatically speaking, subject to other-initiated movement and thus occur as sentential subject. The same explanation holds for all those F/G-configurations in which G is used as a reified entity:

(76)   *The workers' demands centred around pay and conditions* (COBUILD)

It is obvious that we cannot present any particulars as to the quantitative aspects of this F/G-relation, but if we take account of the discussion related to the local domain of this *(a)round*-instance, we are able to deduce from this that, for example, the workers' demands on the employer have to be conceptualized as a "greater" entity than that around which they are centered. Likewise, we may speculate upon the qualitative aspects of this F/G-configuration: Of the large number of workers' demands those are most important which lie in the center of their demands, i.e. payment and working conditions.

Semantic extensions from this schema comprise *(a)round*-instances, in which *looks* or *glances*, as parts of a deep semantic structure, may be identified as F and direct object. The underlying metaphoric formula would then have the wording X SENDS LOOKS/GLANCES (A)ROUND G and would be realized as:

(77)   *The house prefects snoop around the dormitories at night* (ODCIE)
(78)   *It took us two hours to see right round the Boat Show* (ODCIE)

In most of the instances, G is lexicalized and denotes entities which are conceptualized as extended. Around these entities, a number of single entities become *looks* or *glances* if seen in their entirety. It is this entirety and its visual access to extended entities which conveys the idea of a more detailed picture of the observed entity.

A quantitative relationship between F and G *in nuce* is provided by all those instances from the LOB-corpus in which F stands for (pro-)nouns which comprise "quantifiable" entities. Concrete and abstract nouns for F range from *transporters* to *population*, to *prices*, *shares* or *average*. G is represented by numerals such as:

(79)   *the latest bulk transporters costing around 5,000* (LOB)

(80)   *successful title defence. A capacity crowd of around 30,000 in the Areneta Coliseum gave their local* (LOB)

Again, all the entities for F are not conceptualized in their single occurrences, but, as to their extension as a whole, as an indeterminate phenomenon which adds up to a whole, centered around G. It is now irrelevant whether F is seen as a larger entity than G; what is central here is that F in its occurrence is very similar to that of G. While F here stands for entities to which a quantitative value may be ascribed, we are able to discern additional *(a)round*-instances, in which F represents events, to which a particular point of time with a quantifiable value may be attributed. The events are conceptualized as having substantial extension, thus centering around G (as point of time) as amorphous gestalts:

(81)   *It was round about 1931 that he told me he was about to form a new* (LOB)

(82)   *But the morning after Thornie dined with him, around midday, he met Mrs. Longdon - Lorristone coming from* (LOB)

It is striking that F, grammatically speaking, may be represented either by (pro-)nouns or by clauses whereas G, as part of an optional prepositional phrase, stands for nouns with dates, either quantifiable (as in *around 5 p.m.*) or non-quantifiable (as in *around midday, around late August*). But again, in these instances, emphasis is not placed on the path covered by F; rather, F first approaches G from all sides and then, second, encloses G in its entirety.

3.2.   *Image-schema II: The less prototypical core meaning of* (a)round

Here, *(a)round* profiles F/G-relations with F and G as differently conceptualized entities: F is seen as a dimensionless entity which can be located or moves on a two-dimensional entity. Again, the prototypical *(a)round*-instance has F in self-initiated movement.

3.2.1.   Use type: "All over a place"

To begin with, F and G are components of a relation profiled against various bases which can, however, be attributed to the cognitive domain "oriented physical space". The bases comprise "travel" in:

(83)   *I just bummed around northern Europe for a few months*
        (COBUILD)

or "walk" in:

(84)   *At 4.30 we three went to Lula's and wandered round the garden till*
        Acheson turned up, when Clare and he (LOB)

or "strolling" in:

(85)   *We prowled around the second-hand music shops for hours*
        (COBUILD)

or "activity" in:

(86)   *He was bustling around the kitchen cooking up a huge pot of stew*
        (COBUILD)

Common to all these F/G-configurations is the idea of F in self-initiated movement, the movement itself, however, not being understood as goal-oriented or purposive. This "aimless" schema is grammatically realized by (pro-)nouns for F which denote persons and which occur as sentential subject, and it is realized by (pro-)nouns for G which designate two-dimensional areas or areas which are conceptualized as two-dimensional; nouns of this type include *kitchen, museum, room, shop, house, street, village, stage, corridor, garden* or *country* and the corresponding proper names for these. These nouns are explicit (i.e. lexicalized) components of a prepositional phrase the occurrence of which is assumed to be prototypical for this use type. Metonymically, this schema "extends" to:

(87)   *She had a new defiance, and her eyes wandered round the hall*
        confidently (LOB)

and leads to the conclusion that extensions of this type are very rare, at least in the LOB-corpus.

(A)round-instances in great number occur when G as part of the configuration has to be inferred by the language user. In general, (a)round then evokes bases and domains which are similar or even identical to those mentioned above. The "missing" prepositional phrase (i.e. G is not lexicalized) is nevertheless interesting because of its role in metonymic and metaphoric transfers. The lack of the explicit expression of G does not mean that G is absent from our conceptualization of the event pattern, as can be seen in:

(88)   *He's bumming around since he left college* (ODCIE)

Here, the attribute "idleness" marks an event pattern in which the idea of aimless movement becomes insignificant. Similar schemata are realized with the help of a number of verb-particle-constructions such as *loiter around, slouch around, wait around, stand around, loaf around, loll around, moon around, potter around* or *slop around*. The same constructions are used when physical objects are further specified as being a person so that we here get the opportunity to express a diversity of experiences with non-human entities in terms of human activities and characteristics:

(89)   *Catherine looked at the books lying around his room* (LOB)

The attribute "disorder" comes to the fore when an imaginary observer considers F's movement aimless, as in:

(90)   *There were hundreds of boys and girls milling around on the lawn* (COBUILD)
(91)   *At least two more were flitting around* (LOB)

The attribute "foolishness", however, is emphasized in:

(92)   *Now stop buggering around, Charlie. I've got work to do* (ODCIE)
(93)   *He loved to horse around with them in the compound* (COBUILD)

While the concept of movement is largely irrelevant in the above samples, it is non-existent in the following. Here, F is conceptualized as having reached his/her goal so that F is understood as a static entity. This non-deictic reading results in an (a)round-instance such as:

(94)   *Barbara - now there's a girl that's been around* (ODCIE)

and evokes the idea that F successively occupies various positions in an area, which, in an overall view, appears as an unstructured whole of different locations; thus, the different locations of F constitute a two-dimensional area, so that the lexicalization of G becomes dispensable. The fact that F stands for (pro-)nouns which in general not only denote human beings, but also women in particular, adds a more sexist nuance of meaning to this instance so that, again, (94) has to be interpreted as a semantic extension to the local variant.

The idea of F as an area-constituting entity is typically supported by all those samples in which the parallel use of *in* and *(a)round* conveys the picture of an area-enclosed entity:

(95)   *are to promote the serious study of cinema in and around the Leningrad area and it does not duplicate the work* (LOB)
(96)   *spending my own working hours in and around the English Tripos and some of my happiest evenings in* (LOB)

Once more, G is not explicit, while F takes the place of (pro-)nouns which denote the successive occurrence of single entities or the simultaneous occurrence of some entities. But also the occurrence of abstract nouns suggests that entities in their multiplex occurrence are designated; the corresponding nouns include, for example, *geese, rocks, relief, study, people, deaths*, etc.

The majority of *(a)round*-instances discussed so far regards F as being in (supposedly) self-initiated movement. F in (supposedly) other-initiated movement is discernible in all those cases in which it is grammatically realized as direct object. The bases and the domain evoked by particular F/G-configurations here are identical to those above. Thus, the base "disorder" is elicited by:

(97)   *He just litters his stuff around* (ODCIE)
(98)   *and there were women's magazines scattered round. There were also pieces of bread* (LOB)

Here, F stands for (pro-)nouns which denote objects, the occurrence and arrangement of which disturb the idea of an orderly room. In very similar samples, F may also, via (pro-)nouns, denote persons who are subject to (supposedly) aimless movement:

(99)   *The fat girl stared at him; pulling him around the floor as if he were*
       a sack of something (LOB)
(100) *It was intolerable that those two fat slobs could order her around*
       (COBUILD)

The other-initiated movement of F does not, however, necessarily result in the "aggressive" treatment of F; the corresponding schema may also be marked by a supporting element as in:

(101) *Her father proudly took her round his little garden, for,*
       next to philosophy, gardening (LOB)

Identifying F as sentential object necessitates mentioning the causative variant which centers around *look* or *glance*; contrary to the functions of F in the preceding use types, F is now sent (supposedly aimlessly) across a two-dimensional area and results in samples such as:

(102) *in the afternoon. Today I'm simply looking round".*
       Gus led the way, showing him what had been Mark's
       (LOB)

The interpretation given here depends largely on the covert existence of G; i.e. G as an explicit marker and in combination with F profiles different relations which are then attributable to different use types.

3.2.2.   Use type: "From one person/place to another"

Closely connected to the previous use type is this one, for F, once again, is conceptualized as a moving entity across a two-dimensional area; the F/G-relationship, however, is of a different nature. The "local" instance interprets F as represented by (pro-)nouns which denote human beings in self-initiated motion. Apart from F's conceptualization as an indeterminate entity, G in its single occurrence is also seen as indeterminate; the decisive factor here, however, is the multiplex occurrence of G which, seen as a whole, thus constitutes a conceptually two-dimensional entity.

To summarize: We are faced with two different types of G, the one representing a singular entity, the other representing a whole group of single entities. This observation is paralleled by G's occurrence as grammatically pluralized constituents, as in:

(103) *Walking arm in arm in a long procession round the rooms. They were at the back of the party, too far* (LOB)
(104) *were strolling, Lord Undertone and I, on sentry-go, round the tents and we caught sight of Mr. Septimus looking* (LOB)

These F/G-configurations no longer convey the idea of F's aimless advancing, but rather the idea of his/her purposive processing, the successive element of his/her motion being encapsulated in the pluralized instance of G. The conceptual parsing of temporally extended motion into different consecutive parts is reiterated in relations which evoke the base "shopping" in:

(105) *We'll shop around the building societies to find the best terms* (COBUILD)
(106) *Before you start ordering oil for the central heating ring around the suppliers to see who will offer you the best terms* (ODCIE)

the last example being a semantic extension from the previous one. The single entity is then expressed by nouns such as *department store, boutique, workshop, studio, atelier, office*, etc. which offer possibilities for F to do his/her shopping. Another extension comes to the fore when G stands for human beings who lack essential foodstuffs such as coffee, rice, champagne, etc. or who lack essential objects such as books. All these essential goods are represented by F, F occurring as a sentential subject and thus incorporating an agentive function as in:

(107) *How can India possibly find enough rice to go round these millions of refugees* (ODCIE)

The same domain and base are evoked if G remains covert as in:

(108) *There's enough coffee to go round* (ODCIE)

We have to keep in mind, however, that there is no real one-to-one relationship between F/G-configurations, with G either as a lexicalized entity or a non-lexicalized one; rather, the covert "existence" of G is very often responsible for a different interpretation of the F/G-relation involved. Thus, the base "sexuality" is dominant in:

(109) *She treated me right, she didn't let me down. But I wasn't satisfied, I had to turn around* (ODCIE)

The "metaphoric" movement of F can also be found in samples in which the basically local concept of motion recedes into the background in favor of further derived schemata. While the link between "local" and "metaphoric" movement is still evident in:

(110) *You can't go around making up things about being assaulted by people who don't exist* (ODCIE)

it is less evident in passivized constructions, as in:

(111) *It doesn't take long for such stories to be whispered around this neighbourhood* (ODCIE)

Common to all these samples is the idea of F's purposefully caused movement which not only signals change of location, but also, and parallel to the change, the conveyance of ideas, opinions or prejudice. Thus, all the constructions including F which stands for nouns such as *news*, *words*, *story* or *rumor* convey the idea of a supposedly self-initiated movement of F, which seems to be difficult to stop:

(112) *Word went round that something important was in the offing, so the meeting was well attended* (ODCIE)
(113) *Some jokes go round year after year* (COBUILD)

All the "materialized" entities are metadiscursive entities, the dissemination of which obviously and supposedly cannot be controlled by the language users. The concept of other-initiated movement (real or false) is reflected grammatically by the role of the direct object which F can assume. This concept yields F/G-configurations with G either explicit or not, as in:

(114) *Town give me a ring at this number and I'll take you round the pubs where most of the work is done* (LOB)
(115) *his mother, so when Michel was born, I took the baby round to show, and tried to make things up between them* (LOB)

These F/G-configurations may be characterized as relations against the base "company" which includes the cognitive domain "oriented physical space". Here, F "naturally" denotes human beings. But again, there are also other configurations in which F denotes objects which are "transmittable". Samples such as:

(116) *Just take a light and pass the matches round* (COBUILD)

extend from the local interpretation into less local ones, whenever F stands for (pro-)nouns such as *text* or *author*, as in:

(117) *I like "Treasure Island". We read it round the class last term* (ODCIE)

Here, G is not only realized by, grammatically speaking, pluralized nouns, but also, from a more semantic point of view, by collective nouns the referents of which stand for a quantity of more than one element, i.e. the referents being multiplex in nature (Talmy 1988: 176). Thus, the "local" idea inherent in these samples is that F is successively transmitted from one individual to another.

Finally, we should like to refer to *(a)round*-instances which are marked for their high degree of metaphoricity. These evoke the base "collecting money" and are verbalized in different ways. On the one hand, we find constructions such as:

(118) *I'll whip round and raise a few pounds for the office party* (ODCIE)

in which F stands for human beings; on the other hand, F as sentential direct object is exclusively represented by the noun *hat* as in:

(119) *When George died, they passed the hat round to pay for the wreath* (ODCIE)
(120) *Whenever someone retires from this office we pass the hat round* (COBUILD)

4. Retrospect and prospect

In this study, we have examined, from the standpoint of Cognitive Grammar, the polysemous character of *(a)round*; we have discussed in some detail the internal structuring of the preposition's semantic representations and have shown, in many cases, how individual *(a)round-*senses group together into more complex coherent wholes, i.e. use types and image-schemata. We have also demonstrated how particular *(a)round*-instances take on specialized meanings within specific bases and domains. Our investigation yields two different image-schemata for *(a)round* and supports the view that the process whereby we code what we want to say about the world is (in-)directly mediated by general conceptual schemata which restrict how we make sense of the world. Moreover, these two schemata support a highly experiential view of representation and meaning, since our only access to entities and events in the external world is presumed to be through our experience of them.

Apart from arguing that *(a)round* is intrinsically meaningful and that its primary function in the prepositional realm (i.e. on the phrasal level) is to relate, at most, two noun phrases (in the prototypical instance), we suggest that the other major function of *(a)round* (on the clausal level) should not be neglected: to indicate how the entities or participants involved in an event profiled by a verb (or some other clausal predicate) are related to each other (Smith 1987: 296ff, Rice 1987: 71ff). The abstract model resulting from our general conceptual experience should then explicate patterns of word order, designation of grammatical relations, choice of voice, aspects of transitivity and causality, etc.

Notes

1.   We are grateful to the anonymous referees who made a number of useful comments and suggestions. They are, of course, not responsible for whatever faults remain.
      Thanks are also due to Richard Brunt for casting a critical eye over the English of this paper.
2.   For a more comprehensive treatment and documentation of *(a)round*, cf. Schulze (1990).
3.   As a matter of fact, the ensuing characterization of the bases and domains does not exhaust the interpretative possibilities. While the reader may legitimately ask for some independent, "objective" motivation for the bases and domains as descriptive constructs, the only argument which can be stated in our own defence is that we now assume these constructs to be preliminary approximative descriptors for the purposes of our argument and that we fully recognize the need to motivate these constructs in a further paper.
4.   One of the referees has pointed out that, at least in American English, (24) is ambiguous, i.e. F's being turned around could equally well be located in the cognitive domain "marketing", strongly suggested by the

presence of the attribute "profitability". Moreover, the phrasal verb is assumed to refer to the process involving production, delivery to a market and ultimate sale to a customer.

References

I.   Corpus

Cowie, Anthony Paul & Ronald Mackin
      1975   *Oxford dictionary of current idiomatic English*. Vol. 1: *Verbs with prepositions & particles*. Oxford: Oxford University Press.
Hofland, Knut & Stig Johansson
      1986   *The tagged LOB corpus: KWIC concordance* (microfiches). Bergen: Norwegian Computing Center for the Humanities.
Sinclair, John (ed.)
      1987   *Collins COBUILD English language dictionary*. London: Collins.

II.   Works consulted

Bennett, David C.
      1975   *Spatial and temporal uses of English prepositions: An essay in stratificational semantics*. London: Longman.
Bennis, Hans, Ronald Prins & Jan Vermeulen
      1983   "Lexical-semantic versus syntactic disorders in aphasia: The processing of prepositions", *Publikaties van het instituut voor algemene taalwetenschap* 40: 1-32.
Brugman, Claudia M.
      1981   The story of *over*. [Unpublished MA thesis, University of California, Berkeley.]
Chomsky, Noam
      1981   *Lectures on government and binding*. Dordrecht: Foris.
Cresswell, Max J.
      1978   "Prepositions and points of view", *Linguistics and Philosophy* 2: 1-41.
Eijkman, Leonard Pieter Hendrik
      1894   "*Round, around, about, among, between, amid*", *Tijdschrift 'De Drie Talen'* 10: 108-113.
      1920   "*Round, around*", *Tijdschrift 'De Drie Talen'* 36: 4-6.
Fawcett, Robin P., M.A.K. Halliday, Sydney M. Lamb & Adam Makkai (eds.)
      1984   *The semiotics of culture and language*. Vol 1: *Language as social semiotic*. London: Pinter.
Fodor, Jerry A.
      1983   *The modularity of mind*. Cambridge: MIT Press, Bradford Books.
Fries, Norbert
      1988   *Präpositionen und Präpositionalphrasen im Deutschen und Neugriechischen: Aspekte einer kontrastiven Analyse Deutsch-Neugriechisch*. Tübingen: Niemeyer.

Givón, Talmy
1989   *Mind, code and context: Essays in pragmatics.* Hillsdale, N.J.: Erlbaum.
Gläser, Rosemarie
1988   "The grading of idiomaticity as a presupposition for a taxonomy of idioms", in: Werner Hüllen & Rainer Schulze (eds.), 264-279.
Hawkins, Bruce W.
1985   *The semantics of English spatial prepositions.* (L.A.U.T. Papers, series A 142.) Trier: Linguistic Agency of the University of Trier.
Herskovits, Annette
1986   *Language and spatial cognition: An interdisciplinary study of the prepositions in English.* Cambridge: Cambridge University Press.
Hottenroth, Priska-Monika
1986   Die Semantik lokaler Präpositionen: Ein prototypen-semantisches Modell für die französische Präposition *dans* mit einer Analyse der Beziehungen zwischen den Präpositionen und den Objektbezeichnungen in den Präpositionalsyntagmen. [Unpublished *Habilitationsschrift*, University of Constance.]
Hüllen, Werner & Rainer Schulze (eds.)
1988   *Understanding the lexicon: Meaning, sense and world knowledge in lexical semantics.* Tübingen: Niemeyer.
Ikegami, Yoshihiko
1984   "How universal is a localist hypothesis? A linguistic contribution to the study of 'semantic styles' of language", in: Robin P. Fawcett, Michael A.K. Halliday, Sydney M. Lamb & Adam Makkai (eds.), 49-79.
Jarvella, Robert J. & Wolfgang Klein (eds.)
1982   *Speech, place and action: Studies in deixis and related topics.* Chichester: Wiley & Sons.
Kessel, Frank S. (ed.)
1988   *The development of language and language researchers: Essays in honor of Roger Brown.* Hillsdale, N.J.: Erlbaum.
Lakoff, George
1987   *Women, fire, and dangerous things: What categories reveal about the mind.* Chicago: University of Chicago Press.
Lakoff, George & Mark Johnson
1980   *Metaphors we live by.* Chicago: University of Chicago Press.
Langacker, Ronald W.
1987   *Foundations of cognitive grammar.* Vol. 1: *Theoretical prerequisites.* Stanford: Stanford University Press.
1988   "An overview of cognitive grammar", in: Brygida Rudzka-Ostyn (ed.), 3-48.
Leisi, Ernst
1961   *Der Wortinhalt: Seine Struktur im Deutschen und Englischen.* (2nd edition). Heidelberg: Quelle & Meyer.
Lindner, Susan
1981   A lexico-semantic analysis of English verb-particle constructions with *up* and *out*. [Unpublished Ph.D. dissertation, University of California, San Diego.]
Lindkvist, Karl-Gunnar
1976   *A comprehensive study of conceptions of locality in which English prepositions occur.* Stockholm: Almqvist & Wiksell.

Lutzeier, Peter Rolf
1988　　　　　"A proposal for spatial event patterns", in: Werner Hüllen & Rainer
　　　　　　　Schulze (eds.), 367-379.
Quirk, Randolph, Sydney Greenbaum, Geoffrey Leech & Jan Svartvik
1985　　　　　*A comprehensive grammar of the English language*. London: Longman.
Rauh, Gisa
1981　　　　　"On *coming* and *going* in English and German", *Papers and Studies in
　　　　　　　Contrastive Linguistics* 13: 53-68.
Rice, Sally Ann
1987　　　　　Towards a cognitive model of transitivity. [Unpublished Ph.D.
　　　　　　　dissertation, University of California, San Diego.]
Rosch, Eleanor
1988　　　　　"Coherences and categorization: A historical view", in: Frank S. Kessel
　　　　　　　(ed.), 373-392.
Rudzka-Ostyn, Brygida (ed.)
1988　　　　　*Topics in cognitive linguistics*. Amsterdam: Benjamins.
Schmid, Wolfgang P.
1986　　　　　"Eine revidierte Skizze einer allgemeinen Theorie der Wortarten", in:
　　　　　　　Pierre Swiggers & Willy van Hoecke (eds.), 85-99.
Schulze, Rainer
1990　　　　　Sprachliche Raumwahrnehmung: Untersuchungen zu ausgewählten
　　　　　　　Präpositionen des Englischen im Rahmen der Kognitiven Grammatik.
　　　　　　　[Unpublished *Habilitationsschrift*, University of Essen.]
Schulze, Rainer & René Dirven
1989　　　　　*Extended bibliography of cognitive linguistics*. (L.A.U.D. Papers, series
　　　　　　　A 278.) Duisburg: Linguistic Agency University of Duisburg.
Smith, Michael Brockman
1987　　　　　The semantics of dative and accusative in German: An investigation in
　　　　　　　cognitive grammar. [Unpublished Ph.D. dissertation, University of
　　　　　　　California, San Diego.]
Sweetser, Eve Eliot
1984　　　　　Semantic structure and semantic change: A cognitive linguistic study of
　　　　　　　modality, perception, speech acts, and local relations. [Unpublished
　　　　　　　Ph.D. dissertation, University of California, Berkeley.]
Swiggers, Pierre & Willy van Hoecke (eds.)
1986　　　　　*Mot et parties du discours / Word and word classes / Wort und
　　　　　　　Wortarten*. Leuven: Peeters and Leuven University Press.
Talmy, Leonard
1988　　　　　"The relation of grammar to cognition", in: Brygida Rudzka-Ostyn
　　　　　　　(ed.), 165-205.
Trier, Jost
1968　　　　　*Altes und Neues vom sprachlichen Feld*. (Duden-Beiträge Heft 34.)
　　　　　　　Mannheim: Bibliographisches Institut.
Wierzbicka, Anna
1988　　　　　*The semantics of grammar*. Amsterdam: Benjamins.

The semantics of giving in Mandarin

John Newman

1. Introduction[*]

The Mandarin verb *gěi* has as its basic meaning the sense of 'give'. The same form (and character in the Chinese writing system) can also figure in a number of constructions where it does not have the sense of 'give', as illustrated below:

(1) a. *Tā   gěi   wǒ   qián.*
    he   give   me   money
    'He/she gave me money.' (*gěi* = 'give')

b. *Wǒ jì-le   yì   fēng   xìn   gěi   tā.*
    I   mail-ASP   one   CL   letter   to   him/her
    'I mailed a letter to him/her.' (*gei* = 'to')

c. *Tā   gěi   wǒ   zào-le   yì   dōng   fángzi.*
    he   for   me   build-ASP one   CL   house
    'He/she built a house for me.' (*gei* = 'for the benefit of')

d. *Wǒ   yàu   kàn,   tā   jiǔ   gěi   wǒ   kàn.*
    I   want   look   he/she   then allow   me   look
    'If I want to look, he/she will let me.' (*gěi* = 'to permit')

e. *Jīnyú   gěi   māo   chī-le.*
    goldfish   by   cat   was eaten-ASP
    'The goldfish was eaten by the cat.'
    (*gěi* = agent marker in the passive construction)

At first glance, *gěi* presents a bewildering range of uses.[1] The uses in (1b) and (1e) appear in fact to be almost polar opposites: in the former *gěi* indicates that the following noun phrase is the recipient of a transaction, while in the latter it indicates that the following noun phrase is the agent or instigator of an action. Despite the initial impression of unrelatedness between some of these uses, I believe it is reasonable to consider them as related. In other words, the uses (1a) - (1e) represent polysemy rather than homonymy.[2] The naturalness of the relationships among 'give', 'to', and 'for' has indeed been remarked upon elsewhere (see, in particular, the discussion of verb -> preposition reanalysis in African languages in Givón 1975), but the naturalness of these semantic relationships tends to be taken for granted rather than explained. My goal here is meant to be explanatory in that it seeks cognitively based motivations for the full range of meanings evidenced by gěi. Furthermore, the relationships between the meanings will be investigated from a synchronic point of view. I would hope that the synchronic account offered here will turn out to be easily reconcilable with the historical facts, to the extent these can be known, but I do not make any claim about the historical evolution of the meanings.

2.   Theoretical background

My account will draw upon concepts and styles of representation developed by Langacker in publications extending over a number of years, but which appear in perhaps their most definitive and comprehensive form in Langacker (1987). It is this work which I will rely on most in my attempts to articulate semantic structure. The main goal of this paper, however, is the elucidation of the meanings of gěi, rather than the exposition of a full-blown theory of semantic representation. I will proceed, therefore, by discussing each of the meanings, introducing ideas and diagrammatic conventions based on Langacker's work when the need arises. Nevertheless, it may be helpful to describe in general terms what Langacker's approach entails in order to better prepare the reader for what follows.

As suggested by the name given to this approach, i.e. "cognitive grammar", this framework makes a serious attempt to understand linguistic structure as far as possible in terms which have general cognitive significance. In cognitive grammar, the task of carrying out an analysis of linguistic structure is seen as part of the larger enterprise of characterizing cognitive events, and recognition is given to our general cognitive and perceptual experience in describing the functioning of language. While an appreciation of the cognitive basis of language is valuable in analyzing most aspects of grammar, it appears to be quite indispensable when one is dealing with polysemy. It is of some interest to note that it is a problem of polysemy (in this case, the various meanings of the verb keep) which Jackendoff (1983: ix) uses to illustrate the need for a more cognitively based approach which seeks to understand the structure of the concepts. (Jackendoff's further comment (p. ix) is apropos: "... I found myself frustrated at every turn trying to incorporate my findings into existing theories of semantics.") As examples of the cognitive orientation in Langacker's approach, one can cite the reliance on notions of imagery, modes of scanning objects in space, and figure vs. ground, all of which are key concepts in this approach. This is contrasted with an approach which posits (and proliferates) entities which are unique to linguistic theory and which have no counterparts in cognition.

A strong theme running throughout cognitive grammar is the desire to provide an integrated account of language phenomena. Any sharp dichotomy between, say, syntax and semantics is rejected in favor of an approach in which language structures from the smallest morpheme to the largest grammatical construction are all viewed as symbolic units of varying complexity. Since meaning is crucial to the characterization of all symbolic units, an account of syntactic phenomena in "autonomous syntax" terms, independent of semantic description, would be seen as largely misguided. Consequently, when I say that I am attempting to provide an account of the semantics of *gěi* within the cognitive grammar framework, it should be understood that such an account will incorporate much of what could well be called syntax.

In cognitive grammar there is a serious interest in capturing the relationships which hold among different senses of a morpheme. This interest can also be seen in works such as Lindner (1981) and Brugman (1981), where the full range of senses of a lexical item (literal and figurative) is explored by carefully analyzing the nature of the relations among these senses. These two works are all the more interesting because the lexical items investigated (*out, up, over*) have important syntactic significance. What at first sight may appear to be merely a study in lexical semantics or metaphor turns out, upon closer study, to have ramifications for the analysis of sentence structure. Here, too, this approach contrasts sharply with the dominant view, summed up neatly in an introductory textbook on semantics in the following way: "In this area, as indeed everywhere where one is dealing with the notion of sense, one has to ignore metaphorical and figurative interpretations of sentences. We are dealing with the strictly literal meanings of predicates" (Hurford & Heasley 1983: 191). (At the same time this textbook contains extended discussions of truth tables, rules of inference leading from one proposition to another, the logic of connectives such as *and, or, if,* modus ponens, etc.)[3] It should not be thought, however, that the neglect of metaphor and figurative language is merely an omission on the part of introductory textbooks, since neither of these areas receives any attention in a more definitive work such as Katz (1972), in which there is no reference to either of them even in the subject index. Nor is there any reference to metaphor and figurative language among the fifteen phemonena identified in Katz (1972: 4ff) as characterizing, even at a pretheoretical level, the field of semantics. Metaphor and, more generally, figurative language of all kinds are given due recognition in cognitive grammar as reflecting important and fundamental characteristics of language use. The investigation into the polysemy of *gĕi* undertaken here could also be seen as an investigation into metaphor, where the metaphorical extensions are "frozen" and of a mundane nature. (Cf. the discussion of the pervasiveness of metaphor in ordinary language in works such as Lakoff & Johnson (1980) and Lakoff (1987).)

Formalization of semantic properties in the form of predicate-calculus type expressions is viewed as inappropriate and in any case premature, given the state of our knowledge about the semantic properties being investigated. A statement of the form "F(x,y)" to represent the sense of 'x is the father of y' contributes very little to an understanding of either the literal or metaphorical senses of the word *father*, though such a representation may have advantages when it comes to studying purely logical aspects of the word, such as transitivity, symmetry, and reflexivity as understood in predicate calculus. The use of predicate calculus to express what one wants to say about semantics is of course tied closely to the delimitation of the field of semantic inquiry to just those aspects of language which have some interest to logicians. Predicate calculus may suit the needs of those concerned with truth values and rules of inference (namely, logicians and those linguists who are bound by the formal logic tradition), but it seems equally clear that it is not suited to explicating the properties of the bulk of ordinary words and morphemes in any linguistically interesting way. Most of the points which I wish to make concerning semantic properties and relationships can be made with the help of relatively simple diagrams which are more revealing, more immediately intelligible, and for linguistic purposes (as opposed to philosophical purposes) considerably more useful than the formal expressions of predicate calculus.

3.   Uses of gĕi in the spatio-temporal domain

I will begin by explicating those senses of *gĕi* where there is a relatively clear implication that something has been handed over. This includes the uses of *gĕi* which are translated as 'give' and 'to', as well as various other uses to be discussed below. It is natural to group these uses together for a number of reasons: they are probably the most common uses of *gei*; they occur easily and frequently with each other; and one does not need to resort to metaphorical extensions of meaning to explain the different uses. The various uses in this section represent alternative ways of encoding linguistically what is essentially the same scene with the form *gěi* being used to encode different chunks of information within this scene. In other words, these uses stand in a relationship of metonymy to one another. In calling the relevant domain "spatio-temporal", I mean to background the role of emotions, attitudes, and other more complex dimensions of these uses, though I do not mean to imply that they are not present at all. On the contrary, certain psychological conditions are typically present in the persons participating in the handing over of an object. However, it will not be necessary to enter into detail about these less tangible factors until we come to deal with other uses of *gei* in section 4.

3.1.   G̲ěi̲: *'give' and 'to'*

A natural starting point for an analysis of the meanings of *gei* is to characterize the typical scenario involving the act of giving: there is a person who has some thing and this person passes over the thing with his/her hands to another person who receives it with his/her hands. Such a description by no means exhausts all the possible scenes which could be appropriately described by Mandarin *gěi* (or English *give*), nor is it intended to. Rather it describes the key features of the most typical situations referred to by *gěi* in its GIVE senses. (I will use capital letters to indicate meanings which play an important part in the present discussion.) It is furthermore a very common scene, playing itself out in numerous variations in the daily lives of most people. Routines of this sort have been labelled in many ways in recent literature, such as *frame, scene, schema, script, idealized cognitive model*. Here I will simply refer to it as (a part of the) frame invoked by the most typical use of *gěi*. I have qualified my description as only "a part" of a larger frame, since there are many ways in which the frame could be further elaborated - persons function in many related routines and typically act for certain reasons with certain goals in mind; acts of giving may be part of established rituals (birthdays, Mother's Day, etc.), possibly accompanied by ritualistic speech acts and involving presents of a certain type wrapped in a certain way, etc. The existence of such interconnections, though virtually impossible to document fully, is real and in the "encylcopedic" approach adopted here contributes to the meaning of GIVE-type verbs. A frame, then, is made up of numerous domains (spatial, temporal, sensory, causal, socio-historical, etc.), though for convenience some of these can be backgrounded at different points in the discussion. The frame which I begin with is that defined by the spatio-temporal domain in which a person hands a thing to another person, as shown in Figure 1:

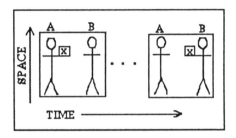

Figure 1: The spatio-temporal frame of giving

The frame shown in Figure 1 constitutes the *base* of GIVE-type predicates, i.e. it is the context within which the GIVE senses of Mandarin *gěi* (as well as English *give*) are defined. It bears comparison with the scenes assumed for verbs of buying, selling, paying, etc. in Fillmore (1977). As a way of simplifying the diagrammatic representations of the relationships between the entities of the base, I will adopt some conventions introduced by Langacker and add some of my own, leading to Figure 2.

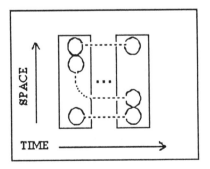

Figure 2: The spatio-temporal base for GIVE-type predicates

A circle is used to indicate a thing-like entity, representing here either the giver (the top circle), the object passed (the circle in the middle), or the receiver (the bottom circle). The movement of the object is indicated by the change in position from the beginning point of time to the end point of time. The dotted lines represent *lines of integration,* indicating the continuity or identity of the entities joined up through time. Admittedly, a considerable amount of information about the base is not directly expressed in Figure 2 (or Figure 1). As mentioned above, I am not attempting in this section to give an account of all the factors involved in such a scene. The whole act of giving, for example, is in a sense controlled by the giver, though this is not reflected in the diagrams. Consequently, Figures 1 and 2, as they stand, also represent the spatio-temporal frame of related acts such as receiving, stealing, etc. Later, it will become important to consider such factors as the control over the event, which differentiate these various acts. For the present, however, Figure 2 is a convenient simplification and does capture, I believe, the essence of what is involved in the spatio-temporal specification of GIVE-type predicates.

The base just described, though relevant to all the uses of *gěi,* cannot simply be equated with any of its meanings. Rather, the base provides the context within which the various GIVE-type meanings can be defined. A particular use of *gěi* will impose additional structure on the base. This will include a profile, referring to selected parts (either things or the interconnections between things) of the base which are designated by the "predicate" (here used to refer to the semantic pole of any morpheme). In the case of simple nouns like *dog, house, skin,* etc., the profile will be some thing, whereas for relational predicates like verbs the profile may include things and the relations between these things. Furthermore, within the profile of a relational predicate, one of the entities will be described as the *trajector,* which prototypically moves (or is located) relative to one or more *landmarks.* These terms capture a cognitively based asymmetry in relations between profiled entities, a special case of which is the distinction between syntactic subject (one type of trajector) and object (one type of landmark). The notions of trajector and landmark are most easily appreciated in the case of predicates referring to a single entity moving with respect to a fixed point, where the moving entity functions as the trajector and the fixed point as the landmark. Other scenes in which there is more than one moving entity or in which there is no moving entity may not have such obvious asymmetries, though particular predicates in a language may impose a trajector-landmark asymmetry on such scenes. The trajector-landmark distinction can be understood as a manifestation of *figure-ground* relationships fundamental to perception and cognition generally. Following Langacker (1987:120): "Impressionistically, the figure within a scene is a substructure perceived as 'standing out' from the remainder (the ground) and accorded special prominence as the pivotal entity around which the scene is organized and for which it provides a setting." It is important to note that the organization of a scene into figure-ground or trajector-landmark is not something automatically provided by the scene, although there are scenes in which there is a strong tendency for relations to be construed in particular ways. It is a feature of human cognition that one and the same scene can be construed with different figure-ground relationships, or different *images*. The reader is referred to Langacker (1987:120ff, 217ff) for further discussion of this generalized interpretation of the figure-gound distinction. (Cf. also a more restricted application of the figure-ground distinction in Talmy (1975, 1985).)

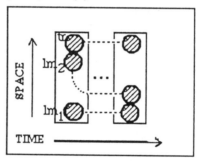

Figure 3: GIVER *gěi* RECIPIENT THING

We return to (1a):

(1)   a.   *Tā   gěi   wǒ   qián.*
           he   give   me   money
           'He/she gave me money.'

Figure 3 is a representation of this meaning of *gěi.* It is by no means the only conceivable way of imaging a GIVE-type scene, nor is it the only way in Mandarin, as we shall see. The profiled portion of the base includes the circles representing the persons giving and receiving and the object being passed. To simplify the metalanguage used in talking about these diagrams, I will refer to the circle representing the person who is doing the giving as the GIVER, the circle representing the object passed as the THING, and the circle representing the receiver as the RECIPIENT. Also, this predicate designates a sequence of distinct configurations which evolve through time, rather than being simply a static unchanging spatial configuration. This dimension of the meaning of the predicate will also be included in the overall profile. These profiled parts of the base are shown in darker outlines (as for all the cognitive grammar diagrams in the present discussion), with the darker time axis indicating that a passage of time is a crucial part of the structure of this predicate, i.e. it has a temporal profile. In addition, the GIVER is labelled as tr (trajector) and the RECIPIENT and THING each as lm (landmark).[4] There is good reason to distinguish between the RECIPIENT as the primary landmark lm_1 and the THING as the secondary landmark lm_2 in characterizing this use of $g\check{e}i$, though a full justification cannot be given here. (The distinction is comparable to that of "2" vs. "2-chomeur" in Relational Grammar.) One obvious reason for making the distinction is the word order, where the RECIPIENT noun phrase occurs in the same position as noun phrases functioning as the solitary landmark or direct object, i.e. immediately after the verb. Shading of the circles is used to indicate that those entities need to be elaborated or "filled in" to make a complete clausal structure. To simplify matters, detailed information about what kinds of entities can elaborate these positions has been omitted from the diagram. As mentioned earlier, it is understood that the top circle stands for a person, the middle circle for a thing, and the bottom circle for another person.

Consider now (2), involving what may be called a "double $g\check{e}i$" construction (an alternative word order *Tā gěi wǒ gěi qián* is also allowed by some speakers):

(2)   *Tā*   *gěi*   *qián*   *gěi*   *wǒ.*
       He/she   give   money   to   me
       'He/she gave money to me.'

I have glossed the $g\check{e}i$ occurring before the RECIPIENT phrase as 'to' as is commonly done, following the structure of the English translation. I believe, however, that such a translation does not do justice to the Mandarin structure. Instead, I believe that the two uses of $g\check{e}i$ in such sentences reflect senses of $g\check{e}i$ which are much closer than *give* and *to* are in English, consistent with the fact that in Mandarin it is the same form realizing both senses. For a start, the implication in such a translation that the two uses of $g\check{e}i$ reflect two quite different parts of speech, a verb and a preposition, is unjustified. A common test for verb-like properties in Mandarin is the possibility of co-occurrence with aspect markers such as the perfective marker *le*; this marker can occur with either instance of *gěi* in the double *gěi* construction:

(3) a *Tā gěi-le qián gěi wǒ.*
  b. *Tā gěi qián gěi-le wǒ.*
  c. *Tā gěi-le qián gěi-le wǒ.*

Mandarin speakers seem unable to find any differences in meaning, even a difference in nuance, among these alternatives. It should be mentioned, though, that some Mandarin speakers find (3c) stylistically less than ideal, citing the two occurrences of *le* as awkward.

On the basis of the sentences in (3), there seems no reason to analyze the two *gěi*'s as belonging to different parts of speech. This view is further supported by the existence in Mandarin of a common serial verb construction, in which a verb is repeated (called "verb copying" in Li & Thompson 1981: 442ff) with different complements. This construction is illustrated in (4), quoted from Li & Thompson (1981: 447):[5]

(4) *Bāba guà màozi guà zài yī jiàzi shang.*
  Papa hang hat hang at clothes rack on
  'Papa hangs hats on the clothes rack.'

Sentences like those in (4) lend support to the feasibility of treating the double *gěi* construction as a repetition of a verbal predicate *gěi*.

I propose to treat the double *gěi* construction as a sequence of semantic variants of *gěi*, differentiated by slightly different stuctures. The two *gěi*'s are diagrammed in Figure 4, which is a preliminary attempt to represent the construction. While the same entities (GIVER, THING, RECIPIENT) enter into the overall profile of each variant, they do so in slightly different ways. The first *gěi* elaborates the THING, while the second *gěi* elaborates only the RECIPIENT. Since there is only one instance of the GIVER in the whole construction, I have shown the GIVER in the first predicate as the sole elaboration site for this, although this position is also integrated with the GIVER position of the second predicate, as indicated by the lines of integration between the two predicates. One might settle for this difference in elaboration sites as the only difference between the two variants. In Figure 4, however, I have posited a further difference between the two variants in the relative prominence of the two landmarks in the profile. The first *gěi* gives slightly more prominence to the THING (treating it as the primary

landmark), while the second *gěi* gives slightly more prominence to the
RECIPIENT and treats it as the primary landmark. Nothing crucial
hinges on this distinction, but it has the virtue of allowing us to uphold
the generalization about Mandarin that the noun phrase immediately
following two-place predicates is the primary landmark. The two *gěi*'s,
then, represent different versions of a predicate, characterized by
different structures imposed upon one and the same base.

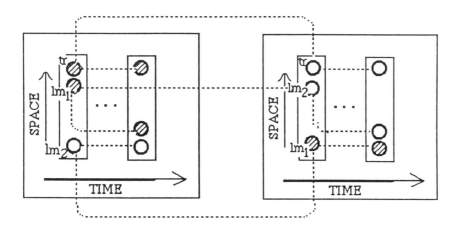

Figure 4: GIVER *gěi* THING *gěi* RECIPIENT

The kind of *profile shift* evident in the two versions of *gěi* is not an
idiosyncracy of this particular predicate. I see the relationship between
the two versions of *gěi* as being comparable, in varying degrees, to the
relationship holding between pairs of verbal predicates such as: *teach
English - teach college students, kick the ball - kick a goal, shoot live
bullets - shoot a person, load hay - load the wagon, credit money (to one's
account) - credit one's account (with money), carve wood - carve a statue,
grind wheat - grind flour*. The first predicate of each pair foregrounds the
interaction between an agent and a (possibly abstract) thing, while the
second predicate foregrounds the relationships between the agent and
an entity associated with the result of the interaction between the agent
and the thing. Each pair has its own constraints in terms of exactly what
predicates may elaborate the *tr* and *lm* sites, but all of them point to the
existence of a fairly pervasive schema in English which relates an
interaction and the result of the interaction by allowing for two versions
of a verbal predicate with alternative profiling.[6]

Figure 5 shows the effect of integrating the two predicates into a larger construction. It is as though the two diagrams representing the two versions of *gěi* are overlaid, so that the GIVER, THING, and RECIPIENT are all elaborated in the resulting profile of the whole construction. In order not to clutter up the diagram too much, I have omitted the lines of integration connecting the two predicates which go to make up the construction. Typically, the parts which make up a construction stand in an *autonomous-dependent* relationship, with one of the parts construed as conceptually dependent, i.e. requiring the presence of some other entity, and the other conceptually autonomous, i.e. not requiring the presence of any other particular entity. Nouns, for example, are autonomous in this sense compared with verbs which are relatively dependent. In the construction under discussion, however, it is extremely difficult to identify what is autonomous and what is depen-

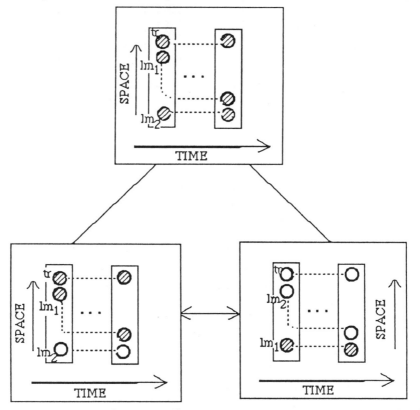

Figure 5: GIVER *gěi* THING *gěi* RECIPIENT (integrated representation)

dent. It is as though each *gěi* complements the other, with each equally dependent on the other. In other words, each *gěi* elaborates the other. Any decision about autonomous vs. dependent entities in this case would appear to be rather arbitrary and so I will simply treat the two predicates as dependent on each other, indicated by < --> between the two predicates. Another aspect of constructions is that one of the component parts of the construction typically functions as a *profile determinant*, i.e. the profile of one of the parts determines the profile of the integrated structure. So, for example, the profile of the expression *the lamp above the table* is that of *the lamp*. Once again, however, it is difficult to see just one of the *gěi* predicates as the only profile determinant of the construction. Each seems to contribute equally to the final profile which incorporates the profiles of both predicates. It is similar to the example discussed in Langacker (1987: 290), *The axe is outside in the backyard near the picnic table*, where the component relations *outside*, *in the backyard*, and *near the picnic table* are all simultaneously profiled as multiple landmarks in the profile of the composite structure. Nevertheless, within the resulting profile, the THING is designated as lm_1 and the RECIPIENT as lm_2, on the basis that the chronological priority of the THING in the sequencing suggests that this element is a more salient landmark than the RECIPIENT.

By comparing Figures 3 and 5, one is now able to appreciate the similarity and the difference between the semantic structures of (1a) and (2):

(1)   a.   *Tā gěi wǒ qián.*
(2)   *Tā gěi qián gěi wǒ.*

The semantic structure of (1a) involves the elaboration of the single predicate *gěi*, whereas (2) is a composite structure made up of the integration of two relational predicates, each one a different version of *gěi*. The result in each case is a clausal structure in which the GIVER, the THING, and the RECIPIENT are all profiled and elaborated, albeit with slightly different landmarking, but this same effect has been achieved through different ways of "imaging" the same scene.

Also, one can bring out quite nicely the difference in semantic structure between (2) *Tā gěi qián gěi wǒ* and the corresponding English sentence which was given above as the translation of (2), namely *He/she gave money to me*. The English sentence is diagrammed in Figure 6. Here, the predicate *to* is shown as profiling the movement of a trajector to a landmark which needs to be elaborated in order to complete the prepositional phrase. English *to* plots the spatial path towards a goal regardless of whether the trajector is an agent or an object sent by an agent to a goal. In this it differs from the use of *gěi* which is used only to plot the path of an object sent by an agent, never to plot the path of an agent moving towards a goal. So, for example, one can not use *gěi* to translate *to* in the sentence *She walked to the shop.* Hence, the diagram for *to* has only two salient entities in its base, some entitity which moves (i.e. the trajector) with respect to some other entity (i.e. the landmark), whereas the diagram for the second *gěi* in the double *gěi* construction has the same base as GIVE-type predicates which includes a GIVER, a THING, and a RECIPIENT.

Another point of difference concerns the profiling of the spatial dimension with *to* (indicated by the darker line of the spatial axis) compared with *gěi* in which the spatial dimension is not profiled. I have decided on this way of representing *to* on the basis of uses which do not have any obvious temporal dimension, such as *the road to the beach, the distance to the township.* It could be argued that the path mapped out by *to* in such cases can be thought of as a movement through time through successive points, but I believe this is a less obvious interpretation of *to* and I will not pursue that approach here.

I have shown the *to* predicate as an elaboration of a (shaded) subsection of the *give* predicate which is functioning as a secondary landmark. This landmark is the spatial path leading to the RECIPIENT. Also, *give* is conceptually dependent on *to*, in so far as *give* cannot be described without crucial reference to a RECIPIENT who receives a THING (the part elaborated by *to* in English). *To*, on the other hand, does not crucially make reference to GIVE-type predicates in its semantic structure. In a sense, both of the predicates "need" some other predicate in order to make a syntactically complete clause, but I am referring here to a notion of conceptual dependence rather than syntactic dependence (cf. Langacker 1987: 300ff).

Finally, I have enclosed the *give* predicate in a darker box, indicating that this is the profile determinant of the whole construction. The construction which results from integration of the predicates will have the profile of a temporal process (like *give*) rather than that of a spatial path (like *to*).

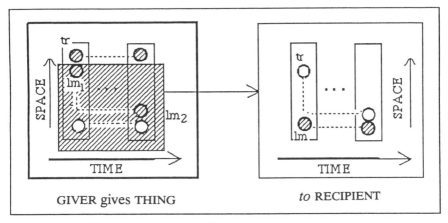

Figure 6.   GIVER gives THING *to* RECIPIENT

3.2.   Gěi: 'to' with verbs other than *gěi*

The use of *gei* to mark a following noun phrase as RECIPIENT is more general than is suggested by the discussion of the double *gěi* construction in the preceding section. The RECIPIENT use of *gěi* is found in fact with many GIVE-type predicates which include in their bases a RE-CIPIENT. Some examples are given in (5), involving the predicates *jì* 'mail, send' and *huán* 'return (something)'. Other verbs which function in the same way include: *chuán* 'pass on', *jiāo* 'hand over', *mài* 'sell', *shǎng* 'bestow', *tuō* 'trust', *shū* 'lose', *fù* 'pay'.

(5) a.   *Wǒ   jì-le   yi   fēng   xìn   gěi   tā.*
   I   mail-ASP   one   CL   letter   to   him/her
   'I mailed a letter to him/her.'
  b.   *Wǒ   huán-le   nèi   běn   shū gěi   tā.*
   I   return-ASP   that   CL   book to   him/her
   'I returned that book to him/her.'

The semantic structures of *jì* and *huán* are diagrammed in Figures 7 and 8 respectively. In the case of *jì*, one can see the movement of a THING from a SENDER (the top circle) to a RECIPIENT (the bottom circle). There is, however, an additional entity, shown as POST in the diagram, which intervenes as RECIPIENT and, subsequently, SENDER. In this way, the diagram gives some indication of the additional structure present in *jì*, although it is still incomplete in all its detail. Omitted from the diagram are various features of the base associated with the predicate: typically, the THING is a letter; POST has a complex internal structure involving more than one person or machine acting as RECIPI-ENT and SENDER; the THING has physical marks added to its cover by POST; some money is paid by the SENDER to POST; the duration of the whole event is typically a matter of days or weeks rather than seconds, etc. All this information is present in the base, but for convenience is omitted from the present diagram. Again, the profiled part containing the trajector and landmarks is indicated by darker lines. In diagram-ming the basic form of a predicate, as here, I will not indicate which are the elaboration sites, since the number and nature of these may vary depending on exactly what construction the predicate enters into. Shaded elaboration sites will be indicated, however, in actual construc-tions. *Huán* involves in its base one act of giving followed by its reversal, although it is only the "reversal" process which is profiled, indicated by the darker outline of the second half of the time axis. It is clear from an inspection of these diagrams that both are more elaborate instantiations of the same base configuration that underlies *gěi*, namely Figure 2. This is why Figure 2 is more appropriately named as the base for "GIVE-type" predicates rather than just the base for *gěi*. Figure 2 represents what is common to all the GIVE-type predicates and may be described as schematic for GIVE-type predicates.

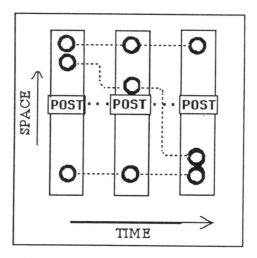

Figure 7: jì 'mail, send'

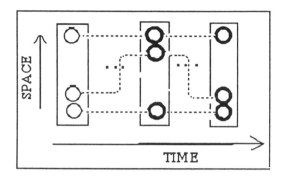

Figure 8: *huán* 'return (a thing)'

The more general form of the construction involving such predicates followed by *gěi* + RECIPIENT may be represented as in Figure 9. The construction consists of a semantic half (the upper part showing the semantic structure) and a phonological half (the lower half). The phonological part is left partly unspecified with V representing the phonological shape of any appropriate GIVE-type verb, while the phonological shapes of the nominals are completely unspecified. Lines of correspondence show how the elements of the semantic structure correspond to elements of the phonological structure. The semantic structure corresponding to V in Figure 9 must now be understood as the schematic form of GIVE-type predicates, rather than any particular predicate. (Although the V structure does appear identical to that of the particular predicate *gěi*, this is because I have omitted some of the more peripheral aspects of the base of *gěi*.) In other words, Figure 9 says that any GIVE-type predicate can be combined with *gěi* + RECIPIENT to form a larger construction. To show a particular instance of this construction, I have diagrammed the semantic structure of the GIVER *huán* THING *gěi* RECIPIENT construction in Figure 10. The general schematic form of the construction appears in the lower half of this diagram. An arrow points from the V structure to *huán*, indicating that *huán* elaborates the schematic V part of the construction. To simplify matters, I have once again omitted some of the lines of integration showing the correspondences between the elements of *huán*, V, and the *gei* predicate. After the *huán* structure replaces the schematic V, *huán* and *gěi* combine in the same way as the two predicates in the double *gěi* construction. The net result of all this is the new, composite semantic structure at the top of the diagram, in which all three entities (GIVER, THING, RECIPIENT) are elaborated.

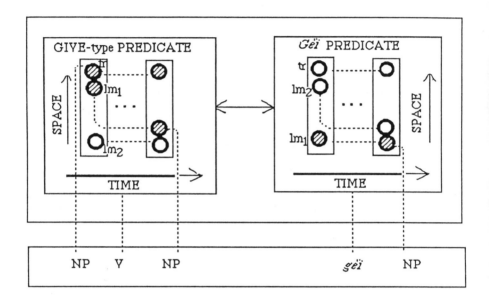

Figure 9: The *gěi* + RECIPIENT construction (schematic representation)

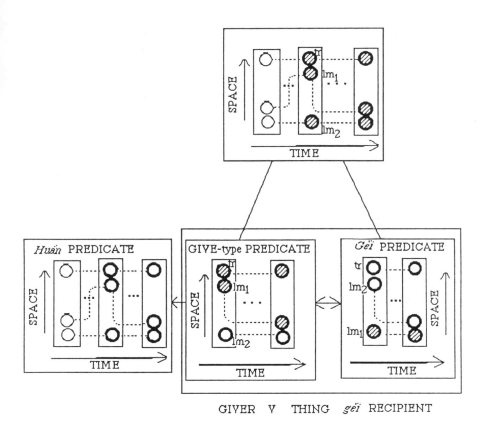

Figure 10: GIVER *huán* THING *gěi* RECIPIENT

The use of the morpheme meaning GIVE as the marker of RECIPIENT is found in other languages as well. (6) and (7) illustrate this phenomenon in Thai and Yoruba (from Pulleyblank 1987: 989):

(6) a. *Chán   hâi   nǎnsɨ̌   kὲ: dèk.*
         I   gave   book   to   child
         'I gave a book to a child.' (*hâi* = 'give')
     b. *Chán   sòng   nǎnsɨ̌   hâi   dèk.*
         I   sent   book   to   child
              'I sent a book to a child.' (*hâi* = 'to')

(7) a.   *ó*   *fún*   *mi*   *ni*   *owó.*
          he/she   gave   me   money
          'He/she gave me some money.' (*fún* = 'give')
     b.   *ó*   *tà*   *á*   *fún mi.*
          he/she   sold   it   to me
          'He/she sold it to me.' (*fún* = 'to')

Here too, I would analyze the 'to' use of such predicates in a similar way to what was done for Mandarin *gěi*. Pulleyblank (p. 989) explicitly rejects an analysis of *fún* in (7b) as a preposition in favor of an analysis of it as a verbal predicate (it can take object clitics and can be nominalized, just like verbs), consistent with the analysis of *gěi* here. It is also relevant to note that the serial verb construction which helped to motivate the analysis of *gěi* is also characteristic of both Thai and Yoruba. English *give* in fact shows up in a RECIPIENT sense in some English-based pidgins and creoles of Africa, parallel to the way *fún* is used in Yoruba (cf. Hall 1966: 78f).

There are GIVE-type predicates in Mandarin which can occur in either of the two constructions dealt with in this section, one introducing the RECIPIENT phrase with *gěi* and the other treating the RECIPIENT as the primary landmark. *Sòng* 'to present' is one such verb:

(8) a.   *Tā*   *sòng-le*   *yì*   *fēn* *lǐwù*   *gěi*   *wǒ.*
          He/she   present-ASP   one   CL   present   to   me
          'He/she gave a present to me.'
     b.   *Tā*   *sòng-le*   *wǒ*   *yì*   *fēn* *lǐwù.*
          He/she   present-ASP   me   one   CL   present
          'He/she gave me a present.'

In the approach adopted here, these two uses of *sòng* 'to present' reflect two different ways of imaging a scene and involve two different versions of the *sòng* predicate - the first one treating the THING as a primary landmark, the second one treating the RECIPIENT as the primary landmark. The predicates which participate in both construction types include *shǎng* 'to bestow', *tuō* 'to entrust', *huán* 'to return', *shū* 'to lose' (as in *to lose money to someone*) and *fù* 'to pay' and, of course, *gěi*. (The (8b) construction is not possible, however, for the predicates *chuán* 'to pass on', *jiāo* 'to hand over', *mài* 'to sell', among others. Cf. Tang (1988) for a classification of GIVE-type verbs into various classes depending on their participation in the different construction types.)

Pairs of sentences like those in (8) are familiar as examples of Dative Shift or 3-to-2 Advancement in the literature, whereby the structure underlying (8a) is in some way "basic" and is changed into the structure underlying (8b).[7] In the approach adopted here, the construction illustrated in (8b) is not "derived" in any sense from that of (8a). Rather, the two constructions in (8) are based on two versions of the verbal predicate, differing slightly in their profile characteristics. Nor is the difference between the two constructions to be understood as a peculiarly syntactic phenomenon characterized in terms unique to syntactic theory. Instead, the relationship between the two constructions can be accounted for using the same cognitively based concepts which account for pairs such as *carve wood* and *carve a statue*, as explained in section 3.1.

3.3. Suffixal gěi

There is yet another (atonal) use of *gěi* related closely to the 'give' and 'to' uses discussed above, whereby *gěi* stands in the position V - *gěi* - RECIPIENT - THING. Consider the following sentences:

(9) a.   *Tā   jiè   gěi   wǒ   shí   kwài   qián.*
          He/she   lent   to   me   ten   dollars money
          'He/she lent me ten dollars.'

     b.   *Tā   sòng   gěi   wǒ   yì   fēn   lǐwù.*
          He/she   present to   me   one   CL   present
          'He/she gave me a present.'

For convenience, I have glossed *gěi* in these sentences as 'to', but this is misleading in that it suggests that *gei* is functioning like a preposition, introducing the phrase *gěi wo*. In point of fact, *gěi* functions like a verbal suffix in such sentences.[8] The unit-like nature of the verb + *gěi* in such cases is supported by facts about the distribution of the perfective aspect marker *le* and the negative morpheme *bù* (with changeable tone). *Le* may occur after the simple verb *sòng*, as in (10a), or after the complex verb *sòng-gěi*, as in (10b). Mandarin speakers have difficulty finding any difference in meaning between these two alternatives. Usually, however, it is not inserted between *sòng* and *gěi* in (10c), as one might have expected if there were a major constituent break between the two morphemes, with *gěi* analyzed as a preposition.[9] (11a) and (11b) illustrate the use of the negative morpheme *bù* in the yes-no interrogative construction involving V *bù* V. Notice that either the simple verb *sòng* or the complex verb *sòng-gěi* can function as the V in this construction, again without any meaning difference (although (11b) is more preferable in spoken rather than written Mandarin). One does not, however, find *gěi* repeated (cf. 11c) after *sòng*, indicating that that *gěi* is not functioning as a verb here. The simplest account of these distributional facts is to say that *gěi* is functioning as a verbal suffix attached to *sòng*.

(10) a. *Tā*   *sòng-le*   *yì*   *fēn*   *lǐwù*   *gěi*   *wǒ*.
         He/she   present-ASP   one   CL   present   to   me
         'He/she gave a present to me.'

   b. *Ta sòng-gěi-le wǒ yì fēn lǐwù.*

   c. **/?Tā sòng-le gěi wǒ yì fēn lǐwù.*

(11) a. *Tā*   *sòng*   *bú*   *sòng-gěi*
         He/she   present   NEG   present-SUFFIX
         nǐ   *yì*   *fēn*   *lǐwù?*
         you   one   CL   present
         'Is he/she going to give you a present?'

   b. *Tā sòng-gěi bú sòng-gěi nǐ yì fēn lǐwù?*

   c. **Ta sòng-gěi bú gěi nǐ yì fēn lǐwù?*

As a verbal suffix, then, *gěi* has the function of modifying the profile of the verb to which it is attached, as diagrammed in Figure 11. This is a schematic diagram of the V - *gěi* construction, in which the semantic structure of a GIVE-type verb is transformed into a new structure in which the RECIPIENT is now the primary landmark and the THING the secondary landmark. This reflects the fact that the RECIPIENT phrase occupies the immediate post-verbal position, just like the landmark of a simple transitive verb. This transformation is indicated by the broken arrow in the diagram. The semantic structure associated with V in this diagram is schematic for any predicate which includes this structure as part of its more elaborate structure.

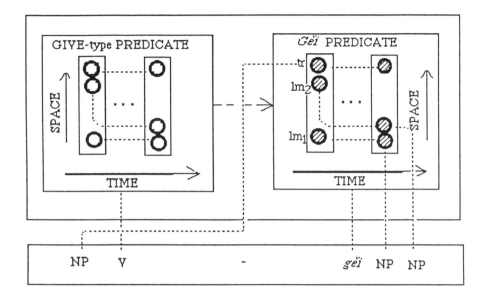

Figure 11: The V-*gěi* construction (schematic representation)

To illustrate the *sòng* ... *gěi* ... and the *sòng-gěi* constructions, I have diagrammed these two constructions in Figures 12 and 13 respectively. Figure 12 is an instantiation of the general schema V ... *gěi* ... with V elaborated by *sòng*, while Figure 13 is an instantiation of the V-*gěi* schema. In these diagrams *sòng* appears in a simplified form which makes it appear identical to the V schema, though in fact the structure of *sòng* is more complex.

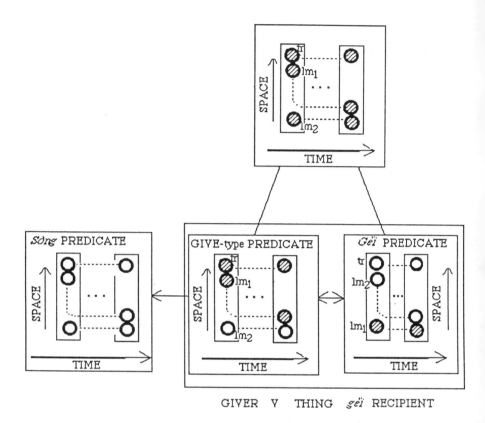

Figure 12: GIVER *sòng* THING *gěi* RECIPIENT

In terms of which elements of the base are profiled, the *sòng* ... *gěi* ... construction is identical to the *sòng-gěi* construction, but they differ in the way in which the whole is built up from the parts. They also differ in the relative salience of the two landmarks. Taken together, Figures 12 and 13 represent a cognitive grammar account of what in Relational Grammar terms would be analyzed as 3-2 Advancement in which the Advancement is marked by a verbal suffix. This phenomenon is widely documented and has received considerable attention in linguistic theory, especially in the RG literature (see for example Givón (1984: 177-185) and Perlmutter (1983)). The pairs of sentences in (12) and (13), taken from Givón (1984: 178) and Crain (1979), illustrate this construction in Kinyarwanda and Chamorro respectively:

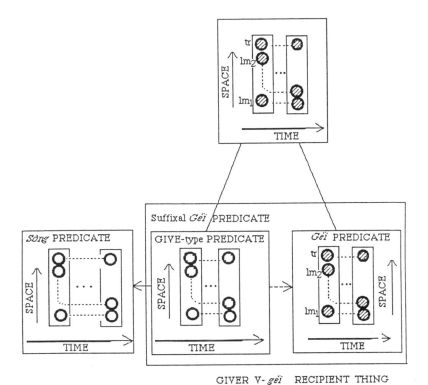

GIVER V-*gěi*   RECIPIENT THING

Figure 13: GIVER *sòng-gěi* RECIPIENT THING

(12) a. *umugore   y-ooher-eje   umubooyi   ku-isoko.*
         woman   she-sent-ASP cook   to-market
         'The woman sent the cook to the market.'

      b. *umugore   y-ooher-eje-ho   isoko   umubooyi.*
         woman   she-sent-ASP-SUFFIX   market   cook
         'The woman sent the cook to the market.'

(13) a. *Ha-sangan   i   istoria   pära   si   Margarita.*
         3SG-tell   the story   to   Det Margarita
         'He/she told the story to Margarita.'

      b. *Ha-sangan-i   si   Maragarita*
         3SG-tell-SUFFIX   Det   Margarita
         ni   i   istoria.
         Preposition   the   story
         'He/she told the story to Margarita.'

In my approach, affixation of the suffix to the verb in such cases results in new profiling characteristics of the verb. This is not fundamentally any different from the way in which the addition of a prepositional phrase, when "added" to a verbal group leads to a new construction. Thus, one version of *gěi* can be combined with a verb like *sòng* to build up *sòng-gěi* and another version of *gěi* can be combined with *sòng* to create the *sòng ... gěi ...* construction. The change brought about by the suffixation of *gěi* is well motivated, since *gěi* as a suffix is imposing the same kind of profiling onto the verbal predicate as we find in the *gěi* RECIPIENT THING construction. In RG terms, on the other hand, the presence of a rule of 3-to-2 Advancement in a language is quite independent of considerations of polysemy among morphemes (which is not a consideration at all in RG). In other words, it is a purely coincidental fact in RG that the verb suffix marking 3-to-2 Advancement in Mandarin should be identical in form to the morpheme marking final 3's. It is true that in some languages there is no relatedness between the 3-marking and the 3-to-2 Advancement marking, as in Kinyarwanda and Chamorro. But this does not mean that where a language does show some relatedness between these forms, this will be irrelevant to understanding the nature of the construction. If one can motivate the form and meaning of the verbal suffix, then the most satisfying account of that suffix will incorporate such motivation. Unlike RG, cognitive grammar captures in an explicit way the relatedness between different versions of a morpheme, thereby establishing a degree of motivation completely absent from RG (and other autonomous syntax accounts).

4.   Uses of gěi in benefactive and control domains

To appreciate the relatedness between the senses of *gěi* discussed in section 3 and its other senses, one must return to the someone-gives-something-to-someone frame. As already explained, the depiction of the frame in Figure 1 represents no more than a part, though obviously a salient part, of the multifaceted complex which provides the backdrop to understanding the act of giving. While the purely temporal-spatial dimensions highlighted in Figure 1 appear to be sufficient to enable us to appreciate the relatedness between the GIVE and RECIPIENT senses of *gěi*, one must bring into focus more of this larger frame in order to understand the relatedness between GIVE and the additional senses. Figure 14 sketches some additional domains relevant to giving. Figure 1 now takes its place as just one of the domains which are present in the more complete frame.

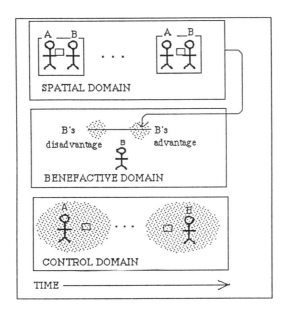

Figure 14: An enlarged frame of giving

In this enlarged frame, I have attempted to indicate in the box marked as BENEFACTIVE DOMAIN that the act of giving falls within that set of events which are to the RECIPIENT's advantage. The scenario whereby giving something results in some kind of benefit to the RECIPIENT is a natural and frequent occurrence in human experience, which deserves to be incorporated into the frame of giving. Figure 14 gives explicit recognition to the "beneficiary" role of the RECIPIENT.

Another domain of the enlarged frame is the one labelled CONTROL DOMAIN, which summarizes information about the degree and extent of control which persons exert over objects or other persons. The notion of control subsumes as particular cases various types of possession. It is not uncommon to analyze GIVE-type verbs as involving a transfer of possession, as is done for example in Miller & Johnson-Laird (1976:568ff). However, as pointed out by Miller and Johnson-Laird (pp. 558-565), there is no simple definition of possession which one can appeal to in characterizing GIVE-type verbs. Any one of "inherent", "accidental", and "physical" types of possession may be involved, and it is not clear which one, if any, should be taken as a prototype. Since the term *possession* is strongly associated with a legal interpretation, I consider it best to avoid this word and use instead *control over* and *control domain*, which are conveniently vague as to whether one is actually the legal owner of what one has control over. In the diagram, the area of control, or "sphere of influence", of each person is indicated by a shaded area around each figure. It can be seen that the THING being passed lies inside the GIVER's area of control at the beginning of the giving act, whereas by the end of the giving act it is located within the RECIPIENT's area of control. It is of course perfectly possible for A to give something to B without A relinquishing control over the thing passed. Person A can, for instance, give a photo to B in order for B to look at it, but the photo may remain the property of A, and B is expected to return the photo to A. While A in such a case maintains ultimate control over the photo, A cedes to B a kind of temporary and limited control. In the more prototypical instances of giving, however, the transfer of control is more definite and irrevocable, and it is this form of giving which is reflected in Figure 14.

With this expanded view of the giving frame in mind, we are in a better position to approach the remaining meanings of *gěi*.

4.1.   G̲ě̲i̲ in the benefactive domain

We return now to the use of *gěi* as a BENEFACTIVE marker, as illustrated in (1c):

(1)   c.   *Tā   gěi   wǒ   zào-le   yì   dōng   fángzi.*
          he/she   for   me   build-ASP   ne   CL   house
          'He/she built a house for me.'

"BENEFACTIVE" is used here to refer to the person for whose sake or on whose behalf some act was (intentionally) done, consistent with the use of the term in linguistics generally. With "true" BENEFACTIVE phrases, there does not need to be anything actually given to the BENEFACTIVE (*I peeled the potatoes for her, I walked the dog for our neighbor* etc.). In most cases, however, there is at least a weak implication that the BENEFACTIVE is also a RECIPIENT. Consider sentences like *I sang a song for her, I wrote a poem for her*, where *her* can be construed as a kind of RECIPIENT of the song/poem, as well as a BENEFACTIVE. In (1c), too, the BENEFACTIVE can also be construed as a RECIPIENT of the builder's help and presumably of the completed house itself. Rather than see the RECIPIENT and BENEFACTIVE senses as either present or not present, it is more natural to view these as either more or less prominent, along a continuum :

mainly RECIPIENT > RECIPIENT or BENEFACTIVE > mainly BENEFACTIVE

The purely BENEFACTIVE use and the purely RECIPIENT use of *gĕi* represent limiting cases along this continuum, relatable through the common experiential association between RECIPIENT and BENEFACTIVE in the the frame of giving.

Figure 15 diagrams the semantic structure of BENEFACTIVE *gĕi*. It assumes a base just like the benefactive domain which forms part of the enlarged GIVE-frame, but makes reference to a larger class of acts (hence the label ACT), rather than just the particular act of giving. There are, after all, numerous acts which can bring benefits to persons. Just as the RECIPIENT of giving is the landmark, so here the person on whose behalf the act is done is the landmark, while the act itself functions as the trajector.

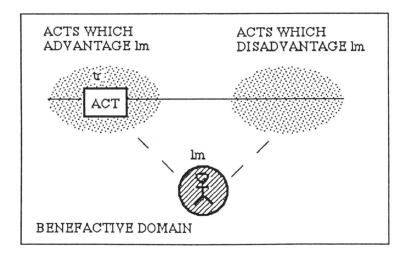

Figure 15: BENEFACTIVE *gĕi*

The close association between RECIPIENT and BENEFACTIVE is evidenced not only in Mandarin but in other languages as well, where these senses may attach to the same form. The use of the morpheme meaning GIVE as a marker of RECIPIENT as well as a BENEFACTIVE marker is common in Southeast Asian languages, including Thai, Cambodian, and Vietnamese. The sentences in (14) illustrate this in Vietnamese. I rely on Nguyen Dang Liem (1979: 57) for information about the ambiguity in (14b).

(14) a. *Bố*   *cho*   *con*   *tiền*   *ạ!*
          father   give   child   money   please
          'Please give me some money, Dad.' (*cho* = 'give')
     b. *Ông ấy*   *bán*   *sách*   *cho*   *tôi.*
          He   sold   books   to/for   me
          'He sold books to me.' or:
          'He sold books for me.' (*cho* = 'to' or 'for')

Compare, too, the following examples from Siya, a Central-Togo language of Ghana, taken from Dakubu & Ford (1988: 144):

(15) a. *ákɔ*   *bɛ*   *kúki*   *mɛ́.*
          he   it   give   me
          'He gave me it.' (*kúki* = 'give')
     b. *átsá*   *kibɔ́ɛ̀*   *kúki Kòfi* *kúki*   *mɛ́.*
          he-paid   money give Kofi   give   me
          'He paid the money to Kofi for me.' (*kúki* = 'to' and 'for')

In these cases, one finds the same three-way polysemy between GIVE, RECIPIENT marking, and BENEFACTIVE marking as with *gěi*, but there may be more limited polysemy involving just RECIPIENT/BENEFACTIVE marking. In Chamorro, the same form *pära* marks RECIPIENT as well as BENEFACTIVE, as illustrated in (16), though it is never used as a verb GIVE:

(16) a. *Hu-na'i* *i*   *lebblu*   *pära*   *i*   *taotao.*
          I-gave   the   book   to   the   man
          'I gave the book to the man.' (*pära* = 'to')

b. *Man-ma'cho'chu*   *i*   *famagùun*   *pära*
    PL-work   the   children   for
    i   *atungu'-niha.*
    the   friends-their
    'The children worked for their friends.' (*pära* = 'for')

In Japanese, although there is no RECIPIENT/BENEFACTIVE polysemy, there is nevertheless an interesting relationship which holds between the verb *ageru* 'give' and BENEFACTIVE marking. *Ageru* preferentially appears as part of a larger verbal complex when there is a benefactive phrase in the same clause, as in (17b). (*Ageru* is not used, however, to mark RECIPIENT.)

(17) a. *Watashi*   *wa*   *piano*   *o*   *hiita.*
         I   TOPIC   piano   OBJ   played.
         'I played the piano.'
     b. *Watashi*   *wa*   *kanojo*   *notameni*   *piano*
         I   TOPIC   her   for   piano
         o   *hiite*   *ageta.*
         OBJ   played   gave
         'I played the piano for her.'

Examples like these from different and unrelated languages provide good support for recognizing a natural association between GIVE, RECIPIENT, and BENEFACTIVE.

In the case of Chamorro, the position of *pära* in the clause is the same regardless of whether it is used in the sense of RECIPIENT or BENEFACTIVE. It will be noticed, however, that *gěi* in the BENEFACTIVE sense occurs before the main verb (which I will refer to as the preverbal position), whereas *gěi* marking RECIPIENT occurs after the main verb (the postverbal position). I repeat the relevant sentences below:

(1) b. *Wǒ*   *jì-le*   *yì*   *fēng*   *xìn*   *gěi*   *tā.*
         I   mail-ASP   one   CL   letter   to   him/her
         'I mailed a letter to him/her.' (*gěi* = 'to')
    c.   *Tā*   *gěi*   *wǒ*   *zào-le*   *yì*   *dòng*   *fángzi.*
         he   for   me   build-ASP   one   CL   house
         'He/she built a house for me.' (*gěi* = 'for the benefit of')

There is thus a restriction on the preverbal use of *gěi* to mark BENE-FACTIVE and the post-verbal use of *gěi* to mark RECIPIENT, though this statement needs some qualification (see below). To understand why the difference in word order should be associated with this semantic distinction, we need to consider these facts against the background of other facts about word order in Mandarin. The relevant facts are insightfully discussed in Tai (1985) and include the following: a "source" locative occurs to the left of a "goal"; the order of clauses reflects the temporal order of the events they refer to; adverbial adjuncts to the right of the main verb are construed as resulting from the action associated with the main verb.These facts are exemplified in the Mandarin sentences (18) - (20), some of which are taken from Tai.

Order of predicates reflects order of events:

(18) a. *Zhāngsan   dào   túshūguǎn   ná   shū.*
        John   arrive   library   take   book
        'John went to the library to get the book.'

   b. *Zhāngsan   ná   shū   dào   túshūguǎn.*
        John   take   book   arrive   library
        'John took the book to the library.'

Main predicate + postverbal adjunct reflects cause + effect:

(19) a. *Tā   pǎo lèi-le.*
        He/she   run   tired
        'He/she is tired from running.'

   b. *Tā   lèi   de bù   néng   shuō huà le.*
        He/she   tired   NEG   able   speak
        'He/she is so tired that he/she cannot speak.'

"Source" occurs to the left of "goal":

(20) a. *Zhāngsan   cóng   Chicago   dào   New York.*
        John   from   Chicago   arrive   New York
        'John arrived in New York from Chicago.'

   b. **Zhāngsan dào New York cóng Chicago.*

These facts point to the existence in Mandarin of a larger iconic relationship between the notions of "before" and "after" in conceptual space to "before" and "after" in the linear arrangement of phrases within the clause. Spatial source vs. goal, earlier vs. later in a temporal sense, and cause vs. effect can all be seen as instantiations of an ordering between entities involving some kind of starting or "prior" point and some kind of end or "subsequent" point.

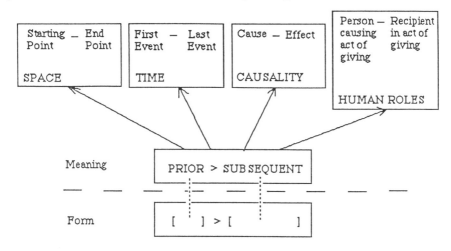

Figure 16. General schema of PRIOR-SUBSEQUENT iconicity in Mandarin with four instantations

The word order restrictions on the use of *gěi* (preverbal use to mark BENEFACTIVE, postverbal use to mark RECIPIENT) may be seen as another instantiation of this iconic relationship (although Tai does not go this far in his own discussion of iconicity in Mandarin). While it is clear how a RECIPIENT can be equated with the "subsequent" end of the "prior-subsequent" schema (representing the endpoint of the giving), it may not be so clear why a BENEFACTIVE phrase should be equated with the "prior" point. To appreciate this, one needs to bear in mind the full meaning of BENEFACTIVE. In order not to clutter up the representation of the frame too much, I omitted from Figure 14 a further aspect which is of crucial importance, namely the GIVER is intentionally acting for the express benefit of the RECIPIENT. BENEFACTIVE thus refers to a person who plays a crucial part in the genesis of some act, who constitutes in a way the *motivation* for some act. This facet of giving is the key to understanding the word-order restrictions on *gěi* as a BENEFACTIVE marker. Viewed as part of the motivation of the act, a BENEFACTIVE phrase can naturally be equated with a starting point or the "prior" part. There is therefore a large PRIOR-SUBSEQUENT schema at work in Mandarin, sketched in Figure

16, and the word-order facts about *gěi* are consistent with this larger schema.

The preverbal vs. postverbal distribution requires some qualification. There is a kink in the pattern of distribution in that one can find with certain main verbs a *gěi* phrase in the preverbal position which has either a RECIPIENT or BENEFACTIVE interpretation, as in (21), from Li & Thompson (1981: 387):

(21) *Wǒ gěi   tā   xiě-le   yì   fēng xìn.*
       I   for/to   him/her   write-ASP   one CL   letter.
       'I wrote a letter to him/her.' or:
       'I wrote a letter for him/her.'

Other verbs which allow such ambiguity (or vagueness!) include *dǎ diànhuà* 'to telephone' and *mài* 'to sell'. Native speakers may not always agree about the preferred interpretation (cf. Tang 1978: 90, who reports that native speakers disagreed about whether sentences like (21) contain a RECIPIENT or BENEFACTIVE *gěi* phrase). It is interesting to compare (21) with (22), which according to Li & Thompson (1981: 388) carries only the BENEFACTIVE sense of *gěi*:

(22) *Wǒ gěi   tā   jì-le   yì   fēng xìn.*
       I   for/*to her/him   mail-ASP   one CL   letter
       'I mailed a letter for him/her.'

One is led to ask, then, why the verbs 'to write' and 'to telephone' allow a RECIPIENT reading of preverbal *gěi*, but 'to mail' does not. I believe a reason for this difference may be found in the status of the RECIPIENT in the frames for these predicates, although I do not pretend to have a full explanation for the difference. It does seem to me, however, that the RECIPIENT functions as a more salient part of letter-writing and telephoning than it does for mailing letters. In writing a letter and telephoning, the agent is communicating with the RECIPIENT of the message, even if the RECIPIENT is not physically present in either case. In the case of mailing a letter, however, the agent is not thereby communicating with the RECIPIENT. The communication with the RECIPIENT takes place at the time of writing the letter, with the RECIPIENT as a kind of invisible dialogue partner, or at the time of receipt of the letter, where the writer is the invisible communicator. That is, the RECIPIENT plays a more prominent role in the case of writing and telephoning, and this may explain why a RECIPIENT sense of *gěi* occurs so readily in construction with the verbs 'to write' and 'to telephone'.[10] The pair of verbs *mài* 'to sell' and *mǎi* 'to buy' also contrast in this way: 'sell' allows a RECIPIENT interpretation of a preverbal *gěi*, whereas 'buy' does not. Again, there is a difference in the status of a RECIPIENT in the frames of the two verbs: selling involves a more obvious path to a RECIPIENT than does buying (cf. *sell something to someone* but not **buy something to someone*). Buying, on the other hand, involves a more obvious path from the GIVER (or seller). There may be a separate RECIPIENT in the buying frame (as in *to buy x to give to her* or Mandarin *mǎi x gěi tā*), but this is more peripheral in the case of buying than in the case of selling. The relative salience of a path to the RECIPIENT in the selling frame provides some explanation for why the RECIPIENT sense of *gěi* is always possible with the verb *mài* 'to sell'.

It appears much more difficult to interpret a postverbal *gěi* phrase as benefactive. Li & Thompson (1981: 387) note that it is "possible but not preferable" with some verbs, including *sòng* 'to present'. The BENEFACTIVE reading in such cases can be seen as a vagueness, attributable to the weak two-way implication between BENEFACTIVE and RECIPIENT discussed above. The distribution of (clear) BENEFACTIVE and RECIPIENT meanings of *gěi* is thus lopsided: the preverbal position can be associated with RECIPIENT or BENEFACTIVE, whereas the postverbal position is more definitively associated with RECIPIENT. In addition to the considerations advanced in the preceding paragraph, this state of affairs is also consistent with some further facts relating to the conceptual schema of Figure 16. The most basic and obvious instantiation of the PRIOR-SUBSEQUENT schema is surely the instantiation of it in the spatial domain. It turns out that the distributional kink noticed in the case of RECIPIENT vs. BENEFACTIVE is characteristic also of the spatial instantiation of the schema. As illustrated in (23)-(24), *dào* DESTINATION phrases may occur either before or after the main verb, whereas *cóng* DEPARTURE phrases occur only before the main verb:

(23)   *Tā*   *zuótiān*   *lái*   *dào*   *Měiguó*   or:
         he/she   yesterday   come   to   America
         Tā   *zuótiān*   *dào*   *Měiguó*   *lái.*
         he/she   yesterday   to   America   come
         'He/she left for the USA yesterday.'
(24)   *Tā*   *cóng*   *Zhōngguó lái.*
         he/she   from   China   come
         (**Tā*   *lái*   *cóng*   *Zhōngguó.*)
         'He/she came from China.'

The oddness in the distribution of RECIPIENT vs. BENEFACTIVE interpretations of *gěi* is thus paralleled by the behavior of *cóng* and *dào*: the
preverbal position in both instances allows somewhat more latitude in
its interpretation than does the postverbal position. By recognizing the
interrelatedness of the parts of the conceptual schema represented in
Figure 16, one can see some additional motivation for the RECIPIENT
vs. BENEFACTIVE distribution being lopsided in just the way it is.

4.2. Gei in the control domain

At the beginning of section 4, I opted for the term *control* instead of
possession in introducing additional aspects of the giving frame. One
way in which *control* and *possession* are differentiated is in terms of
what one can control or possess: one can have control over events as
well as objects, whereas possession is restricted to objects. Clarifying
this wider sense attaching to *control* is a convenient starting point in
one's attempt to analyze the relatedness between the senses of *gěi* in
(1a) and (1d):

(1)   a.   *Tā   gěi   wǒ   qián.*
           he   give   me   money
           'He/she gave me money.'
      b.   *Wǒ   yàu   kàn,   tā   jiǔ   gěi   wǒ   kàn.*
           I   want   look   he/she then   allow   me   look
           'If I want to look, he/she will let me.'

The meaning of *gěi* in (1a) includes the idea of a transfer of control
over money, possibly involving in this case the transference of actual legal possession. In (1b), on the other hand, *gěi* refers to the transfer of
control over the act of looking, as a result of which I have the authority
to look.[11] Both possession of objects and authority to perform acts are
expressions of control in human behavior and represent elaborations of
a general schema of control, one being an elaboration with respect to
objects and the other an elaboration with respect to actions. It is this
parallelism between the conceptual structures embodied in possession
and authority to act which motivates the co-existence of these two
senses of *gěi*.[12] Construing the act of giving in terms of transfer of
control, rather than just transfer of possession, allows us to make this
conceptual link. Figure 17 represents the PERMIT sense of *gěi*. In this

diagram only the trajector and landmarks of *gěi* are indicated. The primary landmark of *gěi*, the NP immediately following *gěi* in the construction) is also functioning as the trajector with respect to the second predicate (typically the predicate *kàn* 'look at' or *ting* 'hear'). The second predicate, which functions as the secondary landmark of *gěi*, is represented in a schematic way, following the conventions of cognitive grammar. This use of *gěi* is defined with respect to several interacting and complex domains (including the control domain), not just the spatio-temporal domain, and I have not attempted to label all these domains in Figure 17. Instead, I have simply used the label PERMIT in the diagram as a shorthand way of referring to the type of interaction involved.

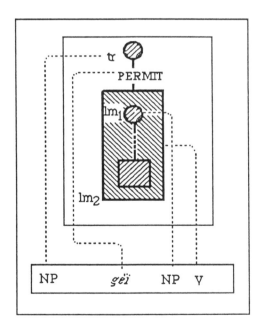

Figure 17: NP *gěi* NP Y (*gěi* = PERMIT)

The GIVE/PERMIT polysemy found with *gěi* occurs in some other languages. The sentences in (25) and (26) illustrate the same phenomenon in Russian and Finnish:

(25) a. *Ya   dal   yemu   dyen-gi.*
         I   gave   him   money
         'I gave him money.' (*dat'/davat'* = 'give')

     b. *Yemu   nye   davali   govorit'.*
         him   NEG   (they)-permit speak
         'They didn't permit him to speak.' (*dat'/davat'* = 'permit')

(26) a. *Annoin   hänelle   10 markaa.*
         (I)-gave   him/her   10 mark
         'I gave him/her 10 mark.' (*antaa* = 'give')

     b. *Annoin   hänen   mennä   elokuviin.*
         (I)-permit   him/her   go   to the pictures
         'I permitted him/her to go to the pictures.'
         (*antaa* = 'permit')

Note also how the phrase *Give me a look* can be more or less equivalent to a request for permission to look, showing that even in English *give* can be seen to function in a sense of PERMIT.

Another related construction with GIVE-type verbs involves their use with a verb of cognition like *think, know, understand*, etc., where the sense of the whole construction is 'to cause someone to think, know, etc.' This is found in English *give to understand* and Malay *beri tahu* 'tell, inform' (literally 'to give to know'). Here one is not granting permission, but there is still a sense in which a person shares out the control over something, in this case control over a body of knowledge.[13] The senses of GIVE, PERMIT and INFORM are all, therefore, particular instantiations of a more general notion of transfer of control (in the case of INFORM it is a sharing out, rather than actual transfer). Transfer of control in the domain of purely three-dimensional space amounts to passing over an object to another person; in the domain of interpersonal power relationships, it manifests itself as the granting of permission to someone to perform an act; in the domain of intellectual activity, it is manifested as the passing on of knowledge to another person. The relationships between these types of control are diagrammed in Figure 18.[14]

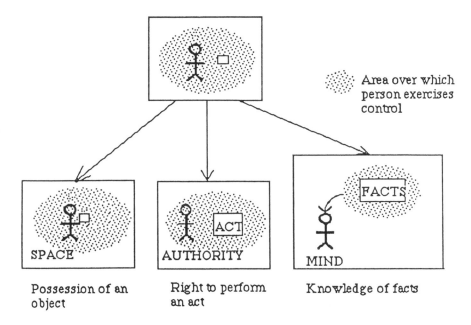

Figure 18. Schematic diagram of the control domain and three instantations

4.3. Gěi: 'agentive marking' in the passive construction

We turn now to the use of *gěi* as a marker of the agent in a passive construction. I repeat here example (1e):

(1) e. *Jīnyú   gěi   māo   chī-le.*
         goldfish   by   cat   was eaten-ASP
         'The goldfish was eaten by the cat.'

There is, in a sense, a reversal of roles of the noun phrases flanking *gěi*, when one compares this use of *gěi* with the GIVE use. In (1e), the referent of the noun phrase preceding *gěi* has no control over the eating and it is the referent of the noun phrase following *gěi* that has control. In the GIVE use of *gěi*, on the other hand, it is the referent of the noun phrase before *gěi* which controls the giving. Accounting for this apparent reversal of roles in the control domain is not an easy task and I do not claim to have arrived at an entirely satisfactory solution.

Nevertheless, I can make some suggestions which I believe throw light, however dim, on the appearance of *gěi* in this construction.

Firstly, one must recognize the possibility of a more complex multiplicity of roles attaching to the RECIPIENT than is suggested even in the enlarged frame of giving in Figure 14. Typically, the RECIPIENT in the act of giving goes on to do something with the THING received. Like most of our actions in the real world, we give things for a purpose, to be used in some meaningful way. Not unexpectedly, then, we find GIVE-type predicates followed by other predicates elaborating on the way in which the RECIPIENT is supposed to use, or otherwise interact with, the THING handed over. Both English and Mandarin allow a second verbal predicate of this sort to be tagged on to a GIVE clause, as in (27):

(27)   *Tā*   *gěi*   *wǒ*   *dōngxi*   *chī.*
       he/she   give   me   something   eat
       'He/she gave me something to eat.'

In (27), *dōngxi* is functioning as one of the landmarks of the predicate *gěi* at the same time as it is functioning as the trajector of the second verbal predicate, just as in the English translation, *something* is a landmark of *gave* and a trajector of *to eat*. The (not infrequent!) occurrence of the construction shown in (27) with *gěi* is one small step towards the *gěi* passive construction insofar as the noun phrase following *gěi* in both (27) and the passive is functioning as a trajector.

Secondly, one must bear in mind the historical fact about Mandarin already alluded to in section 3, namely that there has been a general trend in the history of Mandarin involving a word-order shift from SVO to SOV (cf. Li & Thompson 1975: 185). Where there is a sequence of verbal predicates in a clause, the trend has been for the second predicate to be construed as the main verb and the first predicate as part of the complement of the main verb. One manifestation of this trend has been the depletion of semantic content of the first verbal predicate in a series and the simultaneous enhancement of semantic content of the second predicate (cf. Givón 1975: 93ff). This larger fact about the history of Mandarin syntax is surely relevant to an account of the *gěi* passive, though I do not mean to suggest that passive construction must have emerged out of GIVE uses simply by a gradual semantic shift. I stress that more than one factor needs to be considered in accounting for the passive construction. Nevertheless, this historical fact about Mandarin takes us further towards our goal by providing some motivation for the weakened semantic bonds between *gěi* and the noun phrases which flank it in the passive construction.

Thirdly, there is a certain slipperiness to the semantic role played by a noun phrase at the beginning of a sentence in Mandarin, related no doubt to a pervasive topic-comment structure in the language. In particular, it is possible for initial noun phrases to be interpreted as either the trajector or the landmark of the following verbal predicate. Contextual and pragmatic factors usually result in only one possible interpretation and the frequency of actual ambiguities like this in the real world is therefore relatively low. Nevertheless, ambiguity is possible with the right choices of lexical items, as illustrated in the following example from Chao (1968: 72):

(28)   *Zhèi*   *yú*   *bù*   *néng*   *chī*   *le.*
        This   fish   NEG   can   eat   PARTICLE
        'This fish cannot be eaten any more.' or:
        'This fish cannot eat any more (it is sick)'.

This variability in the semantic function of the initial noun phrase in Mandarin would obviously help to smooth the way for a transition from a *gěi* clause in which the initial noun phrase is a trajector to a clause in which the initial noun phrase functions as a landmark (as in the passive construction).

Fourthly, one can make a conceptual link between a PERMIT sense and passive constructions. As a way of appreciating this link, consider the range of meanings of English *let*. As with other verbs of permission, *let* can have a "strong permission" sense (A expressly authorizes B to do something) or a "weak permission" sense (A does nothing to prevent B from doing something). Both of these senses typically involve an animate being capable of volition as the permitter. But there is another marginal use of *let* which one might call "extra-weak permission", as in *This tarpaulin is too worn - it'll let the rain come in.* Here there is no question of the tarpaulin exercising volition or "doing" anything. All the clause means is that the tarpaulin is such that the rain will come in. Instead of introducing an act which is authorized, *let* simply announces what the rain will do to the tarpaulin. The "manipulative" content of *let* has been bleached out and there is no longer any real sense in which control is transferred. The erosion of meaning which is found in the case of *let* is comparable to the well-known distinction between "root" and "epistemic" senses of the English modals, as in the case of *may* which can refer to either permission or possiblity. We see, then, a connection between the semantic content of the expressions in (27):

(27) a.   *A* EXPLICITLY PERMITS *B* TO DO SOMETHING.
      b.   *A* TOLERATES *B*'s DOING SOMETHING.
      c.   *A* IS SUCH THAT *B* DOES SOMETHING.

When the action that *B* carries out affects *A*, then (27c) becomes "*A* IS SUCH THAT *B* DOES SOMETHING TO *A*", which is the sense of a passive construction.

While I recognize the naturalness of the transition in (27), I am reluctant to rely on this semantic shift as the primary explanation for the emergence of the passive construction with *gěi*. My skepticism is due to the limited role of *gěi* in the PERMIT sense, as mentioned in footnote 12. In particular, *gěi* in the PERMIT sense does not seem to allow a second predicate where the action affects the permitter, unlike English *let* in sentences such as *She$_i$ let me kiss her$_i$.* Since it is exactly this type of sentence which is presumably relevant to the transition to the passive construction, its non-occurrence with *gěi* lessens the force of this argument.

Fifthly, and finally, one can point to the existence of cognitive similarities between an agent role in a passive construction and BENEFACTIVE. (Note that the BENEFACTIVE use of *gěi* occurs in the same position in the clause as the agent-marking use, i.e. immediately before the main verbal predicate.) I have already had occasion in section 4.1 to discuss the way in which a BENEFACTIVE phrase is typically also the motivation for an act, i.e. the NP in the BENEFACTIVE *gěi* + NP phrase refers to a person who not only benefits from some act but who is also, in a sense, the instigator of the act. It is this aspect of the BENEFACTIVE sense which makes it comparable to the agentive sense. The agent of an act and the person for whose benefit an act is carried out both play a part in setting the act in motion.

I offer these five considerations, then, as an attempt to relate the use of *gěi* in the passive construction to other facts about *gěi* and the structure of Mandarin. No one of these seems to completely explain away the *gěi* passive construction, but when taken together, I believe these considerations do help to make the existence of this construction understandable.

Before attempting to represent this use of *gěi* diagrammatically, some words about the constituent structure of the passive construction are in order. Because one can translate *gěi* in this construction as 'by', there is a strong temptation to treat the sequence *gěi* + NP as a prepositional phrase. This imposes an English type of analysis on Mandarin which may have some practical, pedagogical value but fails to do justice to the structure of Mandarin (cf. my remarks on *gěi* meaning 'to' above in section 3.1). Just because the passive use of *gěi* is not fully verbal (it cannot take aspectual suffixes for example), one should not conclude that it is therefore simply a preposition, on a par with English prepositions. All the discussions of such "coverbs" in Mandarin indicate the need to recognize a continuum between verb-like and preposition-like categories (cf. Liang 1971 and Li & Thompson 1981: 356-369), however reluctant linguists have been to face up to the reality of such a continuum. Treating passive *gěi* as a "semantically bleached" or "empty verb" rather than as a "full preposition" is a more natural analysis for Mandarin and this is how I will proceed with *gěi* in the passive construction. In Mandarin, verbal predicates such as 'to permit', 'to advise', etc. enter into "pivotal" constructions with ambiguous constituenthood, as in (28a) or (28b). In cases like this, the object of the higher predicate can be taken as either a noun phrase or a "small s". A neat way of handling this in cognitive grammar is to treat both the pivotal NP and the small clause as landmarks, as was done in my representation of the PERMIT sense of *gěi* in Figure 17. The consituenthood of the passive construction in Mandarin seems to be equally ambiguous, as shown in (29):

(28) a.   *Wǒ*   [*quàn*   *tā*]   [*zǒu*].
      b.   *Wǒ*   [*quàn*]   [*tā*   *zǒu*].
            I   advise   he/she go
            'I advised him/her to go.'
(29) a.   *Wǒ*   [*gěi*   *tā*]   [*dǎ-le*].
      b.   *Wǒ*   [*gěi*]   [*tā*   *dǎ-le*].
            I   PASSIVE   he/she   hit-ASP
            'I was hit by him/her.'

Figure 19 is a representation of passive constructions with *gěi*. The initial NP of the construction is the trajector, while the second NP is the primary landmark. As explained in the preceding paragraph, the only true verbal predicate of the construction functions as a secondary landmark of *gěi*. The primary landmark of *gěi* functions also as the trajector with respect to this verbal predicate, though I have not included this information in the diagram.

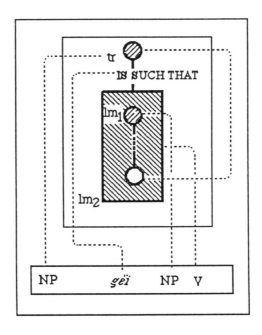

Figure 19: The *gěi* passive construction (the NP following *gěi* corresponds to the agent)

Again, I have relied on a shorthand way of suggesting the role of the trajector in this construction by using the label IS SUCH THAT. In overall appearance, Figure 19 is not unlike the representation of the PERMIT sense of *gěi* in Figure 20, but note the dotted line connecting the trajector with the landmark of the verbal predicate. As with other lines of integration, this line indicates the identity of the connected entities. That is, the trajector of the whole construction is to be identified as the landmark of the verbal predicate. Since this entity appears overtly only once, only one elaboration site (at the site of the trajector) is shown. The landmark of the verbal predicate is left unfilled.

4.4. *Prefixal* gěi *in passive constructions*

There is yet another way in which *gěi* turns up in passive constructions, namely as an atonal prefix to the main verb. This use is illustrated in (30):

(30)   *Ta*   *gěi-mà-le.*
        He/she   PASSIVE-scold-ASP
        'He/she was scolded.'

Virtually all transitive verbs can enter into this type of construction, as with the *gěi* passive of the preceding section, though the trajector or agent of the transitive verb is not elaborated in this construction. Although it might appear as if (30) is simply a case of the NP *gěi* NP V passive with the agentive NP following *gěi* deleted, this is not so. As with suffixal *gěi* discussed in section 3.3, the (atonal) *gěi* here forms an integrated syntactic unit with the main verb, resulting in a complex verb with passive meaning.

A familiar strategy from Generative Grammar and Relational Grammar suggests itself: a morpheme *gěi* is prefixed to the verb as a marker of the application of a Passive rule. In such an account, it is entirely coincidental and irrelevant that the verb prefix has the same form as the agentive marker in the passive construction of 4.3. In cognitive grammar, however, a similarity in the senses which attach to one form reflects a form-meaning unity which is natural and expected, though not without its exceptions. The representation of the meaning of *gěi* as a prefix will therefore reveal much similarity of structure with the passive construction diagrammed in Figure 19.

Figure 20 represents the meaning of *gěi* when used as a passive prefix. Like the suffixal variant, the prefix *gěi* transforms the profile of the base verb and changes it into a new verbal predicate. In this new structure, the trajector is to be identified as the same entity as the landmark of the original verb. The new landmark is the verbal predicate to which *gěi* attaches.

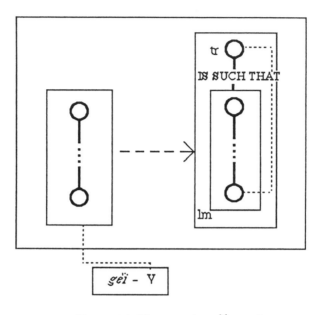

Figure 20: The passive *gěi*-prefix

There is an overall similarity with the representation of the passive construction of Figure 19, as one would expect. I have omitted in Figure 20 the shaded elaboration sites. The simplest way to elaborate the schema, apart from filling in a verbal predicate, is to fill just the trajector position with a noun phrase, giving rise to a clause like (30) above. There is, however, another interesting possibility involving the additional elaboration of the agent by means of another (... surprise!) *gěi*, illustrated in (31):

(31)   *Wǒ -de   biǎo   gěi   tā   gěi-diū-le.*
        My   watch   PASSIVE him/her   PASSIVE-lose-ASP
        'My watch was lost by him/her.'

Here we see *gěi* as an agent marker (although it is not to be simply equated with a preposition) and *gěi* as a passive prefix on the verb. In general, transitive verbs can form passives in Mandarin in any one of three ways:

(a)   with a preceding *gěi* + agent,
(b)   with a *gěi* - prefix on the verb and no overt agent, or

(c)   with a preceding *gěi* + agent and a *gěi* - prefix on the verb.

Given the characterization of the prefix in Figure 20, one can see how the transformed profile of the verb will integrate readily with the structure of the passive construction of Figure 19. A separate constructional schema, not unlike that shown in Figure 19, will license this additional construction type.

5. Conclusion

The range of meanings which attach to *gěi* is not predictable just from considerations of the basic meaning GIVE. But neither is the range of meanings arbitrary. In between these two extremes there is the additional possibility of a semantic extension which can be motivated but not predicted. The preceding discussion has shown that the range of meanings of *gěi*, though unpredictable, can indeed be motivated. I have done this by connecting the various senses of *gěi* in a natural way. In most cases, the semantic extension brings into focus some facet of the basic human experience of giving something to someone, the GIVE frame. Unless one recognizes this experiential basis and all that is associated with it, the relationships between the various meanings of *gěi* cannot possibly be appreciated. Langacker's cognitive grammar approach, built as it is upon concepts which have broad cognitive significance, provides a natural framework for the investigation of such relationships.

In exploring the semantics of *gěi* I have been guided by a desire to establish a unity among the various meanings, reflecting a tacit acceptance of what is sometimes referred to as the "isomorphism hypothesis" (see Haiman 1985: 14, 21ff), i.e. the idea that one form corresponds to one meaning. Obvious cases of homonymy immediately falsify any strong version of this hypothesis, but one can nevertheless propose the principle as a pervasive tendency in language even if it cannot be taken as an absolute. When one accepts the isomorphism hypothesis even in its weak version, then one must confront polysemy head on and face up to the task of accounting for the semantic relatedness, reducing the polysemy to some coherent whole. A research program of this kind presents a formidable challenge, requiring as it does a radical re-orientation in linguistic semantics. Nevertheless, it is a challenge which I believe must be taken up if we are to make progress in understanding the semantic properties of language.

Notes

*   I would like to thank Ron Langacker and the reviewers of this volume
        for helpful comments on an earlier version of this paper. Thanks also
        to Li Ning, Tung Ya Ping, Jock Hoe, and Fumio Kakubayashi for their
        help as informants.
        I will write the Mandarin word for 'give', 'to', etc. as *gěi* with the tone
        mark throughout the discussion, although in some of its uses this mor-
        pheme may lose its tone. This is particularly the case when it is used as
        a prefix or suffix, as discussed in sections 3.3. and 4.4. For the sake of
        typological consistency the inherent tone of the morpheme will always
        be indicated.

1.   There is yet another use of *gěi*, as a direct object marker:

        (i)   *Tāmen*   *gěi*   *nèi*   *běn*   *shū*   *ná*   *zǒu-le.*
              they   D.O.   that   CL   book   take   go
              'They took away that book.'

        Since there was some disagreement among my informants about the
        acceptability of sentences of this type, I have not included this use of
        gěi in the main body of the discussion. *Bǎ*, literally 'to take, hold
        something by the hand', is the preferred direct object marker in such
        constructions and possibly *gěi* has taken on the object marking function
        (for some speakers) by analogy with *bǎ*. Certainly the extension of a
        verb "to take" to an object marking function is familiar from other
        languages, as discussed in Givón (1975). While Givón provides many
        examples from African languages of the reanalysis of "take, get" verbs
        as markers of direct objects (arising out of serial verb constructions),
        he does not cite any example of a "give" verb being reanalyzed in this
        way.
        It may be more appropriate to explain this use of *gei* by drawing an
        analogy with the use of English *give* in expressions such as *give the car a*
        wash, *give the water a stir*, *give the woman a kiss*, etc. In these cases, *give*
        is used to convey the notion of an action proceeding from an agent to a
        patient, representing an extension of its more basic meaning where a
        physical object is passed from an agent to a recipient. The semantic
        extension to something like "a flow of energy from an agent to a pa-
        tient" may be a better way to understand how *gěi* comes to be used as a
        direct object marker in sentences such as (i) above.

2.   Some encouragement for thinking along these lines comes from the
        treatment of *gěi* in a contemporary dictionary of Mandarin, such as
        Wang (1967), where all the uses exemplified above appear as part of
        the meaning description of the one entry for *gěi*. It should be noted that
        this dictionary does distinguish homonymy and polysemy in the usual
        way by writing homonyms as separate entries. So, for example, the
        form *lǐ* can have the meaning 'principle, reason, rationale for doing
        something' and the meaning 'make a gesture or speak to a person in
        order to have a relationship'. In this case the dictionary has two
        separate entries (unlike the one entry for *gěi*), reflecting presumably
        the lexicographer's reluctance to see the senses of *lǐ* as related. It is
        true that *gěi* in all its uses is written as the same character, but this is
        not a criterion (at least not a major criterion) for deciding what goes

into a lexical entry in the dictionary - the two *ĭ* entries referred to above, for example, are both associated with the same character and yet are treated as separate entries. One must conclude that Wang, in compiling the dictionary, perceived, however vaguely, some kind of unity in the range of uses of *gĕi*. To establish convincingly, rather than by fiat, that the uses of *gĕi* are related, one must of course carry out a semantic analysis of *gĕi* in its various uses such that the similarity between the uses becomes evident.

3.   Typical of the formalist-philosophical orientation throughout this text-book is the way in which the authors explain the oddity of the sentence *This idea is red* (p. 192). The reader is required to construct a chain of deduction, as in a formal logic problem, appealing to various meaning postulates and tautologies leading to a final line of the form *p & -p*, thereby establishing the contradictoriness of the original sentence. Obviously, one does not need to go through such a tortuous exercise in order to appreciate the oddity of describing an idea as *red*.

4.   One should note that in Talmy's more traditional and restricted use of the terms "figure" and "ground", the moving object would appear to be always construed as the figure. So, for example, Talmy (1985: 67) calls the THING the "figure" and the GIVER and RECIPIENT both "agents" in discussing *give*. Cf. Talmy's definitions (p. 61): "The Figure is a moving or *conceptually* mov*able* object whose path or site is at issue; the Ground is a reference-frame, or a reference-point stationary within a reference-frame, with respect to which the Figure's path or site is characterized."

5.   It should be noted, however, that there are some constraints on verb copying construction as described in Li & Thompson (1981: 442) which do not hold in the case of the double *gĕi* construction. According to Li and Thompson, the first verb in the verb copying construction does not typically co-occur with aspect markers; also the direct object of the first verb is typically interpreted as non-referential. I claim only that the double *gĕi* construction is similar to the verb copying construction, not that the double *gĕi* construction represents a prototypical instance of it.

6.   Cf. the discussion of "resultative" profiling in Bennett (1975: 50ff) and Lakoff (1987: 440f). In Newman (1981) the discussion of resultative profiling is extended to "patient subject" constructions like *the clothes washed clean* and *seem/appear* constructions.

7.   Hashimoto (1976) analyzes the *gĕi tā qián*, i.e. *gĕi* RECIPIENT THING, construction in Mandarin and other Chinese dialects as being derived both historically and in an abstract syntactic way from the *gĕi qián gĕi tā* construction. Historically, the developments are seen by Hashimoto as involving a change from a Tai type to an Altaic type of word order. Generative grammar accounts of *gĕi* constructions can be found in Hashimoto (1971) and Liang (1971).

8.   Such an analysis is assumed in Wang (1967), where the sequence of the verb *sòng* and *gĕi* is written as one word *sòngei* (with *gĕi* marked as atonal). *Gĕi*, used in this way, is called a "post-verb" by Wang.

9.   Tang (1978: 88) also notes that *le* is normally suffixed to the verb + *gĕi* and not just the base verb, though Tang insists on treating *gĕi* as a preposition even in such cases. The possibility of suffixing *le* to *gĕi* is attributed to the claim that it "may deep structurally as well as

historically derive from the the full verb *gĕi* 'give' ". I would say that *gĕi* in such constructions is functioning as a verbal suffix, even though it bears historical and semantic relationships with the use of *gĕi* 'give'. The appeal of the cognitive grammar framework is that it can bring out the similarities and the differences between different versions of a morpheme.

10.   Related no doubt to the greater prominence of the RECIPIENT in the writing and telephoning frames is the possibility of having the RECIP-IENT as the sole landmark, as in English *I wrote him* and *I telephoned her.* This is not as possible with *mail* : **I mailed her.* It is more possible, however, in special contexts such as *We have mailed all the business corporations,* in the context of an election campaign.

11.   The expression "control over an act" is interpreted in slightly different ways, depending on whether it applies to the granter of permission or the grantee. The granter has control in the sense that he/she has the power to determine who can perform the act. The grantee is given the right to perform the act, but not the power to determine who else can perform the act. What is granted, then, is a right which is closely re-lated to, but not identical with, the rights of the granter.

12.   It should be mentioned that the use of *gĕi* in the sense of PERMIT is quite restricted, in ways that English *permit* is not. So, for example, some speakers are willing to use *gĕi* in this sense only with the predi-cates *kàn* 'look at, see' and *tīng* 'listen, hear'. None of my informants accepted an attempt to translate *Let me kiss you* as *Gĕi wŏ qīnqin nǐ.* The fact that there are these rather severe collocational restrictions on this use of *gĕi* does not diminish the need to explicate the semantic relationships involved.

13.   Unlike handing over gifts, the passing on of knowledge does not mean that the giver of the knowledge no longer possesses this knowledge. Knowledge can be shared, but not forfeited. As in the case of the granting of permission (cf. note 11), one must recognize slight variations in the structure of the transfer of control, depending on the domains to which it is being applied.

14.   The person who transfers control in either the GIVE or PERMIT sense is clearly bringing about a new state of affairs, and there is inherent in both GIVE and PERMIT a notion of causation involving the predicate CAUSE. Cf. the explicit formalizations of these predicates in Miller & Johnson-Laird (1976: 511, 569). It is therefore not surprising that in some languages the sense of CAUSE is a well-developed extension of GIVE-type verbs. This is the case in Thai, Cambodian, and Finnish, for example, where the GIVE-verb is used as a causative (cf. Finnish *antaa jonkun korjata jokin* lit. 'to give someone (Gen.) to repair something' = 'to have someone repair something'). Even in the case of *give to understand*, the semantic contribution of *give* amounts to little more than CAUSE. Although Mandarin *gĕi* does not appear to have any clear CAUSE sense, there is a use of *gĕi* as a kind of "purposive" predicate connecting two clauses, as in (i):

(i)   *Tā   shuō gùshi gĕi   wŏmen   tīng.*
      He/she   tells story ?   we   listen
      'He/she told a story for us to listen to.'

It is unclear just how one should analyze the *gĕi* in this construction. Poteet (MS:7ff) sees it as a connective meaning 'so that', which is reasonable. One could also see the construction as an elaboration of a BENEFACTIVE, RECIPIENT or even PERMIT sense of *gĕi*. This seems to be the closest Mandarin *gĕi* comes to a CAUSE sense.

References

Bennett, David C.
    1975   *Spatial and temporal uses of English prepositions: An essay in stratificational semantics*. London: Longman.
Brugman, Claudia
    1981   Story of *over*. [Unpublished M.A. thesis, University of California. Available from the Indiana University Linguistics Club.]
Chao, Yuen Ren
    1968   *A grammar of spoken Chinese*. Berkeley: University of California Press.
Cheng, Robert L., Ying-Che Li & Ting-Chi Tang (eds.)
    1978   *Proceedings of the symposium on Chinese linguistics, 1977 Linguistic institute of the Linguistic Society of America*. Taipei: Student Book Co.
Cogen, Cathy, Henry Thompson, Graham Thurgood, Kenneth Whistler & James Wright (eds.)
    1975   *Proceedings of the first annual meeting of the Berkeley Linguistics Society*. Berkeley Linguistics Society, University of California, Berkeley.
Cole, Roger W. (ed.)
    1977   *Current issues in linguistic theory*. Bloomington: Indiana University Press.
Comrie, Bernard (ed.)
    1987   *The world's major languages*. New York: Oxford University Press.
Crain, Catherine
    1979   "Advancement and ascension to direct object in Chamorro", in: Philip L. Hubbard & Peter M. Tiersma (eds.), 3-32.
Dakubu, M.E. Kropp (ed.)
    1988   *The languages of Ghana*. (African Languages, Occasional Publication No. 2, International African Institute.) London: Kegan Paul.
Dakubu, M.E. Kropp & K.C. Ford
    1988   "The Central-Togo languages", in: M.E. Kropp Dakubu (ed.), 119-154.
Fillmore, Charles J.
    1977   "Topics in lexical semantics", in: Roger W. Cole (ed.), 76-138.
Givón, T.
    1975   "Serial verbs and syntactic change: Niger-Congo", in: Charles N. Li (ed.), 47-112.
    1984   *Syntax: A functional-typological introduction*. Vol. 1. Amsterdam: John Benjamins.
Haiman, John
    1985   *Natural syntax*. Cambridge: Cambridge University Press.
Haiman, John (ed.)
    1985   *Iconicity in syntax*. Amsterdam: John Benjamins.

Hall, Robert A. Jr.
1966   *Pidgin and creole languages.* Ithaca: Cornell University Press.
Hashimoto, Anne Y.
1971   "The Mandarin syntactic structures", *Unicorn* 7: 84-93.
Hashimoto, Mantaro J.
1976   "The double object construction in Chinese", *Computational Analyses of Asian and African Languages* 6: 33-42.
Hawkins, Bruce W. & William D. Davies (eds.)
1981   *Linguistic notes from La Jolla,* No. 8. Available from Linguistics Department, University of California at San Diego, San Diego, California.
Hubbard, Philip L. & Peter M. Tiersma (eds.)
1979   *Linguistic notes from La Jolla,* No. 6. Available from Linguistics Department, University of California at San Diego, San Diego, California.
Hurford, James R. & Brendan Heasley
1983   *Semantics: A coursebook.* Cambridge: Cambridge University Press.
Jackendoff, Ray
1983   *Semantics and cognition.* Cambridge: M.I.T. Press.
Katz, Jerrold J.
1972   *Semantic theory.* New York: Harper and Row.
Lakoff, George
1987   *Women, fire, and dangerous things: What categories reveal about the mind.* Chicago: University of Chicago Press.
Lakoff, George & Mark Johnson
1980   *Metaphors we live by.* Chicago: University of Chicago Press.
Langacker, Ronald W.
1987   *Foundations of cognitive grammar.* Vol. 1. Stanford: Stanford University Press.
Liang, James Chao-Ping
1971   Prepositions, co-verbs, or verbs? A commentary on Chinese grammar - past and present. [Unpublished Ph.D. Dissertation, University of Pennsylvania.]
Li, Charles N. (ed.)
1975   *Word order and word order change.* Austin: University of Texas Press.
Li, Charles & Sandra A. Thompson
1981   *Mandarin Chinese: A functional reference grammar.* Berkeley, California: University of California Press.
Lindner, Susan
1981   A lexico-semantic analysis of verb-particle constructions with *up* and *out.* [Unpublished Ph.D. Dissertation, University of California, San Diego. Available from the Indiana University Linguistics Club.]
Miller, George A. & Philip N. Johnson-Laird
1976   *Language and perception.* Cambridge: Belknap Press/Harvard University Press.
Newman, John
1981   "Perception predicates", in: Bruce W. Hawkins & William D. Davies (eds.), 25-40.
Nguyen Dang Liem
1979   "Cases in English and Southeast Asian languages, and translation", in: Nguyen Dang Liem (ed.), 43-66.

Nguyen Dang Liem (ed.)
    1979   *Southeast Asian Linguistic Studies*, Vol. 3. Canberra: Department of
                Linguistics, Research School of Pacific Studies, Australian National
                University.
Perlmutter, David M. (ed.)
    1983   *Studies in relational grammar 1*. Chicago: University of Chicago Press.
Poteet, Steve
                "The meaning(s) of giving: A study of Mandarin *gěi*". [Unpublished
                manuscript.]
Pulleyblank, Douglas
    1987   "Yoruba", in: Bernard Comrie (ed.), 971-990.
Shopen, Timothy (ed.)
    1985   *Language typology and syntactic description III*. Cambridge: Cambridge
                University Press.
Tai, James H-Y.
    1985   "Temporal sequence and Chinese word order", in: John Haiman (ed.),
                49-72.
Talmy, Leonard
    1975   "Figure and ground in complex sentences", in: Cathy Cogen et al.
                (eds.), 419-430.
    1985   "Lexicalization patterns: Semantic structure in lexical forms", in:
                Timothy Shopen (ed.), 57-149.
Tang, Ting-Chi
    1978   "Double-object constructions in Chinese", in: Robert L. Cheng, Ying-
                Che Li & Ting-Chi Tang (eds.), 67-95.
Wang, Fred Fangyu
    1967   *Mandarin Chinese dictionary*. Taipei: Mei Ya Publications.

Agentivity in cognitive grammar

Yoshiki Nishimura

1. Theoretical background[1]

The term *cognitive grammar* is intended here to cover some independently developed theories and frameworks that share essentially the same set of assumptions regarding linguistic semantics.[2] What makes cognitive grammar unique is the way it departs from the traditional view of meaning. This latter can be summarized as follows: Meaning resides in objective reality and thus exists independently of human cognition and understanding. Like many old traditions that die hard, this view (hereafter objectivism) seems to persist in and constitute part and parcel of the tacitly assumed framework for much current linguistic work. Cognitive grammar, on the other hand, forms an entirely different conception of meaning: Meaning is mediated and organized by cognitive processing and is thus based on human cognition and understanding. Let us refer to this novel view as *conceptualism* or *experientialism*.[3]

One might object that the contrast between objectivism and conceptualism is not relevant to linguistics proper in spite of its possible philosophical significance. After all, dominant trends in current linguistic theory have produced results that deserve the attention of anyone interested in language, regardless of the position he or she takes on what counts as meaning. So why care about the alleged contrast? This objection, however, does not hold. As we will observe in what follows, whether to adopt one view or the other has ramifications which one cannot afford to ignore if one is to seek truly revealing accounts of linguistic phenomena.

Before we go into specific analyses, some preliminary remarks are in order on the kind of difference which exists between the two conceptions of meaning in the way certain linguistic phenomena are construed and explained.

First, we would like to see how figurative language such as metaphor and metonymy will be treated.[4] Objectivism views rhetorical phenomena as a matter of peripheral interest. This is because figurative expressions, as conceived in objectivism, are used when one chooses to express in effective or aesthetically pleasing ways what could otherwise be represented straightforwardly. In other words, objectivism assumes that figurative expressions are meaningful only via their relations to independently definable objective meanings. Moreover, according to objectivism, the objective meaning associated with a figurative expression must always be distinct from its literal meaning, since it is this distinction that qualifies it to be so called. Thus, the very fact of being figurative renders an expression deviant.

Viewed from the conceptualist perspective, figurative language assumes paramount significance. Conceptualism maintains that figures of speech often serve as patterns for creative cognition, that is, as the (only) means to understand and give expression to otherwise unfathomable realities and thoughts.

Furthermore, rhetoric, in the conceptualist account, permeates everyday normal expressions that are not oriented toward special effects. Figurative language as it is understood in conceptualism thus constitutes a crucial part of creativity characteristic of our linguistic competence. Any theory which downplays figurative language runs the risk of limiting its scope to its disadvantage.

Let us now turn our attention to the domain with which linguistics has been primarily concerned - nonfigurative language. Our discussion here will center around the claim known as the autonomy of syntax. A typical objectivist argument in support of this claim takes the following form: (1) One (type of) extralinguistic situation can syntactically be represented in alternate ways and (2) different types of extralinguistic situations can syntactically be represented in one way. Thus, since there are cases where (1) one and the same (type of) meaning corresponds to distinct syntactic patterns and (2) one and the same (type of) syntactic pattern corresponds to distinct (types of) meanings, meaning does not provide reliable evidence to draw upon in the linguist's attempt to explain formal regularities on a principled basis. Hence the autonomy of the syntactic component.

Although the type of argument outlined above makes perfect sense for anyone committed to objectivism, it simply does not hold water in cognitive grammar, which builds on conceptualism. The point is that cognitive grammar calls into question the objectivist view of meaning on which the above argument largely depends. To be specific, cognitive grammar does not accept the equivalence objectivism assumes to exist between the identification of an objective situation and the semantic characterization of the sentence(s) used to describe that situation. Even if one were to assume the feasibility of the objective identification of a situation to be described by more than one (type of) sentence - a highly dubious assumption, given the conceptualist reinterpretation of figurative language mentioned above - conceptualism would argue that the situation itself is not to be equated with the meaning of the sentence(s) put to descriptive use. It is the way the speaker construes a situation - his or her way of understanding a situation - that really matters in determining the meaning of the sentence(s) with which he or she chooses to delineate it. Consequently, there certainly arise cases where (1) one situation lends itself to alternate construals and is accordingly assigned two (or more) syntactic patterns associated with those construals and (2) different (types of) situations are unified under one and the same type of construal and are accordingly assigned a syntactic pattern associated with that type of construal. Thus, a passive sentence and its active counterpart, for instance, may differ in meaning, though they share a situation as common material to be construed.[5] Similarly, translatability preserving truth conditions does not necessarily guarantee commonality of meaning; mutually translatable sentences of different languages are not always synonymous.[6] The conceptualist argument so far, if valid, leads to the conclusion that syntax is not autonomously organized but inextricably bound up with meaning. In fact, cognitive grammar contends that it is no less gratuitous to purge syntax of meaning than to design a lexicon without semantic information.[7]

Unlike most of the previous frameworks, cognitive grammar seeks to explain linguistic phenomena in a natural and revealing way, that is, to account for formal regularities in terms of human cognition and understanding. What constitutes its keynote is its conception of language: language manifests the way human beings attach meaning to, construe, and make sense of the external world. In what follows, we will see how cognitive grammar allows us to explain certain syntactic and/or lexical regularities in terms of semantic principles, which in turn are founded on human cognition and understanding. Our discussion will center around the reformulation of the thematic relation Agent: We will be addressing ourselves to the task of charging this semantic role with explanatory power, an aim that would be unattainable (and in fact unimaginable) for the standard case grammar and its offspring. To the extent that our specific analyses turn out to be convincing and revealing, the general framework of cognitive grammar and the conception of language on which it rests will gain empirical support.

2.   Thematic relations

Much current linguistic theory makes use of such terms as Agent and Theme to characterize the semantic relations which hold between the predicate verb as the pivotal element in the sentence and the array of arguments it requires. In many cases, however, these semantic roles (henceforth thematic relations) have been invoked either as mere descriptive devices without explanatory power or as extremely theory-laden terms, whose precise definition theorists do not seem to care about. In either way, this trend is largely due to objectivism, according to which, as we have noted, situations to be described by language are distinctly organized independently of human cognition and understanding, not to mention the way they happen to be linguistically represented. Thus, if objectivism were right, the thematic relation assignment as regards a given sentence would be tantamount to the objective characterization of the situation that the sentence is intended to describe.

We will take issue with objectivism on the assignment of thematic relations. Specifically, we will try to demonstrate that cognitive grammar can bring the thematic relation Agent to bear on the task of explaining (rather than just describing) some regularities in syntactic and lexical structure. If we succeed in this attempt, we will have shown that, as far as thematic relations are concerned, the relationship between meaning and form is motivated rather than arbitrary and that, moreover, this motivation is grounded not so much in the external world as in the way we construe and understand it.

2.1.   Agent vs. Instrument

In this section, we will be concerned with pairs of sentences like the following:

(1)   a.   *Bill broke the window with a stone.*
       b.   *A stone broke the window.*
(2)   a.   *Bill killed Jane with poison.*
       b.   *Poison killed Jane.*
(3)   a.   *John removed a persistent stain on his shirt with a new detergent.*
       b.   *A new detergent removed a persistent stain on John's shirt.*
(4)   a.   *John calculated the cost in a minute with a computer.*
       b.   *A computer calculated the cost in a minute.*

2.1.1.   Objectivist approach

As far as these data are concerned, naive realism, a notable manifestation of objectivism, is all that most versions of case grammar have to go
on to determine how to assign thematic relations.[8] Thus, although the
same verb appears in much the same syntactic structure in each pair,
the subject in (b) is generally assigned Instrument, a thematic relation
distinct from Agent, which is assigned to the subject in (a). This
distinction may seem reasonable at first blush. For each of the subjects
in (b) is inanimate and therefore cannot be considered capable of
intentional action leading to the effect in question (e.g. Jane's death)
unless personification is intended. One might even be tempted to argue
that there is evidence for the assignment of Instrument to the subjects
in (b) by pointing out that (a) and (b) in each pair can be used to
describe one and the same situation with the *with*-phrase unmistakably
marked as Instrument.[9] It is to be noted at this juncture that this
argument will be valid if and only if the following premise based on
naive realism holds: each situation (to be described by language) is
unequivocally organized prior to linguistic description, with the result
that the role played by each participant in a given situation is
determined independently of language and can be uniquely identified.

The validity of the analysis we have just outlined and the objectivist
premise on which it rests have been taken for granted in most versions
of case grammar and have seldom been challenged. In fact, they seem
to form a basis for further arguments and generalizations.

In their attempt to use syntactic evidence to define semantic notions,
Deane and Wheeler (1984) go so far as to claim that "Agent and
Instrument can be isolated by their participation in the following
syntactic patterns":

[AGENT   [...   [with INSTRUMENT]]]
[INSTRUMENT   [...   [for AGENT]]

They characterize their method, *correlation analysis*, as follows:

First, identify a syntactic distributional fact. Then ascertain if
the fact is associated with a *demonstrable semantic property*.
If it is, then the syntactic configuration is semantically relevant and can be used to gain access to the meaning of the
lexical item [emphasis added].

Thus, in the case at issue, the "demonstrable semantic property" for them is the unique role played both by the subject in (b) and by the corresponding *with*-phrase in (a) in each pair. In other words, they tacitly base their identification of an "intuitively reasonable semantic category" on the objectivist premise of naive realism.

Foley and Van Valin (1984) posit logical structures like the following for (1a) and (1b):

(1')　a.　[[DO (Bill, [do' (Bill)])] CAUSE [do' (stone)]] CAUSE
　　　　 [BECOME broken' (window)]
　　　b.　[do' (stone)] CAUSE [BECOME broken' (window)]

Here the assumption is that *(with) a stone* in (1a) and *a stone* in (1b) share the role of unintentionally performing some action (in their term, "effector"), difference between them, if any, being attributed to the additional assignment of the role Actor only to the latter.[10]

In a similar vein, Starosta (1978) defines Instrument as "the entity which is perceived as the immediate effective cause of the action or event referred to by the main predicator" in contrast to Agent as "the nonimmediate perceived causer of the action of the verb". (Cf. (1'a) and (1'b).) Despite his criticism of the "once a case relation, always a case relation" methodology and "the use of paraphrase evidence" for establishing case roles, Starosta assumes, with Fillmore (1968, 1977) and others, that once something is perceived as Instrument (the *with*-phrase in (a) in each pair), it must always be perceived as Instrument (the subject in (b) in each pair) unless the one-instance-per-clause constraint is violated (see below).

Fillmore (1968) attributes the unacceptability of sentences like (1c) to a violation of the constraint that only instances of the same thematic relation are coordinated, assuming of course that *Bill* in (1a) and *a stone* in (1b) are respectively marked as Agent and Instrument:

(1)　c.　*Bill and a stone broke the window.*

The unacceptability of sentences such as (3c) is explained, again according to Fillmore (1968), by the constraint that only one token of each thematic relation is permitted per proposition:

(3)　c.　*A new detergent removed a persistent stain on John's shirt
　　　　 with soap.*

Thus (3c) is unacceptable because it has two instances of one and the same thematic relation Instrument, thereby violating the one-instance-per-clause constraint.

To sum up, objectivists claim that, in each pair, the subject in (b), unlike the subject in (a), is to be assigned the same thematic relation as the *with*-phrase in (a). Consequently, the analysis in this subsection, if valid, would indicate that the use of the same lexical item (in this case, the same verb) in the same syntactic structure (NP V NP (PP)) in each pair was a mere accident: the formal regularity did not reflect any semantic regularity. No further explanation (rather than mere description) in semantic terms would follow. Analyses of this kind, it should be noted, can readily be taken to lend support to the autonomous-syntax hypothesis.

2.1.2.   Conceptualist approach

Let us now consider how cognitive grammar would deal with the same set of data.

Note first that cognitive grammar cannot take for granted the assignment of distinct thematic relations to the subjects in (a) and (b) in each pair, because, as we have just mentioned, the use of the same verb in the same syntactic structure (a generalization about the syntax and the lexicon) would then be left unexplained. Cognitive grammar has to seek an alternative analysis unless there is evidence to the contrary. Moreover, the evidence that objectivists adduce for the assignment of Instrument to the subjects in (b) would cease to be such in cognitive grammar. For the objectivist premise in 2.1.1. based on naive realism simply would not hold. To recapitulate the relevant tenet of cognitive grammar mentioned in 1, let us see what Langacker, one of the leading exponents of this framework, has to say:

> the meaning of an expression is not determined in any unique or mechanical way from the nature of the objective situation it describes. The same situation can be described by a variety of semantically distinct expressions that embody different ways of construing or structuring it. Our ability to impose alternate structurings on a conceived phenomenon is fundamental to lexical and grammatical variability (Langacker 1987a: 107).

In other words, cognitive grammar assumes, following Lyons, that

> there are certain universal principles of cognition and per-
> ception (which may or may not be innate) and that the appli-
> cation of these principles to the situations that are described
> by language permits a considerable range of variation in the
> way in which the situations can be categorized (Lyons 1977:
> 499).

Thus one and the same situation[11] may be susceptible to more than one
way of categorization: ambiguity may arise as to the assignment of thematic relations to the linguistic expressions referring to the participants
in a given situation. If we succeed in demonstrating that (a) and (b) in
each pair represent different ways of organizing one and the same situation and that unlike the *with*-phrase in (a), the subject in (b) is to be
marked Agent just like the subject in (a), then cognitive grammar will
have the upper hand over the objectivist analysis in the preceding subsection.

The difference in acceptability between (2b) and (5b) constitutes
prime evidence for a conceptualist approach:[12]

(5)   a.   *Bill killed Jane with a red-hot icepick.*
      b.   **A red-hot icepick killed Jane.*

If *poison* in the perfectly acceptable (2b) were marked Instrument, (5b)
would also be impeccable, since, on the objectivist premise, its subject
would be categorized on a par with its *with*-phrase counterpart in (5a).
The fact is, however, (5b) is unacceptable except under rather abnormal
circumstances (e.g. where the icepick fell from a great height).[13] The
cause for this difference will not be difficult to detect if one gives up
naive realism. The point is that *poison* can be conceived of not only as
mere Instrument entirely subordinate to *Bill* but also as Agent that
brought about Jane's death on its own, whereas to regard *a red-hot
icepick* as Agent would be rather far-fetched, requiring powerful contextual support. In other words, *poison* in (2b), unlike *(with) poison* in (2a),
is to be marked Agent just like *Bill* in (2a). To feel secure about this
line of argument, compare (4b) and (7b) with (6b) and (8b), respectively. (Once again, let us assume for the sake of argument that each
pair of sentences is intended for one and the same situation.)

(6) a.   *John calculated the cost in a minute with an abacus.*
     b.   **An abacus calculated the cost in a minute.*
(7) a.   *The terrorist killed him with a bomb.*
     b.   *A bomb killed him.*
(8) a.   *The terrorist killed him with a stick.*
     b.   **A stick killed him.*

Here again the difference in acceptability is explicable in terms of the plausibility of categorizing *a computer* and *a bomb*, on the one hand, and *an abacus* and *a stick*, on the other, as Agent in these particular situations.[14]

Those people who commit themselves to objectivism may find it uncomfortable to see the term Agent being applied to such inanimate entities as poison and a bomb. For cognitive grammar, on the other hand, there is no a priori reason for requiring that the applicability of Agent be strictly limited to "an animate entity that intentionally and responsibly uses its own force, or energy, to bring about an event or to initiate a process".[15] As suggested in 1, human beings must make creative use of the limited conceptualizing devices with which they are equipped by their languages and other cognitive systems in order to structure and understand ever increasing novel situations, either actual or hypothetical. Consequently, semantic structures must now and again be applied to situations for which they were not originally meant (i.e. non-paradigm situations). This is where rhetoric (such as metaphor) as a means of creative cognition comes in. Key concepts in cognitive grammar, such as prototype and typicality condition, also fit in here. Thus, in this particular case, what is involved is "personification" in a properly expanded sense.[16] Each of the subjects in (1b)-(4b) and (7b) is conceptualized as Agent in spite of its failure to meet such typicality conditions as animateness and intentionality.

The difference in acceptability between (2b), (4b), and (7b), on the one hand, and (5b), (6b), and (8b), on the other, poses a serious problem for objectivist semanticists. As long as they stick to the objectivist premise, they will have little chance to distinguish (2b), (4b), and (7b) from (5b), (6b), and (8b), respectively. The only way out would be to argue, as some objectivists actually do,[17] that a distinction should be drawn between Instrument 1 and Instrument 2, such that Instrument 1 can be promoted to subject position, *preserving the thematic relation*, whereas Instrument 2 cannot.

Apart from the fact that this blatantly ad hoc argument will "diminish the value of Fillmore's proposed realization rule",[18] it can be refuted on factual grounds. The only point in arguing for the alleged distinction is to keep the objectivist premise from collapsing by claiming that the *permissible* "instrumental" subject, which is somehow marked as Instrument 1, plays the same role as the corresponding *with*-phrase. The difference between (1"a) and (1"b) or (2'a) and (2'b) serves to disprove the claim. (Suppose once again that (a) and (b) in each pair are used to report on the same event.)[19]

(1") a. *The window was broken with a stone.*
           (passive counterpart of (1a))
      b. *The window was broken by a stone.*
           (passive counterpart of (1b))
(2') a. *Jane was killed with poison.*
           (passive counterpart of (2a))
      b. *Jane was killed by poison.*
           (passive counterpart of (2b))

If the objectivist remedy were on the right track, the *with*-phrase and the *by*-phrase in each pair would serve the same function (i.e. Instrument 1). Actually, however, their functions are not quite the same. In (1"a) and (2'a), *a stone* and *poison* are understood as subordinate to some other entities (probably persons) that did the breaking and the killing. Those other entities could be made explicit by adding the *by*-phrases corresponding to the subjects of the active counterparts of (1"a) and (2'a). Thus,

(1''') a. *The window was broken with a stone by Bill.*
(2'')   a. *Jane was killed with poison by Bill.*

In (1"b) and (2'b), on the other hand, *a stone* and *poison* are understood as *primarily responsible* for the broken window and Jane's death, respectively: they are construed as doing the breaking and the killing. The persons who used them do not count as main participants of the conceived situations; they are, at best, actors in byplays incidental to the main actions. Accordingly, they could only be expressed in subordinate clauses, as illustrated below:[20]

(1''') b. *The window was broken by a stone which Bill threw at it.*
(2'')   b. *Jane was killed by the poison which Bill had slipped into her coffee.*

We are thus led to the conclusion that in each pair the *by*-phrase (and its subject counterpart), on the one hand, and the *with*-phrase, on the other, should be marked distinct from each other, that is, as Agent and Instrument, respectively.

Also to be noted here is the unfoundedness of the characterization of the Instrument *with*-phrase as a performer of its own action (Foley & Van Valin 1984) or as the (immediate) effective cause of an event in its own right[21] (Starosta 1978). It should be clear from the discussion so far (especially the preceding paragraph) that the participant represented by the *with*-phrase (i.e. Instrument), unlike its subject or *by*-phrase counterpart, is understood as a subsidiary entity entirely subordinate to another entity (i.e. Agent) and incapable of acting on its own (in the construal of the situation associated with the sentence in question). Thus, as DeLancey (1984) argues, "an instrument does not count as a mediating cause because it makes no independent contribution to the event - it functions only as an extension of the agent's will". Viewing the Instrument *with*-phrase this way allows us to capture the essence of Agent: Agent is "a single cause from which an unbroken chain of control leads to the effect" (DeLancey 1984). This covers not only the prototypical Agent[22] represented by the subjects in (a) or their *by*-phrase counterparts (e.g. *Bill* in (1a) or (1'''a)). The discussion so far will have made it sufficiently clear that it also applies to the subjects in (b) or their *by*-phrase counterparts (e.g. *a stone* in (1b) or (1''b)), each being viewed as the primary cause of the event in question. In other words, *a stone* in (1b), for instance, is felt to bear sufficient family resemblances to *Bill* in (1a).

As another piece of evidence that (a) and (b) in each pair represent different ways of structuring the same situation (if it can be defined at all), consider the following pairs:

(9) a. *Bill killed Jane by throwing a stone at her.*
     b. *A stone killed Jane by hitting her right on the head.*
(10) a. *Mary killed Tom by shooting him with his own gun.*
     b. *A bullet fired from his own gun killed Tom by penetrating his heart.*

(Suppose for the sake of argument that (a) and (b) in each pair are used to report the same murder case.) Note first that the *by*-phrase in each sentence designates the way in which the subject performed the action denoted by the main VP. Notice furthermore that the gerundive phrase itself refers to an action performed by the subject and that the relation between the two actions is such that the performance of the lower-level action leads to the realization of the higher-level action. Let us call a sequence of actions involving this relation a coherent action sequence (hereafter CAS).[23] It is readily observable that different CAS's pertaining to a given situation represent different ways of organizing that situation: (a) and (b) in each pair structure the same situation in terms of different images. Thus, in (9a), for instance, Bill is cast as the main actor who performs some requisite action leading to Jane's death, whereas in (9b) the same murder is viewed as stemming from an action performed by *a stone*. Consequently, exchanging the *by*-phrases results in unacceptable sentences - incoherent action sequences - as *reports of the same murder case in question*:[24] [25]

(9')   a.   *Bill killed Jane by hitting her right on the head.*
         b.   **A stone killed Jane by throwing a stone at her.*
(10')   a.   **Mary killed Tom by penetrating his heart.*
         b.   **A bullet fired from his own gun killed Tom by shooting him with his own gun.*

The notion of CAS can solve otherwise formidable problems for cognitive grammar (and the objectivist framework, for that matter). Consider (1c), repeated here as (11), again:

(11)   **Bill and a stone broke the window.*

Fillmore (1968) claims to have explained the unacceptability of (11) as a violation of his constraint on coordination, on the assumption that *Bill* and *a stone* are respectively marked as Agent and Instrument. Since, however, we have rejected the assumption, we have to look elsewhere for an explanation. Moreover, the following sentences are acceptable (at least marginally) in spite of their failure to meet Fillmore's constraint:

(12)   *The window was broken once by John and once by a car fender.*
(13)   *Did the locksmith or the key open the door?*
(14)   *Hurricanes and marauding bands devastated the region (at different times).*

This seemingly recalcitrant series of data can be accounted for by a plausible constraint like this: Distinct CAS's for one and the same situation cannot be collapsed into one CAS. What this constraint means is that different ways of structuring a given situation cannot be activated simultaneously to produce a single coherent image. (11) violates the constraint by collapsing different CAS's for one and the same situation (represented by (11') and (11") below) into one CAS:[26]

(11')   *Bill broke the window by throwing a stone at it.*
(11")   *A stone broke the window by going right through it.*

(12), (13), and (14), on the other hand, each represent two (or more) distinct situations, each of which is organized by a single CAS. Loosely put, they result from contracting (12'), (13'), and (14'):

(12')   *The window was broken once by John and it was broken*
           once by a car fender.
(13')   *Did the locksmith open the door or did the key open the*
           door?
(14')   *Hurricanes devastated the region and marauding bands*
           devastated the region.

It is obvious then that none of (12), (13), and (14) violate the constraint in question.

Fillmore's attempt to explain the unacceptability of sentences like (3c) is also misguided. There are hosts of counterexamples like the following:

(15)   *A new detergent removed a persistent stain on John's shirt with its*
          enzyme.
(16)   *My car hit the garage roof with its radio antenna.*
          (Chomsky 1972)
(17)   *The tree fell and brushed the house with its topmost branches;*
          however, no damage was done. (Croft 1984)
(18)   *The tsunami inundated Kapiolani Park with a towering wall of*
          water. (Starosta 1978)

Fillmore (1968) argues that these acceptable sentences should be derived from underlying representations such as the following:

(16')   [V, hit],[obj, the garage roof],[instr, my car's radio antenna]

But as Chomsky (1972) and Dougherty (1970) point out, this move does not add up, either. First, a pair of sentences that purport to be derived from the same underlying representation of this sort are not always synonymous. Compare (16) with (16"):

(16")   *My car's radio antenna hit the garage roof.*

Chomsky (1972: 177) suggests that "some sort of 'agency' is associated with the subject position" in (16) and (16"). Secondly, within Fillmore's case grammar, a single surface sentence which is "unambiguous can be derived from two distinctly different basic structures" (Dougherty 1970), certainly an undesirable side effect. (19), for example, can be derived either from (19') or from (19"):

(19)   *Caruso broke the window with his voice.*
(19')   [V, break],[obj, the window],[instr, Caruso's voice]
(19")   [V, break],[obj, the window],[instr, his voice],[agent, Caruso]

But (19) is not ambiguous in the relevant way. In our terms, of course, all the subjects in (15)-(19) (and (16"), for that matter) are to be marked Agent, with each sentence following the one-instance-per-clause constraint.

Before concluding the somewhat arduous argument that has been presented in this subsection, I would like to show that the notion of "perspective" in Fillmore (1977) cannot help improve the prospects for objectivist semantics, at least not as much as it is expected to. "Perspective" is intended to cope with some earlier drawbacks of case grammar, most of which have to do with the undeniable semantic contribution of grammatical relations such as subject and object. The revised version of case grammar equipped with perspective, as I understand it, has two stages of semantic role assignment. The first stage corresponds to the case role assignment in the earlier version and the second pertains to the semantic effects on some of the case roles accruing from or, conversely, resulting in their syntactic realizations as subject or object. Thus the dual semantic role assignment can be stated as follows:

1.   *Case role assignment*
     Given a situation, case roles are to be determined uniquely (i.e. unambiguously) and independently of whatever linguistic

expressions the speaker happens to use to describe the situation, which is assumed to be inherently organized.

2.   *Perspective choice*
Choice of perspective determines the way case roles as assigned in 1. are to be syntactically realized.

One might be inclined to argue that the difference in perspective serves to explain away whatever semantic difference there is between the roles played by the *with*-phrase in (a) and the subject in (b) in each pair, as well as the lower frequency of occurrence of (b). The argument would go like this: In (a), the unmarked perspective choice applies, with the result that Agent, which is in perspective, gets realized as subject, whereas in (b), a somewhat unusual perspective is selected, resulting in leaving Agent out of perspective in favor of Instrument, which in turn gets realized as subject. So far, so good. But a serious problem remains: How can one define "perspective" in such a way as to allow some instances of Instrument to be brought into perspective and keep others out of perspective? It is hard to imagine, for example, why it is that *a red-hot icepick* cannot normally be brought into perspective while *poison* can in describing situations where they were used to kill people. Unless furnished with more substance, the newly contrived notion of "perspective" will not get to serve as a truly explanatory device.

Reformulated in our terms, perspective choice would come to assume a role centrally relevant to the assignment of thematic relations (corresponding to Fillmore's case roles). In fact, it is arguable that perspective choice determines the way a given situation is linguistically organized, different perspectives on one and the same situation representing different ways of structuring (and understanding) that situation. Thus, given the task of describing the situation where Bill killed Jane with poison, for instance, if we choose to present *Bill* rather than *poison* in perspective (the unmarked choice), the resulting picture is that of Bill's acting as Agent to bring about Jane's death. If we choose for some special reason to bring *poison* in perspective (a marked choice), a picture emerges where poison, vested with agentivity, acts of its own accord, as it were, with the primary responsibility for Jane's death attributed to it. In short, the choice of perspective under discussion directly ties up with or is even equivalent to the assignment of Agent; a perspective is not something which is superimposed on an independently definable thematic structure. From this conception of perspective naturally follows the anomaly of sentences like (5b). (5b) is odd-sounding simply because it manifests the inclusion of *a red-hot icepick* in perspective, which results in a picture in which a red-hot icepick, vested with a certain degree of agentivity, performs some sort of action leading to Jane's death, certainly an anomolous picture.[27]

In connection with the reformulation of the notion "perspective" in cognitive grammar, it is worthwhile reconsidering the use of the term *cognitive meaning*. Despite its common use, this term seems never to have been defined clearly. Indeed, it looks as if linguists generally assume that its content is self-evident and therefore needs no clarification. However, cognitive meaning is not at all a transparent notion definable across different frameworks. Does perspective choice, for example, affect cognitive meaning? For objectivists, it apparently does not. In fact, we may safely say that reference has seldom been made to a perspective-like notion in objectivist analyses, Fillmore (1977) being a rare exception. As we have just seen, even if it is referred to, perspective choice is regarded as somewhat peripheral compared with the identification of case roles. In other words, what we have referred to as stage 1 determines part and parcel of the cognitive meaning of a sentence and what we have called stage 2 takes care of whatever is left over. In cognitive grammar, on the other hand, the cognitive meaning of a sentence crucially involves a particular choice of perspective. We may even go one step further and say that perspective choice determines cognitive meaning.[28] It certainly is not a matter of taste whether to adopt one conception or the other of cognitive meaning. On the contrary, it is an empirical issue around which the whole discussion of the present study revolves.

To summarize the main line of argument in this subsection, we have demonstrated that the so-called instrumental subject is to be assigned the thematic relation Agent (albeit somewhat atypical) unlike the corresponding *with*-phrase. This means that in each of the pairs (1)-(4) and numerous others, the same verb is used with the same thematic structure, i.e. (Agent, Theme (Instrument)).[29] A set of formal regularities has been shown to reflect a semantic-cognitive principle.

2.1.3.   More on agentivity and causation

The discussion in 2.1.2. has probably made it clear that the so-called instrumental subject is semantically close to the inanimate subject which is commonly referred to as *Force*, another somewhat peripheral variant of Agent. Compare (20) and (21) below:

(20)   *Poison killed him.*
(21)   *Cancer killed him.*

We have demonstrated that *poison* in (20) is understood as having brought about his death on its own[30] or as being primarily responsible for it,[31] whoever might have used the poison retreating to the background or being excluded from the perspective. Obviously, this is also true of *cancer* in (21), for which it is absurd from the outset to ask who used the cancer in question to kill him. Whatever difference there is between (20) and (21) in terms of markedness depends on the relative naturalness of regarding poison and cancer as the ultimate or primary cause of his death, at least at the moment of utterance. It is to be expected that (20) needs more contextual support to be judged acceptable in the intended interpretation. Observe the following to see how contexts (as well as our general knowledge) help to make intelligible otherwise contrived-sounding sentences of this kind:

(22)   *The poison which she had slipped into his coffee killed him.*
(23)   *The axe fell off the shelf and broke the window.* (DeLancey 1984)
(24)   *The lawn mower threw up a stone and broke the window.*
        (DeLancey 1984)
(25)   *A stone scored a hit on her head and killed her.*
(26)   *A bullet fired from his own gun penetrated his heart and killed him.*

We can further argue that the distinction between the two types of inanimate Agent is tenuous and in fact extraneous to an appropriate characterization of Agent as such. After all, as we have repeatedly pointed out, some inanimate entities that human beings use to bring about events can be conceived as Agent precisely because they can be viewed as having a force of their own which enables them to perform certain actions comparable to those typically associated with their manipulators (i.e. prototypical instances of Agent). Whether or not a given inanimate entity is considered to be *intrinsically* capable of acting on its own, it is this conceived possession of force that permits it to be categorized as Agent. (To the extent that the entity in question is understood to be inherently potent, it is regarded as close to the so-called Force. Conversely, it is to be expected that the harder it is to view an inanimate being as inherently equipped to act on its own, the more contextual support it requires to qualify as Agent). Thus, once contextually furnished with force, any inanimate entity can be conceived to be on an equal footing as typical instances of Force. At the very least, there is no nonarbitrary demarcation line beyond which Force ceases to be an appropriate label: the distinction between Force and non-Force, if any, is not a hard-and-fast one.

Having established a close connection between the so-called instrumental subject and the subject marked as Force, we would like to point out their intimacy with the notion of cause, in the hope of suggesting that causality in general be incorporated, at least from one point of view, into a schema of agentivity. Recall first that *cancer* in (21) is still understood as capable of acting on its own. Hence the plausibility of the term *Force*. But the same event can be reported by using (27) below:

(27)   *He died of cancer.*

Here *cancer* is certainly looked on as the cause of his death on a par with *old age* in (28):

(28)   *He died of old age.*

Thus, inanimate instances of Agent are susceptible to recategorization as cause. Conversely, it will not be difficult to turn the tables and reinterpret causes as Agent: it is quite conceivable that the cause of a given event is understood in an actional mode as the agent that brings about the event. For example, it is but a step from (21) to (29):

(29)   *Excessive drinking killed him.*

In fact, it is arguable that the syntactic and lexical devices in English designed for situations involving prototypical tokens of Agent serve as templates, as it were, for the description of situations in cause and effect terms. What motivates this extension is the obvious fact that the prototypical Agent constitutes the most salient instance of cause (i.e. the most readily observable cause).

In this connection, the discussion on causality presented in Hiromatsu (1988: 2.2) is worth special attention. Hiromatsu points out that although event A must necessarily be followed by event B in order for the sequence of events A-B to be said to involve causality, necessary sequence alone does not qualify a pair of events to instantiate causality. This is because we do not want to say, for instance, that day is the cause of night simply because night necessarily follows day. What then is the essential property of causality? Hiromatsu argues quite convincingly that it is the operative relation in which a cause *produces* an effect. In other words, in order to identify an event or an entity as the cause of another event (i.e. an effect), we must be able to project on the former a force that permits it to perform a certain action leading to the latter. Thus the notion of causality itself crucially involves personification, as far as its everyday use is concerned.

There is no lack of stimulating ideas and hypotheses that point in the same direction. Lyons (1977: 490), for instance, observes as follows:

> what is of importance from the linguist's point of view is the fact that, although causality conceived as a relation between two situations is logically distinguishable from agency, there is what would appear to be a natural connexion between them; and both the grammatical and the lexical structure of English (and other languages) reflect this connexion in several ways. We can say of a given situation that it was produced, or brought about, by an agent. But we can also say, no less naturally, that it was produced by some prior event or process in which there was no agent involved.

Lakoff and Johnson (1980) attempt to demonstrate that "the concept of CAUSATION is based on the prototype of DIRECT MANIPULATION, which emerges directly from our experience" (chap. 14). Direct manipulations, it should be noted, definitely involve prototypical instances of Agent.[32] Kuroda (1975: chap. 11) argues to the same effect and maintains that causality involving Agent is the basis of causality as a relation between two events, not the other way around. Finally, DeLancey (1984: 207) characterizes the prototypical transitive event and deviations from this as follows:

> the prototypical transitive event is one which can be traced back to a single cause from which an unbroken chain of control leads to the effect. This ultimate cause can only be an act of volition on the part of a (thus defined) prototypical agent. This act of volition directly engenders an action on the part of the agent, which may in turn be extended through an instrument, and then impinges directly upon the outside world. Both nondirect causation and inactive causation are

deviations from this prototype ... inactive causation because the chain of causation can not be traced back to a comprehensible ultimate cause. Thus poison, for example, is an identifiable cause of death, but it is not a satisfactory ultimate cause, since some external cause must be sought for its entry into the victim's system.

It should be clear now that the thematic relation Agent (at least for English) covers a spectrum with a volitional entity directly effecting an event (the prototypical Agent) at one extreme and an inanimate or abstract entity as ultimate or relevant cause of an event at the other. We have also suggested that the former may well be the notional foundation on which the latter develops.

2.1.4.   Implications for contrastive linguistics

It would be interesting from the viewpoint of contrastive linguistics to note that while English sentences like (20), (21), and (29), in which inanimate or abstract nominals are marked Agent, are quite natural (at least under appropriate circumstances), their literal Japanese translations sound highly unidiomatic. This suggests that Agent in English and Agent in Japanese differ substantially, though they do seem to coincide in their prototypical applications where typicality conditions such as animateness - most typically, humanness - and intentionality are met.

The meaning of a verb denoting a goal-directed action (including, as we have noted, causation in an actional mode) can generally be decomposed into the action component and the goal-achieving component. In prototypical cases, both components are fully activated: a person performs a certain action with a view to achieving a certain goal, with the result that the goal is actually achieved. In nonparadigm instances, however, one or the other of the two components may be suppressed.[33] If the goal-achieving component remains latent, the resulting picture is one in which an action is performed without any effect. If the action component remains inactive, only the achievement of the goal can be focused on. The suppression of one or the other of the two components may take place in varying degrees. Thus, in (20) and (21), for instance, where *poison* and *cancer* can still be conceived as being capable of action, the action component is suppressed to some extent but not completely. In (29), on the other hand, the degree to which the action component is activated is close to zero, though, as suggested in 2.1.3., it is the possible attribution of force that underlies the conceptualization of an inanimate entity as Agent. In the latter case, then, the action component is invoked almost vacuously, that is, to pave the way for us to highlight the external force that brought about his death. English and Japanese show a marked contrast in the way one or the other component is more likely to be brought into focus.

As we have already seen, English tends to extend the coverage of Agent to such an extent that an inanimate or abstract nominal can occur comparatively freely as the subject of verbs of action. Since an inanimate or abstract entity is more or less incongruous with the notion of action, the semantic focus of the English verbs of action tends to shift from the action component to the goal-achieving component. In fact, the achievement of the goal is almost invariably a necessary condition for an inanimate or abstract entity to be viewed as Agent: it is precisely because some observable effect is conceived to have been produced by the entity that the latter can be credited with the force that qualifies it as Agent. This is especially true of cases where abstract nominals are assigned Agent. Consider the following pair:

(30)　a.　*Bill taught Jane how to behave.*
　　　b.　*The experience taught Jane how to behave.*

In (30a), in which *Bill* is Agent, one can focus on the action per se that *Bill* performed, leaving open the question whether or not *Jane* actually learned how to behave. (The preferred reading is that the intended goal was actually achieved.) On the other hand, since *the experience* as Agent is almost incompatible with the notion of action (in other words, the activation of the action component is minimal), (30b) can focus only on the achievement of the goal. Hence the difference in acceptability between (30'a) and (30'b):

(30')　a.　*Bill taught Jane how to behave, with few results.*
　　　b.　**The experience taught Jane how to behave, with few results.*

The situation is quite the opposite in Japanese. Japanese tends to keep intact the action component of the meaning of a verb denoting a goal-directed action by restricting the applicability of Agent to animate, typically human, nominals. Thus unidiomatic sentences will come out if English sentences like (20) and (21) are translated verbatim into Japanese. In fact, as Ikegami (1981a) points out, Japanese verbs denoting a goal-directed action have a tendency to focus on the action rather than the achievement of the goal. One can even say, "(I) burned (it), but (it) didn't burn" in Japanese. An interesting question to be asked now is how Japanese manages to express the achievement of a goal without recourse to the extension of Agent available to English. The answer seems to be that while English tends to structure an event resulting in a change of some kind in terms of the Agent-Theme schema, Japanese prefers to bring to the fore the change itself undergone by Theme in the same event, whatever cause there may be being left unexpressed or at most relegated to the periphery. This contrast can be schematized as follows:

English: Agent CAUSE [Theme GO TO X]^{34}
Japanese: Theme GO TO X (OF Cause)^{35}

This is exactly a manifestation of the contrast that is aptly characterized by Ikegami (1981b) as DO-language vs. BECOME-language. Another way of characterizing the contrast between the two languages may be Agent-oriented vs. Theme-oriented.^{36}

2.2.   Agent vs. Experiencer

This section is intended to throw new light on the semantic structure underlying sentences like the following:

(31)   *John broke his leg.*
(32)   *Taro wa   ashi o   otta*
         Taro-topic   leg-object   broke (vt.)
         'Taro broke his leg.'

What is special about sentences of this kind is that the subject is normally interpreted as being affected by the event in question rather than as acting as full-fledged Agent to bring it about, as is usually the case with verbs of action such as *break* and *oru*.

2.2.1.   Objectivist analyses and their problems

Okutsu (1983) proposes a derivation (33) --> (34) --> (32), which is mediated by a transformation-like operation of "possessor float" or "P-float":

(33)   *Taro no*   *ashi ga*   *oreta.*
       Taro-possessive   leg-subject   broke (vi.)
       'Taro's leg broke.'
(34)   *Taro wa*   *ashi ga*   *oreta.*
       Taro-topic   leg-subject   broke (vi.)

This analysis is based on the assumption that (32), (33), and (34) have the same cognitive meaning. Okutsu (1983) goes on to account for the raison d'être of P-float from a functional point of view. In short, (32) differs from (33) in that the former puts *Taro* into perspective.[37] ((34) also stands midway in this respect.)[38]

This analysis may seem plausible enough in cases where inalienable possession (e.g. the relation between *Taro* and *ashi* in (32)) or something similar to it (e.g. the relation between *Taro* and *boshi* in (35)) is involved:

(35)   *Taro wa*   *kaze de*   *boshi o*   *tobashita.*
       Taro-topic   wind-by   hat-object   flew (vt.)
       'Taro got his hat blown off by the wind.'
(36)   *Taro no*   *boshi ga*   *kaze de*   *tonda.*
       Taro-possessive   hat-subject   wind-by   flew (vi.)
       'Taro's hat got blown off by the wind.'
(37)   *Taro wa*   *boshi ga*   *kaze de*   *tonda.*
       Taro-topic   hat-subject   wind-by   flew (vi.)

As Inoue (1976: vol. 2, p. 95) points out, however, *Taro* in (32) does not serve the same function as *Taro* in (33). It is consequently not appropriate to *derive* (32) from (33) transformationally (i.e. through P-float). Moreover, there are sentences, such as (38) and (39) below, which are similar to (31) and (32) despite their inaccessibility to P-float.

(38)   *John broke the window while playing baseball.*
(39)   *Taro wa*   *yakyu o*   *shiteite*
       Taro-topic   baseball-object   playing-and

mado o   *kowashite*   *shimatta.*
window-object   break (vt.)   perfect
'Taro broke the window while playing baseball.'

Inoue (1976: ch. 4) and Shibatani (1978: ch. 6) assign the thematic relation Experiencer to the subjects of lexical causative sentences like (32), (35), and (39) as well as grammatical causative sentences like (40) and (41) below. (As we will see presently, though, there are complications regarding (38) and (39)).

(40)   *Hahaoya wa*   *kotsujiko de*   *kodomo o*
        mother-topic   traffic accident-by child-object
        shinaseta.
        die-causative-past
        'The mother had her child killed in a traffic accident.'

(41)   *Hahaoya wa*   *kodomo ni*   *kaze o*
        mother-topic   child-dative   cold-object
        hikasete shimatta.
        catch-causative perfect
        '?The mother had her child catch cold.'

The alleged reason for this treatment is that the subject in each sentence is understood not as bringing about the event in question deliberately but as being affected by it. Moreover, (40), for instance, sounds more or less synonymous with (42) in the intended interpretation:

(42)   *Hahaoya wa*   *kotsujiko de*   *kodomo ni*
        mother-topic   traffic accident-by child-dative
        shinareta.
        die-passive-past
        'The mother had her child killed in a traffic accident.'

It is generally agreed that *hahaoya* in (42), an instance of the so-called adversative passive, is marked Experiencer. Inoue (1976: 4.12.) and Inoue (esp. 4.1. and 4.2.) use what she calls agentive contexts to show that Experiencer never appears in these contexts.[39] Consider, for instance, the following, in which (32) in the intended reading is put into the agentive contexts:

AC-1   **Taro wa wazato ashi o ot-ta.*
        (Taro intentionally broke his leg.)

AC-2   *Taro wa ashi o ot-te-mi-ta.*
          (Taro broke his leg as a trial.)
AC-3   inapplicable
AC-4   *Taro ni wa ashi ga or-e-ta.*
          (Taro was able to break his leg.)
AC-5   *Taro ga ashi o or-oo to shi-ta.*
          (Taro tried to break his leg.)
AC-6   *Taro ga ashi o ot-ta. Jiro mo soo shi-ta.*
          (Taro broke his leg. Jiro did so, too.)
AC-7   *?Taro ga shi-ta koto wa ashi o oru koto dat-ta.*
          (What Taro did was break his leg.)
AC-8   *Ashi o orinasai.*
          (Break your leg.)

Obviously, this analysis, making crucial use of Experiencer, is free from the first criticism directed to Okutsu (1983).

In a similar vein, Marantz (1985) proposes the following underlying pattern for causative sentences like (40) and (41):

TO (Z, HAPPEN (Y...

(43) then is the "d-structure" for (40):

(43)

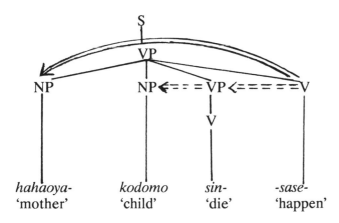

Notice that *sase* is here interpreted as 'happen' and that consequently, at least at the "d-structure" level, (40) is indistinguishable from (42).

Although there may at first seem to be nothing wrong with the kind of analysis exemplified by Inoue (1974, 1976), Shibatani (1978), and Marantz (1985), closer examination shows that it is quite inadequate in many respects.

First, this analysis cannot explain in a principled way why many verbs of action and causation presuppose as their subjects Experiencer as well as Agent. In other words, this analysis, if valid, would indicate that the use of the same verb in the same syntactic structure is a mere accident, unless a revealing account is provided of the semantic relation between Agent and Experiencer.

Secondly, the thematic relation Experiencer is too vague to be invoked even as a descriptive device. Even if we were to admit that cases like (31) and (32) involved Experiencer, we could not help feeling hesitant about assigning this thematic relation to *John* in (38) or *Taro* in (39), for instance, simply because the action is not intentional. In fact, Inoue (1976: ch. 4), while regarding *Jon* in (44) as Experiencer, characterizes *John* in (45) as Cause:

(44)   *Jon wa*   *omowazu*   *mado ni*   *te o*
        John-topic   involuntarily   window-to   hand-object
        tsuite,   *mado o*   *kowashite*   *shimatta.*
        touch   window-object   break (vt.)   perfect
        'John inadvertently touched the window and broke it.'
(45)   *John broke the window by hitting it accidentally.*

However, we cannot see any reason why we should not assign them one and the same thematic relation, whatever it is. On the other hand, if we were to assign them Cause, we would then be unable to capture their obvious similarity in function to *John* in (31) and *Taro* in (32).

One may object that there is a difference between (31) and (32), on the one hand, and (38) and (39), on the other. *John* in (31) or *Taro* in (32) may be interpreted either as performing some action that accidentally leads to his injury or as only passively involved in an accident. The latter interpretation is impossible for (38) or (39). One might then suggest restricting the applicability of Experiencer to the latter and regarding the former as involving Cause. This suggestion not only necessitates proliferation of thematic relations, which may preclude any significant generalization. It also leaves another problem unresolved: it cannot explain why the Experiencer interpretation so delimited only applies to cases where a certain kind of relation (typically, (inalienable) possession) holds between the subject and the object. Consider, for example, the following contrasts:

(46) a. *Taro wa*   *kono aida no*   *kaji de*
          Taro-topic   the other day-possessive   fire-by
          jisho o   *yaite*   *shimatta.*
          dictionary-object   burn (vt.)   perfect
          ??'Taro burned his dictionary in the fire that broke out the other day.'

      b. **Taro wa*   *kono aida no*   *kaji de*
          Taro-topic   the other day-possessive   fire-by
          gakko o   *yaite*   *shimatta.*
          school-object   burn (vt.)   perfect
          *Taro burned his school in the fire that broke out the other day.
          (in the narrowly circumscribed Experiencer interpretation, in which *Taro* was unfavorably affected by the school's destruction)

(47) a. *I broke my leg in the accident.*
      b. **I broke his leg in the accident.*
          (in the narrowly circumscribed Experiencer interpretation, in which *I* was unfavorably affected by his injury)

(46b) might be acceptable if *Taro* were the principal of the school. (47b) could only mean that a certain action of mine (accidentally) led to his injury. There is, however, nothing in the newly defined Experiencer that prevents the generation of sentences such as (46b) and (47b).

The final point reveals another irremediable inadequacy inherent in this analysis. Either (40) or (42) can describe a situation where a mother, while doing the housework, lost her child in a traffic accident caused by an unspecified total stranger. Under this interpretation, one might be tempted to assign Experiencer to both occurrences of *ha-haoya*, as Inoue (1974, 1976), Shibatani (1978), and Marantz (1985) actually do.[40] This assignment, however, creates a serious problem. It predicts that both (40') and (42') below will be applicable to a situation where the roles of the participants are, as it were, reversed. (Suppose, for instance, that while the child was at school, his mother was killed in a traffic accident caused by a total stranger on her way to a department store.) The actual use contradicts this prediction: only (42') can be used to report on an event like that. (40') positively implies either that the child himself was directly responsible for the accident or at least that he

failed to take appropriate measures that could have prevented the un-
happy incident:

(40')   *Sono   kodomo wa   kotsujiko de*
        the   child-topic   traffic accident-by
        hahaoya o   shinaseta.
        mother-object   die-causative-past
        'The child had his mother killed in a traffic accident.'
(42')   *Sono   kodomo wa   kotsujiko de*
        the   child-topic   traffic accident-by
        hahaoya ni   shinareta.
        mother-dative   die-passive-past
        'The child had his mother killed in a traffic accident.'

2.2.2.   Conceptualist approach

Cognitive grammar would assign Agent (albeit noncentral) to the subjects in (31), (32), (35), (38), (39), (40), (41), (44), (45), (46a), and (47a).
Each of these subjects is regarded as having been in a position to control the occurrence of the event in question (e.g. the death of one's
child). Thus, since the event did in fact occur, by being credited with responsibility, he or she is conceived of as Agent who (directly or indirectly) brought it about (even though against his or her will).[41][42]

The relevance of the notion of "control" or that of "responsibility"
can be justified by observing (1) that in many of the cases under discussion, the object is the subject's inalienable property (cf. (31), (32), and
(47a)) or something sufficiently similar to it (cf. (35), (40), (41), and
(46a)) and (2) that adverbs such as *omowazu* 'in spite of oneself, inad-
vertently' and *accidentally* often co-occur (cf. (44) and (45)). One is held
to be in full control of an object of one's (inalienable) possession; one is
therefore held responsible for whatever may happen to it. Adverbs such
as *omowazu* and *accidentally* imply that the subject could have prevented the event from occurring if he or she had exercised sufficient
care - there was a lapse of control on the part of the subject.

The difference in acceptability between (40) and (40') as applied to
the above-mentioned situations further corroborates the relevance of
"control" or "responsibility". In Japanese at least,[43] the mother is responsible for whatever happens to her child - she is viewed as being in a
position to control whatever becomes of her child (in however remote a
way). The reverse, however, is not usually the case.

It will not be difficult to realize that the analysis outlined above from a conceptualist viewpoint overcomes all the shortcomings of the analyses in 2.2.1., while keeping their merits intact. In fact, the problematic phenomena for the objectivist analyses have naturally been incorporated into the cognitive grammar analysis as natural consequences of the new conception of Agent crucially involving the notion of responsibility. The effect of the P-float analysis put forward by Okutsu (1983), for instance, can be obtained without recourse to the spurious transformation-like operation. In our terms, (32) and (33) do not have the same "cognitive" meaning; as we noted in 2.1.2, perspective choice determines cognitive meaning. Specifically, placing *Taro* in perspective with respect to the action schema of the transitive *oru* 'break' means crediting *Taro* with agentivity through attribution of responsibility. Thus our analysis automatically accounts for the difference between (32) and (33) both in terms of perspective and as to the assignment of thematic relations.

Let us now turn our attention to the merits and demerits of the Experiencer analysis to see how they mesh nicely with our analysis. How are we to explain, for instance, why the noncentral variant of Agent under discussion never occurs in the agentive contexts given in Inoue (1974, 1976)? The important thing to note here is that most of her contexts pertain to the notion of intentionality. Consequently, it is only natural that the noncentral instances of Agent in this subsection, which fail to meet the typicality condition "intentional", should not appear in these contexts. Once again, as we pointed out in 2.1.2, we have no apriori reason for assuming that "intentionality" is a necessary condition rather than a typicality condition for somebody or something to be regarded as Agent. To regard those unintentional beings as Agent in spite of their failure to meet this typicality condition allows us not only to capture otherwise arbitrary form-meaning correlations (the first defect of the Experiencer analysis) but also to cope with the other faults of the Experiencer analysis.

John in (38) and *Taro* in (39) are certainly to be marked as Agent because they are unmistakably looked on as responsible for their actions that (directly) caused the windows to break. If they had not performed the actions in question, the windows would not have been broken. We could also say that they could have prevented the windows from breaking if they had exercised sufficient care. The difference in acceptability between (46a) and (47a), on the one hand, and (46b) and (47b), on the other, depends on whether or not the subject is held responsible for what happened to the object. One's own dictionary and, more obviously, one's own leg are considered to be under one's control, while the school one happens to go to and someone else's leg normally are not.[44] Note that if the school in question were in the possession of Taro (for (46b)) and if I had performed some action leading accidentally to his injury (for (47b)), acceptability would go up. Finally, as we have already observed, the difference in acceptability between (40) and (40') stems from the presence or absence of responsibility on the part of the subject. We have also noted that (40') would be acceptable if the child were interpreted either as directly responsible for the accident (e.g. if the child himself had caused the accident) or as having failed to take suitable measures that could have prevented the tragedy (and being held at least partly responsible for it accordingly).

To sum up, we have shown that the subjects in sentences such as (31), (32), (35), (38), (39), and (40) should be marked as Agent (albeit noncentral) and that the notions of "control" and "responsibility" are crucially involved in the definition of this noncentral Agent. We have also demonstrated that the syntactic operation P-float and the thematic relation Experiencer as conceived in 2.2.1. should be dispensed with in favor of the thematic relation Agent with its extended coverage.[45] [46]

2.2.3.   More on responsibility

Let us have a closer look at the notion of responsibility. Note first that as far as human beings who are consciously involved in situations[47] are concerned, (primary) responsibility (in the strict sense of the term) is the minimum requirement to be met in order for them to qualify as Agent.[48] Consider the following:

(48)   *John broke the window in order to wake up Mary.*
(49)   *John broke the window while playing catch.*
(50)   *John broke his leg in a traffic accident.*

In (48), *John* brought about the event (i.e. the breaking of the window) on purpose by performing some action (e.g. by throwing a stone at the window). In (49), *John* performed a certain action (e.g. threw a ball in the direction of a friend) which accidentally caused the window to break. In (50), *John* was only passively involved in an accident without any intention or action on his part. Employing the terminology in Ikegami (1982a), we can characterize each *John* as follows:

	Intender	Actor
John in (48)	+	+
John in (49)	–	+
John in (50)	–	–

Now it is obviously the case that if one is regarded either as Intender or as Actor (or both), one is automatically looked on as bearer of the responsibility in question (in this case, the responsibility for the broken window). To be more specific, (1) one is held responsible for whatever he intends to result from his own action (Intender plus Actor) and (2) one is held responsible for whatever his action (for which he is certainly responsible) (directly) leads to (Actor). In case (2), one is regarded as responsible because without his action, the effect in question (e.g. the broken window) would not have been produced. Thus the following redundancy rule suggests itself:

Intender or Actor ---> Bearer of Responsibility

This rule applies to (48) and (49). In cases where one is regarded neither as Intender nor as Actor as in (50), one is required to be understood as bearer of the responsibility for the event in question (e.g. his injury) in order to qualify as Agent. As we saw in 2.2.2, one is responsible for whatever happens to his inalienable property (e.g. his leg). If one fails to meet this minimum requirement – the bearer of the responsibility in question – he no longer qualifies as Agent and therefore cannot be allowed to appear as the subject of verbs of action or causation, which, in our theory, requires Agent as subject. Hence the unacceptability of (51) in the interpretation in which John was unfavorably affected by Mary's injury, without any responsibility on his part:

(51)   *John broke Mary's leg in a traffic accident.*

As we noted, (51) could only mean that John performed some action which (accidentally or otherwise) led to Mary's injury. To sum up, we have the following table indicating the degree of agentivity:[49]

	Intender	Actor	Resp. Bearer	
I	+	+	+	= prototypical Agent
II	+	–	+	= less typical Agent (1)
III	–	+	+	= less typical Agent (2)
IV	–	–	+	= least typical Agent
V	–	–	–	= non-Agent

It is also to be noted that "responsibility" is closely related to the so-called permissive Agent. According to Ikegami (1981b), for example, a permissive Agent is one who does not exercise his (potential) ability to prevent an event, with the result that the event actually happens. It should be obvious that a permissive Agent thus characterized is most likely to be viewed as the bearer of the responsibility for the relevant event. In fact, the English verbs *let* and *allow*, which are commonly used as hypothetical permissive causative verbs, allow instances of the least typical Agent (-Intender, -Actor, +Responsibility Bearer) to appear as their subjects.[50] Thus,

(52)   *Don't let it bother you.*
(53)   *Don't let yourself be affected by what that ninny said.*
(54)   *My husband sometimes lets his temper get out of hand.*
(55)   *People allow themselves to be duped into buying things they don't really need.*
(56)   *She (= Ruth Benedict) allows value judgments to creep into her ideas.*

(52), for instance, is used to tell the addressee to prevent the possible occurrence of *it* bothering him, which will most likely come about if he lets things ride. Here the addressee is conceived to be in a position to control the occurrence of the event in question; he is held responsible for it. Likewise, in (56), for instance, *she* is viewed as responsible for the creeping in of value judgments precisely because she (or anyone else in scholarly work) is expected to keep them out (in other words, she is regarded as capable of keeping track of her own ideas) but fails to do so. There would be no denying that the use of *let* and *allow* discussed here is strikingly similar to the uses of *break* in (50) and *shinaseru* 'cause to die' in (40). We thus have further supporting evidence for the assignment of (permissive) Agent to the subjects in these latter sentences, which one might find hard to accept as causative.

Finally, the close relation between "responsibility" and "cause" is worth noting. It is intuitively clear that seeking the bearer of the responsibility for an event is one notable way of trying to identify the cause of the event. Thus it is very natural for a responsibility bearer (a noncentral Agent) to appear as the subject of a causative verb. The noncentral Agent discussed in this section then shares the essence of Agent with the prototypical Agent and another noncentral Agent - the inanimate Agent - we dealt with in 2.1.: Agent is "a single cause from which an unbroken chain of control leads to the effect" (DeLancey 1984). It is interesting to note in this connection that the English word *responsible* and the Japanese expression *no seide*, both of which are primarily associated with the notion of responsibility properly so called, are commonly used to refer to the cause of an event. Consider the following:

(57)   *The cold weather is responsible for the influenza epidemic.*
(58)   *Samui   tenko   no seide   infuruenza ga*
        cold   weather   owing to   influenza-subject
        hayatte iru.
        raging   is
        'Owing to the cold weather, the flu is raging.'

3.   Concluding remarks

We have attempted to show that cognitive grammar allows (or even re-quires) us to reformulate the notion of agentivity in such a way as to ac-count for some formal regularities. We hope that the discussion has brought to light the difference between objectivist semantics and con-ceptualist semantics as to the assignment of thematic relations. The former determines what relation to assign to a given argument entirely on the basis of naive realism, without paying enough attention to syntac-tic and/or lexical regularities. This approach evidently goes hand in hand with the autonomous-syntax hypothesis: syntactic uniformity and variation can (and should) be studied independently of semantic fac-tors. The latter, on the other hand, tackles the same task with a view to explaining formal regularities from the viewpoint of semantics - and ul-timately in terms of human cognition and understanding. It seeks se-mantic-conceptual principles underlying formal generalizations; auton-omy of syntax cannot be taken for granted. We have attempted to demonstrate the superiority of conceptualist semantics (inherent in cognitive grammar) over objectivist semantics (assumed in most other frameworks). If we have succeeded in this attempt, we will have pro-vided empirical support for (1) the general framework of cognitive grammar (internalizing prototypicality, imagery, etc.) and (2) the particular conception of language and meaning on which the framework rests.

Notes

1.   I am greatly indebted to Yoshihiko Ikegami for his invaluable comments on earlier versions of this paper. My equally deep thanks go to René Dirven for sending me detailed comments on its L.A.U.D. version. (I am sure I will regret not being able to revise it drastically, taking his advice more seriously.) I cannot thank John Bester, a world acclaimed translator, enough for taking time to practice "mental gymnastics" with me. I would also like to express my gratitude to Andrew Jones, who was kind enough to read the whole manuscript and point out some spelling and stylistic errors. Brygida Rudzka-Ostyn made a number of comments and suggestions, which helped me immensely to prepare the final version. I wish to take this opportunity to thank Hirotaka Tomozawa for listening to me patiently on numerous occasions when I needed help and coming up with insightful suggestions on most of them. Jeff Alton, Isao Hirami, Shungo Shinohara, and Eijiro Tsuboi also helped me a lot. Last but not least, I would like to thank Hisae Nishimura for her moral support.
2.   I am referring to Ikegami (1981b), Jackendoff (1983, 1985a), Lakoff & Johnson (1980), Lakoff (1987), and Langacker (1987a, 1987b) among others.
3.   "Conceptualism" and "experientialism" come from Jackendoff (1985a) and Lakoff & Johnson (1980), respectively. For a critique of objectivism and a revealing and comprehensive account of experientialism, see Lakoff (1987).
4.   See Lakoff & Johnson (1980), Lakoff (1987), Sato (1978, 1981, 1986, 1987) for detailed accounts of rhetorical phenomena from the conceptualist viewpoint.
5.   See Ikegami (1981b: 213 ff) and Langacker (1982).
6.   A stimulating discussion of this matter is given in Lakoff (1987: chap. 18) in connection with the Sapir-Whorf hypothesis.
7.   This position is vigorously advocated by Langacker (1987a). Note that this is where Langacker (1987a) disagrees with Jackendoff (1983), who assumes an autonomous syntactic component. What is responsible for Jackendoff's reluctance to give up the autonomous-syntax hypothesis is probably the fact that the attempt known as generative semantics, which did not postulate syntactic deep structure, ended in failure. I believe, however, that the biggest stumbling block to generative semantics was not so much its failure to admit the existence of syntactic deep structure as its tacit reliance on formal logic for the representation of meaning. At any rate, whether or not to opt for autonomous syntax is an empirical issue that should not be taken lightly. One's position on it, as we will observe in 2, is likely to have ramifications in the way one looks at linguistic phenomena.

8.   For a detailed account of traditional case grammar, see Yamanashi (1983). Cf. also Fillmore (1968) and Chomsky (1972).

9.   Cf. the following passage from Fillmore (1977):

> A reason for feeling sure that the two roles (i.e., the role of *John* in (a) and the role of *this key* in (b)) are distinct is that the same two nouns, *preserving their case roles*, can also occur together, with *open*, in a single sentence, as in (c) [emphasis mine]:
>
> (a)   *John opened the door.*
> (b)   *This key opened the door.*
> (c)   *John opened the door with this key.*

This also shows that even at this stage Fillmore is not free from naive realism.

10.   This is reminiscent of the introduction of the notion "perspective" in Fillmore (1977). See 2.1.2.

11.   Just for the sake of argument, let us assume the validity of the notion "one and the same situation". Strictly speaking, we have no direct access to "one and the same situation" and what we actually perceive is a (probably infinite) set of situations (unconsciously) organized by linguistic and other cognitive mechanisms, only by way of which "the situation as raw material" can be hypothesized. For full discussions of the "projected" nature of the world as experienced and the falsity of naive realism, see Hiromatsu (1982: Introduction), Jackendoff (1983: ch. 2), and Murakami (1979: ch. 1 sec. 2). Cf. also Ikegami (1982b: 39ff) and Sato (1986: ch. 10) for conceptualist models for linguistic description of "one and the same situation".

12.   The examples are from Anderson (1977), in which a similar view is taken of the thematic structure of (2b). Cf. also Dougherty (1970).

13.   Notice that the role played by *a red-hot icepick* in this bizarre situation is comparable to that of *a stone* in (1b). Compare also the following pair:

(a)   *The tile was broken by the hammer.*
(b)   *The tile was broken with the hammer.*

According to Miller (1985), (a) is appropriate to a situation in which the hammer simply slipped off a table, but (b) is appropriate if someone used the hammer to break the tile (p. 177). Cf. also DeLancey (1984) and Schlesinger (1979) for more examples. Schlesinger (1979) argues that a distinction has to be made between cognitive structures and semantic deep structures on the basis of the assumption that *poison* in (2b) is Agent in the semantic deep structure but Instrument in the cognitive structure. Since we have rejected naive realism, we need not draw such a distinction. *Poison* in (2b), unlike *(with) poison* in (2a), is conceived of as Agent (albeit noncentral).

14.   This is not to say that an abacus or a stick cannot be regarded as Agent in any situations. In fact, as John Bester pointed out to me (personal communication), even a leaf can act as Agent if it is put in the right context. Consider the following text he invented:

After he had eaten the apple, Adam felt ashamed in front of Eve. A leaf from a nearby fig tree solved the problem.

Cf. the discussion in 2.1.3.

15.   A prototypical definition of Agent is given in Lyons (1977: 483). Lyons
       (1977) is right in remarking on the definition as follows:
           Each of the features that have been singled out for mention
           here   - animacy, intention, responsibility and the use of its
           own internal energy-source - is separable, in non-paradigm
           instances,   from each of the others. It is a fair assumption,
           however, that languages are designed, as it were, to handle the
           paradigm instances; and it is only to be expected that the
           applicability of notions like agency should be unclear in non-
           paradigm instances.
16.   Personification "allows us to comprehend a wide variety of experiences
       with nonhuman entities in terms of human motivations, characteristics
       and activities" (Lakoff & Johnson 1980: 33). It should be clear that to
       account for this kind of semantic extension, cognitive grammar must be
       equipped with conditions that are typical but subject to exceptions, that
       is, typicality conditions. It certainly is not the case that we are at liberty
       to suspend typicality conditions. The kind of mechanism that Jacken-
       doff (1983, 1985b) calls a preference rule system is crucially involved in
       the workings of typicality conditions. For further discussions of proto-
       typicality and related topics as they are germane to linguistic phenom-
       ena, see Lakoff (1987) and Langacker (1987a).
17.   In Levin (1985: 45), Wojcik (1976) is quoted as claiming that it is nec-
       essary to distinguish enabling instruments, such as a spoon, from other
       instruments:
       (a)   *Maria ate the cake with a spoon.*
       (b)   **A spoon ate the cake.*
18.   Levin (1985: 45). The realization rule in question can be stated: "An
       argument bearing the instrumental role is expressed in a prepositional
       phrase headed by *with* in the presence of an agent argument but as the
       subject of the sentence in the absence of an agent argument" (op. cit.
       44f).
19.   As far as the data under discussion are concerned, we may safely as-
       sume that the *by*-phrases in (1"b) and (2'b) play essentially the same
       role as the subjects in (1b) and (2b), respectively, since the same se-
       mantic restriction seems to be placed on the subjects and the corre-
       sponding *by*-phrases. See Dougherty (1970). Compare (5b) with (5'b)
       and (6b) with (6'b):
       (5')   b.   **Jane was killed by a red-hot icepick.*
       (6')   b.   **The cost was calculated in a minute by an abacus.*
20.   This was pointed out to me by John Bester (personal communication).
21.   As we will see in reference to sentences (15)-(18), "immediacy", as it is
       employed as a defining property of Instrument in Starosta (1978), does
       not always apply to so-called instrumental subjects, since it is under-
       stood there as objectively and uniquely definable (i.e. it belongs to the
       real world, not the projected world). This forces Starosta (1978) to ar-
       gue that sentences like (3b) are ambiguous between the interpretation
       in which the subject is marked Agent and the interpretation in which
       the subject is marked Instrument. The interpretive choice is claimed to
       depend on whether or not *with*-phrases such as *with its enzyme*, each of
       which is assumed to represent "the immediate effective cause", are un-
       derstood to be omitted. We find this argument extremely ad hoc and

unfounded. Here it suffices to point out that in our account, the Instrument *with*-phrase does not count as a participant directly involved in a causal chain.

22.   It is worth noting that Lakoff and Johnson (1980: ch. 14) argue that the concept of causation is based on the prototype of DIRECT MANIPULATION. See 2.1.3.

23.   This corresponds to the notion "causal generation" in Kuroda (1975: 292). One of his examples is this: *A child kills a bird by firing a gun by pulling the trigger.*

24.   (9'a) would be acceptable if *Bill* were interpreted as doing the hitting. The unacceptability of (9'a)-(10'b) can also be accounted for syntactically, that is, by referring to the incompatibility of the main subject as controller and the PRO subject of the gerundive phrase. This was pointed out to me by Eijiro Tsuboi (personal communication).

25.   Note that (9b) and (10b) each represent a somewhat peculiar way of looking at the murder in question, since the primary responsibility of a murder case is most likely to be attributed to the murderer, with the result that the coherent action sequence performed by him, not the "instrument" he happened to use, is normally selected. Hence the lower frequency of occurrence of sentences like (9b) and (10b). This is also true of most sentences with so-called instrumental subjects. Cf. DeLancey (1984: 4.1).

Notice also that Fillmore (1968) cannot explain why sentences with instrumental subjects are quite limited in their possibilities of occurrence. This is because Fillmore (1968) fails to specify the conditions under which Agent, which, in his theory, is uniquely identifiable given a situation, can be left unexpressed and, consequently, Instrument can be promoted to subject position. He simply posits case frames like [____O(I)(A] with the following rule for the "unmarked" subject choice:

(54)   If there is an A, it becomes the subject; otherwise, if there is an I, it becomes the subject; otherwise, the subject is the O.

One might be tempted to argue that the notion "perspective" in Fillmore (1977) can cope with the problem: leaving the manipulator (Agent) out of perspective in favor of the manipulated (Instrument) is a marked choice. As we will see presently, however, the notion "perspective" has its own problems.

26.   The following examples cited in Lakoff & Johnson (1980: 134) appear to violate the constraint in question:

(a)   Q: Who's gonna stop me?
       A: Me and old Betsy here (said by the cowboy reaching for his gun).

(b)   Sleezo the Magician and his Magic Harmonica will be performing tonight at the Rialto.

Actually, however, they do not. In each example, the coordinates are understood as jointly performing a single CAS. In other words, "old Betsy" and "his Magic Harmonica" are personified to such an extent that they have come to assume agenthood on a par with "me" and "Sleezo the Magician", respectively: personification in the traditional sense of the term is involved.

27.   See note (13), however.
28.   See Sato (1986: ch. 10) for a similar view. Cf. Maruyama (1981: 155), in
       which Saussure is quoted as maintaining the priority of perspective
       over objects. As Brygida Rudzka-Ostyn points out in one of her com-
       ments, the discussion here should not be taken to mean that cognitive
       grammar distinguishes between cognitive meaning and some other
       kind of meaning. In her words, "we simply equate meaning with con-
       ceptualization". My reference to cognitive meaning here is simply in-
       tended to emphasize that the conceptualizer's perspective is inherent in
       the very core of the meaning of any linguistic expression (whatever
       term one chooses to adopt to refer to it), rather than a mere overlay
       which may or may not be placed on an objectively definable meaning.
29.   For similar views of Agent, see Chafe (1970: 10.5, 12.6), Cruse (1973),
       DeLancey (1984), and Jackendoff (1983: 9.3).
30.   This property of Agent is referred to as "potent" by Chafe (1970: 10.5),
       "effective" (e.g. *the axe* in (23)) and "agentive" (e.g. *poison* in (20)) by
       Cruse (1973), and "the use of its own internal energy-source" (e.g. *poi-
       son* in (20)) by Lyons (1977: 483f). Since the property "effective" is
       often merely accidental, contingent upon the entity's position or mo-
       tion at the relevant moment, instances of Agent with nothing but this
       property naturally require more contextual support to be judged ac-
       ceptable than those with the property "agentive" or "the use of its own
       internal energy-source". It is as though inanimate entities were tem-
       porarily furnished with agentivity (i.e. "agentivized") with the help of
       context.
31.   Primary responsibility here is close to the same term used in Lakoff
       (1977) and van Oosten (1977) about the subject of the so-called pa-
       tient-subject construction (e.g. *The car drives easily*). Van Oosten ob-
       serves that "properties of the patient bear the *responsibility* for the oc-
       currence of the action of the verb" (emphasis mine).
       Cf. also Lyons (1968: 8.2.13) and Kunihiro (1970: 207f) for similar ac-
       counts of the activo-passive construction. Responsibility as a typicality
       condition for Agent will be focused on in the next section, where we
       will be primarily concerned with responsibility as it pertains to human
       beings (i.e. responsibility in the strict sense of the term).
32.   See Lakoff & Johnson (1980: 70f) for a set of properties characterizing
       prototypical direct manipulations. Cf. also Lakoff (1987: 54f).
33.   Therefore, these two components are typicality conditions.
34.   GO is intended to cover the whole spectrum of change, ranging from
       the most concrete type (i.e. physical motion) to the most abstract type
       (i.e. change in condition). Cf. Ikegami (1981b), Jackendoff (1983: ch.
       10) and Langacker (1987: 4.3.2).
35.   OF is intended as a general marker of cause.
36.   Cf. Tai (1984) for a similar characterization of the contrast between
       English and Chinese. He visualizes the contrast as follows:
       English: Agent (action) ----------->
       Chinese: <---------- Patient (result)
37.   Note that the notion "perspective" here is more or less equivalent to
       the same term in Fillmore (1977), since perspective choice is assumed
       to have no effect on cognitive meaning.

38.   The status of sentences such as (34) and (37) raises a couple of interesting questions. One of the questions to be asked is how we are to derive those sentences. Specifically, are their topics to be transformationally or otherwise derived from ordinary case-marked nouns (in this
case, perhaps, from possessive nouns)? This kind of (transformational)
derivation is reminiscent of the analysis advanced by Mikami (1960) for
sentences of the following kind:

Zo wa   *hana ga*   *nagai*
elephant-topic   trunk-subject   long
'An elephant has a long trunk.'

Zo no   *hana ga*   *nagai*
elephant-possessive   trunk-subject long
'An elephant's trunk is long.'

In spite of its appeal, this analysis lacks generality and accuracy, as is
pointed out by Kitahara (1981). In my opinion, the alternative analysis
put forward by Kitahara (1981) is not insightful enough. The simplest
analysis advanced in Ikegami (1981b: 200ff) seems to me to be the best
one and we will assume its validity in what follows. Ikegami observes
that the topic specifies the location (either concrete or abstract) where
an event takes place or in relation to which a state of affairs obtains. In
other words, the topic simply sets up a frame in which an event occurs
or a state of affairs exists. The "logical" connection between the topic
and the rest of the sentence, if any, is expected to be recovered or re-
constructed by the hearer on the basis of his knowledge of the language
(e.g. the thematic structure or valence of the verb), the linguistic and
nonlinguistic contexts in which the sentence is used, and his general
knowledge about what could happen in the world. This conception of
topic has a far-reaching effect in that it allows us to dispense with the
transformation called topicalization and consequently to capture the
similarity of those sentences to the following famous (or notorious)
sentence:

Boku wa   *unagi da.*
I-topic   eel   be
lit. I am (an) eel.

See Ikegami (1981: 35ff) and Onoe (1977, 1981) for stimulating discussions of this and related matters.

39.   Shibatani (1978) utilizes AC-6 as criterion for identifying Agent.

40.   Inoue (1974) does notice a semantic difference between the following
two examples, attributing it to the contrast between Agent-Experiencer
(*Taro* in (a)) and Experiencer (*Taro* in (b)).

(a)   (= her 33)   *Taroo ga*   *tuma o*   *ryuukan de*
                      Agent-Exp.   wife   flu of
                      sin-ase-ta.
                      die-Cause-Past
(b)   (= her 34)   *Taroo ga*   *tuma ni*   *ryuukan de*
                      Exp.   wife   flu of
                      sin-are-ta.
                      die-Passive-Past

But Inoue (1976: ch. 4) somehow chooses to give up Agent-Experiencer. Cf. especially Inoue (1976: 4.10). Similarly, Shibatani (1978)
does notice the notion of responsibility involved in sentences like (41).

But he simply dismisses it as irrelevant to the semantic relation assigned to the subjects of those sentences by marking *hahaoya* in (40),
for example, as Experiencer. Cf. note (41).

41.   Ikegami (1982) identifies the notion "responsibility", as it is being used
here, as a prominent property of the noncentral instances of Agent under discussion. He proposes the following "semantic transformation":
De-agentivized Act   Agentivized Act
X NOT PREVENT something $=$ X CAUSE something (through
                                                      ATTRIBUTION OF RESPONSIB.)
This is a radically different treatment of "responsibility" from Inoue
(1974) and Shibatani (1978). Cf. note (40). It is evidently the former,
not the latter, that is justified in laying claim to an explanatory semantic theory. Our aim here is to give further support to Ikegami (1982).

42.   Cf. DeLancey (1985) for the significance of the notion *control* as the
defining property of Agent (for Lhasa Tibetan in particular). Consider,
for example, the following pair:
a.   *k'o-s*   *deb*   *brlags*   *son*
      he-ERG   book   lost   PERF/EVIDENTIAL
      'He lost the book (first-hand knowledge).'
b.   *k'o-la*   *deb*   *rned* *sori*
      he-dative   book   find   PERF/EVIDENTIAL
      'He found the book (first-hand knowledge).'
DeLancey (1985: 55) observes that
        The significant difference between losing and finding is that
        finding must be a fortuitous event, while losing can be
        controlled. That is, one cannot guarantee finding a lost object;
        one can only look and hope. One can, however, guarantee not
        losing something; someone who exercises sufficient care will
        not lose things, so that the carelessness which results in loss
        constitutes a lapse of control.

43.   Ikegami (1982) points out that Japanese stretches the thematic relation
Agent much further than English as far as this type of sentence is concerned. Thus sentences such as (40), (41), and (46a) cannot be directly
translated into English in their intended interpretations. According to
John Bester, the following sentence, for example, clearly implies that
she is to blame for her child's death (e.g. she was too careless):
She allowed her child to be drowned in the river.
By contrast, in Japanese, "anyone involved in the event, one with or
without authority, can be represented as a causer, provided that the responsibility for what happens can be attributed, in however remote a
way, to him" (Ikegami 1982).

44.   See note (43).

45.   This should not be taken to mean that the thematic relation Experiencer is entirely dispensable. Following Ikegami (1981b: 188), we
would like to confine its use to cases such as the subjects in (42) and
(42').

46.   Okutsu (1983) employs P-float to account for the neutral meaning of
seemingly indirect passive sentences - what he calls P-float Passives.
The assumption behind this is that the semantic difference between the
direct passive and the indirect passive is reflected in deep structure: the
so-called non-uniform theory of passives is taken for granted. How-

ever, as Kuno (1983) has shown quite convincingly, there is good reason to favor the uniform theory. (For further arguments, see Kuno (1986).) There is thus no supporting evidence for the operation P-float, Okutsu's argument notwithstanding.

47. This proviso is necessary to distinguish the peripheral variant of Agent focused on in this section from cases where instances of another non-central Agent in 2.1. happen to be human, though the two can be unified in a more schematic characterization of "responsibility". Consider the following:

007 had a lot of difficulty breaking the window. He threw at it every object available in the room. Finally, the Russian spy he had knocked down unconscious was thrown through, breaking it.

Another simpler example was pointed out to me by E. Tsuboi:

John fainted and broke the window.

48. Cf. the following remark in Lakoff (1977):

> VOLITION and CONTROL need not be present in agent-subject constructions, but PRIMARY RESPONSIBILITY is always present. Examples are cases like: *John hit Mary (accidentally)*, *John dropped the dish (accidentally)*, etc. In each case there is no volition or control on John's part, but John does bear primary responsibility for what happened.

49. Here we do not deal with II (i.e. +Intender, -Actor). A couple of examples are given below:

(a) *John built a new house.* (in its primary interpretation)

(b) *Nixon bombed Hanoi.*

(b) is cited in Lakoff & Johnson (1980) as an example of the CONTROLLER FOR CONTROLLED metonymy. They comment on (b) as follows:

> Nixon himself may not have dropped the bombs on Hanoi, but via the CONTROLLER FOR CONTROLLED metonymy we not only say *Nixon bombed Hanoi* but also think of him as doing the bombing and hold him responsible for it. Again this is possible because of the nature of the metonymic relationship in the CONTROLLER FOR CONTROLLED metonymy, where responsibility is what is focused on.

It will be interesting to note at this point that the sentences we discussed in 2.1. can be understood as examples of the CONTROLLED FOR CONTROLLER metonymy, the reverse of the CONTROLLER FOR CONTROLLED metonymy here under discussion. As we have shown, *poison* in *Poison killed him*, for example, is thought of as doing the killing and is held responsible for it, whoever might have used it being excluded from the perspective. See Lakoff (1987), Sato (1978: ch. 3) and Seto (1986: ch. 3) for full discussions of the functions of metonymy.

50. However, see note (43).

References

Anderson, John M.
  1977   *On case grammar.* London: Croom Helm.

Chafe, Wallace L.
    1970   *Meaning and the structure of language*. Chicago: Chicago University Press.
Chomsky, Noam
    1972   *Studies on semantics in generative grammar*. The Hague: Mouton.
Croft, William
    1983   "Grammatical relations vs. thematic roles as universals", *CLS* 19: 76-94.
Cruse, D.A.
    1973   "Some thoughts on agentivity", *Journal of Linguistics* 9: 11-23.
Deane, Paul & Rebecca S. Wheeler
    1984   "On the use of syntactic evidence in the analysis of word meaning", *Papers from the Parasession on Lexical Semantics, Chicago Linguistic Society*, 95-106.
DeLancey, Scott
    1984   "Notes on agentivity and causation", *Studies in Language* 8: 181-213.
    1985   "On active typology and the nature of agentivity", in: Frans Plank (ed.), *Relational typology*. Berlin: Mouton.
Dougherty, Ray C.
    1970   "Recent studies on language universals", *Foundations of Language* 6: 505-561.
Fillmore, Charles J.
    1968   "The case for case", in: Emmon Bach & Robert T. Harms (eds.), *Universals in linguistic theory*. New York: Holt, Rinehart & Winston.
    1977   "The case for case reopened", in: Peter Cole & Jerrold M. Sadock (eds.), *Syntax and semantics 8: Grammatical relations*. New York: Academic Press.
Foley, William A. & Robert D. Van Valin, Jr.
    1984   *Functional syntax and universal grammar*. Cambridge: Cambridge University Press.
Hiromatsu, Wataru
    1982   *Sonzai to Imi* [Existence and meaning]. Tokyo: Iwanami Shoten.
    1988   *Shin Tetsugaku Nyumon* [New introduction to philosophy]. Tokyo: Iwanami Shoten.
Ikegami, Yoshihiko
    1981a   "Activity - accomplishment - achievement: A language that can't say, 'I burned it, but it didn't burn' and one that can", Trier: LAUT Series A 87.
    1981b   *'Suru' to 'Naru' no Gengogaku* [Linguistics of DOING and BECOMING]. Tokyo: Taishukan.
    1982a   "'Indirect causation' and 'de-agentivization': The semantics of involvement in English and Japanese", *Proceedings of the Department of Foreign Languages, College of General Education, University of Tokyo*, Vol. 29, No.3.
    1982b   *Kotoba no Shigaku* [Poetics of language]. Tokyo: Iwanami Shoten.
Inoue, Kazuko
    1974   "Experiencer", *Studies in Descriptive and Applied Linguistics* 7: 139-62.
    1976   *Henkei Bumpo to Nihongo* [Transformational grammar and the Japanese language]. Tokyo: Ta i shukan.
Jackendoff, Ray
    1983   *Semantics and cognition*. Cambridge: MIT Press.
    1985a   "Information is in the mind of the beholder", *Linguistics and Philosophy* 8: 23-33.
    1985b   "Multiple subcategorization: The case of *climb*", *Natural Language and Linguistic Theory* 3: 271-95.

Katz, Jerrold J.
1981   *Language and other abstract objects*. Oxford: Basil Blackwell.
Kitahara, Yasuo
1981   *Nihongo no Sekai 6: Nihongo no Bumpo* [The world of Japanese 6: Grammar of Japanese]. Tokyo: Chuokoronsha.
Kunihiro, Tetsuya
1970   *Imi no Shoso* [Aspects of meaning]. Tokyo: Sanseido.
Kuno, Susumu
1983   *Shin Nihon Bumpo Kenkyu* [A new study of Japanese grammar]. Tokyo: Taishukan.
1986   "Ukemibun no imi" [The meaning of passive sentences], *Nihongo Gaku* 5, 2.
Kuroda, Wataru
1975   *Keiken to Gengo* [Experience and language]. Tokyo: Tokyo University Press.
Lakoff, George
1977   "Linguistic gestalts", *CLS* 13: 236-287.
1987   *Women, fire, and dangerous things: What categories reveal about the mind*. Chicago: University of Chicago Press.
Lakoff, George & Mark Johnson
1980   *Metaphors we live by*. Chicago: University of Chicago Press.
Langacker, Ronald W.
1982   "Space grammar, analysability, and the English passive", *Language* 58: 22-80.
1987a   *Foundations of cognitive grammar*. Vol. 1: *Theoretical prerequisites*. Stanford: Stanford University Press.
1987b   "Nouns and verbs", *Language* 63: 53-94.
Levin, Beth
1985   "Lexical semantics in review: An introduction", in: Beth Levin (ed.), *Lexical semantics in review*. Cambridge: MIT Press.
Lyons, John
1968   *Introduction to theoretical linguistics*. Cambridge: Cambridge University Press.
1977   *Semantics*. Cambridge: Cambridge University Press.
Marantz, Alec
1985   "Lexical decomposition vs. affixes as syntactic constituents", *Papers from the Parasession on Causatives and Agentivity, Chicago Linguistic Society*.
Maruyama, Keizaburo
1981   *Sassure no Shiso* [Thoughts of Saussure]. Tokyo: Iwanami Shoten.
Mikami, Akira
1960   *Zo wa Hana ga Nagai*. Tokyo: Kuroshio Shuppan.
Miller, Jim
1985   *Semantics and syntax*. Cambridge: Cambridge University Press.
Murakami, Yoichiro
1979   *Kagaku to Nichijosei no Bunmyaku* [Contexts of science and everyday life]. Tokyo: Kaimeisha.
Nishimura, Yoshiki
1986   Aspects of conceptual semantics. [Unpublished M.A. Thesis, University of Tokyo.]

Okutsu, Keiichiro
    1983   "Fukabunri Shoyu to Shoyusha Ido - Shiten no Tachiba kara" [Inalienable possession and the possessor float - from the viewpoint of perspective], *Todai Ronkyu* 20.
Onoe, Keisuke
    1977   "Teidairon no Isan" [Legacy of the theories of topic], *Gengo* 6, 10.
    1981   "'Zo wa Hana ga Nagai' to 'Boku wa Unagi da'", *Gengo* 10, 2.
Sato, Nobuo
    1978   *Rhetoric Kankaku* [The sense of rhetoric]. Tokyo: Kodansha.
    1981   *Rhetoric Ninshiki* [Rhetorical cognition]. Tokyo: Kodansha.
    1986   *Imi no Dansei* [Elasticity of meaning]. Tokyo: Iwanami Shoten.
    1987   *Rhetoric no Shosoku* [Whereabouts of rhetoric]. Tokyo: Hakusuisha.
Schlesinger, I.M.
    1979   "Cognitive structures and semantic deep structures: The case of the instrumental", *Journal of Linguistics* 15: 307-324.
Seto, Kenichi
    1986   *Rhetoric no Uchu* [The universe of rhetoric]. Tokyo: Kaimeisha.
Shibatani, Masayoshi
    1978   *Nihongo no Bunseki* [Analysis of Japanese]. Tokyo: Taishukan.
Starosta, Stanley
    1978   "The one per cent solution", in: Werner Abraham (ed.), *Valence, semantic case and grammatical relations*. Amsterdam: Benjamins.
Tai, James H.-Y.
    1984   "Verbs and times in Chinese: Vendler's four categories", *CLS Lexical semantics. Chicago Linguistic Society*.
Van Oosten, Jeanne
    1977   "Subjects and agenthood in English", *CLS* 13: 459-471.
Yamashi, Masaaki
    1983   "Kakubumpo Riron" [Case Grammar], in: Minoru Yasui et al., *Eigogaku Taikei* 5: *Imiron* [Outline of English linguistics 5: Linguistic semantics]. Tokyo: Taishukan.

Cases as conceptual categories: Evidence from German

Michael B. Smith

1. Introduction

Cognitive linguists generally agree that the study of language can offer rich insights into the general nature of human conceptualization and categorization. The question of how conceptual categorization is reflected in language (via linguistic categorization) is thus a fundamental issue in linguistic theory. An especially interesting aspect of this issue is the question as to whether conceptual categories can be marked not only by vocabulary items in languages but also by the grammars of the languages themselves. Lakoff (1987: 91) notes that the grammaticization of conceptual categories is common and states furthermore that "conceptual categories marked by the grammars of languages are important in understanding the nature of cognitive categories in general". The present paper is a contribution to this general line of inquiry in its challenge to the usual assumption that morphological cases are mere grammatical markers without inherent semantic content. On the contrary, I will show how the dative (DAT) and accusative (ACC) cases in German can be analyzed as meaningful in encoding fundamental cognitive categories.

The analysis is grounded in and presupposes the theoretical framework of Langacker's *cognitive grammar* (CG). I will briefly describe here the constructs to be employed in this paper, but readers wishing a more detailed introduction to the theory can read Langacker (1987a) or Langacker (1988). Cognitive grammar assumes a conceptual view of meaning, wherein semantic structure is equated with conceptual structure and meaning is assumed to equal conceptualization. Grammatical constructions in cognitive grammar represent the grammaticization of *conventional imagery* - they structure or construe situations in a particular fashion for linguistic purposes.

In cognitive grammar linguistic predications are defined through the imposition of a figure/ground organization on one or more cognitive domains (i.e. knowledge structures of varying complexity). Within a given domain (or *base*) taken as salient for characterizing a linguistic predication, aspects are singled out for *designation* by the predication (the *profile*). The relation between the profile and the base of a predication determines the semantic value of an expression. In this paper I will be concerned with relational predications such as verbs and prepositions, which profile interconnections between entities. Every relational profile has a *trajector* (TR) (the figure in a relational profile) and one or more *landmarks* (LM) (salient entities in the profile other than the trajector which often provide a point of reference with respect to which the TR moves or is located).

Taking as a starting point a basic prototype semantics and the assumption that each case defines a complex category within which a constellation of senses joins to form a network of interrelated meanings, I will propose prototypical meanings for each case and show how these meanings can motivate less prototypical senses as extensions from the prototype (where some but not all features of the extension are incompatible with the prototype). The use of the cases differs slightly (though significantly) from one construction type to another, so in order to achieve a full picture of the system, the paper samples the array of meanings manifested by each case across representative construction types in German, with the distribution of DAT and ACC shown to reflect a subtle semantic patterning which is not immediately apparent.[1]

Before proceeding to the analysis proper, it is worth briefly considering potential problems of attributing meaning to grammatical markers such as cases: the abstractness of the meanings and the lack of predictability in many usages of a particular case. Doubters might claim, for example, that any meaning which could be attributed to a grammatical marker such as a case would be so abstract as to be essentially devoid of meaning for practical purposes. Such an objection disappears in a cognitively-based analysis, where abstractness of meaning is expected, given that some concepts can serve as schemata which sanction other more specific concepts (see Langacker 1987a: 68ff, 132ff for a thorough discussion of this notion). In addition, Lakoff (1987: 308) notes that some parts of the conceptual system are inherently more fundamental than others. Such concepts are often used in many other concepts and tend to be grammaticized because of their basic importance to the linguistic system. They may be so fundamental that speakers use them automatically and unconsciously, without having everyday awareness of them. To use Lakoff's terminology, such concepts are used "in" thought (rather than as objects of thought) and actually help to structure how speakers look at events (Lakoff 1987: 335). It is thus reasonable to claim that grammaticized concepts, which are more fundamental than lexical items, indeed have semantic import. The fact that such concepts are used unconsciously does not imply that they have no semantic validity. In such a view, entrenchment of use does not imply lack of meaning, but rather implies the central importance of the concepts in the linguistic system (and by implication in the conceptual system in general).

What about the lack of predictability of many uses of the cases? Some might claim that the lack of choice in case in many constructions (after certain prepositions, for example) indicates that the cases contribute no independent meaning to the construction and that they are thus meaningless grammatical markers. Indeed, notes Langacker, "the standard criterial-attribute model of categorization...exemplifies an expectation of absolute predictability" (Langacker 1987a: 49). But it is now recognized within cognitive linguistics that the adoption of the prototype model of categorization requires a relaxation of the expectation that the semantic import of certain grammatical markers be linked to absolute predictability in their use, since rule applicability tends to depend on prototype effects. Also, absolute predictivists fail to note the possibility that in some construction types the meaning contributed by a grammatical marker such as a case may simply coincide with (or overlap) the meaning of some other part of the construction (such as a preposition or verb). This is not the same thing as saying that the case has no independent meaning of its own.

2.   The prototypical meanings of DAT and ACC in German

The array of data I will survey in this paper supports the claim that the prototypical meaning of ACC centers on the fundamental conceptual notion of one entity coming into physical contact with another entity. In CG terms, ACC case signifies, in its prototypical sense, the physical movement of a TR along a path which makes contact with a significant aspect of the LM (i.e. either the LM itself or a region associated with the LM). I will refer to this notion as the *contact image*, which is grammaticized via ACC case. This prototypical meaning is assumed to be a psychologically basic-level category similar to what Lakoff calls a kinesthetic image-schematic structure. Such structures are directly meaningful and "constantly recur in our everyday bodily experience" (Lakoff 1987: 267; see also Johnson 1987 for detailed discussion). Abstract conceptual structures can be semantically extended from basic-level structures and are "indirectly meaningful", notes Lakoff; "they are understood because of their systematic relationship to directly meaningful structures" (Lakoff 1987: 268). Basic-level categories may also be schematic for more specific instantiations of the categories, as will be noted directly. We will see in the following sections that the contact image lends itself to a rich array of semantic extensions in both the prepositional and clausal realms. Given that this image is fundamentally rooted in our everyday experience, it is not surprising to find it playing a part in the grammatical system of German (and doubtless many other languages, as well).

We will also see that DAT reflects the fundamental importance of the contact image in its general use in signifying a conceptually significant "departure" from the contact image (or one of its extensions). This "departure from ACC" sense of the DAT may be manifested by a variety of possible instantiations (depending on the verbs or prepositions with which it is used) which will be discussed presently, including its prototypical use in the clausal realm to encode the *experiencer* participant in conceived events.

3. Two-way prepositions

We begin our survey with a brief look at how DAT and ACC function following the set of German prepositions which can govern either case (two-way prepositions).[2] It is in this realm where the semantic motivation for case selection is most evident and least problematic. All prepositions generally introduce locative configurations which give information as to the spatial setting within which verbally designated processes take place. In the two-way prepositional realm, ACC denotes that the TR of the preposition is conceived to move along a path which brings it into contact with some salient aspect of the LM of the preposition. Under other circumstances DAT is used. This account, sometimes known traditionally as the *motion vs. location* analysis, can be stated more precisely as follows in CG terms:.

DAT designates the confinement of the TR of the preposition to a set of points satisfying the locative specifications of the preposition. This set of points is called the *search domain* (SD) of the preposition.

ACC designates the fact that the TR of the preposition is not always confined to the SD of the preposition, but enters the SD at some point along a path.

The following examples illustrate these definitions for the two-way preposition *in* (whose SD is equivalent to the boundary of the LM itself):[3]

(1) a. *Hans   geht   in   den   Garten.*
         Hans   goes   in   the-ACC   garden
         'Hans goes into the garden.'
     b. *Hans   sitzt   im   Garten.*
         Hans   sits   in-DAT   garden
         'Hans is sitting in the garden.'
(2) a. *Wir   wanderten   in   die   Berge.*
         we   wandered   in   the-ACC   mountains
         'We wandered into the mountains.'
     b. *Wir   wanderten   in   den   Bergen.*
         we   wandered   in   the-DAT   mountains
         'We wandered (around) in the mountains.'

Note that in (2) the traditional motion vs. location analysis still holds in spite of the fact that the TR is in motion in both variants. DAT is motivated in (2b) since the path of the TR is conceived to be confined throughout to the locative configuration specified by the preposition. Verbs like those in (2) can be thought of as *neutral motion verbs*, because the path (or in abstract domains the activity) profiled by the verb is neutral with respect to whether it can be conceived as located totally within a given locative configuration (as specified by the preposition) or whether it can be conceived to enter the configuration from without.

Concrete spatial examples like those exemplified above can be found for all of the two-way prepositions. Rather than give a complete list here, I simply note a few additional examples involving selected two-way prepositions with neutral motion verbs, as in the following:

(3) a. *Das Auto   steht   hinter   dem   Baum.*
         the car   stands   behind   the-DAT   tree
         'The car stands behind the tree.'
     b. *Hans   stellte   das Auto   hinter   den   Baum.*
         Hans   placed   the car   behind   the-ACC   tree
         'Hans parked the car behind the tree.'
(4) a. *Der Hund   schläft   unter   dem   Tisch.*
         the dog   sleeps   under   the-DAT   table
         'The dog is sleeping under the table.'

    b.   *Er   legte   den   Teppich   unter den   Tisch.*
         he   laid   the   carpet   under the-ACC   table.
         'He laid the carpet under the table.'

(5)   a.   *Das Flugzeug prallte   auf*
         the   airplane bounced on
         dem   Wasser   auf.
         the-DAT   water   on.
         'The airplane hit the water.'
         (with a bouncing motion along the surface
         of the water)

    b.   *Das Flugzeug prallte   auf   das   Wasser.*
         the   airplane bounced on   the-ACC water
         'The airplane hit the water.'
         (downplay bouncing motion, more force involved)

(6)   a.   *Er   schloß   sein   Fahrrad*
         he   locked his   bicycle
         an   dem   Zaun   an.
         to   the-DAT   fence on.
         'He locked his bicycle to the fence.'
         (it was already there)

    b.   *Er   schloß   sein   Fahrrad*
         he   locked his   bicycle
         an   den   Zaun.
         to   the-ACC   fence.
         'He fastened his bicycle to the fence.'
         (by moving it there)

(7)   a.   *Sie   sind   in   der   Bank   eingebrochen.*
         they   are   in   the-DAT bank   broken-in
         'They broke into the bank.'
         (they were already in the bank and then
         broke through the floor (or the safe, etc.))

    b.   *Sie   sind   in   die   Bank   eingebrochen.*
         they   are   in   the-ACC bank   broken-in
         'They broke into the bank.'
         (i.e. the building)

(8)   a.   *Sie   führten   ihn   in   einer   neuen*
         they   led   him in   a-DAT   new

> *Gesellschaft*   *ein.*
> society   in
> 'They introduced him into a new society/club.'
> (implies a more personal relationship, where the member is already conceived to be a member when the sentence is spoken)
> b. *Sie   führten   ihn   in   eine   neue*
>   they   led   him   in   a-ACC   new
>   *Gesellschaft*   *ein.*
>   society   in
>   'They introduced him into a new society/club.'
>   (implies a new member is inducted into a club where he was not previously a member)

The SDs of the prepositions in the above sentences are the region behind the tree in (3), the region under the table in (4), the area surrounding the surface of the water in (5), the surface of the fence in (6), the bank building in (7), and the society in (8), respectively.

Note that the actual senses of DAT and ACC vary slightly depending on the configurational properties associated with the prepositions with which they are used, so that even the relatively explicit prototypical characterizations of DAT and ACC given above must be taken as schematic for particular instantiations of the cases with particular two-way prepositions. In (3-5) the SDs of the prepositions are regions distinct from the actual LMs, and ACC is motivated not only by contact of the TR with the SD's boundary but also by the movement of the TR into the SD (since movement of the TR into the SD is part of the meaning of the preposition). In (5), for example, DAT signifies that the TR of the preposition (*Flugzeug*) is conceived to remain within the horizontally-oriented ṣD of the preposition as it bounces along fairly close to the surface of the water, whereas the ACC signifies the intrusion of the TR on the conceptually relevant boundary of the SD.

In other circumstances the SD of the preposition may not be distinct from the LM. In (6), for example, the vertically-oriented SD of the preposition *an* is equivalent to the LM itself - thus, the movement of the TR so that it comes into contact with the LM is sufficient to motivate ACC, and the location of the TR on the LM is sufficient to motivate DAT. In (7-8) the SDs are again equivalent to the LMs of the preposition *in*. These specific differences within each case category, though admittedly minor, nevertheless reflect differences in imagery (and thus in meaning), and represent slight semantic variants serving as instantiations of the DAT and ACC prototypes. We can still assume that the characterizations of the basic-level DAT and ACC prototypes given in section 2 above are reasonable candidates for the prototypical meanings of the cases.

Now we come to two-way prepositional data which pose a problem for the traditional motion vs. location accounts, because they extend the use of DAT to situations not involving neutral motion verbs. The traditional motion vs. location analysis is insufficient as it stands to account for data like the following, where the path profiled by the verb is conceived to enter the SD of the preposition in both the DAT and ACC variants:

(9) a.   *Die   Sonne   versank   in   dem   Abenddunst.*
          the   sun   sank   in   the-DAT   evening mist
          'The sun sank in the evening mist.'
          (it is enveloped or swallowed up in the haze)
     b.   *Die   Sonne   versank   in   den   Abenddunst.*
          the   sun   sank   in   the-ACC   evening mist
          'The sun sank in the evening mist.'
          (stresses the movement of the sun into the mist
          (as if it drops into it))
(10) a.   *Die   Mutter   hat   das   Kind   in   der*
          the   mother   has   the   child   in   the-DAT
          Decke   eingewickelt.
          blanket   wrapped-in
          'The mother wrapped the child in the blanket.'
          (stresses the end result of the action)
     b.   *Die   Mutter   hat   das   Kind   in   die*
          the   mother   has   the   child   in   the-ACC
          Decke   eingewickelt.
          blanket   wrapped-in
          'The mother wrapped the child in the blanket.'
          (stresses the progression of the wrapping activity
          up to its final state)

Note how the DAT variants draw attention to the end result or final state of the path or activity profiled by the verbs. Such verbs will be referred to as *endpoint focus verbs* in order to characterize their ability to co-occur with DAT in situations where the endpoint is particularly salient.[4] The use of DAT can be motivated in these examples by proposing that DAT reinforces the saliency of the endpoint of the path profiled by the verb, as can be seen from the indicated native speaker interpretations for the DAT variants. In other words, DAT establishes a focal point within the verbal profile through its own profiling of that segment of the path profiled by the verb that is within the SD of the preposition. Given the notion of endpoint focus with such German verbs, the distinction between using DAT to highlight the endpoint of a profiled path crossing the boundary into the LM's SD vs. the use of ACC to highlight the entire path itself can still be accounted for via a type of location vs. motion analysis, in an extended sense. While this set of data does not illustrate a meaning extension of DAT case per se (since DAT still designates that portion of the path confined to the preposition's SD), it nevertheless represents an extension in the application of DAT to situations departing from those first discussed above.

Another type of endpoint focus data illustrating a meaning extension of both DAT and ACC can be seen in the following examples:

(11) a. *Das Pulver ging in dem duftenden*
the powder went in the-DAT fragrant
Schaum auf.
foam on
'The powder is gone (has disappeared) in the
fragrant foam.'

b. *Das Pulver ging in den duftenden*
the powder went in the-ACC fragrant
Schaum auf.
foam on
'The powder turned into fragrant foam.'

(12) a. *Die Tablette löst sich in dem*
the tablet dissolves REFL in the-DAT
lauwarmen Wasser auf.
lukewarm water on
'The tablet dissolves in (is hidden in) the lukewarm water.'
(water a medium)

b. *Die Tablette löst sich in das*
the tablet dissolves REFL in the-ACC
lauwarme Wasser auf.
lukewarm water on
'The tablet dissolves (turns) into lukewarm water.'

Here neither sentence involves the objective movement of the TR of the preposition along a path into the preposition's SD, but rather the notion of the TR moving from one state to another (i.e. change of state). The

DAT versions stress the final state of the TR of the preposition (i.e. the endpoint of the conceived change), whereas the ACC versions accentuate the change from one state to another (i.e. a type of abstract movement from solid to liquid). These data, in which DAT and ACC signify unchanging state vs. change of state, respectively, can be motivated as extensions from the prototypical senses of the cases if we reinterpret the path notion in abstract terms as "movement" from one state to another.[5]

Finally, consider the following data, where the endpoint focus analysis breaks down completely. In these data the use of DAT and ACC to signify no change vs. change has been extended even further, in that they now refer to the unchanging vs. changing state of the LM (as opposed to the TR) of the preposition:

(13) a.　*Ich　werde　die　Briefmarke*　　*in*　　*meiner*
　　　　　I　　will　　the　stamp　　　　in　　my-DAT
　　　　　Sammlung　aufnehmen.
　　　　　collection　take-on
　　　　　'I'll add the stamp to my collection.'
　　　　　(the collection is finished except for a missing stamp
　　　　　(for which a place was left))

　　　b.　*Ich　werde　die　Briefmarke*　　*in*　　*meine*
　　　　　I　　will　　the　stamp　　　　in　　my-ACC
　　　　　Sammlung　aufnehmen.
　　　　　collection　take-on
　　　　　'I'll add the stamp to my collection.'
　　　　　(the collection is expanded to include a new section)

(14) a.　*Hast　du　die　Steinchen*　　　*in*　　*diesem*
　　　　　have　you　the　little stones　in　　this-DAT
　　　　　Mosaik　eingefügt?
　　　　　mosaic　added-in
　　　　　'Have you added the little stones to this mosaic?'
　　　　　(put the stones into a prearranged place in the otherwise
　　　　　finished mosaic)

　　　b.　*Hast　du　die　Steinchen*　　　*in*　　*dieses*
　　　　　have　you　the　little stones　in　　this-ACC
　　　　　Mosaik　eingefügt?
　　　　　mosaic　added-in
　　　　　'Have you added the little stones to this mosaic?'
　　　　　(increase the size of the mosaic by putting in new stones)

In these data, the no change vs. change senses of DAT and ACC are paramount. In the DAT versions the LMs of the prepositions are conceived to be finished wholes with fixed boundaries into which the TRs are inserted into prearranged positions. In the ACC versions the LMs are not conceived as complete wholes, but rather expand (change) to accommodate the newly inserted TRs.

It is readily apparent from the small sample of data given above that the DAT and ACC cases in the two-way prepositional realm illustrate both prototypical meanings and their instantiations as well as senses which can be motivated as extensions from the prototypes. The notion of change vs. no change within a conceived situation emerges as an especially important meaning extension which has been overlooked by the traditional accounts.

Note finally that the categorizing judgment which enables speakers to motivate the extended senses of the cases from the prototypical senses leads to the increased salience of their perceived similarity as a schema in its own right. The general notion of no change vs. change thus subsumes the more concrete senses of two-way prepositional DAT and ACC given at the beginning of this section, given that the movement of the TR of a two-way preposition across the boundary of the preposition's SD can be thought of as a type of change, with the lack of such movement signifying no change with respect to the configuration set up by the preposition.

4.   One-way ACC prepositions

Recall that the meanings of the cases tend to vary depending upon the lexical items they combine with in grammatical constructions. The basic-level ACC configuration is rich in conceptual possibilities and is open to myriad interpretations which can be exploited as semantic motivators for ACC. Thus, aspects of the contact image isolated as motivating ACC in the two-way prepositional realm may play a lesser role in other realms, where other aspects of the image may be focussed on as particularly relevant. The goal of this section will be to show that, with a few minor adjustments in imagery, the contact image proposed as the prototypical sense of ACC in the two-way prepositional realm also serves to motivate the use of ACC with the set of one-way ACC prepositions in German.

It is important at this point to note a fundamental difference between the two-way and one-way groups of German prepositions. Although the contact image motivates ACC in both groups (for those prepositions taking ACC), they differ with respect to the type of contact involved. As we have seen, the notion of an SD is necessary to account for the case-marking properties of the two-way prepositions, for which the use of ACC requires contact of the TR with the SD of the LM of the preposition as it passes from outside the SD to within the SD. But in the one-way prepositional realm it is the contact (either actual or implied) of the TR with the LM itself (not an SD associated with the LM) which is criterial for motivating ACC and its extensions.

An aspect of the contact image which emerges as particularly important with the one-way ACC prepositions is the notion of the TR of the preposition making forceful, directed physical contact with the LM, which is often perceived as a type of *goal*. This can be exemplified by the following concrete situation involving the preposition *gegen*:

(15)   *Das Auto   fuhr   gegen   einen Baum.*
        the   car   drove   against a-ACC tree
        'The car drove against a tree.'

In more abstract senses the LM-as-goal sense emerges even more clearly, as in the following sentence, where the TR is conceived to be a remedy or force directed against an illness (LM):

(16)   *Wir haben ein   gutes   Mittel   gegen*
        we   have   a   good   remedy   against
        diese   Krankheit.
        this-ACC   sickness
        'We have a good remedy against (for) this sickness.'

Another one-way ACC preposition which evokes the LM as goal sense is the preposition *für*, the domain of which is generally more abstract than the configurational/spatial domains considered up to this point. The goal-oriented sense of *für* is obvious, though, as illustrated in the following data:

(17)   *Hans arbeitet   für   seine   Familie.*
        Hans works   for   his-ACC   family
        'Hans works for (the sake of) his family.'
(18)   *Die Mutter   sorgt   für   ihr   Kind.*
        the mother   cares   for   her-ACC child
        'The mother cares for her child.'

Note that the activities profiled by the verbs in (17-18) are conceived to be directed toward the LMs in a benefactive sense. Consider now the following example:

(19)   *Für   seine   Krankheit   gibt   es*
         for   his-ACC   sickness   gives   it
         kein   Mittel.
         no   remedy
         'For his illness there is no cure.'

Sentence (19) illustrates the use of *für* in contexts involving the remedy sense discussed above for *gegen*.

Another ACC preposition manifesting a clear goal-directed sense is *bis*, as illustrated in the following:[6]

(20)   *Hans   fährt   bis   Stuttgart.*
         Hans   drives   until-ACC   Stuttgart
         'Hans is traveling as far as Stuttgart.'

Note that the LM of *bis* is taken to be a region representing the goal of the travel. In the temporal domain the LM of *bis* can be understood as a temporal benchmark which represents the endpoint or goal of the activity profiled by the verb:

(21)   *Wir   bleiben   bis   Weihnachten.*
         we   stay   until-ACC   Christmas
         'We'll stay until Christmas.'

In all of the examples up to this point we see, therefore, that the ACC case is compatible semantically with verbs and prepositions involving activities conceived as directed towards a goal (LM). The goal-oriented sense represents an extension from the prototypical ACC contact image in its emphasis not only on contact between the TR and LM of the preposition, but also on interpreting the LM as the goal of the clausal activity.

In addition to the goal-oriented sense, other one-way ACC prepositions may invoke a *completeness* sense which is also semantically compatible with ACC, since contact with the LM of the preposition by the TR implies the completeness of a goal-oriented path. The preposition *durch* illustrates one way in which the completeness sense can be manifested:

(22)   *Der Dieb geht durch das   Fenster*
        the thief goes through the-ACC window
        ins   Haus.
        in-the   house
        'The thief goes into the house through the window.'
(23)   *Hans hat durch die   Wand   geschossen.*
        Hans has through the-ACC wall   shot
        'Hans shot through the wall.'

The notion of LM as goal is insufficient to account fully for the meaning of these sentences, since if the TR of the preposition stopped upon making contact with the LM (and thus reaching its goal), the meaning of the preposition would not be satisfied. The completeness sense of *durch* makes special reference to all the boundaries of the LM and requires that the TR of the preposition move all the way through the LM, rather than simply make contact with it. This sense is even more apparent in the following examples:

(24)   *Der Vogel fliegt durch   die   Luft.*
        the bird flies through the-ACC air
        'The bird flies through(out) the air.'
(25)   *Das Blut fließt durch   den   Körper.*
        the blood flows   through the-ACC body
        'The blood flows through(out) the body.'

In (24) the motion of the bird has no specified goal, but the flying activity is conceived to effectively suffuse the space designated by the LM. In (25) the completeness sense is even more pronounced in the conception of the LM as a container up to whose boundaries the TR flows. Note that neither (24) nor (25) particularly evokes the goal sense evident in the previous data.

Data like the following show how directional/goal-oriented and completeness senses can have varying importance even within the same clause:

(26)   *Wir sind durch   den   Wald   gegangen.*
        we are   through the-ACC woods   gone
        'We went through the woods.'

Sentence (26) can have either the interpretation of wandering around all parts of the woods (the completeness sense), or it can evoke the sense of moving straight through the woods from one side to the other (which involves both completeness and directionality).

The goal-oriented and completeness senses of *durch* can also be detected in temporal and abstract domains of various sorts:

(27) *Er   ist   gut   durch   die   schweren*
      he   is   well through   the-ACC   difficult
      Jahre   hindurchgekommen.
      years   come-through
      'He got through the difficult years well.'

(28) *Er   ist   durch   alle   Schwierigkeiten*
      he   is   through   all-ACC   difficulties
      hindurchgekommen.
      come-through
      'He got through all the difficulties.'

The preposition *um* also evokes both goal-oriented and completeness senses, as illustrated in the following:

(29) *Die Planeten   gehen   um   die*
      the planets   go   around   the-ACC
      Sonne   herum.
      sun   around
      'The planets go around the sun.'

The goal-oriented sense of *um* follows from the fact that the TR of the preposition follows a directed path which completely encircles the LM. The original starting point of the TR can be interpreted as the goal once the TR has made a complete circuit around the LM. Returning to the starting point thus also evokes the sense of completeness, which in some situations may be paramount:

(30) *Die Straße geht   um   die   Stadt.*
      the street goes   around   the-ACC   city
      'The street goes around the city.'

(31) *Um   den   Brunnen   herum   ist   Kies.*
      around   the-ACC   fountain   around   is   gravel
      'Around the fountain there is gravel.'

Sentences like (30) and (31) exemplify situations in which the path sense of the preposition is regarded as fully instantiated at all points around the LM. The image of the TRs fully surrounding the LMs emphasizes the completeness sense. Data like the following show that *um* can also be used to indicate abstractly oriented aim or purpose:

(32)   *Wir   spielten   um   (das)   Geld.*
      we   played   around   (the-ACC)   money
      'We played for money.'

(33)   *Die   Mutter   kümmerte   sich   um*
      the   mother   looked   after REFL   around
      ihre   Kinder.
      her-ACC   children
      'The mother looked after her children.'

We can see in both (32) and (33) how the LMs are centers of attention, surrounded as it were by entities or processes which are clearly goal-oriented.

Finally, we come to the last one-way ACC preposition, *ohne*, which is illustrated in the following sentence:

(34)   *Ohne   das   Geld   kann   man nicht leben.*
      without   the-ACC   money   can   one   not   live
      'Without money one cannot live.'

(35)   *Ich   kann   die   Suppe   ohne   einen   Löffel*
      I   can   the   soup   without   a-ACC   spoon
      nicht   essen.
      not   eat
      'I can't eat the soup without a spoon.'

This preposition seems to evoke exclusively the completeness sense as a motivation for ACC. That is, we can plausibly account for the semantic compatibility of ACC with this preposition if we note that the LMs of *ohne* are completely excluded from participating in the activity of the clause. While this analysis is admittedly far removed from the prototypical ACC contact image, we have already seen how completeness can be plausibly derived from that image to motivate ACC with some senses of other ACC prepositions (where the contact sense is still at least weakly evident). The next logical step would be to use the notion of completeness itself, apart from its contact-image source, to motivate ACC with *ohne*.

The discussion in this section has shown that there are at least two conceptually significant extensions of ACC which occur in the realm of the one-way ACC prepositions: the notions of *goal* and *completeness*, both of which are derivable from the prototypical contact image.

5.   One-way DAT prepositions

The prepositions taking only DAT are quite varied in meaning. The data show that the semantic notion uniting the use of DAT with this group of prepositions is that DAT signifies a conceptually significant departure from the ACC prototype, that is, the absence of a directed path followed by the TR of the preposition which results in contact with the prepositional LM itself. I will divide the DAT prepositions into three main groups, each of which represents an instantiation of the DAT prototype.

5.1.   *DAT prepositions confining their TRs to static locations*

By far the largest group of one-way DAT prepositions isolate their TRs to static locations in some domain relative to the LM, regardless of individual meaning differences between particular prepositions. Consider first the following sentences containing the prepositions *bei* and *gegenüber*:

(36)   *Hans   stand   bei   mir.*
         Hans   stood   near   me-DAT
         'Hans stood near me.'
(37)   *Gegenüber   dem   Bahnhof   steht   ein   Hotel.*
         opposite   the-DAT   station   stands   a   hotel
         'Opposite the railroad station stands a hotel.'

It is obvious that the prepositions in these sentences have meanings reminiscent of the DAT interpretations of the two-way prepositions discussed earlier.

Consider now a set of data involving the preposition *mit*:

(38)   *Inge   beschäftigt   sich*
         Inge   occupies   herself

mit   der   Mathematik.
with   the-DAT   mathematics
'Inge occupies herself with mathematics.'

(39)   *Ich   bin   mit   ihm   gefahren.*
I   am   with   him-DAT   traveled
'I traveled with him.'

(40)   *Er   fährt   mit   dem   Auto nach München.*
he   travels with   the-DAT   car   to   Munich
'He travels by car to Munich.'

Note that *mit* may be used either with verbs which profile activities usually conceived to occur in one place (38) or with verbs which profile paths (39-40) along which the TR and LM are conceived to move. Each sentence with *mit* involves some kind of connection between the TR and LM of the preposition, which may be understood in terms of accompaniment (39) or instrument (40). What is crucial in motivating DAT in (39-40) is that the TR and LM are not conceived to move relative to each other, although they are moving relative to some other fixed point.

The preposition *nach* is a DAT preposition which evokes a kind of proximity relation between its TR and LM. It differs from *mit* in that this relation prototypically involves sequentiality in some domain, as illustrated by the following:

(41)   *Hans   ging   nach   dir.*
Hans   went   after   you-DAT
'Hans went after (subsequent to) you.'

This sentence can be interpreted in either spatial or temporal terms. The proximity sense is most clear in its spatial reading, where the TR and LM of *nach* are conceived to be moving relative to some fixed observer, but not relative to each other. The proximity sense is of lesser salience in its temporal reading, where the LM is conceived to go before the TR. Note, however, that the temporal sense still departs from the ACC contact image (in that the TR is not conceived to make contact with the LM).

Consider next the following use of *nach*:

(42)   *Nach   dem   Direktor   ist   er*
next to the-DAT   director   is   he

der   wichtigste   *Mann*   *in*   *der*   *Fabrik.*
the   most important   man   in   the   factory
'Next to the director he's the most important man
in the factory.'

In this sentence the TR and LM of *nach* are located sequentially on a
scale of value, with the TR (*er*) conceived to be a step lower than that of
the LM (*Direktor*). Once again the absence of a path directed towards
the LM motivates ACC.

The preposition *nach* also appears in sentences like the following,
where the LM of the preposition is taken as a model with respect to
which some activity is performed:

(43)   *Er*   *zeichnet*   *nach*   *der*   *Natur.*
       he   draws   after   the-DAT   nature
       'He draws from (according to) nature.'

This sentence evokes the temporal sequential sense of *nach* discussed
previously, in that the LM (i.e. the model) must exist prior to the activity
it inspires.[7]

Next consider a sentence with the preposition *seit*:

(44)   *Ich*   *wohne*   *seit*   *dem*   *ersten*   *Mai*
       I   live   since   the-DAT   first   May
       in   *meiner*   *neuen*   *Wohnung.*
       in   my   new   apartment
       'I've been living in my new apartment since the first of May.'

In (44) *seit* relates the TR of the preposition (here understood as the
process profiled by the verb) to the point in time profiled by the LM.
More specifically, the temporal relationship described in this sentence
involves locating the TR process wholly within the span of time following the LM (including the present).

5.2. *DAT prepositions with separation senses*

The next main group of one-way DAT prepositions consists of three
prepositions manifesting separation senses of various types. In each of
these sentences the TR of the preposition is conceived to be removed in
some sense from the LM. Let us first consider the preposition *aus*:

(45)   *Hans   geht   aus   dem   Haus.*
        Hans   goes   out   the-DAT   house
        'Hans is going out of the house.'

(46)   *Dieser   Ring   ist   aus   purem   Gold.*
        this   ring   is   out   pure-DAT   gold
        'This ring is (made) out of pure gold.'

(47)   *Sie   zeigte   uns   Bilder*
        she   showed   us   pictures
        aus   ihrer   Kindheit.
        out   her-DAT   childhood
        'She showed us pictures from her childhood.'

In (45) the separation of the TR along a path from the LM is rooted in the concrete spatial domain, while in (46-47) the path sense is only implied. Sentence (46) involves the metaphor for the manufacturing process as a path followed by the TR as it goes away from the LM (the raw material which can be interpreted as the source for the TR). Sentence (47) involves the temporal separation of the TR (*Bilder*) from the LM (*Kindheit*), and is very similar to the following sentence involving the preposition *von*:

(48)   *Der   Brief   ist   von   meinem   Vater.*
        the   letter   is   from   my-DAT   father
        'The letter is from my father.'

Note that (48) differs from (47) in evoking spatial (rather than temporal) separation along an implied path of the TR from its source (LM).

In (49) we have a situation involving *außer* in which the LM is conceived to be separated or isolated from the TR rather than the other way around:

(49)   *Außer   dir   war   niemand   gekommen.*
        besides   you-DAT   was   no one   come
        'Besides you no one came.'

Note, however, that this separation sense still departs from the ACC configuration, which motivates the use of DAT with this preposition.

5.3   A preposition involving a path approaching the LM: zu

Finally, we come to the last member of this group, the preposition *zu*. Consider the following sentences:

(50)   *Ich   bin   zu   Hause.*
          I   am   to   house-DAT[8]
          'I'm at home.'
(51)   *Hans   fährt   zu   seinen   Eltern.*
          Hans   drives   to   his-DAT   parents
          'Hans is driving to his parents.'
(52)   *Ich   möchte   mich*
          I   would like   me
          zum   Studium   anmelden.
          to-the-DAT   study   register
          'I'd like to register for study.'

Sentence (50) illustrates the locational sense of *zu*, which is similar to the first set of one-way DAT prepositions discussed earlier. Sentences (51-52), however, would appear to pose a problem, since the TR of the preposition in each is conceived to move along a path (which is abstractly construed in (52)) towards a goal-like LM. In order to accommodate the use of DAT with this sense of *zu* we must recall the point made earlier in section 4 that, in the one-way prepositional realm, ACC is only compatible with prepositions which involve actual or implied contact of the TR with the boundary of the LM itself. Note that in (51) actual contact with the LM is not implied - the TR is only construed to enter a region associated with the LM. In order to satisfy the meaning of *zu* in this sentence the TR of the preposition need only get close to the LM. In (52), the ACC configuration is not met because the LM is construed as a relatively diffuse or abstract region without well-defined boundaries. In effect, any contact made by the TR with the LM in (52) is of lesser salience than the terminus of the implied path in the vicinity of the LM (which motivates DAT). Generally speaking, the semantics of *zu* departs significantly enough from the ACC prototype to plausibly motivate DAT.

To sum up this section, note that the use of DAT with the three subtypes of prepositions reflects three subtypes of DAT, all of which variously instantiate the prototypical DAT sense which signifies a departure from the ACC prototype. I do not take these three subtypes as meaning extensions per se, since the DAT prototype as I defined it at the beginning of the paper is broad enough to subsume each subtype.

6.   Clausal uses of DAT and ACC case

In the clausal realm DAT and ACC indicate how various entities are conceived to interact with each other in domains involving actions profiled by verbs rather than in locative relationships profiled by prepositions. The purpose of this section is to survey how the ACC and DAT prototypes proposed earlier can be used to motivate the meaningfulness of the cases across a representative sampling of construction types in the realm of actions and events.[9] I will focus on justifying the semantic notions of *asymmetry* and *bilateral involvement* as the primary motivators of ACC and DAT, respectively, in the clausal realm (though contact and completeness are still relevant in motivating clausal ACC in many situations).

Let us first briefly consider how speakers look at actions and events on the clausal level. They prototypically conceive of interactions among entities to involve the transferal of energy from one participant to another along a chain of asymmetrical interactions, which are conceived to occur within a setting of some type (though whether the setting is linguistically specified depends on the situation). Langacker (1987b) introduces the notion of an *action chain* as a speaker-constructed model of how entities interact in the world or in the realm of mental experience. Action chains represent the flow of force and energy from one participant to another in a conceived event.

Identifying the participant role status (such as agent, patient, experiencer) of the entities in a conceived sequence of interactions along the action chain is the crucial first step in imposing order on an event. Once this has been accomplished, part of the action chain is selected for profiling (and thus designation via linguistic coding). Simple finite clauses usually profile processes construed as constituting single events which can be isolated within a complex series of participant interactions along the chain, although occasionally a finite clause will restrict itself to only a portion of a single event (depending on the particular imagery involved).

In German, as in many other languages, both case marking and grammatical relations can indicate information about relationships between entities in the profiled portion of the action chain, with the cases generally assigned as follows: nominative case (NOM) tends to mark agents in canonical active clauses, DAT prototypically marks experiencers (more about which later), and ACC tends to mark patients in prototypically asymmetrical actions.[10]

As was the case with the completeness notion, the *asymmetry* notion is also derivable from the prototypical ACC contact image schema, since it is apparent that the path traced by a TR as it comes into contact with a LM in the prepositional realm (which essentially describes the prototypical ACC contact image) is conceptually similar to the asymmetric flow of force along an action chain from one entity to another. That is, ACC-marked prepositional LMs are conceptually related to the ACC-marked participants (direct objects) which are conceived as maximally-affected patients (as opposed to agents) in highly asymmetrical interactions. The asymmetry sense evoked by clausal ACC thus represents a semantic extension from the prototypical ACC image to a new and more complex domain. The asymmetry sense in turn serves to sanction the use of ACC in situations not strongly evoking physical contact between TR and LM.

I use the term *bilateral involvement* to refer to the two-sided nature of DAT participants in the clause: i.e. the tendency of clausal DAT to mark participants which are less patient-like and therefore either actually or potentially capable of independent action in their own right, a state of affairs which diverges substantially from the clausal ACC notion. The bilateral involvement notion, which is schematic for a variety of instantiations in different construction types within the clause (especially the *experiencer* prototype in ditransitive constructions), is itself yet another instantiation of the prototypical DAT notion (i.e. departure from ACC in general).

6.1. Clausal ACC

Concrete examples like the following can help to illustrate how prepositional and clausal ACC are related:

(53)   *Der   Mann   hat   den   Tisch   geschlagen.*
       the   man   has   the-ACC   table   hit
       'The man hit the table.'

(54)   *Der   Junge   hat   den   Ball   geworfen.*
       the   boy   has   the-ACC   ball   thrown
       'The boy threw the ball.'

(55)   *Das   Kind   hat   das   Glas   zerbrochen.*
            the   child   has   the-ACC   glass   broken
            'The child broke the glass.'

As was the case with the TRs and LMs of prepositions, the fact that the
TRs of the action verbs in these data are conceived to make *contact* with
the LMs is a crucial factor in motivating ACC marking on the LMs, which
are conceptually similar here to prepositional LMs. But whereas in the
prepositional realm the notion of contact is primary, in the clausal
realm other factors derivable from the notion of contact may arise as
equally important in motivating ACC to mark verbal LMs. The above
data illustrate important aspects of these additional factors, in that each
sentence additionally evokes the flow of force from the TR along a path
(or action chain), which results in the transfer of energy to the passively
construed LM. The type of effect exerted by the TRs upon the patient-
LMs varies in each example, however: no effect in (53), change of
position in (54), or change of state in (55). It should be noted, however,
that any movement or change on the part of the LMs is strictly
involuntary (resulting from the energy transmitted from the TRs) and is
not attributable to any independent potential within these entities.

   The notion of asymmetry which is derivable from the contact images
evoked in (53-55) reflects the fact that there are substantial differences
between the participants with regard to volitionality, inherent energy
potential of the TRs relative to the LMs, and their ability to transfer this
energy, etc. In each of the clauses these agent-like characteristics are
the exclusive possession of the TRs, while the LMs are conceived as
inherently passive recipients of the action instigated by the TRs. The
profiled interactions are thus highly asymmetrical.

   The asymmetry notion is important in the clausal realm because it is
schematic for a wide variety of interactions in more abstract contexts,
especially in those where overt physical contact is either downplayed or
completely absent, but where agent-patient asymmetry is nevertheless
evident. An instantiation of the asymmetry notion in which the sense of
a path-like TR making overt contact with the LM is downplayed can be
seen in the following clause:

(56)   *Ich   habe   einen   Brief   geschrieben.*
            I   have   a-ACC   letter   written
            'I wrote a letter.'

Here ACC is semantically compatible with a situation where the LM (an effected object) is conceived to be created via the TR's exertions. In this sentence the asymmetry between the energetic TR and the passive object of his creation is more important than the contact between TR and LM.

In even more abstract contexts, such as the realm of mental thoughts and events, the asymmetric notion of transference of energy from TR to LM is still evident, albeit in a figurative or abstract sense:

(57)   *Hans*   *erzählte*   *eine*   *Geschichte.*
           Hans   told   a-ACC   story
           'Hans told a story.'

(58)   *Der Linguist*   *hat*   *einen*   *Satz*   *formuliert.*
           the   linguist   has   a-ACC   sentence   formulated
           'The linguist formulated a sentence.'

Note in (57) how the asymmetric relationship is one in which the TR is a volitional, intellectual source transferring the passive, inanimate LM to unnamed persons, and in (58) the LM is conceived as an abstract effected object.

The asymmetry notion also plays a role in abstract situations not necessarily evoking energy transfer per se, where the TR is conceived as a type of experiencer (coded in NOM) which engages in some sort of mental activity:

(59)   *Wir*   *haben*   *einen*   *guten*   *Film*   *gesehen.*
           we   have   a-ACC   good   film   seen
           'We saw a good film.'

(60)   *Der Student*   *versteht*   *die*   *Aufgabe.*
           the   student   understands   the-ACC   exercise
           'The student understands the exercise.'

In these data the TRs of the verbs are experiencers conceived as origins of mental activity which is directed from the experiencer along a perceptual path which makes abstract contact with the objects of perception (the LMs). The LMs themselves (inanimate entities) are not conceived to be potential agents or loci of physical or mental energy.[11]

Data like the following illustrate how the completeness notion developed earlier can also motivate clausal ACC:

(61)   *Hans   ging   einen   langen   Weg.*
         Hans   went   a-ACC   long   way
         'Hans went a long way.'

(62)   *Ich   habe   den   ganzen   Tag   gearbeitet.*
         I   have   the-ACC   whole   day   worked
         I worked the whole day.'

The ACC-marked noun phrases in these sentences represent the overt coding of the *setting* within which the profiled activities take place. It is clear from the meanings of the sentences that not only are the activities conceived to occur within the indicated settings, but that they are conceived to extend throughout the space (61) or time (62) designated by the postverbal noun phrases. We can think of the activities in these sentences as continuing (in a directed sense) until they terminate at the boundaries of the settings. The conception that the activities fill up the settings evokes the completeness sense of ACC.

A similar analysis can account for the ACC noun phrases in cognate object constructions like the following:

(63)   *Er   lebt   ein   trauriges   Leben.*
         he   lives   a-ACC   sad   life
         'He lives a sad life.'

(64)   *Er   schlief den   Schlaf   des   Gerechten.*
         he   slept   the-ACC   sleep   the   just
         'He slept the sleep of the just.'

The cognate object phrases in these sentences describe in nominal form the processes profiled by the verbs themselves. We can thus construe a cognate object as a setting for the process profiled by the verb in the limiting case where the setting is identical to the process itself. ACC is motivated because the process is conceived to extend up to the limits of its own boundary (evoked by the cognate object). The extent of the process is trivially co-terminal with its own endpoint.

6.2.   Clausal DAT

The function of DAT in the clausal realm appears to center around the role of *experiencer*, perhaps the most frequent instantiation of the bilateral involvement notion in the clausal realm. This role serves as a clause-level prototype in its own right for a variety of participants in conceived events which display experiencer-like characteristics, but which may diverge somewhat from prototypical experiencers. Prototypical experiencers tend to be animate, human, and actual or potential loci of either physical or mental energy/activity of various sorts which themselves are conceived to be affected in some way by the flow of energy along the action chain. It is this two-sided nature of experiencers which instantiates the bilateral involvement notion.

In this section I will survey the occurrence of DAT in three main varieties of constructions, each with participants coded in DAT which evoke the notion of bilateral involvement.

6.2.1.   Three-place constructions involving DAT

The following data illustrate the use of DAT in ditransitive (three-place) constructions in which the DAT participant is conceived as a possessor:

(65)   *Hans   gab   mir   ein   Buch.*
        Hans   gave   me-DAT   a-ACC   book
        'Hans gave me a book.'

(66)   *Hans   erzählte   mir   eine   Geschichte.*
        Hans   told   me-DAT   a-ACC   story
        'Hans told me a story.'

(67)   *Inge   hat   mir   Geld   genommen.*
        Inge   has   me-DAT   money   taken
        'Inge took money from me.'

Possessors are good examples of experiencers because their active and passive qualities are fairly easy to identify. In each clause the DAT entities are conceived to exert control over their immediate spheres of influence (active property) while simultaneously being acted upon (passive property) by the perceived movement of something along the action chain either into (65-66) or out of (67) that control.

The next sentence illustrates a slightly different type of experiencer, especially with regard to its active characteristics:

(68)   *Fritz   öffnete   der   Dame die   Tür.*
        Fritz   opened   the-DAT   lady   the-ACC   door
        'Fritz opened the door for the lady.'

Here the active aspect of the DAT participant is a sphere of interest which is less intense than a sphere of control or possession, but which nevertheless is of importance to the person. The passive sense of being affected by the verbal activity is essentially analogous to that discussed in (65-67).

Sometimes DAT experiencers may be coded alternatively in ACC, with a concomitant difference in meaning:

(69) a.   *Der   Lehrer   fragt   dem   Kind*
           the   teacher   asks   the-DAT   child
           die   Wörter   ab.
           the   words   from
           'The teacher quizzes the child on the words.'
           (the teacher may not know what the child knows and
           asks the child to inform him)
     b.   *Der   Lehrer   fragt   das   Kind*
           the   teacher   asks   the-ACC   child
           die   Wörter   ab.
           the   words   from
           'The teacher quizzes the child on the words.'
           (the teacher knows the answer and quizzes the child,
           as if in a test situation)

This example nicely illustrates how a difference in imagery can be reflected by choice in case. In both versions the teacher is the agent who initiates the questioning activity, with the child affected by this activity (passive property). The DAT and ACC variants differ with respect to the knowledge held by the child. The use of DAT in (69a) accentuates the bilateral involvement of the child in the situation, in that it plays up the possibility that the child has an active potential (i.e. knows something) not available to the teacher. The upshot is that in the DAT version the relative power of the teacher and child is more balanced than in the ACC version, wherein the use of ACC in (69b) accentuates the asymmetrical nature of an interaction in which a highly potent agent exerts an affect on a powerless patient.

6.2.2.   Two-place constructions involving DAT

Data of the following type involve DAT-marked experiencer nominals in two-place constructions which differ from the three-way constructions considered earlier in that they are static and do not involve the transmission of energy along the action chain:

(70)   *Das Buch   gefällt   mir.*
         the   book   pleases   me-DAT
         'The book pleases me.'
(71)   *Das   ist   mir   ein   Rätsel.*
         that   is   me-DAT   a   riddle
         'That is a riddle to me.'

The relation holding between the DAT experiencer and the other nominal in the clause is not asymmetrically construed in these examples. The DAT experiencers are bilaterally involved to the extent that they perceive some other entity in their immediate proximity which then invokes an involuntary reaction in the form of psychological or mental activity of some sort. Note that it is not easy here to identify which aspects of the experiencers are active and which are passive (as was done earlier for the experiencer prototype). This represents a slight extension from the prototype which abstracts away from the importance of the active/passive dichotomy to the simple fact of the two-sided participation of the experiencer in the clausal profile, which is encoded by DAT.

The following examples are similar to (70) and (71), except that processes or activities (rather than just entities) are conceived to affect the experiencers:

(72)   *Dem   Kind   brennt   der   Rücken.*
         the-DAT   child   burns   the   back
         'The child's back burns (is sunburned).'
(73)   *Mir   schmilzt   das   Eis.*
         me-DAT   melts   the   ice cream
         'My ice cream is melting.'

Again, the activity profiled by the verb exerts an effect upon the experiencer which produces a reaction of some sort, with both the effect and the reaction relevant for coding. Thus, the bilateral nature of the experiencer's role in the clause is marked by DAT.

Not all uses of DAT in the clausal realm necessarily stem from the experiencer prototype. A number of German verbs with the prefix *ent-* have clear separation senses and take DAT objects, as illustrated by the following:

(74)   *Hans   entstammt   einer   großen   Familie.*
       Hans   comes from   a-DAT   big   family
       'Hans comes from a big family.'

(75)   *Das Wort   ist   ihm   entfallen.*
       the   word   is   him-DAT   escaped
       'The word escapes him (he can't remember).'

In these sentences the verb profiles a relation in which the TR becomes separated from the LM, which is a clear departure from the ACC contact image (recall the one-way prepositional data with *aus* and *von*). In a somewhat similar vein, the following sentence also departs from the ACC prototype, but slightly differently than in (74-75) above:

(76)   *Der Zug   näherte   sich   dem   Bahnhof.*
       the   train   approached   REFL   the-DAT   station
       'The train approached the station.'

Here the path followed by the verbal TR is never conceived to make actual contact with the LM.

Many other uses of DAT are clear extensions from the experiencer prototype. Data like the following, in which the DAT participants are not construed as passive or patient-like but rather as actually or potentially potent in their own right, illustrate two types of extension:

(77)   *Der Polizist   folgt   dem   Dieb.*
       the   policeman   follows   the-DAT   thief
       'The policeman is following the thief.'

(78)   *Der Mann   hilft   mir.*
       the   man   helps   me-DAT
       'The man is helping me.'

In these sentences the DAT nominals are entities which receive or are affected by energy (transmitted by the NOM agents) which stimulates some type of reaction in them, though the reaction is not necessarily psychological (as it tends to be for experiencers). In (77) the reaction is one of movement on the part of the DAT entity, which is conceived to move on its own. Thus, some experiencers are conceived as *movers*. In (78) the stimulation exerted on the DAT entity by the NOM agent results in the former's ability to effect some further activity on its own. Such extensions can be thought of as *secondary actors*. Again, both movers and secondary actors are types of extensions from the experiencer prototype.

Another type of extension from the experiencer prototype is illustrated in the following data, wherein the verbs evoke situations involving the exertion of power over an individual and that individual's response to that power or control. Note that in spite of the fact that they receive some type of abstract energy from the subjects of the verbs, the DAT entities are not construed as wholly passive or patient-like, but as inherently higher in status than the NOM entities (the subjects) with respect to trustworthiness (79) or power (80):

(79)   *Ich   glaube   dir.*[12]
        I-NOM   believe   you-DAT
        'I believe you.'
(80)   *Der   Mann   gehorcht   ihr.*
        the-NOM   man   obeys   her-DAT
        'The man obeys her.'

Rather than profiling the asymmetrical exertion of power or influence from the higher status entity to the lower status entity, these verbs profile a complementary relation in which some aspect of the reaction of the lower status entity to this control is designated. Thus, in (79) the TR of the verb (the NOM entity) attributes a greater degree of knowledge or ability to the LM (the DAT entity) than it assumes for itself. This attribution involves the transmission of abstract energy by the TR towards the LM, which is conceived as a goal of the TR's mental activity of believing. Thus, one aspect of the DAT entity's bilateral involvement in this interaction (i.e. its patient-like aspect) is that it is conceived to be affected by the TR's mental activity. The other, non-patient-like, aspect of the DAT entity's bilateral involvement is its perceived higher status or potency in the interaction. Similarly, the situation in (80) is one in which, objectively speaking, the NOM entity is actually conceived to be under the control of the DAT entity, but the verb *gehorchen* profiles the aspect of the relationship taken from the less powerful participant's point of view. The use of DAT (as opposed to ACC) to mark the LMs of these verbs accentuates their inherent greater potency in comparison to the TRs.

Finally, consider data like the following involving resemblance between two entities:

(81)   *Der Mann ähnelt   seinem   Vater.*
       the   man   resembles   his-DAT   father
       'The man resembles his father.'

The use of DAT plays up the essentially equal status of the two entities, as well as the lack of an asymmetrical relation holding between them.

6.2.3.   One-place constructions involving DAT

In this final section I will discuss a few examples illustrating the use of DAT in one-place constructions (commonly called impersonal experiencer constructions), which employ verbs evoking psychological feelings or attitudes on the part of the experiencer:

(82)   *Es   ist   mir   kalt.*
      it   is   me-DAT   cold
      'I'm cold.'   (lit. it's cold to me)
(83)   *Es   ist   mir   angst   und   bange*
      it   is   me-DAT   fear   and   afraid
      'I'm afraid.'   (lit. it's scary to me)
(84)   *Es   schwindelt   ihm.*
      it   dizzies   him-DAT
      'He is dizzy.'
(85)   *Es   graut   mir   vor   der   Prüfung.*
      it   scares   me-DAT   before   the   test
      'I'm scared of the test.'

The general sense in each sentence is that the DAT entity undergoes a psychological experience which is externally induced and is not intentional.

    Note that except for the pronominal subject *es* 'it', the DAT entities in these data are the only nominals not governed by prepositions. The pronominal *es* is often regarded as a meaningless filler item (a dummy subject) whose purpose is purely grammatical: to keep the conjugated verb from occurring in initial position in neutral statements.

    If the pronominal *es* in these constructions is analyzed to be meaningful, then it is the plausible source of the inducing stimulus. The most plausible way of attributing meaning to this element is to propose that it profiles the *setting* (in its most abstract sense) within which the indicated activities are conceived to take place (cf. Bolinger 1973). My claim is that in constructions of this sort speakers construe the setting as an actual participant in the action. This participant - a maximally unspecified energy source - is conceived to impose a type of abstract outside force on the experiencer which in turn induces an internal feeling, reaction, thought, etc. within the experiencer.

Given these points, the bilateral involvement on the part of the DAT entity is obvious: it is affected from without by the abstract force represented by *es* and exhibits internal psychological reactions which depend on this stimulus.

7. Conclusions

I hope to have shown how DAT and ACC can be motivated as meaningful across a representative sampling of construction types in German. I think the weight of evidence is convincing that the cases encode conceptual categories which play a crucial part in structuring how speakers construe actions and events. Such results cast serious doubt on linguistic theories which assume the autonomy of grammar and help support the essential correctness of the cognitive program.

Notes

1. This paper overviews the main topics from my doctoral dissertation (Smith 1987), aspects of which appeared in a preliminary version in Smith (1985). The reader should note that space limitations for the paper required the elimination (or at most cursory treatment) of much detail and supporting discussion which strengthen the points made. For a cognitive analysis of cases in Czech and Russian, see Janda (1988), as well as Jakobson ([1971]) for a classic treatment of the Russian case system in the verbal realm.
2. See both Smith (1987) and Smith (1988) for a more detailed account of the topics in this section.
3. Note that in the data cited I will omit any identifying grammatical material (such as cases, tense, etc.) in the interlinear glosses which is not specifically under discussion. Note also that certain English translations of the German examples may seem stylistically awkward. In such cases I have tried to render as accurately as possible the meaning of the German examples according to my native informants' intuitions, rather than strive for good English.
4. See Smith (1987: chap. 2), for discussion of yet another class of verbs in German (*restricted profile verbs*) which are compatible only with DAT. I omit them here because the sense of DAT with these verbs is essentially the same as for the endpoint focus verbs.

5.   See Langacker (1986) for more detailed discussion of abstract motion.
6.   Note that no overt case marking occurs with *bis*, but native speaker intuition confirms that ACC is implied.
7.   Readers familiar with German will probably wonder about yet another use of *nach*, one which does seem to evoke a path-like sense from TR to LM. This is its use in sentences like *Hans fährt nach England* 'Hans is traveling to England'. While there is no overt case morphology following *nach* in sentences of this type, native speaker intuition holds that it still "feels DAT". What seems to be going on is that this apparent goal-oriented use of *nach* departs significantly from the prototypical ACC contact image, in that the LM is a large geographical location without sharply defined boundaries, in contrast to earlier examples involving ACC prepositions with smaller, or more discrete LMs with clearly defined boundaries. In addition, *nach* seems to evoke a directional path without a clear-cut sense that the goal is actually reached (in contrast to the ACC preposition *bis*). The interested reader is directed to Smith (1987) for a more fully developed treatment of *nach*.
8.   Note that in this example DAT is marked on the noun *Haus* (by the vowel *-e*) rather than on an article.
9.   Anderson's book (1971) is an insightful precursor to my analysis of clausal case, as is Jakobson ([1971]).
10. I omit here discussion of how the cases correlate with grammatical relations, as well as analysis of the *nominative* case, which I will simply assume to mark the most prominent participant in the clause. See Langacker (1987b) and Smith (1987) for more detailed discussion of these matters.
11. Cf. data in section 6.2.2. below for a different sort of imagery involving DAT rather than NOM experiencers.
12. Note that it is also possible to say *Ich glaube sie* 'I believe it' (where *glauben* takes an ACC object) if the object pronoun refers to an inanimate object, such as *Geschichte* 'story'. The use of ACC to mark an inanimate object with this verb is completely consistent with the analysis presented here, since one would expect ACC for LMs conceived as passive recipients of the action instigated by the verbal TR.

References

Anderson, John M.
1971   *The grammar of case: Towards a localistic theory*. Cambridge: Cambridge University Press.
Bolinger, Dwight
1973   "Ambient it is meaningful too", *Journal of Linguistics* 9: 261-270.
Jakobson, Roman
1936   "Beitrag zur allgemeinen Kasuslehre: Gesamtbedeutung der russischen Kasus", *Travaux du Cercle Linguistique de Prague* 6: 240-283.
[1971]   [reprinted in *Selected writings II*. The Hague: Mouton, 23-71].
Janda, Laura A.
1988   "Pragmatic vs. semantic uses of case", *Chicago Linguistic Society* 24, Part I, 189-202.

Johnson, Mark
   1987   *The body in the mind: The bodily basis of meaning, imagination, and reason*. Chicago: University of Chicago Press.

Lakoff, George
   1987   *Women, fire, and dangerous things: What categories reveal about the mind*. Chicago: University of Chicago Press.

Langacker, Ronald W.
   1986   "Abstract motion", *Berkeley Linguistics Society* 12, 455-471.
   1987a   *Foundations of cognitive grammar*, Vol. 1. *Theoretical prerequisites*. Stanford: Stanford University Press.
   1987b   "Transitivity, case, and grammatical relations: A cognitive grammar prospectus". Duisburg: LAUD Series A 172.
   1988   "A view of linguistic semantics", in: Brygida Rudzka-Ostyn (ed.), *Topics in cognitive linguistics*. (Current Issues in Linguistic Theory 50) Amsterdam: Benjamins, 49-90.

Smith, Michael B.
   1985   "Event chains, grammatical relations, and the semantics of case in German", *Chicago Linguistic Society* 21, Part 1, 388-407.
   1987   The semantics of dative and accusative in German: An investigation in cognitive grammar. [Unpublished Ph.D. Dissertation, University of California, San Diego.]
   1988   "The semantics of case-assignment by two-way prepositions in German: Toward an empirically more adequate account", in: Elmer H. Antonsen & Hans Henrich Hock (eds.), *Germanic linguistics II: Papers from the second symposium on Germanic linguistics* (University of Illinois at Urbana-Champaign, 3-4 October 1986). Bloomington: Indiana University Linguistics Club, 123-132.

A cognitive account
of Samoan <u>lavea</u> and <u>galo</u> verbs

Kenneth William Cook

1. Introduction

This paper presents a cognitive analysis of Samoan *lavea* and *galo* verbs.[1] These two verb types have previously been grouped together under the rubric of "stative verbs", but there is both semantic and syntactic evidence that they form two separate classes. The paper is organized as follows: The latter part of this section introduces some of the assumptions, claims, and constructs of Cognitive Grammar; section 2 applies some of these constructs in a brief description of Samoan intransitive, middle, transitive, and passive clauses; 3 establishes that *galo* and *lavea* clauses (i.e. clauses containing *galo* and *lavea* verbs) differ one from the other both semantically and syntactically; 4 analyzes *galo* clauses and proposes that certain of these clauses are instances of what Langacker (1986, 1987c, 1989) calls "the setting subject construction"; 5 describes *lavea* clauses and contrasts them with passive clauses; 6 gives an account of Clitic Placement and Equi (phenomena which distinguish *galo* and *lavea* clauses) based on semantic roles rather than grammatical relations; 7 summarizes the main points of these analyses and concludes with comments concerning the approach taken in this paper.

The assumptions, claims and constructs of the framework of Cognitive Grammar (Langacker 1982, 1987a, 1987c, 1989) that are relevant to the present discussion are given in (1).

(1) a. Encyclopedic (rather than truth-conditional) semantics is assumed.

   b. A prototype (rather than a criterial) model of linguistic meaning is assumed.

   c. The meaning of any linguistic expression (even a single morpheme) is referred to as a *predication*.

   d. Predications are characterized in terms of *cognitive domains*. Any conceptualization or knowledge system can function as a cognitive domain.

e.   The semantic value of a predication includes both its con-
      ceptual content and *imagery*, which is defined as how that
      content is construed. Active and passive pairs provide
      examples of situations construed in alternate ways. *The
      enemy destroyed the village* and *The village was destroyed by
      the enemy* have the same conceptual content but differ in
      how their content is construed.
f.   The *base* (or *scope*) of a predication is the portion of a
      domain relative to which the predication is characterized.
g.   Every predication *profiles* (or *designates*) some substructure
      as maximally prominent with respect to the base. This de-
      signated substructure is referred to as the *profile* of the
      predication.
h.   *Relational predications* (i.e. verbs, adjectives, and pre-
      positions) profile the interconnections among different fa-
      cets of a conceived situation.
i.   Relational predications also single out one entity involved in
      a profiled relationship and make it the most prominent ent-
      ity within the profile. This entity is referred to as the *trajector*
      and is hypothesized to be the *figure* (as in *figure/ground
      organization*) within the relational profile. At the clausal
      level, the trajector (or figure) is the *subject*.
j.   The notions of transitivity, case, voice, and grammatical
      relations are characterized with respect to the *canonical-
      action model* diagrammed in (k). In this model, discrete,
      mobile *participants* interact with one another in a stable,
      inclusive *setting*. The general claim here is that our under-
      standing of grammatical relations, etc. is grounded in our
      everyday experience of the interaction of entities in the
      world around us (Langacker 1987c, 1989).

k.

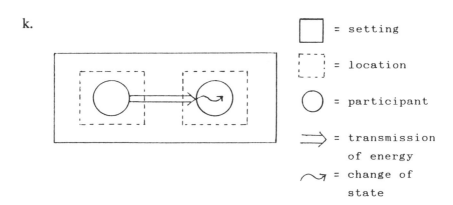

☐ = setting

⌐ ¬ = location
⌐ ¬
☐
L _ ⌐

◯ = participant

⟹ = transmission
of energy

∿ = change of
state

l.   In a *canonical action*, a human *agent* moves towards, makes contact with, and transmits energy to an inanimate *patient* which absorbs energy from the agent and thereby undergoes a change of state.

m.   A *prototypical transitive clause* codes the agent and patient of a canonical action as subject and object, respectively. Departures from this prototype involve either a noncanonical action or a marked coding of the action. Examples of departures from a canonical action include events which occur in a domain of perception or social interaction rather than in a physical domain.

n.   In both transitive and passive clauses, the entire path from what DeLancey (1981) calls the *initial participant* (IP) to the *terminal participant* (TP) is profiled by the verb. (Profiling is indicated with darker lines.) A *transitive clause* codes an IP as subject and a TP as object. A *passive clause* codes a TP as subject and an IP as optional oblique (i.e. neither subject nor object). Passive provides an example of a marked coding in that the TP rather than the IP is chosen as subject. Diagram (2a) corresponds to transitive clause (3a), and (2b) to passive clause (3b).

(2)   a.   IP   TP

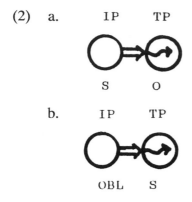

S   O

   b.   IP   TP

OBL   S

(3)   a.   *The enemy destroyed the village.*
      b.   *The village was destroyed by the enemy.*

2.   Samoan clause types

I will now describe Samoan intransitive, middle, transitive, and passive clauses, using some of the constructs introduced in the last section. With respect to Samoan case marking and grammatical relations, I will be assuming the statements in (4) throughout this paper.[2]

(4)   a.   Case marking indicates semantic roles. In Samoan, absolutive and ergative are "macro semantic roles". An *absolutive* is a theme, i.e. a patient, experiencer, mover, or zero (an entity that does not act or have an experience and is not acted upon). An *ergative* is a profiled participant at the head of a path leading to an absolutive.
      b.   Word order is determined by grammatical relations. Samoan word order is Verb Subject Object Oblique.
      c.   Every clause (with the exception of subjectless weather and temporal clauses) has a subject.[3]

In (5-8), we have examples of Samoan intransitive, middle, transitive, and passive clauses and their corresponding construals. In (5), which is intransitive, a mover moves towards a location. The single arrow indicates motion.

Middle clauses contain middle verbs, i.e. verbs of emotion, perception, cognition, communication and social interaction. In middle clause

(6), an experiencer directs attention towards a zero TP. The dotted arrow in (6) represents a path of perception. The events profiled by middle verbs are "middle" in that they share characteristics with both transitive and intransitive events. Like transitive events, they profile a path from an initial to a terminal participant, but unlike transitive events, they do not profile transmission of energy. They share this lack of transmission of energy with intransitive events. The subject of a middle clause is in the absolutive and the complement is in the locative or directional case.

Both transitive and passive clauses (7) and (8) profile a transitive event, but they differ in how such an event is construed. Transitive clause (7) codes the IP of the event as subject and passive clause (8) codes the TP as subject. The word order and morphology of the clause types in (5-8) are summarized in (9).

(5) a.   *E   alu   le   tama   'i   le   fale'oloa.* (intrans.)
           IMP   go   the   boy   DIR   the   store
           'The boy is going to the store.'

     b.

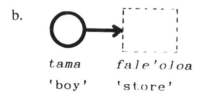

       tama   *fale'oloa*
       'boy'   'store'

(6) a.   *'O lo'o   fa'alogo   le   amu 'i   le   faiâ'oga.* (mid.)
           PROG   listen   the   boy DIR   the   teacher
           'The boy is listening to the teacher.'

     b.

       tama   *faiâ'oga*
       'boy'   'teacher'

(7) a.   *Na   tipi   e   le   tama le   ufi.* (trans.)
           PAST   cut   ERG   the   boy the   yam
           'The boy cut the yam.'

b.

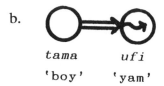

    tama   ufi
    'boy'   'yam'

(8) a. *Na   tipi   le   ufi   e   le   tama.* (passive)
         PAST   cut   the   yam   ERG   the   boy
         'The yam was cut by the boy.'

b.

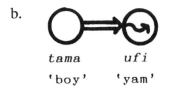

    tama   ufi
    'boy'   'yam'

(9) a. intransitive   verb subject
                           absolutive
     b. middle   verb subject   compl.
                    absolutive dir/loc
     c. transitive verb subject   object
                    ergative   absolutive
     d. passive   verb subject   oblique
                    absolutive ergative

My reasons for believing that (7) and (8) are transitive and passive, respectively, concern word order and the Samoan version of Quantifier Float. As illustrated in (10), in clauses with a full nominal subject, the general tendency is for the subject to immediately follow the verb, except for the possible intervention of short adverbial phrases as in (10a). This observation, which is in agreement with assumption (4b), suggests that the first nominal after the verb in (7) and (8) is also the subject. If (7) and (8) are, respectively, transitive and passive, then their analysis as given in (9c) and (9d) will conform to this word order generalization.

(10) a. *'Ua   ô   mai   tamaiti   mai*
         PERF   come   hither   children   from
         le   â'oga.
         the   school
         'The children have come from the school.'

b.   *'O lo'o   tâ'a'alo   tamaiti   i   le   paka.*
     PROG   play   children   LOC   the   park
     'The children are playing in the park.'

c.   *Na   'ote   le   faiâ'oga   'i   le   tama.*
     PAST   scold   the   teacher   DIR   the   boy
     'The teacher scolded the boy.'

My second reason for believing that (7) and (8) are, respectively, transitive and passive has to do with the Samoan version of Quantifier Float, which is given in (11):

(11)   Quantifier Float: subjects and absolutives can be
         bound by the postverbal quantifier *'uma* 'all'.[4]

Given (11), if a nominal cannot be bound by postverbal *'uma*, it is not a subject (nor is it an absolutive). (12a) and (12b) illustrate that ergatives in verb-erg-abs clauses such as (7) can be bound by postverbal *'uma*, but those in verb-abs-erg clauses such as (8) cannot. Hence, the ergative in a verb-erg-abs clause is a subject and the ergative in a verb-abs-erg clause is not. (12c) and (12d) illustrate that absolutives can be bound by postverbal quantifier *'uma* in both verb-erg-abs and verb-abs-erg clauses. The facts of (12) are summarized in (13).[5]

(12) a.   *E   uli   'uma$_i$ e   a'u   uô$_i$*
       IMP   drive   all   ERG   my   friend
       la'u   ta'avale.
       my   car
       'My friends all drive my car.'

     b.   **E   uli   'uma$_i$ la'u   ta'avale   e*
       IMP   drive   all   my   car   ERG
       a'u   uô$_i$.
       my   friend
       (My car is driven by all my friends.)

     c.   *Na   'ave   'uma$_i$ e   le   tama   tusi$_i$.*
       PAST   take   all   ERG   the   boy   book
       'The boy took all the books.'

     d.   *Na   'ave   'uma$_i$ tusi$_i$ e   le   tama.*
       PAST   take   all   book   ERG   the   boy
       'The books were all taken by the boy.'

(13) a.   transitive   verb   SUBJECT   OBJECT
                                        ERGATIVE   ABSOLUTIVE
     b.   passive   verb   SUBJECT   oblique
                                        ABSOLUTIVE   ergative
           [CAPS = can be bound by postverbal *'uma*]

My reasoning as to why (9c) is passive is specifically as follows. If every clause has one (and only one) subject, and subjects and absolutives can be bound by postverbal *'uma*, then if only one nominal in a clause can be bound by postverbal *'uma*, it must be the subject. Thus since only the absolutive of a clause like (9c) can be bound by postverbal *'uma*, it must be the subject, and the clause, according to the definition of a passive clause in (1n), must be passive.

3.   Differences between <u>lavea</u> and <u>galo</u> clauses

In addition to the clause types in (9), there are at least two other types, those containing *lavea* verbs and those containing *galo* verbs. *Lavea* means 'be hurt' and *galo* means 'forget' or 'be forgotten'. (14a) and (14b) give examples of *galo* and *lavea* clauses.

(14) a.   *'Ua   galo   le   tusi   i   le   tama.*
           PERF   forget   the   book   LOC   the   boy
           'The book has been forgotten by the boy.'
     b.   *'Ua   lavea   le   teine   i   le   tama.*
           PERF   hurt   the   girl   LOC   the   boy
           'The girl has been hurt by the boy.'[6]

These two classes of verbs have previously been grouped together under the rubric of "stative verbs". However, as I have pointed out in Cook (1987, 1988), there is evidence that these verbs do indeed form two separate classes.

Semantically, the two verb-types differ in that *lavea* verbs profile events that affect a patient or experiencer or the state that results from such an event, while *galo* verbs are verbs of understanding, forgetting and responsibility. (15) gives a list of *galo* verbs:

(15) *galo* verbs

mâlamalama	'be bright (as the sun is bright), understand'
manino	'be clear, understand'
masino	'know, be known exactly'
galo	'forget'
nimo	'forget, disappear'
lilo	'disappear, be beyond one's comprehension'
pa'û	'fall (said of a responsibility)'
pogai	'stem from, be due to, be caused by'
mâfua	'originate from, be caused by'

Most *galo* verbs have other (more basic) meanings and/or can be used in other clause types. For example, *mâlamalama* 'bright' and *manino* 'clear' can also be used as adjectives and as middle verbs. *Pa'û* literally means 'fall' and is regularly used in that sense. *Galo* itself is probably cognate with *gâlo* 'disappear'. *Nimo* and *lilo* literally mean 'disappear'. Thus the general situation here is that the basic meaning of some verb or adjective is extended from a physical domain of objects disappearing, lighting up, etc. to more abstract ones of mental experiences and responsibilities.[7] (16) lists *lavea* verbs:

(16)

noun/adjective		*lavea* verb	
lavelave	'tangled'	*lavea*	'be hurt'
fa'alavelave	'complication'	*fa'alavelavea*	'be busy'
afâ	'storm'	*afâtia*	'be struck by a storm'
papa'u	'shallow'	*pâ'ulia*	'run aground'
pô	'night'	*pogia*	'be overcome by night'
timu	'rain'	*timu'ia*	'be rained on'
ua	'rain'	*uaina*	'be rained on'
savili	'wind'	*saviligia*	'be affected by the wind'
lâ	'sun'	*lâina, lâ'ia*	'be exposed to the sun'
tîgâ	'pain'	*tîgâina*	'suffer'
pagâ	'trouble'	*pagâtia*	'be troubled'
manû	'good luck'	*manuia*	'be lucky, successful'
mamafa	'heavy'	*mâfatia*	'be overcome'
matapogi	'look frightening'	*matapogia*	'faint'

As pointed out in Cook (1988: 113ff), the suffix *Cia* ((Consonant)(*i*)*a* or *ina*) is involved in the derivation of many *lavea* verbs. (16), therefore, also gives the noun or adjective to which *Cia* is suffixed in the derivation of *lavea* verbs. *Lavea* verbs, however, are not limited to these derived forms. *(Ma'i)tô* 'get or be pregnant' and *manu'a* 'be wounded' are examples of *lavea* verbs that are not derived by means of the *Cia* suffix.

Lavea verbs are syntactically intransitive and, as mentioned above, they profile events that affect a TP or the states that result from such events.[8] The TP of a *lavea* clause is coded as an absolutive subject, and if the entity which is responsible for the state or event is coded, it is in the locative case, and not the ergative. This is illustrated in (17a). The entity which is responsible for the event is often the entity referred to by the noun that forms the stem of the *lavea* verb. For example, a storm (*afâ*) in (17b) is responsible for the event experienced by the traveling party. Such responsible entities are usually not prototypical agents. Most of the processes profiled by *lavea* verbs adversely affect the absolutive, but not all do: for example, *manuia* 'to experience good luck' (from *manû* 'good luck') designates an event in which the absolutive is favorably affected.

(17) a. *Na*   *lavea*   *le*   *teine*   *i/*e*   *le*   *tama.*
          PAST   hurt   the   girl   LOC/ERG   the   boy
          'The girl was hurt by the boy.'

     b. *'Ua*   *afâtia*   *le*   *malaga.*
          PERF   struck-by-storm   the   traveling party
          'The traveling party has been struck by a storm.'

Galo and *lavea* clauses also differ syntactically. (18) illustrates the fact that *galo* clauses are acceptable with both verb-loc-abs and verb-abs-loc word order. *Lavea* clauses with verb-abs-loc word order, however, are unacceptable:

(18) a. *'Ua*   *galo*   *le*   *tusi*   *i*   *le*   *tama.*
          PERF   forget   the   book   LOC   the   boy
          'The book has been forgotten by the boy.'

     b. *'Ua*   *galo*   *i*   *le*   *tama*   *le*   *tusi.*
          PERF   forget   LOC   the   boy   the   book
          'The boy has forgotten the book.'

     c. *'Ua*   *lavea*   *le*   *teine*   *i*   *le*   *tama.*
          PERF   hurt   the   girl   LOC   the   boy
          'The girl has been hurt by the boy.'

     d. *'Ua*   *lavea*   *i*   *le*   *tama*   *le*   *teine.*
          PERF   hurt   LOC   the   boy   the   girl
          The boy has hurt the girl.

(19) and (20) show that the absolute of a *lavea* clause undergoes Clitic Placement while that of a *galo* clause does not. Clitic Placement "moves" a particular postverbal pronoun into a position between the tense/aspect marker and the verb. In some cases the pronoun undergoes phonological reduction:

(19) a. 'Ua   lavea   a'u   i   le   masini.
         PERF   hurt   I   LOC the   machine
         'I have been hurt by the machine.'
     b. 'Ua   'ou   lavea   i   le   masini.
         PERF   I   hurt   LOC the   machine
         'I have been hurt by the machine.'
(20) a. 'Ua   galo   'oe   i   lou   'âiga.
         PERF   forget you   LOC your   family
         'You have been forgotten by your family.'
     b. *'Ua   'e   galo   i   lou   'âiga.
         PERF   you   forget LOC your   family
         (You have been forgotten by your family.)

As exemplified in (21), the absolute of a *lavea* clause can undergo Equi with the governing verb *mana'o* 'want', but the absolute of a *galo* clause cannot. In other words, the absolute of the embedded clause in (21a) can be omitted on the basis of identity with the matrix subject, but that in (21b) cannot:

(21) a. E   lê   mana'o   le   teine   e   lavea
         IMP   NEG   want   the   girl   INF   hurt
         i   le   tama.
         LOC   the   boy
         'The girl doesn't want to be hurt by the boy.'
     b. E   lê   mana'o   le   teine
         IMP   NEG   want   the   girl
         e   galo   *('o   ia)   i   le   tama.
         INF   forget   ABS   she   LOC   the   boy
         'The girl doesn't want to be forgotten by the boy.'

I will now consider it established that *galo* and *lavea* verbs form separate classes, and I will proceed to analyze *galo* and *lavea* clause types individually.

4.   <u>Galo</u> clauses and the setting subject construction

To facilitate the presentation of my analysis of *galo* clauses, I will first review Langacker's (1986, 1987b, 1989) analysis of the setting subject construction. I will then propose that certain *galo* clauses involve a similar construction. Clauses (22a) and (22b) and their corresponding diagrams in (23a) and (23b) are relevant for our discussion of the English version of the setting subject construction:

(22) a.   *Fleas are crawling all over my cat.*
      b.   *My cat is crawling with fleas.*

(23) a.   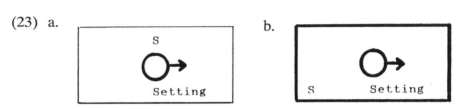   b.

Clause (22a) represents the unmarked choice of a participant as subject. The participant (the fleas) is chosen as subject, and the cat, which is the setting for the activity of the participant, is coded as an oblique. This is represented in diagram (23a). (The arrow represents the fact that the fleas are moving.) Clause (22b) is an instance of the setting subject construction. In this clause type, a marked choice of subject is made in that the setting (rather than the participant) is coded as subject. Since the setting is chosen as subject, it is naturally part of the verb's profile (cf. 23b). The verb then means something like 'be the setting for crawling'. The participant (the fleas) is part of the verbal profile in both construals.

One may ask at this point whether or not the participant in (22b) is a grammmatical object. If we make the standard assumption that a clause containing a subject and an object can passivize, the fact that clause (22b) cannot passivize provides evidence that the participant is not an object. This point is illustrated in (24):[9]

(24)   **Fleas are being crawled with by my cat.*

I propose that *galo* clauses have structures similar to those of (22a) and (22b). As stated above, *galo* verbs are verbs of understanding, forgetting, and responsibility. The entity which is forgotten, etc. is por-

trayed as a thematic participant that disappears, clears up, etc. within a
setting in the cognitive domain of mental experience or responsibility.
(25a) and (25b) illustrate the fact that this setting may be the person or
mind in which the understanding, etc. takes place, or it may be the locus
of responsibility for some state or event. As a setting, this locus of
cognition or responsibility is coded in the locative case.[10] The entity
that is forgotten, etc. is coded in the absolutive case. Schematically,
then, the construal associated with a *galo* clause can be represented as
in (26):

(25) a.   *'Ua*   *galo*   *i*   *lo'u*   *mâfaufau*   *le*   *mea*
         PERF   forget   LOC my   mind   the thing
         na   *tupu.*
         PAST   happen
         'My mind has forgotten what happened.'

     b.   *Na*   *mâfua*   *iate ia*   *le*   *fa'alavelave.*[11]
         PAST   originate   LOC him   the   trouble
         'He caused the trouble.'

(26)

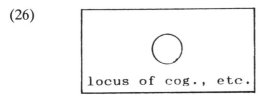

As shown above, *galo* clauses allow both verb-abs-loc and verb-loc-
abs word order. These two clause types, illustrated in (27), correspond
to the construals in (28). In (27a), the absolutive participant is coded as
subject. In (27b), the setting, i.e. the locus of cognition, is chosen as
subject. Only the participant is profiled in (28a), but in (28b), both the
participant and the locus of cognition are included in the profile:

(27) a.   *'Ua*   *galo*   *le*   *tusi*   *i*   *le*   *tama.*
         PERF   forget   the book   LOC   the boy
         'The book has been forgotten by the boy.'

     b.   *'Ua*   *galo*   *i*   *le*   *tama*   *le*   *tusi.*
         PERF   forget   LOC the boy   the book
         'The boy has forgotten the book.'

(28) a. 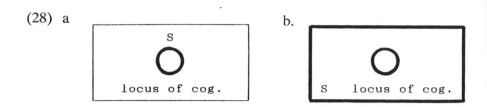 b.

My reasons for believing that the absolutive of (27a) and the locative of (27b) are subjects have to do with the assumptions and observations made above and repeated in (29):

(29) a.   All Samoan clauses (with the exception of subjectless weather and temporal clauses) have a subject.
   b.   Samoan word order is Verb Subject Object Oblique.[12]
   c.   Quantifier Float: subjects and absolutives can be bound by postverbal *'uma*.

Putting the assumptions and observations in (29) together leads to the test for subject given in (30):

(30) a.   If only one nominal of a clause can be bound by postverbal *'uma*, it is the subject.
   b.   If more than one nominal of a clause can be bound by postverbal *'uma*, the first nominal after the verb that can be bound by postverbal *'uma* is the subject.

As we have already seen, *galo* clauses occur in both verb-abs-loc and verb-loc-abs word order. The facts concerning *galo* clauses and Quantifier Float are illustrated in (31) and summarized in (32):

(31) a.   *'Ua   galo   'uma$_i$ tali$_i$ i   le   tama.*
         PERF   forget   all   answer   LOC   the   boy
         'The answers have all been forgotten by the boy.'
   b.   *'Ua   galo   'uma$_i$ i   le   tama   tali$_i$.*
         PERF   forget   all   LOC   the boy   answer
         'The boy has forgotten all the answers.'
   c.   *'Ua   galo   'uma$_i$ i   tamaiti$_i$ le   tali.*
         PERF   forget   all   LOC   children the   answer
         'The children have all forgotten the answer.'

d. *'Ua   galo   'uma_i   le   tali   i
    PERF   forget   all   the   answer   LOC
    tamaiti_i.
    children
    (The answer has been forgotten by all the children.)

(32) a.   verb   ABSOLUTIVE   locative
                       subject
     b.   verb   LOCATIVE   ABSOLUTIVE
                       subject
           [CAPS = can be bound by postverbal *'uma*]

Applying our test for subject given in (30) to the observations concerning word order and Quantifier Float in (32), we see that according to (30a), the absolutive of verb-abs-loc clauses must be the subject because it is the only nominal of that clause type that can be bound by postverbal *'uma*, and in accordance with (30b), the locative of verb-loc-abs clauses must be the subject of that clause type because it is the first nominal after the verb which can be bound by postverbal *'uma*.[13]

Now since clauses with the pattern in (32b) contain a subject and an absolutive, the question might come up as to whether the absolutive of such a clause is an object. I would say that it is not. If the absolutive of such a clause were an object, then the variant of *galo* that occurs in such a clause would be transitive, but I would not analyze *galo* as a transitive verb since there is evidence that it is not. One thing that distinguishes transitive from intransitive verbs in Samoan is that intransitive verbs tolerate the causative prefix *fa'a*, while transitive verbs do not. Thus we have *fa'agoto* 'cause to sink' from the intransitive verb *goto* 'sink' but not **fa'afufulu* 'cause to clean' from *fufulu* 'clean'. Significantly, several *galo* verbs tolerate the causative prefix *fa'a*, which indicates that they are intransitive rather than transitive.[14]

5. Lavea clauses

As mentioned above, *lavea* clauses are syntactically intransitive. The absolutive is the subject and the locative is an oblique. (33) shows that only the absolutive of a *lavea* clause can be bound by postverbal *'uma*. The locative cannot be bound even if it appears in immediate postverbal position. Applying our test for subject in (30), the absolutive of a *lavea* clause must be the subject because it is the only nominal of the clause that can be bound by postverbal *'uma*. This analysis is corroborated by the fact that when the two nominals follow the verb, they occur in verb-abs-loc word order (cf. (18) above). If the absolutive is subject and the locative an oblique, then this word order conforms to the verb-subject-object-oblique word order statement in (29b).

(33) a.   *'Ua*   *lâvevea*   *'uma*_i   *teine*_i   *i*   *le*   *tama.*
      PERF   hurt (PL)   all   girl   LOC   the   boy
      'The girls have all been hurt by the boy.'

b.   **'Ua*   *lavea*   *'uma*_i   *le*   *teine*   *i*   *tamaiti*_i.
      PERF   hurt   all   the   girl   LOC   children
      (The girl has been hurt by all the children.)

c.   *'Ua*   *'ou*   *lavea*   (**'uma*_i)   *i*   *tamaiti*_i.
      PERF   I   hurt   all   LOC   children
      'I have been hurt by (all) of the children.'

Since *lavea* clauses are passive-like, it is worth briefly contrasting them with "true" passive clauses. (34) and (35) illustrate that *lavea* clauses profile only the tail end of the path of a transitive event. A passive clause profiles the entire path. Since, as stated in (4a), an ergative is a profiled participant at the head of a path leading to an absolutive, then the IP of a passive clause is in the ergative case. The IP of a *lavea* clause, which is not in the profiled portion of the path, is in the locative case (rather than the ergative). Like the locative of a *galo* clause, the IP of a *lavea* clause is a locus of responsibility (and hence in the locative case):

(34) a.   *Na*   *lavea*   *le*   *teine*   *i/*e*
      PAST   hurt   the   girl   LOC/ERG
      le   *tama.*   (*lavea*)
      the   boy
      'The girl was hurt by the boy.'

b.

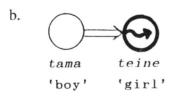

     tama   teine
     'boy'   'girl'

(35) a. *Na   tipi   le   ufi   e*
          PAST   cut   the   yam   ERG
          le   tama.   (passive)
          the   boy
          'The yam was cut by the boy.'

b.

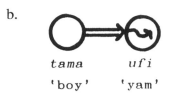

        tama   *ufi*
        'boy'   'yam'

6.   Clitic Placement and Equi with the governing verb <u>mana'o</u>

As previously observed, *lavea* and *galo* clauses differ with respect to
which nominals (if any) can undergo the rules of Clitic Placement and
Equi with the governing verb *mana'o*. I will now discuss how I account
for these differences. The standard assumption concerning Clitic
Placement is that clitics are subjects. If we apply our test for subject to
clauses like (36a) and (36b) which contain a clitic and an intransitive or
middle verb, this assumption seems to be correct. Only the clitic can be
bound by the postverbal quantifier *'uma*, which indicates that the clitic
is the subject:

(36) a. *Na   lâtou$_i$ ô   'uma$_i$'   i   atunu'u*
          PAST   they   go (PL)   all   DIR   country
          o   le   lalolagi.
          of   the   world.
          'They all went to the countries of the world.'
          (NOT: They went to all the countries of the world.)
      b. *Lâtou$_i$ te   âlolofa   'uma$_i$ 'i   tamaiti.*[15]
          they   IMP   love (PL)   all   DIR   children
          'They all love the children.'
          (NOT: They love all the children.)

Applying the same test to clauses containing clitics with transitive
verbs, however, yields different results. As we can see in (37a) and
(37b), the postverbal quantifier *'uma* can be bound by the absolutive

but not by the clitic. (In clauses with transitive verbs, ergatives cliticize but absolutives do not.)

(37) a. *Lâtou   te   uli-a   'uma*$_i$ *a'u   ta'avale*$_i$.
         they   IMP   drive-*Cia*   all   my   car
         'They drive all my cars.'
         (NOT: They all drive my cars.)

   b. *Na   lâtou   'ave-ina   'uma*$_i$ *tusi*$_i$.
       PAST   they   take-*Cia* all   books
       'They took all the books.'
       (NOT: They all took books.)

These data indicate that the absolutive (and not the clitic) is the subject of a clause containing a transitive verb and a clitic. Assuming that both the IP (the clitic) and the TP (the absolutive) are in profile, and given that the absolutive is the subject of clauses like (37a) and (37b), such clauses must be passive.[16]

Now what is relevant to the present discussion is that the clitic in clauses like (37a) and (37b) is not the subject of the clause. If a clitic cannot be characterized as a subject, then what is its proper characterization? I propose, as stated in (38), that a clitic codes the most active of the non-zero profiled participants.[17] A zero is a participant that does not act or have an experience, nor is it acted upon. Non-zero participants are agents, patients, movers, and experiencers.

(38)   A clitic codes the most active of the profiled non-zero
        participants.

The participants referred to by the subjects of predicate adjectives are zeros; hence, they fail to cliticize:

(39) a. *E   sa'o   'oe!*
         IMP right   you
         'You are right!'

   b. **'E   te   sa'o!*
       You   IMP   right
       (You are right!)

The absolutive participants of *galo* clauses are also zeros. They do not move, have an experience, or receive energy from an agent. Therefore it comes as no surprise that such absolutives do not cliticize even if they are coded as subjects:

(40) a.   '*Ua*   *galo*   '*oe*   *i*   *lou*   '*âiga.*
            PERF   forget   you LOC your   family
           'You have been forgotten by your family.'
    b.   *'Ua*   '*e*   *galo*   *i*   *lou*   '*âiga.*
            PERF   you   forget   LOC your   family
           (You have been forgotten by your family.)

Clitic Placement is limited to participants. Therefore the setting subjects of *galo* clauses do not cliticize:

(41) a.   '*Ua*   *galo*   *iate*   *a'u* *le*   *tusi.*
            PERF   forget   LOC   I   the   book
           'I have forgotten the book.'
    b.   *'Ua*   '*ou* *galo*   *le*   *tusi.*
            PERF   I   forget   the   book
           (I have forgotten the book.)

As specified in (38), a participant must be in profile in order to be coded as a clitic. With respect to *lavea* clauses such as those in (42), the participant coded as absolutive is in profile and it is non-zero in that it is a patient. The participant coded in the locative case is conceivably more active than the patient but since it is not in profile, it fails to cliticize. Thus the absolutive is the most active of the profiled participants and qualifies for Clitic Placement:

(42) a.   '*Ua*   *lâvevea*   *teine*   *i*   *tamaiti.*
            PERF   hurt (PL)   girls   LOC children.
           'The girls have been hurt by the children.'
    b.   '*Ua*   *lâtou*   *lâvevea*   *i*   *tamaiti.*
            PERF   they   hurt (PL)   LOC children.
           'They have been hurt by the children.'
    c.   *'Ua*   *lâtou*   *lâvevea*   *teine.*
            PERF   they   hurt (PL)   girls
           (They have hurt the girls.)

Finally, if a construal contains two or more non-zero participants, only the one which is most active cliticizes. For example, only the IP of a middle clause cliticizes:

(43) a. *Na*   *tautala* *le*   *faiâ'oga*   *'i* *le*   *tama.*
         PAST   speak   the   teacher   DIR the   boy
         'The teacher spoke to the boy.'

   b. *Na*   *ia*   *tautala* *'i* *le*   *tama.*
       PAST he   speak   DIR the   boy
       'He spoke to the boy.'

   c. **Na*   *ia*   *tautala* *le*   *faiâ'oga.*
       PAST   he   speak   the   teacher
       (The teacher spoke to him.)

Transitive verbs (in both active and passive clauses) profile both an
IP and a TP. Since the IP is the more active of the two profiled non-zero
participants, it cliticizes, and the TP does not:

(44) a. *Na*   *opo*   *e*   *le*   *tama*   *le*   *teine.*
         PAST   hug   ERG   the   boy   the   girl
         'The boy hugged the girl.'

   b. *Na*   *ia*   *opo-ina*   *le*   *teine.*
       PAST   he   hug-*Cia*   the   girl
       'He hugged the girl.'

   c. **Na*   *ia*   *opo(-ina)*   *e*   *le*   *tama.*
       PAST   she   hug-*Cia*   ERG   the   boy
       (She was hugged by the boy.)

(45) states that the constraints on Equi with the governing verb
mana'o 'want' are the same as those on Clitic Placement: only the most
active of the profiled non-zero participants can undergo this version of
Equi:[18]

(45)   The most active of the profiled non-zero participants
        can undergo Equi with *mana'o*.

Equi with *mana'o* affects exactly the same nominal types as Clitic
Placement. I will summarize what those nominal types are: the absolutive subjects of intransitive and middle verbs:

(46) a. *E   mânana'o   tamaiti   e   ô'*
         IMP   want (PL)   children   INF   go (PL)
         i   Sâmoa.
         DIR   Samoa
         'The children want to go to Samoa.'

 b. *E   mana'o   le   faiâ'oga   e   tautala*
         IMP   want   the   teacher   INF   speak
         'i   le   tama.
         DIR   the   boy
         'The teacher wants to speak to the boy.'

The absolutive subjects of *lavea* clauses but not the those of *galo* clauses:

(47) a. *E   lê   mana'o   le   teine   e   lavea*
         IMP   NEG   want   the   girl   INF   hurt
         i   le   tama.
         LOC   the   boy
         'The girl doesn't want to be hurt by the boy.'

 b. *E   lê   mana'o   le   teine*
         IMP   NEG   want   the   girl
         *e   galo   *('o   ia)   i   le   tama.*
         INF   forget   ABS   she   LOC   the   boy
         'The girl doesn't want to be forgotten by the boy.'

And the ergatives (but not the absolutives) of transitive clauses:

(48) a. *E   mana'o   le   tama   e   opo le   teine.*
         IMP   want   the   boy   INF   hug the   girl
         'The boy wants to hug the girl.'

 b. *E   mana'o   le   teine   e   opo *('ov ia)*
         IMP   want   the   girl   INF   hug ABS she
         e   le   tama.
         ERG   the   boy
         'The girl wants to be hugged by the boy.'

7. Summary and conclusion

This paper has presented both semantic and syntactic evidence that *galo* and *lavea* verbs, which have previously been grouped together as "stative verbs", form two separate verb classes in Samoan. The two differ semantically in that *galo* verbs are verbs of forgetting, understanding, and responsibility; *lavea* verbs describe what happens to a terminal participant. The clauses in which these verbs occur differ syntactically with respect to the rules of Clitic Placement and Equi with the governing verb *mana'o* 'want'. It was argued that *galo* clauses with verb-locative-absolutive word order are instances of Langacker's (1986, 1987b, 1989) setting subject construction. It was claimed that *lavea* clauses differ from passive clauses in that *lavea* clauses profile the terminal phase of a transitive event while passive clauses profile the entire event. Clitic Placement was given a new characterization in terms of semantic roles rather than grammatical relations. Finally, it was claimed that the semantic constraint that holds for Clitic Placement also holds for Equi with the governing verb *mana'o*.

By way of conclusion, I will comment on certain aspects of the approach taken in this paper. To begin with, it is unusual to assume, as I have done in my analysis of Samoan, that case marking uniquely indicates semantic roles (i.e. it does not indicate grammatical relations). The fact that this assumption (along with the assumption that word order is determined by grammatical relations) leads to a cohesive analysis of the array of clause types presented in this paper argues for this approach, and it suggests that this approach may shed light on related phenomena in other languages which have previously been seen as problematic.

A similar observation can be made about my analysis of Clitic Placement. The fact that this phenomenon is best characterized in terms of semantic roles rather than grammatical relations suggests that semantically-based analyses may be in order for other phenomena which have previously been accounted for in terms of grammatical relations.

Lastly, in support of claims concerning the syntax of different clause types, I have employed a form of syntactic argumentation that resembles that of relational analyses found in previous works such as that of Chung (1976, 1978) or Cook (1987). With the advent of every paradigm there is the impulse to throw out the old and start anew. My personal opinion is that we cannot simply "throw out" phenomena such as Equi and Quantifier Float (phenomena upon which I have based my arguments) for they need to be dealt with in any theory that professes to describe syntax. Ideally, cognitive explanations for these phenomena would be given, but for the present such explanations can only be seen as the result of future work within the theory.

Notes

1. This paper summarizes and slightly revises certain sections of Chapter 3 of Cook (1988).
2. The Samoan I am describing here is that of Milner's (1966) dictionary and of my American Samoan informants who reside in Southern California. Long vowels in this paper are marked with a circumflex rather than a macron. The abbreviations used in the glosses are as follows:

ABS:	absolutive	LOC:	locative
DIR:	directional	NEG:	negative
ERG:	ergative	PERF:	perfect
IMP:	imperfect	PL:	plural
INF:	infinitive	PROG:	progressive

3. Mosel (1987) has proposed that Samoan does not have the category subject. Her definition of subject as a "grammaticalized topic within the clause" is different from mine. As per (1i), I am defining subject as the most prominent entity within the clausal profile. An entity may be prominent whether or not there is a host of rules which refer to it (Langacker 1989). Mosel, in her search for subject in Samoan, does not find that grammatical rules consistently pick out one nominal type or a conflation of nominal types (e.g. intransitive absolutives and ergatives). She does not, however, consider the analysis argued for in Cook (1988) and assumed here that different nominal types (i.e. ergatives, absolutives, and locatives) are subjects when they occur in particular clause types, nor does she have anything to say about Quantifier Float, which I employ as part of a test for subject (see below). My analysis, of course, also differs from the more traditional one by Chung (1976, 1978) in which case marking indicates grammatical relations. The following are examples of subjectless weather and temporal clauses:

    (i)   'Ua   timu.
          PERF   rain
          'It is raining.'

    (ii) 'Ua   o'o   'i   le   Aso   Sâ.
          PERF arrive   DIR   the   day   sacred
          'It is (lit. has reached) Sunday.'

4. Some speakers extend Quantifier Float to recipient objects that precede absolutives in the dative shift construction (Cook 1988: 46ff).
5. Nominals without determiners are plural. Barbara Voigt (personal communication) reports that her Western Samoan informants allow Quantifier Float with ergatives in verb-abs-erg clauses. See note 2.
6. One consultant notes that there is a strong connotation associated with (14b) that the offense involved is sexual.
7. For some speakers, *galo* is a transitive verb occurring with erg/abs case marking (Chung 1978: 205). The portrayal of forgetting, understanding, etc. coded in *galo* clauses is reminiscent of that of certain English idioms like *it slipped my mind* and *it dawned on me*.
8. Tuitele, et al. (1978: 160ff) analyze *lavea* itself as intransitive and the following *lavea* verbs, which are listed in (16), as transitive: *afâtia*, *pogia*, *timu'ia*, *saviligia* and *lâ'ia*. I consider the treatment of these

verbs as transitive an innovation, since those of my consultants whose judgments are otherwise more conservative treat these verbs as intransitive. Note also that this innovation may be running along the lines of adjective vs. noun (*lavea* is derived from an adjective while the other verbs mentioned here are derived from nouns).

9.   Notice that it is not the verb + preposition sequence per se that makes (24) bad. Such a sequence is permitted in the cases of so-called pseudo-passives. Compare, for example, *This issue has not been dealt with by the president.*

10.   (i) illustrates that *pa'û* 'fall' takes a locus of responsibility in the directional case rather than in the locative. Presumably this difference adds a dimension of directionality in the sense that the entity for which one is responsible "falls into" one's domain of responsibility. For ease of exposition, I will ignore this fact in this discussion and treat *galo* verbs as if they all took a locus of cognition, etc. in the locative case.

(i)   *'Ua*   *pa'û*   *'iate*   *'oe*   *le*   *tausiga*
      PERF   fall   DIR   you   the   care
    o   *tamaiti.*
    of   children
    'The care of the children has fallen on you.'
    (i.e. You are responsible for the children.)

The use of the directional case in (i) makes the structure of such a clause look very similar to the dative subject constructions which can be found in other languages (particularly those of Southern Asia).

11.   The locative case marker *i* takes the shape *iate* before pronouns.

12.   This statement ignores certain facts concerning clitic pronouns that will be presented below.

13.   Chung (1976: 194-198) attempts to account for the fact that the locative of a clause like (31c) "triggers Quantifier Float" by extending this rule to "animate obliques in immediate postverbal position", but as (i) shows, some animate obliques in immediate postverbal position do not trigger Quantifier Float. In addition, (ii) and (iii) illustrate that Quantifier Float affects some inanimate obliques in immediate postverbal position, and (for some speakers) certain animate obliques that are not in immediate postverbal position. (The percent sign in (iii) indicates that this sentence type is good only for some speakers.)

(i)   *'Ua*   *'ou*   *lavea (*'uma$_i$)*   *i*   *tamaiti$_i$.*
      PERF   I   hurt   all   LOC   children
    'I have been hurt by (all of) the children.'

(ii)   *'Ua*   *galo*   *'uma$_i$*   *i*   *o*   *mâtou*
      PERF   forget   all   LOC   of   us
    mâfaufau$_i$ *le*   *mea*   *na*   *tupu.*
    mind   the   thing   PAST   happen
    'Our minds have all forgotten what happened.'

(iii)   *%Na*   *ta'u*   *'uma$_i$*   *e*   *Sina*   *'i*
      PAST   tell   all   ERG   Sina   DIR
    tamaiti$_i$ *le*   *tali.*
    children   the   answer
    'Sina told all the children the answer.'

14.   The *galo* verbs in (15) that tolerate the *fa'a* causative prefix are *mâlamalama, manino, masino, galo, lilo,* and *pa'û.*

15.   Clitics appear before (rather than after) the imperfect tense/aspect marker *te*.
16.   Although clauses like (37a) and (37b) are passive in structure, I have glossed them in the active since passive sentences such as *By them my car is driven* sound very unnatural in English. The unnaturalness of such translations (among other things) has probably kept scholars from analyzing such clauses as passive. See Cook (1988: 155ff, 190) for more on the role of the *Cia* suffix in such clauses.
17.   In Cook (1988) I used the term "interactive" rather than "non-zero", but I now believe that "non-zero" is more appropriate. The problem with the term "interactive" is that some absolutives that cliticize do not interact in any obvious sense with other participants.
18.   If the governing verb is one like *alu* 'go' which takes an agentive subject rather than one like *mana'o* 'want' that takes an experiencer subject, then the restrictions on what can undergo Equi are more rigid. (Only an agentive profiled participant can undergo Equi with *alu*). Therefore, neither nominal of a *lavea* or *galo* clause undergoes Equi with *alu*. Since this version of Equi does not point out any difference between these two clause types, I will not discuss this version in this paper. Nor will I discuss Raising with *mafai* 'can', which has the same restriction as that of Equi with *alu*.

References

Chung, Sandra
    1976   Case marking and grammatical relations in Polynesian. [Unpublished Ph.D. Dissertation, Harvard University.]
    1978   *Case marking and grammatical relations in Polynesian.* Austin: University of Texas Press.
Cook, Kenneth W.
    1987   "A new relational account of Samoan quantifier float, case marking and word order", *Proceedings of the Annual Meeting of the Berkeley Linguistics Society* 13: 53-64.
    1988   A cognitive analysis of grammatical relations, case, and transitivity in Samoan. [Unpublished Ph.D. Dissertation, University of California, San Diego.]
DeLancey, Scott
    1981   "An interpretation of split ergativity and related phenomena", *Language* 57: 626-657.
Langacker, Ronald W.
    1982   "Space grammar, analysability, and the English passive", *Language* 58: 22-88.
    1986   "Settings, participants, and grammatical relations", *Proceedings of the Annual Meeting of the Pacific Linguistics Conference* 2: 1-31.
    1987a   *Foundations of cognitive grammar,* Volume I: *Theoretical prerequisites.* Stanford: Stanford University Press.
    1987b   "Grammatical ramifications of the setting/participant distinction", *Proceedings of the Annual Meeting of the Berkeley Linguistics Society* 13: 383-394.

1987c   "Transitivity, case, and grammatical relations: A cognitive grammar prospectus", Linguistic Agency, University of Duisburg.
1989   *Foundations of cognitive grammar*, Volume II: *Descriptive application* (preliminary draft).
Milner, George B.
1966   *Samoan dictionary*. London: Oxford University Press.
Laycock, Donald C. & Werner Winter (eds.)
1987   *A world of language: Papers presented to Professor S.A. Wurm on his 65th birthday*. (Pacific Linguistics C-100).
Mosel, Ulrike
1987   "Subject in Samoan", in: Donald C. Laycock & Werner Winter (eds.), 455-479.
Tuitele, M.T., M.Z. Sâpolu & J. Kneubuhl
1978   *Lâ tâtou gagana: Tusi muamua* [Our language: Book I]. Pago Pago: Bilingual/Bicultural Education Project of American Samoa.

"Locations", "paths" and the Cora verb

Eugene H. Casad

1. Introduction

In this paper I discuss the cognitive basis for the categories Locative, Source, Goal and Path as far as I can discover it from an examination of data from Cora, a Uto-Aztecan language spoken in the state of Nayarit, Mexico. Various aspects of this language are described in some detail in Casad (1977, 1982, 1984, 1988) and in Casad & Langacker (1985).[1]

Although not particularly central to the interests of many linguists, the kinds of phenomena that I have been describing are widely distributed among the world's languages (cf. Friedrich 1970; Casad 1982; Svorou 1987). A careful and comprehensive analysis of such data can go a long way toward elucidating many theoretical issues, helping us to better frame believable and realistic models of grammatical structure.

In recent linguistic theory, the notions Locative, Path, Source and Goal are variously construed as kinds of case or role markers. These construals include the terms *deep cases* (Fillmore 1977), *local cases* (Anderson 1971) and *orientational semantic roles* (Grimes 1975). They are usually associated with nouns and prepositions and are commonly analyzed as primitive functional elements of a grammar.[2]

Data from Cora show that these four notions are neither tied to particular morphological categories, nor are they primitive grammatical elements.[3] Instead, they form part of the semantic representations of both verbal prefixes and verb stems. Essentially, they designate various aspects of a conceptual complex, the Directed Path Schema.

In many respects, the results of this study converge on various recent proposals by Talmy (1975, 1987, 1988), Miller and Johnson-Laird (1977), Jackendoff (1978; 1983), Bybee (1985), Dahl (1985), Traugott (1985), Lakoff (1987) and Geeraerts (1988).

For example, Miller and Johnson-Laird (1977) discuss the perceptual basis of paths, basing much of their discussion on analyses by Bennett, Leech and others (1977: 383). For Miller and Johnson-Laird, the path, with a salient beginning point and a salient end point, constitutes the conceptual core for characterizing motion. Basically, Miller and Johnson-Laird see the path notion as a conceptual plan with beginning and end points that are connected by a set of intermediate points (1977: 405f), the viewpoint that I also take in this paper (Casad 1982: 371; cf. also Hawkins 1984: 66f; Traugott 1985: 49 and Lakoff 1987: 275, 282f).

Talmy (1975) gives a typology of the path notion and relates it to a universal characterization of what he calls "the motion situation". As the data in this paper will show, the path concept is relevant to much more than just the motion situation.

Of interest is Talmy's discussion of Atsugewi suffixes. He notes that there are "several score" of them and that they "almost exhaustively partition into as many areas the whole semantic realm of paths oriented with respect to ground objects" (op. cit.: 193).

Bybee (1985) discusses motion verbs briefly, recapitulating Talmy's typology of motion. She associates the notion of "path" only with respect to the semantics of verbs, however. She notes that some verbs are used to express both motion and location and goes on to state that shape is loosely associated with motion and is actually compatible with both motion and location (1985: 14), which is perfectly correct. Talmy (1988) cites the pair of sentences in (1) in which the preposition *through* occurs following verbs that indicate differently shaped paths, making the interesting, but vague, claim that a "cross-linguistic spot check of closed-class elements suggests that they largely have this further topological property of being 'shape-neutral'" (Talmy 1988: 170):

(1)   a.   *I zig-zagged through the woods.*
      b.   *I circled through the woods.*

Talmy may be correct in saying that the meaning of *through* does not specify a particular configuration to the path it corresponds to. But that does not mean that there are no closed-class elements whose meanings do entail such a specification. Nor does it mean that no kind of configurational information is relevant to the usages of English prepositions, as the examples in (2a) through (2c) suggest (cf. also Talmy 1987: 104):

(2)   a.   *I zig-zagged around the woods.*
      b.   *I zig-zagged to the woods.*
      c.   *I zig-zagged by the woods.*

These examples suggest strongly that each English preposition is based on one or more distinct image schemata with own network of related configurations (cf. Lindner 1981; Hawkins 1984, Leys 1986; Brugman 1986; Taylor 1988). The data in this paper show that the semantic effects of the locative prefixes is often precisely to specify the shape of the path that extends through space or time, whether motion is involved or not. Clearly, these prefixes do represent small closed-classes. On the other hand, the analysis that I present here supports Talmy's finding that such grammatical elements are neutral with respect to rate of motion, the "medium" involved and sensorimotor characteristics. Finally, these data also show that the Path and Area schemata are distinct (cf. Hawkins 1984: 85). Functionally, area schemata are seen to be the base or domain in terms of which path schemata receive their orientation and structuring.

2. The cognitive framework

The analysis presented in this paper is based on Langacker's Cognitive Grammar, which views the meanings of lexical units as conventional-ized conceptual structure (cf. also Jackendoff 1978, 1983). Recognizing that language use is grounded in cognitive processing in general, Cognitive Grammar attempts to characterize the kinds of cognitive events that constitute mental experience (Langacker 1986: 3, also cf. Lamb 1971: 101, 120; Jongen 1985: 124; Lakoff 1987: 582; Paprotté 1988: 447).[4] Informally, the most salient aspects of meanings can be modelled as contextually defined configurations organized into networks in se-mantic space. The Directed Path Schema is one such configuration. In its prototypical processual instantiation in language, "path" designates the movement of one entity from one location to another within the domain of the topography. Nonprototypical instantiations are motivated by numerous factors (cf. Lakoff 1987: 153).

2.1.   On the nature of grammar

In his approach to Cognitive Grammar, Langacker suggests that a grammatical unit could easily have several variant meanings which can best be related in a network (1986: 5). Of these meanings, one might be prototypical, providing the ground for certain extended meanings. Certain other ones might be schematic for distinct subparts of the network. The schematic ones summarize the commonalities that speakers per-ceive to exist among semantically related sets of words (1987: 371, 411).

Although such a position represents a distinct alternative to and, possibly, a clear departure from established theories (Langacker 1986a:

3), a moment's reflection on observations made by Stockwell and associates, Anderson, and Grimes all suggest that there is nothing at all counterintuitive or unscientific about the claim that notions such as "subject" and "direct object" are semantically complex (cf. Stockwell, Schacter & Hall Partee 1968: 957; Anderson 1971: 218f; Grimes 1975: 119). Both Fries and Pike also noted the multiple functions of subjects (cf. Grimes 1975: 116).[5]

Langacker's point of view is partly based on two assumptions of Cognitive Grammar. For one, Cognitive Grammar views all grammatical structure as a set of symbolic units, each of which pairs a semantic representation with a phonological one (1987: 76). Grammar itself consists of patterns for grouping morphemes into successively larger configurations, with grammar and lexicon forming a continuum of symbolic structures (1986a: 17). Grammatical constructions are therefore also meaningful; their meanings can even be characterized in much the same terms as the meanings of individual lexical items, e.g. as complex symbols forming a categorizing network, the nodes of which differ in cognitive salience, some being more schematic than the rest, others representing prototypical values. The values in such a network are both distinct and interrelated (1986a: 17; 1987: 382). Langacker analyzes the notions "subject," "direct object," "finite clause" and "transitivity" in these terms.

Grammatical constructions themselves structure conceptual scenes in various ways depending on the particular components of the scene that they select for comment, the relative degree of salience that they attribute to the interacting entities, the vantage point from which the event is viewed and the degree of detail that they specify for describing the relevant scene.[6]

Verbal processes play a special role in this structuring of conceptual scenes. In particular, the structuring of scenes by a verbal predicate allows autonomous entities to be brought into an entire construction at differing levels of analysis. In addition, the physical extent of subject and object nominals can be construed as trajectors and landmarks at given levels of analysis (Langacker 1986b: 6). This range of potential for choices of lexicalization also turns out to be the base for instantiating the schematic location provided by the meaning of the prefix sequences.

Scope relations, which are inherently variable, are operative (Casad & Langacker 1985: 273-8). Furthermore, shapes of things change from domain to domain as do scope relations (cf. McLaury 1989: 126f). Frequently, with a restricted scope of attention paid to the situation, the schematic location extends throughout only a subconfiguration within the physical expanse of the entity that the subject or object nominal designates. In such situations, the relevant entity (either Trajector or Landmark) constitutes a more extended base that pragmatically subsumes the restricted location. This sets up the possibility for the schematic location to be attributed to the entire entity when the nominal gets integrated into the composite structure of a linguistic expression. This part-to-whole extension in the meanings of locative prefix + verbal stem construction is another salient valence feature of such structures. This observation jibes well with the suggestion of Dirven (1985), Rudzka-Ostyn (1985), Lakoff (1987) and Traugott and König (1988) (among many others) that metonymy is an important factor in grammaticalization (cf. Traugott & König 1988: 23). Since some Cora Locative Prefix + Stem constructions are possessives, this metonymical function also explains how the possessor can be construed as an "animate" place (Clark 1978: 89).

2.2. A cognitive model of the canonical event

Langacker's characterization of the structure of a canonical event, an important aspect of clause structure, is particularly relevant at this point. The conceptual framework includes the viewer of an event, the participants in that event, the setting within which the event unfolds and the interactions highlighted by the event. He sets up the Idealized Cognitive Model (cf. Lakoff 1987: 68ff) given in Figure 1, which can be construed as a representation for prototypical events.

Figure 1 implies a "chunking into discrete events of temporally contiguous clusters of interactions observed within a setting" (Langacker 1986a: 6). The viewer is positioned outside the setting and is thus not himself a participant in the event, although his perspective on the scene is crucial. (This represents the unmarked third-person case).

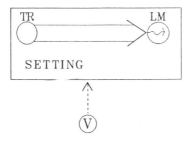

Figure 1: Structure of the canonical event (Langacker in press)

The model makes a clear distinction between the setting for an event and the participants in it.[7] The setting encompasses sufficient area to take in the participants, but is not itself essentially involved in the interactions among the participants. Usually, setting elements are peripheral to clause structure, but in the Cora data that I discuss here, the setting has taken on special salience so that it is often essential to the interactions and relationships specified by a given verb. Cora Locative Prefix + Verb Stem constructions are thus non-prototypical structures in terms of Langacker's characterization of the canonical event given in Figure 1.

Finally, the notions "subject" and "direct object" find their prototypical characterization in terms of this model. The double shafted arrow between the two participants represents the transfer of energy from the left-most participant to the right-most one in what Langacker terms "an action chain" (1986a: 9). The wavy arrow within the confines of the right-most participant represents the change of state occasioned in him by the interaction (Langacker 1986a: 10). The prototypical value of "subject," then, is as the "volitional energy source" who initiates the activity in the action chain, whereas the prototypical value of the "direct object" is as the "energy sink" (or Goal) of the action chain (Langacker 1986a: 7).[8]

2.3.   The Cora situation and event structure

Langacker describes both nonprototypical and schematic values of subjects and direct objects in terms of Figure 1, but it is beyond the scope of this paper to summarize them here. Instead, I focus on the role of the "setting" elements which have come to take on special salience with respect to the verb. In addition, the typical example in this paper will illustrate one of two nonprototypical versions of a single link of the "action chain". These data also show how the categories Locative and Path form networks of semantically interrelated meanings. In short, the locative prefix plus stem combinations fit well into the structure of Langacker's Idealized Cognitive Model of the canonical event, at the same time that they represent an explicit modified version of it.[9]

In particular, the function of the locative prefixes is to specify in schematic (= underspecified) terms the setting within which events transpire or qualities exist, a function important to language in general (cf. Grimes 1975: 122; Rudzka-Ostyn 1985: 211; Langacker 1986b, 1987: 212; Janda 1988: 327; Talmy 1988: 188). This role is carried out jointly by as many as four locative prefixes, although, more commonly, a sequence consists of just two or three prefixes. These relate as a unit to verb stems, incorporated noun roots or adjective stems, forming a unit that internally is like a serial verb in which a pair of sub-processes is strung together as a single event which has the same trajector all the way through. The one event is schematic and is elaborated in various ways by the other event. All of this is summarized in Figure 2, which gives a schematic representation of a finite clause in Cora that consists of a locative prefix sequence plus a motion verb:

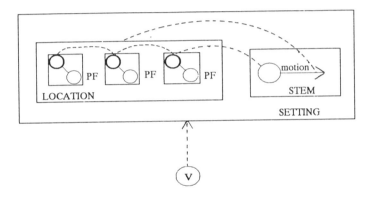

Figure 2: Finite clause: Locative Prefixes + Motion Verb

Each prefix is represented in Figure 2 as a schematic stative relation, i.e. an unspecified relation between two entities that remains unchanged through time. Each stative relation is grounded in a distinct cognitive domain or subdomain and represents a distinct structuring of semantic space. The related entities are symbolized by small circles, whereas the schematic stative relation is symbolized by a straight line connecting them. The vast majority of Cora verbs are structured in this way. Diagrams such as Figure 2 play a heuristic role in helping to display graphically one set of relations in the semantic representation of grammatical constructions (cf. Langacker 1987: 111).

The prototypical linguistic relation is asymmetric (Langacker 1987: 231). This is shown in the semantic representation of the prefixes by foregrounding one of the entities. The most salient entity is the trajector of the relation. The backgrounded entity functions to locate the trajector in some way within a given cognitive domain and is therefore called the landmark (Langacker 1987: 217). The box marked STEM gives a schematic representation of a motion verb, in which the motion is indicated by a labelled arrow and the trajector in the motion situation is indicated by a circle at the tail end of the arrow. This link of the action chain, then, is non-prototypical since there is no salient transfer of energy from a trajector to another entity who would undergo a subsequent change of state. Instead, the relevant change in the case of motion verbs is a change of the trajector's position relative to one or more landmarks.

The dotted lines connecting the trajectors of each of the stative relations with the trajector of the motion verb are lines of integration (Langacker 1987: 96) and serve to indicate that one entity is identical to another one in some other component relation within the structure. The implication of these lines of integration is that there is actually only a single trajector in the composite (overall) semantic structure of the Locative Prefix + Motion Verb clause. The integration line that connects the LOCATION constituent as a whole to the schematic path in the representation of the motion verb is construed as depicting the joint role of the prefixes in the sequence to specify, in particular detail, information about the shape of the path that the trajector takes in moving from one location to another.

Note that the box enclosing the prefix sequence in semantic space is labelled LOCATION and is set off from the more general SETTING of the entire clause. This distinction is necessary because other adverbial elements can occur elsewhere in the sentence and these additional elements elaborate in one way or another the locative prefix sequence that occurs with the verb stem (cf. Secs. 3.2.1 and 3.2.2). Another purpose of this paper, therefore, is to substantiate this distinction and characterize it in reasonably explicit terms.

Figure 3 gives a very similar graphing of the relations implied by the semantics of the Locative Prefix + Stative Verb construction. As before, the trajector of each relation represented by a single prefix is equated with all the others and with the trajector in the stative relation that the stative verb or adjective stem designates. Again, the schematic stative relations, which are filled out in more detail by particular prefixes and stems, are symbolized by a single line between the trajectors and the landmarks of the corresponding relations. Finally, the viewer's canonical vantage point is depicted as impinging on the entire structure from the outside. In particular cases, this vantage point is very relevant for the semantic structure of the construction. As a first approximation, I assume that the individual trajectors of the coordinate locative stative relations are all equivalent to the trajector of the verbal process or state profiled by the clause. Particular examples will show that this relation does not always hold.

Figure 3 includes a schematic representation of the phonological pole of this construction to show the reader the bipolar nature of this linguistic unit in which particular semantic elements relate in precise ways to phonological strings through the symbolization relation:

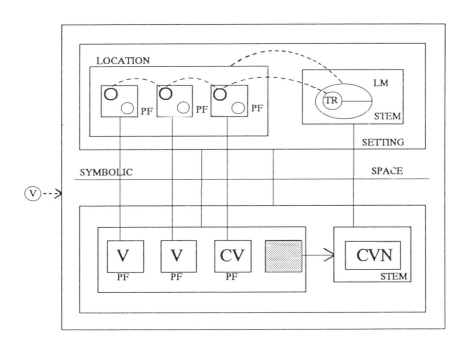

Figure 3: Finite clause: Loc PF + Stative V

At the phonological pole, the diagram shows a string of three prefixes with the canonical shapes of V, V and CV, respectively, and a stem that has a canonical CVN shape. The left to right order of phonological elements in this example matches the left to right order of semantic elements. This is indicated by the vertical symbolization lines that specify the correspondence between units in semantic space (upper large box) and units in phonological space (Langacker 1987: 77). These correspondences are stated, not only for each of the three prefixes and the stem, but also for the locative unit as a whole and for the entire construction.

The small square with hashmarks inside the LOCATIVE box is an elaboration site (Langacker 1987: 304ff). This site is a schematic part of the meaning of the locative sequence which must be filled out in fuller detail by some other entity in order for it to function as a unit at a higher level of grammatical structure. This is due to the fact that the locative constituent is a dependent unit that makes inherent salient internal reference to that other unit. The unit that further specifies the schematic part of the LOCATIVE's meaning is shown at the head of the arrow originating at the e-site. In this case, the e-site is elaborated by the stative verb. Notice also that Semantic Space and Phonological Space represent two discrete (but not autonomous) areas of Symbolic Space.

With this preliminary introduction into both the notational devices of Cognitive Grammar and the complexities of the linguistic structure of the Cora Locative Prefix + Verb combinations behind us, we can now move on to a more detailed analysis of the data. For ease of representation, the rest of the diagrams in this paper will depict only the semantic pole of these constructions. The phonological forms of morphemes are given in slashes above their corresponding predicates in order to help the reader keep track of which predicate corresponds to which morpheme and to emphasize the fact that these diagrams are in no way claiming that semantic structure is autonomous.

3.   The path notion in Cora

In its most concrete form, a path can be thought of as how one gets from one point in three dimensional space to a second point in that same space. As I mentioned previously, I take this characterization to be the prototypical version. In a more schematic sense, I take the term to refer to a conceptual schema (or, in Lakoff's terms, an image schema (1987: 275)) that has salient end points, the Source and the Goal, and a set of intermediate points that constitute the extension of the path over an unspecified base. The differential end points give the path an inherent orientation that has its basis in a set of related concepts such as the natural movement of an entity through space or the typical posture that a perceiving entity assumes for viewing a scene. The image schema, then, is given in Figure 4. The initial point on the path is labelled "Source" (S), whereas the final point is labelled "Goal" (G). In addition, the path itself is situated within an unspecified Base, and the canonical viewing point is located at a neutral point at the middle, but spatially removed from the path itself.

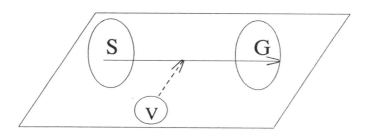

Figure 4: The Directed Path Schema

3.1. *Differential lexicalization of the path notion*

Both the path notion itself and its individual components are coded into the semantics of a great variety of linguistic units in Cora. In particular, as the analyses of the data given in this paper will show, there is no single morpheme or grammatical class in Cora which can realistically be labelled "Path," "Source," "Goal" or "Locative".[10] Instead, each of these notions can be found coded into the semantic representations of particular locative adverbs, directional prefixes, postpositions, locative nouns, motion verbs, and stative adjectives. Further complicating the picture, is the fact that each of these four notions can potentially be coded into the variant meanings of practically any one of these grammatical elements (cf. Talmy 1987: 57). Finally, each of these notions can take on varying degrees of salience from usage to usage; i.e. the path notions reveal a gradient in the degree of lexicalization that they display in particular usages (cf. Talmy 1987: 122ff).

3.1.1.   Meaning of the verb includes a path

Different prefixes, characterizing distinct path shapes, occur with the same stem.[11] For stems whose meanings include a path configuration, the prefix imposes a further specification on the nature of that path. I begin to illustrate these points with a consideration of the semantic representation of the verb stem *-nʸe* 'to arrive at X location/to pass by X location'. This motion verb includes the idea of a typically animate trajector following a path that terminates at a general location whose characteristics are unspecified. The goal of the path is particularly salient to the meaning of *-nʸe*, which in other intransitive forms has the meaning 'to appear/to come on the scene'. In Figure 5, the path component of *-nʸe* is located on a schematic horizontal base. The trajector's movement along that path is indicated by three circles labelled "TR" at distinct locations along that path. That the motion is actually a gradual one that passes through an indeterminate set of intermediate points is indicated by the sets of dots that occur between the explicitly specified "TR" locations. This is simply an abbreviatory convention for summarizing the totality of positions that the trajector passes through on his way from one point to another. Finally, the oval that encloses "TR" in his position at the head of the path is construed as meaning that the trajector's final position is the most salient one in the situation to which *-nʸe* applies.

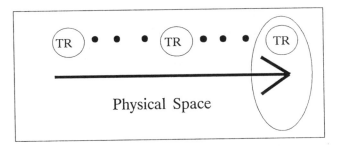

Figure 5. The intransitive stem *-nʸe* 'to arrive at X'

The examples in (3a) and (3b) present two distinct prefix sequences that occur with *-nʸe*:

(3)   a.   *saɨh á-h-nʸeh ɨmuu-ra'a-n*
           one outside-slope-arrive ART head-his-ABS
           'One of his heads popped up out of the water.'

      b.   *a-vé'e-nʸe*
           outside-back-arrive: PAST
           'He came back here from behind the rim of the canyon.'

As the glosses of (3a) and (3b) suggest, each distinct prefix sequence + -*nʸe* combination correlates with a distinct meaning structure. In (3a) the prefix sequence *ah* signals that the trajector is following a vertically-oriented path which ends in the trajector's coming out into the open air from underneath the surface of the water which acts as a barrier to visual accessibility. To be even more specific, the trajector of the prefix *a*- is represented as a distinct entity, i.e. *muura'an* 'his head'. The particular version of *a*- selected in this usage is the one in which visual accessibility is afforded to the viewer by virtue of the fact that the trajector is located at the viewer's side of a barrier that would otherwise put limits on his field of vision (cf. Casad & Langacker 1985: 265). The prefix *h*- designates location along a vertical path which takes its orientation from the viewer's normal standing position and his typical viewing stance vis-à-vis ground level. The viewer in the representations of both *a*- and *h*- is equated with the speaker as viewer, whereas the trajector of *a*- is equated with the trajector of -*nʸe*, but is separate from the speaker of the sentence. All these elements are combined into a single compacted, composite representation in Figure (6b):

(a)

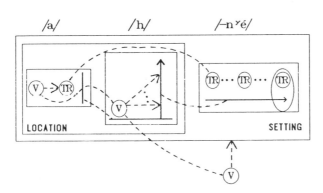

(b)

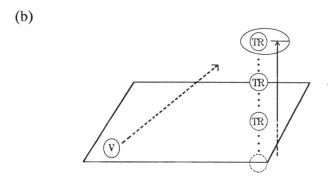

Figure 6: *a-h-nʸeh*

A real topographic base is involved in the situation that (3b) describes. In this example, the use of *a-ve'e-* indicates that the trajector is understood to have followed a path coming from down in a canyon on up over the canyon rim and ending at some place visually accessible to the speaker. The rim of the canyon is thus a barrier to visual accessibility.

Finally, the examples in (3a) and (3b) illustrate alternate views of the shape and orientation of the path forming part of the semantic representation of *-nʸe*. Thus, the semantic force of the prefixes is that of heightening the salience of some particular aspect of that path.

3.1.2.   Meaning of the verb subsumes an area

Path notions are even associated with verb stems whose basic meanings imply an area. In these cases, the meanings of the prefixes bring an adjustment into the nature of the physical extension designated by the stem (cf. Talmy 1988: 183). This semantic effect is seen clearly in the usages of the locative prefixes with stative stems such as *-nʸeeri-'i* 'be illuminated' which designates an area. The intransitive stem *-nʸeera* designates the diffusion of an effect, i.e. illumination, throughout an area. This illumination can be thought of as following an indefinite number of virtual paths, represented by a broken double-shafted arrow in Figure 7. The circular pattern of dots suggests that these virtual paths are indefinite in number and are not discrete perceptually, i.e. the path is a diffuse one. The suffix -*i* is an ablauting STATIVE suffix; since -*i* designates a resultant stative relation that holds between a trajector and an area, the process of illumination is itself the trajector.

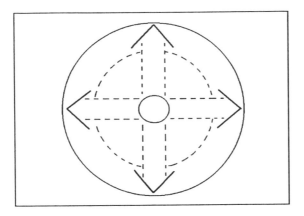

Figure 7: -nʸeeri'i

As (4a) through (4d) show, the semantic force of the prefixes is to impose a particular image of location and directionality to the illumination that -*nʸeeri-'i* designates. Four very distinct images are presented by these sentences:

(4) a.   *a-h-ká-nʸeeri-'i*
           outside-slope-down-visible-STAT
           'From a string of lights along the top, the wall is all
           lit up going downwards to its foot.'
    b.   *a-n-tá-nʸeeri-'i*
           outside-top-across-visible-STAT
           'From a source at one side of the river, it is all
           lit up going across the water to the opposite bank.'
    c.   *a-n-tʸí-nʸeeri-'i*
           outside-top-up-visible-STAT
           'It is all lit up around there at the top of the hill.'
    d.   *a-ii-ré'e-nʸeeri-'i*
           outside-path-corner-visible-STAT
           'By a source coming from behind the house, it is
           all lit up at the corner of the house.'

The situation illustrated by (4a) is that of a string of lights anchored along the top of a wall so that they jointly cast their light down and along the vertical face of that wall. The typical speaker vantage point for this usage of *ah-ka-* is a lateral view from near one end of the string of lights. The verticality of the wall is indicated by the use of the prefix sequence *ah-*, whereas the downward orientation of the illumination is signalled by *ka-*.

The view in mind for (4b) is that of light being cast across the surface of the water in a river, the surface itself being construed as an "upper" one, as indicated by the use of *an-* 'on top'. The use of the prefix *ta-* 'across' signals that the dispersion of the illumination extends across the total expanse of the water from one side of the river to the other. Here, the typical vantage point for the viewer is from the same side of the river as the source of the illumination.

The body of a hill forms the broad topographical context for sentence (4c). In this case, the illuminated area does not involve a salient path, but rather designates a resticted zone at the extreme upper area of the hill. Whereas the prefix *an-* 'on top' designates an upper surface of some kind, the prefix *t^{y}i-* 'up' places salience on the notion 'above the speaker's level'. Taken together, the entire sequence, then, is conventionally construed as meaning 'at the upper extremity of X', which , in the domain of the lay of the land, is the very top of a hill (cf. Casad 1988: 352, figure 3). This is a fairly clear case in which the location designated by the locative prefix sequence subsumes only a part of the overall setting.

The situation that *a-i-re'e-n^{y}eeri-'i* in (4d) depicts involves both a salient directionality to the illumination that it designates and a particular speaker vantage point. The speaker's vantage point is at one corner of the house, looking along the side toward a back corner. The source of illumination is around that back corner and out of the speaker's visual field. The prefix *re'e-* thus traces a complex path that includes an abrupt change point on its way between the source and the speaker. That abrupt change point delimits in one dimension the range of the speaker's field of visual accessibility. The prefix *ii-* 'this way' imposes a directionality on the path; i.e. the path comes toward the speaker. In addition, the prefix *a-* reinforces the notion of visual accessibility, which is a salient part of the situation that *-n^{y}eeri-'i* designates.

All of these elements are explicitly indicated in Figures (8a) and (8b). Figure (8a) gives an exploded graphing of the salient component elements in the meaning of *a-i-re'e-n^{y}eeri-'i* and their interrelationships, whereas Figure (8b) presents a composite, compacted representation that shows the particular image that emerges from combining the individual linguistic units. Both the exploded representation and the compacted one are needed in order to give a reasonably adequate account of a linguistic construction (Langacker 1987: 75).

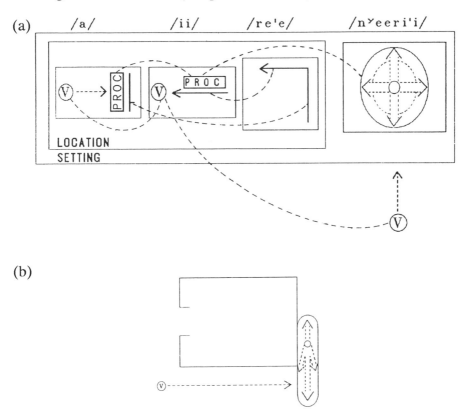

(a)   /a/   /ii/   /re'e/   /nʸeeri'i/

(b)

Figure 8: a-i-re'e-nʸeeri-'i

3.1.3.   Meaning of the prefix designates a path

The path notion is common to the full set of prefixes and prefix combinations. The sentences in (5a) through (5c) are typical:

(5) a.   *ŧʸ-úh-tutáh-mee ɨ huye*
          up-REFL-curve-COLL ART road
          'The road curves back and forth on itself going uphill.'
     b.   *ká-sinuuri mɨ hɨri hece*
          down-slide ART hill at
          'He is sliding down the side of the hill.'
     c.   *wa-tá-vi-vɨ*
          EXT-across-RDP-hang
          'The wires are strung horizontally from side to side across
          the wall.'

Example (5a) *ŧʸ-uh-tutah-mee* includes an incorporated noun *tutah* 'curve' as the stem of the verbal construction. A path component, of course, is the salient part of the meaning of *tutah*, which can be glossed 'curvilinear entity'. That a multiplicity of curves are combined into a single string is intimated by the use of the COLLECTIVE suffix *-mee*. The "back and forth" notion given by the gloss finds its grounds in the use of the REFLEXIVE prefix *uh-* (a metathesized form of *ru-*) and can be alternatively glossed 'back upon itself'. The directional prefix *ŧʸ-* 'up' (a truncated form of *ŧʸi-*) anchors the string of curves along an uphill trajectory and provides the axis in terms of which to calculate the notion 'back upon itself'.

The verb stem *sinuuri* of (5b) also includes the notion of a path. In this case, the trajector is involved in a general movement in which his normal ambulatory faculties are out of control and his motion is provided by an external force, i.e. gravity. The directional *ka-* anchors this unintentional movement to a topographical base, i.e. the side of a hill, as does *ŧʸ-* in (5a). The prototypical vantage point for both *ŧʸ-uh-tutah-mee* and *ka-sinuuri* is from near the foot of the hill. However, the location signalled by *ŧʸ-* in (5a) takes in a broader range of the general setting than does that signalled by *ka-* in (5b). In addition, *ŧʸ-uh-tutah-mee* presents the path as an extended, but bounded area, whereas *ka-sinuuri* profiles an indeterminate and intermediate expanse of the slope which is the context for the event.

The situation described by *wa-ta-vi-vɨ* (5c) is located within a walled-off area such as a room. The prefix *wa-* designates the total (horizontal) expanse of this bounded area, placing salience on the boundedness, whereas the prefix *ta-* saliently designates a simple linear path extending from a point at one side of the enclosed area to a point on an opposite side. Neither point is more salient than the other, a point that is also illustrated by *ta-cʸapʷa*, below in (7a).

Additional views on the path come from the fact that speakers have the choice of whether to focus on some internal configuration within the path schema, or whether to view it as a discrete entity, making no reference whatsoever to its internal structure, i.e. the path may be viewed as a bounded whole. In one version of the perspective of a path as a bounded whole, it is viewed as being extended throughout a bounded area. This is clear from the meanings of certain stative stems such as -$t^{y}ee$ 'it is long'. This stem takes 3-dimensional physical space as its domain and includes in its meaning the notion of the calibration of the extension of some entity throughout some subarea of that space. This calibration also includes the implicit notion of some standard of normal extendability within that space such that extension between the starting point of the calibration and that norm is considered "not long" (= short) and every perceptible extension beyond that norm is considered "long".[12]

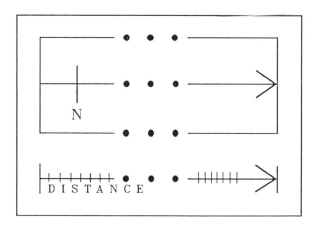

Figure 9: -$t^{y}ee$ 'It is long.'

These relationships are represented graphically in Figure 9. The base is a neutral surface, and the extended entity under discussion is located all along an arrow that goes from one side of the base to the opposite side. Both the arrow and the upper and lower sides of the base are interrupted by a series of three dots which signal indefinite extension along a given dimension. Beneath the base is shown a calibration scale with the location of "Normal" extension indicated by "N" at the left third of the scale. The Origin and Goal points of the scale anchor the full expanse within the base.

Two distinct prefix sequences are shown in combination with -t^yee in (6a) and (6b). Again, distinct prefix sequence choices entail greatly different semantic content and distinct imagery:

(6)   a.   *a-n-t^yí-t^yee*
            outside-top-up-long
            'It is a long way up to the top of the cliff/hill/tower.'
       b.   *wa-tá-t^yee*
            EXT-straight-long
            'It is a long way.'

The alternate glosses of *an-t^yi-t^yee* (6a) illustrate typical usages of *ant^yi-* to designate the uppermost extremity of some entity which is substantially above the normal horizontally directed line of sight of the speaker. In this case, *ant^yi-* again designates an area that constitutes only a subpart of the base that the entire locational setting includes.

The situation designated by *wa-ta-t^yee* (6b) is described by the simple statement that, according to the speaker, the distance between his location at the time of speaking and a distal reference point is substantial. The pertinent relationships are graphed in Figure 10. The prefix *wa-* treats the quantity of distance as a bounded area throughout whose entirety some entity is distributed. The entity is the state of quantified linear extension, i.e. relative distance. The prefix *ta-* adds salience to the linear relation bounded by *wa-* by detailing the path that extends from a point at one side of its base to a corresponding point at the opposite side. This base is also represented as a bounded area. In the structure that results from combining these two prefixes, the base of *wa-* is equated with the base of *ta-*, whereas the extended state associated with *wa-* is equated with the path of *ta-*. Both the boundedness of the bases of *wa-* and *ta-* and the full extension of the path of *ta-* are equally salient to the composite representation of *wa-ta-t^yee* given in Figure 10 (b). In contrast to *ant^yi-*, *wa-ta-* encompasses the entire locational setting appropriate to the use of *wa-ta-t^yee*:

(a)   /wa/   /ta/   /t^{y}ee/

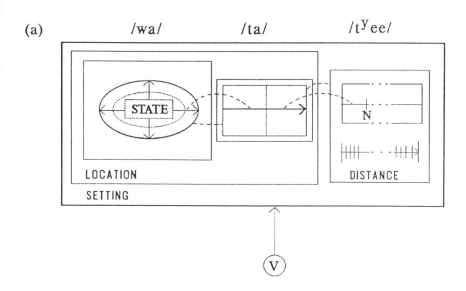

(b)

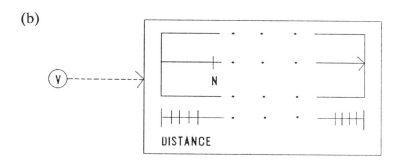

Figure 10: *watat^{y}ee* 'It is a long way off.'

Notice from Figure 10 that both *wa-* and *ta-* are unmarked for the viewer's vantage point. This backgrounding of the speaker's vantage point is the cognitive basis for the usage of *wa-ta-* to apply to situations in which *wa-ta-* is employed whenever the speaker wishes to leave unspecified the particular locational information normally associated with the usage of certain verb stems, such as *-tu'a* 'to hit'. The peculiarities of both *wa-* and *ta-* also lend themselves to making extensions into syntax which I discuss later in Section 4.

3.2. Location vs. setting

Given that the typical means of locomotion for the Coras has been on foot or by burro or horseback until the last two or three decades, at least, and that the Coras have lived in rugged mountainous terrain for hundreds of years, the topography has been the background to much of their daily life and it should be no surprise to find a reasonably developed set of adverbial concepts coded into their language (Casad 1977: 239; cf. also Geeraerts 1988: 222; Dirven & Taylor 1988: 381). Adverbials, however, are generally peripheral elements in clause structure, whereas the prefixes we have observed thus far are seen to be highly relevant to Cora verb structure. The prefixes of location and direction occur closer to the verb stem than do the subject and object prefixes. Furthermore, they are not separable as are the verbal prefixes of Indo-European languages. This extent of elaborate locative marking on the verb is typologically odd for Uto-Aztecan, a feature Cora shares with Huichol. In turn, both of these reflect a preoccupation with space that is similar in many ways to that displayed by Tarascan (cf. Casad 1982: 14-22), but is very different from the body-part systems of Oto-Manguean (cf. Hollenbach 1983) or the suffixal systems of Mixe-Zoque. All this cries out for an adequate explanation as to how the present system might have become grammaticalized. In the following sections of this paper, I show how the relation between the global setting of events and the particular locational constituent of the verb word relate to one another in terms of Langacker's model of the canonical event and in terms of the notions of prototypicality, scope variation and domain shift, among other things.[13]

To begin discussing the justification for the distinctions between the global setting for events and the locative constituent that provides a schematic characterization of the specific locational setting for those events, I give the examples in (7a) and (7b), in which either a topographic adverb or a locative particle occurs in construction with Locative Prefix + Stem sequences:

(7)   a.   *án-tan pú tá-cʸapʷa*
            top-across SUBJ straight-footprint river
            'There is a line of footprints on the far side,
            following the river.'

       b.   *ú=nú=a'-a-ráa-me*
            there=I=DISTAL-outside-face-go: SG
            'I am going to come back down the river from there.'

The overall setting of the scene that (7a) describes is specified by the topographic adverb *an-tan* 'off there on top across the river'. The line of footprints described at the far side of the river opposite the speaker's viewing point, is neutral with respect to the directionality of the river's flow; it merely follows along the river's edge. The role of *an-tan* to locate *ta-cʸapʷa* within a larger global setting suggests strongly that the LOCATION component of this construction is indeed distinct from the SETTING.[14] It also suggests that the structure of the LOCATION element itself may include an e-site.[15] However, since this construction includes only a single locative prefix, there is not sufficient evidence to demonstrate this clearly.

On the other hand, the multiplicity of locative markers in (7b) *u nu a'-a-raa-me* does lend support to this. The speaker uses *u* to designate a particular location where he will be at some time in the future. He situates this location at a distal location upriver from the location where he is found at the time of saying *u=nu=a'araame* (7b). The prefix *a'-* 'off yonder' designates the location from which he begins his return trip back to his present location from that distal point, whereas the prefix sequence *a-ra-* anchors his path to the natural direction of the flow of the river. The role of the prefix *a-* 'outside' is likely to represent the future motion along the path back to where the speaker is at the moment, i.e. back onto the present scene. To conclude, in *u=nu=a'-a-raa-me*, the sentence inital particle *u* establishes the most remote location within the setting for the event, whereas the prefix complex *a'-a-raa-* specifies the shape of the motion the trajector follows in returning to his location occupied as speaker. This same functional relationship will be observed in other examples that I discuss in the paper. In the following sections, I illustrate some of the more obvious relationships that occur between the role of the LOCATION constituent and the global setting.

3.2.1.   Setting is co-extensive with location

Certain uses of the prefix sequences appear to show that the location that they designate is equivalent to the global setting for the event expressed by the verb stem. This is especially easy to see in those cases in which the locational prefixes designate areas or configurations on a discrete object such as a clay pot, as in (8):

(8)   *a-uu-tá-tap^w a mɨ sa'ɑ̈ri*
       outside-that way-across/straight-broken ART pot
       'The clay pot is broken in half.'

The situation in view in (8) is that of a clay cooking pot that has gotten broken into roughly two equal parts. As the multiple morphemic gloss suggests, there are two possible resultant states, each of which can be appropriately designated by *a-uu-ta-tap^w a*. The line of fracture could either have been oriented horizontally with respect to the natural sitting position of the pot, or it could have divided the pot into halves along a line going from top to bottom. This double possibility is based on the indeterminacy of the meaning of the prefix *ta-* with respect to any particular orientation to the fracture line. The prefix *a-* 'outside' places the fracture on a visually accessible surface of the pot, the prefix *uu-* 'that way' designates the path that the fracture line follows, and *ta-* contributes the notion that the fracture line cuts clean across the physical expanse of the pot. To conclude, the location designated by *a-uu-ta-* is co-extensive with the setting for *-tap^w a* 'broken'.

A more abstract version of the location and setting is illustrated by the contrastive pair of sentences in (9):

(9)   a.   *á=a'-i-ré'e-n^y á-a*
             there = DISTAL-path-corner-arrive-PRTC
             'He arrived back at the primary center of activity.'
       b.   *á=a'-u-ré'e-n^y á-a*
             there = DISTAL-EXT-corner-arrive-PRTC
             'He arrived back at the place he had left from earlier.'

The pair of examples *a=a'-i-re'e-n^y aa* and *a=a'-u-re'e-n^y aa* (9a-b) present contrastive complex movements within the context of a folklore text in which the narrator is viewing the scene as though he were actually looking on from a distance. Crucially, both of the locations designated by the locative constituents *a'-i-re'e-* and *a'-u-re'e-* are defined in terms of the same global base which is needed for defining the particle *a* 'off there'.

The elaborate clitic and prefix sequence *a=a'-i-re'e-* of (9a) designates a textually-defined spatial setting for the arrival event. In this case, the particle *a* designates a primary point of reference as defined by the narrative text, i.e. the place where the initiating events are staged. The sequence is conventionally construed as meaning that the named participant has followed a complex path that earlier led away from that primary point and later turned back to it. The locative prefix *a'-* specifies the location reached by the trajector that is most distally removed from the primary reference point. In other words, the particle *a* anchors the most salient end of the complex path that the trajector follows, whereas the prefix *a'-* anchors the other end of the unilinear extension of that path. Note that the base needed for defining the location specified by the locative particle is equivalent to the global locational setting of the entire event.

The contrastive movement of *a=a'-u-re'e-n^yaa* (9b) vis-à-vis *a=a'-i-re'e-n^yaa* is indicated by the locative prefix *uu-* 'that way'. In this case, the trajector's movement is away from the primary narrative vantage point to the distal area from where the trajector was summoned to come to the stated center of activity mentioned in the text. In both cases, the trajector is viewed as completing a round-trip. In both cases also, the entire movement designated by the prefix sequences encompasses the entire area taken in by the global setting, which, in turn, is the base for defining the locative particles that co-occur with the prefix sequences. This notion of a mutually-shared base is a common feature of many of the constructions I examine in this paper.

3.2.2.   Location is only a part of the setting

A somewhat different version of the relation between the LOCATION constituent and the global setting involves the case in which the location is only a portion of the global setting.

(10) a. *án-t^yi á'-u-h-ru-pi*
          top-up-uphill DISTAL-inside-slope-enter PAST
          'He went off to the top of the hill.'
      b. *á-h-t^yap^wa a'-u-tá-ru-pi*
          outside-slope-upriver DISTAL way-that-straight-enter-PAST
          'He went off somewhere upriver.'

Examples (10a) and (10b) show, for one, that the speaker has options for characterizing upwards going motion even within the same domain. Thus, in (10a), *uh-* designates upward motion within the hill domain, whereas in (10b) *a-uu-ta-* designates upward motion within the domain of the river. These two domains, in turn, are subsumed in a more generalized topographic domain or base (Casad 1982: 135; 1988: 349). In (10a), the end of the path located in this domain is indicated by the

free topographic adverb *an-tʸi* 'up there at the top of the hill', whereas
the prefix sequence used on the verb is *uh-* 'inside-slope', which
contrasts with the *ah-* of *ah-nʸeh* (3a). This contrast is based on the
notion of a canonical viewer's position at the foot of a hill. The viewer
typically is facing toward the slope of the hill. The *u-/a-* distinction,
then, is determined with respect to a line of sight that follows the
vertical axis of the hill up to its uppermost extremity. Locations that lie
along this line of sight are 'inside', whereas those that lie perceptibly off
to one side or to the other are characterized as 'outside' locations
(Casad 1982: 101; Casad & Langacker 1985: 261ff). In general, within
the domain of the hill, locations that are straight upslope from the
viewer are *uh-*, whereas those that are oblique to the slope are *ah-*.

All these relations are graphed in Figure (11a). The prefix *a'-* locates
the trajector at a distal point out of the immediate vicinity of the
viewer; *u-* traces the viewer's line of sight upslope, crossing the horizontal long axis of the hill or range; *h-* places the motion of the trajector
within the slope, and the past tense *-rupi* 'he entered into X' places the
end of the motion within a circumscribed area, which is elaborated by
the adverb *an-tʸi*, which takes as its base the entire hill domain. Functionally, *an-tʸi* designates the end point of the path within the domain of
the hill, whereas the prefix sequence *uh-* designates the shape of the
path within that domain. The two grammatical elements thus fill in
complementary aspects of the conceptual scene, but they both have the
same global setting in terms of which they are defined. This is the prototypical use of the LOCATION constituent in its relation to both the
global setting and an accompanying topographic adverb or locative particle. The complementary semantic roles played by the LOCATION
constituent are graphed clearly in the compacted composite representation of Figure (11b):

(a)   /a'/   /u/   /h/   /rupi/

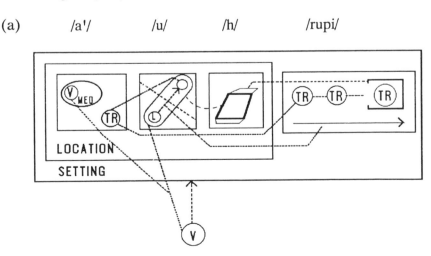

(b)

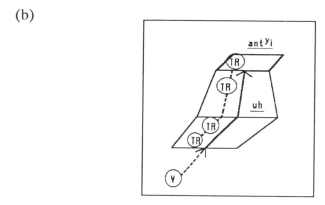

Figure 11: *a'-uh-rupi* 'He climbed the hill.'

The same relationship between topographic adverb and prefix sequence is illustrated by *ah-t^yap^wa a'-u-ta-ru-pi* (10b). In this example, the scene is localized within the river subdomain of topographic space. The adverb *ah-t^yap^wa* 'outside-upriver' designates the end, or goal, of the trajector's path, which runs counter to the natural direction of the river's flow. *Ah-t^yap^wa*, then, provides a finer specification of the distal point designated by the prefix *a'-* "DISTAL". It designates an upriver location that is off out in the slope that parallels the river. On the other hand, the prefix sequence *uu-ta-* 'that way-upstream' details the directionality of the trajector's movement within the river domain (it contrasts with *uu-ra-* 'that way-downstream'). This complementary relationship of semantic roles for the LOCATION constituent vis-à-vis the global setting for the entire event will be obvious from additional examples that I discuss later in this paper.

3.3. Speaker's vantage point relative to setting

The model of the canonical event, given earlier in Figure 1, explicitly includes an observer and his perspective on the relevant scene. In its prototypical sense, the observer's vantage point is a specific location in space from which he looks out over a developing situation located within his field of vision. In the section that follows, I present an analysis of data which suggest strongly that the speaker's vantage point is indeed a crucial aspect of the semantic structure of Cora LOCATIVE PREFIX + STEM constructions.

Cora employs a set of orientational prefix sequences *ii-* 'this way' and *uu-* 'that way' to locate a path in distinct ways with respect to a speaker's conceptual primary reference point (or the Deictic Center, cf. Serzisko (1988: 433)).

The primary reference point, in many cases, is the viewer's actual position when he comments on a situation that he is observing. When motion is involved, the path can, in the examples I discuss here, be construed as coming toward the primary point, as in (11a), (11c), and (11d).

As these examples show, the orientation towards the speaker's location is determined by the use of the prefix *ii-* 'this way'. Additional aspects of the path's orientation are signalled by the other prefixes that co-occur with *ii-*:

(11) a.   *a-ii-ká-suuna háih hece*
            outside-this way-down-pour cliff at
            'Water is pouring down the cliff facing the observer.'
      b.   *a-n-ká-suuna*
            outside-top-down-pour
            'Water is pouring down over the edge of the cliff.'
      c.   *a-í-h-n^{y}eeri-'i*
            outside-this way-slope-visible-STAT
            'From a source at the foot of the slope, it is all
            lit up along the slope coming up this way to the top.'
      d.   *a-ii-tá-t^{y}ee ayun hece*
            outside-this way-across-long back here to
            'It is a long way across the river to back on this side.'

A waterfall is in view in both *a-ii-ka-suuna* (11a) and *an-ka-suuna* (11b). In (11b) *an-ka-suuna*, the speaker views the situation from the top of the cliff over which the waterfall spills. This usage of *an-* is close to its prototypical topographically based version in which it designates the region at the head of a slope. The prefix *ka-*, then, designates the natural downward flow of the water under the influence of gravity toward the base of that cliff. The speaker's vantage point is at the top of the cliff over which the water pours and he is typically close enough to the edge of the cliff to see the downward flow of the water.

In the contrasting situation of *a-ii-ka-suuna* (11a) the viewer is somewhat spatially removed from the foot of the waterfall. He may even be clear across the canyon from it. The important aspect of this scene to keep in mind is that his viewing point for appropriately using *a-ii-ka-suuna* is clearly distinct from his viewing point for appropriately using *an-ka-suuna* (11b), in which he must be near the top of the fall, looking over the edge toward the base of the cliff.

In *a-ii-ka-suuna*, the prefix *a-* 'outside' places the entire scene within the scope of the viewer's visual field, whereas the prefix *ii-* 'this way' traces the water's trajectory along a path basically oriented toward the viewer's vantage point. Pragmatically, this probably allows the viewer's visual field to take in a perceptible stretch of the river above the fall or, at least, the perceived motion of the water gives the orientation of the path in this scene. Finally, *ka-* traces the normal fall of the water from the top of the cliff to its base.

The role of the prefix *ii-* to determine a marked vantage point is also evident in *a-i-h-n^yeeri-'i* (11c). In this case, the situation concerns the effects of some source of illumination located at or near the foot of a hill. This source, then, is lighting up the hillside with a distinct orientation coming from the foot of the hill all the way up to near the top of that hill at the viewer's position. Once again, the use of *a-* 'outside' places the entire scene within the scope of the viewer's visual field, whereas *ii-* signals the orientation of the trajector (i.e. the process of illumination) toward the viewer's position. Finally, the prefix *h-* places the entire path within the face of the slope. This situation, then, clearly contrasts with that described earlier for *an-t^yi-n^yeeri-'i* (4c), in which the viewer's canonical viewing position is at the foot of the hill and the illuminated area is at the top, with the intermediate slope backgrounded to the rest of the scene.

The example *a-ii-ta-t^yee* (11d) provides a third instance in which *ii-* allows us to see a clear contrast in vantage point with that associated with another prefix sequence. The relevant situation in this case finds the speaker looking across a river and gauging its width as being rather substantial. This is no little brook.

In contrast to *an-ta-n^yeeri-'i* (4b), however, the speaker's primary point of focus for construing this situation is some point at the side of the river opposite his own position, as shown in Figures (12a) and (12b). The use of *a-* 'outside' again places this point within his visual field. The use of *ii-* 'this way' shows that the speaker is calculating the extension of the trajector (i.e. DISTANCE) along a path that starts at the far side of the river and ends at the viewer's position. The prefix *ta-*, in turn, traces the extension totally across the width of the river. The fact that *ta-* in *an-ta-n^yeeri-'i* (4b) also highlights the total width of the river shows that

(a)

/a/   /ii/   /ta/   /-tʸee/

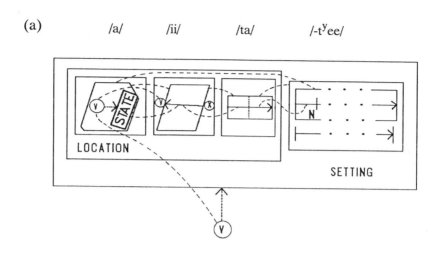

(b)

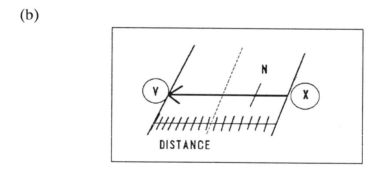

Figure 12: *a-ii-ta-tʸee* 'It's a long way over to here.'

ta- is neutral with respect to vantage point. This is also true of its use in *wa-ta-vi-vɨ* (5c) and in *ta-cʸapʷa* (7a). These facts, then, support Hawkins' notion of an "undirected" path (1984: 77). I take the "undirected" path to be a specialization of the "directed" one.

On the other hand, motion away from the speaker's position is indicated by the use of the prefix *uu-* 'that way,' as illustrated by (12a) and (12b):

(12) a.   *y-áa pú ú-ɛ̃ʸapʷa*
            here-outside SUBJ that way-footprint
            'From here, there is a string of footprints leading off yonder.'

      b.   *á-úu-na'a-ra*
            DISTAL-that way-burn-CAUS
            'Go and make a fire!'

The scene related to *yaa=pu=uɛ̃ʸapʷa* (12a) finds the speaker
looking at a string of footprints in the ground that leads off from his position to some point an unspecified distance away. The particle *yaa* locates the entire scene within an unenclosed area anchored to the
speaker's position, indicated by the initial *y*. The subject particle *pu* is
the topic pivot for the fronted locative particle *yaa*. The nominal *ɛ̃ʸa-*
pʷari appears here in its incorporated form without the absolutive suffix
-ri and the prefix *uu-* indicates that the line of footprints follows a path
leading directly away from the speaker's position.

The use of *uu-* in *a-uu-na'ara* (12b) also indicates movement along a
path from the speaker's location to an unspecified goal, yet the use of *a-*
'outside' probably limits the extension of the path to a location within
eyeshot of the speaker. The fact that this form is an imperative and
designates a common domestic activity lends support to this interpretation of *a-*.

The prefix *uu-* has also become grammaticalized, taking on the intentive meaning 'go to do X'. I discuss this in Section 4.2. Occasionally,
a given use of a locative prefix sequence carries with it an unexpected
vantage point. For example, the verb *-kɨh* 'go: PL' usually designates
motion along a path away from the speaker's location or along some intermediate stretch of a path. Thus one might expect that *ma-ku-ra'a-*
kɨh-ší might mean 'they went off in all directions'. However, as the gloss
in (13) shows, it means just the opposite, i.e. 'they came from everywhere around'. In this instance, the prefix sequence *ku-ra'a-* 'around-
corner' designates the starting point on the path that the trajector follows, whereas *-kɨh* designates the end point of that path:

(13)   *ma-ku-rá'a-kɨh-ší*
        they-around-corner-go: PAST-DISTR: PAST
        'They came from everywhere around.'

The speaker's vantage point for *ma-ku-ra'a-kɨh-ší* (13) is prototypically at the center of the scene. This is based partly on the gloss 'came

from all directions'. The plural subject marker *ma-* indicates that an unspecified number of trajectors are involved in the motion. The notion of multiple trajectors is highly salient to this construction, as it is also marked by the suppletive plural form of the verb stem that means 'go'. The individuality of the trajectors that are jointly involved in the motion is signalled by the use of the DISTRIBUTIVE suffix -*ši*. The locative prefix *ku-* 'around' then specifies a circle along whose perimeter the individuals pass over on their way to a common goal point from distinct starting points. The verb stem *kih* gives the individual paths their origins from somewhere beyond the limits of the perceptual field to the prototypical vantage point at the center of the scene. Although the verb -*me/-hu'u* does not normally single out a particular facet of the path as the salient one, in this case, the conventional understanding that it designates the initial point on the path may be forced by the fact that the otherwise expected reading, i.e. 'they went off in all directions' has been co-opted by *m-a'-u-kih-ši*. Whereas the prefix *ku-* 'around' summarizes the set of points along the individual trajectors' paths at which they are conventionally construed as collectively appearing on the scene, the perimeter of the circle itself can be construed as constituting the abrupt changepoint in the path associated with *ra'a-* 'around a corner'. The expanse then, between the outer limit of the perceptual field and the center point can be construed as the perceptually accessible side of the configuration that defines the "corner" around which the trajector's path comes. All these facets of the meaning of *ma-ku-ra'a-kih-ši* are represented graphically in Figure 13:

(a)

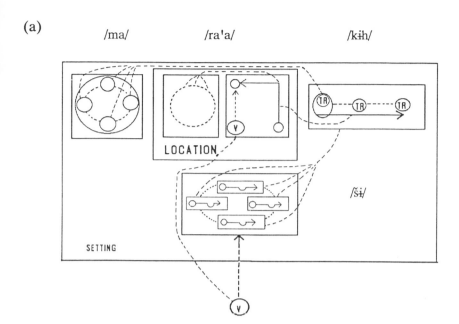

(b)

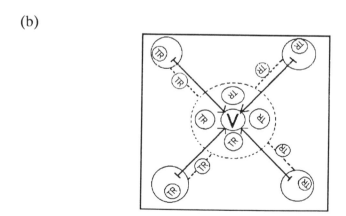

Figure 13: *ma-ku-ra'a-kɨh-sɨ* 'They came from all sides.'

The final example that I cite in this section to illustrate the role of the speaker's vantage point in determining the usage of a sentence also exemplifies a version of a complex path within three-dimensional geometric space. The form is *u-ve'e-re'e-n^{y}e* 'he came here from back around the corner' (14):

(14)   *u-ve'e-ré'e-n^{y}e*
       inside-back-corner-arrive
       'He came back from around the corner to where I was.'

In this construction, the prefix *u-* 'inside' anchors the starting point of the trajector's path to a location outside the speaker's visual field, whereas the prefix *ve'e-* imposes a directionality on that complex path, anchoring its goal point to the viewer's actual position. The role of *ve'e-* in this example is analogous to that of *ii-* 'this way' in such forms as *a-ii-ka-suuna*, *a-i-h-n^{y}eeri-'i*, and *a-ii-ta-t^{y}ee* (11a) through (11c), which I discussed earlier. The difference between *ii-* and *ve'e-* is simply that they are defined in terms of two distinct conceptual bases (or ICM's), with *ve'e-* being defined in terms of a three dimensional base, whereas *ii-* is defined in terms of a two dimensional one.[16] Finally, the role of *u-* and *ve'e-* to orient the complex path designated by *ra'a-* is an additional suggestion that the prototypical structure associated with *ra'a-* is neutral with respect to how the path is oriented in relation to the speaker's vantage point.

To summarize, in this section I have discussed several prefix sequences that fall into contrastive pairs with other prefixes in which they are distinguished by the speaker's vantage point for viewing a conceptual scene. This suggests strongly that an explicit mention must be made of this vantage point if one is to formulate a credible cognitive model of Cora Locative Prefix + Verb/Adjective Stem constructions.

These data, moreover, suggest other aspects of the Directed Path Schema that I have only briefly touched on thus far, i.e. its characterization as a network that includes prototypical instances, as well as non-prototypical ones. In addition, it contains schematic versions of various sorts. The next section of this paper examines several non-prototypical examples of path notions in which domain shifts are a key factor.

4.   Non-prototypical versions of LOCATION

Although the locative prefixes primarily serve to specify the locational settings for processes and relations, their conventionalized usages show that they extend semantically into other domains of the grammar as well. In certain cases, they lexicalize in ways that make them quasi-aspectual in their function.[17]

One motivation for their lexicalization in such ways is that frequently, the spatial setting of an activity is viewed differently depending on whether that activity is viewed as one in progress or as one already completed or at the end of its temporal evolution (cf. Claudi & Heine 1986: 320).

One of the subsequent developments of the creation of LOC PREFIX-VERB constructions has been the selection of particular prefix combinations for conveying distinct situational configurations associated with alternate aspectual usages of Cora verbs.[18] In such instances, certain prefix combinations become so consistently associated with aspectual choices that one can say that the prefix combinations themselves carry "semantic aspectual distinctions" (cf. Comrie 1976: 7). This is especially true for cases in which one member of the normal set of markers that indicate aspectual distinctions is zero, or the aspectual marker per se is semantically ambiguous.

4.1.   The heightened Perfective wa-ta-

The prefixes *wa-* 'extensive' and *ta-* 'across' are frequently used, either singly or together, to mark PERFECTIVE aspect. This gives rise to the PERFECTIVE-IMPERFECTIVE contrast given in (15a) and (15b) in which the Perfective notion is encoded by the prefix sequence *wa-ta-* 'extensive-across/straight' and the contrasting Imperfective notion is marked by *a-ve'e-* 'back across a front surface':

(15) a.   *ka=pú wa-ta-nʸúu*
            NEG = SUBJ EXT-straight-respond
            'He did not answer back.'
      b.   *ka=pu a-vé'e-nʸuu*
            NEG = SUBJ outside-back-respond
            'He is not answering.'

The ordinary completive use of *wa-* is shown in (16a), whereas its uses in combination with *ta-* are illustrated by (16b) and (16c). The prefix *ta-*, like *wa-ta-*, has an extended use as a marker of perfective processes. In particular, *ta-* contributes a sense of immediacy to the event reported on (16b) or heightens the intensity of the thoroughness of the effects of an event (16c) (cf. Grimes (1964: 90), for the same extension of Huichol *ta-*):

(16) a.   *wa-mɨ'ɨ*
            COMPL-die
            'He died.'
      b.   *wa-ta-mɨ'ɨ*
            COMPL-PERF-die
            'He up and died.'
      c.   *wá-ta-'i-mɨ'ɨ*
            COMPL-PERF-drink-DESID
            'It gets one really thirsty.'

There is a straightforward connection between the meanings of *wa-* and *ta-*, given in configurational terms for their spatial usages, and for their extended meanings as markers of aspectual notions. In both (16b) and (16c), *wa-ta-* indicates an intensified perfective view of things. As we have noted before, the "perfective" view of an event considers it as a totality, i.e. a bounded whole. Thus it does not need to look at any particular subconfiguration within the temporal profile of a process, although it may focus on either the beginning or on the end point of the process (cf. Comrie 1976: 3). Instead, the temporal profile can be viewed as a simple path, with the duration of that event being construed as setting bounds on the length of that path.

It is significant that bounded areas are part of the configural representations of both *wa-* and *ta-*. Whereas an undirected path is a salient subconfiguration in the representation of *ta-*, as shown by the righthand box of Figure 14a, the limit on the expansiveness of an area is salient in the representation of *wa-*, given in the lefthand box of the exploded representation of *wa-ta*. When the two prefixes are combined, as the integration lines show, the bounded area in the base of wa- typically coincides with that in the base of *ta-* and even reinforces the relative salience of that boundary area in the composite representation. This gives a version of *wa-ta-* in which both the bounded area and the undirected path are foregrounded (Figure 14b). I have indicated in Figure 14b the temporal relation of the occurrence of the event in mind (t_0) to the time of speaking (t_i). I also include the representation of a schematic event as the trajector of the heightened perfective *wa-ta*.

(a)   /wa-/   /ta-/

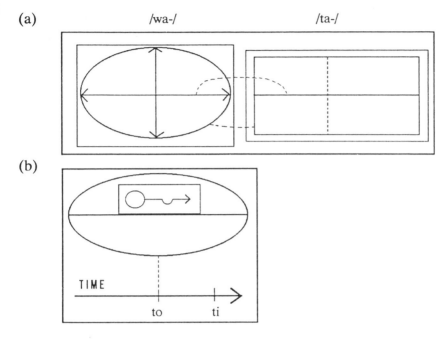

(b)

Figure 14. The heightened Perfective *wa-ta-*

To close, the configurations in Figure 14a at least partially explain the extension of these spatial prefixes into the domains of time and aspect. The semantic result of thoroughness or intensity of action can be construed as an iconic reflection of the salience placed on both the path of *ta-*, which goes all the way from one side of a bounded area to an opposite side, and the boundary of *wa-*, which encompasses the entire area within the scope of the speaker's attention.

4.2.   The intentive uu- 'go to do X'

Some Cora locative prefix combinations show a marked degree of grammaticalization in that they mark schematic patterns for locating events in distinct ways within a global setting. Although they are highly grammaticalized, they are still decidedly meaningful (cf. Langacker 1987: 12). This suggests that the move from free lexical item to grammatical functor does not always entail a complete loss of meaning. In this section, I discuss only one example, that of the Intentive use of *uu-* 'that way'.

uu- may refer to a horizontally-oriented path totally within the confines of a bounded area, as in (17a). Its horizontal orientation is clearly established by the semantic contrast between (17b) and (17c):

(17) a. *ú-kun*
          inside: horizontally-hollow
          'There is a hole (doorway) in there between the rooms of the house.'
      b. *uu-rúh-tʸi-ʼi*[19]
          inside: horizontally-slope-enter-CAUS-STAT
          'It is plugged into the wall socket.'
      c. *u-h-rúh-tʸi-ʼi*
          inside-slope-enter-CAUS-STAT
          'It is plugged into the ceiling.'

When used with motion verbs or predicates of extension to refer to locations within the domain of the topography, *uu-* simply means 'straight off to the edge of the horizon', as in (18a). In other contexts it means 'directly away from the viewer's position', as in (18b):

(18) a. *á-h-kaʼi a-úu-ru-pi*
          outside-slope-hillside DISTAL-inside: horiz
          -enter-PAST
          'He went off to the side of the hill.'
      b. *y-áa=pú ú-ɛʸapʷa*
          here-outside-flat=SUBJ=inside: horiz-footprint
          'The footprints go leading off from right here.'

The examples in (18a) and (18b) illustrate two path-oriented versions of *uu-*. Their respective image schemas are given in Figures 15a and 15b:

(a)   (b)

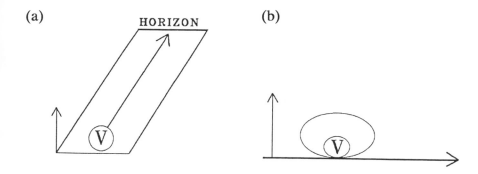

Figure 15.   *uu-* 'there: in the flat' vs. *uu-* 'that way'

Sentence (18a) establishes the horizontality of the path associated with *uu-*, whereas the locative particle in (18b) provides evidence that a potential viewer's canonical vantage point anchors that path, thus giving *uu-* the meaning 'that way'.

One extension of *uu-* that is based on the schematic of Fig. 15 functions productively in the combination of *uu-* with verb stems. The *uu-* plus stem construction has the generalized meaning of 'to go off and do X', as in the examples in (19). This version of *uu-* may well represent the grammaticalization of a conversational implicature, since, in order for someone to do something that he intends to do at a remote location, under normal circumstances he must first go there and establish his presence.

(19) a.   *n-úu-m^Wasa-p^Wa*
           I-that way-deer-PRIV
           'I'm going off to hunt deer.'
      b.   *n^Yí yéewí sa-n-úu-m^Waari-n*
           Q QUOT you: PL-me-that way-visit-FUT
           'Are you not going off to visit me
           [i.e. go off to where I live]?'

4.3.   *The temporals* a-uu-ta- *and* an-t^Yi-

In this section I begin to show how the schema behind certain strictly spatial usages of the prefixes transfers to a pair of prefix sequences with usage in the additional domain of time.

Greenberg (1985: 282) notes the naturalness attached to the way that speakers of natural languages extend the spatial usages of grammatical elements to temporal usages and relates this to several pragmatic factors, including the visual field and the participants involved in the events being discussed. To this I would add the speaker's conceptual field and abilities, as well as the sanctioning potential of the grammar itself and the implicit limitation on the range of mental models that can be employed from domain to domain, these limitations arising from the fact that space itself, with the entities that occupy it, is not always structured the same way across domains (cf. McLaury 1989). As we might expect from the discussion thus far, the LOCATIVE PREFIX + VERB combinations also show such extensions. Traugott (1985) details the various sorts of schemata that underly extensions into the temporal sphere. These include a front and back orientation, an up versus down one, and an open versus closed field (Traugott 1985: 26-30). Our data show that the full range of schemata that she mentions are operative in Cora grammar. In this section of the paper I illustrate only two of them and show how the speaker's potential for viewing situations in distinct ways and for selecting distinct domains for discussion has led to conventionalized forms of expression.

The first example that I discuss involves the use of the prefix sequence *a-uu-ta-* 'going all the way around the circumference', which, in the domain of the human body, traces a path all the way around a joint of the finger, arm or leg and the waist, as in (20a). It can also designate the circumference of a cooking pot, as in (20b). Thus, *a-uu-ta-*, in its temporal usages can be construed as instantiating one version of the closed field view of time.

(20) a.   *n-a'-u-ta-pí-p^{w}a*
            I-outside-that way-straight-RDP-skinny
            'I'm as skinny as a rail.'
      b.   *a-uu-tá-tap^{w}a mí sa'ari*
            outside-that way-straight-broken ART pot
            'The clay cooking pot is broken in two.'
      c.   *t^y-á'-u-te-'it^{y}é-n í ineeru*
            DISTR-DIST-that way-straight-count-PRTC ART January
            'at the beginning of January'

In particular, the temporal use of *a-uu-ta-*, illustrated in (20b), is sanctioned by the image schema in which *a-uu-ta-* designates a complete circular path that its trajector follows as it traverses a closed surface in three-dimensional space. In Figure 16, this surface is shown as part of a cylindrical base that I depict standing on one of its flat ends. The path in question runs horizontally around the base at its middle. The hashmarks represent the successive stages arrived at by counting, whereas a somewhat restricted area near the tail of the area of the directed path is an iconic representation of the "beginning" region of the monthly cycle. In short, *a-uu-ta-* is appropriate here because the months are counted cyclically, with an ascending order that comes back around to the starting point for beginning a new month. This starting point is identified as Referential Time (T_x) on the neutral timeline below the cylindrical base.

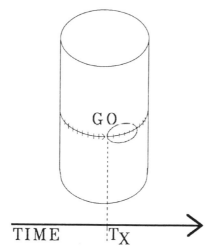

Figure 16: a-uu-ta-: A closed field version of time

The final example I discuss here illustrates an up and down orientation employing the locative prefix sequence *an-t^yi-* 'at the top of the hill'/'at the tip of' (21):

(21)   *an-t^yi-p^wá'ara-ka'a*
        top-up-end-PAST PERF
        'Time's up.'

In the domain of the topography, *an-t^yi-* designates the very top of a hill, as examples (4c), (7) and (9a) illustrate. In other domains, it designates things like the top of a tree, pole, tower or church steeple, and even the tines of a fork or the tips of one's fingers. These extended usages of *an-t^yi-* involve the fading out of the verticality notion and the highlighting of any prominent projection at all (cf. Casad 1982: 267f; 1988: 354ff).

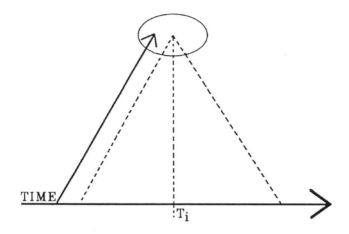

Figure 17: An upwards view of time: *ant^yip^wa'araka'a*

In (21) *an-t^yi-* designates the very end point of a temporal path, giving time a backgrounded topographic orientation such that it is seen marching toward the top of a hill (Figure 17). In this construction, the verb stem *-p^wa'are-* 'to end' specifically highlights the end point of the time period; the prefix sequence *an-t^yi-* augments the end point with its "up" orientation. The perfective suffix *-ka'a* indicates that the entire event is viewed as having been realized in recent past time; i.e. practically speaking, this phrase is used to refer to events that have terminated just prior to the time of speaking.

5.   Implications

An analysis of Locative Prefix + Verb Stem constructions in Cora shows that paths can be part of the semantic representations of both verb stems and locative prefixes, no single one of which can be simply glossed 'path' or 'source' or 'goal', although some combinations such as *an-t^yi-* are more goal-oriented than others such as *a-uu-*, which often indicates a path in its linear extension. Often enough, the same prefix sequence can indicate either Source, Goal or Path, depending on any of a number of considerations. All this suggests that the notions of Source,

Path and Goal are not really "local cases", "deep structure cases" or grammatical case-markers, but are rather aspects of a basic cognitive complex, the Directed Path Image Schema (Miller & Johnson-Laird 1977; Casad 1982; Jackendoff 1978, 1983; Hawkins 1984, Traugott 1985; Lakoff 1987).

The prototypical usage of these constructions is to orient the interlocutors of the speech event to the physical settings in which events are realized. The adverbials used select particular domains for discussion, whereas the prefixes specify the shape (or orientation) of the path within that domain. The fact that so many different orientations and shapes are conventionally employed by Cora speakers suggests the importance of mental imagery to grammatical structure, which is based on the operations of the cognitive abilities of human speakers (cf. Lamb 1971; Langacker 1979, 1987; Jongen 1985; Lakoff 1987).

The observation that the same scene may be structured in several different ways shows that scenes are not given objectively, but rather are structured by the viewer in particular ways for linguistic expression (cf. Fillmore 1977; Nöth 1985; Langacker 1987; Lakoff 1987). In particular, a specification of the role of the vantage point of the speaker is seen to be necessary for adequately characterizing many of the usages of these constructions.

It is very clear from the analysis that I present here that a prototype model, with all of its implications for complex relationships within a category, fits well with these data (cf. Dahl 1985; Rudzka-Ostyn 1985; Brugman 1986; Lakoff 1987; Langacker 1987; Geeraerts 1988). Location, Source, Goal and Path can all be treated as complex categories in their own right, while the Directed Path Schema can be construed as a superordinate category that unites Source, Path and Goal in a single schematic framework (cf. Casad 1982; Traugott 1985). In short, the Directed Path Schema represents a radial category of the nature discussed by Lakoff (1987: 84).

A simplified version of such a network is given in Figure 18. It represents the Directed Path Schema as the most abstract version of the entire network, serving as the hub that relates six families of more specific variants of the path schema. These variants differ from each other in the details of the schema itself, in the domains against which the schema is judged and in the morphological and syntactic correlates of the semantic differences among them. The first of the families consists of Topographic Paths. These include up, down and across paths within the domain of the River, and up, down and over paths within the Hill domain. The over paths may be either simple or complex.

The Adverbial paths consist of those grammaticalized sequences which have taken on the schematic meanings 'Go to do X,' 'Did X off yonder,' and 'Went, did X and came back'. The Geometric Paths include minimal paths, reflexive paths and several kinds of configurational paths that are defined rather abstractly within general three-dimensional space. These variants include upwards, downwards and horizontal paths. Horizontal paths may be either simple or complex, and, in addition, may be non-directed. For purposes of this study, non-directed paths are a specialization of the Directed Path Schema (cf. Hawkins 1984: 78, 81).

The family of Oriented Paths consists of those in which the viewer's canonical vantage point plays a crucial role in the calculation of particular relationships. This involves relations such as toward the speaker, leaving the speaker (= away from), source-oriented, goal-oriented and forwards-looking. The family of Aspectual Paths includes perfective uses versus imperfective ones. The perfective usages either highlight the final stage of the event or present the totality of the event in a heightened perspective.

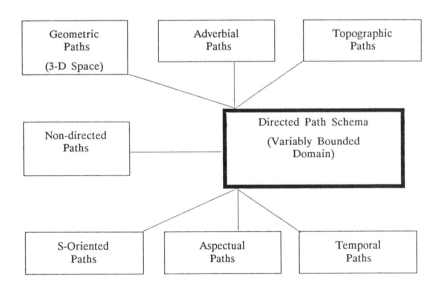

Figure 18: Directed Path Schema as hub of Radial Category

Finally, Temporal Paths include either a forwards or a backwards perspective on the scene, as well as present the scene as occurring within either an open or closed field. Temporal usages may also display an upwards orientation. To conclude, the resulting network illustrates nicely Lakoff's notion of Radial Category, the hub of which is constituted by the Directed Path schema itself and the families of which are themselves subsystems (cf. Lakoff 1987: 91, 287). The six sets of subsidiary networks relate to the hub in a configuration that is reminiscent of, but more complex than, the "family resemblances" schema illustrated by Dahl in his paper on "Case grammar and prototypes" (Dahl 1985: 22). These variants are not predictable in any strong sense of the word from prototypical values, but they are all motivated in the Lakovian sense (1987: 107).

Jackendoff rightly treats "paths" and "locations" as conceptual entities that are part of semantic structure (1978: 204; 1983: 163). Regarding prepositional phrase constructions whose meanings involve such notions, he comments that "to achieve even observational adequacy, a theory of semantics will have to include a rich set of projection rules to map these constructions into the information they convey; moreover, it is hardly obvious what the nature of that information is" (Jackendoff 1978: 206).

To begin to answer Jackendoff, I suggest that the analysis of the data in this paper shows that the following kinds of considerations are relevant for characterizing the information encompassed by the meanings of both morphemes and constructions:

1. Which cognitive domain is the speaker using for his frame of reference? Physical space? Temporal Space? Abstract Logical Space (cf. Traugott 1985)? This specification is only the first step, however.
2. How is the path oriented within a particular domain? For topography, it could be uphill, downhill, going around behind the hill, upriver, downriver or going across the river, as in the Cora system of topographic adverbs (Casad 1977, 1982). In general three-dimensional space, when the speaker grounds a path to his canonical position and orientation for viewing his surroundings, the path he describes could be oriented upwards, downwards, straight ahead, from side to side, toward a point, away from a point, coming from within an enclosure or going through an entrance into an enclosed area. For the temporal domain, it could be coming from around behind the corner, going along a straight line horizontally, or coming up to the uppermost point of a vertically oriented path.

3. What options does the Speaker have available to him for characterizing the role of a path or location within the scene the Speaker is describing? Often, he has more than just a single choice. This latitude of choice is what brings nonobjectivity into semantics.
4. Closely related to (3), how is the path notion lexicalized? As a verb stem? As a locative prefix or suffix? As some other grammatical element? Is the particular path notion salient to the semantic representation of the morpheme in question? Or is it backgrounded to the rest of that representation (cf. Talmy 1987)?
5. How does the course of the path relate to the Speaker's position? Does it come toward him, move away from him? Or come back toward him after the entity in motion makes an abrupt change in direction at a distal additional reference point?
6. Is the Speaker conceived as following the path himself? Or is the path being treated in a more "objective" fashion?
7. What is the nature of the path? Is it simple? Complex? Multiplex?
8. Which aspect of the path does the Speaker wish to select for comment? "Source"? "Goal"? Does he view the entire path as an extended entity, or as a single minimal point? Or is he simply focussing on some intermediate point within the extension of the path?[20]

6. Conclusion

Language is a highly organized and flexible system used by human speakers who continuously employ numerous cognitive facilities for enriching their own expressiveness. The faculty for linguistic expression finds its basis in the nature of cognizing individuals. In characterizing the usages of numerous examples from the Cora language of northwest Mexico, I have tried to show how these cognitive abilities have helped determine specific linguistic forms. In doing so, I have drawn heavily on the model of grammatical structure that is being elaborated by Ronald W. Langacker and his associates.

My analysis of these Cora data suggests strongly that Langacker's model of the finite clause (or event structure) is essentially correct in insisting that both the settings of events and the speaker's vantage point for viewing them are both relevant and crucial in accounting for the forms and usages of Cora Locative Prefix + Verb Stem constructions.

A consideration of these data, however, has shown clearly that, in order to provide a descriptively adequate account of these Cora data, it is necessary to include in a model of the Cora finite clause a locative constituent which provides a schematic characterization of the spatial framework within which events transpire and states occur. This locative constituent is distinct from the global setting of the event , but is not autonomous from it (cf. Langacker 1989: 7ff). In fact, its relationship to it is organic and variable. The prototypical topographic use, for example, invokes either a topographic adverb or a locative particle that enters into construction with a verb that includes one of six conventionally established prefix sequences. In this construction, the external adverbial designates a location within a specific domain, whereas the prefix sequence designates the shape of the trajector's path within that domain. The semantics of both the adverbial and the prefix sequence is defined within a common base. In other versions, the area designated by the prefixes may be only a subpart of the entire global setting that the path covers. Even more abstract versions occur.

Finally, an examination of the categorization intrinsic to all these usages shows that the concepts Path, Source and Goal are not semantic primitives, but rather are aspects of a superordinate category which I call the DIRECTED PATH SCHEMA, which serves as the hub for an entire set of interrelated subnetworks of contextually defined path-related notions.

Notes

1.   The data on which this paper is based were collected during the period beginning February 1971 and continuing until the present during the course of field investigations being carried out under the auspices of the Summer Institute of Linguistics. These data are culled from elicited materials such as word lists, extracted from texts and even gleaned from active conversations with Cora speakers. The data are almost entirely from the Jesus Maria dialect. I would like to thank numerous Cora speakers, who continue to be my teachers in their language. I would like to thank Ronald W. Langacker for his help on both the original version of this paper and on the present one. I would also like to thank Barbara Hollenbach for her very helpful critique of that early draft. Finally, comments by David Tuggy, Brygida Rudzka-Ostyn and an anonymous reviewer have been helpful in completing this paper.

2.   The following abbreviations are used in this paper:

APPLIC:	Applicative
ART:	Article
BASE:	Base
CAUS:	Causative
CNJ:	Conjunction
COLL:	Collective

COND:	Conditional
DEM:	Demonstrative
DIST:	Distal
DISTR:	Distributive
DUR:	Durative
EXT:	Extensive
FUT:	Future
HAB:	Habitual
IMPERF:	Imperfective
LOC:	Locative
MED:	Medial
NARR:	Narrative
NEG:	Negative
PASS:	Passive
PAST:	Past
PAUS:	Pausal
PERF:	Perfective
PERIP:	Peripatetic
PL:	Plural
PRIV:	Privative
PROCOMP:	Procomplement
PRTC:	Participle
QNT:	Quantifier
QUOT:	Quotative
RDP:	Reduplication
REFL:	Reflexive
STAT:	Stative
SUBJ:	Subjunctive
SUBR:	Subordinator

3.   A respectable summary of this topic is beyond the scope of this paper. However, in a longer version, I have summarized some of the key studies, focussing largely on those that have adopted case notions from Fillmore's Case Grammar (1968) and have tried to accommodate these notions within Generative theory. One interesting tendency has been for authors to explicitly treat these notions as semantically primitive, but admit openly that they are not conceptually simple (cf. Stockwell, Schachter & Hall Partee 1968: 957; Anderson 1971: 81, 218f; Grimes 1975: 119).

4.   Lamb (1971) expressed a very similar point of view when he stated that the purpose of his theory was "to provide a model of the information system that enables a person to speak his language (1971: 99)". Lamb also outlines in this paper what such a theory must contain, i.e. what a person knows about his environment, his culture, his own personal history, in short, his encyclopedic knowledge in toto (1971: 119).

5.   In a recent paper, Janda describes uses of the Russian prefix *pere-*, gives a unified account of these uses in terms of a cognitive network, and suggests that the grammatical relations "subject" and "object" are actually complex concepts (1988: 343). For a more general critique of the "primitiveness" and "universality" of semantic features, cf. Casad 1982: 37-41; Svorou 1987: 86-90; Lakoff 1987: 115f; Langacker 1987: 19-22; Dirven & Taylor 1988: 394.

6. A similar point of view, that scenes are relativized to grammatical patterns is given in Fillmore (1977).

7. Grimes expresses an identical point of view when he categorizes notions such as "Source", "Goal" and "Range" as Orientational Roles that help establish setting for events (1975: 120ff).

8. The term "action chain" can be viewed as part of the more general domain of "Force Dynamics" discussed in Talmy (1985). In part, Talmy characterizes Force Dynamics as a system for organizing conceptual structure via schematic models that relate physical, psychological and social phenomena.

9. The non-prototypicality of the Cora clause structure I discuss here is neither a surprise, nor a problem, for Cognitive Grammar. As Langacker notes, there can be many versions based on the model of Figure One, both because speakers can construe situations in alternate ways and because they have various grammatical devices for expressing their thoughts (Langacker 1986a: 22; 1989: 7-2, 7-5).

10. The only exceptions to this are the prefix *ii-* 'this way/in a path', whose gloss I shorten to 'path' in the morpheme by morpheme gloss lines of some of the examples I use in this paper, and the verb form *a'a*, which I gloss as 'be: LOC'. I also use the gloss "Locative Base" for the proclitic use of *a-uu.*

11. Thus, Cora prefixes display an interesting functional parallel to the Dutch and Polish prefixes discussed by Rudzka-Ostyn (1985). On the other hand, the Cora LOCATIVE PREFIX + VERB construction contrasts typologically with both the Atzugewi and English examples discussed by Talmy (1987: 102ff).

12. Note that Dirven and Taylor also use the notion of a norm in their analysis of German *hoch* 'high/tall' and *lang* 'long' and in their English counterparts (1988: 385). Svorou also treats the norm as one part of a conceptual complex (1987: 66-7).

13. An important part of the story, to be sure, requires a detailed historical study of the Southern Uto-Aztecan languages, and, especially, of the verbal systems of Cora and Huichol, since 9 of the 11 Huichol prefixes that Grimes (1964) cites are clearly related to the Cora prefixes by regular sound change and semantic structure. In two cases, a pair of Huichol prefixes have apparently fallen together in Cora. I am just beginning to write up this part of the story.

14. The *ta* in *antan* may be the historical source for the grammaticalization of the prefix *ta-.*

15. The notion "e-site" is based on the assumption that semantic units combine in pairs such that one member is autonomous, whereas the other is dependent. The dependent one is said to make inherent internal reference to the autonomous unit via the e-site, which is actually a substructure within the dependent unit that corresponds to the profile of the autonomous unit. In turn, the autonomous unit elaborates the e-site in detail (Langacker 1987: 304). Notice that the individual prefixes, however, contain no e-sites. They thus represent nonprototypical semantic structures (cf. Casad 1982: 86; Langacker 1987: 304).

16. Geeraerts distinguishes between Dutch *vernielen* and *vernietigen* on the basis that they relate to distinct prototypical semantic structures (1988:

214f, 217). See also Taylor (1988: 309) for the difference between Italian *su* and *sopra*.

17.   Cf. Jackendoff (1983: 209), who comments on the spatial and temporal basis of thematic relations in English.

18.   Cf. Rudzka-Ostyn (1985) for an illuminating discussion of Dutch *uit* and Polish *wy*.

19.   Note that *uu-* has the shortened form *u-* in (17a) and (17c). This reflects a common process in Uto-Aztecan languages in which long vowels are shortened in word-initial position. The underlying length of *u-* is preserved in initial position when it is followed by the retroflexed forward tap /r/.

20.   For a similar listing of information relevant to the adequate description of prepositions, see Taylor (1988: 304f).

References

Anderson, John M.
    1971   *The grammar of case: Towards a localistic theory*. Cambridge: Cambridge University Press.
Bennett, David C.
    1975   *Spatial and temporal uses of English prepositions*. London: Longman.
Brugman, Claudia
    1983   "The use of body-part terms as locatives in Chalcatongo Mixtec", in: Alice Schlicter, Wallace L. Chafe & Leanne Hinton (eds.), *Reports from the survey of California and other Indian languages*, No. 4. Berkeley: Survey of California and Other Indian Languages.
    1986   *The story of over: Polysemy, semantics, and the structure of the lexicon*. New York: Garland.
Bybee, Joan
    1985   *Morphology*. Amsterdam: Benjamins.
Casad, Eugene H.
    1977   "Location and direction in Cora discourse", *Applied Linguistics* 19: 216-241.
    1982   Cora locationals and structured imagery. [Unpublished Ph.D. Dissertation, University of California, San Diego.]
    1984   "Cora", in: Ronald W. Langacker (ed.), *Southern Uto-Aztecan grammatical sketches*. Arlington, TX: The University of Texas and the Summer Institute of Linguistics, 152-459.
    1988   "Conventionalization of Cora locationals", in: Brygida Rudzka-Ostyn (ed.), 345-378.
Casad, Eugene H. & Ronald W. Langacker
    1985   "'Inside' and 'outside' in Cora grammar", *IJAL* 51: 247-281.
Clark, Eve V.
    1978   "Locationals: Existential, locative and possessive constructions", in: Joseph H. Greenberg (ed.), *Universals of human language*, Vol. 4. Stanford: Stanford University Press, 85-126.
Claudi, Ulrike & Bernd Heine
    1986   "On the metaphorical base of grammar", *Studies in Language* 10: 297-335.

Comrie, Bernard
1976   *Aspect*. Cambridge: Cambridge University Press.
Dahl, Östen
1985   "Case grammar and prototypes", Duisburg: Linguistic Agency University of Duisburg.
Dirven, René & John R. Taylor
1988   "The conceptualization of vertical space in English: The case of *tall*", in: Brygida Rudzka-Ostyn (ed.), 403-427.
Fillmore, Charles J.
1977   "The case for case reopened", in: Peter Cole & Jerrold M. Saddok (eds.), *Syntax and semantics*. Vol 8: *Grammatical relations*. New York: Academic Press, 59-81.
Friedrich, Paul
1970   "Shape in grammar", *Language* 46: 379-407.
Geeraerts, Dirk
1988   "Where does prototypicality come from?", in: Brygida Rudzka-Ostyn (ed.), 207-229.
Greenberg, Joseph H.
1985   "Some iconic relationships among place, time and discourse deixis", in: John Haiman (ed.), *Iconicity in syntax*. Amsterdam: Benjamins, 271-287.
Grimes, Joseph E.
1964   *Huichol syntax*. The Hague: Mouton.
1975   *The thread of discourse*. The Hague: Mouton.
Hawkins, Bruce W.
1984   The semantics of English spatial prepositions. [Unpublished Ph.D. Disserta-tion, University of California, San Diego.]
Hollenbach, Barbara E.
1983   Semantic extensions of Copala Trique body-part nouns. [Unpublished manuscript.]
n.d.   Semantic extensions from space to time in Copala Trique. [Unpublished manuscript.]
Jackendoff, Ray
1978   "Grammar as evidence for conceptual structure", in: Morris Halle, Joan Bresnan & George A. Miller (eds.), *Linguistic theory and psychological reality*. Cambridge: MIT Press, 201-228.
1983   *Grammar and cognition*. Cambridge: MIT Press.
Janda, Laura A.
1988   "The mapping of elements of cognitive space onto grammatical relations: An example from Russian verbal prefixation", in: Brygida Rudzka-Ostyn (ed.), 327-343.
Jongen, René
1985   "Polysemy, trope and cognition or the non-Magrittian art of closing curtains whilst opening them", in: Wolf Paprotté & René Dirven (eds.), 121-139.
Lakoff, George
1987   *Women, fire, and dangerous things: What categories reveal about the mind.* Chicago: University of Chicago Press.

Lamb, Sidney
1971   "The crooked path of progress in Cognitive Linguistics", in: Richard J.
                O'Brien (ed.), *Linguistics: Developments of the sixties - Viewpoints for
                the seventies*. (Georgetown University Monograph Series on Languages
                and Linguistics. No. 22.) Washington, D.C.: Georgetown University
                Press, 99-123.
Langacker, Ronald W.
1979   "Grammar as image", *Linguistic Notes from La Jolla* 6: 87-126.
1986a   "An introduction to Cognitive Grammar", *Cognitive Science* 10: 1-40.
1986b   "Settings, participants and grammatical relations", *Proceedings of the
                Annual Meeting of the Pacific Linguistics Conference* 2: 1-31.
1987   *Foundations of Cognitive Grammar*. Vol I. *Theoretical prerequisites*.
                Stanford: Stanford University Press.
1989   *Foundations of Cognitive Grammar*. Vol II. *Descriptive application*. (To
                appear) Stanford: Stanford University Press.
Leys, Odo
1986   "Some remarks on spatial prepositional structure". [Unpublished
                manuscript.]
Lindner, Susan
1981   English verb-particle constructions with *up* and *out*. [Unpublished
                Ph.D. Dissertation, University of California, San Diego.]
McLaury, Robert E.
1989   "Zapotec body-part: Prototypes and metaphoric extensions", *IJAL* 55:
                119-154.
Miller, George A. & Philip N. Johnson-Laird
1977   *Language and perception*. Cambridge: Harvard University Press.
Nöth, Winfried
1985   "Semiotic aspects of metaphor", in: Wolf Paprotté & René Dirven
                (eds.),
                1-16.
Paprotté, Wolf
1988   "A discourse perspective on tense and aspect in Standard Modern
                Greek and English", in: Brygida Rudzka-Ostyn (ed.), 447-505.
Paprotté, Wolf & René Dirven (eds.)
1985   *The ubiquity of metaphor: Metaphor in language and thought*.
                Amsterdam: Benjamins.
Rudzka-Ostyn, Brygida
1985   "Metaphoric processes in word formation: The case of prefixed verbs",
                in: Wolf Paprotté & René Dirven (eds.), 209-241.
Rudzka-Ostyn, Brygida (ed.)
1988   *Topics in cognitive linguistics*. Amsterdam: Benjamins.
Serzisko, Fritz
1988   "Bounding in Ik", in: Brygida Rudzka-Ostyn (ed.), 429-445.
Stockwell, Robert P., Paul Schachter & Barbara Hall Partee
1968   *Integration of transformational theories on English syntax*. Bedford:
                United States Air Force.
Svorou, Soteriu
1987   "The semantics of spatial extension terms in Modern Greek", *Buffalo
                Working Papers in Linguistics* 87: 56-122.

Talmy, Leonard
1972   Semantic structures in English and Atsugewi. [Unpublished Ph.D. Dissertation, University of California, Berkeley.]
1975   "Semantics and syntax of motion", in: John Kimball (ed.), *Syntax and semantics*. Vol. 4. New York: Academic Press, 181-237.
1985   "Force dynamics in language and thought", *Papers from the Parasession on Causatives and Agentivity at the Twenty-first Regional Meeting of the Chicago Linguistic Society*, 293-337.
1987   "Lexicalization patterns: Semantic structure in lexical forms", in: Timothy Shopen (ed.), *Language typology and syntactic description III: Grammatical categories and the lexicon*. Cambridge: Cambridge University Press, 57-149.
1988   "The relation of grammar to cognition", in: Brygida Rudzka-Ostyn (ed.), 165-205.
Taylor, John R.
1988   "Contrasting prepositional categories: English and Italian", in: Brygida Rudzka-Ostyn (ed.), 299-326.
Traugott, Elizabeth Closs
1978   "On the expression of spatio-temporal relations in language", in: Joseph H. Greenberg (ed.), *Universals of human language*. Vol 3. Stanford: Stanford University Press, 369-400.
1985   "'Conventional' and 'dead' metaphors revisited", in: Wolf Paprotté & René Dirven (eds.), 17-56.
Traugott, Elizabeth Closs & Ekkehard König
1988   "The semantics and pragmatics of grammaticalization revisited". [Unpublished manuscript.]

Part IV

A broader perspective:
Discursive, cross-linguistic, cross-cultural

Patterns of mobilization:
A study of interaction signals in Romance

Béatrice Lamiroy and Pierre Swiggers

0. Introduction

In addressing his audience a speaker invites an addressee to participate in the discursive event. He acts upon his interlocutor or, in other words, "mobilizes" him for discursive interaction: this mobilization concerns the linguistic capacities, the encyclopedic knowledge and, of course, the psychological (and characterological) properties of his audience. In acting on his public, the speaker - whatever type of discourse he is producing - uses organization schemes which are functional in both the production of his message and its reception.

This concept of "mobilization" seems interesting to us in that it opens vistas for the construction of a comprehensive theory for the description of communicative events. Programmatically sketched, this theory can be visualized as follows:

(1)   Communicative event:

propositional content	--->	verificationism
modalizing perspective	--->	extended logic (modal/relational logic)
imagery/"envisagement"	--->	cognition + perception + personality theory
mobilization	--->	philosophy of action

A communicative event - that is, a conceptually complex symbolic unit involving also a sensory and emotive aspect - comprises in our view four dimensions: propositional content, a modalizing perspective, imagery (French *schèmes d'envisagement*), and strategies of mobilization. We take the term *imagery* in the sense defined by Langacker (1988a, 1988b: 63), as referring to our "amazing mental ability to structure or construe a conceived situation in many alternate ways". As rightly stressed by Langacker, this ability has largely been neglected, whereas it is "crucial to a revealing account of either semantic or grammatical structure, and provides the necessary foundation for a subjectivist theory of meaning".

This view, centered on the communicative event, implies an integrated conception of language as an activity involving a multifunctional instrument. Linguistic theorizing has very often dissociated content and context, or system and use (the latter opposition underlies Chomsky's critique of Wittgenstein's view of language). Saussurean linguistics, Bloomfieldianism and generative grammar have emphasized the "inner form of language" - and an important contribution has thus been made, from various viewpoints, to a better grasping of language structures - but have on the other hand largely neglected language as used in context. This approach is a very limited one, since - as cognitive grammar has convincingly shown - the language system itself can only be properly understood from the point of view of the uses to which it is put. In such a view, the language system should be defined as a *dynamic* configuration of *functional positions* of elements and structures. The dynamics of the system is manifest from its contextual adaptations, from its synchronic variation and from its diachronic restructuring. Focusing the description on functional positions of elements and structures - instead of on the elements and structures themselves, as is customary in the various forms of taxonomic linguistics - implies that the descriptive concern is with the *use* of forms, viz. their use in a discursive chain and within a communicative context, and with the *shifts* from one functional position to another. In this paper, we want to study a particular type of functional shift, involving the use of imperative forms. Our analysis hinges on the need to transcend a content-based approach and to integrate contextual features within the description.

Linguistic theory and description have too often been confined to the *content*-dimension. For this, there is no principled justification, but only a practical motivation (seldom explicitly admitted): viz. that this is the dimension which is most easy to describe, and for which there have been long-standing models. Propositional content has most often been dealt with in terms of (absolute/relative) completeness, and especially in terms of truth and falsity (see Plato's *Sophist*, Aristotle's *Peri Hermeneias*, the speculative grammars of the Middle Ages, 18th-century analyses of *propositions,*[1] and the propositional logic-based accounts since the second half of the 19th century). This type of analysis can be subsumed under the principles of *verificationism*, and more specifically under the assumption of some kind of "Lavoisier" dictum with application to the proposition: *Rien ne se perd, rien ne se crée* ['Nothing is lost, nothing is created']. This means complete reversibility between *synthesis* and *analysis*: in other words, the proposition is the perfect composition of its constituent parts (cf. also Frege's compositionality principle; Dummett 1973: 152ff). But anyone who is familiar with the analysis of discourse fragments, with the study of spoken language, or with the analysis of metaphor (metonymy) and polysemy knows how much of this Lavoisier picture is true (or how much of it is false - to use the dimension of imagery).

In fact, a first problem for this type of analysis is the modalizing perspective imposed upon the propositional content. Scope of negation (e.g. with verbs of attitude), obligation, desire, volition and interrogation have made us aware that the verificationist approach is not always fully satisfactory: often "truth" and "falsity" are completely irrelevant for the study of utterances (as we already know from Austin's 1962 study of speech-act verbs), and there is no point in appealing to a compositionality principle, as is illustrated by examples such as the following:

(2)   *Men are men, and women are women.*
(3)   *Why is this so, daddy? Well, because (it is so).*
(4)   *Qu'   est-ce   que   c'est que   cette salade?*
        What   is   this   that   is   this salad?
        'What's all this about?'

Now it is true that some of the aspects not captured by a classical propositional approach have been accounted for in terms of a type of extended logic (mainly modal and relational logic), which allows one to deal with other than truth values. Nevertheless, these types of analysis cannot tell us anything about the difference between:

(5)   *John is Peter's nephew.*
(6)   *Peter is John's uncle.*

Nor can these types of extended logical analysis tell us anything about the differences among:

(7)   *Michael married Susan on September 6.*
(8)   *Susan married Michael on September 6.*
(9)   *Michael and Susan married on September 6.*
(10)   *Susan and Michael married on September 6.*

What we have here are expressions of different *schèmes d'envisagement* (or different modes of imagery) which can be reduced to a single cognitive or perceptual event, or better, which can be "digitalized" (or standardized)[2] into a single content. This content is, by necessity, much poorer and less accurate than the expressions corresponding to the *schèmes d'envisagement*: the latter involve specific cognitive, emotive and sensory values which are lost in the digitalized standardization. These *schèmes d'envisagement*, for which Langacker uses the term *imagery*, correspond to what Chafe calls *directionality*. In our opinion, they are basic ingredients of linguistic communication and of linguistic competence, and the best proof of it can be found in a linguistic activity that up to now has been neglected too much, viz. *paraphrase*.[3] Imagery is essential to our understanding of how messages or utterances are construed: its study involves a theory of cognition and of perception, and a theory of personality.

It has been customary to distinguish between semantics and pragmatics in terms of semiotic relationships: semantics is then defined as the study of signs (semiotic units) in their relationship to meanings/denotata, whereas pragmatics would be the study of signs in their relationship to (a community of) users. It is clear that this distinction has only a limited theoretical justification: the semantics of a semiotic system such as natural language is determined by the history of the system as used by generations of speakers, and it is analyzable only insofar as the descriptivist can "translate" the pragmatic competence of a speech community into a (reductive) set of semantic correspondences. Within a cognitive framework, it is hard to see how semantics and pragmatics can be kept separate, especially if one wants to study language in its synchronic and diachronic variation. The only way to save the distinction - but for what purpose? - is to reduce semantics to an abstract theory of semantic primes (which leaves us with another problem, viz. whether this is still a semantic description of language systems). The view underlying this paper is that semantics of forms in discourse cannot be separated from pragmatics. A useful distinction to maintain, however, which parallels Langacker's distinction between *content* and *meaning*, is that between the mere lexical meaning of an item (which, if necessary, can be called "bare semantics") and the discursive (pragmatic or interactional) meaning of items in their contextual use.

But there is more to the picture. We have already seen that in language indeed *quelque chose se crée*, the newly created aspect being relevant to the audience, to the addressee. We have just mentioned the necessity of bringing in a theory of personality, but a theory of personality floats in the air when it is not integrated within a theory of behavior, or better, a theory of (human) action.[4] A theory of action is a philosophical construct taking as its subject matter the strategies and purposes of (human) activity, in its relationship to society and individual data. The latter can be subsumed under the term *personality*, as referring to psychological states and moral attitudes developed in interaction with other persons and with the outer world. Studying all this from a linguistic vantage point implies a descriptive departure from linguistic behavior and from linguistic strategies used to establish contacts, to achieve particular goals, to avoid undesirable consequences, etc. Historians and especially philosophers of history have recently become aware of the basic importance of "action patterns" in history.[5] These, and not facts, are the principal components of history - at least if one views it as a dynamic process, as one should. Action patterns have also been recognized as essential objects of biological research (e.g. processes of morphogenesis,[6] of epidemicization and immunization, etc.).

In language there exist conventionalized patterns for mobilization purposes. We will focus here on a particular type of discourse signal, viz. imperative forms used as pragmatic markers (or "mobilization" signs). In studying these forms, it will be necessary to abandon the formalist conception of syntax that has characterized much of recent linguistic thinking (see the survey in Lamiroy 1990). In analyzing patterns for mobilization, we are dealing with communicative competence, and this goes well beyond (rule-governed) grammatical competence as studied in generative grammar. The present paper aims at clarifying one aspect of communicative competence which is interesting from a triple point of view:

(a)   as a particular instance of a reflexive attitude of the speaker towards his utterance;
(b)   as an example of functional "displacement" of a particular word class;
(c)   as a case of diachronic "emptying" of word meaning(s), and, indirectly, as an illustration of the secondary nature of word meaning.

The aspect of communicative competence that will be studied here is mobilization (of the audience) through the use of specific organization schemes. Among these schemes we have selected a particular conventionalized type, viz. imperative forms used as discourse signals. The

imperative forms *voyons* 'let's see' and *allez* 'go' in the following examples illustrate this:

(11)   *Arrête de   dire   des bêtises,   voyons.*
       Stop   talking   nonsense,   let's see.
       'Stop talking nonsense, you.'
(12)   *Allez,   tout   ira   mieux   demain.*
       Go,   everything will go   better   tomorrow.
       'Come on, everything will go better tomorrow.'

Our examples are taken from Romance languages, French in
particular, but occasionally parallels with other languages will be noted.
We will try to provide a typology and an analysis of these forms, but
before taking up these points, a few words about the notion of discourse
signals are in order.

1.   Discourse signals and the "mobilization" of the addressee

Discourse signals are linguistic symbols which subsume forms with a
rather heterogeneous morphosyntactic status sharing a discourse-con-
necting and a "mobilizing" function. By *function* we understand here
external function, which concerns the relation between language units or
sequences and language users. The latter function is in fact a way of
mobilizing the potentialities offered by the *internal* function, which relates language units to the language system (Saussure's notion of
valeur).

Let us first illustrate some of the specific features of verb forms used
as mobilization signals. Take the following passage in Capus's play *La
bourse ou la vie*:

(13)   PLESNOIS: *Mme Herbault n'a pas trouvé grâce devant ses
                   petites perfidies.*
                   'Mrs. Herbault has not found mercy for her
                   little treacheries.'
       JACQUES: *Tiens! Tiens! Il dit que ma femme a un amant?*
                   'Well, well, is he saying that my wife has a lover?'

This exchange involves a (repeated) use of *tiens* (literally 'hold', imperative singular of the verb *tenir*), which is remarkable in a number of respects:

(a)   although formally an imperative (singular), the verb is not used here to convey an order;

(b)   the verb shows no congruity with either the "direct participant" (turned into a third person role: *il dit que ma femme a un amant*), or the implicit or "indirect" participants (viz. the audience);

(c)   the verb has a specific function: it brings about the change of what normally would count as an observation (*il dit que ma femme a un amant?*) into an emotive reaction (one of surprise, and perhaps also one of indignation).

This example can be regarded as a nice illustration of the fact that the speaker is in the first place an actor playing with his utterance, before an audience upon which he acts. It is our conviction that the study of mobilization signals will contribute to our knowledge of this aspect of linguistic conceptualization as a symbolic activity, including conceptual, sensory and emotive aspects. Let us briefly illustrate this with example (13) above.

The non-congruity of the imperative with the grammatical number/person of the addressee is a sufficient proof of its functional displacement. The form is no longer used as the expression of an order, but as a polyvalent linking element which can be attached to verbal forms (of whatever mood, including the imperative), or can be used as full utterances by a speaker, or as a reaction to a non-linguistic stimulus:

(14)   *Tiens! c'est vrai.*
'Hey, that's true.'

(15)   *Tiens, dis-moi ce que tu en penses.*
'By the way, tell me what you think of it.'

(16)   (Marguerite to René:)   *J'ai finalement décidé de me marier.*
'I've finally decided to get married.'
(René:)   *Tiens!*
'No kidding!'

(17)   [Marguerite drops her glass at a party when she sees René]
(René:)   *Tiens!*
'Ah!'

Finally, the use of *tiens* (or of the plural *tenez*) in examples such as (14)-(17) testifies to the loss of the core meaning 'to hold'. Whereas one might claim a meaning-conserving origin of functionally displaced discourse and mobilization signals, it is very hard - especially in view of the possible absence of grammatical congruity - to invoke in a straight-forward way the semantic correlation with *tenir* 'hold', although from a formal point of view *tiens* and *tenez* fit within this paradigm.

Mobilization of the audience involves, as one of its most fundamental organization schemes, forms with an explicitly signalizing function, e.g. imperatives. The forms we will discuss here can only be accounted for in a satisfactory way if one does justice to their mobilizing function. We will try to show that these forms have lost a number of their syntactically and semantically coded properties in taking the value of a discourse and mobilization signal.

The term *signal* should not be taken in the Bühlerian sense, as an interlocutor-oriented sign or sign-value, opposed to *symptom* (speaker- or ego-oriented sign or sign-value) and to *symbol* (referent- or reality-oriented sign or sign-value). Bühler's model, useful as it may be, is deficient in that it overlooks the essential discursive relation of signs to their larger context, and in that it neglects one of the fundamental features of discursive behavior, the integration or fusion of functions (e.g. integration of symptom and signal, as reflecting the interaction between speaker and hearer). Our use of *signal* is a more neutral one, in that it refers to the relationship between a sign and its discursive context, without making specific claims as to boundedness to speaker, hearer or "outer world".

Discourse signals have been neglected to a large extent in linguistic description. They have been studied mostly from the point of view of conversational analysis, but very few systematic studies have been devoted to their linguistic status and functioning which involve an analysis of their semantic and syntactic features. The extant literature on discourse signals is very often restricted to their "textual" properties (articulation of the speech event; signalling of the participant's role; conversational strategies). In this paper, however, we want to focus on the grammatical features of discourse markers (more specifically, imperative forms) with direct reference to their interactional function, thus continuing the recent linguistic interest in discourse signals.[7] In our view, the scarcity of linguistic analyses of discourse signals is probably due to the following reasons:

(a)   Discourse signals do not constitute a paradigmatic class (defined in terms of morphosyntactic and/or semantic properties). In fact, it turns out that forms with a variegated morphosyntactic status function as discourse and mobilization signals (see below), and consequently there is no corresponding "word class" for such signals.

(b)   Discourse and mobilization signals do not correspond to a particular syntactic behavior (contrary to auxiliaries, relative pronouns and conjunctions): they even seem to function almost outside of the syntactic pattern of the sentence (cf. Rubattel 1982: 59), and it is very difficult to assign a particular syntactic function to this composite class.

(c)   Discourse and mobilization signals are not amenable to an overall semantic description (i.e. they do not fit into a semantic field or domain). For some of them, no semantic description can be given, and for most of the others (surface) semantic descriptions hardly help to explain their use.

The status of these signals is a very problematic one, to judge from synchronic grammars or partial descriptions.[8] They are conspicuously absent from historical and comparative grammars, except for a few interesting forms such as the imperatives of verbs which mean 'to see' or 'to listen', and in synchronic work they have a variety of labels, ranging from *briseurs de chaîne* 'chain interruptors' to *Gliederungssignale* 'articulation signals' or *connecteurs* 'connectives'.[9] We will propose as a working definition the following:

Discourse and mobilization signals are pragmatic units of a variegated grammatical nature (non-lexemes, words, syntagms) that can function either in complete isolation (i.e. as totally free elements, equivalent to a sentence or to a set of sentences), or in isolation from the pattern of actants (*schème actanciel*) of the sentence in which they are inserted. They do not introduce a new actantial pattern and are not subject to a number of phrase-structure operations (such as passivization or topicalization).

2.   A typology of discourse signals

Typologically speaking, these discourse signals can be divided into different morphological types. As we have just mentioned, no full inventories of discourse signals are available in the linguistic literature. We have drawn tentative lists for French, Spanish and Italian.[10] As a starting principle, we excluded very little from these lists, i.e. we registered sounds like *aïe, hé* as well as phrases like *je t'en prie* (lit. 'I beg you'; 'please'), *tant qu'à faire* (lit. 'so much as to do'; 'while you are at it'), etc.

We excluded only punctuation signs which have a connective use in written language, vulgar expressions and certain open series of signals, especially those with temporal indications. Examples of the latter would be: Fr. *à demain* 'till tomorrow', *à après-demain* 'till the day after tomorrow', *à demain matin* 'till tomorrow morning', Sp. *hasta la vista* 'see you', *hasta luego* 'see you later', It. *a più tardi* 'see you later', *a questo pomeriggio* 'till this afternoon', etc. We made one exception here, viz. when a new pragmatic meaning arises which is different from that of the original discourse signal. Two examples are Fr. *bonjour* 'hello' and Sp. *adiós muy buenas* 'farewell', 'good afternoon' in the following sentences:

(18)   *S'il faut faire ce travail manuellement, bonjour!*
        'If one has to do the job manually, forget it!'
(19)   *Acabó el trabajo en 5 minutos, y ¡adiós muy buenas!*
        'He finished the job in five minutes, and that was it!'

In (18) *bonjour* no longer means 'hello', but something like 'forget it!' and in (19) *adiós muy buenas* should be translated as 'and that was it'.

As the primary typological criterion, we use the possibility of morphological segmentation. This yields two classes, A (non segmentable signals) vs. B (segmentable ones). The second criterion is that of the existence or non-existence in class B of a syntagmatic relation between the morphemes (subclass B.1. vs. B.2.). Finally, we take as the third criterion the existence or non-existence in class B.1. of a paradigmatic alternation with other signals (subclass B.1.1. vs. B.1.2.). This gives us the following classes:

A.   Not morphologically analyzable discourse and mobilization signals

Examples are:
Fr. *aïe* 'ah', *chut* 'hush', *bof* 'oh well', *bien* 'well', *certes* 'sure', *ouf* 'phew'...
Sp. *hola* 'hello', *olé, bueno* 'well'...
It. *beh* 'well', *toh* 'look', *anzi* 'rather', *dai* 'come on', *ebbene* 'well', *ecco* 'look'...

B.   Morphologically analyzable signals

B.1.   *Signals not manifesting a syntagmatic relation*

B.1.1.   Absence of paradigmatic alternation

Examples are:
Fr. *absolument* 'absolutely', *chic* 'fine', *chapeau* 'hats off', *adieu* 'farewell'...
Sp. *francamente* 'frankly', *dios* 'my god', *jesús* 'Jesus', *ojo* 'careful'...
It. *altrimenti* 'otherwise', *certamente* 'certainly', *diavolo* 'devil', *poiché* 'since'...

B.1.2.   Presence of paradigmatic variation

Examples:
Fr. *va, allez* 'go' 2d sg./plur., *allons* 'let's go', *dis, dites* 'say' 2d sg./plur., *tiens, tenez* 'behold' 2d sg./plur.
Sp. *anda, ande* 'go' 2d sg./3d sg. polite form, *digo* 'I say', *diga* 'say' 3d sg. polite form, *oye, oiga* 'listen' 2d sg./3d sg. polite form, *va, vaya* 'go' 2d sg./3d sg. polite form
It. *scusa, scusate, scusi* 'excuse' 2d sg./plur. and 3d sg. polite form, *capisci* 'you understand', *capito* 'understood'.

B.2.   *Signals involving a syntagmatic relation*

Examples:
Fr. *après tout* 'after all', *au contraire* 'on the contrary', *somme toute* 'all in all', *au demeurant* 'after all', *à quoi bon* 'what for'...
Sp. *por lo tanto* 'therefore', *sin embargo* 'nevertheless', *al fin y al cabo* 'in the end', *venga y dale* 'there we go again'...
It. *ciò non toglie* 'nonetheless', *come per caso* 'as if by chance', *considerato che* 'given that', *mamma mia* 'mother'...

This typology must be supplemented by a number of observations. First, we notice that a number of these signals can be identified as formally belonging to a particular lexical or grammatical category, but that they do not show the characteristic use of their category. As a matter of fact, most of the nouns included here are used as discourse and mobilizing signals only in the singular form: *chapeaux* (hats), *cieux* (heavens), *hombres* (men) do not have a connective use, although some exceptions exist, e.g. both *demonio* 'devil' and *demonios* 'devils' can be used as signals. As an example of a form not showing the characteristic use of the corresponding grammatical category, we can mention Fr. *par contre* (lit. by against), 'however', *sur ce* (lit. on this), 'thereupon', which never appear as a PP:

(20) a. *Il   est tombé   sur   ce.*
        He   fell   on   this.
     b. *Sur ce, il est parti.*
        'Thereupon he left.'
(21) a. *Il   s'est arrêté   par   contre   un   arbre.*
        He   stopped   by   against a   tree.
     b. *Par contre, il s'est arrêté.*
        'However, he stopped.'

A second remark to be made is that the morphological classification proposed here yields different natural (or intuitive) classes. The morphologically unanalyzable class contains "inarticulate sounds", conjunctions and adverbs. The first subclass of the morphologically analyzable group is constituted of nouns and adjectives and a particular type of conjunctions and adverbs: conjunctions with *que* and adverbs which end in *-ment* (Sp. *-mente*, It. *-mente*). The second subclass, on the other hand, contains only verb forms which are all imperatives. And the last subgroup consists of only phrases. This group is the most heterogeneous because the phrases belong to various syntactic categories, ranging from NPs (*somme toute* 'sum total'), AdvPs (*jamais de la vie* 'never in my life') to small clauses (*cela étant* 'this being so'), clauses (*s'il te plaît* 'if you please') and sentences (*je t'en prie* 'I beg you').

A third fact to be noted is that a number of forms can be regarded as "doublets" or metaphors of lexical items, deviating from the mere lexical meaning of the item. For example, Fr. *chapeau*, used as a discourse or mobilization signal, means 'well done' or 'congratulations', but not 'hat', although one can still make the link with the appreciative gesture of taking off one's hat. Similarly, Sp. *ojo* (lit. eye) means 'be careful' when it is used as a mobilization signal (one can think of the gesture of pointing to one's eye in order to warn the interlocutor; compare more explicit formulae such as Engl. *watch out* or Dutch *kijk uit je ogen* (lit. watch out of your eyes)). The doublet hypothesis also applies to adverbs, e.g. Fr. *franchement* and Sp./It. *francamente*:

(22) a. *Max a parlé franchement.*
          'Max spoke frankly.'
      b. *Franchement, Max a parlé comme un dieu.*
          'Frankly, Max spoke like a god.'

Whereas *franchement* in (22a) is synonymous with *avec franchise* 'with frankness', this equivalence does not hold for (22b). The same applies to PPs, e.g. Fr. *au fond*, Sp. *en el fondo* (lit. at the bottom), 'in fact', and VPs, e.g. Fr. *allons* (lit. let's go), 'come on', Sp. *vaya* (lit. go), 'well, well':

(23) a. *Max a trouvé la bague au fond du tiroir.*
          'Max found the ring at the bottom of the drawer.'
      b. *Au fond, c'est Max qui a trouvé la bague.*
          'In fact, it was Max who found the ring.'
(24) a. *Soyons gentils et allons vite voir notre grand-mère.*
          'Let's be kind and go see our grandmother.'
      b. *Allons, soyez gentils.*
          'Come on, be kind.'

In (23a) *au fond* could be replaced by *au bout (du tiroir)* 'at the back of the drawer' without a change in meaning: but this substitution would in the case of (23b) result in an unacceptable sentence:

(23) c. ?**Au   bout,   c' est   Max   qui   a trouvé   la   bague.*
          At   the back   it was   Max   who   found   the   ring.

Similarly in (24a) *allons vite (voir)* can be replaced by *courons (voir)*, but not in (24b):

(24) c. ??*Courons,   soyez   gentils.*
          Let's run,   be   kind.

The latter sentence, if grammatical, has a totally different meaning 'please run with me/us'.

   This idea leads to the view that discourse and mobilization signals are lexical elements which have undergone a process of semantic change, analogous to the well-known process of grammaticalization. In our case, however, the meaning of the words does not necessarily fade, but it changes, sometimes radically, and the new function of these expressions extends beyond the boundary of the proposition.

The "doublet" hypothesis gets further support from the fact that many signals not only differ in meaning from their homonymous counterparts, but also show a different syntactic behavior. In (23b) for example, *au fond* does not allow a nominal complement after it:

(25)   *Au fond du tiroir, c'est Max qui a trouvé la bague.*
        At the bottom of the drawer it was Max who found the ring.

Similarly, *allons* allows a locative complement in (26a), but not in (26b):

(26) a.   *Soyons gentils et allons à la maison voir notre grand-mère.*
           'Let's be kind and go home to see our grandmother.'
     b.   *?Allons   à la maison,   soyez   gentils.*
           Let's go   home,   be   kind.

The latter sentence is acceptable only in a reading where *allons* is used as a verb of motion.

Although the doublet hypothesis accounts for several signals of all lexical categories, it is irrelevant to a number of them. Various discourse signals do not have a non-pragmatic equivalent from which they could be derived. In other words, many discourse and mobilization signals are used exclusively with that function. Cases in point are, among many others, Fr. *certes* 'certainly', *assurément* 'for sure', *en fait* 'in fact', Sp. *en suma* 'in sum', *de hecho* 'as a matter of fact', It. *infatti* 'indeed', *suvvia* 'come on', etc. It should also be noted that in certain cases where both a lexical and a pragmatic use exist, it may be the case that the pragmatic use is the primary one from which the lexical is derived, and not vice versa. A discourse signal such as *bonjour* 'hello', for example, may occur as an NP within a sentence:

(27)   *Remettez-lui mon bonjour.*
        'Give him my best regards.'

But in this case, the NP is "secondary" with respect to the discourse marker.

So much for the typology of discourse and mobilization signals. We will now proceed to the analysis of a particular subclass of signals, viz. imperative forms.

3. Properties of imperative discourse signals

The discursive function of verb forms in the imperative subsumes a number of morphological, syntactic and semantic properties.[11] The morphological properties come from the imperative (sub)paradigm to which they belong. As such, these forms also fulfil the basic function of imperative modalization, viz. that of calling upon someone. Their syntactic properties will be studied in detail below, but from the outset we can define three basic characteristics:

(a)   Imperative signals are inherently modalizing and are therefore not capable of higher-level modalization;
(b)   these signals are minimally referential (there is no "fit" to the world, in Searle's (1979) sense), and hence the idea of graduality or scalarity as expressed by changes in tense, person or voice disappears;
(c)   verb signals appear as syntactically autonomous elements, loosely adjoined to the rest of the sentence, or as separate utterances.

3.1. As one of the main functions of discourse signals is that of modalizing discourse, it is not easy to impose upon them modalizations of a higher level. This is why the combination of an adverbial with a discourse signal usually yields an ungrammatical sentence. As pointed out by Rubattel (1982), the fact that a modifier (*assez* in example 28) is allowed in one case but not in the other constitutes the difference between the predicative adverb and the discourse signal:

(28)   a.   *Arthur a assez justement agi.*
           'Arthur acted quite correctly.'
       b.   *Justement, Arthur a eu tort d'agir ainsi.*
           'Quite so, it was wrong for Arthur to behave like that.'
       c.   **Assez justement, Arthur a eu tort d'agir ainsi.*
           Enough rightly, it was wrong for Arthur to behave like that.

Examples (29)-(31) show that the same applies to verbal discourse signals in general (note that the modifiers cannot be excluded on semantic grounds), and to imperatives in particular:

(29)   a.   **Tout   compte   bien fait,   je   reste.*
           Every   count   well made,   I   stay.

    b.   *Réflexion tout à fait faite, j'ai décidé d'acheter une voiture.*
          Thought completely made, I have decided to buy a car.

    c.   *Cela déjà dit, elle fait ce qu'elle veut.*
          This already being said, she does what she wants.

    d.   *Arthur est crétin, n'est-ce pas du tout?*
          Arthur is stupid, isn't it at all?

(30) a.   *Voyons vite si Arthur a gagné au lotto.*
          'Let's see quickly whether Arthur won in the lotto.'

    b.   *Arthur ne gagnera jamais au lotto, voyons!*
          Arthur will never win in the lotto, let's see.
          'Arthur will never win in the lotto, that's for sure!'

    c.   *Arthur ne gagnera jamais au lotto, voyons vite!*
          Arthur will never win at the lotto, let's see quickly.

(31) a.   *Va, n'exagérons rien.*
          Go, let's not exaggerate!
          'Come on, let's not exaggerate!'

    b.   *Va un peu dire aux voisins qu'ils exagèrent.*
          Go a bit tell the neighbors that they exaggerate.

    c.   *Va un peu, n'exagérons rien.*
          Go a bit, let's not exaggerate.

3.2. Verbal discourse and mobilization signals, which are minimally referential, are not subject to morphological variation according to tense, person, voice, etc., as the following examples show:

(32) a.   *Tant qu'à faire, il peut aussi bien vendre le tout.*
          So much that to do he might as well sell the whole thing.
          'While he is at it, he might as well sell the whole thing.'

    b.   *Tant qu'à avoir fait...*
          So much that to have done...

    c.   *Tant qu'à être fait...*
          So much that to be done...

(33) a.   *Il avait, si tu veux, un don spécial.*
          'He had, if you will, a special gift.'

    b.   *Il avait, si tu voulais, un don spécial.*
          He had, if you would, a special gift.

    c.   *Il avait, si je veux, un don spécial.*
          He had, if I will, a special gift.

In the case of imperatives, agreement in person with the addressee is not obligatory:

(34) a. *Voyons,   les enfants,   soyez   raisonnables.*
Let's see,   children,   be   reasonable.
'Come on, children, be reasonable.'

    b. *Voyons, Arthur, sois raisonnable.*
'Come on, Arthur, be reasonable.'

(35) *Tiens,   vous   ici!*
Behold (2d sg.),   you (2d plur.)   here!

(36) a. *Allons, ne sois pas ridicule!*
'Come on, don't be ridiculous!'

    b. *Allez, arrête ces bêtises!*
'Come on (2d plur.), stop (2d sg.) this nonsense!'

The low degree of referentiality of verbal signals also accounts for the fact that they cannot be negated:

(37) a. *Allons,   ne   pleure pas.*
Let's go,   don't   cry.
'Come on, don't cry.'

    b. **N'allons   pas,   ne   pleure pas.*
Let's   not go,   don't   cry.

(38) a. *Tenez,   voilà   mon   grand-père.*
Behold,   there's   my   grandfather.
'Look, there's my grandfather.'

    b. **Ne   tenez pas,   voilà   mon   grand-père.*
Don't   behold,   there's   my   grandfather.

3.3. We will now study the syntactic behavior of imperative forms as mobilizing elements, first in terms of constructional properties, then in terms of linear ordering. Incidentally, the latter investigation is in our view important not only in terms of categorization following from positional features (cf. Hymes' (1955) work on positional analysis of linguistic categories), but also because discourse and mobilization signals have a specific *locus*: it is important to know not only what and how something is said, but also when it is said.

    The constructional properties that will be examined here are valency, embedding, coordination and scope of negation. All four of these properties show that the mobilizing elements are not integrated in the actantial or predicative pattern of the verb, but rather have an adjoined status.

3.3.1.   As the following examples show, verbal discourse and mobilization signals in the imperative do not show up in a valency pattern, as opposed to imperative full predicates:

(39) a.   *Voyons, ne sois pas ridicule.*
            'Come on, don't be ridiculous.'
      b.   *Voyons   cela,   ne   sois pas   ridicule.*
            Let's see   that,   don't   be   ridiculous.
      c.   *Voyons cela en détail, nous trouverons peut-être une solution.*
            'Let's look at that in detail; maybe we'll find a solution.'
(40) a.   *Dis donc, tu as une chance inouïe!*
            'Say, you're incredibly lucky!'
      b.   *Dis-le donc, tu as une chance inouïe!*
            Say it, you're incredibly lucky!
      c.   *Dis-le donc (= avoue): tu as une chance inouïe!*
            'Admit it: you're incredibly lucky!'

3.3.2.   Similarly, they do not allow embedding:

(41)   *Il a répondu que dis/dites donc où ils allaient.*
            He answered that say (2d sg./plur.) where they were going.
(42)   *Il a répondu que va/allez/allons il ne fallait pas exagérer.*
            He answered that go (2d sg./2d plur./3d sg.) one should not exaggerate.
(43)   *Il a répondu que tiens/tenez donc son voisin était là aussi.*
            He answered that behold (2d sg./plur.) his neighbor was there too.

This is hardly surprising. As a matter of fact, several scholars (e.g. Blumenthal 1980: 131) consider it a defining property of discourse signals that they cannot appear in an embedded sentence. Indeed, we have:

(44) a.   *Il a répondu: justement.*
            'He answered: precisely.'
      b.   *Il   a répondu que   justement.*
            He   answered that   precisely.
(45) a.   *Il a répondu: cela dit, je suis prêt à recommencer.*
            'He answered: this being said, I am ready to start again.'

b.   *Il a répondu que cela dit, il était prêt à recommencer.
He answered that this being said, he was ready to start
again.

3.3.3.   Another characteristic of verbal discourse signals is that
coordination with another verbal form of the same type is impossible
when the form has its pragmatic meaning. Coordination becomes
possible, however, when the verbal form recovers its literal meaning.
For example:

(46) a.   Voyons, soyons raisonnables.
'Come on, let's be reasonable.'
b.   *Voyons   et   soyons   raisonnables.
Let's see   and let's be   reasonable.
c.   Voyons cela de plus près et prenons ensuite une
décision raisonnable.
'Let's look at this from closer up and then make a
reasonable decision.'

(47) a.   Tiens, tu me rends mon livre!
'Look, you're giving me my book back!'
b.   *Tiens   et   rends-   moi   mon   livre.
Behold   and   give   me   my   book back!
c.   Tiens-le et rends-le-moi tout à l'heure.
'Keep it and give it back to me later on.'

This observation seems to apply to the entire class of verbal discourse
signals:

(48) a.   *Cela   étant   et   ne   changeant pas...
This   being   and   not   changing...
b.   *Tant   qu'   à   faire   et   à   dire...
So much that   to   do   and   to   say...
c.   *Si   tu   veux   et   souhaites...
If   you   want   and   wish...
d.   *Tout   compte   fait   et   refait...
Every   count   made   and   remade...

3.3.4.   That these forms function as adjoined elements, loosely
attached to the sentence, can be inferred from the fact that they never
fall under the scope of negation of the main verb. This is a well-known
property of sentential adverbs, as the following example shows:

(49) a.   *Justement, il a agi comme il fallait.*
            'Precisely, he acted as he should have done.'
      b.   *Justement, il n'a pas agi comme il fallait.*
            'Precisely, he didn't act as he should have done.'

The same holds for our verb forms:

(50) a.   *Dis donc, tu as de la chance!*
            'Say, you're lucky!'
      b.   *Dis donc, tu n'as pas de chance!*
            'Say, you're not lucky!'
(51) a   *Allez, discutez!*
            'Come on, discuss it!'
      b.   *Allez, ne discutez pas!*
            'Come on, don't discuss it!'
(52) a   *Réflexion faite, j'aurais dû partir.*
            'With that thought, I should have left.'
      b.   *Réflexion faite, je n'aurais pas dû partir.*
            'With that thought, I shouldn't have left.'

Since the four syntactic properties examined so far are essential characteristics of verbal (predicative) behavior, the fact that verbal discourse signals in the imperative are incompatible with all of them suggests that they have undergone a process of functional change, from a syntactic to a pragmatic function.

3.4. We now turn to the positional analysis of imperative signals. In general, discourse and mobilization signals occur either in initial or, less often, in final position:

(53) a   *Tant qu'à faire, elle pouvait aussi bien acheter le tout.*
            'While she was at it, she might as well have bought the whole thing.'
      b.   *Elle pouvait aussi bien acheter le tout, tant qu'à faire.*
            'She might as well have bought the whole thing, while she was at it.'
(54) a.   *Arthur a eu tort de partir, n'est-ce pas?*
            'Arthur shouldn't have left, should he?'
      b.   **N'est-ce pas, Arthur a eu tort de partir?*
            Should he, Arthur shouldn't have left?

Some of them can even appear in the middle of the sentence:

(55) a.   *Arthur a eu tort de partir, tout compte fait.*
           'Arthur shouldn't have left, in fact.'
      b.   *Tout compte fait, Arthur a eu tort de partir.*
           'In fact, Arthur shouldn't have left.'
      c.   *Arthur, tout compte fait, a eu tort de partir.*
           'Arthur, in fact, shouldn't have left.'

Position sometimes allows disambiguization, as in:

(56) a.   *Justement, il a agi.* (discourse signal)
           'Precisely, he acted.'
      b.   *Il a agi justement.* (adverb)
           'He acted correctly.'
      c.   *Il a agi, justement.* (discourse signal)
           'He acted, indeed.'
      d.   *Il a justement agi.* (adverb)
           'He acted correctly.'
      e.   *Il a, justement, agi.* (discourse signal)
           'He indeed did act.'

For the imperative forms the possibilities are as follows (I = initial; M = medial; F = final):

Table 1

	I	M	F
dis (donc)	+	-	+
dites (donc)	+	-	+
va	+	-	+
allons	+	-	+
allez	+	-	+
voyons	+	-	+
tiens	+	-	+
tenez	+	-	+

As Table 1 shows, verbal discourse signals in the imperative specifically appear at the opposite ends of discursive units:

(57) a.   *N'insulte pas   ton   père,   voyons.*
            Don't insult   your   father,   let's see.
            'Come on, don't insult your father.'
      b.   *Voyons,   n'insulte pas   ton   père.*
            Let's see,   don't insult   your   father.
            'Come on, don't insult your father.'
      c.   **N'insulte pas,   voyons,   ton   père.*
            Don't insult,   let's see,   your   father.

Interestingly enough, the pragmatic meaning of a mobilization signal can change according to its position in the sentence:

(58) a.   *Tiens, Arthur n'est pas venu.* (expression of surprise)
            'Well, well, Arthur hasn't shown up.'
      b.   *Arthur n'est pas venu, parce qu'il ne voulait pas
            venir, tiens.* (*tiens* as the pragmatic "tail" of an argument)
            'Arthur hasn't shown up, because he didn't want to come,
            you see.'
(59) a.   *Voyons, qu'est-ce que tu as à me raconter?*
            'Let's see, what do you have to tell me?'
      b.   *Mais tu ne fais que raconter des bêtises, voyons!*
            (mild reproach)
            'But you are merely talking nonsense, you!'

And finally, it should be noted that the mobilization signals in the imperative form can occur independently, as the equivalent of a full utterance, a fact that confirms their autonomous status within discourse. Their discursive function is therefore twofold: they establish a link between speaker and hearer (as does a vocative form), and they also "connect" segments within an utterance (unlike vocatives in most languages).[12]

4. Conclusions

Before formulating several conclusions, we will briefly summarize our findings about imperative mobilizing elements.

4.1. As one of the organization schemes of discursive mobilization, these forms appear at the edges of sentences or utterances. This is their specific *locus* of action, and it testifies to the relative autonomy (or better, the specific function) of mobilization. This property is even more manifest in those cases where the imperative forms are used absolutely (e.g. *allons!, tiens!*).

Furthermore, these forms have "de-activated" a number of their morphosyntactic possibilities, such as variation in tense, mood, voice, actantial integration, and scope liability. In a way, one could say that they have been subject to a functional displacement which has turned them into basic pragmatic functors.

Imperative forms are in fact mobilizing elements *par excellence*. They retain their basic semantic-syntactic value, that of prompting the involvement of the addressee, of stimulating him. It is interesting to note that verb signals constitute a proper subset among discourse signals, in which there is a remarkable functional distribution:

- first-person singular forms, e.g. Fr. *je vous en prie* 'I beg you', Sp. *digo* 'I say', It. *mi raccommando* lit. I recommend myself, are used to put into evidence the "enunciative" role (*instance d'énonciation*);
- first-person plural forms, e.g. Fr. *mettons* 'let's put [it this way]', *disons* 'let's say', Sp. *aclarémonos* 'let's be clear', *entendámonos* 'let's understand each other', It. *intesi* 'understood' - past participle plural, are used to mark the solidarity between speaker and hearer as speech partners;
- second-person forms, including our imperative forms, e.g. Fr. *tu sais* 'you know', *dis donc* 'say', *penses-tu* 'do you think', Sp. *no veas* lit. don't see, *qué te parece* 'what do you think', *no fastidies* 'you must be kidding', It. *se vuoi* 'if you want', *che mi dici* 'what are you telling me', solicit the cooperation of the addressee;
- third-person forms serve to mark, in one way or other, the enunciative content or its particular linguistic form, e.g. Fr. *soit* 'it be so', *peu importe* 'it does not matter', *n'est-ce pas* 'isn't it', Sp. *es decir* 'that is', *así es que* 'so it is that', *qué importa* 'what does it matter', It. *non ti pare* 'doesn't it seem to you', *può darsi* 'it may be the case', *tanto vale* 'it doesn't matter'.

4.2. Another positive fact that results from the analysis of the verbal discourse signals is that they are taken from frequently used verbs relating to the spheres of motion, perception and speaking (linguistic production). It appears that these fields are most liable to prompt the interlocutor's cooperation, either by bringing him into movement, which is a way of "encouraging" him (compare the formulae used to encourage someone: Fr. *allez* 'go' 2d plur., Sp. *va* 'go' 2d sg., It. *ma va* 'go' 2d sg., Dutch *komaan* 'come on', Eng. *come on*, etc.) or by appealing to his capacities as a prototypical speaker (some imperatives by inviting the interlocutor to speak have the discursive function of changing pragmatic roles), or simply by inviting him to observe (listen to or watch) what is going on, e.g. Fr. *voyons* 'let's see', Sp. *oiga* 'listen', It. *vediamo un pò* 'let's see', Dutch *luister 'ns* 'listen', Eng. *look*, etc. Here we find confirmation of our view of speech events as actions, to which both speaker and hearer contribute, and it is no surprise that in some languages verbs of giving or contributing are also used with a mobilizing function, e.g. It. *dai* originally: 'give him', Russian *davaj/davajte* 'give' + infinitive.

It seems that the shift in functional position of these elements is not idiosyncratic, but is linked to general properties of metaphorization. In the present case, the cognitive perspective allows us to explain how "concrete" verbs associated with the semantic spheres of motion, perception and speaking can be used to mobilize the audience,[13] to invite the addressee to participate in the speech event. It is interesting to note that these strategies have an underlying cognitive appeal, as can be gathered from the analogous interactional use of verbs with a primarily "reflective" meaning (e.g. Eng. *you know [what]*, Polish *wiesz*). The latter forms are used, then, not to make a statement of fact, but to point to the exchange of information involved in the discursive event (e.g. Eng. *you know* or Fr. *tu sais*, as discourse markers, are used with the meaning 'I am telling you now'. Finally, one should note the fact that certain signals combine several of these domains into complex mobilizing signals, e.g. Sp. *venga y dale* 'come and give him' (motion and giving), Dutch *zeg luister 'ns* 'say, listen' (speaking and perception), *zeg kom* 'say, come' (speaking and motion), etc.

4.3.   Our analysis has tried to convey an idea of the nature and importance of a linguistic-pragmatic approach. We believe that a pragmatic view is extremely useful for the description of linguistic categories (and not only for the study of discursive strategies). Such a view can be coherently articulated throughout the following levels:

-       that of the sentence: a sentence is not only a string of words or a result of a combination of rules and principles. It is also, and perhaps primarily, a way of conveying views, attitudes, feelings, and of interacting with others. We have tried to show that sentences contain specific signals for this function, and that a systematic account can be given of a particular subclass of these signals;

- that of linguistic competence: linguistic competence is not merely a matter of grammatical knowledge; it is primarily an integrated system of strategies involving the use of linguistic units in order to perform functionally diversified speech acts;
- that of language: language is much more than an inventory of elements and rules; it is essentially a battery of forms, extensions, and hierarchical sets - all allowing for various groupings - coupled with an array of (socially) stratified functions, and relating to a speech community's experiences of the world.

In sum, the pragmatic view adopted here should be embedded in a linguistic theory that analyzes linguistic units in terms of their contribution to the discursive event, while focusing on the *use in context* of linguistic forms. It seems to us that here lies a field of investigation open to cognitive linguistics. The latter framework has the advantage of flexibility and extensibility (see Rudzka-Ostyn 1988), and gives a central place to the speaker as a conceptualizing subject. Our purpose has been to show that the "conceptualizing perspective" should include the pragmatic aspects of the speech event. This enlarged perspective cuts across the traditional distinctions of grammatical and semantic theories; it also shows to what extent pragmatic exploitations "transform" the core meaning of single items (too often studied in isolation from their use in context). Finally, it allows us to view the speech event as a communicative setting, involving the essential interaction between speaker and hearer, and implying specific strategies which turn lexical and grammatical structures into "effective" speech.

Notes

*   We would like to thank Brygida Rudzka-Ostyn and two anonymous referees for their comments and suggestions on a previous version of this paper.
1.   On the history of the description of propositional content, see Nuchelmans (1973, 1983), Land (1974), and Swiggers (1984, 1988, 1989).
2.   On digitalization as a semiotic-linguistic process, see Hiż & Swiggers (1990).
3.   Paraphrase has been used as a descriptive device, both in a more rigid way (see Harris 1981: 293-351) and in a less rigid way (see e.g. Fuchs 1982; Mel'čuk 1984-1988; Bès & Fuchs 1988).
4.   A philosophy of action has been developed, along divergent lines of thinking, by Davidson (1980) and Apostel (1979).
5.   See e.g. the essays in Yovel (1978).

6.   This field shows some interesting analogies with language viewed as a capacity and as a process (see, e.g. Thom 1974).
7.   See e.g. Berrendonner (1983), Danlos (1988), Gülich & Kotschi (1983), Nølke (1988), Roulet (1987), Rubattel (1982), Van Dijk (1979). For Italian, there are a number of recent studies: Bazzanella (1986), Beretta (1984), Biasci (1982), Conte (1972, 1977), Conte, Petöfi & Sözer (1989), Jacqmain (1973), Lichem (1981), Manili (1986), Mara (1986), Stammerjohann (1977).
8.   See our remarks in Lamiroy & Swiggers (1990); for Italian, see Bazzanella (1985).
9.   See Berrendonner (1983), Danlos (1988), Gülich (1970), Hagège (1982).
10.   In the following we will offer only a selective sample. The full lists can be obtained from the authors upon request.
11.   For a more detailed study of these properties, see Lamiroy & Swiggers (1990).
12.   The status of the vocative as a discourse signal should be studied on a wider cross-linguistic scale. Although it does not seem that vocatives constitute a "syntactic connective" within utterances, it appears that the pragmatic-interactional behavior of vocatives strongly varies among languages. West European languages, for instance, seem to use vocatives in speech events to mark off full discursive contributions (with the vocatives - appealing to the addressee - mostly occurring as the initial segment and sometimes also as the final segment of a complete discursive unit). But in Slavic languages (e.g. Polish) vocatives occur within discursive contributions, thus assuring a reinforcement of the appeal to the addressee, and their repetition has the same value as some of the "conative" discourse signals involving a verb form (such as Eng. *you know*, Fr. *tu sais*, Dutch *weet je*, Pol. *wiesz*).
13.   This "intralinguistic" dimension can be superimposed on the cross-linguistic relevance of imagery, as a factor of significant differentiation; on the cross-linguistic aspect, see Langacker's (1988a: 36) pertinent observation: "Languages make different inventories of symbolic resources available to their speakers, who consequently say comparable things in different ways. To convey roughly the same content, the speakers of two languages may be forced, by the constructional schemes at their disposal, to employ expressions that differ in such factors as how precisely they specify some parameter (e.g. definiteness, number, gender), the amount of redundancy they incorporate, or the nature of the compositional path through which they arrive at the composite semantic structure. In short, semantic structure is not universal when imagery is properly taken into account, so the non-identity of grammatical markings across languages does not itself demonstrate their semantic irrelevance."

References

Apostel, Leo
    1979   *Communication et action*. Gent: Communication & Cognition.

Austin, John L.
1962   *How to do things with words*. Oxford: University Press.
Bazzanella, Carla
1985   "L'uso dei connettivi nel parlato: Alcune proposte", in: A. Franchi de
            Bellis & L.M. Savoia (eds.), *Sintassi e morfologia della lingua italiana
            d'uso: Teorie e applicazioni descrittive*. Roma: Bulzoni, 83-94.
1986   "I connettivi di correzione nel parlato: Usi metatestuali e fatici", in:
            Klaus Lichem, Edith Mara & Susanne Knaller (eds.), 35-45.
Beretta, Monica
1984   "Connettivi testuali in italiano e pianificazione del discorso", in:
            Lorenzo Còveri (ed.), *Linguistica testuale*. Roma: Bulzoni, 237-254.
Berrendonner, Alain
1983   "Connecteurs pragmatiques et anaphore", *Cahiers de linguistique
            française* 5: 215-246.
Bès, Gabriel & Catherine Fuchs (eds.)
1988   *Lexique et paraphrase* (*Lexique* 6). Lille: Presses Universitaires de
            Lille.
Biasci, Claudia
1982   *Konnektive in Sätzen und Texten*. Hamburg: Buske.
Blumenthal, Peter
1980   *La syntaxe du message: Application au français moderne*. Tübingen:
            Niemeyer.
Chafe, Wallace
1971   "Directionality and paraphrase", *Language* 47: 1-26.
Casad, Eugene
1988   "Conventionalization of Cora locationals", in: Brygida Rudzka-Ostyn
            (ed.), 345-378.
Conte, Maria Elisabeth
1972   "Vocativo e imperativo secondo il modello performativo", in: *Scritti e
            ricerche di grammatica italiana*. Trieste: LINT, 159-179.
Conte, Maria Elisabeth (ed.)
1977   *La linguistica testuale*. Milano: Feltrinelli.
Conte, Maria Elisabeth, Janos Petöfi & Emel Sözer (eds.)
1989   *Text and discourse connectedness*. Amsterdam: Benjamins.
Danlos, Laurence
1988   "Connecteurs et relations causales", *Langue française* 77: 92-127.
Davidson, Donald
1980   *Essays on actions and events*. Oxford: Clarendon Press.
Dummett, Michael
1973   *Frege: Philosophy of language*. London: Duckworth.
Edmondson, Willis & Juliane House
1981   *Let's talk and talk about it*. Munich: Urban & Schwarzenberg.
Fuchs, Catherine
1982   *La paraphrase*. Paris: Presses Universitaires de France.
Gülich, Elisabeth
1970   *Makrosyntax der Gliederungssignale im gesprochenen Französisch*.
            München: Fink.
Gülich, Elisabeth & Thomas Kotschi
1983   "Les marqueurs de la reformulation paraphrastique", *Cahiers de
            linguistique française* 5: 305-351.

Gumperz, John
 1982   *Discourse strategies*. Cambridge: Cambridge University Press.
Hagège, Claude
 1982   *La structure des langues*. Paris: Presses Universitaires de France.
Harris, Zellig S.
 1968   *Mathematical structures of language*. New York: Wiley.
 1981   *Papers on syntax*. Edited by Henry Hiz. Dordrecht: Reidel.
Hiż, Henry & Pierre Swiggers
 1990   "Bloomfield, the logical positivist", *Semiotica* 79: 257-270.
Hymes, Dell
 1955   "Positional analysis of categories: A frame for reconstruction", *Word*
             11: 10-23.
 1972   "On communicative competence", in: J.B. Pride & Janet Holmes
             (eds.), *Sociolinguistics: Selected readings*. Harmondsworth: Penguin,
             269-293.
 1974   *Foundations in sociolinguistics: An ethnographic approach*.
             Philadelphia: University of Pennsylvania Press.
Jacqmain, Monique
 1973   "Vicende dell'imperativo", *Studi di grammatica italiana* 3: 231-248.
Keller, Eric
 1979   "Gambits: Conversational strategy signals", *Journal of Pragmatics* 3:
             219-238.
Lamiroy, Béatrice
 1987   "Verbes de mouvement: Emplois figurés et extensions
             métaphoriques", *Langue française* 76: 41-58.
 1990   "Des *Aspects de la théorie syntaxique* à la *Nouvelle syntaxe*
             chomskyenne: rupture ou continuité?", in: Pierre Swiggers (ed.),
             Moments et mouvements dans l'histoire de la linguistique (Cahiers de
             l'Institut de Linguistique de Louvain-la-Neuve 16:1). Louvain: Peeters,
             101-124.
Lamiroy, Béatrice & Pierre Swiggers
 1990   "The status of imperatives as discourse signals", in: Suzanne
             Fleischman & Linda Waugh (eds.), *Discourse-pragmatic approaches to
             the Romance verb*. London: Croom-Helm.
Land, Stephen K.
 1974   *From signs to propositions: The concept of form in eighteenth century
             semantic theory*. London: Longman.
Langacker, Ronald W.
 1987   *Foundations of cognitive grammar*. Vol. 1: *Theoretical prerequisites*.
             Stanford: Stanford University Press.
 1988a   "An overview of cognitive grammar", in: Brygida Rudzka-Ostyn (ed.),
             3-48.
 1988b   "A view of linguistic semantics", in: Brygida Rudzka-Ostyn (ed.), 49-
             90.
Lichem, Klaus
 1981   "Bemerkungen zu den Gliederungssignale im gesprochenen
             Italienisch", in: Christoph Schwarze (ed.), *Italienische Sprachwissen-
             schaft*. Tübingen: Narr, 61-82.
Lichem, Klaus, Edith Mara & Susanne Knaller (eds.)
 1986   *Parallela, 2*. Tübingen: Narr.

Manili, Patrizia
    1986   "Sintassi dei connettivi di origine verbale", in: Klaus Lichem, Edith Mara & Susanne Knaller (eds.), 165-176.
Mara, Edith
    1986   "Per un'analisi dei segnali discorsivi", in: Klaus Lichem, Edith Mara & Susanne Knaller (eds.), 177-189.
Mel'čuk, Igor
    1984-1988   *Dictionnaire explicatif et combinatoire du français contemporain.* (2 vols.) Montréal: Presses de l'Université.
Nølke, Henning (ed.)
    1988   *Opérateurs syntaxiques et cohésion discursive.* Copenhagen: Akademisk Forlag.
Nuchelmans, Gabriel
    1973   *Theories of the proposition: Ancient and medieval conceptions of the bearers of truth and falsity.* Amsterdam: North Holland.
    1983   *Judgment and proposition from Descartes to Kant.* Amsterdam: North Holland.
Roulet, Eddy
    1980   "Stratégies d'interaction, modes d'implication et marqueurs illocutoires", *Cahiers de linguistique française* 1: 80-103.
    1987   "Complétude interactive et connecteurs reformulatifs", *Cahiers de linguistique française* 8: 111-140.
Rubattel, Christian
    1982   "De la syntaxe des connecteurs pragmatiques", *Cahiers de linguistique française* 4: 37-61.
Rudzka-Ostyn, Brygida
    1988   "Semantic extensions into the domain of verbal communication", in: Brygida Rudzka-Ostyn (ed.), 507-553.
Rudzka-Ostyn, Brygida (ed.)
    1988   *Topics in cognitive linguistics.* Amsterdam: Benjamins.
Schiffrin, Deborah
    1987   *Discourse markers.* Cambridge: Cambridge University Press.
Searle, John R.
    1979   *Expression and meaning: Studies in the theory of speech acts.* Cambridge: Cambridge University Press.
Silverstein, Michael
    1978   "The three faces of 'function'", in: Maya Hickmann (ed.), *Proceedings of a working conference on the social foundations of language and thought.* University of Chicago.
Sirdar-Iskandar, Christine
    1983   "'Voyons!'", *Cahiers de linguistique française* 5: 111-130.
Stammerjohann, Harro
    1977   "Elementi di articolazione dell'italiano parlato", *Studi di grammatica italiana* 6: 109-120.
Swiggers, Pierre
    1984   "Théorie grammaticale et définition du discours dans le *Sophiste* de Platon", *Les Etudes Classiques* 52: 15-17.
    1986   "La linguistique fonctionnelle du Cercle de Prague", *Philologica Pragensia* 29: 76-82.
    1988   "Grammatical categories and human conceptualization: Aristotle and the Modistae", in: Brygida Rudzka-Ostyn (ed.), 621-646.

1989   "Structure propositionnelle et complémentation dans l'histoire de la
            grammaire: La théorie de Beauzée (1767)", *Lingua e Stile* 24: 391-407.
Tannen, Deborah
1983   *Conversational style: Analyzing talk among friends*. Norwood: Ablex.
Tannen, Deborah (ed.)
1984   *Coherence in spoken and written discourse.* Norwood: Ablex.
Thom, René
1974   *Modèles mathématiques de la morphogenèse*. Paris: Union générale
            d'éditions.
Van Dijk, Teun A.
1979   "Pragmatic connectives", *Journal of Pragmatics* 3: 447-456.
Yovel, Yishai (ed.)
1978   *Philosophy of history and action*. Dordrecht: Reidel.

Interaction and cognition:
Speech act schemata with <u>but</u> and their interrelation with discourse type

Gerda E. Lauerbach

1. Introduction

A shift in focus can be observed in recent studies in cognitive linguistics. While the early semantic studies concentrated on lexical items referring to physical and sensory domains, and drew on the interaction of human agents with their *physical* environment in order to discover the underlying conceptual principles, a growing body of work is being directed at items that can only be analyzed if the interaction of humans with their *social* environment is taken into account. Examples are Dirven et al. (1982) on *speak, talk, say,* and *tell*; Rudzka-Ostyn (1989) on *ask,* and Wierzbicka (1989) on pragmatic meaning and prototypical human relationships. Coleman and Kay (1981), in their analysis of *lie*, introduce speakers' beliefs and intentions directed at addressees. They pose the question if, since "lying is inherently a social act ... an investigation of the word *lie* might (not) lead naturally into a full-scale investigation of communicational and interactional sociology" (p. 42). While they deny this and hold fast to the distinction between linguistic meaning and language use, Sweetser (1987), in a follow-up study, develops a model of linguistic communication as a general cognitive model needed for other areas of grammar, but constitutive of the meaning of the word *lie*.

Conjunctions are another area of language where pragmatics intrudes upon grammar, and as such they received early attention in the syntax/semantics/pragmatics debate. Rutherford (1970) noted that the dependent clauses under (b) in the following examples do not modify their main clauses but have to be seen in relation to an underlying performative clause, as in (c):

(1)   a.   *He beats his wife because I talked to her.*[1]
      b.   *He beats his wife, because I talked to her.*
      c.   *I (can) say, because I talked to her, that he beats his wife.*

(2)   a.   *He sings well, if he remembers the notes.*
       b.   *He sings well, if I remember correctly.*
       c.   *I say (truthfully) if I remember correctly, that he sings well.*

While the performative analysis, for various reasons that need not be gone into here, is no longer being entertained as a viable model of linguistic description and explanation, the facts remain. Other researchers have described the clauses in question as qualifications of illocutionary acts and have derived them from general conditions on verbal interaction, in particular from conditions on speech acts, Gricean maxims and principles of politeness.

In recent work, I have termed such constructions *speech act schemata* (Lauerbach (1989) on *but*). In the following, I will briefly spell out the conditions on verbal interaction from which they can be derived, and then describe some schemata involving *but*. I will also show that different speech act schemata are systematically associated with different discourse types. In conclusion, I will argue that the scope of cognitive linguistics has to be extended beyond the focus on monadic (but identically wired) human experiencers, perceiving and coding their perceptions of physical reality (e.g. into category names, deep cases, etc.), in order to be able to account for the way in which social (inter-) actors perceive, make sense of and interactively construct through language their social reality.

2.   A model of verbal communication:
   Constitutive rules, normative rules, and discourse type

In a paper entitled "This is just a first approximation, but", Baker (1975) deals with what she calls "*but*-prefaces". These prefaces are "comments about the speech acts which follow them" (1975: 44), and they can be addressed to rules of politeness (3), to Gricean maxims (4), and to "impression management rules" (5):

(3)   *I don't want to rush you, but let's try to catch the next bus.*
(4)   *This is just a first approximation, but...*
(5)   *I don't want to sound chauvinistic, but...*

Lakoff (1973), in an early paper on politeness and grammar, formulated two overarching "Rules of Pragmatic Competence":

(6)   a.   *Be clear.*
      b.   *Be polite.*

The "Rules of Clarity" are taken to be principles such as Grice's maxims; politeness is further differentiated:

(7)   a.   *Don't impose.*
      b.   *Give options.*
      c.   *Make A feel good - be friendly.*

Lakoff (1973: 297f) notes that in the case of conflict between clarity and politeness, politeness tends to be preferred:

> It seems to be the case that, when Clarity conflicts with Politeness ... Politeness supersedes: it is considered more important in a conversation to avoid offense than to achieve clarity. This makes sense, since in most informal conversations, actual communication of important ideas is secondary to merely reaffirming and strengthening relationships.

One of the questions to be addressed in this paper is whether the preference for politeness in informal conversation can be considered prototypical for verbal interaction in general, or whether it is subject to constraints imposed by discourse type (see below).

In a very influential paper, Brown and Levinson (1978) defined politeness from a social-psychological perspective. They assume a rational social actor who pursues his/her goals intentionally, while at the same time paying attention to "face".

Face is differentiated into positive and negative face and incorporated into two rules of politeness, which I name *normative rules* (see Table 1):

Table 1.   Rules of politeness or normative rules

(a)   attend to *positive face*: the positive consistent self-image or personality (crucially including the desire for this self-image to be appreciated and approved of) claimed by interactants
(b)   attend to *negative face*: the basic claim to territories, personal preserves, rights to non-distraction, i.e. to freedom of action and freedom from imposition (cf. Brown & Levinson 1978: 66).

Some speech act types intrinsically threaten face (see Table 2). By introducing the concept of face-threatening act (FTA), Brown and Levinson make their overarching rules of politeness sensitive to types of speech acts:

Table 2.   Types of face-threatening acts (FTAs)

(a)   regarding hearer's negative face: requests, threats, etc.
(b)   regarding hearer's positive face: criticism, contradictions, etc.
(c)   regarding speaker's negative face: thanks, apologies, etc.
(d)   regarding speaker's positive face: admissions of guilt, etc.

In Brown and Levinson's framework, clarity-modifying *but*-prefaces such as (4) or (8a) through (8c) will have to be taken as protective of the speaker's positive face, since vagueness, conversational incoherence or the imparting of unreliable information reflect negatively on the speaker:

(8)   a.   *I know this will sound rather vague, but...*
       b.   *I don't want to sidetrack the discussion, but...*
       c.   *I don't remember exactly, but I think...*

This means, however, that "social face" and what I call "communicative identity" ought to be one and the same thing. Yet all things being equal, and *pace* Lakoff, in verbal interaction it is not altogether essential for one to be liked and appreciated. It is, however, absolutely indispensable for interactors to be mutually understood and believed. The Rules of Clarity and the Rules of Politeness are not on the same level, and neither do social face and communicative identity coincide: it is possible to imagine or encounter very face-conscious liars.

Indeed, interactors may lie because they are unduly attentive to their positive face. By submitting to an excessive need to be appreciated and admired, they put their positive communicative identity at risk. On the other hand, there are discourse types such as small talk, discourse sequences such as routine openings or speech acts such as compliments, where lying, if not actually expected, is at least not sanctioned. Yet the very concept of lying is only possible as the violation of a set of assumed constitutive rules (or rules of clarity) that the speech community at large adheres to.

Constitutive rules are the ground rules interlocutors must follow if verbal communication is to be possible at all. According to Habermas (1981, I: 369ff), such rules provide for the fact that interactants must make their utterances *comprehensible* to their interlocutors, that they must be able to provide *evidence* for the *truth* of their assertions, for the *legitimacy* of their directives and for the *authenticity* of their expressive utterances. Thus with each utterance, speakers raise a "validity claim" that these conditions are fulfilled. Addressees, on the other hand, are expected to accept or challenge these claims and to react with appropriate verbal or non-verbal action.

Habermas calls this the "binding force" of speech acts. Habermas' validity claims can be related to Grice's maxims and his cooperative principle (cf. Lauerbach 1989: 28), as well as to Searle's (1969) conditions on speech acts. All three approaches posit an *ideal model* of verbal interaction in which rational, intentional social subjects interact, accept responsibility for their actions as defined above, and mutually expect each other to do so. It is to the protection of this rational, responsible, intentional subject that clarity-modifying *but*-prefaces are addressed.

What distinguishes Habermas' approach from that of Grice or Searle is that in his model of the "ideal speech situation", the acceptance, rejection and negotiation of the validity claims is a necessary condition for achieving a true consensus in discourse (a fact on which he bases his consensus theory of truth and a critical theory of society). In order for this to work, a further condition has to be satisfied: all interlocutors must enjoy equal rights and opportunities as participants of the discourse, and no participant may impose his or her opinion on others by means of higher status and/or greater power.

On the basis of these "contrafactual conditions on the ideal speech situation" (Habermas 1971) and in analogy with Brown and Levinson's rules of politeness (or *normative rules*), we can now attempt to formulate two general rules of clarity (or *constitutive rules*). Unlike the normative rules which apply to *all* social interaction, the rules formulated in Table 3 are *specific* to verbal interaction: they have to be, since they encode its constitutive conditions:

Table 3.   Rules of clarity, or constitutive rules,

(a)   attend to *positive identity*: the positive, consistent, communicative identity claimed by interactants as rational, responsible interlocutors able to produce evidence for their validity claim if challenged, and to be taken seriously as competent, truthful, non-usurping and authentic communicators

(b)   attend to *negative identity*: the basic claim to appropriate reaction and equal discoursal rights and opportunities, in particular the freedom from infringement of discoursal space (in "fair" turn-taking)

Just as with face, some speech acts intrinsically threaten communicative identity. Such "identity-threatening acts" (ITAs) are given in Table 4:

Table 4.   Types of identity-threatening acts (ITAs)

(a)   regarding hearer's positive identity:
       corrections; challenges with regard to being incomprehensible, uninformative or irrelevant; accusations of raising invalid claims - of lying, misrepresenting, misleading, etc., of usurping illegitimate status or power, of being insincere.
(b)   regarding hearer's negative identity:
       monopolizing the floor; not providing the appropriate reaction; interrupting.
(c)   regarding speaker's positive identity:
       admissions of lying, etc.; of having been or being imprecise, mistaken, etc.
(d)   regarding speaker's negative identity:
       apologies for violating another's discoursal rights, for not paying attention (on the part of S); not paying attention (on the part of H).

There exists an interesting asymmetry between clarity and politeness, at least for Western cultures, in that with respect to clarity it is the positive dimension of identity which is the more important; with respect to politeness, it seems to be the negative dimension of face that receives more explicit attention.[2]

We are now in a position to return to the issue of when interlocutors are preferentially oriented to clarity and when to politeness in a discourse situation. Both possibilities exist: that of modifying clarity for the sake of politeness and that of neglecting politeness for the sake of clarity; attending to face at the expense of identity, and insisting on identity to the detriment of face. The two are interrelated, but their relationship is a complex one. While in some situations, honesty is the best policy, the person staunchly clinging to positive identity may not be the most sought-after conversational partner in others. The balance achieved by interlocutors between face and identity in any encounter will depend on the "weightiness" of the threatening acts[3] - but only to the extent that the constraints of discourse type allow for variance.

Lakoff's statement about the preference for politeness is valid for the informal situations she mentions. It also holds for situations in which business is being transacted and status and power relations are important, but for some reason veiled. In other situations, especially in those that have become institutionalized for the purpose of fact-finding (e.g. courtroom interrogations), clarity is the governing principle.

Levinson presents examples for the way in which the type of speech event provides for certain participants in certain roles and constrains the choice of certain types of speech actions. Expectations are thereby generated as to what can come next, and these in turn influence the interpretation of what is said. I use *discourse type* instead of Levinson's term *activity type* in order to indicate that my approach is owed primarily to a concern with linguistics, and not with sociology. This does not prevent me from adopting Levinson's characterization of activity type as "a fuzzy category whose focal members are goal-defined, socially constituted, bounded events with *constraints* on participants, setting, and so on, but above all on the kinds of allowable contributions" (Levinson 1979: 368).

I hope to show below that discourse type also constrains particular preferential orientations between clarity and politeness on the part of participants, particular strategies to be followed and particular speech act schemata to be used.

However, the question of which orientation is required by which discourse types is not one that can be dealt with by the rational reconstruction of universal pragmatic principles, nor can it be decided by evaluating constructed examples. It is an empirical question that can only be answered by the analysis of actually occurring discourse.

3.   Speech act schemata with <u>but</u>

Theoretically, speech act schemata involving *but* could be described and explained as conventionalized compromise solutions to recurring conflicts of orientation between constitutive and normative rules of interaction, where the *but*-preface carries a mitigating act that softens the threat to face or identity contained in the head act. Taking attending to and threatening face or identity as the basic orientations of the speech acts in preface and head, and adding S and H as the basic objects of these acts, we get four basic patterns:

attend to H	*but*	threaten H
attend to S	*but*	threaten S
threaten H	*but*	attend to H
threaten S	*but*	attend to S

This number has to be doubled to take care of the positive and negative aspects of face and identity, which gives us eight. These eight can interact with each other (e.g. threaten S, but threaten H), which gives us 64 schemata for each face and identity domain, 128 in all. However, face and identity can also interact, e.g. *I hate to interrupt* (addressed to H's negative identity), *but your argument doesn't make sense* (addressed to H's positive face). This last interaction will yield a total of over 16,000 possible patterns. Obviously, they are not all conventionally realized.

Some combinations can be excluded from the start, because they conflict with a logic of practical reasoning from goals to means, others due to presuppositions about reasonable human goals and action motivations. Still others will be excluded by concentrating on *typical* goals and motives. However, such a calculus, if it existed, would still predict more combinations than are usual in a speech community.

The method of discovering the typical schemata is likewise an empirical one, to be supplemented by the relevant concepts from linguistics, universal pragmatics, speech act theory, linguistic discourse analysis and the ethnomethodological analysis of conversation, social psychology, and from wherever else one is able to glean insights into the interdisciplinary object known as "verbal communication". In a procedure aimed at theory building, rules are then formulated on the basis of the data; classes and subclasses are abstracted and defined, and principles stated. As soon as one tries to apply this theoretical apparatus to a new body of data, one encounters its resistance to theory. This situation leads to modification of the theoretical apparatus, renewed attempts at application, and so on.

Shuttling backwards and forwards between theory and data, one comes to realize that the ideal of a close fit between the two is a chimera and has to be abandoned without, however, having to abandon the theory. Interactants orient to different principles to varying degrees at one and the same time. They compromise between politeness and clarity, between face and identity, and between their positive and negative dimensions in ways that are only partially predictable and that resist all-or-nothing categorizations, since interlocutors move freely on a gradient of orientation - as freely as the constraints imposed by discourse type permit. This principle has to be made part of the theory.

The most promising way to do this at present is through a combination of prototype theory with schema theory as developed by Rumelhart and Ortony.[4] Rumelhart and Ortony (1977: 101) define *schema* as follows:

> Schemata are data structures for representing the generic concepts stored in memory. They exist for generalized concepts underlying objects, situations, events, sequences of events, actions, and sequences of actions. Schemata are not

atomic. A schema contains, as part of its specification, the network of interrelationships that is believed to generally hold among the constituents of the concept in question.

Schemata have four characteristics - they have variables, they embed, they exist on different levels of abstraction, and they represent knowledge not definitions. The variables of a schema become bound by different values when the schema is activated on a particular occasion. The relations between them, however, remain constant and impose constraints on what type of object can fill the variable. Some "fillers" are more typical than others; some are prototypical. The fact that schemata embed is important for the topic of this paper in as far as speech act schemata embed in discourse schemata. The latter have their own network of interrelations, and impose constraints on the variables they accept prototypically. Not all speech act schemata can go in all discourse schemata in the unmarked case. Of the possible levels of abstraction, those of speech act and discourse type will be relevant here. That schemata represent what is normally, typically true, but not what is necessarily true, means that they tolerate deviations, vagueness, imprecision and inconsistencies.

Rumelhart and Ortony also discuss the functions of schemata in language comprehension, in memory and in making inferences. It is this latter function which is of particular interest here. Since schemata are structures with variables and constraints on variables and since, in the prototypical case, they represent stereotypes of experience, once part of a schema is instantiated, the rest can be inferred.[5] The inferences of some *but*-schemata will be explored in detail below.

In this section, I will present two *but*-schemata of compromise abstracted from my data and illustrate them with extracts in which interlocutors can be shown to employ a cognitive model of such schemata as rough and context-sensitive blueprints of their production. I use the term *speech act schema* in a provisional manner to refer to a fairly abstract, complex and dynamic cognitive model for speech production and interpretation. This model incorporates linguistic, interactional and cultural knowledge in a characteristic structure; it conventionally carries a set of inferences and a cluster, or perhaps an ordered complex, of interactional functions.

My data base consists of the transcripts of two types of discourse. One is an elicited role-play interaction between a British native speaker and a German student of English, the native speaker being in a position of institutional authority over the student in an assumed educational-administrative setting. In accordance with modern educational and management theory, the native speaker endeavours not to express his authority directly but to obscure it rhetorically to varying degrees. The second discourse is Oliver North's testimony before the U.S. Congressional committee set up to investigate the Iran-Contra affair during 1987. Again, institutional authority is one of the issues, but the overriding concern is to discover the truth about the events in the Iran-Contra affair. Not surprisingly, it is the commitment to truth that is obscured rhetorically to varying degrees by the person being interrogated, Oliver North. For both types of rhetoric veiling, *but*-schemata are used in abundance.

There are various well-known semantic and pragmatic uses of *but*. I shall restrict myself here to two types of speech act schemata - the "disarm schema" and the "appease schema".

3.1.   The disarm schema

The disarm schema consists of a *but*-preface in which the forthcoming violation of a constitutive or a normative rule is announced, and a speech act following the preface that contains the violation. It differs from the schemata dealt with in the next section in that the first part of the schema makes more or less explicit reference to either norms of clarity or of politeness. Its structure is: (pre-head) - *but* - (head). Its function is twofold. The *but*-preface, first, forestalls a negative response by the addressee, such as an objection or a challenge to the act which follows. Aptly named "response controlling prefaces" by Baker (1975), these devices thus "disarm" the addressee by blocking the obvious objection. At the same time they serve, second, to protect the speaker, as shown in examples (9) and (10):

(9)   A: *I don't want to bother you, but could you just check
             this translation for me.*
         B: **Don't bother me with this.*
(10)   A: *I don't want to sound like a chauvinist, but I think we
             should seriously consider the implications to the job
             market of giving women access to higher paid jobs.*
         B: **That's a very chauvinistic remark* (cf. Baker 1975: 44).

The potential of the schema for "addressee control" (Baker 1975) is, however, not due only to the announcement of the forthcoming violation of a pragmatic rule. The schema has far more power than merely to block the most obvious negative response. This power rests essentially not in what is *said*, but in what is *implied* (see below).

3.1.1.   Schemata addressed to rules of politeness

In the disarm schema addressed to politeness, the violation of, or at least a negative attitude to, a normative rule of interaction is signalled in the preface, while the following speech act is a face-threatening act, i.e. an act touching on positive self-image or freedom from imposition (see Table 5):

Table 5.   Structure and content of the disarm schema (politeness)

Preface		Head
Expression of negative attitude towards violating a normative rule of interaction, specifically towards performing an FTA	*but*	Violation of the rule, specifically by performing the FTA mentioned or alluded to in the preface

The preface is oriented to hearer's positive or negative face, while the head act threatens hearer's face, positive or negative (see Table 6):

Table 6.   Orientation of the disarm schema (politeness)

Preface		Head
Attention to H's face (positive or negative)	*but*	Threat to H's face (positive or negative)

A typical disarm schema addressed to politeness carries at least the types of inferences listed in Table 7:[6]

Table 7.   Types of inferences of the disarm schema (politeness)

(a)   The preface signals the forthcoming violation of a normative rule of interaction and thereby implies the speaker's *determination* to perform the disclaimed act.

(b)   S implies that s/he has contextually derivable *valid reasons* for violating the normative rule, reasons that are stronger than his/her reluctance to do so (e.g. circumstances beyond of his/her control) and that thereby *oblige* him/her to do so.

(c)   These overriding reasons *justify* S's violating the normative rule.

(d)   The disclaimer in the preface may not be sincere, and is in fact regularly taken to be *mere lip-service* to a normative rule. It is, however, virtually unchallengeable and *leaves S free to perform implicit FTAs* without having to accept responsibility for their social acceptability.

(e)   By virtue of (b), (c) and (d), the schema functions to protect S's positive face.

These inferences are part of the schema, and it is due to their implicit nature that the schema is such an effective strategic device.

The following two extracts are taken from the first day (July 7th, 1987) of Oliver North's testimony before the Select Committee on Secret Military Assistance to Iran and the Nicaraguan Opposition. In this early phase of his 13-day testimony, we find some rare instances in which North shows himself to be oriented not predominantly to truth and limitations of memory (see below), but to social rules. In Extracts 1 and 2, it is not communicative identity that is being negotiated, but social face and individual freedom within a context circumscribed by rigid institutional norms:[7]

Extract 1

Nields: And these operations - they were covert operations?
North: Yes, they were.
Nields: And covert operations are designed to be secrets from our enemies?
North: That is correct.
Nields: But these operations were designed to be secrets from the American people?
North: Mr. Nields, I am at a loss as to how we could announce it to the American people and not have the Soviets know about it. *And I'm not trying to be flippant, but I just don't see how you could possibly do it* (North, p. 9).

Extract 2

Nields: Did - where are these memoranda?
North: Which memoranda?
Nields: The memoranda that you sent up to Admiral Poindexter seeking the President's approval.
North: Well, they're probably these books to my left that I haven't looked through yet and I'm going - if I try to guess I'm going to be wrong. But I think I shredded most of that. Did I get 'em all? *I'm not trying to be flippant but I'm just* - (scattered laughter)
Nields: Well, that was going to be my very next question, Colonel North, "Isn't it true that you shredded them?"
North: I believe I did (North, p. 19).

In Extract 1, Nields embarks on the first of his numerous attacks on the concept and reality of "covert operations". Our concern here is not with Nield's *but* that introduces his third turn (a straightforward across-turn speech-act use), but with the schema used by North: *And I'm not trying to be flippant, but I just don't see how you could possibly do it.* In jockeying for position in the opening bouts of his televised testimony that was to make him a national hero, North, the expert, gives the amateur Nields a patronizing crash course in covert operations. When he realizes that he may have gone too far and that he may have used the wrong register, thereby disrespectfully threatening Nields' positive face, he follows this up with a typical disarm schema, thus forestalling a possible rebuke like: *Col. North, this is no place to be flippant.* What is not said but contextually inferred, and therefore not officially challengeable information, is his scathing criticism: *Your question was so simplistically stupid* (valid reason for FTA) *that I could not but* (obligation to do FTA) *answer it in a slightly flippant manner - even in this very serious context of which I am, of course, aware and - unless provoked* (justification of FTA) *- observant.*[8]

In Extract 2, our concern is again not with *But I think I shredded most of that,* but with the incomplete disarm schema *And I'm not trying to be flippant, but I'm just....* As in the first extract, the preface of the schema is - on the surface - addressed to a social norm, the style of speaking (*Did I get 'em all?*). And again, the really important message is being transported implicitly and prophylactically - that the shredding of documents (shortly before North's office was searched by Attorney General Edward Meese) was necessary, right, correct, even laudable as an action that averted damage from the President and the nation at large. North thus implicitly protects S's positive face, even before he is being attacked.

3.1.2.   The disarm schema addressed to rules of clarity

In analogy to the disarm schemata addressed to politeness, in those addressed to clarity it is the infringement of a *constitutive* rule of interaction that is signalled in the preface of the schema, while the following speech act is just such an infringement and thereby an act threatening the speaker's or hearer's communicative identity, or ITA (cf. Table 4 above and Table 8 below):

Table 8.   Structure and content of the disarm schema (clarity)

Preface		Head
Expression of negative attitude towards violating a constitutive rule.	*but*	Violation of the rule by performing an ITA.

In expressing reluctance to violate a constitutive rule in the preface, s is attending to H's negative identity (the right to expect an appropriate reaction). Yet in violating the constitutive rule in the head, s threatens H's negative identity. The orientation is as in Table 9:

Table 9.   Orientation of the disarm schema (clarity)

Preface		Head
Attention to H's identity	*but*	Threat to H's identity
(positive or negative)		(positive or negative)

The following Extracts 3-5 are typical of the strategy consistently followed by Oliver North in his testimony, a strategy which prompted Daniel Schorr to remark in his introduction to the transcripts, when writing about reporters' on-the-spot reactions: "We noted, also, how often a renowned steel-trap memory went vague, or forgetful, or, in an effort to provide an instant answer, slipped into misstatement" (North, p. viii).

The extracts are taken from a stretch of discourse dealing with the summaries, or chronologies, of the United States Government's involvement in arms sales to Iran that North had been asked to prepare:

Extract 3

Nields: And were drafts of these sent to Admiral Poindexter?
North: I honestly can't tell you whether this specific draft, the drafts - various drafts of these chronologies were sent to Admiral Poindexter, and I believe to others within the administration. *And I can't absolutely testify to that, but I will tell you that* I got back to my office versions of these chronologies, and this is but one of many that had the writing of other people that I did not recognize on those margins, and cross-ins and line-outs - I did not recognize the handwriting: I did know that it was not Admiral Poindexter's (North, pp. 39f).

Extract 4

Nields: Did you say to Mr. McFarlane, "That's not the truth?"
North: I don't have a specific recollection of that conversation. I do know that at one point, in trying to determine who was where and when, I had in my office General Secord. When General Secord saw that version - and I, *again I may not be recalling it correctly, but I think Mr. McFarlane may well have been there at that point* - General Secord said, "That's not true, I'm not going to help anymore in this. I'm leaving (North, p. 43).

Extract 5

Nields: My question, sir: Did you raise with Mr. McFarlane or any other person
           the fact that this version of the chronology was false?
North: Well, I believe I did. Again, *I do not recall the specific discussion, but I*
           came to be believe [sic] *- or came to be convinced that there were good and*
           sufficient reasons why that version had to go the way it was (North, pp. 43f).

The three disarm schemata illustrated in Extracts 3-5 are indirectly
protective of the speaker's positive communicative identity.[9] Each of
the prefaces contains a caveat as to the reliability, or factual truth, of
the information supplied in the head act, to the effect that S does not
have sufficient information to answer the question satisfactorily (3),
may not be recalling correctly (4) or does not recall a specific event (5).
In this manner, the prefaces serve to forestall possible attacks on S's
positive identity such as, *You are not answering the question* (3), *This is*
untrue/too vague (4) or *Please, be more precise* (5).

The above is the usual analysis of prefaces like the ones under review. However, just as with schemata addressed to politeness, there is
more to them than meets the eye. Yet while the disarm schema addressed to politeness is a highly effective device for the transmission of
implicit, inferential information, this does not seem at first sight to be
the case with the one addressed to clarity.

But what is the *point* of North's filibustering? Is he just evading
Nield's questions? Is he merely avoiding an answer? Why then does he
not just say, *I don't remember, I'm afraid*?

Well, first of all, because almost certainly he would not be believed.
Secondly, because he would appear to be obstructing the truth-finding
process of the Congressional committee. Both alternatives would be a
threat to his positive communicative identity. So in offering a reconstruction of the events to the best of his recollection, he appears to be
cooperating in the institutional purpose of the encounter by attempting
to answer the counsel's questions. North cannot refuse his institutionally
required cooperation, but what he can avoid doing with impunity is
raising validity claims for the statements he is forced to make. He
thereby creates a situation in which he is at liberty to put his own interpretation on events, select them, weigh them and present them in a certain light. Having renounced full communicative responsibility, he is
free to misrepresent, mislead, or perform other identity-threatening
acts, such as incriminating others, without appearing to do so.

The purpose of the discourse type "interrogation" is thereby defeated: Mr. Nields is not getting straight answers to his questions. If he

wants to take North's verbose replies as answers, he can only do so on the basis of the inferences derived from them - that Admiral Poindexter probably did not see the drafts (which very likely is untrue) (Extract 3); that McFarlane knew that the chronologies were false (Extract 4); that McFarlane may even have told North that they had to be false (Extract 5). Thus it is only on the surface that *a renowned steel-trap memory went vague, or forgetful* (North, p. viii). In providing the material that is to serve as the basis of his listeners' inferential processes, North's memory works in lucid detail. In the end, Poindexter and North are in the clear, and McFarlane has been chosen to be the fall-guy.[10]

The clarity-oriented disarm schema is not the only device whereby the above strategies can be implemented. There are other formulations in English that serve the same purpose, such as the numerous ones in the following passage:

Extract 6

(Mr. Nields has asked a question about North's involvement in the first shipment of arms to Iran).

North: *I'm working without refreshed recall. Let me do the best I can to remember back to that period of time.* I had had several meetings with Mr. Ledeen which led to a meeting or two with two Israeli citizens, private citizens. And then a subsequent meeting, *as I recall*, with Mr. Ghobanifar. That in turn led to a meeting with Mr. Kimche. And *I believe* all of these took place prior to the September shipment. Mr. Kimche and Mr. McFarlane then had a meeting, *as I recall*. And I was aware, *I think*, by virtue of the sensitive intelligence at the time that the Israelis were indeed involved in the transaction. I did not know at the time the exact nature of that, *I don't think*. But I did know that as a consequence an American hostage or two was expected to be released (North, pp. 67f).

What the schema does, however, is to condense, within the unit of one complex speech act, what in the case of devices like the ones illustrated in Extract 6 must be taken to be a property of the coherence of texts. Also, by being of the form *I don't remember - BUT ...*, the schema codes a contrast, a certain tension, between impaired memory and what is offered as information in spite of this. This contrast is officially absent in Extract 6, although it is carried by the textual sequence of what should be studied as a particular paragraph schema. Basically, we have the same phenomenon, but coded differently in different linguistic units.

Table 10 is a preliminary attempt to list the types of inferences carried by the clarity-oriented disarm schema:

Table 10. Types of inferences of the disarm schema (clarity)

(a)   The preface signals the forthcoming violation of a *constitutive rule* of interaction.
(b)   S implies that s/he has (contextually derivable) *valid reasons* for violating the constitutive rule (e.g. yielding to constraints of situation and/or discourse type), reasons that are stronger than his/her reluctance to violate a constitutive rule and that thereby *oblige* him/her to violate the rule.
(c)   These overriding reasons *justify* S's violating the constitutive rule.
(d)   The modifier in the preface may not be sincerely meant, but it *leaves s at liberty to perform implicit ITAs* without having to accept responsibility for their communicative validity.
(e)   By virtue of (b), (c) and (d), the schema functions to protect S's positive identity.

3.2.   The appease schema

In this schema, the first of the two speech acts connected by *but* is one that in some manner mitigates, atones for, or is balanced against the face- or identity-threatening act performed in the second. The mitigating speech acts in the preface are in some way supportive of H's face or identity, or they are in some way detrimental to S's face or identity.

3.2.1.   The appease schema addressed to politeness

In the appease schema addressed to politeness, the appeasing speech act in the preface is addressed to face. The following extracts will serve to illustrate some possible combinations of types of speech acts within the schema. They are taken from elicited conversations between a British native speaker and a German student of English before and after the latter went to England for a year to work as an assistant teacher at a public school in London. The student is acting in the role of assistant teacher (AT), the native speaker in the role of headmaster of the school (HM). AT has come to see HM about permission to take his upper 6th on an evening's excursion to the National Film Theatre to see a Faßbinder film in German. Unbenownst to AT, HM is fully informed about the last such outing, which ended rather merrily in a pub:[11]

Extract 7

HM: so you went after the/the cinema with twelve pupils from this school into a pub in London?
AT: yeah, for sure

HM: well, *I don't know if you quite understand my point of view on this but . I'm afraid that . it's a school rule that alcohol is not allowed under any circumstances here*
AT: Oh, is it really? (HM 2/2: 3).

Extract 8

(AT has tried to justify taking the pupils to the pub and has apologized.)
HM: Okay, we/*I might have done the same thing if I'd been in London. I might have gone into the pub as/as well, but . I'm afraid HERE, Mr. Holland, there's a very strict rule that pupils are not allowed under any circumstances to drink alcohol, and they're certainly NOT allowed to go into any/any public houses, particularly not with a member of the staff of the school* (HM 2/7: 3).

In both Extracts 7 and 8, the headmaster takes over the perspective of the assistant teacher in the preface by guessing at his state of knowledge (7), or by proclaiming affinity to his dispositions (8). These hearer-supportive acts of empathy are then followed by acts of reprimand - by the statement of school rules that the assistant teacher should have known about and has acted against. Also, there is a certain balance: the more supportive the act of empathy, the stronger the reprimand.

In Extracts 9-11, acts of qualified agreement and of appreciation are followed by acts of injunction, of refusing permission, and of granting qualified permission, respectively:

Extract 9

HM: Hm, yeah, I take your point, *it's/it's very interesting to have this discussion, uhm, but I'm afraid, as far as the next trip to the theatre is concerned, we/we/we can't possibly have a teacher going into a pub with pupils* (HM 2/7: 6).

Extract 10

(Towards the end of the conversation, AT has renewed his request.)
HM: Well, in principle, certainly, I/I/ as I said before, *excursions like these are very valuable, but as a result of this unfortunate experience the last time I don't think I can allow them to do this again so soon* (HM 2/2: 7).

Extract 11

(Context as in 10)
HM: Well, in principle I would say yes, certainly, *we are very pleased to encourage outside visits like this, and it's very good that you're willing to spend some of your free time doing this, the pupils'll benefit a lot from it, but/the only problem really, you know, in this country people tend to go to bed earlier, we don't stay out very late, do you think you could make sure that the pupils get back straight after the film* (HM 1/7: 4).

The following two extracts differ from the ones given above in that the speech act in the preface is an act touching negatively on the speaker's positive face. In (12), the headmaster admits to an omission, while in (13), he apologizes for the rigidity of the British public school system - or at least expresses regret that it must appear so to the assistant teacher:

Extract 12

(This is a direct sequel of Extract 7.)
HM: You sound surprised
AT: yes, I ʌ.M . well, I/I never had problems with things like that in Germany when we had our discussions after evenings like that
HM: well, *perhaps we should have made you aware of this before, but we're responsible for these pupils all around the clock, and this means we're responsible to the parents, and that means that what the pupils are allowed to do is what WE decide they're allowed to do, and alcohol, I'm afraid, is not one of those things* (HM 2/2: 3).

Extract 13

(Towards the end of the conversation, HM has suggested that AT and the pupils come straight back to school after the film and have a talk about the film in the common room, where matron will provide some tea. He is now summing up.)
HM: Okay, I'll speak to the caretaker about keys but/alright, I'm glad that you see it from my point of view, *I'm sorry that our system seems very rigid to you but, if you don't mind, this is the way we have to do it* (HM 2/7: 8).

Table 11 summarizes structure, content, and orientation of this schema:

Table 11.   Structure, content and orientation of the appease schema (politeness)

Preface		Head
Act protective of	*but*	Act threatening
H's positive face,		H's face
or threatening to S's positive face		

The appease schema is a speech act schema as defined earlier in that the *but*-clause does not modify the main clause of the construction. It is not the propositional contents of two clauses which are being contrasted but the illocutionary forces of two types of speech acts. Similar inferences to those carried by the disarm schema addressed to politeness are generated by the appease schema (cf. Table 12):

Table 12.   Types of inferences of the appease schema (politeness)

(a)   The preface signals the *forthcoming violation of a normative rule*, and thereby implies the speaker's *intention* to perform an FTA.
(b)   S implies that s/he has (contextually derivable) *valid reasons* for violating the normative rule that *oblige* him/her to do so.
(c)   These overriding reasons *justify* S's violating the normative rule.
(d)   The hearer-supportive act in the preface may be meant sincerely, or not. However, it provides S with an opportunity of performing an implicit face-oriented act to the effect that s/he is performing the FTA in the head reluctantly.
(e)   By virtue of (b), (c) and (d) the schema functions to protect S's positive face.

About (a): In Extracts 7-13, an expectancy is set up by the acts of empathy, praise, and apology in the preface for the occurrence of an FTA in the head. About (b): The headmaster, in spite of his understanding of the assistant teacher's motives, of his being appreciative of his work and effort, of being sorry about the rigidity of the British public school system, implies that he has to enforce school rules. He skillfully sets up and exploits a tension between his understanding and tolerance as an individual, and the constraints of his institutional role as a person of authority and power. It is the latter which obliges him to reprimand, forbid, and order. About (c): It is the acceptance of the predominance of institutional norms that justifies the headmaster's violation of interactional norms. About (d): Since the headmaster implies that he is obliged to enforce institutional norms, it may be further inferred that he does so unwillingly.[12] About (e): (b), (c) and (d) combine to protect S's positive face. We can take the manifestations of the appease schema in this context as the embodiment of non-authoritarian leadership style.

3.2.2.   The appease schema addressed to clarity

It is easy to confuse the schema presented in this section with the *yes, but*-schema (cf. Lauerbach 1989: 46f), with its structure of "agree, but disagree". However, the *yes, but*-schema is a schema addressed to face and as such a subtype of the politeness-oriented appease schema, which is at the same time protective of and threatening to the hearer's face. The appease schema addressed to clarity, on the other hand, is oriented to the negotiation of identity. In the extracts I present in this section, it is negative identity that is at risk and being negotiated - in particular the freedom from infringement of discoursal rights. I will again quote from Oliver North's testimony.

We have already seen that North makes ample use of the disarm schema addressed to clarity in order to protect his positive communicative identity as a rational, responsible, and above all, truthful interlocutor. In fact, he went into the Committee's hearings with this identity very much in question. Previous witnesses had severely discredited him as a trustworthy person, and Assistant Attorney General Charles J. Cooper had said, under questioning and just before North's appearance before the Committee, "that he would not believe the testimony of North whether or not under oath" (North, p. vii). We can define the whole context of North's testimony as one in which his positive identity was continuously on the stand and had to be defended.

This is not so with his negative identity. In the context of a Congressional committee's hearing, the constraints of institution and discourse type provide quite clearly for discoursal rights and obligations - who performs what type of speech act when and addressed to whom. Thus it is Nields' role as counsel to ask the questions, and North's to answer them. An institutional threat to North's negative identity is thus built into this discourse type. It cannot, therefore, be further threatened in the ongoing interaction. The situation is different with Nields' negative identity. Nields is supposed to be in full discoursal control, and this position, though institutionally secured, is nevertheless open to attack and may have to be defended.

We have seen above how North, after a clarity-disarming preface, tends to be rather prolix in his answers, and to present and above all select information according to his best judgment of what is relevant but was not asked. Since the decision as to what counts as relevant when is exclusively made by the interrogating counsel, such behavior is apt to infringe on the latter's discoursal rights and thereby threaten his negative identity. Nields, for his part, operates under two contradictory strategic goals: to retain control of the proceedings on the one hand, (and be *seen* as retaining control; there is face involved here, too), and to let North talk on the other - in the hope that he will entangle himself in the web of his own rhetoric, get caught up in contradictions, or let something slip which was supposed to remain hidden. Interestingly, the device Nields uses to compromise between these contradictory strategies, to have his cake and eat it too, is another *but*-schema, and one well suited to defense and counter-move: the clarity-oriented appease schema in responsive position, as illustrated by Extracts 14-17:

Extract 14

Nields: (question about a paragraph in the false chronology)
North: There is much in that paragraph that is false, and it was false because we were
         at that point in time making an effort to disassociate ourselves with the earlier
         Israeli shipments.
Nields: For what reason
         (long reply)
Nields: Colonel North, *I am going to ask you in a while to tell us the story of this
         transaction. But, just for the moment my question was more limited.* I think
         you've answered it, and I will put another one to you. I think you may have
         answered this, too (North, pp. 40f).

Extract 15

North: (long reply to earlier question)
Nields: I want to return - *we'll come to these subjects in a minute, Col. North. But I'd
         like to return* to the chronologies and to the question of who it was in the
         Administration that decided that the false version of the facts should be put
         forward (North, p. 47).

Extract 16

Nields: I take it this call was from Mr. Rabin?
North: It was.
Nields: And what was the problem?
North: (long reply; 1 1/2 pages of transcript)
Nields: *Yeah, I'll come back to some of these issues, but I take it* there was
         originally contemplated to ship more than 18 Hawks (North, pp. 72f).

Extract 17

Nields: What was your authority for using that money for the Contras?
North: Well, I don't know that I actually had any, in specifics. By the end of January
         and early February, we had come to a conclusion that we were going to
         proceed to use funds generated by the sale of arms to Iran to support this
         initiative. And we came that-to that through a rather circuitous route. And if
         you like, I can lay that out for you. And it is important to the whole decision
         process on the use of residuals or profits.
Nields: *We will want to hear your testimony on that I can assure you but for the moment
         I'd like to stay with the $1 million* (North, pp. 78f).

What Nields does in these extracts is to weakly support North's
positive identity as communicator by acknowledging his replies as not
altogether irrelevant in the preface, and to strongly attack his negative
identity as equal interaction partner by explicit acts of discoursal control
in the head (see Table 13):

Table 13.   Structure, content and orientation of the appease schema
            addressed to clarity

Preface		Head
Act protective of	*but*	Act threatening H's
H's positive identity		negative identity

However, we stated above that, in this institutional context, North's negative identity is not really at issue, is not up for negotiation. We have also noted that this is, on the other hand, very much the case regarding his positive identity. By openly attacking North's negative identity (and thereby defending his own), Nields implicitly shows North up as having violated the norms of the discourse type they are both engaged in, be it from ignorance, disregard, or strategy. He dismisses North's replies as too prolix (14), relevant, but not at the moment (15), not answering the question fully (16), and leading away from the question (17).

The tokens of the schema quoted here thus carry the inference that North is either incompetent, uncooperative, or devious as a communicator - or all of these. These inferences are a strong, albeit implicit, threat to North's positive identity.

Apart from this type of inference, which is peculiar to the schema, its other inferences are similar to the ones generated by the schemata dealt with already (see Table 14):

Table 14.   Types of inferences of the appease schema (clarity)

(a)   The preface signals the *forthcoming violation of a constitutive rule* of interaction.
(b)   s implies that s/he has *valid* (contextually derivable) *reasons* for this violation (e.g. upholding constraints of discourse type) that *oblige* him/her to violate the rule.
(c)   The overriding reasons *justify* s's violating the constitutive rule.
(d)   The hearer-supportive act in the preface may be meant sincerely or not. However, it provides s with the opportunity of performing an implicit identity-oriented act with the effect of calling into question the positive identity of the addressee, i.e. his/her cooperativity, sincerity and/or competence as a communicator.
(e)   By virtue of (b), (c) and (d) the schema functions to protect s's negative identity.

The types of inference described under (d) and (e) in Tables 7-10, 12 and 14 account for what in speech-act theory used to be dealt with (or rather, not dealt with) as perlocutionary effects. In the appease schema addressed to clarity, while the official threat to the hearer's identity in the head act is a threat to negative identity (freedom from infringement of discoursal rights), the perlocutionary effect of the schema as a whole is a threat to the hearer's positive identity (cooperativity, sincerity, and competence as a communicator), and a boost to s's negative identity. (Such feats have consequences on the social plane: s's positive face is enhanced.) Like the other (d) and (e)-inferences, these effects are conventionally associated with the schema in that type of discourse. Couched in Austinian terms, they would be "perlocutionary objects" rather than "perlocutionary sequels". The enhancement of Nields' positive face would be a perlocutionary sequel.

The fact that Nields had cause to defend his discoursal rights by questioning North's communicative cooperativity and competence is strikingly illustrated by Extract 18 (Sullivan is North's counsel):

Extract 18

North:	...
Nields:	I don't think there is a question pending to which you are responding, sir.
Sullivan:	I think there is.
North:	But, I want to clarify the question for you, Mr. Nields (North, pp. 28f).

It is, however, common knowledge that Nields' strategy did not work equally well for all addressees involved.[13] The majority of the TV audience, as distinct from the members of the Congressional committee, did not perceive a counsel who, in pursuit of the truth, was trying to disperse North's smoke screens, but a valiant patriot who stood his ground against an agressive interrogator and a hostile committee - witness the bags of fan mail and other symptoms of "Ollie-mania".

4.   Summary and open questions

In this paper, I have presented two types of *but*-schema, the disarm schema and the appease schema, in their orientation to rules of clarity and politeness, to face and identity. I have described their structure, content and orientation, and the inferences they generate; and I have illustrated these schemata with tokens of their occurrence in different discourse types.

The structure of the schema is complex: two speech acts connected by *but*. In both parts of the structure, the speech acts used are essentially linked to face and/or identity of speaker and hearer. These concepts are defined in a model of verbal interaction that rests on constitutive and normative rules, and which has to supplement the definition of speech-act schemata. Such a model is, however, needed not only for pragmatics and discourse analaysis, but also for part of the grammar proper, such as speech-act verbs, and for other boundary areas, such as other conjunctions (e.g. speech-act schemata with *if*: *Your paper is plagiarized, if you don't mind my saying so*, cf. Lauerbach 1979).

What sorts of acts can go into the two structural slots of the schema may vary, depending on the preferred orientation towards face or identity, towards speaker or hearer, and towards the positive or negative dimensions of face and identity. It is likely that the schema is a universal model underlying language use, and that the preferred orientations and what counts as a speaker or hearer protecting or threatening act is culture-specific.

The analysis further shows that what is oriented to as protective or threatening depends not only on culture-specific value systems but also on discourse type. In a highly institutionalized discourse type like a Congressional committee hearing, the communicative roles of the participants as well as the global purpose of the encounter are rigidly prescribed, and this leads to different dimensions of communicative identity being potentially vulnerable for different participants - negative identity for the interrogator, positive identity for the witness.

Different roles and priorities are in force in the headmaster-teacher discourse. Thus a certain preferred distribution of protective and threatening acts is, as it were, preprogrammed for the participants.[14] This is part of participants' knowledge about the discourse types of their culture, knowledge which has to be taken to underlie actual language use and which must also be stored in a cognitive structure, or "discourse schema".

The inferences carried by the schemata are of different types and arise on different levels of abstraction. Inferences of justification for threatening acts, as well as the general perlocutionary effects of discoursal manipulation and control, and of enhancement of face and identity are context- and culture-independent. What counts as valid reasons and the particular perlocutionary effect achieved are culture-, discourse- and situation-specific. It is by exploiting the potential of such inferences that participants have a certain leeway in the negotiation of face and identity, even if the constraints imposed by discourse type are very rigid. Context-independent inferences may be viewed as generalized in a Gricean sense, context-specific ones as particularized (cf. Lauerbach 1989).

There is also the question of whether all of the inferences generated by *but*-schemata (and there are likely to be many more context-specific ones than the typical ones listed here) are consciously present in all speakers and hearers. There may be a prototypical core for production and another one for comprehension, both depending crucially on mode of discourse - whether writing/reading or speaking/listening - and on the sophistication of interactants. However, this is not really a problem for cognitive linguistics, which can stop at accounting for the stereotypical and prototypical knowledge that is represented in such schemata. An interesting question in this respect is whether the perlocutionary inferences are peripheral, that is, furthest from the prototypical core, or not. My intuition is that, since it is these effects that make the schemata strategically so effective, they should be very salient and therefore central. This, however, is something else which requires empirical study. For this reason, any attempts at formalization of schema constituents and their interrelations, beyond the ones given, would still be premature.

Much of what has been presented in his paper is provisional; all is in need of further refinement and theoretical underpinning. Other schemata have to be looked for in other discourse types with other conjunctions. The question of schemata in initiative and responsive position, as well as that of paragraph-schemata, has only been touched on in passing. In addition, the question of universality needs to be studied empirically.

However, in spite of these caveats, I believe there is sufficient evidence to posit a level of socio-linguistic-cognitive organization that lies between language system and language use, a level that Coseriu (1970) has called *Norm*. This level comprises the conventional realizations within a speech community of the potential provided by the language system. *It does not exhaust the possibilities offered by the system on the one hand, and it goes beyond the system by using principles other than linguistic ones on the other.* Such a level has been shown by Coseriu to exist in phonology, morphology, syntax and semantics. The facts presented in this paper are evidence for its existence in pragmatics, too. This level of conventionalization provides speakers and hearers with cognitive models that are different from but every bit as effective as those assumed for the language system. As such, it is a bonafide and important new field of study for cognitive linguistics. For if we can find in texts and discourses evidence for this third level of conventionalization, a level that supplies language users with a variety of "rhetorical" schemata, with context-sensitive blueprints for their functional orientations, schemata that are not created afresh in every linguistic encounter but are activated as automatic or at most half-conscious routines, then the units of such a level should have strong cognitive reality. To restrict enquiry to the properties of language systems alone, without accounting for the cognitive schemata that underlie systems of use and conventionally govern functional selections from the potential of language systems, would mean settling for only half the truth about cognition in language.

Notes

1.   The sexist example is typical of linguistic discourse at that time.
2.   For an argument that the concept of positive and negative politeness have to be modified for Japanese, cf. Matsumoto (1988).
3.   Cf. Brown & Levinson (1978). The "weightiness" of an FTA is a function of the power relations between interlocutors, their social distance, and the degree of imposition on the addressee intrinsic to the act.
4.   These researchers acknowledge a debt not only to Bartlett (1932/1967), as most workers in modern psychology do, but surprisingly also to Kant (1787). In this, they have a prominent predecessor: H. Paul Grice, who, tongue in cheek, formulated his maxims of Quantity, Quality, Relation and Manner in analogy to Kant's four categories of reason. For an overview on frames, scripts, schemata, scenarios and mental models, cf. Brown & Yule (1983: 233ff).
5.   This can lead to "interferences" or "inter-schema inference transfer", cf. Lauerbach (1989). Thus, very strikingly, once you hear someone say *I don't want ...*, *but*, an inference is generated to the effect that that's exactly what he or she wants, and this inference may "linger", even if the subsequent input does not manifestly confirm that expectation.
6.   These inferences are worked out in detail in Lauerbach (1989: 41f) for the "double-bind schema".
7.   John Nields is the House Committee counsel. References are to the transcripts of the North testimony provided by the Federal News Service, Washington, D.C., and published in 1987 by Pocket Books, Simon and Schuster, New York, as *Taking the stand: The testimony of Lieutenant Colonel Oliver North*. Extracts are labelled "North, p. x".
8.   See inferences (a) to (d) in Table 7.
9.   The tokens of the schema contained in Extracts 3 and 4 deviate from the definition initially given for speech-act schemata, namely that the dependent clauses do not modify their main clauses:
      (3)   *I can't absolutely testify to that but I will tell you...*
      (4)   *I may not be recalling it correctly, but I think...*
      (3) makes the speech act of giving information explicit. In (4) the *but*-clause contains an additional modification of S's commitment to his truth claim (*I think*). These phenomena will have to be acccounted for in a comprehensive analysis, but can be neglected for the time being.
10.   McFarlane is Poindexter's predecessor as National Security Advisor, and as such North's former boss.
11.   The orthography and punctuation in these transcripts conform to normal conventions, with one exception: one full stop stands for a short pause, two for a longer one; etc.

12.   The contrast between individual disinclination and externally imposed obligation is also a theme of the "double-bind" schema *I don't want to ..., but ...*, where the unwillingness is starkly expressed; however cf. Lauerbach (1989).

13.   With utterances addressed to multiple hearers with diverging interests, diverging illocutionary points and perlocutionary effects can arise; cf. Lauerbach (1989), Clark & Carlson (1982).

14.   In this paper, I have used the terms *preferred*, *preference*, and *preferential* in their everyday use and pre-theoretical meaning. Unfortunately, this meaning connotes a psychological dimension of needs and motivations, and is not to be confused with the concept of preference organization as used in conversation analysis (cf. Bilmes 1988). It would take another paper to show how psychological motivation evolves into structural organization, and another one yet to study the relation of preference organization and prototypicality in discourse.

References

Baker, Charlotte
      1975   "'This is just a first approximation, but...'", *Papers from the Eleventh Regional Meeting of the Chicago Linguistic Society*, 37-47.
Bartlett, Frederick
      1932-1967   *Remembering*. Cambridge: Cambridge University Press.
Bilmes, Jack
      1988   "The concept of preference in conversation analysis", *Language in Society* 17: 161-181.
Brown, Gillian & George Yule
      1983   *Discourse analysis*. Cambridge: Cambridge University Press.
Brown, Penelope & Stephen Levinson
      1978   "Universals in language usage: politeness phenomena", in: Esther Goody (ed.), *Questions and politeness: Strategies in social interaction*. Cambridge: Cambridge University Press, 56-289.
      1987   *Politeness: Some universals in language usage*. Cambridge: Cambridge University Press.
Clark, Herbert & Thomas Carlson
      1982   "Hearers and speech acts", *Language* 58: 332-373.
Coleman, Linda & Paul Kay
      1981   "Prototype semantics: The English verb *lie*", *Language* 57: 26-44.
Coseriu, Eugeniu
      1970   "System, Norm und Rede", in: Uwe Petersen (ed.), *Sprache, Strukturen und Funktionen*. Tübingen: Narr, 53-72.
Dirven, René, Louis Goossens, Yvan Putseys & Emma Vorlat
      1982   *The scene of linguistic action and its perspectivation by SPEAK, TALK, SAY and TELL*. Amsterdam: John Benjamins.
Fillmore, Charles J.
      1988   Varieties of conditional sentences. [Unpublished MS.]
Geeraerts, Dirk
      1989   "Introduction: Prospects and problems of prototype theory", *Linguistics* 27: 587-612.

Goffman, Erving
1955   "On face-work: An analysis of ritual elements in social interaction",
            Psychiatry 18: 213-231.
Grice, H. Paul
1975   "Logic and conversation", in: Peter Cole & Jerry Morgan (eds.),
            Syntax and semantics, Vol. 3: *Speech acts*. New York: Academic Press,
            41-58.
Habermas, Jürgen
1971   "Vorbereitende Bemerkungen zu einer Theorie der kommunikativen
            Kompetenz", in: Jürgen Habermas & Niklas Luhmann: *Theorie der
            Gesellschaft oder Sozialtechnologie*. Frankfurt/Main: Suhrkamp, 101-
            141.
1981   *Theorie des kommunikativen Handelns*. 2 vols. Frankfurt/Main:
            Suhrkamp.
Heringer, James T.
1971   Some grammatical correlates of felicity conditions and
            presuppositions. [Unpublished Ph.D. Dissertation, Ohio State
            University.]
Kant, Immanuel
1781/1787   *Critique of pure reason*. (Translated by N. Kemp Smith). London:
            Macmillan [1963].
Kenny, Arthur J.
1966   "Practical inference", *Analysis* 26: 65-75.
Lakoff, Robin
1971   "*If*'s, *and*'s and *but*'s about conjunction", in: Charles J. Fillmore &
            Terence D. Langendoen (eds.), *Studies in linguistic semantics*. New
            York: Holt, Rinehart and Winston, 115-150.
1973   "The logic of politeness; or, minding your p's and q's". *Papers from the
            Ninth Regional Meeting, Chicago Linguistic Society*, 292-305.
Lauerbach, Gerda
1979   *Form und Funktion englischer Konditionalsätze mit 'if': Eine
            konversationslogische und sprechakttheoretische Analyse*. Tübingen:
            Niemeyer.
1989   "'We don't want war, but...': Speech act schemata and inter-schema-
            inference transfer", *Journal of Pragmatics* 13: 25-51.
Levinson, Stephen
1979   "Activity types and language", *Linguistics* 17: 356-399.
Matsumoto, Yoshiko
1988   "Reexamination of the universality of face: Politeness phenomena in
            Japanese", *Journal of Pragmatics* 12: 403-426.
North, Oliver
1987   *Taking the stand: The testimony of Lieutenant Colonel Oliver North*.
            With an introduction by Daniel Schorr. New York: Simon and
            Schuster.
Ross, John R.
1968   "On declarative sentences", in: Roderick A. Jacobs & Peter S.
            Rosenbaum (eds.), *Readings in English transformational grammar*.
            Waltham: Blaisdell, 222-272.
Rudzka-Ostyn, Brygida
1989   "Prototypes, schemas, and cross-category correspondences: The case
            of *ask*", *Linguistics* 27: 613-661.

Rumelhart, David E. & Andrew Ortony
  1977   "The representation of knowledge in memory", in: Richard Anderson
              & William Montague (eds.), *Schooling and the acquisition of
              knowledge*. Hillsdale, N.J.: Lawrence Erlbaum, 99-135.
Rutherford, William
  1970   "Some observations concerning subordinate clauses in English",
              Language 46: 97-115.
Sacks, Harvey
  1975   "Everyone has to lie", in: Mary Sanders & Ben G. Blount (eds.),
              Sociocultural dimensions of language use. New York: Academic Press,
              57-80.
Sacks, Harvey, Emanuel Schegloff & Gail Jefferson
  1974   "A simplest systematics for the organisation of turn-taking for
              conversation", *Language* 50: 696-735.
Searle, John
  1969   *Speech acts*. Cambridge: Cambridge University Press.
Sweetser, Eve
  1984   Semantic structure and semantic change: A cognitive linguistic study of
              modality, perception, speech acts, and logical relations. [Unpublished
              Ph.D. Dissertation, University of California.]
  1987   "The definition of *lie*: An examination of the talk models underlying a
              semantic prototype", in: Dorothy Holland & Naomi Quinn (eds.),
              Cultural models in language and thought. Cambridge: Cambridge
              University Press, 43-66.
Van Dijk, Teun
  1979   "Pragmatic connectives", *Journal of Pragmatics* 3: 447-457.
Wierzbicka, Anna
  1989   "Prototypes in semantics and pragmatics: Explicating attitudinal
              meanings in terms of prototypes", *Linguistics* 27: 731-769.

Syntactic, semantic and interactional prototypes: The case of left-dislocation

Ronald Geluykens

1. Introduction[1]

This paper deals with a specific problem which is one of the central issues in cognitive linguistics, viz. that of the fuzziness of linguistic categories, both from a functional and a formal point of view. We will attempt to show that syntactic constructions defy strict categorization, but are prototypically organized. As a case in point, we will investigate empirically a sample of one particular construction, viz. left-dislocation.

In his recent study about categories and prototypes, Lakoff (1987: 582) draws several conclusions about the nature of language, among which are the following:

- "Prototype-based categorization occurs in grammar. Radially structured categories exist there, and their function is to greatly reduce the arbitrariness of form-meaning correlations."
- "Syntactic categories are not autonomous, nor are they completely predictable from semantic considerations. Instead, their central subcategories are predictable from semantic considerations, and their noncentral subcategories are motivated extensions of central subcategories."
- "A great many syntactic properties of grammatical constructions are consequences of their meanings."

The present paper, apart from providing evidence for these claims from naturally occurring conversational discourse, tries to take this reasoning one step further, by showing that certain syntactic constructions are not only prototype-based, but cannot be properly explained, on a functional level, except by reference to their interactional discourse properties. The discourse-functional behavior of these constructions is in itself prototype-based.

More specifically, as a case in point, the rest of this paper will be devoted to an analysis of a construction which is usually labelled "left-dislocation" (following Ross 1967; henceforth LD) in the literature. The pattern we mean is exemplified by (1):

(1)   *John, he likes Mary.*

As a formal characterization of what constitutes an LD, we can define it as a concatenation of on the one hand an NP which is "bare" - i.e. which is not the argument of any preceding verb - and on the other hand a syntactically complete clause which has as one of its verbal arguments a pronominal element which is coreferential with the preceding bare NP. If we label (following the terminology in Geluykens 1988a, 1988b) the bare NP the "referent" of the LD (or REF for short), and the subsequent clause the "proposition" (or PROP), while referring to the coreferent pronoun within the PROP as the "gap", the typical formal structure of an LD can be represented as follows:

(2)   LD: [REF$_i$] + [...[GAP$_i$]...PROP]

What we will argue, in the remainder of this paper, is that a strict formal characterization of LD in terms of necessary and sufficient characteristics is not an appropriate solution on a discourse level. First of all, although a syntactic analysis may of course be possible in theory, such a strict definition does not allow us to account for the semantic and functional similarities between what could be labelled "core" LDs (as defined in (2)) and related structures such as the ones listed in (3-10):

(3)   *To Duisburg, I used to go there.*
(4)   *As for John, he likes Mary.*
(5)   *Living in London, that seems nice.*
(6)   *To live in London, that seems nice.*
(7)   *That he lives in London, that's what I said.*
(8)   *There's this guy John, he likes Mary.*
(9)   *You know this guy John, he likes Mary.*
(10)   *Talking about this guy John, he likes Mary.*

Secondly, apart from certain syntactic and semantic similarities among all these constructions (cf. section 3.), there are outspoken functional parallels between them which would be swept under the carpet in a purely categorial approach to LD. As we will show in section 2., LD and LD-like structures all occur in specific discourse conditions, viz. they are used to introduce a new referent (i.e. irrecoverable (Geluykens 1988c) from the previous discourse record) into the conversation in a collaborative manner (cf. Geluykens 1988a, 1989b); this referent is then developed as a new discourse topic (cf. Geluykens 1988b). Thirdly, from a functional, interactional point of view it will be shown that it also makes sense to think about the discourse function of LD in terms of prototypes. That is to say, we will attempt to show that the interactional strategy labelled "LD" can be reduced to a three-stage prototypical process on which less prototypical variations are possible.

2. Left-dislocation (LD) as a collaborative strategy

2.1. LD as a three-stage process

Elsewhere (Geluykens 1988a, 1988b, 1989a, in press), we have already claimed that what is usually labelled LD in the literature is in fact the outcome of an interactional process, whereby a new referent is introduced into the discourse. This introductory process can be schematically represented as follows:

(11)   - stage 1 (speaker):
                referent-introduction (= REF)
                [+ optional elaborative material]
         - stage 2 (hearer):
                referent-acknowledgment (explicit or implicit)
         - stage 3 (speaker):
                establishment of referent as topic (= PROP)

LD in English conversation can thus be shown to be a reflection of a three-stage interactional process rather than being a variation on the SVX order. In the first stage of this process (the REF), a new referent is introduced into the discourse; in a second stage, this introduced referent is acknowledged, either verbally or implicitly, by the hearer; the third stage (the PROP), finally, establishes the referent in the discourse. The stages can thus be referred to as Introduction, Acknowledgment, and Establishment, respectively. As an exemplification of this interactional process, consider (12-14):[2]

(12)   A: *and that table tennis room of mine*
        a: *mhm*
        A: *it's always cold in there .*
              because you know we don't live in it .
              (S.1.7.119.1)[3]

In this example, the speaker produces the referent *that table tennis room*, after which the hearer gives a short acknowledgment noise, indicating that he is prepared to accept the new referent into the discourse; after this, the speaker goes on to produce the second part of the LD, viz. the PROP *it's always cold in there*.

(13)   B: *ahm - and - well the British Academy frankly ahm*
        a: *well they haven't got very much money .*
        B: *well you know they have this new grant which started*
              last year - (...)
              (S.2.1.40.2)
(14)   B: *all right then Salad Street you know where I put you down*
              this morning .
        A: *yeah *yeah**
        B: **or .* I'll tell you what I'll just wait in that bay there .*
              (S.7.2.d14.7)

Instances (13) and (14) are slight variations on this process. In (13), acknowledgment is carried out by means of an entire clause rather than a short agreement signal; in (14), the speaker adds some extra elaborative material to the REF, in order to facilitate the hearer's referent-identification.

In instances (12-14), there is explicit acknowledgment of the new referent (cf. the hearer-turn); in (15-16), acknowledgment is tacit (cf. the pause between REF and PROP):

(15)   A: *- then the drainage well -- I don't know how long that'll*
              take more
              (S.1.9.88.4)
(16)   B: *ah yes but then the gift tax - [ə:] it was essential to do*
              that
              (S.1.13.123.3)

In these cases, the speaker produces a REF (*the drainage* and *the gift tax*, respectively), then pauses for acknowledgment. The fact that the hearer does not explicitly object to the new referent can then be read by the speaker as a tacit acknowledgment signal (in addition, there may of course be other, non-verbal acknowledgment signals, such as gestures, nods of the head, and the like; the nature of the database does not permit us to check on these).

From a cognitive, informational point of view, LDs in English are argued to be topic-introducing, by which we mean the following. First of all, with regard to the preceding context, the introduced referent is *irrecoverable*, i.e. is not derivable from the previous discourse record (Geluykens 1988c). An example will make this clear:

(17)   A: *(5 syllables) register*
        B: *hello .*
        A: *hello Daphie*
        B: *could you have a look [ə] you know that file I left on Mrs Boyle . Miss *Boyle**
        A: **file* you left on Miss Boyle **yeah***
        B: ***yeah** the brown one . it's got a number on the front . could you look on it and tell me what the number is -* (S.7.3.h2.5)

This LD comes from the opening sequence of a telephone conversation; it is clear, therefore, that the REF *that file* cannot be recovered from the previous discourse context, since there is no such context. Most LDs in our database are of a similar nature.

Secondly, with regard to the subsequent context, it is argued that LD-referents are *topical*, i.e. they recur, or "persist", in the immediately following discourse context (Geluykens 1988b). Again, an example will illustrate this:

(18)   A: *yes . [ə:m] Randolph . when he drove us up to London . from after skiing - .*
        a: *yeah*
        A: *he went all . round the houses trying to find it *and**
        a: **m**
        A: *he hadn't the slightest idea where the . M 23 . new M 23 was . in relation to Gatwick .*
        c: *m*
        A: *and he knew it had been opened (...)* (S.1.11.b7.8)

In this exchange, the new referent *Randolph*, which is introduced by the LD, recurs in both speaker-turns following the LD (cf. *he* in the fifth and seventh turns), and is thus employed as a topical referent.

Our findings on the informational function of LD in English are confirmed by related work on LD in narrative discourse; according to Givón (1983), LD is:

> Used to return topics back into the register over long gaps of absence, thus high ref. distance, and also consequently fairly high interference values; often associated with major thematic breaks in discourse structure, i.e. typically a paragraph-initial device (Givón 1983: 32).

Another study on LD, with an emphasis on spoken discourse, is Ochs & Schieffelin (1983). An important feature of their work is that they appear to be aware of the interactional implications of LD:

> ...the Referent + Proposition constructions look more like discourses (a sequence of communicative acts) than a single syntactically bound communicative act (Ochs & Schieffelin 1983: 172).

They also point out the possibility of prosodic breaks and interruptions between Referent and Proposition.

We can conclude two things from this. First of all, from a cognitive point of view, LD is shown to introduce entirely new (i.e. irrecoverable) discourse topics. Secondly, from an interactional point of view, we have shown LD in English to be a rather direct reflection of a three-stage communicative process, a process which is probably subject to syntactization (cf. Geluykens 1989c). In the following sections, we shall see that there are interactional variants on this pattern which can be related to the prototypical process outlined in (11).

2.2.   Five-stage variants on the prototypical patterning

In a number of cases, the interactional exchange between speaker and hearer is more complicated than the process outlined in the previous section; this section will discuss three such instances in some detail. The point we want to make is that these variant exchanges are reducible to the basic interactional schema presented in (11), in that there are some additional discourse factors which necessitate a more complex interactional pattern. In other words, these are interactionally less prototypical variants of the basic three-stage process outlined in 2.1.

A first example of such a five-stage variant is given in exchange (19) below, which we will analyze in some detail:

(19)   B: *this Polly . you know that girl whom I've mhm mhm*
               presented a rather absurd report in a way that genuinely
               represented what I felt I said she *might* fail
        A: **who's that**
        B: *or get a two A do you remember at the end I thought*
               she's **get further than two B do you know her**
        A: ***oh yes . yes well (3-4 syllables)***
        B: *she's a very funny girl* (S.1.4.58.12)

What appears to happen here is the following: after producing the new referent *this Polly* (the REF), the speaker decides to give some elaborative material to enable the hearer to identify the intended referent (turn 1). After this, the hearer is still not able to identify the referent, hence is unable to acknowledge it as a potential new discourse topic; he thus asks for yet more elaboration (turn 2). In turn 3, the speaker duly provides this elaboration, after which the hearer acknowledges the new referent (turn 4); note that there is some overlap between these two stages of the exchange. Finally, in turn 5, the speaker can establish the referent by producing a PROP. We thus get the following interaction:

(20)   -   stage 1 (speaker B):
                     referent-introduction (REF) +
                     elaborative material
        -   stage 2 (speaker A):
                     request for more elaboration
        -   stage 3 (speaker B):
                     further elaboration
        -   stage 4 (speaker A):
                     acknowledgment of referent
        -   stage 5 (speaker B):
                     establishment of referent as topic (PROP)

It can easily be seen how this pattern is a more complex variant of (11) above.

Another instance of a five-stage exchange, albeit for a different reason, is (21):

(21)   A: *yes I see . yes . yes - ahm . one other thing Sam - ahm -*
              *Delaney a Canadian *who graduated - **
        B: **ah where did you* put those things just one . let me put this*
              in my bag or I'll walk away without it ---
        A: *Delaney's the Canadian . student remember last year*
        B: *mhm*
        A: *ah he should have had his dissertation in at the beginning*
              of May
              (S.1.1.5.2)

In this case, the speaker's new referent (*Delaney*) fails to get acknowledged by the hearer in turn 2, due to the fact that he is busy with something else (viz. looking for his bag); this gives rise to a short side sequence (Jefferson 1972). The speaker is thus forced to have another go at introducing his referent (turn 3), after which acknowledgment (turn 4) and establishment (turn 5) take place. Interactionally, we thus get the following:

(22)   - stage 1 (speaker B):
              referent-introduction (REF)
        - stage 2 (speaker A):
              failure to acknowledge referent ("side sequence")
        - stage 3 (speaker B):
              second attempt at introducing REF
        - stage 4 (speaker A):
              acknowledgment of referent
        - stage 5 (speaker B):
              establishment of referent as topic (PROP)

Again, this pattern is a less prototypical variant of (11) above.

Thirdly, and finally, we will look at a five-stage exchange which is due to different discourse factors still:

(23)   B: ***well the sessional question** -*
        A: *what*
        B: *on the sessional question*
        A: **yes**
        B: **have you* got it* (S.5.11.a16.2)

Whereas in (19) the delay of the acknowledgment stage was due to the hearer's identification problems, and in (21) to the hearer being involved in a side sequence, the delay in (23) appears to be caused by a simple perception problem: the hearer has not heard what the speaker was saying, has thus missed the new referent, and asks for repetition. The exchange can be summarized as follows:

(24)   - stage 1 (speaker A):
                      REF: topic-introduction
        - stage 2 (speaker B):
                      request for repetition
        - stage 3 (speaker A):
                      second mention of REF
        - stage 4 (speaker B):
                      acknowledgment
        - stage 5 (speaker A):
                      PROP: topic-establishment

Once again, apart from the complexity caused by the specific problem spot, this variant can be reduced to the prototype schema in (11).

2.3.   Two-stage variants on the prototypical patterning

There are also LDs which, rather than having three distinct interactional stages, have only two. We will try to show here that, in the majority of cases, such two-stage exchanges are non-prototypical variants on the prototype three-stage pattern. We will concentrate on one clear example, viz. (25):

(25)   A: *(...) about those seminars that Millicent was talking about*
              are they in fact conducted by him .
        C: *he does this five fifteen on a Wednesday one (...)*
              (S.1.5.59.3)

In this instance, the REF *those seminars* is immediately followed by the PROP *are they in fact conducted by him*, without an intervening acknowledgment-stage (neither explicit nor implicit. It is important to note, however, that this LD functions as a question. Assuming the hearer to be cooperative, there will be an onus on him to supply a response to this question. In doing so, he thus implicitly acknowledges the new referent, but after the entire REF + PROP structure has been produced rather than right after the REF. Should the hearer decide not to acknowledge the REF, he still has a chance of doing so at this later stage. The process underlying (25) is thus something along the lines of (26):

(26)   - stage 1:   Question:
                      REF + PROP (referent-introduction)
        - stage 2:   Answer:
                      (topic-establishment)

Once again, then, a non-prototype use of LD can be explained with reference to the prototype three-stage use, allowing for the special discourse context in which it occurs.

2.4.   Alternative outcomes of the topic-introducing process

If LD, on a functional level, is the outcome of a process rather than being a construction, one would logically expect there to be alternative, less straightforward developments of this process. If we regard the exchange represented in (11) above as the prototypical interactional exchange, the variants discussed in sections 2.2. and 2.3. are already less prototypical, from an interactional point of view, as they only occur to deal with specific discourse conditions. The speaker-hearer interaction may, moreover, yield even less prototypical results, which will be discussed in this section.

First of all, it would not be very far-fetched to assume that the Introduction-Acknowledgment-Establishment sequence may be distributed differently over speaker and hearer. That is to say, after the speaker has introduced a new referent, and this has been acknowledged by the hearer, the hearer rather than the speaker may go on to establish the new referent by means of a PROP (we will stick to the LD terminology here). We do in fact find instances of this in the database, such as (27):

(27)   A: *starting at about seven tonight*
        B: *yes I . may be a few minutes late *but . don't know**
        A: **yes . the girls'* final* -
        B: *yes - I want to see that*
        A: *yes - well that's . we're . hoping to start at seven - . or as near as possible* (S.7.3.e7.3)

What happens here is that speaker A produces a referent (*the girls' final*) and pauses for acknowledgment; speaker B duly acknowledges the referent (cf. *yes*). After that, it is speaker B rather than speaker A who establishes the REF by producing the PROP *I want to see that*. What we have here, then, is a structure (*The girls' final, I want to see that*) which would be a straightforward core LD, were it not for the fact that the REF and the PROP are produced by different speakers.

Rather than saying - as one would be forced to do in a categorical account - that (27) cannot possibly qualify as an LD, a prototype approach enables one to recognize (27) as a less prototypical instance of the LD-generating process outlined in (11). The reason why (27) would be less typical is a straightforwardly interactional one: if a speaker takes the trouble to introduce a new referent into the discourse, it is much more natural to assume that it will also be this speaker who will go on to establish this new referent; the fact that the hearer carries out establishment is interactionally less to be expected. That is also the reason why exchanges like (27) are relatively rare.

One other good example of such a non-prototype process, which can be explained by looking at the surrounding interactional context, is (28):

(28)   a: *sorry you were saying - * - about .
        A: *Elisabeth's man*
        a: *I don't know anything about him* what do you know about
              him --
              (S.2.12.2.8)

In (28), we get the same distribution of REF and PROP over two different participants. Here, however, it is relatively easy to see why this should be the case, since it is participant "a" who has prompted the introduction of the new referent *Elisabeth's man* in the first place, by producing *sorry you were saying about*. Since it is the hearer who, interactionally speaking, lies at the origin of the REF being introduced, it becomes less surprising that the same hearer also establishes the referent by producing the PROP *I don't know anything about him*.

From the procedural nature of LD it also follows that sometimes the referent-introductory process may fail to be successful, the new referent not being accepted into the discourse by the hearer. In other words, a sequence along the lines of the constructed exchange in (29) seems very well possible:

(29)   A: *and that table tennis room of mine* -
        B: *oh just shut up - I couldn't care less* ---
        A: *ahm - well - as I was saying (...)*

The reason that, in practice, these sorts of exchanges hardly ever occur need not surprise us, given the workings of the cooperative principle (Grice 1975) in discourse, whereby participants will strive towards maximum cooperativeness. In other words, unless there are very outspoken reasons for him not to do so, there is a distinct onus upon the hearer to acknowledge the new referent, thereby attempting to be as cooperative as possible. The immediate effect of a rejection of the referent as in (29), as most people would agree, is a breaking of the normal pragmatic principles of politeness and tact (see Brown & Levinson 1987; Leech 1983).

Another reason why the LD process may not be carried through to the end is that the introduction of a new referent might give rise to another, related referent which is being concentrated upon instead. This is the case in (30):

(30)   A: *but as for ahm Australia - I don't know now because ahm - (.coughs) you know my . little cousin - girl*
        a: *which one*
        A: *the one that's married and got a kid*
        a: **oh yeah . mhm**
        A: **and a husband in trouble* - ahm he nearly killed himself in a car accident - like he had a head injury*   (S.2.12.19.7)

In this sequence, the speaker introduces the referent *my little cousin girl* which, after some elaboration, gets acknowledged by the hearer (turn 4). After this has been done, however, the speaker chooses not to establish this referent, but uses it as a kind of jumping board to start talking about the closely related referent *a husband* (turn 5). It is obvious that this second referent is closely linked to the first one by virtue of belonging to the same frame (Fillmore 1975) or scenario (Sanford & Garrod 1981), and that the original REF thus does serve some purpose. However, strictly speaking, the result of this exchange is an "unfinished" LD, viz. a REF (*cousin girl*) which is not followed by a PROP. As with the previous example, though, careful analysis reveals the interactional similarity to those exchanges which we did label as LDs in section 2.1. A protoype account is able to deal with these similarities, in that these exchanges can be shown to be non-prototypical developments on the core interactional schema proposed in (11).

2.5. Summary of interactional account

We have now reached a stage where we can summarize our findings on the interactional behavior of LDs and their variants (table 1).

Table 1: Summary of interactional variants of LD process

	Stage 1	Stage 2	Stage 3	Stage 4	Stage 5	e.g.
prototype	Intro [REF]	Ackn turn/pause	Establ	[PROP]		(12)
5-stage	Intro	query	Elabor	Ackn	Establ	(19)
5-stage	Intro	(side sequence)		Ackn	Establ	(21)
5-stage	Intro	query	Repet	Ackn	Establ	(23)
2-stage	Intro	"Establ"	Ackn			(25)
hearer	Intro	Ackn + Establ				(27)
short-circ.	Intro	(no ackn.)				(29)
short-circ.	Intro	Ackn	(no establ.)			(30)

The important thing to conclude here is that an analysis in terms of prototype properties allows us to account for the similarities as well as the differences among all these interactional possibilities, whereas an account in terms of necessary and sufficient conditions fails to do justice to the functional richness of the database. In the following section, we will attempt to show that, from a syntactic and semantic point of view, the same prototype approach to LD is the only tenable one.

3.   Syntactic and semantic prototypes

In this section, we will attempt to show that from a formal point of view, the LD phenomenon cannot be clearly delineated either, but shows prototype properties. We will concentrate here on two aspects in which constructions may differ from what could be called "core" LDs, viz. the "bare-ness" of the REF-component, and the REF's being another type of constituent than a NP. In addition, we will look at a particular type of construction with existential *there* which is also similar to LD. Finally, we will discuss instances which are semantically non-prototypical, in that they do not exhibit the coreference characteristic associated with core LDs.

3.1. Syntactically non-prototypical LD phenomena

In all the following instances, one could argue, to a greater or lesser degree, that the REF is not really a bare NP at all, but is embedded in a clausal framework. Since we have taken this bareness aspect of the REF as one of the defining characteristics of core LD, this would mean that none of these instances would qualify as an LD. In fact, we will argue that these cases provide evidence that the LD category cannot be easily (i.e. categorially) delineated on syntactic grounds, and that the instances discussed below merely form syntactically less prototypical cases of the same LD phenomenon.

First of all, let us consider the following examples, in all of which the REF is preceded by the discourse marker *you know*:

(31)   C: *(...) but . you know <u>the big desk</u> . in the . room in the big room . <u>that has . a file drawer</u> (...)* (S.7.1.a56.2)

(32)   A: *(...) . you know <u>this man . he's advertised</u> . (. coughs) . apparently it's in the Lady as well* (S.2.12.57.2)

In (31) and (32), one could argue that the REFs are not bare, but are syntactically the direct object of the immediately preceding verb *know*. In actual fact, these cases do not present that much of a problem, since *you know* can be considered purely as a discourse particle whose function is exclusively an interactional one. That would mean that the REF is not really the object of *know* at all, but is merely preceded by a discourse marker.

A similar line of reasoning would apply to (33) below, where the REF could, strictly speaking, be considered to be the object of the preceding verb *mean*:

(33)   A: *(...) I mean . mhm - <u>general medicine</u> . [ə] people don't [?] . ((it's very)) <u>interesting</u> everybody knows what*

a general surgeon is (S.2.9.68.9)

Here as well, a solution could be to regard *I mean* purely as a discourse particle, which it clearly is in these instances, and which thus does not really have a direct object.

In the following instances, however, the REF cannot but be regarded as the direct object of a preceding verb:

(34)   B: *[ə] before I forget about it in the chatter. [ə] you remember - <u>the [ə:m]</u> - what do you call it [ə:m] - <u>cricket commentary</u> . <u>there was a manuscript of that</u>.* (S.7.1.a1.11)

(35)   A: **well you know talking* about Greek tragedy <u>you remember the [ə]</u> (8 Greek syllables)*

       B: *yes -*

       A: *<u>I found in Seneca a chorus that almost echoes that</u>* (S.1.4.28.5)

(36)   A: *I know nothing of art but [ə:m] . <u>thinking of [ə:m] - [ə:] people like [ə:ə:] Michaelangelo</u> and so on the . [ə:m o:] all their sketch stuff*

       b: *mhm .*

       A: *well <u>they might have been done yesterday</u>* (S.4.4.62.1)

In all these instances, the REF is the object of some preceding verb (*remember, remember* and *thinking of,* respectively), and thus cannot be regarded as a bare NP. On the other hand, however, the similarity to the core LDs discussed earlier is striking: not only is there a coreference link between the two parts of the "LD" but, more importantly, there is a very strong functional similarity, in that (34-36) are also three-stage interactional exchanges employed for topic-introducing purposes. A strict categorial account would not enable us to account for this similarity; if we regard (34-36) as syntactically less typical variants of LD, however, the problem is resolved.

In the following three instances, the REF is not an NP, but another type of constituent, respectively a PP in (37), an adverb in (38), and a gerundial clause in (39):

(37)   B: *and I suspect <u>with . quite a number of the American -- foundations they</u> - probably put ((the)) <u>citizenship as a sort of you know . prerequisite</u>* (S.2.1.64.10)

(38)   A: *no . no <u>North of Crawley</u> that's it . <u>there's an interchange</u>*

> *there (...)*
> (S.1.11.b11.8)

(39)   A: *mhm --- but [ə:m] -- <u>doing linguistics</u> apart from these
              lectures I gave*

        B: **mhm**

        A: <u>*it takes you out of this*</u> *[ə:m] . out of the literary scene at all
              - quite a bit .*
              (S.5.9.92.1)

Once again, there is a very strong similarity to structures with a NP-REF,
in that these exchanges are also topic-introducing, and consist of three
interactional stages. We can thus also regard these structures as non-
prototype variants of LD.

3.2. LD-like strategies with existential <u>there</u>

A very specific subset of LD-like constructions is formed in instances
where a referent is introduced by means of an existential *there*-clause of
the following type:

(40)   *There's this guy I know, he likes Mary.*
(41)   *There's this guy I know and he likes Mary.*

It is relatively clear that this structure is close to the straightforward LD
This guy I know, he likes Mary, and can be used for the same
communicative purpose, viz. the introduction of a new referent onto the
discourse scene.

    In order to show this, let us turn to a concrete exchange like the one
in (42):

(42)   C: *[ə:] there's <u>there was [u:] [ə:] one other man</u> that I I [ə:] -
              wondered about and this was the one with [thi:]
              Polish name *((like Puvsky))**

        A: **oh yes* [si si] Semigodsky or **some** such name*

        C: ***yes** and he <u>he's doing a thesis on Sidney</u>* (S.2.6.122.3)

In this instance, the referent *one other man* is introduced for the first
time by speaker C, gets acknowledged in the second turn by speaker A,
and is finally established in the third turn of the exchange by means of a
proposition with a coreferential pronoun. In other words, we get the

typical three-stage interactional schema discussed in section 2. In addition, we get a structure which resembles the REF + PROP structure of core LDs, but formally also differs from it in some respects. A categorical account of LD would not be able to account for the formal and functional similarities between LDs and these *there*-constructions, whereas in a prototype approach the latter can simply be regarded as syntactically non-prototypical instances of a functionally similar process.

In order to show that the interactional similarities of these constructions to proper LDs are very outspoken, we have included two more examples:

(43)   C: *I mean <u>*there was* one person</u>*
         B: *that's right*
         A: **mhm**
         C: who did **an** awful lot of things *-* Edward
         B: *Edward*
         D: oh **yes yes**
         G: **oh Edward** yes yes
         C: and I mean . and <u>he used to organize all these things</u> (...)
               (S.3.3.105.3)
(44)   A: (...) ((cos)) there's some friends of [m] <u>there's a friend of</u>
               <u>mine</u> that wants to do surgery - now . <u>he has the greatest</u>
               <u>difficulty with drugs</u> (...) (S.2.9.83.2)

In (43), we get a five-stage elaboration (introduction - acknowledgment - elaboration - acknowledgment - establishment) of the three-stage process very similar to the one outlined in section 2. In (44), the acknowledgment-part of the introductory process is tacit rather than explicit, resulting in a pause rather than a turn between REF and PROP.

3.3. Non-coreferential semantic links between REF and PROP

The coreference feature adopted for our characterization of LD in section 1. also gives rise to a number of non-prototype variants, this time of a semantic nature. Consider the following examples:

(45)   *As for the conference, I like the papers.*
(46)   *As for the photos, I've ruined the negatives.*

In these instances, there is no pronominal element in the PROP which is a candidate for coreference with the REF. However, it is clear that there is an element in the PROP (*papers* and *negatives*, respectively) which is semantically very strongly linked to the REF (*conference* and *photos*, respectively), by virtue of belonging to the same frame or scenario.

A few concrete examples will make clear that, once again, there is a strong functional parallel between such structures and core LDs, in that the former are also used for introducing new topics into the discourse. Take, for instance, (47) below:

(47)   A: *you know Professor Kalapandy where *oh**
          B: *I know *him* by sight . and I've heard him - talking in the*
                  *refectory ((but)) I've heard him lecture - **mhm***
          A: *charmer an **abso**lute charmer is Kalapandy -- and . a*
                  wonderful lecturer -- [thi] this phonology I'm doing [ə] -
                  apart from the fact ((of having)) done quite a lot before I
                  came here I'm still relying on some of Kalapandy's notes .
                  (...) (S.1.6.112.9)

In this example, the REF *this phonology* is obviously semantically closely linked to the NP *Kalapandy's notes* (i.e. *notes of his phonology*) in the PROP. Another instance:

(48)   A: *I mean I don't want to stay there forever . obviously . or*
                  else it'll be terribly bad for me - I mean it's been bad
                  enough for me as it is I think really . in lots of ways but
                  [ə:m] -- [ə:] as far as the archaeology is concerned which
                  is really much more my thing now
          B: *yes*
          A: *until I've finished digging Cartmel and Torsearton - . and*
                  until I've finished ((the)) drainage book .
                  ((you know)) I couldn't have a better centre . (...)
                  (S.1.9.79.1)

The resemblance, in this example, to a core LD like, say, (49) (with coreference between the REF and *it*) is very striking:

(49)   *The archaeology, I couldn't have a better centre for it.*

In fact, the latter structure could fit equally well into the context of (48), since it would serve equally well the topic-introducing purpose for

which the latter is employed. There is thus a compelling functional argument to regard (48) as a less prototypical variant of LD, despite the
lack of an overt pronominal, coreferential Gap in the PROP *I couldn't
have a better centre.* A strictly categorial account would not be able to
deal with the similarities between (48) and (49).

4. Conclusion

By way of conclusion, we will try to see where the findings in sections 2.
and 3. lead us. Considering that LD has prototypical properties from
syntactic, semantic, and functional points of view, core LDs could be
described as the cross-section between these three radial categories. If
we try to present this diagrammatically, the result might look somewhat
like table 2:

Table 2: LD as a cross-section of syntactic, semantic and
interactional prototypes

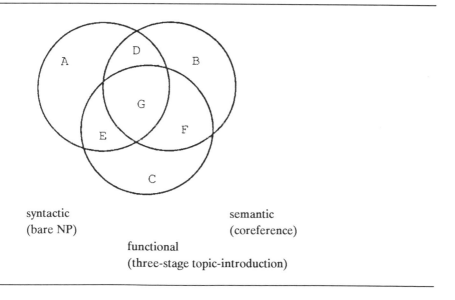

syntactic   semantic
(bare NP)   (coreference)
         functional
        (three-stage topic-introduction)

In section G of the diagram, we get what we have called a "core LD"
(the prototype form from a syntactic, semantic and functional point of
view), that is to say: the REF has the form of a bare NP, there is a strict
coreference link between REF and PROP, and the LD exhibits three-

stage interactional features. Sections D, E, and F represent cases which are non-prototypical in one of the three respects. Section D groups together the non-three-stage LDs (but which have a bare NP-REF and a coreference link); section E the non-coreferent NPs (with a bare NP and three-stage); section F the LDs with a non-bare-NP REF (three-stage and coreferent). Sections A, B, and C, finally, represent those instances which are even less prototypical, in that they deviate in two out of three respects from the prototype structure. In section A, the LD has a bare NP-REF, but has no coreference, nor a three-stage interactional structure; in section B, there is a coreference link, but the REF is not a bare NP, the LD also being non-three-stage; in section C, finally, the LD is three-stage, but without a coreference link, the REF not being a bare NP.

The theoretical repercussions of this study are quite far-reaching. First of all, it has been shown that the syntactic category "LD" has prototype properties. Secondly, what is called LD is in fact the cross-section of three distinct radial categories (see table 2). Thirdly, we hope to have shown that syntactic categorization can be dependent not only on the construction's meaning, but also on its discourse function.

Notes

1.   This paper was first presented at the Cognitive Linguistics Symposium, University of Duisburg, Spring 1989. Thanks are due to Louis Goossens, Brygida Rudzka-Ostyn, Sandy Thompson, René Dirven, Anna-Brita Stenström and Mia Vanrespaille for their comments. Some of the findings are also discussed, in a different context, in Geluykens (1988a, 1988b).

2.   The data used in this study are taken from the conversational files of the Survey of English Usage, based at University College, London. We are indebted to Sidney Greenbaum for allowing us access to these data. References are to Survey slip numbers, e.g. "S.1.7.119.1" refers to spoken file S.1.7, slip 119, line 1.

3.   Transcription conventions:
-    speaker identity:
      A, B, C, ... (surreptitious)
      a, b, c, ... (non-surreptitious)
-    overlapping speech: *...*; **...**
-    pauses: . (very brief); - (brief); -- (longer); --- (long)
-    intranscribable or dubious: ((syll))
-    phonetic transcription: [...]
-    LD: <u>underlined</u>

References

Brown, Penelope & Stephen C. Levinson
    1987   *Politeness*. Cambridge: Cambridge University Press.
Chafe, Wallace L.
    1987   "Cognitive constraints on information flow", in: Russell S. Tomlin
                (ed.),
                21-55.
Clark, Herbert H. & Deanna Wilkes-Gibbs
    1986   "Referring as a collaborative process", *Cognition* 22: 1-39.
Cole, Peter & Jerry L. Morgan
    1975   *Syntax and semantics 3: Speech acts*. New York: Academic Press.
Fillmore, Charles H.
    1975   "An alternative to checklist theories of meaning", *Proceedings of the
                First Annual Meeting of the Berkeley Linguistic Society:* 123-131.
Geluykens, Ronald
    1988a   "The interactional nature of referent-introduction", *Papers from the
                24th Regional Meeting, Chicago Linguistic Society:* 141-154.
    1988b   Left-dislocation in English discourse: A functional analysis, with
                special reference to conversation. [Unpublished Ph.D. Dissertation,
                University of Antwerp.]
    1988c   "Five types of clefting in English discourse", *Linguistics* 26: 823-841.
    1989a   Referent-introduction as an interactional process: A case study.
                [Unpub-lished MS.]
    1989b   "Referent-tracking and cooperation in conversation: Evidence from
                repair", *Papers from the parasession on Language and Context, 25th
                Regional Meeting, Chicago Linguistic Society.*
    1989c   "The syntactization of interactional processes: Some typological
                evidence", *Belgian Journal of Linguistics* 4.
    in press   *From discourse process to grammatical construction*. Amsterdam:
                Benjamins.
Givón, Talmy
    1983   *Topic continuity in discourse: A quantitative cross-language study.*
                Amsterdam: Benjamins.
Grice, H. Paul
    1975   "Logic and conversation", in: Peter Cole & Jerry L. Morgan (eds.), 41-
                58.
Jefferson, Gail
    1972   "Side sequences", in: David Sudnow (ed.), 294-338.
Lakoff, George
    1987   *Women, fire, and dangerous things: What categories reveal about the
                mind.* Chicago: University of Chicago Press.
Leech, Geoffrey
    1983   *Principles of pragmatics*. London: Longman.
Levinson, Stephen C.
    1983   *Pragmatics*. Cambridge: Cambridge University Press.
Ochs, Elinor & Bambi B. Schieffelin
    1983   *Acquiring conversational competence*. New York: Academic Press.

Ross, John R.
    1967   Constraints on variables in syntax. [Ph.D. Dissertation, MIT, published
                as Ross (1986).]
    1986   *Infinite syntax!* Norwood, N.J.: Ablex.
Sacks, Harvey, Emanuel A. Schegloff & Gail Jefferson
    1974   "A simplest systematics for the organization of turn-taking in
                conversation', *Language* 50: 696-735.
Sanford, Anthony J. & Simon C. Garrod
    1981   *Understanding written language*. Chichester: Wiley and Sons.
Sudnow, David (ed.)
    1972   *Studies in social interaction*. New York: Free Press.
Tomlin, Russell S. (ed.)
    1987   *Coherence and grounding in discourse*. Amsterdam: Benjamins.

Scenes and frames
for orders and threats

Savas L. Tsohatzidis

0. Introduction

The purpose of this paper is to draw attention to a common mistake in the analysis of two speech act names, and to show that a particular application of the distinction between foregrounded and backgrounded elements in conceptual organization is useful in correcting that mistake, in explaining its origins, and in throwing light on some apparently independent phenomena as well.[*]

1. The standard analysis of orders and threats

Speech act theorists who make explicit claims about the analysis of both orders and threats usually present them as belonging to strictly independent categories of illocutionary acts. Furthermore, they take their analysis to be a relatively simple matter, once the primitive members of the categories of illocutionary acts to which they respectively (and exclusively) belong is known. The theory of speech acts recently formalized by Searle and Vanderveken (1985; hereafter SV) faithfully reflects received opinion on both of these matters, and since it is the best developed theory of speech acts now available, it provides an appropriate frame of reference for the present discussion.

In that theory, there are claimed to be just five mutually irreducible categories of illocutionary acts, namely, assertives, directives, commissives, expressives and declaratives, and all individual speech act types realizable in natural languages are supposed to be uniquely derivable from one or another of the primitive members of these five categories by means of a limited number of operations. Orders are assigned to the category of directive illocutionary acts, which are defined as acts whereby a speaker tries to make a hearer do something. Threats are assigned to the category of commissive illocutionary acts, which are defined as acts whereby a speaker undertakes the commitment to do something himself. Orders are then derived from primitive acts of directing, by specifying that they are acts of directing whose distinctive feature is that their speakers occupy a position of authority vis-à-vis their hearers. And threats are derived from primitive acts of commitment, by specifying that they are acts of commitment whose distinctive feature is that their content is supposed to represent something bad for the hearer. (For more details, whose omission does not affect the points to be made below, see SV: 193, 201.)

It seems to me that this theory does not provide everything one would need to know in order to understand what an order or a threat is; and this, of course, would not be a particularly important defect if the missing elements could be specified without disturbing its overall structure. But it also seems to me that the particular elements that I have in mind cannot be expressed by the theory unless SV abandon their central claim that their five categories of illocutionary acts generally determine non-overlapping classes of speech act names.[1]

2.   What is not right about the standard analysis

Let us take orders first. I assume that everyone will agree that an utterance like (1) is odd in a way that an utterance like (2) is not:

(1)   *?There is nothing that I intend to do against you in case you decide to leave, but I order you to stay.*

(2)   *There is nothing that I intend to do against you in case you decide to leave, but I request of you to stay.*

Since (1) ceases to be odd when *order* is replaced by a primitive directive speech act name like *request*, it follows that the reason for the oddity of (1) cannot be that its utterer violates some condition concerning directive illocutionary acts in general. The reason must rather have something to do with a condition applying specifically to orders, and it is not difficult to figure out what that condition is: It is that you cannot order someone to do something and at the same time disclaim any intent to *punish* him (or, more generally, to do something or other *against* him) if he does not do what you are telling him to do.

The problem with this condition, however, is not only that it is absent from SV's analysis, but also that it cannot be incorporated into that analysis without implying that, contrary to what SV contend, orders are simultaneously directive *and* commissive illocutionary acts. For saying that one cannot order someone to do *p* and at the same time disclaim any intent to do something against him if he does not do *p* is surely no different from saying that one cannot order someone to do *p* without *committing oneself* to do something against him if he does not do *p*. The correct analysis of ORDER (x,y,p), therefore, would have to include, at the very least, two components: one component to the effect that *x* requests *y* to do *p*, and one component to the effect that *x* commits himself to do something or other against *y* in case *y* does not do *p*. And since these components refer, respectively, to what SV would recognize as a directive and a commissive illocutionary point, it follows that a minimally satisfactory analysis of orders would have to represent them as being simultaneously directive and commissive illocutionary acts.

Let us now turn to threats, where a very similar pattern will emerge. I trust everyone will agree that an utterance like (3) is odd in a way in which an utterance like (4) is not:

(3)   *?I know this will not make you do any of the things I want you to do, but I intend to send you to prison - that's a threat.*
(4)   *I know this will not make you do any of the things I want you to do, but I intend to send you to prison - that's a commitment.*

Since (3) ceases to be odd when *threat* is replaced by a primitive commissive speech act name like *commitment*, it follows that the reason for the oddity of (3) is not that its utterer violates some condition concerning commissive illocutionary acts in general. The reason must rather have something to do with a condition applying specifically to threats, and it is not difficult to guess what that condition is: It is that you cannot threaten to do something to someone and at the same time disclaim any intention of trying *to make him do* certain other things which, if done, would be regarded by you as sufficient for not realizing the threat in question.

The problem with this condition, however, is not only that it is absent from SV's analysis, but also that it cannot be incorporated into that analysis without implying that, contrary to what SV contend, threats are simultaneously commissive *and* directive illocutionary acts. For saying that you cannot threaten someone without at the same time trying to make him do something that you would regard as sufficient for not realizing your threat is surely no different from saying that you cannot threaten someone without at the same time asking him, urging him, suggesting to him, or otherwise *directing* him to do something that you would regard as sufficient for not realizing your threat. Therefore, an adequate analysis of THREATEN (x,y,p) would have to include, at the very least, two components: one component to the effect that x commits himself to do a certain thing p against y, and one component to the effect that x directs y to do something or other that x would regard as sufficient for not doing the thing p against y. And since these components refer, respectively, to what SV would recognize as a commissive and a directive illocutionary point, it follows that a minimally satisfactory analysis of threats would have to represent them as being simultaneously commissive and directive illocutionary acts.[2]

3.   What is not strange about the standard analysis

The fact that SV were mistaken in supposing that one can analyse an order or a threat by invoking just one kind of illocutionary intention seems difficult to deny. What, however, may appear puzzling about the multiple illocutionary intentions we have been invoking is that they are very much *the same* for orders and threats. If it is true that a person who gives an order directs a hearer to do something and commits himself to harming the hearer if he does not do the thing in question, and if it is also true that a person who issues a threat commits himself to harming a hearer and directs him to do something in order to avoid the harm, then it seems that people who give orders and people who issue threats are, in a non-trivial sense, doing fundamentally the same kind of thing. But if this is so, then we must somehow explain why SV as well as so many other speech act theorists have been led to believe that the only common property of people who issue threats and of people who give orders is that they both use language in meaningful ways.

It seems to me that the solution to this puzzle comes from a basic insight of what Fillmore (1977a) has described as the "scenes and frames" approach to questions of meaning - the insight, namely, that two superficially non-synonymous (or, more generally, semantically unrelated) words may in fact require, in order to be understood, reference to fundamentally the same situation (usually referred to as the "scene"), but may give the *appearance* of being unrelated because each of them *foregrounds* different elements of that common situation in different ways. Consider, to take Fillmore's (1977b) own example, the verbs *sell*, *spend*, and *cost*. In order to understand what any of them means, one has to know what a commercial transaction is - and, in particular, that it obligatorily involves such elements as buyers, sellers, goods, and money (as well as their interrelationships). What distinguishes these verbs from each other, however, is not that each is associated with some *further* situational element not present in the commercial transaction scene that they all evoke. It is, rather, that each of them *foregrounds* a different element (or a different combination of elements) from that common scene, while leaving the others in the background. When one uses the word *cost* one has to speak about goods and money and one can linguistically (though not conceptually) ignore sellers and buyers. When one uses the word *spend* one has to speak about buyers and money, and one can linguistically (but not conceptually) ignore goods and sellers. When one uses the word *sell* one has to speak about sellers and goods, and one can linguistically (though not conceptually) ignore buyers and money. These three words, then, may well give the appearance of referring to different sorts of situations, whereas what they in fact do is perspectivize the very same situation in three different ways.

If this is so, however, it does not seem particularly difficult to explain why speech act theorists have been led to suppose that the words *order* and *threat* refer to products of quite different sorts of activities, whereas in fact they do not: Their basic semantic unity can be expressed by saying that both evoke fundamentally the same scene - namely, the scene of a *choice* that a hearer faces between satisfying a speaker's wishes and suffering the consequences of an action that the speaker undertakes to perform against him. The fact that they nevertheless *appear* to name radically different things can then be traced to the fact that each of them *foregrounds* a different element of the common scene. When one speaks of an *order*, one focuses on a speaker's asking a hearer to satisfy certain wishes, and one is not, grammatically speaking, required to *say* that the speaker in question purports to present the hearer with a choice between satisfying those wishes and eliciting unwelcome actions on the speaker's part. When, on the other hand, one speaks of a *threat*, one focuses on a speaker's undertaking to perform certain unwelcome actions against a hearer, and one is not, grammatically speaking, required to *say* that the speaker in question purports to present the hearer with a choice between suffering those unwelcome actions and satisfying certain wishes of the speaker. However, what one is not grammatically required to say is not what one can conceptually afford to ignore: Understanding what *order* means is understanding that it names utterances made not only with the intention of making hearers do things, but also with the intention of presenting them with a choice between doing those things and having unwelcome things done to them. Understanding what *threat* means is understanding that it names utterances made not only with the intention of announcing to hearers a speaker's commitment to do unwelcome things to them, but also with the intention of presenting them with a choice between having those unwelcome things done to them and doing certain other things themselves. In short, understanding either orders or threats requires reference to fundamentally the same *choice situation*. The difference is that, in the case of orders, the content of the speaker's directive intention is foregrounded, and everything else (including the content of his commissive intention) remains in the background; whereas in the case of threats, the content of the speaker's commissive intention is foregrounded, and everything else (including the content of his directive intention) remains in the background. And this difference suffices for explaining - though, of course, it hardly justifies - the mistaken assumption that orders and threats have nothing in common apart from the trivial property of being illocutionary acts.[3]

4.   A wider perspective

If the choice situation to which we have been referring is conceptually required in order to grasp the meaning of *order* and *threat*, and if it is also true that conceptual requirements can exert their influence *across* linguistic levels, then it might also be necessary to refer to a similar choice situation in order to explain apparently unrelated linguistic constraints. I would like to mention just one constraint of this kind.

It is generally the case that disjunctive coordination between sentences requires the coordinated sentences to be of the same grammatical type. In particular, sentences of the form "S_1 or S_2" are not, in general, admissible, if, say, S_1 is an (unquoted) imperative sentence and S_2 an (unquoted) indicative sentence, or conversely. However, there are certain uses of *or* where this restriction appears to be freely suspended. Thus, sentences like those in (5) are grammatical whereas sentences like those in (6) are not (even though the communicative intentions of a non-native speaker uttering the latter might be as transparent to us as the communicative intentions of a native speaker uttering the former):

(5)   a.   *Come with me or I'll kill you.*
       b.   *Don't touch her or you are dead.*
(6)   a.   **Come with me or I am sad.*
       b.   **Don't touch her or you are rude.*

It seems to me that any adequate characterization of the relevant grammatical constraint would have to refer to a conceptualization of a choice situation similar to the one just described. It would have to say, that is, that the permissible coordinations of imperative and indicative sentences by means of *or* require the simultaneous satisfaction of three conditions: first, that the imperative be taken to express directly or indirectly a future state of affairs whose realization the speaker presents as falling under the responsibility of the hearer; second, that the indicative be taken to express directly or indirectly a future state of affairs whose realization the speaker regards as harmful to the hearer; and third, that their coordination be taken to present the hearer with a choice between assuming the responsibilities assigned through the imperative and suffering the harms announced through the indicative. But if this is so, it means that a scene quite similar to the one that we would need to refer to anyway in order to better understand the semantics of *order* and *threat* and the pragmatics of orders and threats would also be helpful in order to better understand an apparently unrelated constraint concerning the distribution of *or*. And this in turn means that, just as orders and threats are more similar activities than they might appear to be, grammatical and conceptual problems are not as dissimilar as they might be taken to be.[4]

5. A narrower perspective

Since it is to similarities, rather than to differences, between orders and threats that this paper has primarily given attention, the apparently obvious difference that the former, but not the latter, presuppose that the speaker occupies a position of authority over the hearer, has not been singled out for special comment. Let me conclude, then, by expressing my belief that the notion of authority that one has the tendency to invoke in this connection is not precise enough to be of real discriminatory value, and that the differences that one would purport to elucidate by invoking it would be better expressed by making specific further distinctions *within* the choice situation scene that orders and threats commonly evoke. Viewed from this perspective, the relevant difference between orders and threats would be (roughly) that, although they both present hearers with a choice between doing certain things and suffering certain other things, orders assume, whereas threats do not necessarily assume, that hearers have tacitly or explicitly *agreed* to suffer things of certain sorts if they do not do things of certain other sorts. Once such an analysis is fully worked out, it will give, I suggest, a precise sense to the intuition that ordering is an activity that is somehow tied to conventions in a way in which threatening is not. But the task of fully working it out I will leave for another occasion.

Notes

*   I would like to thank Brygida Rudzka-Ostyn for commenting on an earlier draft.

1.   The spirit of SV's claim, as applied to orders and threats, would not be substantially affected even if one were in a position to redefine commissives and directives - following an early suggestion of Searle's (1975: 356) that he himself abandons - as two distinct species of a more inclusive category of illocutionary acts: the claim would then be that there is no overlapping *between* the two species. It is also worth noting that the same spirit is present not only in the analyses (which represent the majority) that follow SV in allocating orders to directives and threats to commissives, but also in the few analyses (e.g. Fraser 1975, Katz 1977) which, while characterizing orders and threats in essentially SV's way, prefer to regard the former as directives and the latter as assertives: the implication is always that no overlapping between categories needs to be postulated in order to analyze either the ones or the others.

2.   The idea that there are types of speech acts whose analysis shows that there is overlapping between SV's five basic categories is accepted by SV themselves for certain speech acts other than orders and threats (see, e.g. SV: 197), but they obviously regard these cases as sufficiently marginal so as not to necessitate a revision of their system. Further cases of such overlapping are proposed in Bach & Harnish (1979: 50f), but neither orders nor threats are counted among them. The closest approximation to the idea that threats do involve a combination of commissive and directive components (in SV's sense of these terms) occurs in Wierzbicka (1987: 178f), though her way of expressing this cannot easily be translated into SV's idiom. Unfortunately, Wierzbicka's analysis of orders is not similarly sensitive to (and thus cannot adequately cope with) the fact that the same combination of commissive and directive components is present in them as well.

3.   As used above, the *foreground/background* distinction refers to a process whereby, given a set of elements that are conceptually required for the interpretation of a linguistic form, some of them are provided with appropriate formal exponents while others are not. The same terminology is also frequently used for a different purpose namely, to refer to a process whereby, given a set of conceptually required elements all of which possess formal exponents in the above sense, some are perceived as more salient than others. Langacker (1987: 116-126) describes these two processes as two different types of "focal adjustment" and proposes that possible confusion between them could be avoided by reserving the term *foregrounding* for the latter, and by adopting the term *profiling* for the former.

4.   Fillenbaum (1977) has assembled a good deal of evidence suggesting that other coordinating and subordinating conjunctions besides *or* behave in grammatically unexpected ways. I suspect that constraints similar to the one formulated above might prove necessary in accounting for at least some aspects of such behavior.

References

Bach, Kent & Robert M. Harnish
    1979   *Linguistic communication and speech acts.* Cambridge: MIT Press.
Fillenbaum, Samuel
    1977   "Mind your p's and q's: the role of content and context in some uses of *and*, *or*, and *if*", in: Gordon H. Bower (ed.), *The psychology of learning and motivation.* Vol. II. New York: Academic Press, 41-100.
Fillmore, Charles J.
    1977a   "Scenes-and-frames semantics", in: Antonio Zampolli (ed.), *Linguistic structures processing.* Amsterdam: North-Holland, 55-81.
    1977b   "The case for case reopened", in: Peter Cole & Jerrold M. Sadock (eds.), *Syntax and semantics, Vol 8: Grammatical relations.* New York: Academic Press, 59-81.
Fraser, Bruce
    1975   "Warning and threatening", *Centrum* 3: 169-180.
Katz, Jerrold J.
    1977   *Propositional structure and illocutionary force.* New York: Thomas Y. Crowell.
Langacker, Ronald W.
    1987   *Foundations of cognitive grammar.* Vol 1. *Theoretical prerequisites.* Stanford: Stanford University Press.
Searle, John R.
    1975   "A taxonomy of illocutionary acts", in: Keith Gunderson (ed.), *Language, mind and knowledge.* (Minnesota Studies in the Philosophy of Science 7) Minneapolis: University of Minnesota Press, 344-369.
Searle, John R. & Daniel Vanderveken
    1985   *Foundations of illocutionary logic.* Cambridge: Cambridge University Press.
Wierzbicka, Anna
    1987   *English speech act verbs: A semantic dictionary.* Sydney: Academic Press.

Tenses and demonstratives:
Conspecific categories

Theo A.J.M. Janssen

0. Introduction[*]

The aim of this paper will be to argue that tenses and demonstratives can be conceived as cognitively conspecific. If tenses and demonstratives could be shown to be analyzable as variants of one linguistic category, there is no doubt that this would lead to a much more coherent theory of deixis.[1] For describing both categories as instances of *demonstratio actualis* versus *disactualis* I will use three tools of analysis: the notion of the speaker's vantage point, the notion of salience of the event or entity referred to, and the notion of the speaker's actual versus disactual referential concern for the event or entity at issue. The tense analysis put forward in this paper hinges basically on the latter notion, which will replace the time relation in the traditional approach of tense, namely the relation between the time of speech and the time of the event referred to by means of the verb. Therefore the argumentation will start with an appraisal of the traditional tense analysis in terms of time.

In section 1, I will argue that in Dutch the present and past-tense forms must be considered to be the only tenses and as such the only deictic verb categories. The deictic character of the "compound tenses" will be shown to be based on the finite auxiliary in its present or past-tense form. Furthermore, tense analyses based on an event coordinate in the time dimension will be rejected as merely referential and thus as covering just one of the possible usage types. In section 2, the categorical meaning of the present and past tense will be characterized by an analysis based on an event coordinate in the dimension of actual versus disactual referential concern. In section 3, this coordinate will be shown to be related to an object coordinate (*deze/dit* 'this' versus *die/dat* 'that' and *hier* 'here' versus *daar* 'there').

1.   Tense and time

In this section I will argue that Dutch shows a systematic semantic distinction between two classes of "tenses": in one class the finite form of the "tenses" is the present-tense form; in the other it is the past-tense form. The present and the past-tense forms are the only deictic categories. The other forms, the so-called "compound tenses", consist of a deictic part, involving the finite - present or past - auxiliary, and a nondeictic part, involving one or more nonfinite verbs.

The distinction between the present and the past tense class can arguably be motivated by strong cooccurrence restrictions on the finite forms and some adverbials with a temporal (i.e. chronological) reference. Such restrictions could be used to justify a traditional analysis in terms of time. However, the cogency of the cooccurrence relations at issue will be explained as a conjunction of two different factors: on the one hand tense deixis, being basically nontemporal, and on the other deixis of adverbials with temporal reference.

1.1.   Two classes of "tenses"

In Dutch verbs or verb formations show a systematic semantic distinction with regard to their temporal use. Table 1 shows the division: in one class the finite form is the present-tense form, in the other the past-tense form.

Although I will argue for a distinction between two classes of verbs and verb formations on the basis of their temporal use, I assume that the distinction reflects in principle the general semantic difference between the classes which can account for other types of use as well. Consider first sentences (1)-(4). These sentences, each consisting in three coordinate clauses, show a strong cooccurrence relation between the adverbial *nu* 'at this moment in the present' and the tense of the finite verb, whether it is a main verb or an auxiliary. The question mark indicates that I cannot provide a plausible interpretation here, and I will use the same symbolism in the rest of the paper.

Table 1. *Classification of the "tenses" (two tenses and six "compound tenses") in Dutch*

grammatical form tense/"compound tense"	finite form	auxiliary *zullen*	auxiliary *hebben/zijn*	main verb
	PRESENT			
1. praesens	*vertrekt* 'leaves (/is leaving)'			--
2. perfectum	*is* 'has		--	*vertrokken* left'
3. futurum	*zal* 'shall/will	--		*vertrekken* leave'
4. futurum exactum	*zal* 'shall/will	--	*zijn* have	*vertrokken* left'
	PAST			
5. praeteritum	*vertrok* 'left (/was leaving)'			--
6. plusquamperfectum	*was* 'had		--	*vertrokken* left'
7. futurum praeteriti	*zou* 'was (about) to	--		*vertrekken* leave'
8. futurum exactum praeteriti	*zou* 'was (about) to	--	*zijn* have	*vertrokken* left'

(1)   a.   *Nu is Tom vertrokken,*
               'Now (at this time) Tom has left,
       b.   *vertrekt Dick en*
               Dick is leaving and
       c.   *zal Harry vertrekken.*
               Harry will leave.'

(2)   a.   *?Nu was Tom vertrokken,*
             lit. Now Tom had left,
       b.   *vertrekt Dick en*
             Dick is leaving and
       c.   *zal Harry vertrekken.*
             Harry will leave.
(3)   a.   *?Nu is Tom vertrokken,*
             lit. Now Tom has left,
       b.   *vertrok Dick en*
             Dick left and
       c.   *zal Harry vertrekken.*
             Harry will leave.
(4)   a.   *?Nu is Tom vertrokken,*
             lit. Now Tom has left,
       b.   *vertrekt Dick en*
             Dick is leaving and
       c.   *zou Harry vertrekken.*
             Harry was still to leave.

The reason for the contrast between the interpretability of sentence (1) and the uninterpretability of sentences (2)-(4) must be that it is only in sentence (1) that the finite verbs are comparable with respect to their interpretation. In this sentence, the adverbial *nu* can be regarded as the modifier of the finite verb in each of the three coordinate clauses, but not as the modifier of the nonfinite verbs in the (a) and the (c) clause. As a matter of fact, we can observe in the case of sentence (1) that Tom's departure precedes the time specified by the adverbial *nu*, while Harry's departure follows the time thus specified. Only in sentence (1) can the finite verbs be considered to be of a type quite distinct from the class of past-tense forms.

Obviously, coordinated sentences introduced by the adverbial *nu* must share the same type of finite verb. Such a strong cooccurrence relation of the finite verb and the adverbial *nu* can also be observed between the initial temporal adverbial *toen* 'at that moment in the past' and the finite verbs of a coordinated sentence like (5), shown here in comparison with sentences (6)-(8):

(5)   a.   *Toen was Tom vertrokken,*
             lit. Then (at that time in the past) Tom had left,
       b.   *vertrok Dick en*
             Dick was leaving and

c. *zou Harry vertrekken.*
Harry was still to leave.

(6) a. *?Toen is Tom vertrokken,*
lit. Then Tom has left,

b. *vertrok Dick en*
Dick was leaving and

c. *zou Harry vertrekken.*
Harry was still to leave.

(7) a. *?Toen was Tom vertrokken,*
lit. Then Tom had left,

b. *vertrekt Dick en*
Dick is leaving and

c. *zou Harry vertrekken.*
Harry was still to leave.

(8) a. *?Toen was Tom vertrokken,*
lit. Then Tom had left,

b. *vertrok Dick en*
Dick was leaving and

c. *zal Harry vertrekken.*
Harry will leave.

I assume on the basis of the contrast between the interpretability of (5) and the uninterpretability of (6)-(8) that the finite verbs of the coordinated sentence (5) share one significant aspect of meaning. In this sentence the adverbial modifies the finite verbs only. As we saw before with regard to sentence (1), it does not modify the nonfinite verbs in the (a) and the (c) clause; Tom's departure precedes the time specified by means of the adverbial *toen*, while Harry's departure follows the time specified by means of *toen*. Therefore it can be assumed that it is only in sentence (5) that the finite verbs are all of one type, quite distinct from the class of present-tense forms.

The "tenses" 1-3 and 5-7 in Table 1 are thus shown to be classifiable in two coherent present and past tense categories. Examples (9)-(12) illustrate that "tenses" 4 and 8 in Table 1 can be categorized in the same way:[2]

(9) *(Nu Tom eindelijk vertrokken is,) nu zal ook Harry spoedig*
vertrokken zijn.
lit. Now that Tom has left at last, now Harry will also have left soon.

(10)   *?(Nu Tom eindelijk vertrokken is,) nu zou ook Harry spoedig
       vertrokken zijn.*
       lit. Now that Tom has left at last, now Harry would also have
       left soon.
(11)   *(Toen Tom eenmaal vertrokken was,) toen zou ook Harry spoedig
       vertrokken zijn.*
       lit. Once Tom had left, then Harry would also have left soon.
(12)   *?(Toen Tom eenmaal vertrokken was,) toen zal ook Harry
       spoedig vertrokken zijn.*
       lit. Once Tom had left, then Harry will also have left soon.

Examples (9)-(12) show that a correspondence is required between the
adverbials *nu* or *toen* on the one hand and the finite verb on the other.
In both sentences (9) and (11) Harry's departure follows the time of the
finite verb specified by means of the respective adverbials *nu* and *toen*.

1.2.   Tense and deixis

"Compound tenses" (2-4 and 6-8 in Table 1) consist of a deictic part,
the finite (present or past) auxiliary, and a nondeictic part, a nonfinite
main verb or a nonfinite auxiliary together with a nonfinite main verb.
The following texts show how crucial the deictic role of the finite element is (cf. Janssen 1989a: 317ff):

(13)   *In de periode 1899-1900 <u>werkt</u> Grönloh, die later de schrijver
       Nescio <u>zal worden</u>, achtereenvolgens op vijf handelskantoren in
       Amsterdam. En intussen <u>heeft</u> hij ook nog korte tijd op een kan-
       toor in Hengelo <u>gewerkt</u>.*
       lit. In the period 1899-1900 Grönloh, who <u>will</u> later <u>become</u> the
       writer Nescio, <u>works</u> successively at five merchant's offices in
       Amsterdam. And in the meanwhile he <u>has</u> also <u>worked</u> at an of-
       fice in Hengelo for a short time.
(14)   *Waarvoor dienen de onderscheppingsraketten van dit ontwerp?
       Wel, stel je voor dat een kernmacht de oorlog <u>begint</u>. De agressor
       <u>zal</u> zijn arsenaal aan kernraketten dan niet in zijn geheel <u>lanceren</u>,
       want door een deel achter te houden houdt hij een dreiging achter
       de hand tegen de vijandige strijdkrachten die <u>zijn overgebleven</u>.*
       lit. What is the purpose of the interceptive missiles of this de-
       sign? Well, imagine that a nuclear power <u>starts</u> war. The ag-
       gressor <u>will</u> not then <u>launch</u> its whole arsenal of nuclear mis-

siles, because by keeping some part in reserve it <u>preserves</u> a threat to the enemy forces that <u>have survived</u>.

If the present-tense form of the underlined cases in the first text were to be described as a "historical present", then such a form in the second text might be seen as a "futuristic present". What is more, one might even be tempted to use the labels *historical*[3] and *futuristic* for the "compound tenses" as well. Such a proliferation of "tense" types would be absurd. In both texts the interpretation of the "compound tenses" is determined by the interpretation of their finite form, being the deictic base that enables the proliferation of types due to different vantage points. The vantage point of the present-tense forms in examples (13) and (14) is not the speech time, which usually can be assumed by default[4] of a more salient time, or rather a more salient situation. In text (13) the vantage point is a situation earlier than the situation of speech, and in text (14) it is an imaginary situation possibly in the future.[5] With regard to "compound tenses" the following must be stressed: whenever the vantage point of the finite form shifts, the temporal relation between the time of the auxiliary event and the time of the main verb event remains constant. In other words, the cardinal factor in the interpretation is the vantage point to be assigned to the finite form.

The relation between the vantage point and the time of the event mentioned by means of a present-tense verb should not be conceived of as temporal. Later on I will argue that this relation has to be formulated in terms of actual referential concern: even if the event does not coincide temporally with the time the sentence is spoken, the event can be of actual referential concern to the speaker from his vantage point. This can be shown with sentences like the following, in which even a partial simultaneity can be missing; the temporal relation between speaking the sentence on the one hand and the event referred to on the other is merely concomitant:

(15)   *Frits, je wordt geroepen!*
       'Frits, you are being called!'
(16)   *Frits, iemand vraagt naar je.*
       lit. Frits, somebody asks for you.
       'Frits, somebody is asking for you.'
(17)   *Maar Frits, wat zeg je nou toch?*
       lit. But Frits, what do you say now?
       'My dear Frits, what's that you are telling me?'

Viewed strictly temporally, the events of these sentences have already taken place when the sentences are spoken: Frits must have been called, somebody must have asked for him, and he must have said something baffling.

Conversely, in sentences (18) and (19) the present-tense form is used as a "future present":

(18)   *Kom je even?*
        lit. Come you for a moment?
        'Will you come here for a moment?'
(19)   *Ja, ik kom zo.*
        lit. Yes, I come in a moment.
        'Yes, I'll be there in a moment.'

Here the events referred to have yet to take place after the time when the sentences are spoken.

The temporal discrepancies emerging from (15)-(19) cannot be explained coherently in terms of time, although both the speaker's vantage point and the event involved are in principle locatable in time. These entities have a temporal relation from a chronological point of view, but this temporal facet is merely epiphenomenal from the linguistic perspective. The fundamental relation conveyed specifically by the present tense is the speaker's actual referential concern for the event referred to. This concern permits the event at issue to be situated, with regard to the time of utterance, within a broad temporal region in positions that vary significantly.[6]

As we have seen, the present tense can be used in various ways with regard to temporal reference due to the actual referential concern relation and due to the shiftability of the vantage point: for past or future events, (15)-(17) versus (18)-(19), and for "historical" and "futuristic" events, (13) versus (14). Furthermore, the shiftability of the vantage point allows us to use the past tense in order to indicate present events, as is the case in (20) (cf. Kollewijn 1892: 145):[7]

(20)   *Ik moet nu weg, anders zal hij straks vragen waar ik toch bleef.*
        'I have to leave now, otherwise he'll be asking what kept me.'

In (20) the person who must be held responsible for what has been said in the indirect question *waar ik toch bleef* 'what kept me' differs from the speaker of the entire utterance. It is the vantage point of the presumed questioner which is at issue here.

A similar referential variation based on the shiftability of the vantage point can be observed in a type of deictic element other than tense. Consider the use of the adverb *nu* 'now' in the coordinated sentence (21) in contrast with sentences (1)-(4):

(21)   *Nu was Tom vertrokken, vertrok Dick en zou Harry vertrekken.*
        'Now Tom had left, Dick was leaving and Harry was to leave.'

Here the adverbial *nu* must be interpreted as 'at this moment in the past', whereas in sentence (1) the same adverbial must be interpreted as 'at this moment in the present'. Such an example requires an explanatory analysis of the presumably common ground which enables these interpretational differences. Clearly, the adverb *nu* 'now' should not be qualified as temporal, neither in (21) nor in (1). The adverb specifies a salient situation on which the speaker is focusing. In sentence (21) both the vantage point of *nu* and the situation referred to differ from the speech time. In particular, it should be borne in mind with regard to (21) that the vantage point determining the interpretation of *nu* differs from the vantage point determining the interpretation of the past-tense forms, although *nu* specifies the time of the event mentioned referentially by means of the past-tense form.

I will argue in the following subsection for an analysis uniting the interpretationally different usage types of the present and past tense within a categorical meaning ("sense"). Considering the diversity of uses, the tenses should not be termed *present* and *past* but, in a formal semantically neutral way, *first* and *second finite form*. Because of the derivational character of the "compound tenses" attention will be focussed on the finite form types, whether these finite forms are main verbs or auxiliaries.

1.3. Interpretation and meaning

From a chronological point of view, the conditions for describing a future event with a present-tense form in Dutch are rather loose.[8] The future interpretation of a present-tense form is determined by the context or cotext, in particular by an adverbial indicating a future time. As pointed out before, the "future present" should not be regarded as a separate "tense", but as a particular use. The appropriateness of this view can be illustrated with the help of sentences (22) and (23), seen as descriptions of a noniterative, singular case:

(22)   *Je mag wel even meespelen. Maar zodra de vaste man komt, moet*
        je je plaats afstaan.
        'You may join in the game for a while. But as soon as the
        regular man comes, you will have to leave.'
(23)   *Je mocht wel even meespelen. Maar zodra de vaste man kwam,*
        moest je je plaats afstaan.
        'You were allowed to join in the game for a while. But as soon
        as the regular man came, you had to leave.'[9]

In the subordinate clauses of both (22) and (23) the connective *zodra* 'as
soon as' induces a future interpretation: the assumed arrival of the regular man is seen as posterior to your receiving permission to join in.

The symmetry between the present and the past case is important. If
a "future present" is to be seen as a separate tense, then we should postulate a "future past" too.[10] But such a proliferation of "tenses" would
explain nothing (cf. Grewendorf 1982, 1984; Heringer 1983; Ballweg
1984; Lenerz 1986). Moreover, this futurization of both the present and
past tenses cannot be explained away as a metaphorical use, as is done
in the case of counterfactuals (Weinrich 1964), because here we have a
purely referential shift rather than a transfer from one conceptual
domain of use to another.

What I wish to claim is that in (22) the assumed arrival of the regular
man is of actual referential concern to the speaker with regard to his
vantage point, i.e. the situation at the time when he uses the sentence,
whereas in (23) the regular man's arrival is of disactual referential
concern to him. By means of *zodra* 'as soon as' the temporal positioning
of the event is shown to be posterior to receiving permission to join in.
The speaker's actual or disactual referential concern allows, then, that
with regard to the speech time the event at issue can be situated within
a broad temporal region in rather different positions, as discussed
before with respect to sentences (15)-(19).

I assume that all the uses of the present tense as well as all the uses
of the past tense must be covered by one categorical meaning; the
meaning will be based on the notion of the speaker's actual or disactual
referential concern. There is no need for a comprehensive meaning[11]
within the temporal domain, because the adverbials can do the
referential temporal job, as in sentences (22) and (23); otherwise the
context of situation can give the clue for the correct referential
temporal interpretation of a verb, as we saw in sentences (15)-(19).[12]

There is a host of literature dealing with the meaning of the present and past tenses in Germanic languages. Bolinger (1947) sees the simple present tense as "timeless", as "non-committal about time", and as "expressing merely the FACT OF PROCESS".[13] But the past tense is held to be a temporal category. For German and Dutch a similar position has been taken by Heidolph et al. (1981), Koops (1986), Vennemann (1987), Fuchs[14] (1988).

Joos' (1964) semantic distinction between the non-past and the past, termed the "actual" and "remote" tenses respectively, conveys a valuable line of approach with regard to my analysis of the present and past tenses in Dutch.[15] The "remote" tense, which can serve to mark both unreality and past reality,[16] is assigned the meaning that *"the referent* (what is specified by the subject-verb partnership) *is absent from that part of the real world where the verb is being spoken"* (1964: 121).

The meaning assigned by Joos to the "actual" tense can be deduced from the qualification "actual", as well as from the way he characterizes the use of past events in narratives (1964: 131): "the use of actual tense for past events comes naturally to the lips of a man who gets himself involved in what he is talking about". By means of the present tense the speaker expresses what he sees before his eyes as if it were present.[17] A similar analysis of the present tense for "historical" events in narratives is made by Roloff (1921) (quoted in Casparis 1975: 18): "Wo ... das persönliche Interesse des Erzählers an dem Gegenstand seiner Darstellung erwacht, wo er von der Bedeutung seines Gegenstandes selbst ergriffen wird, da sieht er die Dinge gegenwärtig. So kommt er von selbst dazu, im Präsens zu erzählen." Casparis (1975: 22) comments: "[Bauer (1967)] insists that the meaning of the hist. Pres. ... is one of 'Presentness' (*'Vergegenwärtigung'*). He admits that *'Vergegenwärtigung'* is not a result of the hist. Pres. but the hist. Pres. is *'ein (ganz natürliches) Symptom der Vergegenwärtigung....'"* Consequently, Casparis (1975: 23) can state that: "the hist. Pres., being an *atemporal* device, functions as a conscious or unconscious signal, for instance, of the narrator's mood, or his subjective attitude towards the experience he is relating imaginatively or as eyewitness".[18] Therefore, as is often observed, the historical present can have a vivid or dramatic effect, but such an effect is merely an epiphenomenon of the function of the present tense in certain contexts or cotexts.

By means of the present tense, however it is used, the speaker of Dutch expresses the idea that the event is of actual referential concern to him: he envisages the event as taking place in his presence. The sentences in (24) can show that the present tense in Dutch is more than a form expressing the fact of process:[19]

(24) a.   *?Vroeger ben ik nog optimistisch.*
             'In the past I am still optimistic.'
      b.   *Vroeger was ik nog optimistisch.*
             'In the past I was still optimistic.'

The uninterpretability of the (a) sentence can only be explained by assuming that the adverbial *vroeger* 'in the past', interpreted as modifying the finite-verb form of the (a) and (b) sentences, is incompatible with the meaning of the present tense. A similar conclusion can be drawn from the difference between the sentences in (25) and (26);[20] the adverbs *nu* and *toen* are used here as temporal connectives, or rather as free relative adverbs:[21]

(25) a.   *Nu Tom vertrekt, besluit Mary te blijven.*
             'Now that Tom is leaving, Mary decides to stay.'
      b.   *Nu Tom vertrokken is, besluit Mary te blijven.*
             'Now that Tom has left, Mary decides to stay.'
      c.   *Nu Tom zal vertrekken, besluit Mary te blijven.*
             'Now that Tom will leave, Mary decides to stay.'
(26) a.   *?Toen Tom vertrekt, besluit Mary te blijven.*
             lit. At the time in the past when Tom is leaving, Mary
             decides to stay.
      b.   *?Toen Tom vertrokken is, besluit Mary te blijven.*
             lit. At the time in the past when Tom has left, Mary decides
             to stay.
      c.   *?Toen Tom zal vertrekken, besluit Mary te blijven.*
             lit. At the time in the past when Tom will leave, Mary
             decides to stay.

All of the sentences in (25) are interpretable, but none of the sentences in (26) are. The uninterpretability of those in (26) must be caused by a mismatch of *toen* 'at the time in the past when' and the present tense in the *toen* clause.[22]

     Considering these facts, the atemporalists may be right in assuming that the present is noncommittal about time, but as far as its supposed meaning is concerned - namely that merely the fact of process is expressed - the facts prove them to be wrong. How can the apparent incompatibilities in (24a) and (26a-c) be explained? The explanation cannot be found simply and solely in the fact that the adverbials *vroeger* 'in former days' and *toen* 'at the time in the past when' refer to a time in the past, while the present-tense form must refer to an event at the time of speech. This has already been illustrated with the first sentence of (13), *In de periode 1899-1900 werkt Grönloh, die later de schrijver Nescio zal worden, ... in Amsterdam.* [lit. In the period 1899-1900 Grönloh, who will become later the writer Nescio, works ... in Amsterdam.] The phrase *In de periode 1899-1900* refers to a time in the past, while *werkt* and *zal* are present-tense forms.

If the present tense is considered to be a means for presenting events of actual referential concern to the speaker from his vantage point, we can explain both the interpretable and the uninterpretable cooccurrences. In (24), the situation of still being optimistic in the past is not the focus of the speaker's referential concern, as is the case in the sentence of (13) cited above. A similar internal mismatch holds for the sentences of (26). It is not the temporal relation between the vantage point and the event referred to that is of primary relevance, but rather the relation of the speaker's actual referential concern for the event at issue, whether or not the event is simultaneous to the vantage point. This primacy can be illustrated with the following newspaper captions (*De Volkskrant* Friday, 6 October 1989), which provide instances of seemingly opposite deictics: adverbials that can be interpreted as referring to a past interval of time but which nevertheless go together with present-tense forms:

(27)   *Jim Bakker en zijn vrouw Tammy <u>verlaten</u> <u>woensdag</u> het gerechtsgebouw. De jury was toen nog niet tot een uitspraak gekomen, waardoor Bakker nog welgemoed kan wuiven.*
lit. Jim Bakker and his wife Tammy <u>leave</u> the courthouse <u>on Wednesday</u>. The jury had at that point not yet come to a verdict, so that Bakker still can wave in good spirits.

(28)   *De Oostduitse leider Erich Honecker (links op de linkerfoto) <u>inspecteert</u> <u>donderdag</u> Sovjet-soldaten die in paradepas aan hem voorbij trekken tijdens een plechtigheid in Oost-Berlijn. Daar wordt de veertigste verjaardag van de DDR gevierd. <u>Op dezelfde dag</u> <u>arriveren</u> Oostduitse vluchtelingen, zwaaiend met vlaggen en bloemen, uit Praag in het Westduitse Hof (foto rechts).*
lit. The East German leader Erich Honecker (left on the left photo) <u>reviews</u> Soviet soldiers <u>on Thursday</u> who march past him in parade step during a ceremony in East Berlin, where the fortieth anniversary of the GDR is being celebrated. <u>On the</u>

same day East German refugees, waving with flags and flowers, arrive from Prague in the West German town of Hof (photo on the right).

Present-tense forms cooccur with an adverbial indicating a past time in relation to the time of writing: in (27) *verlaten* 'leave' and *woensdag* 'on Wednesday'; in (28) *inspecteert* 'reviews' and *donderdag* 'on Thursday', as well as *op dezelfde dag* 'on the same day' and *arriveren* 'arrive'. If the clue of being captions is not given, sentences containing this type of cooccurrence would hardly be interpretable. I assume that the use of the present-tense forms is induced by the fact that the writer is looking at the photograph. It is from this vantage point that the event in the photograph has been presented as being of actual referential concern to him. This can be illustrated with captions like the following (*NRC* 14 March 1989 and *De Volkskrant* 16 October 1989):

(29)   *Karin Kania (links) leidt op de vijf kilometer nog voor Van Gennip, maar zou later drie seconden na de Nederlandse finishen.*
'Karin Kania (left) is still ahead of van Gennip in the five kilometers, but would later finish three seconds behind the Dutchwoman.'

(30)   *ANC-leider Walter Sisulu omhelst een familielid nadat hij, samen met zeven andere politieke activisten, uit de gevangenis is vrijgelaten.*
'ANC leader Walter Sisulu embraces a relative after he has been released from prison, together with seven other political activists.'

Without a deictic temporal adverbial, these texts form correct captions whenever they have been written or are written with reference to the photographs involved, and on the basis of that the texts retain their correctness of description whenever they are read. Obviously, with respect to tense the situation of looking at a photo can overrule other options for acquiring a suitable vantage point in verbalizing the scene displayed on the photo and can constitute the basis for the "actualness" of the observer's referential concern.[23]

Texts (27) and (28) show that even deictic temporal adverbials like *woensdag* 'on Wednesday' and *donderdag* 'on Thursday' can do their referential job of specifying the time of the events at issue independent of - or, as traditional analyses would have it, in spite of - the tenses involved. The relevant vantage point of adverbials with temporal reference can be different from the vantage point of the tense at issue, as already has been shown in my discussion of sentence (21) with the adverbial *nu* 'now' and the past tense. As a matter of fact, sentence (23) shows a similar difference: the vantage[24] point of *zodra* 'as soon as' is determined by the foregoing event, whereas the vantage point of the tenses is determined by the speech situation.

The question may arise how different deictic coordinates can go together without causing serious interpretive problems. Langacker (1987: 125) shows convincingly that the "notions figure, foreground, and focus of attention do not always coincide, despite the naturalness of their association". I assume that a similar coincidence holds for the time coordinate expressed by means of temporal adverbials and the coordinate of actual and disactual referential concern expressed by means of the present and past tenses respectively.

2.   The meaning of the first and second finite forms

What semantic characterization can unite the finding that the present tense is noncommittal about time and the finding that there are still some incompatibilities between the finite forms and adverbial expressions with temporal reference? What comprehensive meaning could be assumed for the present and past-tense forms to handle them satisfactorily? As argued before, there is no need at all to look for such a meaning in the temporal domain. On the contrary, context or cotext can sufficiently guarantee a temporally suitable interpretation. The semantic function of the present and past-tense forms which I discern is the following:

(31)   *Semantic function of the first and second finite forms*

1.   By using a finite verb, the speaker indicates that the event mentioned by means of this verb is salient to him from his vantage point, which is given either contextually or cotextually,

2.   - by using the first finite form the speaker indicates that from his vantage point the event is of actual referential concern to him (the event is the focus of his referential concern),

    - by using the second finite form the speaker indicates that from his vantage point the event is of disactual

referential concern to him (the event is not the focus
of his referential concern).

In this definition, by delineating the present and past-tense forms as expressions of an indicated event coordinate in the dimension of actual
versus disactual referential concern, three pragmatico-grammatical cognitive notions are assumed. These are given as tools of analysis in (32):

(32)   *Tools of analysis*

1.   The speaker's vantage point.
2.   The salience of an event from the speaker's vantage
point.
3.   The speaker's actual or disactual referential concern for
the event from his vantage point.

Appendix

Provided that tools 1-3 are applied regularly, the hearer can
place the event at issue and can regard it as definite by
inference:

- usually the hearer knows or can construe the speaker's
vantage point,
- the hearer can take into account the fact that the event will
be salient from the speaker's vantage point,
- the hearer can take into account the fact that the event will
or will not be of actual referential concern to the speaker
from the latter's vantage point.

Allen (1966) has put forward definiteness as a characteristic of the
present and past tenses. In my view, this notion is not an atomic
primitive but a composite interpretational tool: the strong feeling or
sense of definiteness in the case of the present and past tenses might be
regarded as an effect. The hearer can take into account (1) the
speaker's vantage point, (2) what the speaker mentions, which is
obviously salient to him, and (3) how the speaker expresses his
referential concern for what he mentions. No certainty is explicitly
offered that the event involved is referentially unique. Such a
requirement would be far too strong. Consider for example sentence
(33):

(33)   *Would you close the window, please?*

Although the room in which the speaker finds himself may have several windows, the hearer will not experience any difficulty in understanding the request if just one window is open and that window has not been mentioned before. The same holds for the use of possessives in sentences like the following:[25]

(34)   *Your shoe is beyond repair.*
(35)   *Have you hurt your finger?*

The entity determined by the possessive will tend to be seen as the only relevant one within the context or cotext involved. In this matter, I see no difference between the use of present and past and the use of the nominals at issue in (33)-(35). Normally, the hearer can discriminate the entity presumably involved as the only relevant one, partly due to the information given by means of the utterance itself and partly due to the context of situation.

   In the following subsections I will comment on the cognitive factors of (32). In 2.4. I will return to Allen's (1966) interesting but controversial view on the definiteness of the present and past tenses in connection with the analysis of the perfect.

2.1.   Tense and vantage point

Distinguishing the speaker's vantage point with regard to tense is relatively uncontroversial, even if it is put forward as a tool that functions contextually as well as cotextually. I have already shown that tenses can be used very variedly due to the shiftability of the vantage point. In this respect, cases like (27)-(30), which contain the present tense for past events, appeared to elucidate the crucial fact that the relevant vantage point is the situation in which the caption editor is visualizing a past event in the photo as being present before his eyes; in this way the past event turns out to be of actual referential concern to him. Between the time of the visualized event and the present tense in these sentences there is no temporal relation of any significance.

   In section 1, a variety of temporal relations emerged between the event mentioned and the vantage point, i.e. the time when the sentence is spoken. One type of temporal divergence is assigned to the shiftability of the vantage point; see (13)-(14), (27)-(30) with regard to the present tense, (20) with regard to the past tense. Another type of temporal divergence is assigned to the strength of the speaker's actual or disactual referential concern for the event presented, allowing a positioning within a broad temporal region (see (15)-(19)).[26]

The latter type of sentence is not merely brought into the discussion here to stress once again that this type shows that tense does not hinge on a temporal relation between the speaker's vantage point and the event referred to by means of the finite verb. Rather, I wish to claim also that other sentence types not mentioned before belong to this type, in particular sentences with present tense that is referred to as gnomic, timeless, omnitemporal, universal, generic, repetitive, iterative, habitual, etc. Considering other deictics, I see no reason why such sentences should be treated as exceptional in their present-tense character because of their more or less unlimited temporal delineation (cf. also Lyons 1977: 679ff). Adverbs like *hier* 'here' (in e.g. *hier in deze wereld* 'here in this world' or *nu* 'now' (in e.g. *nu in deze eeuw* 'now in this century') can cover a region much more extensive than the vantage point relevant to the words involved (Klein 1978: 35; 1983: 294f; Talmy 1988: 168f; Paprotté 1988: 459f). When someone says, for example, *De kat slaapt op de mat* 'The cat sleeps on the mat' at a time when the animal involved is strolling around the neighborhood, there is no overlap between one factual distinct instance of sleeping on the mat within the habitual event, on the one hand, and the speech time, on the other. But such an apparent discrepancy does not make this type of sentence special with respect to tense, because it is not a matter of tense but a matter of event type. The habitual event in its entirety is of actual referential concern to the speaker from his vantage point. The same holds *mutatis mutandis* with regard to a habitual sentence in the past tense, such as *De kat sliep op de mat* 'The cat slept on the mat'.[27] In interpreting sentences like *Doctor, this tooth hurts* (said when there is no pain at the moment), one does not need any additional pragmatic assumption for bridging the speech time and the times of the series of factual discrete instances constituting the habitual event at issue, as Paprotté (1988: 505) would have it.[28] The evoked habitual event is of current relevance in its entirety and is as such of either actual or disactual referential concern to the speaker from his vantage point.

2.2.   Tense and salience

Now let us consider the point of salience. The use of the finite verb, both in the past and present-tense form, indicates that the speaker envisions the event concerned as being salient to him from his vantage point; the event is prominently within his real or mental field of vision. Perhaps this issue does not call for any further remarks with regard to most of the uses of the present tense, but I would like to comment briefly on the use of the past tense. Consider in this respect the (a) and (b) sentences of (36) and (37):

(36)   The doorbell rings. You ask your son to go and see who is there. A minute later you hear the visitor leaving. When your son returns, you ask:
   a.   *Wie was er aan de deur?*
         'Who was at the door?'
   b.   ?*Wie is er aan de deur geweest?*
         'Who has been at the door?'
(37)   You see a man coming to the front door. You ask your son to go and ask what the man wants. A minute later you hear the man leaving. When your son returns, you ask:
   a.   *Wat wilde hij?*
         'What did he want?'
   b.   ?*Wat heeft hij gewild?*
         lit. What has he wanted?

In both cases, only the sentence with the past tense is an appropriate question. The (b) sentence cannot be interpreted as concerning the salient situation the speaker has in mind, the situation directly related to his foregoing request. Let us consider another pair of examples:

(38) a.   *Er was iemand voor je aan de deur.*
           'There was someone at the door for you.'
     b.   *Er is iemand voor je aan de deur geweest.*
           lit. There has someone been at the door for you.
           'There was someone at the door for you.'

Both sentences are perfectly interpretable, but they differ in their use. When one's son comes home at the end of his school day, one will tend to say (38b); (38a) is applicable only to an event well embedded in a given situation, for example when the son left for a minute in order to post a letter. Obviously, in the case of the past tense the requirement that the event in question must be salient to the speaker is rather severe in Dutch: the speaker - and usually his addressee too, otherwise the latter will ask for the intended context - must be in a position to place the event in question within an encompassing, rather closefitting scene.[29] In accordance with my view on "compound tenses" (§1.1.), the absence of salience may be expected in the case of the event mentioned by means of the past participle, because it is the nonfinite part of a "compound tense" and as such a nondeictic element.

With regard to nondeictic elements, a speaker's vantage point, salience and actual or disactual referential concern do not come into play. In Dutch, nonfinite verb forms of "compound tenses" can be modified temporally, as can be demonstrated with the following examples; the adverbials specify the time of the event mentioned by means of the nonfinite main verb, except in sentences (43)-(44), in which the time of the nonfinite auxiliary *zijn* 'have' is specified:

(39)   *Tom is toen zo snel als hij kon vertrokken.*
       lit. Tom has left then as fast as he could.
       'Tom then left as fast as he could.'
(40)   *Tom was toen zo snel als hij kon vertrokken.*
       'Tom had left then as fast as he could.'
(41)   *Harry zal morgen om acht uur vertrekken.*
       'Harry will leave at eight o'clock tomorrow.'
(42)   *Harry zou morgen om acht uur vertrekken.*
       'Harry was to leave at eight o'clock tomorrow.'
(43)   *Jim zal morgen om acht uur vertrokken zijn.*
       'Jim will have left at eight o'clock tomorrow.'
(44)   *Jim zou morgen om acht uur vertrokken zijn.*
       'Jim was to have left at eight o'clock tomorrow.'

The possibility that the nonfinite verb can be modified temporally does not prove that the event mentioned should be viewed as salient with regard to the speaker's actual or disactual referential concern for what is going on in the context of the situation. The irrelevancy of the temporal modification in this respect can be illustrated with the following sentences:

(45) a.   *Er was zojuist iemand voor je aan de deur.*
        'There was someone at the door for you just a minute ago.'

b.   *Er is zojuist iemand voor je aan de deur geweest.*
lit. There has just a minute ago someone been at the door
for you.
'There was someone at the door for you just a minute ago.'

Irrespective of the temporal modification the same interpretive distinction holds as for the sentences in (38). I will return to the issue of salience of nonfinite-verb forms later on.

2.3.   *Tense and actual versus disactual referential concern*

Now we can concentrate on the third tool of analysis: the speaker's actual or disactual referential concern for an event. Let us first consider the sentences in (46):

(46)   My colleague and I try to remedy an obstinate technical failure,
but we cannot solve the problem and need advice from a specialist. I phone Peter, the best expert we know. My colleague
listens and waits for the advice. As soon as I have hung up, he
asks:
a.   *?Wat vond Peter ervan?*
'What did Peter think we should do?'
b.   *Wat vindt Peter ervan?*
'What does Peter think we should do?'

The (b) sentence is far more appropriate than the (a) sentence with respect to its applicability in the given context, where the expert's current opinion is what really matters. From my colleague's vantage point, Peter's advice is of actual referential concern when he asks for it. He therefore prefers the present to the past tense, even though Peter is no longer giving his advice.

Present-tense cases in English comparable to that in (46b) are characterised by Quirk et al. (1985: 181) as follows:[30] "the implication of the present tense seems to be that although the communicative event took place in the past, its result - the information communicated - is still operative". The current notion of operativeness is appropriate with regard to a case like (47) in Dutch:

(47)   *Frits, iemand vraagt naar je. Kom je even?*
lit. Frits, somebody asks for you. Do you come for a moment?
'Frits, somebody is asking for you. Will you come for a
moment?'
(48)   *Frits, iemand vroeg naar je. Kom je even?*
lit. Frits, somebody asked for you. Do you come for a moment?
'Frits, somebody was asking for you. Will you come for a
moment?'

The request to come for a moment makes sense if someone's wish to
see Frits is still valid, that is to say of actual referential concern to the
speaker, as can be indicated with the present-tense form *vraagt* 'is
asking' in text (47). In such a situation, text (48) is rather puzzling. A
similar difference in applicability of the past and present tenses can be
shown with the following examples; this time the first text is rather
incomprehensible:

(49)   *Frits, iemand vraagt naar je. Ik heb maar gezegd dat je niet kon
komen.*
lit. Frits, somebody asks for you. I have just said that you could
not come.
'Frits, somebody is asking for you. I just said that you could not
come.'
(50)   *Frits, iemand vroeg naar je. Ik heb maar gezegd dat je niet kon
komen.*
lit. Frits, somebody asked for you. I have just said that you
could not come.
'Frits, somebody was asking for you. I said that you could not
come.'

Mentioning the pretext *Ik heb maar gezegd dat je niet kon komen* makes
sense only in a situation in which someone's asking for Frits is not relevant any longer, as indicated by means of *Frits, iemand vroeg naar je* in
(50).

2.4.   All tools on deck

The relevance of all three tools - the speaker's vantage point, the
salience of the event, and the speaker's actual versus disactual

referential concern - can be illustrated nicely with the following examples:

(51)   *Er wordt geklopt.*
        lit. There is knocked.
        'There's someone at the door.'
(52)   *Er werd geklopt.*
        lit. There was knocked.
        'There was someone at the door.'
(53)   *Er is geklopt.*
        lit. There has been knocked.
        'There's been someone at the door.'

The circumstances in which these sentences are used might be the following. Imagine a conference room in which a meeting is being held; among the attendants are Tom, Dick and Harry. A noisy buzzing is drowning out almost all other background noises. But somehow Tom hears a knock on the door and tells his neighbor Dick using sentence (51). Then Dick passes the news to his neighbor Harry with the help of sentence (52). And Harry, in his turn, draws the chairman's attention to the event in question with sentence (53).

Of course there are other possibilities. For example, once Tom has drawn his attention to the sound, Dick may realize that he too has heard something that could be the knocking. In this case he, too, could use sentence (51) appropriately, and all the more so if he wants to state that the knocking calls for action by one of the attendants. But, whatever the interpretation of sentence (51), my first assumption is that the speaker regards the event as being salient to him from his vantage point, and second that, from his vantage point, the speaker envisions himself as being strongly involved in the event expressed with the present-tense verb. In the case of sentence (52), again I assume that the speaker regards the event as salient to him from his vantage point, but I assume that, from his vantage point, the speaker sees the event expressed with the past-tense verb as lying beyond his immediate or actual referential concern. The question of whether or not the speaker envisions the event at issue as being entirely within his scope of interest, or as lying beyond it, seems to me the decisive distinction between the use of the present and past tenses.

Thus, with regard to the present-tense case, the speaker envisions the knocking not only as being salient to him, but also as being the focus of his referential concern, even when the sound has already died away and does not recur. With regard to the past-tense case, we can observe that the use of this verb form also involves a salient event envisioned within the discourse context as being aloof from the things actually going on. Again, both the salience and the actual or disactual referential concern are interpreted as being seen from the vantage point of the speaker.

Turning finally to the present-perfect case, in view of my analysis of "compound tenses" we concentrate on the interpretation of the finite verb, because the speaker's vantage point, the salience of the event and the speaker's actual or disactual referential concern do not come into play with regard to the participle. For example, when Harry draws the chairman's attention to the obvious fact that someone is at the door, he is the first one of the trio who cannot relate the report of the knocking to that very event itself, in the strict and actual sense.[31] Indeed, what Harry reports is not this or that knocking, but a certain knocking, the said knocking. Any direct link between the occurrence of the event in question and Harry's own perception is lacking.

It is worth noting here that the present perfect can have a slightly modal (inferential)[32] interpretation in contrast to the past tense. For instance, when leaving the theater and discovering that the streets are wet, one would be much more likely to say (54), with the present perfect, than the very odd (55), with the past tense. Sentence (54) is understood as 'it must have rained':

(54)   *Hé, het heeft geregend.*
        'Hey, it has been raining.'
(55)   *Hé, het regende.*
        'Hey, it rained.'

But when looking at one's parents' wedding photos, the past tense variant is a lot more plausible, if the wedding day was obviously rainy, than the version with the present perfect. In the case of the past tense, the event involved must be salient from the speaker's vantage point. And due to some indications of rain on the photograph the salience is fully guaranteed.

The present-tense auxiliary of the present perfect has an important semantic function which can be deduced from the possibility of modifying the auxiliary temporally, as observed in sentences (1) and (5). The relevance of the auxiliary's own semantic role can be elucidated with the following example:[33]

(56)   *Waar legde je mijn portemonnaie neer?*
        'Where did you put my purse?'
(57)   *Waar heb je mijn portemonnaie neergelegd?*
        'Where have you put my purse?'

The first sentence evokes an action related to a broader scene within the speaker's focus of attention; this scene could be a reconstruction of a theft committed by a person who may or may not yet be identified. But in the second sentence, the act of putting the purse away is not presented as related to an encompassing scenario. What is salient here, due to the present-tense form of the auxiliary *heb* 'have', is the currently relevant or operative situation presented as being of actual referential concern to the speaker, a situation caused by the addressee's having put the purse somewhere. With respect to the function of the auxiliary *heb* 'have', I follow Langacker (1978: 865), who states that "*have* locates within the sphere of relevance a perfect expression, marked with the perfect participle".

Now let us take a closer look at the issue of salience or definiteness of the event mentioned by means of the present and past tenses from a theoretical point of view. McCoard (1978) has made a vigorous attempt to reject the definiteness view of the past tense in English, as put forward by Allen (1966).[34] There are three problems with McCoard's objections. Firstly, the classic tense analysis, which involves associating the event with a certain interval of time, conceived by him as a firm base, has emerged in the foregoing as challengeable. Secondly, and closely related to this point, the connection between tense and adverbials with a temporal reference has also appeared in the foregoing to be rather loose, but when rejecting the definiteness view, McCoard regards this relation as an intrinsic one, as did Allen (1966), for that matter. Finally, the notion of definiteness has crystallized since McCoard presented his objections.

For an important view on definiteness, consider Donnellan's (1978) approach. He shows, with the help of text (58), that definiteness is only loosely tied up with identification:

(58)   *We now had a telephone call from a man high in the inner circle. He asked us to meet him at a certain suburban garage where he would give us confirmation of some of our conjectures. We later decided to give the man the code name "Deep Throat".*

On the basis of the pronoun *he* in the second sentence the reader can try to place the supposed referent: he can relate the supposed referent of *he* to the supposed referent of *a man*. But the pronoun does not serve to make the person in question identifiable: the (supposed) authors of (58) "did not intend that there should be recognition", as Donnellan (1978: 62) points out.[35] Du Bois (1980) also assumes a weak notion of identification with regard to definiteness; his idea that "a reference is counted as identifiable if it identifies an object close enough to satisfy the curiosity of the hearer" (1980: 233) is compatible with Donellan's view.

In this line of approach, I will take the view that the present and past tenses are definite in the sense in which *this* and *that* can be considered definite. Assuming that the speaker has a specific salient event in mind, either of actual or disactual referential concern to him from his vantage point, the hearer can certainly try to place the event in question in the right context or cotext. However, what the speaker expresses is not an instruction for a search, but a signal of what he experiences or envisions. To say this with a variant on Joos' words: the use of the present tense comes naturally to the lips of a man who envisions an event as salient and actual to him from his vantage point; a similar statement applies to the use of the past tense, except that the speaker's referential concern is off-center, so that the event is disactual to him. Of course, the hearer can regard a tense form as a clue for a plausible interpretation, but such a form is just a possibility for a search, rather than an instruction to search for a contextually or cotextually given event salient and of actual or disactual referential concern to the speaker from his vantage point (*pace* Schopf 1987: 186).[36]

3.   Conspecificity of categories: "Demonstratio actualis" versus "disactualis"

In this section I will take a closer look at the dimension of the indicated object coordinate (*dit/deze* 'this', versus *dat/die* 'that') and the dimension of the indicated place coordinate (*hier* 'here', *daar* 'there'). Firstly, it will be shown that demonstratives can be viewed as signalling the speaker's referential concern, while the speaker's accompanying gesture or his vicinity is basically concomitant. It will thus become clear that tenses and demonstratives in fact constitute conspecific categories. Secondly, attention will be paid to the congruity of deictics of both the same and of different types; they will emerge as working in close concert.

3.1.   Demonstratives and actual/disactual referential concern

When uttering the words *dit, deze* 'this' or *hier* 'here' in the following sentences, the speaker will not point to just anything:

(59)   *Dit artikel had niet geschreven kunnen worden zonder hulp van mijn computer.*
'This paper could not have been written without the aid of my personal computer.'
(60)   *Vorig jaar om deze tijd hield ik hier een lezing over regels van gezichtswerk.*
'Last year at this time I gave a talk here about some rules of face work.'

To what might one point in the case of *deze tijd* 'this time' in (60)? A similar question could be put in the case of sentences like (61) and (62):

(61)   *Wie is daar?*
'Who is there?'
(62)   *Is daar iemand?*
'Is somebody there?'

The only factors which can be assumed to determine the use of the demonstratives *dit, deze, hier* and *daar* in (59)-(62) are the three specified in (63):

(63)   *Tools of analysis*

1.   The speaker's vantage point.
2.   The salience of an entity from the speaker's vantage point.
3.   The speaker's actual or disactual referential concern for the entity from his vantage point.

These tools of analysis can be illustrated with the following example. If a doctor is palpating a patient, he may utter (64). The patient might answer as in (65):

(64)   Doctor: *Doet het hier zeer? / Doet het zeer op deze plek?*
                   'Does it hurt here? / Is this where it hurts?'
(65)   Patient: *Ja, daar. / Ja, op die plek.*
                   'Yes, there. / Yes, that is where it hurts.'

The patient's answer shows that the differentiation between the domain of *hier/deze* 'here/this' and *daar/die* 'there/that' cannot be characterized as "in the vicinity of the speaker" and "not in the vicinity of the speaker" (Lyons 1968: 275).[37] The use of the deictic *hier/deze* 'here/this' in the doctor's question depends on the following:

(66)   1.   The vantage point of the speaker: his palpating hand.
        2.   The salience of the place in question with regard to the speaker's vantage point: the place palpated.
        3.   The speaker's referential concern for the salient place with regard to his vantage point: the place palpated, as a matter of fact in the direct environment of his palpating hand, thus of strongly actual referential concern from the speaker's vantage point.

More abstract uses of *hier/deze* 'here/this' and *daar/die* 'there/that' can be handled similarly. Compare, for instance, the use of the demonstratives *this* and *that* in English, as analyzed by Lakoff (1974: 351):

(67)   A: *Dick says that the Republicans may have credibility problems.*
              This is an understatement.
(68)   A: *Dick says that the Republicans may have credibility problems.*
        B: *That is an understatement.*

Here the choice of *this* or *that* can depend on whose turn it is to speak (the use of *that* by the same speaker - compare (70) - is not excluded). In Lakoff's words (1974: 349): "*This* may be used only if the two sentences are uttered by the same speaker", while "*that* can be used by a speaker to comment on an immediately prior remark by another". With *this* the speaker expresses his commitment to the remark, whereas the speaker presents the indicated entity with *that* as removed from his referential concern.

The use of *this* and *that* in cases like (69) and (70) proffered by Lakoff (1974: 346; 350) can be viewed in the same line of approach;

these cases allow a more refined explanation with the help of the distinction between actual and disactual referential concern:

(69)   *The prime minister made his long-awaited announcement*
        yesterday.
        This statement confirmed the speculations of many observers.
(70)   *The prime minister made his long-awaited announcement*
        yesterday.
        That statement confirmed the speculations of many observers.

The demonstratives *this* and *that* have a similar referential function, but as Lakoff (1974: 350) comments: "There seems, however, to be a subtle feeling in [(69)] that the speaker remains involved in his subject, and may well go on to say more about it. *That* [in (70)] distances the speaker from [the minister's] report, making it less likely that he will expatiate on it". How does this difference, especially the presumption that the speaker might dwell on the subject when using *this*, fit in my analysis?

When using *his long-awaited announcement* the speaker reveals that the report is salient to him. Due to this reference the minister's announcement gets hold of the focal position in the speaker's referential concern, as is indeed communicated by means of the demonstrative *this* in *This statement*, which is coreferential with *his long-awaited announcement.* Thus, with *This statement* the speaker gives evidence of having taken the vantage point in which the statement is of actual referential concern to him, as a result of which he may be considered as possibly bringing to the fore some details or circumstantialities. But in the case of *that* in (70) the speaker's vantage point is one of looking back on the occurrence; from that vantage point his initial statement is of removed referential concern.

Sentences like (71) and (72) show a comparable opposition between *hier* 'hier' and *daar* 'there' (cf. Klein 1978; Janssen 1983: 45f).

(71)   *Fred arriveerde in Montreal. Hier hadden zijn ouders al lang naar*
        hem uitgezien.
        'Fred arrived in Montreal. His parents had long been awaiting him here.'
(72)   *Fred ging naar Montreal. Daar moest hij zijn voor een conferentie.*
        'Fred went to Montreal. He had to attend a business meeting there.'

In the *hier*-version the speaker presents the awaiting from the point of view in Montreal, but in the *daar*-version he sees the event at hand from his actual situation outside of Montreal.[38] A similar difference can be seen in sentences (73) and (74) with *nu* 'now' and *toen* 'then' (Janssen 1983: 46):

(73)   *Daar klonk eindelijk het eindsignaal. De overwinning was nu een feit.*
         'There it was, the final whistle at last. Now victory was certain.'
(74)   *Eindelijk klonk het eindsignaal. De spelers beseften toen pas dat ze gewonnen hadden.*
         'At last the final whistle blew. It was only then that the players realized they had won.'

I regard the difference between *nu* and *toen* in these sentences too as a contrast between the speaker's perceiving a situation with actual referential concern and his viewing it as removed from his central referential concern.

No one will have failed to notice that the difference in each of the foregoing pairs of sentences greatly resembles the difference between the narrative use of the present tense as the so-called historical present and the narrative use of the past tense. What did we see in such uses of demonstratives? In the contrastive examples (69)-(70), (71)-(72) and (73)-(74) the use of *dit*, *hier* and *nu* could be interpreted as having a vivid, dramatic effect. However, I assume that it can be regarded as a special interpretive effect, allowed on the basis of the comprehensive meaning of these forms. The present tense has no dramatic effect of its own, as can be illustrated in (75):

(75)   *Op twaalf oktober 1492 ontdekt Christoffel Columbus Amerika.*
         lit. On the twelfth of October, 1492, Christopher Columbus discovers America.

No matter how dramatic the discovery was in itself, the event is presented by means of the present tense in a dry, not distinctly vivid manner.

3.2. The congruity of different deictic types

In using the present tense, the speaker presents a situation as being his central referential concern, even if the factual event is remote in chronological and spatial respects. These seemingly conflicting features can be indicated explicitly within the same sentence; witness the following newspaper caption (*De Volkskrant* 14 March 1988):

(76)   *Aartsbisschop Tutu (links) en dominee Boesak gaan voor in gebed tijdens een dienst die zondag in Kaapstad werd gehouden.*
'Archbishop Tutu (left) and the reverend Boesak lead the prayers during a service which was held in Cape Town on Sunday.'

The main clause of the text relates to what can be viewed as the event of the photograph. This clause is in the present tense, even though the event occurred in the past, as becomes apparent from the subordinate clause. The present tense of the main clause is understood as a presentation of the speaker's actual refcrential concern when looking at the photograph. The caption illustrates nicely that the application of the present tense can be seen as a symptom of the speaker's view that the event at issue is salient to him and is of actual referential concern to him; the speaker sees himself actually confronted with the event. Since the subordinate clause presents an event not displayed with the picture itself, this clause is in the past tense. The past tense functions as the presentation of an event which is salient to the speaker but removed from his actual referential concern.

A second illustration of the congruity of different deictic types is the following newspaper caption (*De Volkskrant* Saturday, 11 November 1989):

(77)   *Oostberlijnse grenswachten kijken naar een bulldozer die vrijdagnacht een deel van de Muur sloopt. Op deze plek komt nog een grensovergang tussen Oost- en West-Berlijn.*
'East German border guards watch a bulldozer which is pulling down part of the Wall on Friday night. Another border crossing point between East and West Berlin will be opened on this site.'

Here the vantage points of the present tenses *kijken* 'watch' and *sloopt* 'is pulling down' differ from the present tense *komt* (here to be read as 'will be opened'). The vantage point of *kijken* and *sloopt* originates from the fact that the writer is observing the photograph. From this vantage point the events mentioned are the caption editor's actual referential concern. The actualness of his concern is not disturbed by the adverbial *vrijdagnacht* 'on Friday night' in the subordinate clause. For this adverbial, we have to assume a different vantage point, as emerges when the caption is read outside the context of the newspaper of Saturday, 11 November 1989. A caption without the adverbial is always applicable whenever the photograph is observed and whenever the caption is phrased.

In the first sentence we see that deictics determined by two different vantage points can cooccur perfectly. In the second sentence we again find a cooccurrence of two deictics, but now the vantage point of the adverbial is anchored in the situation of looking at the photograph, while the vantage point of the present-tense form *komt* (here to be read as 'will be opened') depends on a context which is wider than the foregoing sentence and the photograph. The vantage point of *deze* in *Op deze plek* 'on this site' is the situation of someone who is observing the photograph. The relevance of the site is partly due to the content of the foregoing sentence and partly due to the photo. Due to these facts the site can get hold of the focal position in the editor's referential concern, as he indeed reveals with his use of the demonstrative *deze* in *Op deze plek*. Nevertheless, the vantage point of the present tense in the second sentence is most probably not that of observing the photograph. The information on the future event which the editor has provided in the second sentence cannot be inferred from the photo itself: it is not shown on the picture. He can make his statement on the basis of independent evidence.[39] We can conclude that the editor has the same vantage point in the case of the present-tense forms in the first sentence as in the case of the demonstrative *deze* 'this' in the second sentence.

A symbiosis of the present tense and the deictic adverbial *hier* 'here' sharing the same vantage point can be seen in the following caption (*De Gooi- en Eemlander* 25 November 1989):

(78)   *Hand in hand staan hier Alexander Dubcek (l) en Vaclav Havel op het punt de menigte in Praag toe te spreken.*
        'Standing hand in hand Alexander Dubcek (l) and Vaclav Havel are here about to address the crowd in Prague.'

With regard to both the present tense *staan op het punt* 'be about to' and the demonstrative *hier* 'here', the vantage point relevant to the editor is the situation of looking at the photograph. From this point the event and place displayed are envisioned as being of actual referential concern to him.

4.   Conclusion

In line with Langacker's (1987: 125) observation that figure, foreground and focus of attention need not coincide, I contend that the vantage points of tense and temporal adverbials can differ. This contention is based on arguments for describing the seeming cooccurrence restrictions on tenses and temporal adverbials as epiphenomenal. This idea leads directly to the necessity to disconnect the basic semantic characterization of tense from the notion of time and clears the way for a coherent approach to several deictics.

By examining present versus past tense and in connection with that *nu* 'now, at this moment' versus *toen* 'then' or 'when' and consequently *dit* 'this' versus *dat* 'that' and *hier* 'here' versus *daar* 'there', I have demonstrated that only three tools of analysis are needed: the speaker's vantage point, the salience of the entity in question, and the dimension of actual versus disactual referential concern.

Little attention has been paid to crosslinguistic facts. Differences between English and Dutch in the use of, for example, the past and the perfect - see cases like (38b), (45b) and (53) - might be due to differences in routine perceptions of what is considered salient, and what is considered of actual or disactual referential concern.[40] If this is the case, research on deixis could make an interesting move towards a coherent theory.

Notes

*   I wish to thank Madelein van Baalen, Ellen Ziff, Mike Hannay and two referees for their helpful comments on an earlier draft.

1.   See, for example, the following passing reference in Quirk et al. (1985: 184): "A parallel may ... be drawn ... between the present and past tense, and the 'near' and 'far' reference of the demonstratives *this* and *that*..."; see also Langacker (1987: 127) and Ehrich (1982), who uses basically Reichenbachian analytical categories (speaker's place, denotation place, reference place).

2.   Because the participle *vertrokken* could have an adjectival character (cf. Janssen 1988), one might doubt whether formations like *zal/zou vertrokken zijn* in (9) and (11), presented as futurum exactum and

futurum exactum praeteriti, actually are "tenses". But the following sentences with a reflexive element in them leave no room for doubt about the possibility of the suggested temporal use; both of them can be interpreted to mean that Jim has finished shaving before eight o'clock:

(1)   *Jim zal zich morgen om acht uur geschoren hebben.*
       'Jim will have shaved [himself] at eight o'clock tomorrow.'
(2)   *Jim zou zich morgen om acht uur geschoren hebben.*
       'Jim was to have shaved [himself] by eight o'clock tomorrow.'

3.   See Janssen (1989b: 81f) for criticism on taking "historical future" to be a relevant linguistic category.
4.   For the notion default in a similar case, see Langacker (1987: 127); Klein (1983: 291) proposes the notion "prototypical origo". I use the term *shift* to indicate that a vantage point differs from the one which might be chosen by default, however by no means implying any mental process of shifting from the "prototypical" vantage point to another in interpreting deictic words.
5.   Dinsmore (1987: 15), following Fauconnier (1985), regards the kind of vantage point at issue as the result of a shift to an alternative focus space. The present tense of a newspaper caption like (1) (*NRC* 6 November 1989) can be explained in a similar way:
      (1)   *Zaterdag 4 november. Op de Berlijnse Alexanderplatz heeft de grootste demonstratie in de geschiedenis van de DDR plaats.*
             'Saturday 4 November. On the Berlin Alexanderplatz the largest demonstration in the history of the GDR is taking place.'
      Both the cotextual introduction *Zaterdag 4 november* and the contextual connection of a caption being put under a photograph focus on the event of the happening itself, so that the caption can be interpreted as being of actual referential concern to the observer, although the situation of his vantage point is different from the time of describing the event.
6.   For different views on similar phenomena in the use of the present tense in German, see for instance Rauh (1983: 240f), Fabricius-Hansen's criticism as well as her own approach (1986: 41ff; 56ff), and Ballweg (1988: 48).
7.   For a similar observation with regard to English, see e.g. Jespersen (1932: 163f).
8.   There is a semantic difference between the "future present" and the "future tense" (3 in Table 1); the "future tense" is an explicitly modal expression (cf. Janssen 1989b).
9.   In German, for example, similar temporal relations can be observed:
      (1)   *Du darfst schon kurz mitspielen. Aber sobald der feste Mann kommt, mußt du den Platz räumen.*

(2)   *Du durftest schon kurz mitspielen. Aber sobald*
       der feste Mann kam, mußtest du den Platz räumen.
       For "future action in the past" with regard to French, see Waugh
       (1975: 458f).

10.   See for a case of an "impending event" Hirtle (1967: 97): "George
       dropped in yesterday evening just for a chat. We *were dining* at the
       Jones's, but he simply wouldn't go, so we were terribly late."
       In addition to the "future perfect" we should have to postulate a
       "future past perfect"; see for discussions e.g. Grewendorf (1982: 231),
       Janssen (1989a).

11.   See, for example, Janssen (1986) for a theoretical argument on
       assigning lexical elements a comprehensive meaning.

12.   With respect to German, this point is clearly shown by Heringer
       (1983), who gives three temporally completely different interpretations
       for *Er kommt.* For a similar treatment of the sentence *He's leaving*, see
       Joos (1964: 135).

13.   For a similar view with regard to the present tense in English, see e.g.
       Twaddell (1960) and Langacker (1978); with regard to German, see
       e.g. Vennemann (1987); for a crosslinguistic study, see e.g. Fleischman
       (1989).

14.   With regard to the past tense, Fuchs (1988: 6f) views the temporal facet
       ("zeitrelationale Bezugsfestlegung auf Vorzeitigkeit") as being
       subordinate to the facet of relevance ("Festlegung in der Dimension
       des Relevanzbezugs"). Thus *"Präteritum* signalisiert eine Verlagerung
       des Relevanzbezugs weg von unmittelbar anstehenden 'Belang' ". If the
       facet of the relevance relation (conceived as a relation of disactual
       referential concern) may be taken to be a matter of meaning ("sense")
       and the facet of the temporal relation to be a matter of interpretation
       ("reference"), then I agree, at least as far as the past tense is
       concerned.

15.   See for related views on the distinction between the categories present
       and past e.g. Balk-Smit Duyzentkunst (1963) with regard to Dutch, and
       further Waugh (1975), Wallace (1982: 203, 210), Tobin (1988), and
       Andersson (1989).

16.   In Dutch and in other languages as well, the past tense can have a rich
       variety of uses in addition to past time reference. See e.g. Waugh
       (1975: 451ff) for French, and Fleischman (1989) for a crosslinguistic
       study.

17.   The characterization of the simple present tense as marking an
       eyewitness report needs to be modified with regard to "historic
       narratives" in English, but not in Dutch, German or French. The
       adjustment might be a slight one according to Joos' remark (1964:
       125): "The speaker gets so deeply involved that he forgets where he is
       as he speaks, and tends to place himself rather at the scene he is
       narrating...." See also Langacker (1978: 868f).

18.   The idea of the eyewitnessing function can be found in the literature
       from as early as Jespersen (1924: 258): "The speaker in using [the
       dramatic present] steps outside the frame of history, visualizing and
       representing what happened in the past as if it were present before his
       eyes" up to Quirk et al. (1985: 181): "The historic present describes the

past as if it is happening now: it conveys something of the dramatic immediacy of an eye-witness account."

19.   The argument was originally presented by Grewendorf (1984: 229) with *Früher bin ich noch optimistisch* versus *Früher war ich noch optimistisch*. The first sentence is starred by Grewendorf; I prefer the convention of placing a question mark if a plausible interpretation is not available.

20.   See also in this connection sentences (1)-(4) and (6)-(9). It might be argued that the uninterpretability of (2)-(4) and (7)-(9) is due to the requirement that coordinated finite verbs have to be of the same "tense" class, regardless of the adverbial with temporal reference under which the coordination is construed; witness sentence (21).

21.   The adverbs *nu* and *toen* can function as demonstrative, relative or free relative adverbs. See for example the uses of *toen* in (1)-(3):

 (1)   *toen* used as a demonstrative adverb:
        Toen vertrok Jan.
        'Then Jan was leaving.'
 (2)   *toen* used as a relative adverb in the subordinate clause, and as a demonstrative adverb in the main clause:
        Toen Jan vertrok, toen besloot Marie te blijven.
        lit. When Jan was leaving, then Marie decided to stay.
 (3)   *toen* used as a free relative adverb:
        Toen Jan vertrok, besloot Marie te blijven.
        'When Jan was leaving, Marie decided to stay.'

Toen can be used as a demonstrative for modifying the nonfinite part of the perfect-tense formation as in sentence (4), but used as a relative it cannot normally modify either the nonfinite or the finite part; witness (26b):

 (4)   *Toen is Jan vertrokken.*
        lit. Then Jan has left.
        'Then Jan left.'

In very particular cases the perfect tense is compatible with the free relative adverb *toen* specifying the time of the event mentioned by means of the main verb (Paardekooper 1986: 318), as Albert Sassen pointed out to me:

 (5)   A: *Wanneer kan dat dan geweest zijn?*
             'When can it have been?'
        B: *Toen je geslaagd ben, weet je nog wel!*
             lit. When you have passed, don't you remember!
             'When you passed, don't you remember!'

22.   For the sake of completeness we should also consider the following sentences:

 (1)   a.   *Toen Jan vertrok, besloot Marie te blijven.*
             lit. At that time in the past at which Jan was leaving, Marie decided to stay.
        b.   *Toen Jan vertrokken was, besloot Marie te blijven.*
             lit. At that time in the past at which Jan had left, Marie decided to stay.

      c.   *Toen Jan zou vertrekken, besloot Marie te*
            blijven.
            lit. At that time in the past at which Jan was to
            leave, Marie decided to stay.

(2)   a.   *?Toen Jan vertrok, besluit Marie te blijven.*
            lit. At that time in the past at which Jan was
            leaving, Marie decides to stay.

      b.   *?Toen Jan vertrokken was, besluit Marie te*
            blijven.
            lit. At that time in the past at which Jan had
            left, Marie decides to stay.

      c.   *?Toen Jan zou vertrekken, besluit Marie te*
            blijven.
            lit. At that time in the past at which Jan was to
            leave, Marie decides to stay.

In the case of the (a-c) sentences of (2) the cause of the uninterpretability might be found in the combination of the entire *toen*-clause and the present tense in the main clause, as becomes apparent from the perfect interpretability of the (a-c) sentences of (1). However, it could be argued that clauses connected by temporal connectives (relative adverbs) can never differ in tense (cf. Ritchie 1979: 113), so the sentences of (2) would be odd anyhow. But in Dutch this regularity does not hold absolutely in the case of the perfect; witness (3)-(4):

(3)   *Toen ik je gisteren sprak, heb ik je vergeten te*
        zeggen dat ik niet zal kunnen komen.
        lit. When I had a word with you yesterday, I
        have forgotten to say that I will be unable to
        come.

(4)   *Ze is met roken gestopt toen ze wist dat ze in*
        verwachting was.
        lit. She has quit smoking once she knew that
        she was pregnant.

23.   The use of the present tense which is characteristic of captions can be seen as a variant of the local deixis use (termed *analogical deixis* by Klein 1978; 1983), e.g. when pointing to a map one says: *Here is my house* (Klein 1983: 289).

24.   One can observe that the "orientation time" for *zodra* 'as soon as' in (23) consists in the event of getting the permission, and one might conclude that *zodra*, used as a "relative adverb", is an anaphorical rather than a deictic element. But this would cause a purely artificial distinction between the occurrence of *zodra* in (23) and e.g. its occurrence in (22), where the "orientation" is given by the speech time.

25.   See, for example, Janssen (1975: 11), Hawkins (1978: 180), Du Bois (1980: 232ff, 243, 273).

26.   With regard to the problem of delimiting the regions of actual and disactual referential concern compare Klein's (1983: 290) investigation of where the region of "here" ends and the region of "there" starts.

27.   All these uses of the present tense have past tense counterparts in both Dutch and English (even the gnomic use; witness *Faint heart never won fair lady*).

28. The situation whereby both a single event and a habitual or generic etc.
     event can be expressed by means of the same words is comparable with
     cases like *The beaver builds dams*, which can be read as concerning one
     specific beaver or the class of beavers in general. The relation between
     such readings might be explained by using pragmatic principles (cf.
     Nunberg 1978: 172ff; Declerck 1987: 148ff).
29. Other differences between past and perfect in Dutch are presented in
     Janssen (1989c).
30. See for other illustrations of this use, with regard to English, Lakoff
     (1970) and with regard to German, Fuchs (1988: 13f).
31. As Harweg (1975) points out, a "Hörensagenerzähler" lit.
     'hearsayspeaker' strongly prefers perfect to past in German.
32. See also Comrie (1976: 108ff); with regard to Turkish, see Slobin &
     Aksu (1982).
33. Compare the contrastive examples presented by Quirk et. al. (1985:
     192):
     (1)   *Where did you put my purse?*
     (2)   *Where have you put my purse?*
     The comment runs as follows: "The purpose of both of these questions
     may be to find the purse; but in [1] the speaker seems to ask the
     addressee to remember a past action; while in [2] the speaker
     apparently concentrates on the purse's present whereabouts."
     See Leech (1987) for a mine of excellent information on different uses
     of past and perfect.
34. A related view was already presented by Diver (1963) and more
     recently by Rauh (1983). However, their tense analysis is time based.
35. Klein (1983: 286) lucidly shows that one can refer to entities with a
     definite pronoun without knowing their identity; he starts by giving the
     reader this task:
     "Close your eyes and imagine a little red square. Fine. You are reading
     again, I presume. Now, keep the square, close your eyes again (not yet)
     and imagine a second, identical square beside it (now). Now you can
     open your eyes again."
     His comment runs as follows: "The two squares only exist in your
     imagination. No one but you knows their exact size or their exact
     colour. But I can refer to them. I can say, for example, *Think them
     away.* Then *them* means 'the two little red squares which I asked you to
     imagine.'"
36. For a different view, see Kirsner (1987: 81), who claims "that Dutch
     demonstratives are *instructions to pay attention* rather than *descriptions
     of location*".
37. When rejecting the near/far characterization with regard to the Dutch
     demonstratives, Kirsner (1987: 81) refers to Wierzbicka's (1980: 37)
     argument: *This tooth hurts* does not communicate the message 'The
     tooth which is nearest to me hurts'.
38. Of course, the speaker can actually be in Montreal in the case of the
     here-version, but he need not be for an appropriate use of the sentence.
     See Fuchs (1988: 15) for a different explanation of similar sentences.
39. We should not overlook the possibility that the consecutive and closely
     connected sentences are phrased from the same vantage point.

Compare the following example, in which *komt* is substituted by *zal komen*:

(1)   *Oostberlijnse grenswachten kijken naar een*
       bulldozer die vrijdagnacht een deel van de Muur
       sloopt. Op deze plek zal *nog een grensovergang*
       komen *tussen Oost- en West-Berlijn.*
       'East German border guards watch a bulldozer
       which is pulling down part of the Wall on
       Friday night. Another border crossing point
       between East and West Berlin will be opened
       on this site.'

The vantage point of the present *zal* 'will' coincides - obviously not in a chronological respect - with the vantage point of the present forms in the first one, namely the situation of observing the photograph. The whole text can be viewed as for example a caption in a book recording the memorable days of *glasnost* and *perestroika* with a series of sequential photos. The relevant vantage point of the present-tense form *zal* 'will' is now apparently the situation of the event displayed on the photograph. The caption can be seen as phrased from the situation in which it is evident that the border crossing point will be installed consequent to the demolition of the concerning part of the Wall. Here we have a perfect parallel with the "historical present" and "historical future" as in text (13).

An example of a case in point with the present-tense form *zal* 'will' is the following newspaper caption under a photograph showing a moment of action in a soccer game (*De Volkskrant* 14 March 1988):

(2)   *Rob Witschge haalt uit. De Bossche-doelman*
       Van Grinsven zal de bal over de zijlijn werken.
       'Rob Witschge takes a swing at the ball. The
       Bossche-keeper van Grinsven will deflect the
       ball across the sideline.'

40.   Leech (1987: 38f) even records subtle differences between past and perfect in the varieties of American English (AE) and British English (BE), namely the distinction between *She just arrived* (AE) and *She has just arrived* (BE, also AE) versus *She cut her hands* (AE) and *She has cut her hands* (BE). For similar observations with regards to German, see e.g. ten Cate (1989).

References

Abraham, Werner & Theo A.J.M. Janssen (eds.)
    1989   *Tempus-Aspekt-Modus: Die lexikalischen und grammatischen Formen*
                in der Germania. Tübingen: Niemeyer.
Allen, Robert L.
    1966   *The verb system of present-day American English.* The Hague: Mouton.

Andersson, Sven-Gunnar
1989   "Zur Interaktion von Temporalität, Modalität, Aspektualität und Aktionsart bei den nichtfuturischen Tempora im Deutschen, Englischen und Schwedischen", in: Werner Abraham & Theo A.J.M. Janssen (eds.), 27-49.
Balk-Smit Duyzentkunst, Frida
1963   *De grammatische functie* [The grammatical function]. Groningen: Wolters.
Ballweg, Joachim
1984   "Praesentia non sunt multiplicanda praeter necessitatem", in: Gerhard Stickel (ed.), 243-261.
1988   *Die Semantik der deutschen Tempusformen.* Düsseldorf: Schwann.
Bauer, Gero
1967   "Historisches Präsens und Vergegenwärtigung des epischen Geschehens: Ein erzähltechnischer Kunstgriff Chaucer's", *Anglia* 85: 138-160.
Bolinger, Dwight L.
1947   "More on the present tense in English", *Language* 23: 434-436.
Casparis, Christian P.
1975   *Tense without time: The present tense in narration.* Bern: Francke.
Comrie, Bernard
1976   *Aspect.* Cambridge: Cambridge University Press.
Declerck, Renaat
1987   "A puzzle about generics", *Folia Linguistica* 21: 143-153.
Dinsmore, John
1987   "Mental spaces from a functional perspective", *Cognitive Science* 11: 1-21.
Diver, William
1963   "The chronological system of the English verb", *Word* 19: 141-181.
Donnellan, Keith S.
1978   "Speaker references, descriptions and anaphora", in: Peter Cole & Jerrold M. Saddock (eds.), *Syntax and semantics.* Vol. 9. *Pragmatics.* New York: Academic Press, 47-68.
Du Bois, John W.
1980   "Beyond definiteness: the trace of identity in discourse", in: Wallace L. Chafe (ed.), *The pear stories: Cognitive, cultural, and linguistic aspects of narrative production.* Norwood: Ablex, 203-274.
Ehrich, Veronika
1982   "*Da* and the system of spatial deixis in German", in: Jürgen Weissenborn & Wolfgang Klein (eds.), *Here and there: Crosslinguistic studies on deixis and demonstration.* Amsterdam: Benjamins, 43-63.
Ehrich, Veronika & Heinz Vater (eds.)
1988   *Temporalsemantik.* Tübingen: Niemeyer.
Fabricius-Hansen, Cathrine
1986   *Tempus fugit.* Düsseldorf: Schwann.
Fauconnier, Gilles
1985   *Mental spaces: Aspects of meaning constructions in natural language.* Cambridge: MIT Press.
Fleischman, Suzanne
1989   "Temporal distance: A basic linguistic metaphor", *Studies in Language* 13: 1-50.

Fuchs, Anna
1988   "Dimensionen der Deixis im System der deutschen 'Tempora'", in:
            Veronika Ehrich & Heinz Vater (eds.), 1-25.
Grewendorf, Günther
1982   "Zur Pragmatik der Tempora im Deutschen", Deutsche Sprache 10:
            213-236.
1984   "Besitzt die deutsche Sprache ein Präsens?", in: Gerhard Stickel (ed.),
            224-242.
Harweg, Roland
1975   "Perfekt und Präteritum im gesprochenen Neuhochdeutsch: Zugleich
            ein Beitrag zur Theorie des nichtliterarischen Erzählens", Orbis 24:
            130-183.
Hawkins, John A.
1978   Definiteness and indefiniteness: A study in reference and grammaticality
            prediction. London: Croom Helm.
Heidolph Karl R. et al.
1981   Grundzüge einer deutschen Grammatik. Berlin: Akademie-Verlag.
Heringer, Hans J.
1983   "Präsens für die Zukunft", in: John Ole Askedal et al. (eds.),
            Festschrift für Laurits Saltveit. Oslo: Universiteitsforlaget, 110-126.
Hirtle, W.H.
1967   The simple and progressive forms: An analytical approach. Québec: Les
            Presses de l'Université Laval.
Hopper, Paul J. (ed.)
1982   Tense - aspect: Between semantics and pragmatics. Amsterdam:
            Benjamins.
Janssen, Theo A.J.M.
1975   "Possessieve constructies [Possessive constructions]", De Nieuwe
            Taalgids 68: 1-13.
1983   "Het temporele systeem van het Nederlands: Drie tijden en twee
            tijdscomposities [The temporal system in Dutch: Three tenses and two
            tense compositions]", Glot 6: 45-104.
1986   De betekenis van het Nederlands [The meaning of Dutch]. Amsterdam:
            VU Uitgeverij.
[1987]   [reprinted in: Forum der Letteren 28: 1-23].
1988   "Tense and temporal composition in Dutch: Reichenbach's 'point of
            reference' reconsidered", in: Veronika Ehrich & Heinz Vater (eds.),
            96-128.
1989a   "Tempus: Interpretatie en betekenis [Tense: Interpretation and
            meaning]", De Nieuwe Taalgids 82: 305-329.
1989b   "Die Hilfsverben werden (deutsch) und zullen (niederländisch): Modal
            oder temporal?", in: Werner Abraham & Theo A.J.M. Janssen (eds.),
            65-84.
1989c   "Preteritum of perfectum? O tempora, o sores! [Preterit or perfect? O
            tempora, o troubles]", Neerlandica Extra Muros 59: 50-60.
Jespersen, Otto
1924   The philosophy of grammar. London: Allen & Unwin.
1932   A modern English grammar on historical principles, Part IV: Syntax.
            Volume 3: Time and tense. London: Allen & Unwin.
Joos, Martin
1964   The English verb. Madison: University of Wisconsin Press.

Kirsner, Robert S.
1987   "What it takes to show whether an analysis 'fits'", in: Hermann
             Bluhme & Göran Hammarström (eds.), *Descriptio linguistica*.
             Tübingen: Narr, 76-113.
Klein, Wolfgang
1978   "Wo ist hier? Präliminarien zu einer Untersuchung der lokalen
             Deixis", *Linguistische Berichte* 58: 18-40.
1983   "Deixis and spatial orientation in route directions", in: Herbert L. Pick
             & Linda P. Acredolo (eds.), *Spatial orientation: Theory, research, and
             application*. New York: Plenum, 283-311.
Kollewijn, R.A.
1892   "Het systeem van de tijden der werkwoorden [The tense system]",
             Taal en Letteren 2: 141-147.
Koops, Aaldrik
1986   "Gebruiksgevallen van de 'onvoltooid tegenwoordige tijd' [Uses of the
             present tense]", *Forum der Letteren* 27: 122-128.
Lakoff, Robin
1970   "Tense and its relation to participants", *Language* 46: 838-849.
1974   "Remarks on *this* and *that*", *CLS* 10: 345-356.
Langacker, Ronald W.
1978   "The form and meaning of the English auxiliary", *Language* 54: 853-
             882.
1987   *Foundations of cognitive grammar*. Vol. 1. *Theoretical prerequisites*.
             Stanford: Stanford University Press.
Leech, Geoffrey N.
1987   *Meaning and the English verb*. 2nd ed. London: Longman.
Lenerz, Jürgen B.
1986   "Tempus und Pragmatik - oder: Was man mit Grice so alles machen
             kann", *Linguistische Berichte* 102: 136-154.
Lyons, John
1968   *Introduction to theoretical linguistics*. Cambridge: Cambridge
             University Press.
1977   *Semantics* II. Cambridge: Cambridge University Press.
McCoard, Robert W.
1978   *The English perfect: Tense-choice and pragmatic inferences*.
             Amsterdam: Benjamins.
Nunberg, Geoffrey D.
1978   *The pragmatics of reference*. Bloomington: University of Indiana
             Linguistics Club.
Paardekooper, Piet C.
[1986]   *Beknopte ABN-syntaksis* [Concise syntax of Standard Dutch].
             Eindhoven.
Paprotté, Wolf
1988   "A discourse perspective on tense and aspect in Standard Modern
             Greek and English", in: Brygida Rudzka-Ostyn (ed.), 447-505.
Quirk, Randolph et al.
1985   *A comprehensive grammar of the English language*. London: Longman.
Rauh, Gisa
1983   "Tenses as deictic categories: An analysis of English and German
             tenses", in: Gisa Rauh (ed.), *Essays on deixis*. Tübingen: Narr, 229-275.

Ritchie, Graeme D.
1979   "Temporal clauses in English", *Theoretical Linguistics* 6: 87-115.
Roloff, Hans
1921   Das praesens historicum im Mittelenglischen. [Unpublished Ph.D.
            Dissertation, University of Giessen.]
Rudzka-Ostyn, Brygida (ed.)
1988   *Topics in cognitive linguistics*. Amsterdam: Benjamins.
Schopf, Alfred
1987   "The past tense in English", in: Alfred Schopf (ed.), *Essays on tensing
            in English*. Vol. 1. *Reference time, tense and adverbs*. Tübingen:
            Niemeyer, 177-220.
Slobin, Dan I. & Aylan A. Aksu
1982   "Tense, aspect, and modality in the use of the Turkish evidential", in:
            Paul J. Hopper (ed.), 185-200.
Stickel, Gerhard (ed.)
1984   *Pragmatik in der Grammatik: Jahrbuch 1983 des Instituts für deutsche
            Sprache*. Düsseldorf: Schwann.
Talmy, Leonard
1988   "The relation of grammar to cognition", in: Brygida Rudzka-Ostyn
            (ed.), 165-205.
ten Cate, Abraham P.
1989   "Präsentische und präteritale Tempora im deutsch-niederländischen
            Sprachvergleich", in: Werner Abraham & Theo A.J.M. Janssen (eds.),
            133-154.
Tobin, Yishai
1988   "Modern Hebrew tense: A study of the interface of objective and
            subjective spatio-temporal and perceptual deictic relation", in:
            Veronika Ehrich & Heinz Vater (eds.), 52-80.
Twaddell, W. Freeman
1960   *The English verb auxiliaries*. Providence: Brown University Press.
Vennemann, Theo
1987   "Tempora   und   Zeitrelation   im   Standarddeutschen",
            Sprachwissenschaft 12: 234-249.
Wallace, Stephen
1982   "Figure and ground: The interrelationships of linguistic categories", in:
            Paul J. Hopper (ed.), 201-223.
Waugh, Linda R.
1975   "A semantic analysis of the French tense system", *Orbis* 24: 436-485.
1987   "Marking time with the passé composé: Toward a theory of the
            perfect", *Lingvisticae Investigationes* 11: 1-47.
Weinrich, Harald
1964   *Tempus, besprochene und erzählte Welt*. Stuttgart: Kohlhammer.
Wierzbicka, Anna
1980   *Lingua mentalis: The semantics of natural language*. New York:
            Academic Press.

Articles in translation:
An exercise in cognitive linguistics

Elżbieta Tabakowska

1. Preliminaries

Looking for equivalents of articles in language that do not possess them as a separate grammatical category has long been considered a promising task by linguists of varying orientations. For notoriously articleless languages like Polish, lists of proposed equivalents include such heterogeneous entities as demonstrative and indefinite pronouns, lexical items defined as "referring expressions", sentence stress, word order and, finally, "context of situation", an often shapeless container used to dispose of all troublesome cases which resist attempts at rigorous classification. Most textbooks as well as contrastive studies are based on the assumption that the system of articles in languages like English is governed by grammatical rules which can be formulated and, consequently, memorized to good advantage by language learners, translators and everybody else. Inadequacy of the approach manifests itself in the inadequacy of the resulting performance.

One of the recent publications which appeared on the Polish market, Douglas-Kozłowska's *The articles in Polish-English translation* (1988), disappeared from the bookshops in a few days. The few who managed to get a copy must have been disappointed to find out that, like her predecessors, the author deals, albeit extensively, with several "textbook" categories only; she does not consider any of the problems of usage that torment learners and translators whose native language has "no articles". On the other hand, having assumed that articles cannot be learned, native teachers of English assume that foreigners simply have to make errors and consistently "correct articles" in their advanced learner's speech and writing in a way that leaves them even more baffled. What the teacher considers an error is frequently only an interpretational difference which merely reflects the possiblity of alternative views on reality.

Attempts to formulate explicit rules of article use within systems of (formal) semantics, notably Russell's theory of definite descriptions and its subsequent modifications (Strawson, Donnellan, Grice), as well as certain pragmatically oriented theories in which conditions of article use are relativized either to "shared knowledge" or to a set of possible worlds (notably Hawkins 1978), are only able to cover some cases of article use - mainly those which result from convention or are required by textual cohesion (e.g. coreference and anaphora). Predictably, these are the cases that make up the bulk of textbook examples, even though they constitute but a small fraction of the total usage.

Yet it has also been repeatedly pointed out that the very *raison d'être* of articles, i.e. the notion of (in)definiteness, is a conceptual category and as such it is independent of grammatical theory (cf. Pickering 1981: 1). Like designation and reference, it is first of all a matter of thought and action, and only secondarily a matter of language (cf. the analogous treatment of metaphor in Lakoff & Johnson 1988: 182), and may but need not be grammaticalized. Often neglected in older sources, (in)definiteness has been considered a "semantic category" in recent works by Polish linguists who emphasize its subjective character: "charakterystyka referencyjna obiektów, o których mowa w tekście, jest aktem świadomej intencji komunikatywnej nadawcy tekstu" ['the referential characteristics of objects spoken about in a text is an act of conscious communicative intention of the speaker'] (Topolińska 1984: 311), and as such, it necessarily proves to be "wielkością subiektywną" ['of subjective value'] (Topolińska 1984: 311). It is interesting to observe that this subjective view is applied to an analysis of Polish, where the lack of formal cues systematically results in potential discrepancies between the interpretations intended by the speaker and those actually chosen by the hearer. In fact, Benveniste's *subjectivité* as an intrinsic property of natural language is now generally recognized to be "of the greatest importance" (Lyons 1977: 739) for grammarians; apart from modality, deixis and reference are considered its main domains (cf. Lyons 1981).

Although, to the best of my knowledge, the use of articles has not yet been fully explored within the general framework of cognitive linguistics, the cognitive approach, with its emphasis on the speaker's conceptual freedom and the resulting subjectivity of linguistic expressions, seems for this purpose particulary promising.

2.   Assumptions

The analysis presented in this paper is based on the following assumptions:

(1)   As a notion, (in)definiteness is defined in terms of *interactional* (rather than *intrinsic*) features, namely identifiability, accessibility and recoverability (cf. Beaugrande & Dressler 1983: 151), which implies its basically subjective nature. It must be defined relative to the observer rather than be considered as inherent to the thing that is observed. Hence:

(2)   Article use (in English) is to a large extent conditioned by parameters of scene construal as defined in Langacker (1983: 46 and 1987: 116ff), viz. attention, selection, figure/ground organization, viewpoint (perspective) and the levels of specificity and/or schematicity of reference.

(3)   In English, changes involving the parameters just listed result in corresponding changes in the use of articles. In Polish, they may, but need not, also condition the grammatical structure. The use of lexical markers (pronouns and "referring expressions") in order to activate, for the sake of the addressee, the interactional features ascribed to (in)definite entities either in the physical space or in the "space of discourse" (cf. Lyons 1973) certainly deserves a study of its own. However, at this point I would like to offer a fairly tentative fragmentary discussion of the way in which English and Polish handle the above parameters of scene construal. In Polish, the means at the speaker's disposal (apart from sentence stress and/or intonation, which I will not consider here) are word order and "context of situation" (cf. Szwedek 1974, Topolińska 1984: 311). In this connection, two questions arise. First, what happens in those cases in which syntactic position seems to be irrelevant for the definite/indefinite distinction (cf. Szwedek 1974: 219)? Second, what is the "context of situation" that influences the interpretation of unmarked expressions (Topolińska 1984: 301ff)?

However, since my chief interest is interlingual translation, I would like to look for an answer to yet another question: namely, do differences in linguistic conventions influence the way in which a scene construed by an original author is reconstrued in another language by a bilingual translator?

3. Data

As a sample text, I have chosen an extract from Stanisław Lem's novel *Wizja lokalna*, quoted *in extenso* in the Appendix below. The choice was conditioned by the overtly imagelike character of the text. The paragraph makes up an image in an almost literal sense and enhances the informative aspect of definiteness (exophora), with the cohesive aspect (endophora) being greatly reduced (on the distinction between the two aspects, see Beaugrande & Dressler 1983: 151, fn.12). Markers of text cohesion are grammaticalized and rule-governed in both languages (e.g. the classical rule of "prior mention" for the definite article in English vs. unstressed demonstrative pronoun in postposition in Polish); these linguistic conventions can actually be "learned", which makes them totally uninteresting.

The text was translated into English by two bilingual native speakers of English; two other translations into French (as an instance of a different article language) were subsequently added, to verify and possibly corroborate some of the resulting observations.

4. Analysis

An analysis of all the occurrences of articles in the resulting translations would be too tedious for the reader; therefore I will limit the following discussion to cases which illustrate the points under consideration.

4.1. Viewpoint and perspective

It has frequently been observed (cf. Lyons 1977: chap. 15; Langacker 1983: 33; Lakoff & Johnson 1988: *passim*) that in language use reference point is prototypically equated with the speaker ("ego orientation", or "speaker perspective", cf. also the egocentric use of articles by English-speaking children in Maratsos 1976, or the use of non-standard egocentric demonstrative *taki* 'such' in Polish in Miodunka 1974: 55). Accordingly, the default reading of the analyzed text would require the assumption that the point of view is that of the speaker (or narrator), and obviously not that of the author himself. Yet the application of the transfer principle, where the speaker mentally adopts the vantage point of his addressee (cf. Langacker 1983: 48f, 1987: 140), is encouraged by the appearance in the text of the second *dramatis persona*: *ty* 'you', grammaticalized in the verb forms, familiar singular (cf. the opposition between *tu* and *vous* in French). Like the English *you*, the second person singular may also be used in Polish as a generalized impersonal form; in Lem's text, however, the probability of this interpretation is reduced by the occurrence of dialogic, or polyphonic, expressions which reconstruct within the text some elements of a full-fledged dialogue (e.g. the colloquial *ot* 'here' (line 2) or *proszę* 'well' (line 15), which are both verbalizations of a pointing gesture).

Thus, while for the speaker the scene (image of Switzerland) is mentally accessible and recoverable and consequently calls for definite reference, from the point of view of the *you* it is only gradually construed, with particular entities being just activated. The first image that allows for alternate construals resulting from a particular choice of the vantage point is the view from the window, which offers no grammatical clue as to the viewer; there is no overt verb of seeing, and the only indication of the perspective is the non-proximic demonstrative *tam* 'there', suggesting a (temporarily) external position of the observer in relation to the scene. The possibility of alternate construals is shown by the discrepancy between the two English translations: E2 immediately specifies the viewpoint as that of the *you*, which results in indefinite specification of both NP's (*alpine fields, lilac cows*, line 4), while E1 shifts from ego orientation to the *you* perspective only after the visual field has been established (*the alpine meadow, mauve cows*, lines 3-4).

Interestingly, while F1 establishes the field by definite "category reference" to *les pâturages alpestres* 'the alpine meadows' (line 4), and then adds the unexpected *des vaches couleur lilas* 'mauve cows' (line 4) as ground elements, thus building up the setting from the viewpoint of *tu*, F2 consistently assumes the ego perspective.

4.2.   Perspective: subjectivity and figure/ground organization

As the scene develops, there is a change in the relationship between the scene and the observer; the prototypicality, i.e. the ego perspective as a shared assumption of both the narrator and the reader, is established by the verb *siadasz* 'you sit down' (line 8). So far, the observer was only changing his position in space, "observing" things in a fairly objective sense. (Note the culture-induced addition of the specification *down* in line 6.) From now on, he becomes an active participant in the event. It is he who bites the toast and smells the honey. It is he who perceives the silence and (subjectively) qualifies it as "divine". It is true that the canonical SV word order of the two sentences in:

(1)   *grzanki chrupią*   ...   *miód   pachnie*
       (line 8)
       toasts   snap   honey   smells
E1:   the toast snaps   ...   the honey has an odor ...
       (lines 9-10)
E2:   the toast is crisp   ...   the honey smells ...
       (lines 9-10),

which reflects the prototypical "topic first, comment second" structure, conveys no clues as to the identifiability of the two entities. On the other hand, the VS word order of

(2)   *chrupią   grzanki*   ...   *pachnie   miód*
       snap   toasts   smells   honey

is an instance of the natural order: the sound and the odor become registered earlier than their respective sources. This, however, is not tantamount to definiteness - all NP's in (1) and (2) may be either definite or indefinite.

The OVS structure of:

(3)   *błoga   ciszę   solennie punktuje*
       divine-ACC   silence-ACC   solemnly punctuates
       tykot   szwajcarskich   zegarów   (lines 9-10)
       tic-toc   Swiss-GEN   clocks-GEN
E1:   The divine silence is broken solemnly by the tick-tock of
       Swiss clocks (lines 10-11)
E2:   The sublime silence is marked out solemnly by the tick-tock
       of the Swiss clocks (lines 10-11),

which illustrates the principle of topic-fronting, brings about topicality in the sense of "aboutness". As in (1) and (2), this need not be tantamount to the definiteness of the topicalized entity. Where, then, do the informants get the idea of definiteness? The entities in question in (1) and (3) are interpreted as "definite" because the reader knows that the toast is heard to crunch only when chewed and the honey found to smell of alpine herbs only when sniffed. He also knows that it is the observer-participant who does the chewing and the sniffing. And it is he who also perceives and qualifies the silence. Therefore, seen from the observer-participant's perspective, all these entities must be identified (i.e. made definite) before the predication can be made. In other words, what makes them definite for my English and French-speaking translators is the consistent subjectivization of the scene.

Topicality partially involves what Langacker (1987: 122) defines as figure/ground organization; selection of such factors of a scene as are subsequently dealt with implies their arrangement, so that some are considered pivotal and shown against a setting made up by others. It seems that the main function of topicalization consists in establishing the figure/ground arrangement - pairs of canonical and topicalized structures illustrate their mutual reversal. Thus in the OVS structure of (3) the tick-tock of the clocks is the figure perceived against the ground of the silence, and in:

(4)   *z   cienkiej   porcelany   dymi   szwajcarska*
       from   fine-GEN   china-GEN   smokes   Swiss
       czekolada (lines 5-6)
       chocolate
E1:   the Swiss chocolate smokes in delicate porcelain cups
       (lines 6-7)
E2:   the Swiss chocolate is steaming in the delicate china
       (lines 6-7),

the chocolate is selected as the figure, with the china functioning as an element of the ground.

Yet the figure/ground distinction cannot be considered as tantamount to the definite/indefinite opposition. However, it would be justifiable to assume that elements of the ground might be construed as less specific - or more schematic - than figures. In fact, Langacker (1987: 126ff) seems to view indefiniteness as a feature characteristic of ground construal. On the other hand, it is also conceivable that the speaker will compose his figure/ground arrangement of elements that are well specified, i.e. definite. The possibility of this alternative is indeed illustrated in the translations. While E1 (like F1) chooses not to specify the china (indefinite plural), E2 (like F2) uses the definite article, thus emphasizing the identifiability of the ground.

The treatment of the second instance of topicalization (3) is even more revealing (apart from the obvious choice of the passive; for the passive/active voice opposition and figure/ground reversal, see Langacker 1983: 49). Within the hierarchy of the figure/ground organization, the clocks can be seen as providing the ground for the figure, the tick-tock that breaks the silence. While E2 (and this time also F1 and F2) considers them as particular clocks identifiable by the observer, E1 treats them as indefinite members of a category.

4.3. Abstraction

One of the main functions of articles, emphasized in nearly all traditional taxonomies (e.g. Jackendoff 1972, Karttunen 1976, Maratsos 1976, 1979), is the indication of the level of abstraction, i.e. specificity, or schematicity, of reference. The level is established subjectively, by the speaker who construes (or reconstrues) a given scene; in our text, this is illustrated by the reference to *Neue Züricher Zeitung*. The canonical order of the original Polish sentence:

(5)   *Rozwijasz   świeżutką   "Neue Züricher Zeitung"* (line 10)
        (you) open   very fresh-ACC NZZ
E1:   You unfurl your fresh NZZ (lines 11-12)
E2:   You open up a brand new NZZ (line 12)

allows for alternate interpretations, which indeed is manifested in the English and French translations. Objectivization is possible again. From the position of an external observer, reference can be made either to an unspecified copy of NZZ (E2, and also F2) or to a "typical representative of a class" (Douglas-Kozłowska 1988: 226; cf. the bias of F1, translated by an inhabitant of Switzerland, who later explained his choice by saying that NZZ is "known to everyone there"). Consistent subjectivization of the scene gave rise to E1, where the possessive pronoun expresses the perspective of an observer-participant without necessarily implying the definiteness of reference.

The other discrepancy of this kind, i.e. reference to (the) Swiss cheese:

(6)   *szwajcarski   ser   lśni   gorliwie* (line 6)
        Swiss-NOM   cheese-NOM   shines   eagerly
E1:   Swiss cheese shines eagerly (line 7)
E2:   the Swiss cheese is glistening eagerly (line 7)

in E1 and E2 is even more directly indicative of the possibilities of alternative scene construals. While E2 "sees" a specific quality and quantity of the substance, E1 is satisfied with more abstract reference to substance, with less emphasis on "bounding" (cf. the discussion of bounding in Langacker 1987: 204ff).

4.4. Convention

If we assume (following Lewis 1969) that "convention" in language use is characterized by expectation, regularity and preference, then in our text the "textbook" instances of conventionalization in the use of indefinite and definite articles consist in

1. for indefiniteness: general specification which does not involve identification of a particular class element (cf. the opposition between reference and designation in Langacker 1987: 187; see also Beaugrande & Dressler 1983: 155ff).
2. for definiteness: expression of the "be a part of" relation traditionally defined as the "entailment *the*".

The "noncontroversial" instances of the article use in the English (and French) translations fall within one or the other of the two categories: *the morning, the window, the dining room, the holes [of Emmenthaler], the front page* and *the cantons [of Switzerland],* but *a telescope/diminishing lense,* and *a Swiss clock.*

Yet not even here does convention reign supreme - the translations differ as to whether *bombs* and *casualties* should be interpreted as being "part of" *wars,* or whether they might be conceived of as resulting from, for instance, terrorist actions.

In neither case does the Polish text offer any grammatical clues that might resolve that alternative.

4.5. Instantaneousness

The translations of the text - notably the English ones - illustrate yet another property of the process of scene construal: the observer may look at entities and events as building up an instantaneous configuration, but he can also view the scene as an ever present, recurring pattern. To use a rather trivial metaphor, the difference would parallel that between describing a painting while actually looking at it, as compared to its description, so to speak, *in absentia*, such as in a museum catalog. This, of course, is a distinction that has traditonally been relegated to the chapter on tenses, notably the opposition between simple and continuous tenses.

But the contribution of articles is obvious in a comparison of the two English translations. While the scene in E1 is consistently "recurrent", in E2 it is consistently "instantaneous". Indeed, the Simple Present in E1 contrasts with the Present Continuous in E2 (*smokes* vs. *is steaming*, line 6; *shines* vs. *is glistening*, line 7), but the opposition of tenses is accompanied by significant differences in article use. The "recurrent" picture of *Swiss cheese* in E1 allows for differences in specification on every individual occasion - hence the lack of determination, as opposed to a more natural need for bounding in E2. The possessive adjective in E2 *your fresh "NZZ"* (line 12) (apart from establishing perspective) stresses the habitual character of the action; the indefinite article in E2 *a brand new "NZZ"* (line 12) emphasizes the fact that on this particular occasion the paper cannot yet be referred to as an entity identifiable to the speaker-observer; he has just picked it up. Similarly, the ground *Swiss clocks* that break the silence in the particular situation that E2 describes becomes in E1 an abstract "type of entities", whose particular designates may well differ on different occasions. Within this category, perhaps the most interesting example is provided by the translation equivalents of:

(7)   *odkładasz   więc niedoczytaną   gazetę* (line 17)
         (you) put aside   so   unfinished-ACC   paper-ACC
E1:   you fold a newspaper that you never finish reading (lines 18-19)
E2:   you put aside the unfinished newspaper (18-19)

E2 conforms to the textbook rule of "prior mention": textual reference to an entity mentioned earlier requires definite determination. E1 breaks the rule (which at this point automatically ceases to exist) for the sake of conceptual consistency: on each occasion when his recurrent picture is brought into existence again, the speaker folds a different paper (another "typical representative" of the given class).

5.   Conclusions

To return to the two questions raised earlier, we can now say that

1. word order in Polish is indeed less indicative of the definite/indefinite distinction than is often thought; and
2. the "context of situation", considered decisive for the definite/indefinite distinction in Polish, can in fact be defined in terms of Langacker's parameters of scene construal.

In English these parameters are to a large extent grammaticalized, as their determination is the main function of articles. In Polish, as a rule, analogous grammaticalization does not occur (at least within the limited range covered by the present paper, which deliberately ignores certain crucial aspects of determination, as mentioned above). Predictably, the lack of conventional (decontextualized, cf. Langacker 1987: 63) units determining the parameters of scene construal results in potential interpretational discrepancies (cf. Topolińska 1984: 311). Hence apart from (but often also according to) the communicative intentions of the speaker, a Polish text offers the addressee more freedom, especially in terms of the degree of its subjectivization or objectivization. Although certain aspects may be signalled by grammatical means (recall the obvious connection between topicalization and figure/ground organization above), they are mainly determined through the interaction of all constituents of the text.

The advantage - and requirement - of grammaticalization of the interactional features of determination is the mandatory "narrowing" of the scene as construed by the speaker, followed by the parallel "narrowing" of its reconstrual by the addressee.

It could perhaps be argued that an attempt to look at articles from the point of view of cognitive linguistics does not change people's basic intuitions, as reflected in the many works on the subject. Yet it certainly makes it possible to understand a little better the cognitive mechanisms underlying the usage. These are activated each time Chomsky's "reasonable procedure for translation" (i.e. not requiring extralinguistic information, Chomsky 1965: 30, fn.17) is proved impossible in confrontation with actual translation practice.

6. Relevance for translation

It is a thinly veiled platitude indeed to say that there can be no translation without interpretation. It is perhaps, less trivially, worth looking for an answer to the question of what "interpretation" is. I would like to believe that the analysis presented above constitutes a step towards such a goal.

Interpretation, or "understanding of the original", a necessary prerequisite to translation, can perhaps be seen as a reconstrual by the addressee of the scene structured by the speaker, involving in particular the determination of such parameters as perspective and level of abstraction. The inherently subjective character of this process, conditioned not only by grammar (i.e. structuring and symbolization of semantic content - cf. Langacker 1983, 1987) but also - or perhaps chiefly - by the imposition of the addressee's own focal adjustments, precludes the existence of translational algorithms to the same extent that it renders impossible any formulation of textbook rules (rather than principles) of language use.

The second step of the translational procedure consists in choosing, out of the repertoire offered by the target language, such expressions as the translator may consider appropriate for the actual conceptualization. It may happen - as in the case discussed in this paper - that the target language will show a higher degree of grammaticalization where the source language leaves more conceptual freedom and forces the translator to make choices. It helps if he is conscious of this fact, as it may often escape his attention; at best he can create "another image of the same situation" (Langacker 1987: 110), if only by reducing the number of images latent in the original portrayal of the scene.

Appendix

Polish (P)

1   Ostatecznie zdecydowałem się na Szwajcarię. Od dawna nosiłem w duszy jej obraz. Ot, wstajesz rano, podchodzisz w bamboszach do okna, a tam *alpejskie łąki*, *liliowe krowy z* wielkimi literami MILKA na bokach; słysząc ich pasterskie
5   dzwonki kroczysz do jadalni, gdzie *z cienkiej porcelany dymi szwajcarska czekolada*, a *szwajcarski ser lśni gorliwie*, bo prawdziwy ementaler zawsze się troszeczkę poci, *zwłaszcza w* dziurach, siadasz, *grzanki chrupią*, *miód pachnie alpejskimi ziołami*, a *błoga ciszę solennie punktuje tykot*
10   *szwajcarskich zegarów*. Rozwijasz *świeżutką* "Neue Züricher Zeitung", wprawdzie widzisz na pierwszej stronie wojny, bomby, liczby ofiar, ale takie dalekie to, *jakby za pomniejszającym szkłem*, bo wokół ład i cisza. Może i są gdzieś nieszczęścia, ale nie tu, w sercu terrorystycznego
15   niżu, proszę, na wszystkich stronicach kantony rozmawiają ze sobą przyciszonym bankowym dialektem, odkładasz więc

niedoczytaną   gazetę,   bo   skoro   wszystko   idzie   jak
w szwajcarskim zegarku, po cóż czytać?

English (E1)

1   Finally I chose Switzerland. I had carried its image in my
    heart for a long time. Well, you wake up in the morning and
    go slippered to the window. In the alpine meadow you see
    mauve cows with enormous letters MILKA branded on their
5   flanks. Hearing the tintinabulation of their bells, you glide
    down to the dining room, where the Swiss chocolate smokes in
    delicate   porcelain   cups.   Swiss   cheese   shines   eagerly,
    because real Emmenthaler always sweats a little, especially
    in the holes; you take your place, the toast snaps, the honey
10 has an odor of alpine herbs, the divine silence is broken
    solemnly by the tick-tock of Swiss clocks. You unfurl your
    fresh "NZZ", it is true that on the front page you read about
    wars, the bombs, the number of victims, but all of that is
    like looking through the wrong end of a telescope, because
15 around you there is only order and silence. Perhaps elsewhere
    there is misery, but not here, in the heart of the terrorist-
    depression. Well, in all the pages, the cantons whisper in
    a financial dialect, so you fold a newspaper that you never
    finish reading, because here everything works like a Swiss
20 clock - why read?

English (E2)

1   Finally I decided on Switzerland. For a long time I had had a
    mental image of the country. You get up in the morning, you
    go up to the window in your slippered feet, and there you
    have alpine fields, lilac cows with MILKA in big letters on
5   their sides. Hearing their shepherd's bells, you walk into
    the dining-room, where the Swiss chocolate is steaming in the
    delicate china, and the Swiss cheese is glistening eagerly,
    because real Emmenthaler is always perspiring a little,
    especially round the holes, you sit down, the toast is crisp
10 and the honey smells of alpine herbs, and the sublime silence
    is marked out solemnly by the tick-tock of the Swiss clocks.
    You open up a brand new "NZZ", there you do in fact find in
    page one wars, bombs and casualty numbers, but it is all so
    far away, as if under a diminishing lense, because all around
15 you there is peace and quiet. Perhaps there are calamities
    elsewhere, but not here, in the heart of the terrorist low,
    here we have, on all the pages, the cantons speaking to each
    other in a hushed banking dialect, so you put aside the
    unfinished newspaper, since if everything is like Swiss
20 clockwork, why bother reading?

French (F1)

1   Finalement, je me décidai pour la Suisse. Cela faisait
    longtemps que son image m'habitait. C'est le matin, tu te
    lèves, tu mets tes babouches, et t'approches de la fenêtre;

devant toi, les pâturages alpestres, des vaches couleur lilas
5   avec de grandes lettres MILKA sur les flancs; dans le
tintement des cloches, tu glisses vers la salle à manger où
le chocolat suisse fume dans une fine porcelaine et le
fromage suisse reluit irreprochablement, le veritable
Emmental transpirant toujours le moindre, surtout au fond
10   des trous; tu t'assieds, les toast crissent, le miel sent bon
les herbes des Alpes et le silence béni est cadencé par le
tic-tac des horloges suisses. Tu déplies la "NZZ" toute
fraîche, tu voies bien, certes, à la première page des
guerres, les bombes, les nombres de victimes, mais tout cela
15   est si loin de cet ordre et de ce silence qui t'entourent,
comme sous un verre rapetissant. Peut-être bien que le
malheur existe quelque part, mais pas ici, au coeur de la
dépression terroriste; tiens, on entend à toutes les pages le
chuchotement des cantons qui se parlent dans leur dialecte
20   bancaire; tu deposes alors le journal que tu n'as pas fini
de lire; a quoi bon lire, puisque tout fonctionne comme une
horloge suisse?

French (F2)

1   En fin de compte, je me suis décidé pour la Suisse. Depuis
longtemps déjà, je portais dans mon âme son image. Tu te
lèves le matin, tu t'approches en pantoufles à la fenêtre, et
là, les prés des Alpes, les vaches mauves avec des grosses
5   lettres MILKA sur les flancs; en écoutant leurs grelots, tu
te rends à la salle à manger, où fume le chocolat suisse dans
de la porcelaine fine, et le fromage suisse luit avec
empressement, car un vrai Emmental transpire tourjours un peu,
surtout dans les trous. Tu t'assieds, les toasts
10   croustillent, le miel embaume les herbes de la montagne, et le
silence béat ponctue le tic-tac des horloges suisses. Tu
ouvres une fraîche "NZZ", et bien que tu voies etalées sur la
première page des guerres, des bombes, de nombreuses
victimes, tout cela te semble si lointain, comme sous un
15   verre réduisant, car autour de toi tout est silence et ordre.
Peut-être, quelque part, il y a des malheurs, mais pas ici,
au coeur de la dépression terroriste: voilà que sur toutes
les pages les cantons dialoguent entre eux d'une voix douce,
en jargon bancaire, tu reposes ton journal sans l'achever, a
20   quoi bon le lire, si tout va bien comme dans une montre
suisse?

References

Beaugrande, Robert de & Wolfgang Dressler
    1983   *Introduction to text linguistics*. London: Longman.
Chomsky, Noam
    1965   *Aspects of the theory of syntax*. Cambridge: MIT Press.

Douglas Kozłowska, Christian
1988   *The articles in Polish-English translation*. Warszawa: Państwowe
            Wydawnictwo Naukowe.
Fletcher, Paul & Michael Garman (eds.)
1979   *Language acquisition: Studies in first language development*.
            Cambridge: Cambridge University Press.
Hawkins, John
1978   *Definiteness and indefiniteness: A study in reference and grammaticality
            prediction*. London: Croom Helm.
Jackendoff, Ray S.
1972   *Semantic interpretation in generative grammar*. Cambridge: MIT Press.
Karttunen, Lauri
1976   "Discourse referents", in: James D. McCawley (ed.), 383-387.
Lakoff, George & Mark Johnson
1988   *Metafory w naszym życiu*. (transl. P.T. Krzeszowski) Warszawa:
            Państwowe Wydawnictwo Naukowe.
Langacker, Ronald W.
1983   *Foundations of cognitive grammar*. Trier: LAUT.
1987   *Foundations of cognitive grammar: Theoretical prerequisites*. Stanford:
            Stanford University Press.
Lewis, David
1969   *Convention: A philosophical study*. Cambridge: Harvard University
            Press.
Lyons, John
1973   "Deixis as the source of reference", *Work in progress* 5. Edinburgh:
            Dept. of Linguistics, 92-115.
1977   *Semantics*. Cambridge: Cambridge University Press.
1981   *Language, meaning and context*. Bungay: Fontana Books.
Łozinska, Maria & Ludomir Przestraszewski
1988   *O francuskim rodzajniku i jego ekwiwalentach*. Warszawa: Wiedza
            Powszechna.
Maratsos, Michael P.
1976   *The use of definite and indefinite reference in young children: An
            experimental study of semantic acquisition*. Cambridge: Cambridge
            University Press.
1979   "Learning how and when to use pronouns and determiners", in: Paul
            Fletcher & Michael Garman (eds.), 225-240.
McCawley, James D. (ed.)
1976   *Syntax and semantics*. Vol.7. New York: Academic Press.
Miodunka, Władysław
1974   *Funkcje zaimków w grupach nominalnych współczesnej polszczyzny
            mówionej*. Warszawa: Polskie Wydawnictwo Naukowe.
Pickering, Michael
1981   "Definiteness as a unifying conceptual category in linguistics". [Paper
            presented at the 14th Annual Meeting of SLE, Copenhagen.]
Szwedek, Akeksander
1974   "A note on the relation between the article in English and word order
            in Polish", *Papers and Studies in Contrastive Linguistics* 2: part I, 213-
            220; part II, 221-225.
Topolińska, Zuzanna
1984   "Składnia grupy imiennej", in: Zuzanna Topolińska (ed.), 301-386.

Topolińska, Zuzanna (ed.)
1984   *Gramatyka współczesnego języka polskiego: Składnia*. Warszawa:
Państwowe Wydawnictwo Naukowe.

Source of text:

Lem, Stanisław
1982   *Wizja lokalna*. Kraków: Wydawnictwo Literackie.

What does it mean for a language to have no singular-plural distinction? Noun-verb homology and its typological implication

Yoshihiko Ikegami

0. Introduction

An important perspective offered by cognitive linguistics is that language is not as "arbitrarily" structured (and hence will not as readily lend itself to "formal" analysis) as might be imagined. Language, on the contrary, is very much "motivated" both in terms of the general cognitive capacities of the human beings who use it in their interaction with each other and their environment and in terms of the pragmatic goals they have in mind when they use it and which they intend to achieve effectively and efficiently by its use. The new perspective opens up a possibility that language not only can be described in terms of how it is structured but also can meaningfully be described in terms of why it is that it is so structured. The inquiry along this line has amply demonstrated, for example, that iconicity (together with metaphorization) plays a very basic role as a formative principle in the structure of language.

The purpose of the present paper is to suggest that the cognitive linguistic notion of language as in principle motivated can also profitably be employed in discussing the problem of "holistic" typology - the discussion of which has generally been avoided because of the apparent methodological difficulties involved.[1] We may assume that if language is motivated at all, it is motivated in an integral manner - that is, it will hardly be the case that language is motivated in one way in one part and in an entirely different way in some other part. There will plausibly be an integral principle of motivation recurring in the different parts of language. Such a principle, if definable for a particular language, will serve as a feature which typologically characterizes the language holistically. And if a set of such features, defined for various individual languages, can further be shown to be systematically correlated with each other and with certain cognitive (and perhaps perceptual) propencities of human beings, then we will have a viable theoretical basis for talking about a "holistic" typology in a meaningful way. The following discussion is intended to be illustrative of an approach along such lines.

1.   Construal in terms of "motion" and construal in terms of "transition"

In Ikegami (1989a), it is argued that when an entity is in motion through space, there are two contrastive ways of construing the situation, i.e. in terms of "motion" (or "change in locus") and in terms of "transition" (or "change in state"). The contrast is illustrated by a poem about "cranes flying over the lagoon toward the reedy shores". On one interpretation, the focus is on the flying cranes as they move (or change their locus) through the scene. On the other interpretation, the whole scene (involving the flying cranes) is in focus, so that the construal is in terms of the whole scene, which gradually changes as the cranes fly from one side of the scene to the other. It is suggested that the original text in Japanese is phrased in such a way as to be readily associated with the latter construal, while an English translation of the same passage readily evokes an image opting for the former interpretation.[2]

In order to give a clearer idea of the notional contrast in question, let me illustrate the same point with another concrete example. In *Yukiguni 'Snow Country'*, a novel by Yasunari Kawabata, the 1968 Nobel prize winner for literature, the opening sentence reads as follows:

Kunizakai no	*nagai*	*tonneru*	*o*	*nukeru*	*to,*
border of	long	tunnel	object	pass	when
yukiguni	*de atta.*				
snow-country	was				

An approximately literal translation of the sentence would be something like 'On passing through the long tunnel at the border, (it) was a snow country'. The sentence impresses the Japanese reader immediately as a beautiful prelude to what is about to follow in the novel, but the reaction of a Western reader who knows Japanese is typically one of bewilderment. He asks himself, "In the first half of the sentence there is a verb *nukeru* 'pass through'. But what is it that passed through (the tunnel)?" The sentence makes no mention of it. Also in the second half we are told that "(it) was a snow country". But what exactly is characterized as a "snow country" here is not made explicit.

Very interestingly, the sentence in question is rendered in the translation by the American Japanologist E. G. Seidensticker as 'The train came out of the long tunnel into the snow country'. The English sentence is quite explicit about the agent of *passing through the tunnel* - namely, the train, of which no mention is made in the Japanese original.

The image which Kawabata's sentence in question evokes in the Japanese reader is a sudden switch of the scene - from the rather dark, narrowly confined space in the tunnel to the wider bright perspective of the snow-covered landscape. It is true that a train is involved in the scene (as will be apparent from the ensuing description in the novel), but the train is not focused on, being merged (and eventually lost) in the whole scene. The representation in the Japanese original is made in terms of a change in state of the whole scene. The English translation, in contrast, singles out and focuses on a particular entity, a train in motion; the representation is in terms of a particular individuum undergoing a change in locus.

The article referred to above (Ikegami 1989a) discusses a number of linguistic expressions in English and Japanese which represent either of these two contrasting types of construal and suggests that there is a difference between the two languages as to which of the two types of construal is preferred: English tends towards the "change-in-locus" type, a construal in terms of "motion" or GOING/COMING, and Japanese towards the "change-in-state" type, a construal in terms of "transition" or BECOMING. Thus, faced with a situation to which either type of construal may be applicable, speakers of the two languages tend to behave differently. There is a tendential difference in their linguistic performance.

How can we bring these findings to bear on the problem of holistic typology? Two theoretical links have to be supplied: one concerning the theoretical justification of the pair of contrasting notions proposed and the other concerning the relationship between linguistic performance and lingustic structure.

First, it will not be difficult to see that there is nothing fortuitous about the pair of contrasting notions, "motion" (or "change in locus") and "transition" (or "change in state"). The pair, in fact, represents the "dynamic" counterpart (i.e. the entity in question is in motion) of what is already well known about the "figure"-"ground" relationship. Thus given a scene in which an entity at rest is located in a space, the scene can be construed either in terms of focusing on the particular entity and putting it in relief against the background or in terms of not focusing on the entity in question and letting it merge with the background. Similarly, given a scene in which an entity is in motion through a space, the scene can also be construed in either of the two analogous ways. There is clearly a parallelism between the two contrasts here - one applied to a static situation, the other to a dynamic situation. Integrating the two contrasts at a superordinate level, we propose, as an overall notion, a contrast between the "individuum" schema (with a well-defined boundary distinguishing it from its background and other entities) and the "continuum" schema (with no definite boundary distinguishing it from background and other entities). I assume that processing in terms of the "individuum" schema and processing in terms of the "continuum" schema are both justifiably rooted in human cognition

Second, let us recall one of the theses of cognitive linguistics, namely, that structure is iconic of the function it is supposed to perform. Most of the examples discussed in Ikegami (1989a) concern the preferential difference in the choice of expression forms between English and Japanese speakers at the level of performance. It is reasonable to assume, on the basis of the above thesis, that the structure of each language also iconically reflects the preferential difference in the ways in which the speakers of that language tend to perform. Specifically, we expect to find that English has structural features consonant with the "individuum" schema, while Japanese has structural features consonant with the "continuum" schema. If it is found that such is indeed the case, then the "individuum" schema and the "continuum" schema should qualify as useful parameters for a "holistic" typology. The following sections of the paper will be concerned with illustrating such typological considerations along the lines described above with special reference to Japanese.

2.   Noun-verb homology: construal in terms of the "individuum" schema vs. construal in terms of the "continuum" schema

In the discussion of the interpretation of the poem about flying cranes in Ikegami (1989a), there was a point I did not touch upon. This concerns the linguistic representation of the number of cranes involved. The noun in Japanese is not grammatically marked for singular or plural, and in fact, the English translation, 'The cranes go flying' (with *cranes* in the plural), is at best based on the interpretation which will most plausibly be associated with the kind of scene we have in the poem. In other words, there is nothing in the text of the Japanese poem itself which would exclude the translation, 'A crane goes flying'.

Now the point I would like to raise here is whether it is meaningful to ask why a language like Japanese does not have a number distinction for its nouns. Can such a question be legitimately discussed from a linguistic point of view? Our reaction, quite expectedly, will be rather skeptical. In fact, it does not seem to be clear at all what kind of argument one would have to develop in order to "prove" that the language in question lacks a singular-plural distinction for nouns. It would seem highly improbable that one could ever "explain" a feature of a language like the lack of distinction between singular and plural by invoking a principle which applies universally and which therefore has predictive power.

On the other hand, however, it does seem to me quite possible and very worthwhile to discuss a linguistic feature like the lack of number distinction for nouns in another way, namely, by trying to show that the existence of the linguistic feature in question is not entirely arbitrary in the language, but somehow motivated - by trying to show, in other words, that the feature is not there just by chance.

An exemplary way of arguing in this way is found in a certain type of language play in which one person poses an apparently unanswerable question and another is expected to give a clever reply. Suppose the one challenges the other with the question, "Why is it that Miss Armstrong is named *Armstrong*, when she is so meek and gentle?" Naturally, there is no principled way in which one can account for that being the case. The rule of the game, however, is that an answer will be considered adequate if it succeeds in producing an analogue of what is pointed out as peculiar in the question and thereby showing that what is being questioned is not at all an isolated instance, not something simply so by chance. By producing an analogue, that is, by pointing to the existence of a parallel instance, the challenged person shows that the very instance he is challenged about is not unique as the challenger claims it to be, and thereby relativizes the validity of the claim, and in so doing deprives the challenge of its force. Thus in the case of the particular question referred to above, an answer is called for like "For the same reason that young Mr. Whitehead is called *Whitehead*, despite the fact that he does not have a single white hair on his head".

In Japan, this kind of traditional language play is called "irrational questions and answers". It reminds us of what the French anthropologist Lévi-Strauss once referred to as *bricolage*.[3] Bricolage, according to Lévi-Strauss, is an account which applies reasonably well to a particular case in question and thus more or less serves some present, immediate purpose; it is, on the other hand, not a systematic and principled account applicable generally and predictively. It is thus an attempt at a motivated explanation, whose applicability, however, is highly constrained. Lévi-Strauss considers bricolage characteristic of what he calls *pensée sauvage*; it is "pre-scientific" as contrasted with the systematic account of maximally general applicability aimed at by modern science. Nevertheless, bricolage has interesting things to tell us in its own way. It tells us, above all, how the human mind naturally tends to work. If we consider, for instance, folk etymology as an example of bricolage related to language, we can readily see its relevance.

What we are in need of is a notion which will bridge the gap between simple bricolage and scientific explanation. It seems to me that a very good candidate for this can be found in the notion of "homology". In referring here to homology, I have particularly in mind its use in semiotics. Thus, if a term X behaves in a sphere A in the same way as another term Y behaves in a different sphere B, then we have an instance of such homology. A definition given by Titzmann in his book, *Strukturale Textanalyse* (1977), is somewhat more elaborate than the one just given:

> *Homologie* = Relation der Äquivalenz zwischen (mindestens) zwei (mindestens) zweiteiligen Relationen, die jeweils beliebige Terme derselben oder verschiedener Klassen verknüpfen. ...in einem Bereich A verhält sich also ein Term *a* zu einem Term *b* wie in einem Bereich B ein Term *c* zu einem *d* (Titzmann 1977: 152).

> [Homology = relation of equivalence between (at least) two (at least) two-place relations which link terms of the same or of different classes. ...thus, a term *a* is to a term *b* in domain A as a term *c* is to a term *d* in domain B (Titzmann 1977: 152).]

Essentially the same definition is also found in *Sémiotique: Dictionnaire raisonné de la théorie du langage* by Greimas and Courtés (1979):

> Étant donné la structure A : B :: A' : B', A et A' sont dits homologues par rapport à B et B' (Greimas & Courtés 1979: 174).

[Given the structure A : B :: A' : B', A and A' are said to be homologous with respect to B and B' (Greimas & Courtés 1979: 174).]

The definition of homology just quoted represents a purely structural interpretation of the notion. There is, however, another notion of homology which, in fact, more closely parallels the notion of homology as it was originally used in biology: 'having the same relation to an original or fundamental structure (but not necessarily in function)' (*Oxford English Dictionary*, HOMOLOGY). Thus the dog's forelegs and the grasshopper's wings are *homologous*, because they have developed from the same source, while the grasshoper's wings and the eagle's wings are *analogous*, in spite of their present functional similarity, because they derive from different sources. It seems to me methodologically very useful to reintroduce a genetic implication into the notion of homology. Combining the two interpretations we get the following formulation: When two instances stand in homologous relationship to each other, then we may assume that the two are concrete manifestations of one and the same underlying principle. Thus for the homologous terms X and Y, there is possibly an underlying and more abstract term W, of which the terms X and Y are concrete manifestations in two different spheres.[4]

Applied to the particular question we are concerned with at present, this means the following. We have discussed one particular type of answering a question, namely by giving a parallel instance, and have considered it a "bricolage-like" way of accounting for what is being questioned. Our question concerned the personal names *Armstrong* and *Whitehead* and the answer to the question was that Miss Armstrong need not have strong arms, just as (and because) Mr. Whitehead need not have a white head. Now the two propositions we have here are indeed parallel. However, they hardly strike us as an instance of homology as defined above. The reason for this is that both propositions are concerned with the relationship between names and referents and hence do not belong to different spheres. As long as this is the case, an explanation in terms of a parallel instance remains an instance of simple bricolage. Thus with regard to the singular-plural distinction, we have to ask ourselves whether it will be possible to discover a feature parallel to the lack of singular-plural distinction in a particular language that would satisfy the definition of homology. If it is, we can then claim that the linguistic feature is there not by chance but is motivated, since we now have essentially the same feature recurring in different spheres of the same language.

But will this ever be possible for the lack of the singular-plural distinction? One possibility is the parallelism in behavior between nouns and verbs, of which we already have some discussion and data. The point to be checked now is whether there is any feature in the Japanese verbs that homologically parallels the lack of singular-plural distinction in the nouns.

I suggest that the verb counterpart of this nominal feature is the relatively low degree of transitivity. It is a fact that a number of Japanese verbs of action consistently behave in a different way from the English verbs of action to which they apparently correspond semantically. Thus it sounds contradictory in English to say, "I burned it, but it did not burn", whereas the corresponding Japanese sentence is acceptable, and there are dozens of pairs of English and Japanese verbs that behave in the same way. For detailed discussion, reference is made to Ikegami (1985).[5]

What happens is the following. Action is usually associated with a certain goal to be achieved for which the action is undertaken. Some verbs of action need not imply that the intended goal is achieved. For example, if you *invite* someone to come to the party, he may or may not come. The intended goal here does not have to be achieved. Some other verbs of action, on the other hand, do imply that the intended goal is achieved. Thus if you *kill* someone, he certainly dies. Now when English and Japanese verbs of action which apparently correspond to each other semantically are compared, it is obvious that quite a few pairs of English and Japanese verbs behave in the same way. As we have seen, the English verb *invite* and its Japanese counterpart behave in the same way: neither of them necessarily implies that the intended goal is achieved. Similarly, both the English verb *kill* and its Japanese counterpart behave in the same way: both imply the achievement of the intended goal. There are, on the other hand, other pairs of English and Japanese verbs which do not behave in the same way. And a very remarkable fact in this respect is that whenever they behave differently, it is invariably the English verb which implies the achievement of the intended goal, while its Japanese counterpart does not necessarily imply the achievement. I know of no exeption to this. The English verb *burn* and its Japanese counterpart referred to above are just one example of the case in point. Other examples which behave in the same way include such English verbs as *boil* (as of water), *count* (the number), *help* (a person do something), *persuade* (a person to do s.t.), *thaw* (frozen food), *wake* (a person), and so forth.

We thus have two facts to consider. On the one hand, Japanese nouns behave neutrally as to singular and plural. On the other, Japanese verbs of action tend to behave neutrally with respect to achievement and non-achievement. The former concerns the sphere of grammatical number and the latter the sphere of grammatical aspect. Can we speak of homology here? We know already that the categories number and aspect can be correlated with each other in terms of "boundedness" and "unboundedness".[6] Thus, the singular number of the noun and the achievement sense of the verb go together as both being "bounded", while the plural number of the noun and the non-achievement sense of the verb go together as both being "unbounded".

The distinctive criterion I would prefer to operate with here would rather be in terms of the contrast between "individuum" versus "continuum". While the contrast between "bounded" and "unbounded" is based essentially on positing a plus term and a minus term, the proposed contrast between "individuum" and "continuum" is meant to be a contrast between a marked term and an unmarked term. I would argue that a language like English which has the singular-plural distinction processes the notion of "thing" in terms of an individuum, and the essential distinction made in English is one between a single individuum and a group of individua (which the language represents as singular and plural, respectively). In a language like Japanese which has no singular-plural distinction for nouns, on the other hand, the notion of "thing" is processed essentially in terms of the continuum, an important characteristic of which is that the contrast between the single entity and a collection of entities does not simply apply.

The contrast between "individuum" and "continuum" applies also to the "achievement" versus "non-achievement" distinction. The aspectual distinction between achievement and non-achievement is essentially that between reaching a goal and not reaching a goal. If we employ the prepositions *to* and *toward* in the ideal senses of 'reaching a goal' and 'proceeding toward (but not yet reaching) a goal' respectively, then the aspectual distinction in question can be represented as a contrast between "GO TO a goal" and "GO TOWARD a goal". This contrast, however, can be reinterpreted in terms of whether the goal is conceived of as an individuum or as a continuum. If the goal is conceived of as an individuum, then there is a time point at which one can say that the goal has been reached. If the goal is conceived of as a continuum, however, there will be no definite time point at which one can say that the goal has been reached. What we will have here will be an unending process of going toward a goal. There is thus an equivalence between GO TO-WARD an individuated goal and GO TO a continuous goal. The equivalence, however, is not perfect. What is implied by "GOing TO-WARD a goal" is that the goal is not yet reached. What is implied by "GOing TO a continuous goal" is that the goal is both reached and not quite reached. In other words, the notion of reaching a goal is itself neutralized. And this is all to our advantage, because a characteristic behavior of the Japanese verbs of action is exactly the ambiguity between the achievement and the non-achievement sense. Thus the image of a "continuum" serves rather well to characterize the behaviors of both Japanese nouns and verbs.

The noun-verb parallelism I have just discussed is a case of homology as manifested at the level of linguistic structure. I would like to point out also that homology can be found at the level of linguistic performance as well (as discussed in Ikegami 1989a). For example, when the number is to be mentioned for the thing being talked about, the Japanese speaker characteristically tends to represent it in ambiguous, approximate terms rather than in clear, definite terms. An utterance like *May I have about two ten p. stamps?* would certainly sound odd in English, but the equivalent sentence can be heard quite commonly in Japanese. The psychology behind the preference for this rather oddly ambiguous way of saying things is that by avoiding the mentioning of a definite number, one will sound less demanding, leaving the ultimate decision to the other party, and therefore more polite. This preference is especially characteristic of the speech of elderly ladies. Saying things in this manner contributes to *quantitatively* blurring the extension of the reference.

There is also a preferred way of *qualitatively* blurring the extension of the referent itself. This is observed characteristically in the Japanese speaker's preference for using the equivalent of the English word *such* when actually he means either 'this' or 'that': thus saying something like *I don't know such a man* rather than *I don't know this man* or *You can't say such a thing to me* rather than *You can't say that to me* or speaking of *such things as you can buy at a supermarket* instead of *those things that you can buy at a supermarket*, and so forth. By using the equivalent of *such* rather than the equivalent of *this* or *that*, the Japanese speaker can imply that there may possibly be similar entities that are just as relevant as the entity in question, and thus blur the extension of the entity in question qualitatively. Notice that *such* is ambiguous in two further ways: it neutralizes the contrast between "proximateness" (associated with the word *this*) and "remoteness" (associated with the word *that*) and also the quantitative contrast between "singular" (associated with *this/that*) and "plural" (associated with *these/those*). Thus the word has a special appeal to the mentality of Japanese speakers, and I have heard English and American teachers of English in Japanese schools wondering why students use the word *such* so often in compositions.

What we have just observed is that the Japanese speaker tends to refer to a thing ambiguously, by quantitatively or qualitatively blurring the extension of the referent. It will readily be noticed that here again the notion of "continuum" is relevant. In the continuum, not only the quantitative contrast between singular and plural, but also qualitative contrasts such as "male" vs. "female" and "animate" vs. "inanimate" are neutralized.

Further examples which homologously point to the underlying image-schema of continuum can be adduced in relation to the Japanese language (the interested reader is referred to Ikegami (1991) for further discussion). It seems to me that the images of the clearly articulated individuum and the ambiguously unarticulated continuum form a pair of basic contrastive principles around which language is organized both in structure and use. I hasten to add that the two terms in the proposed contrasts will of course not function to the absolute exclusion of each other. We do not claim, for example, that if a language makes no singular-plural distinction for nouns, then it will necessarily also neutralize the distinction between the achievement and non-achievement senses of verbs of action. Most plausibly, we will have to anticipate a gradience here - a gradience between languages which fit images of clearly articulated individua and languages which fit images of ambiguously unarticulated continua. The whole picture will look very much like the one we are familiar with for the gradience between ergative and accusative languages. It is, furthermore, tempting to conjecture whether the gradual shift from one pole to the other may possibly represent an aspect of language evolution - in the same way that originally ergative languages tend to develop into accusative languages. If any such evolutionary directionality can be posited for the contrast with which we are now concerned, it will most plausibly be from the ambiguously unarticulated continuum to the clearly articulated individuum. At present, of course, this remains mere speculation.

3.   Concluding remarks

Having said this, let me add two further comments in support of the case for homology. The first concerns the relationship between language and culture. Since culture arises essentially out of human semiotic activity, out of the activity of creating signs - "signs" in the broadest sense of entities with which significance is associated - and since language undoubtedly plays a central role in semiotic activity, one can reasonably expect there to be aspects of culture whose structure and function are in homology with language. In fact, it would be highly surprising if we found that the human mind worked one way with regard to language and another way with regard to other aspects of culture. To quote again from Lévi-Strauss:

> If there were no relations [between culture and language] at all, that would lead us to assume that the human mind is a kind of jumble - that there is no connection at all between what the mind is doing on one level and what the mind is doing on another level (Lévi-Strauss 1952 [1963]: 79).

It seems to me that the image of the continuum, in terms of which certain basic features of the Japanese language can be accounted for, also applies very well to certain basic features of Japanese culture. At a very general level, consider the relationship between the individual and the group or that between man and nature. Two poles are conceivable here. At one pole, the individual is clearly articulated and maintains his identity within the group. At the other pole, the individual loses his identity and is dissolved into the group. Similarly, man stands in sharp contrast to nature at one pole, while he merges with nature at the other. It is the image of the continuum that is created in the second pole of either case, and it is to this second pole that Japanese culture seems to tend. More detailed discussion of cultural aspects of the problem can be found in Ikegami (1989b).

My second and final comment concerns the relationship between cognition and perception. It will perhaps have been noticed that the contrast between the individuum and the continuum bears close resemblance to the contrast between the figure and the ground at the level of perception. Here again two poles are conceivable. At one pole, the figure is clearly articulated and stands in sharp contrast to the ground. At the other pole, the figure remains unarticulated and submerges itself in the ground. If, as often suggested, there is a close relationship between perception and cognition - in the sense that the way we perceive has a great deal to do with the way we cognize - it is no wonder that a contrast which is comparable to the one familiar to us at the level of perception can also be found at the level of cognition. Here we have a case of homology again between the two different levels and this fact should also further support the claim in my paper (Ikegami 1989a), namely that a contrast exists between an orientation toward clearer articulation and a focus on the individuum vis-à-vis an orientation toward blurred articulation and a focus on the whole configuration or gestalt and on the continuum.

Notes

1. Cf. "... one might imagine a holistic typology, i.e. some set of typological parameters that are logically independent but in practice correlated so highly with one another that they enable us to typologize the whole, or at least a large part, of the structure of an arbitrary language. ... experience to date is rather against this possibility..." (Comrie: 1981: 37).
2. I may add in passing that the Japanese text is also phrased in such a way as to produce quite naturally the effect of the "subject"-"object" merger (or the merger of the observer and the observed or, more specifically, the merger of the writer/reader and the character in the novel). But this is not our present concern.
3. Cf. Whorf (1956a: 60), where Whorf seems to be referring to exactly the same kind of contrast found in the Hopi language.
4. A detailed discussion of these points is found in Ikegami (1991).
5. Cf. Lévi-Strauss (1962), Chap. 1.
6. For a theoretical discussion and an application of these points, see Ikegami (1989b, 1989c).

References

Comrie, Bernard
    1981   *Language universals and linguistic typology.* Chicago: University of Chicago Press.
Greimas, Algirdas J. & J. Courtés
    1979   *Sémiotique: Dictionnaire raisonné de la théorie du langage.* Paris: Hachette.
Ikegami, Yoshihiko
    1985   " 'Activity' - 'accomplishment' - 'achievement': A language that can't say 'I burned it, but it didn't burn' and one that can", in: Adam Makkai & Alan K. Melby (eds.), 266-304.
    1989a   "What we see when we see flying cranes: motion or transition", *The Japan Foundation Newsletter* 15.5-6: 1-9.

1989b   "Homology of language and culture: A case study in Japanese semiotics", in: Walter A. Koch (ed.) (1989a), 388-403.
1989c   "Culture and semiotics", in: Walter A. Koch (ed.) (1989b), 13-26.
1991   "DO-language and BECOME-language: Two types of linguistic representation", in: Yoshihiko Ikegami (ed.), *The empire of signs: Semiotic essays on Japanese culture.* Amsterdam: John Benjamins.

Koch, Walter A.(ed.)
1989a   *The nature of culture.* Bochum: Brockmeyer.
1989b   *Culture and semiotics.* Bochum: Brockmeyer.

Lévi-Strauss, Claude
1952   "Linguistics and anthropolgy", in: Claude Lévi-Strauss (1963), 67-80.
1962   *La pensée sauvage.* Paris: Librairie Plon.
1963   *Structural anthropology.* Harmondsworth: Penguin Books.

Makkai, Adam & Alan K. Melby (eds.)
1985   *Linguistics and philosophy: Essays in honor of Rulon Wells.* Amsterdam: John Benjamins.

Rudzka-Ostyn, Brygida (ed.)
1988   *Topics in cognitive linguistics.* Amsterdam: John Benjamins.

Talmy, Leonard
1988   "The relation of grammar to cognition", in Brygida Rudzka-Ostyn (ed.), 165-206.

Titzmann, Manfred
1977   *Strukturale Textanalyse.* München: Wilhelm Fink.

Whorf, Benjamin Lee
1956a   "American Indian model of the universe", in: Benjamin Lee Whorf (1956b), 57-64.
1956b   *Language, thought, and reality.* Cambridge: MIT Press.

Subject index